Europe between Democracy and Dictatorship

1900–1945

Conan Fischer

A John Wiley & Sons, Ltd., Publication

Blackwell Publishing was acquired by John Wiley & Sons in February 2007. Blackwell's publishing program has been merged with Wiley's global Scientific, Technical, and Medical business to form Wiley-Blackwell.

Registered Office
John Wiley & Sons Ltd, The Atrium, Southern Gate, Chichester, West Sussex, PO19 8SQ, United Kingdom

Editorial Offices
350 Main Street, Malden, MA 02148-5020, USA
9600 Garsington Road, Oxford, OX4 2DQ, UK
The Atrium, Southern Gate, Chichester, West Sussex, PO19 8SQ, UK

For details of our global editorial offices, for customer services, and for information about how to apply for permission to reuse the copyright material in this book please see our website at www. wiley.com/wiley-blackwell.

Library of Congress Cataloging-in-Publication Data

Fischer, Conan.
    Europe between democracy and dictatorship, 1900–1945 / Conan Fischer.
        p.   cm. – (Blackwell history of Europe)
    Includes bibliographical references and index.
    ISBN 978-0-631-21511-0 (hardcover : alk. paper) – ISBN 978-0-631-21512-7 (pbk. : alk. paper)
1. Europe–History–1871–1918.   2. Europe–History–1918–1945.   3. World War, 1914–1918–Europe.
4. World War, 1939–1945–Europe.   I. Title.
    D424.F55 2011
    940.5–dc22

                                                         2010009758

A catalogue record for this book is available from the British Library.

Set in 11/13pt Dante by SPi Publisher Services, Pondicherry, India
Printed and bound in Malaysia by Vivar Printing Sdn Bhd

1   2011

the last date belo

6075

Blackwell History of Europe

General Editor: John Stevenson

The series provides a new interpretative history of Europe from the Roman Empire to the end of the twentieth century. Written by acknowledged experts in their fields, and reflecting the range of recent scholarship, the books combine insights from social and cultural history with coverage of political, diplomatic and economic developments. Eastern Europe assumes its rightful place in the history of the continent, and the boundary of Europe is considered flexibly, including the Islamic, Slav and Orthodox perspectives wherever appropriate. Together, the volumes offer a lively and authoritative history of Europe for a new generation of teachers, students and general readers.

Published

Europe between Democracy and Dictatorship: 1900–1945
Conan Fischer

Europe's Troubled Peace: 1945–2000
Tom Buchanan

Europe in the Sixteenth Century
Andrew Pettegree

Fractured Europe: 1600–1721
David J. Sturdy

In preparation

Europe: 300–800
Peter Heather

Europe in Ferment: 950–1100
Jonathan Shepard

The Advance of Medieval Europe: 1099–1270
Jonathan Phillips

Europe: 1409–1523
Bruce Gordon

Europe from Absolutism to Revolution: 1715–1815
Michael Broers

Europe's Uncertain Path: 1814–1914
R. S. Alexander

To Mary, Kate and Jane

Contents

List of Maps

List of Figures

Frontispiece: Advertisement in 1927 for Mercedes-Benz, showing Le Corbusier's Double House, Weissenhofsiedlung, Stuttgart (Mercedes-Benz Archive and Collection)

Foreword

Between 1900 and 1945 two world wars and a string of murderous dictatorships called time on an age of European global preeminence, material and moral. They form the main subject matter of this book, but do not dominate it entirely. Interwar Europe also experienced deep-seated and far-reaching changes that testified to human society's powers of innovation and renewal and laid many foundations of the post-1945 world. Contrasting paradigms therefore compete for our attention: an abysmal story of conflict, economic crisis, dictatorship and slaughter which had by 1945 left much of the continent a smouldering wasteland, but against this the fruits and legacy of constructive diplomacy, cultural vibrancy, political and social emancipation, prosperity and technological advance.

The labyrinthine complexity of the European story prevents easy generalization or the full and equal treatment of all themes, places and events. Each author will bring their own perspectives, enthusiasms and expertise to a general history and this work is no exception, laying a degree of emphasis and sometimes a revisionist take on the international diplomacy of a turbulent and warlike age. The book adopts a broadly chronological approach to the general European story, embedding the two great wars within the narrative, but foregrounds selected major events and themes, such as the post-1918 peace settlements, the key revolutionary upheavals, economic crises, and also cultural change. Brief national histories appear at appropriate points and, as far as space has allowed, the "peripheral" and smaller nations of Europe are not ignored. They were no less caught up in the events of the earlier twentieth century than the great powers, even if they more often ended up as victim or prey rather than predator.

Referencing is denser than in many general histories, but the sheer scale of first-rate scholarship on this period must leave the attribution selective. It serves essentially as an entry into a range of specialist and general works. Quotation has been used widely both to provide a flavour of other authors' writing and to lend life and colour to this fascinating period in Europe's history, sometimes exploiting nonacademic sources, occasionally to be taken with a good dash of salt.

The commissioning editors at Wiley-Blackwell, Gillian Kane and Tessa Harvey, have provided encouragement and wise counsel throughout and proved remarkably tolerant as the book outgrew its planned scope and dimensions. I owe a major debt of gratitude to John Stevenson who provided very helpful and much appreciated comments on the finished typescript and also wish to thank many friends and colleagues who have helped me in a variety of ways. Among them, Hartmut Pogge von Strandmann and Volker Berghahn kindly read and commented on some earlier sections of the draft; others, including Simon Adams and Alan Sharp, lent or gave me more esoteric items from their personal libraries. My former Department at the University of Strathclyde generously granted me leave to complete the book, invaluable time for which I am particularly grateful. Finally, once again, I must thank my wife, Mary, and my daughters, Kate and Jane, for their unstinting patience, advice and support during the completion of this book, which has imposed on their lives too much and for too long.

C.J.F., Edinburgh

Chapter One
The European Paradox

At the turn of the twentieth century Europe enjoyed unprecedented prosperity and a vibrant cultural life. The continent was also witnessing a series of scientific inventions and discoveries that were to shape decisively the historical experience of the coming century: wireless, radiation, the petrol engine, aviation and in medicine, to name but a few. International investment and trade underpinned the continent's economic strength and those who could afford to were able to travel freely across the continent, unimpeded by passport formalities or, for that matter, tiresome security checks.

Consumption and leisure were becoming increasingly accessible to society. The growing middle classes of Paris could enjoy shopping in the Bon Marché, Galeries Lafayette or at Au Printemps, Londoners could visit Harrods or from 1909 Selfridges, and the burghers of Berlin soon enough could enjoy a comparable experience in the city's great department store, KaDeWe (Kaufhaus des Westens). The seaside holiday or its equivalent was not just the privilege of the few, even if some traveled in third class railway carriages and lodged in cheap boarding houses, while others could enjoy the splendors of the grand hotels that sprang up along Europe's Atlantic and Mediterranean coasts.

Overcrowding and poverty weighed on many households in Europe's burgeoning cities, but dramatic improvements in public health and sanitation and rapid additions to the housing stock promised a more tolerable future. Modern urban transport networks made the dream of suburban living a reality for many and unemployment was relatively low in the industrialized regions of Europe, which continued to attract a stream of rural migrants. Illiteracy remained relatively widespread in Mediterranean and eastern Europe, but universal primary education had all but eliminated it in the center and northwest of the continent, where government was becoming increasingly accountable to an informed (male) electorate. Much was also changing in the workplace, as the principles of trade union representation and workplace consultation were conceded fitfully and unevenly in the industrialized economies and health and safety regulations were gradually tightened up.

One could embellish or add to this list of achievements almost indefinitely. If a certain fin de siècle, self-indulgent pessimism stalked the salons of the bored and wealthy and premonitions of doom haunted certain hypersensitive artists and intellectuals, this could not sweep away the underlying confidence of mainstream European society. Paris hosted a series of world fairs, at which France and the other exhibiting nations could show off their latest technological and artistic achievements. The 1889 World Fair had seen the construction of Gustave Eiffel's iconic wrought-iron tower, much criticized by architectural purists at the time and originally intended only to serve as a temporary structure for the duration of the fair itself. The 1900 fair was housed largely in the magnificent domed, iron and glass Grand Palais, decorated in art nouveau style, which encapsulated the unmistakable confidence and ambition of the Belle Epoque, the golden age, of the early twentieth century.

Expressionist painters, such as Egon Schiele or Ernst Ludwig Kirchner, may have scandalized their more conservative contemporaries, Pablo Picasso and Georges Braque may have seen their prewar artistic efforts dismissed as "mere" cubism, the first concert performance in Paris of Igor Stravinsky's *Rite of Spring* may have triggered fist fights within the audience, but such work reflected tellingly the accelerating pace of an increasingly urbanized, emancipated and metropolitan society. The French impressionist painters of the previous century had sometimes evoked a romantic past (in a radically novel fashion), but prewar expressionism was decidedly rooted in the present and looked to the future. Culture apart, in 1910 the German electrics giant AEG commissioned the architect and industrial designer Peter Behrens to create the world's first coordinated corporate brand[1] as the evolution of a modern global economy gathered pace. France acknowledged the irresistible force of globalization when finally adopting Greenwich Mean Time in 1911.

Among the continent's prevailing political creeds, liberalism and socialism owed their credibility to an inherent belief in progress, and the willingness of conservatives to concede or even preempt reform spoke volumes. During the nineteenth century this self-confidence had combined with material and military strength to see Europe project its power worldwide, and by 1900 European imperialism neared the peak of its potential, dominating much of the globe. Even where Europeans did not rule directly, the continent's businessmen and financiers were ubiquitous as they invested, for example, in China, Turkey or Argentina, funding governments and developing trade across the globe. The City of London was central to this process, but Paris also played a major role and German capital strove to close the gap with these long-established imperial centers. Only the United States of America, itself the offspring of the European Enlightenment and peopled primarily by European immigrants and their descendants, promised to challenge Europe's position in any meaningful way.

The self-confidence of the age was reflected in a multitude of intimate, often minor, ways. In 1886 a doting uncle, a French bourgeois, sent his niece, Julie, an idiosyncratic wedding present. He admitted that the set of account books lacked somewhat in romantic charm, but insisted that orderly book-keeping should shape and guide Julie's future life. As he continued:

> The second part of this book contains only blank paper. It is for recording at the year's end a detailed inventory of your assets. If all [your marital] expenses are deducted from your total fortune you will have the capital remaining to you when you arrive in Tunis, and which you will be able to add to, year by year, in order to provide your daughters with dowries.
>
> But your fortune will vary not only with the level of your expenditure and receipts, but also with the rise and fall in the value of your investments. In order that you may know your real financial position you must note in this second part of the book each of your investments and its actual value at the time, according to its quoted price on the stock exchange.[2]

Investments could, indeed, fall, indicating that life was not without its risks. The European capitalist edifice had been built through the efforts of many losers as well as winners within an uneasy relationship between risk, struggle and reward. Interpretations of this process found their most extreme expression in the writings of so-called "social Darwinists," who argued that individual fortunes, and indeed the fortunes of entire societies, were defined by struggle and by the survival of the fittest. Such theories could and sometimes did assume racialist overtones that also provided a spurious moral justification for the European colonization of other continents.

Julie's uncle, however, had confined his thoughts to financial prudence. Such was clearly called for, but any investment would have been reduced to a mere gamble unless one held an inherently optimistic view of the future. And indeed, underlying optimism defined the Europe of 1900, shared by countless middle-class and working-class families for whom inheritance, a profession, a trade, or honest labor provided the wherewithal for a morally upstanding life, whether affluent or modest. Most families placed assets, however large or small, on the stock market, in government securities, in cooperative savings banks, building societies, or friendly societies. Urban sophisticates mocked the apocryphal (or not so apocryphal) peasant who simply stashed whatever gold he could accumulate under the mattress without a thought to the returns offered by rational investment. Capitalism, to give this process a name, had become deeply and inextricably embedded in society's wider values. It only remained to be asked what might ensue, if this inherent faith in a calculable form of progress were ever to be fundamentally disrupted.

And soon enough, twentieth-century Europe witnessed a succession of hammer blows that shattered these certainties and much besides. Confidence in the efficacy of reform, the wisdom of compromise or tolerance, and, ultimately, respect for humanity itself buckled and broke. The First World War initiated this

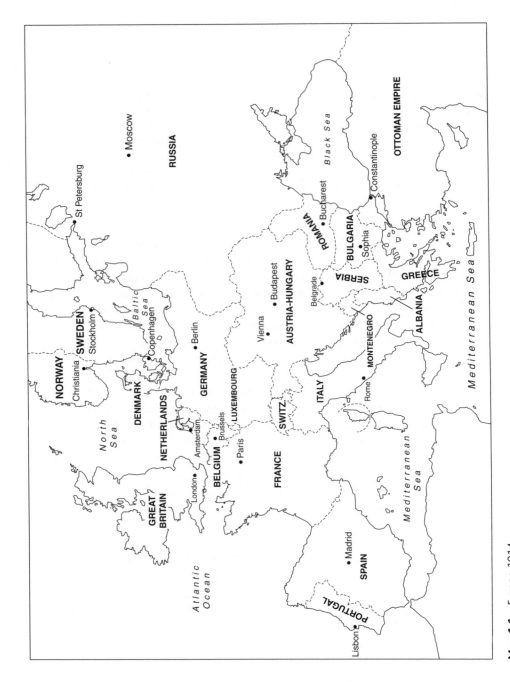

Map 1.1 Europe 1914.

destructive process and the Second World War brought it to its culmination, for which the extermination camps at Auschwitz-Birkenau serve as harrowing short-hand. The devastation wrought by the First World War was rationalized by the hope that this was truly a "war to end all wars," but beyond the unprecedented loss of life the crippling expense of modern warfare had rocked Europe's economy to its foundations. The accumulated wealth of a century or more was dissipated as the value of money melted away and faith in money as a just reward for effort and a secure medium of exchange evaporated. Commentators such as the economist John Maynard Keynes feared for the very existence of liberal capitalist society.

This great inflation was at its most extreme in Germany (and the lands to its east) as pensions earned through a lifetime of hard and honest toil became worthless, as salaries that reflected expertise and professional dedication were reduced to a pittance, and as workers could no longer put bread and meat on the table because their pay packets had lost any meaningful value. During mid-1923 they or their wives struggled to find a trader or shopkeeper willing to accept banknotes that would be worthless within hours. An economic and financial crisis thus became a profoundly corrosive moral crisis, as Gerald Feldman once explained:

> The [German] Republic [came] to be identified with the trauma of all those who had lost out and with the shameful practices of law, equity, and good faith that characterized the period. No less offensive than the misappropriation of money and goods, however, was the sense that there had been a misappropriation of spiritual values and a selling of what the *Bürgertum* [middle class] – above all the *Bildungsbürgertum* [the professional middle class] – held to be holy. The so-called … histories of manners and morals of the inflation were simply an extension of this belief, so that the inflation added a powerful pornographic element to the political culture of Weimar with all the elements of shame and self-disgust and the projections onto others that came with it.[3]

Feldman continued that these traumas and the accompanying social and political disruption contributed to a tolerance of political violence and so of Nazism, with consequences that today are universally understood. After all, even the sordid process of Holocaust denial accepts by default that there is something that needs to be denied.

It is, therefore, tempting in the extreme simply to trace this history of apocalyptic decline to a zero hour or *Stunde nul*, from which life had to begin all over again in 1945. However, contemporary Europe owes far too much to its past to permit such an approach. Its deeper heritage remains profoundly ancient, modified and supplemented over millennia, but also during the decades with which we are concerned. This work will confront the paradox of this history as it traces and evaluates much that shaped and is celebrated in contemporary Europe, but simultaneously confront the successive waves of darkness that enveloped the continent some two generations ago. War and peacemaking, modernity and nostalgic reaction, humanity and barbarity, and, of course, democracy and dictatorship all contributed decisively to the European experience of the earlier twentieth century.

Chapter Two
The Coming of War

2.1 A Balkans War

Austria-Hungary declared war against Serbia on July 28, 1914, and shelled the enemy capital, Belgrade, on the following day. The Third Balkan War of the early twentieth century had begun, but this time the hostilities engulfed Europe within days, drew in the European colonial empires, distant powers such as Japan, and, in 1917, the United States of America. This "Great War" or "World War," as contemporaries named it, swept away ancient empires, unleashed convulsive revolutionary upheavals, and hardly seemed to respect the victors more than it did the vanquished. The catastrophe seemed all the greater and all the more bewildering since it defied an unmistakable improvement in wider European relations during the preceding few years, at any rate away from the Balkans. Even in 1914 the belligerents blamed each other for the mounting carnage and after the war the enduring question of "guilt" – especially German culpability – came to serve as more than an interpretation of the past. It also influenced the history of interwar Europe as countries shaped their foreign and even domestic policies around the assertion or denial of this guilt. As we shall see, the legacy of the Second World War with its history of unprecedented mass murder has since cast even darker shadows that extend back into the history of the pre-Nazi past as much as they still cloud the present.

The initial, regional conflict between Austria-Hungary and Serbia was triggered by a mix of Serbian ambition and Habsburg pessimism. Since 1815 the history of the Austrian (Habsburg) Empire had been punctuated by successive defeats and revolutions which saw Austria driven from much of Italy (1860 and 1867), excluded from the emergent Prussian-dominated German federation (1866–7), and forced to grant Hungary far-reaching autonomy (1867). The Austrian Empire was renamed Austria-Hungary in reflection of this, but Austrian-Hungarian tensions were not definitively resolved. Habsburg statesmen did manage to hold the Empire together and, Italy apart, maintain the boundaries negotiated by Metternich at the

Congress of Vienna in 1814–15, but in 1903 this tenuous equilibrium was disturbed by a coup d'état in Belgrade. King Alexander Obrenovic was assassinated and replaced by King Peter, of the rival Karadjordjevic family, who refused to accept Serbia's erstwhile position as an Austrian satellite. As tensions subsequently rose, Belgrade began to look toward France and Russia for support against Vienna.

This prompted Austria-Hungary to annex outright in 1908 the former Turkish (Ottoman) province of Bosnia-Herzegovina, which it had ruled since 1879, in order to assert its primacy in the region and also block any possible Serb expansion toward the Adriatic coastline. Bosnia, however, contained a sizeable Serbian population and had always been coveted by Belgrade. Regional tension rose further, accompanied by the formation of secret, luridly named Serb terrorist societies such as the Black Hand (otherwise known as Unity or Death). Dedicated to expelling the Austro-Hungarians from all Serbian lands, these societies recruited their membership from the backward, increasingly overpopulated Bosnian countryside, where grinding poverty readily bred widespread resentment against the Habsburg rulers and created a form of political extremism which owed much to the Russian anarchism of that time. Assassination, of course, formed an integral part of its political repertoire.

These tense relations were heightened by two short, sharp wars that broke out in the Balkans in 1912 and 1913. The first saw Greece, Bulgaria and Serbia join forces to drive the Ottoman Empire (already embroiled in a war with Italy over control of Libya) out of southeastern Europe. By the end of October 1912 the Balkan states were victorious, but yet again Austria-Hungary (and for that matter Italy) sought to prevent Serbia gaining a port on the Adriatic, which might provide a base for a rival great power. To block Serb ambitions, Vienna and Rome proposed that the Albanian peoples, who inhabited the coastal region between Montenegro to the north and Greece to the south, be given a state of their own. However, this was more easily said than done. The Serbs pushed on toward the sea, slaughtering Albanians as they went, kidnapped an Austro-Hungarian consular official in Macedonia, and appealed to Russia for support. Russia responded by carrying out a trial mobilization, while Austria-Hungary stiffened its garrisons in Galicia which bordered on Russian Poland. This time, however, war did not spread. By late November it was plain that Russian sympathy for Serbia did not extend to a readiness to use force, and Serbia itself had apologized to Austria for kidnapping an accredited diplomat. The collective of European great powers, or "Concert of Europe," moved to call closure on the crisis. An Ambassador's Conference was convened in London by the British Foreign Secretary, Sir Edward Grey, which confirmed the existence of Albania.

However, despite some hard bargaining in London over Albania's borders with Montenegro and Serbia, which tended to favor the latter two states, Montenegro resented the proposed settlement and invaded northeastern Albania. The Concert of Europe appeared helpless as St Petersburg backed the Montenegrins, while Rome and Vienna backed the Albanians. On May 2, 1913 Austria-Hungary put its troops facing the Montenegrin border on a war footing, prompting the Balkan statelet to withdraw from Albania with alacrity. The Austro-Hungarian military commander, Conrad von Hötzendorf, would have preferred a punitive war against the Habsburgs' southern Slav neighbors, but the Foreign Minister, Count Berchtold, observed that saber rattling had achieved in short order what the Concert of Europe, divided "between hostile Triple Entente colleagues [France, Russia, and Britain] and feeble Triple Alliance colleagues [Germany and Italy]"[1] could not. On May 30, 1913 the Treaty of London brought the upheaval of the First Balkan War to an end.

Within a matter of days, however, the Second Balkan War erupted as Bulgaria and Serbia fell out over their share of the spoils from the first conflict. Greece joined Serbia, and Bulgaria lost. This time the Austro-Hungarians remained onlookers, despite their pro-Bulgarian sympathies, hoping to salvage for their Bulgarian friends as much territory as possible once it came to peace negotiations. However the Habsburg Empire's principal ally, Germany, had other priorities. The Kaiser's brother-in-law sat on the Greek throne and, personal sympathies apart, Berlin was locked in a struggle with Paris for influence in Athens. Greece (and by implication Serbia) could not be offended and the Treaty of Bucharest of August 10, 1913 saw the collapse of Berchtold's pro-Bulgarian policy, enormous resentment in Vienna toward Berlin, Austrian despair over the traditional system of Concert diplomacy, and a growing conviction that further conflict was inevitable. The Emperor of Austria, Franz Joseph, observed bleakly: "The Treaty of Bucharest is untenable and we are moving towards another war. May God grant that it is confined to the Balkans."[2]

This war might have come in October 1913, for the Serbians, in defiance of the two freshly signed Balkans settlements, had again begun occupying Albanian territory. On October 17, without troubling to consult the other major powers, the Austro-Hungarians issued Belgrade with an ultimatum that allowed the Serbs eight days to quit Albania. Despite ruffled feathers in Rome and Paris no great power openly supported Serbia, forcing Belgrade to comply hastily with Vienna's demands. "Independent action," Bridge observes, "seemed after all to be the most effective means of defending the Monarchy's interests,"[3] and in fairness, few alternatives were on offer. Despite a brief outburst of pro-Austrian enthusiasm in October 1913 in the wake of the latest Albanian crisis, Berlin's policy in the Balkans and Turkey was distinct from Vienna's, prompting Franz Joseph and Berchtold to undertake a major diplomatic offensive designed to reclaim German support. As Berchtold complained to his ambassador to Berlin in May 1914: "People in Berlin do not seem to have been able to free themselves … from the idea of a political rapprochement between Austria-Hungary and Serbia – an idea which must be regarded as futile in view of the animosity towards Austria-Hungary deep-rooted in the Serbian national consciousness …"[4] In June he instructed Baron Matschenko, a senior official at the Ballhausplatz (Foreign Office), to set out a long-term diplomatic strategy for the Balkans. On June 24 Matschenko completed his draft, which urged Germany, finally, to coordinate its Balkans policy with that of Austria-Hungary, envisaged a potential Austro-German-Bulgarian-Turkish alliance in the region, and sought to convince Berlin that the differences between Vienna and Belgrade were irreconcilable.

This program sought essentially to stabilize the Balkans through peaceful if robust diplomacy, but within days events were to demand something very different. On June 28, 1914 the heir to the Habsburg throne, the Archduke Franz Ferdinand, and his wife Sophie made an official visit to the Bosnian capital, Sarajevo, where they were killed by students associated with the Black Hand. The initial attempt to kill the Archduke was botched and it was only when one of the failed assassins, Gavrilo Princip, later stumbled on the official motorcade that he succeeded in shooting the royal couple. This outrage radicalized the mood in Vienna so dramatically that the Ballhausplatz's existing diplomatic strategy was immediately rendered redundant. Its shock effect combined with longer term tensions and attitudes to precipitate the outbreak of the Austro-Serbian War on July 28, a war whose approach the respective governments appeared to welcome as much as they feared.

Serbs understood their history as a process of victimhood, martyrdom and ultimate resurrection analogous in some ways to Christ's passion on the cross. As the newspaper *Straza* commented at Easter 1914:

> The year 1908 likewise signifies for us a Good Friday, which was followed in 1912–13 by the Resurrection ... and the Easter festival of the whole Serbian people too, the day of national unification, which will gather into one state all who speak Serbian, is no longer far off. There, across the Save and the Danube ... languish Slavs who look out on today's great Christian festival in sorrow, seeking to discern the gleam of Serbian bayonets, for these form their only hope of a final resurrection.[5]

On June 28 the Serb nation observed the festival of Vivovdan, the anniversary of the great medieval Battle of Kosovo at which the Ottoman Turks had overwhelmed the Serbian kingdom and thereafter placed most of the Balkans under Ottoman rule. Now the Turks had gone, but the Austro-Hungarians threatened at best to retain control over territories claimed by Serbia, at worst to replace the Ottomans as masters of all Serbia. Thus in early 1914 the extreme nationalist journal *Pijemont* described the recent recovery of Kosovo as a "victory of the Serb national consciousness which has preserved the memory of Kosovo and which in the future must conquer in Bosnia just as it conquered in Macedonia."[6]

These ambitions might have been controlled, for although the Serbian Prime Minister Nikola Pašić supported the vision of a south Slavonic, or Jugoslav, federation, he believed its realization to lie a generation or two in the future. For the moment, reconciliation with Serbia's aggravated, northern Habsburg neighbor seemed the most prudent course, especially since the Russians had been reluctant to support Serbia too strongly during the series of recent crises. Unfortunately, however, Pašić's administration was locked in a struggle with the military over who should have primacy in Serbia. The Serbian army chiefs were altogether more hawkish, flushed with recent military success and in some cases fixated on the Jugoslav mission. The head of Serbian Military Intelligence, Colonel Dragutin Dimitrijević, even moonlighted as leader of the Black Hand and, as such, actively fostered terrorist activity on Austro-Hungarian territory. To Pašić's consternation,

Dimitrijević had instructed frontier officials to help two armed students to slip into Bosnia on June 2, prompting the Prime Minister to open a secret inquiry into the spy chief's activities. Meanwhile, the wider struggle between politicians and military culminated in a call for elections, set for August 14. During the ensuing Sarajevo crisis therefore, Pašić found himself caught between the need to concili-ate an enraged Austria-Hungary, and yet indulge in the nationalist rhetoric that any Serbian election campaign demanded. As Mark Cornwall observes, "Serbian prodding of the [Habsburg] tiger continued in the weeks after Sarajevo and even Pašić himself (albeit unwittingly) could not avoid indulging in it."[7]

That said, his little state was hardly in a position to attack its mighty northern neighbor, leaving the decisions for war to be taken in Vienna, not Belgrade. For a century or more Habsburg statesmen had struggled to oppose nationalist chal-lenges to their multinational empire. In 1866 such threats had driven Austria to war against Italy in an effort to retain possession of Venice. As the Foreign Minister, Count Mensdorff, had explained to the British ambassador of the day: "The result of war might be that Austria would be dismembered, perhaps destroyed, but she must defend herself and her rights or fail in the attempt to do so, and was resolved not to acknowledge the principle of nationalities ..."[8] The underlying issues remained unchanged in July 1914 when a comparable form of pessimistic, even fatalistic determination drove Austro-Hungarian policy toward war. "If we must go under, we better go under decently," as the aged Franz Joseph declared, and Conrad von Hötzendorf echoed these sentiments when predicting that: "It will be a hopeless struggle, but nevertheless it must be because such an ancient monarchy cannot perish ingloriously."[9] Even after the event there were few regrets. "We had to die," as Count Czernin later commented, "but we could choose the means of our death, and we chose the most terrible."[10]

These were the sentiments of the handful of senior diplomats, politicians and military men who dominated an empire which, Franz Joseph had observed several months earlier, could not be governed by parliamentary means. In March 1914 the Austrian parliament, or Reichsrat, had been suspended after sustained disruption at the hands of minority nationalities, in particular the Czechs. These decision makers neglected even to consult the economic elite, the country's bankers and industrialists, who remained largely unaware of the gathering storm until they were summoned to the Finance Ministry on 23 July to be briefed and instructed to prevent a stock market panic. That these bourgeois gentlemen favored a peaceful policy of commercial collaboration in the Balkans and beyond was of little interest to Austria-Hungary's political masters; wider political opinion mattered even less so long as it did not disrupt the empire's stability.[11]

Alois Count Lexa von Aehrenthal served as Austro-Hungarian Foreign Minister until his death in late 1912 and had annexed Bosnia-Herzegovina in October 1908. Despite his expansionist Balkan policy and despite his willingness to push things to the brink, Aehrenthal possessed considerable finesse, transferred "decisions over war and peace to his opponents,"[12] and in so doing had managed to avert war alto-gether. A coterie of younger diplomats at the Ballhausplatz had cut their teeth under Aehrenthal's guidance and identified with his longer term program of Habsburg dominance in the Balkans. However, when Berchtold succeeded Aehrenthal, he initially favored a more consensual approach through the tried and tested medium of the Concert of Europe. Berchtold had previously been posted to St Petersburg, where, in 1908, he experienced Russian fury over Aehrenthal's unilateral annexation of Bosnia and Herzegovina at first hand. However, although firmly committed to the Concert of Europe and despite a German ultimatum to Russia in 1909 in support of Vienna, he subsequently became dismayed at the German indifference to Austria-Hungary's vital interests, and even more so at the failure of the Concert to resolve the Balkan crises in a manner and on terms acceptable to the Habsburg Empire. With his country neglected by its fair-weather friends and ill served by wider European diplomacy, Berchtold fell increasingly under the influence of Aehrenthal's protégés, who remained committed to a forward foreign policy, but lacked their mentor's subtle touch. The death of Franz Ferdinand touched Berchtold personally, compounding his sense of despair and wiping away any remaining ability or even desire to counsel moderation.

As war fever swept the Ballhausplatz, Berchtold redrafted the Matschenko Memorandum, transforming it into a case for immediate hostilities against Serbia. Rumors spread, prompting the German ambassador to Vienna to warn Berlin on 30 June: "Here I often hear even serious people expressing the wish that Serbia ... be sorted out once and for all."[13] On July 5 the redrafted memorandum was delivered to Berlin in person by the Austro-Hungarian Chef de Cabinet, Count Alexander Hoyos, and this time his German counterparts did not disappoint. Berlin not only offered unqualified support, but urged Vienna to move swiftly against Serbia (of which more later). This was hugely significant, for the Austro-Hungarians at best feared and at worst expected that this time Russia would back Serbia. Vocal German support promised to hold back the Russians, and it has been argued that had Berlin vetoed the whole adventure at this critical point a European war would have been averted.

However that still begs the question of what Vienna would have done even without Berlin's blessing. Immediately after the war the former Habsburg diplomat Count Andrian-Werburg conceded that: "We started the war, not the Germans and even less the Entente – that I know. ... I myself was in lively agreement with the basic idea that only a war could save Austria."[14] Historians of the Habsburg Empire largely agree, with Evans observing that: "Vienna was certainly not waiting for instructions; indeed, the Habsburg capital exhibited a rare harmony of its military and civil leadership,"[15] or as Fellner remarks: "The will to this third Balkan War dominated the thoughts and actions of Austrian politicians and military men."[16] Ironically, the very assassination of Franz Ferdinand had not merely provided the pretext for war, but also removed from Austrian public life the figure most likely to oppose such a strategy.

Following Hoyos's return from Berlin, the Austro-Hungarian Cabinet met on 7 July to finalize its strategy, and despite serious and sustained misgivings on the part of the Hungarian Minister President, Count Tisza, it decided for war. No one professed to have any faith in future Serbian assurances, for those given after the 1908 Bosnian crisis had now been broken. Radical newspapers in Belgrade had already praised Princip as a martyr, highlighted Habsburg oppression in Bosnia, and deplored the stupidity of Franz Ferdinand in visiting Sarajevo on Vivovdan, of all days, which hardly served to lighten the mood in the Austro-Hungarian capital. Immediately after the Cabinet meeting Berchtold warned the ambassador to Belgrade, Baron von Giesl, that an ultimatum would be prepared and that: "However the Serbs react to [it], you must break off relations and it must come to war."[17] However, in Fellner's estimation there was a grotesque mismatch between Austro-Hungarian belligerence and its actual military preparedness, forcing the Chief of the General Staff, von Hötzendorf, to "beg for at least three weeks' grace in order to take the necessary mobilisation measures."[18] This rendered obsolete Berlin's call on July 5 for swift action, which had been designed to present Europe with a fait accompli and thus resolve the crisis. In the event it was a good fortnight later, on July 23, that the ultimatum (painstakingly designed to be rejected) was finally dispatched. The Serbian reply of July 25 was conciliatory, but "in fact still full of reservations,"[19] for Belgrade had already begun to mobilize and was prepared to run the risk of a localized war rather than return to its pre-1903 status as an Austrian satellite. Serbia had appealed to Russia for help on July 23, but the first material evidence that St Petersburg might support Belgrade militarily only came after the ultimatum had run its course. The Serbian government moved from Belgrade (on the frontier with Austria-Hungary) to Nis, while von Giesl left Belgrade for Vienna as soon as he had presented the ultimatum.

On July 27 Berchtold urged the Emperor to declare war without delay, explaining that it was "not impossible that the Triple Entente Powers might yet try to achieve a peaceful solution of the conflict unless a clear situation is created by a declaration of war."[20] The stage fright exhibited in other major European capitals during these final, fateful days appears to have been altogether lacking in Vienna, with the Austro-Hungarian declaration of war following on July 28. A day later Habsburg forces bombarded Belgrade even though any effective military action was untenable before mid-August. Neither side was blind to the potential international ramifications of their collision course, but Austrian fatalism and Serbian pan-Slavonic ambition drove them to accept these risks, however they might crystallize over the coming days or weeks.

2.2 Why the War Need Not Have Spread

Given that the initial, regional conflict involved Austria-Hungary and Serbia, its spread assumed a seemingly curious pattern.[21] Between August 1 and 4 Germany plunged into war against the Triple Entente of Russia, France, and Britain, with hostilities between Austria-Hungary and the Entente powers only following a week or two later. A. J. P. Taylor once described this wider conflict as the first German war, and whatever its name, Germany is almost invariably regarded as the key player. It was Germany that defeated Russia and imposed a punitive peace on the nascent Soviet Union in 1918; it was the German army that fought the great set-piece battles on the western front and was ultimately defeated there by France, Britain and the USA. Thereafter it is the November 1918 armistice with Germany and the subsequent treaty between Germany and the Allies, signed at Versailles in 1919, which remain fixed in the collective popular and institutional memory and dominate the histories of the period. And Britain for one went to war not to uphold Serbian rights, nor would it ever have done so, but because the Prime Minister and Foreign Secretary of the day were not prepared to see France defeated and subordinated by Germany.

Many historians, therefore, tend to see the Balkans crisis, and particularly the murder of Franz Ferdinand, as incidental, serving as a pretext for wider European or even global conflict that had very different roots from the forces that drove Austria-Hungary and Serbia to war. Hostilities on the grand scale invite comparably grandiose explanations, in this case all the more so given that the origins of the even more devastating 1939–45 war lay partly in this earlier Great War. Capitalism, imperialism, the European alliance system, the arms race, autocracy, or antagonistic relations between different European powers have variously been held to blame. Following the seminal publications of a German historian, Fritz Fischer, in the 1960s and 1970s,[22] attention focused on Germany. The very course of German history, the character of Germany's leadership, of its government and institutions, came to dominate the debate (to the exclusion, some complained, of much else). All of this might appear to leave consideration of any factors that militated against the outbreak of hostilities superfluous at best, but the history of prewar Europe involved more than a conscious or unconscious march to war. The continent was home to many optimists in 1914 and a brief consideration of the case against a wider conflict pays fuller justice to the history of the time, and also offers certain insights into the broader pattern of the twentieth-century European story.

In June 1913, just weeks before his own death, the eminent German Social Democrat August Bebel assured the Second [Socialist] International that the prospects for peace were excellent. No doubt the Bern Meeting of May 1913 was at the back of his mind, when 214 French and German parliamentarians, mostly socialists, had met in the Swiss capital. General declarations of goodwill were followed in November by a joint meeting of the same group in Germany's Reichstag, where they agreed to form a standing committee to work for continued peaceful relations between France and Germany. Little of substance followed, but increasingly close relations had developed within the Second International between the mighty Social Democratic Party of Germany (SPD) and the newly formed (1905) French Section of the Workers' International (SFIO) or French Socialist Party, led by Jean Jaurès.

However, Bebel's optimism had different roots, given that neither in France and still less in Germany did the socialists make foreign policy. Indeed the German constitution explicitly excluded the elected house of parliament, the Reichstag, let alone its socialist members, from determining the country's external relations. That was a matter for the Kaiser and his ministers, the latter not members of the Reichstag. Furthermore, despite vague talk of strikes to prevent any effective mobilization, the International had not managed to articulate any concrete strategy for avoiding a future war, in part to avoid trespassing on national prerogatives and in part because Europe's socialists were, at the end of the day, staunch advocates of a defensive patriotism. It was even suggested by one French delegate (although the notion was repudiated by Jaurès) that the SPD had gone further and bought into the German government's imperialist goals.

Thus Bebel was looking elsewhere, concluding that: "The greatest guarantee for the preservation of the world today is found in the international investments of capitalism."[23] This would have surprised the Russian Bolshevik leader, Vladimir Ilyich Lenin, who in 1916 was to conclude that imperialism, and (as he saw it) the resulting Great War, represented the highest stage of capitalism. Lenin's analysis owed much to an earlier, non-Marxist British work, J. A. Hobson's *Imperialism*,[24] and whatever the historical validity of either analysis, imperialism was widely perceived as a major threat in 1913. Examples there were aplenty, for the war between Britain and the Boer Republics, Russian ambitions in Asia, German resentment at arriving too late at the imperialist feast, and a series of crises in North Africa with French involvement the common denominator had contributed significantly to international tension from the 1880s onward. Germany's burgeoning economic power also provoked hostile reactions from its continental neighbors, whether from France, or from Russia which by 1914 particularly resented Germany's dominant role in its external trade. Much of the resulting angst could be found in Britain where, Paul Kennedy notes, a Social Darwinistic attitude to international economic relations prevailed in prewar political circles. International prowess and internal economic dynamism were regarded as synonymous, with the British Conservative politician Leo Amery commenting: "Those people who have the industrial power and the power of invention and science will be able to defeat all others."[25] Britain, Kennedy observes, had indeed dominated the entire global economy during the earlier nineteenth century, but the race for colonies during the latter half of the century had left it with formal economic and political control over just a quarter of the globe, "which was not a good bargain, despite the continued array of fresh acquisitions to Queen Victoria's dominions."[26]

Politicians and businessmen unwittingly betrayed Britain's relative economic decline when lamenting the allegedly nefarious practices adopted by German competitors in the British home market, and also the German economy's growing global reach. However, complaining was one thing and fighting quite another, for British businessmen understood that the country would suffer devastating material losses in any major European conflict and regarded such a possibility with deep foreboding. The writer Ralf Lane (alias Norman Angell) depicted the economic and financial devastation that any conflict would bring, predicting that under the circumstances war was sustainable for nine months at most.[27] For its part the British financial community feared instability above all else, given its considerable exposure to international debtors and creditors who might default on their debts or repatriate their assets at the first hint of serious trouble. The Bank of England itself was similarly concerned for it functioned as the linchpin of the global financial system, and such was the confidence in its creditworthiness that the Bank had never troubled to hold sufficient gold to cover its liabilities. However, were the threat of war to trigger panicky withdrawals by French and German banks, among others, Britain's finances would be crippled as the Bank's limited supplies of gold were quickly exhausted. As for trade, a quarter of British imports came from Germany and the Baltic, leading official committees of enquiry to conclude in 1911 and 1912 that in a prolonged German war, this trade might have to be resumed to keep the economy going. (No one thought to ask if Berlin would prove so altruistic in these circumstances.) Then there were domestic tensions. A series of major industrial strikes in Britain and an ominous stand-off between nationalists and unionists in Ireland over the issue of Home Rule further convinced government ministers that war could only add to their problems. In 1913 it was agreed that 6,000 regular troops would remain at home to guard key buildings in wartime and 5,000 rifles were reserved for police use. Thus John Morley subsequently remarked in Cabinet on August 2, 1914: "The atmosphere of war cannot be friendly to order, in a democratic system that is verging on the humour of 1848."[28] Governments elsewhere in Europe were similarly uneasy and contemplated the mass arrest of political radicals and other troublemakers should hostilities break out.

Further to these practicalities, British economic life was underpinned ideologically by classical economic liberalism, which had little time for military adventure. Few in Britain would have argued against the maintenance of a powerful navy, given the country's global commitments, but nonetheless the eighteenth-century Scottish political economist Adam Smith had regarded the military as little more than "menial servants" who, lacking any productive role, needed to be maintained at the "lowest level commensurate with national safety."[29] His nineteenth-century English counterpart, John Stuart Mill, went further, arguing that commerce between nations would in any case render war obsolete.[30] For sure a body of very different, early twentieth-century literature accompanied a spy mania as British authors imagined a future German–British confrontation, among which Erskine Childers' *The Riddle of the Sands* is possibly the most famous.[31] Some authors even feared a British defeat, with Ernest Oldmeadow imagining "the Germans wooing their new vassals with universal Christmas gifts and subsidised food. Indeed, the worst atrocities … are the introduction of a diet of sausages and sauerkraut, the correct spelling of Handel's name in concert programmes and Home Rule for Ireland."[32] However, others, including the satirical magazine *Punch*, lampooned this war and spy scare literature, and authors such as H. G. Wells came out against any conflict. And when it came to substantive personal and cultural ties, British society remained closely linked to that of Germany, as witnessed among other things by the German students attending Oxford University in early 1914, or by the connections and intermarriage between British and German middle- and upper-class families. The Anglo-German Schlegel family of E. M. Forster's novel *Howards End*, while obviously fictitious, would not have appeared exceptional to his readers, for as Richard Cobb observes, such liaisons "were much commoner and apparently more generally acceptable than Anglo-French ones" before the 1914 war.[33]

Turning to the continent, such intimate cultural or social links scarcely existed between France and Germany, for the latter's victory in the 1870–1 Franco-Prussian War had left its legacy. National stereotyping was common even in educated circles, with many in France perceiving the German monarchy as inherently bellicose, while Germans feared that their French neighbors remained fixated on revenge for defeat and for the loss of Alsace and northeastern Lorraine to Germany after a century or more of French rule. France's humiliation at the hands of Prussia had certainly left deep wounds, encapsulated in Edouard Detaille's painting, *Le Rêve* (the dream). Finished in 1888, the work depicts French soldiers billeted and asleep at night while on maneuvers, as a ghostly dream-like form of Napoleon's all-conquering Grande Armée sweeps irresistibly across the heavens, banners flying, offering the vision of renewed and restored national glory.[34] "Incidents," involving the likes of hapless lost balloonists or travelers suspected of spying, continued to punctuate the course of relations in the Franco-German borderlands, but that said, the passage of time witnessed a growing acceptance by French opinion that Alsace in particular had lost any real interest in returning to France. The constitutional settlement of May 1911, which granted the provinces greater autonomy within Germany and established a state parliament (Landtag) in Strassburg, appeared to mark the way forward. The French historian Charles Sancerme observed in 1913 that the Alsace, or "das Elsass" as it called itself, had effectively abandoned protest against annexation, instead seeking integration within Germany. "In truth," he remarked, "a protest against its race and real fatherland simply could not go on forever, and furthermore would not even be natural." The future, Sancerme continued, lay in a Franco-German entente which would include an autonomous, but German, Alsace-Lorraine / Elsass-Lothringen as part of the accord.[35]

With the climate easing, some 80,000 Germans had come to reside in Paris before the war, reciprocated by a smaller French presence in Berlin, and complemented by a limited volume of tourism in each direction. Beyond this, the aristocracies of the two countries were interrelated to a degree. During his visit to St Petersburg in July 1914, the French President, Raymond Poincaré, found time to chat with the German ambassador to Russia, Count Friedrich von Pourtalès: "He asked him about the French origins of his family, his wife's relationship to the Castellanes [family], a motor tour which the Count and Countess were proposing to make through Provence and particularly Castellane etc. Not a word about politics," as the

French ambassador recorded in his diary.[36] This conversation, like much of the correspondence between French and German grandees, was conducted in French, still at that time the official diplomatic language and lingua franca of European high society, but it was heavy industry and commerce rather than blood ties or culture that lay at the heart of Franco-German relations before 1914.

In April 1911 the German trade attaché in Paris, Otto Weber, detailed the growing collaboration between the great industrial houses of both nations, their increasing reliance on joint funding initiatives, and concluded that these "companies are delighted at the success of their cooperative ventures."[37] Weber foresaw the day when a united Franco-German metallurgical industry, under German leadership, would take on its North American rivals for dominance in global markets, a notion echoed by the liberally inclined commercial lobbyists of the Hansabund when they advocated closer European cooperation to "enable us and our neighboring countries to safeguard our export markets in competition with extra-European states."[38] The electrical engineering magnate Walther Rathenau similarly advocated a broad central European trading bloc, located within a multilateral global economy, to compensate for Germany's lack of raw materials.[39] Individual German firms were in reality far too busy fighting each other for positions in the French market to unite behind a coherent geopolitical agenda, but egotistical interests did serve to fashion an internationally integrated Franco-German economy by default in which "the process of cooperation rapidly create[d] a situation through which, if one of the two parties is to survive, both must survive; if one perishes, both perish."[40]

The explosive growth of heavy industry in western Germany, most notably in the Ruhr District, the Saarland, and Lothringen (German Lorraine) lay at the heart of this relationship. From 1897 Germany became a net importer of iron ore and individual firms sought to avoid overdependence on existing Swedish suppliers by turning to their western neighbor. Thus in 1900 just 2 percent of German ore was sourced from France, but by early 1914 this proportion had grown to almost a third. The Ruhr steel baron August Thyssen, for one, therefore began to seek out French iron ore fields, in part to serve his huge new blast furnaces at Hagendingen, which stood within a stone's throw of the Franco-German frontier. Thyssen's corporate operations in France extended from the Briey iron ore fields, from where Hagendingen was supplied by an overhead cable railway, to ore fields and smelters south of Cherbourg in Normandy. Thyssen was aware that a symbiotic relationship was developing between France with its rich deposits of iron ore and Germany with its unrivaled deposits of coking coal (vital in the production of steel) and hoped that this would evolve into a European trading economy free from the distractions of national-political rivalries. His French subsidiaries operated under the chairmanship of a Frenchman, Louis de Chatelier, and of de Chatelier's seven directors a maximum of three were Germans from Thyssen itself, the remainder French. This politically astute balancing act was sufficient to reassure the French government that the resulting operation was of private and commercial significance rather than posing any strategic threat, but Thyssen (no doubt with an eye to future profits) aspired to more than this. These collaborative ventures, he hoped, might serve as "the foundation stone of a lasting accord and contribute to the improvement of relations between our two countries,"[41] while his son, Fritz, speaking in Normandy in 1912, similarly hoped that Franco-German economic integration would render war between the two former enemies obsolete. The French nationalist author Louis Bruneau was sufficiently convinced of Thyssen's bona fides to conclude that: "One must grant each activity ... its due and so recognize with complete justice that M. Thyssen's are truly prodigious."[42] Thyssen's French ventures were matched by those of Emil Kirdorf's Gelsenkirchener Mining Company, Paul Reusch's Gutehoffnungshütte (metallurgy), and Hugo Stinnes's Deutsch-Lux (metallurgy) which acquired iron ore holdings in French Lorraine and Normandy, as well as in Luxembourg. The German chemical giants had similarly acquired a significant presence in France through a network of subsidiaries.

Efforts followed by German companies to obtain listings on the Paris bourse, as well as to establish a German chamber of commerce in the French capital. The newspapers *Echo de Paris* and *Le Temps* led a press campaign against these moves, while the French ambassador to London, Paul Cambon, fulminated: "They will take our money, but will remain our enemies."[43] Oblivious to all of this, it seems, French consumers continued to snap up German imports as trade between the two neighbors grew by over 50 percent between 1907 and 1913. However, this trading relationship was less one-sided than its French critics assumed, for by 1912 Germany constituted France's third largest export market and a similar reciprocity applied to wider economic relations. In comparison to France or Britain, Germany had relatively modest volumes of capital at its disposal for overseas investment, thus necessitating the use of French banking houses to fund German investments in France to the tune of 16 billion francs. The servicing of these loans, of course, saw a proportion of German company earnings flow into the coffers of the French financial sector. Furthermore, French industrialists did not pass up the opportunity to invest in Germany and therefore regarded any protectionist or Germanophobic outbursts with deep suspicion. The Comité des Forges de France (metallurgy) dismissed the anti-German press campaign as "the impact of an exaggerated nationalism,"[44] and joined with the Comité des Houillères de France (coal mining) to oppose any government regulation of foreign participation in French industry. Despite some mutual Franco-German economic sanctions in the wake of the Moroccan crises (1905 and 1911), French businesses contrasted the French government's protectionist attitude with the more liberal (and for them preferable) character of the Prussian law of June 1909. Among them was the glass manufacturer St Gobain which had built up a significant holding in Germany. Given their community of interest with German counterparts within a plethora of international consortia, French companies were particularly fearful that their own government's protectionist instincts might provoke comparable countermeasures abroad.

In this regard, high quality coal was the most valuable commodity Germany had on offer. France was becoming increasingly reliant on its eastern neighbor for supplies of hard coal to the point where a rumor did the rounds that France's great eastern border fortresses depended on German coal deliveries to remain operational. Furthermore, by 1913 the French metallurgical industry was almost entirely dependent on the Ruhr District for coke, leading soon enough to French investment in this prime industrial region of Germany. Much of this activity involved the huge, but family-owned de Wendel metallurgical combine, which found itself in a particularly ambivalent position after the 1870 Franco-Prussian war. The revised Franco-German frontier ran (inadvertently) through the very middle of the company's operations in Lorraine, complicating enormously the issue of patriotic loyalty for this staunchly French family. Thus one of the founder's grandsons (Robert) took German nationality, while family members sat in the Reichstag and the French National Assembly respectively. The German authorities looked on the company's largely Francophile politics with some suspicion, but did nothing to hinder the expanding and largely excellent relations between de Wendel and its German counterparts. As massive consumers of coking coal, therefore, the de Wendels extended their operations into the Ruhr and Westphalia, and cooperated there with German companies in various infrastructural schemes, prompting the French journalist Auguste Pawlowski to conclude: "We have interests in German mines. The Germans have the same in French mines. What could be fairer?"[45] Nothing, it would seem, leading Walther Rathenau to write to Chancellor Bethmann-Hollweg shortly after the outbreak of war to urge a speedy and conciliatory peace with France, for "occupation and the transfer of property in France would, in Rathenau's opinion, be more trouble than they were worth."[46]

This Franco-German nexus, which included a new commercial treaty in 1911, appears particularly poignant given the desolate state of affairs from 1914 onward, but German business interests of a comparable kind had been established in most parts of Europe. Thus Hugo Stinnes's ventures extended beyond his investments in Luxembourg and France to include a much wider global network of shipping, mining and electrical generation interests, reaching from the Americas, through Britain, to Russia and the Middle East. His metallurgical and engineering ventures may have profited from Germany's armaments program, but Stinnes remained unconvinced about such business, resenting the damage done to German competitiveness on international markets by the fiscal demands of the government's naval program in particular. The Hamburg banker Max Warburg was among prominent businessmen who expressed similar concerns, contrasting France and Britain's fiscal strength with Germany's fiscal and financial weakness, which led in turn to excessive and potentially ruinous government borrowing. And war itself posed unacceptable risks for the likes of Stinnes, prompting him in 1911 to lecture the leader of the imperialistic and belligerent Pan German League, Heinrich Class, on its futility. Germany's future lay in its economic rather than its military power, Stinnes insisted, explaining that he employed foreigners to front his growing network of overseas operations, among which his Welsh coal mine supplied the Royal Navy and also exported coal to Italy on British ships flying the German flag. Little had changed in 1913, when he took the opportunity to buy up further mining interests in Yorkshire and Nottinghamshire, and in April 1914 Stinnes regarded the business potential of Serbia and Bulgaria as inviting. A decade of peace in the Balkans beckoned, or so he believed. In July 1914 he observed anxiously that war would constitute "an immense financial and economic catastrophe with dangerous social possibilities,"[47] and must have been greatly reassured when his son wrote to him from London on July 22 that British–German relations were on the mend.

Turning to the European powers' imperialist adventures, a series of crises, and also the Russo-Japanese War of 1904–5 over territory in northeastern China and Korea, had defined relations around the turn of the century. In 1898 French and British forces had come close to conflict over control of the southern Sudan (the Fashoda incident), while relations were tense on the boundaries between the British and Russian empires from east to west across the length of Asia. The British attack on the South African Boer Republics and the ensuing Boer War (1899–1902) caused outrage throughout continental Europe, while shortly thereafter in 1905 and 1911 French encroachments on Moroccan sovereignty prompted ill-advised German countermeasures that appeared to threaten the peace of Europe itself.

In the event, however, the European powers invariably sought to mediate colonial disputes rather than resort to force of arms, leading to a situation by 1914 where major disagreements had either been resolved, or set aside. The Fashoda incident, for example, initially led France and Britain separately to consider reaching some form of agreement with Germany, but thoughts quickly turned to mending fences with each other. Commercial relations had been flourishing for some years, and successful visits by Edward VII to Paris in May 1903 and the French President Loubert, Prime Minister Delcassé and Colonial Minister Étienne to London in July were followed by a series of colonial arbitration agreements. The resulting Entente Cordiale of April 1904 regulated spheres of influence in Southeast Asia, off Newfoundland, and across the northern half of the African continent where, in secret clauses, France was given the green light in Morocco in return for Spain acquiring the north coast of that country and for Britain gaining a free hand in Egypt. Thus Fashoda, far from precipitating war, had led swiftly to a far-reaching Franco-British rapprochement. As the Quai d'Orsay (French Foreign Ministry) appreciated (and as we shall see), this promised to draw Britain into continental power rivalries by ranging it alongside France and so against Germany. Few in Britain appreciated this in 1904, but the anti-German dimension of the Entente was strengthened by the conclusion of the Russo-British Entente of 1907 which, on the face of it, merely regulated colonial disputes between the signatories.

The two Moroccan Crises marked the nadir of relations between the European great powers in the years preceding the Great War. Morocco was an independent state in the northwest corner of Africa, from which Europe (Spain) was visible across the Strait of Gibraltar on a fine day. Its public finances and internal stability left something to be desired, but mineral wealth, trade and agriculture offered foreign investors possibilities and an "open door" approach to commercial dealings and trade with Morocco had therefore been agreed between the European powers. France, however, had already annexed neighboring Algeria and Tunisia and now sought to extend its dominions westward to Morocco's Atlantic coast. Italy had resented France's seizure of Tunisia in 1881, but in 1899 Delcassé offered Rome commercial privileges in Tunisia and in 1900 a free hand in the Ottoman province of Tripoli (Libya) if France, implicitly, was allowed a free hand in Morocco. Italy concurred and Paris obtained further reassurances from Rome in November 1902. Meanwhile Delcassé had in secret agreed provisionally with his Spanish counter-part a partition of Morocco in October 1902 which offered Spain the north coast and France the remainder of the country.

The desolate finances of the Sultan of Morocco did the rest. During 1903 and 1904 substantial French loans were advanced to his government, the latter under French supervision and administration and bearing a heavy burden of interest payable over 36 years. With a French foot now firmly wedged in the Moroccan door, Madrid and Paris formalized their partition agreement on October 3, 1904, by which time German suspicions had been aroused. Although Delcassé had been careful to offer Spain, Britain and Italy compensation, he had neglected even to keep Berlin informed, yet in 1904 Germany conducted over 11 percent of Morocco's foreign trade (as against France's 30 percent) and was the second ship-ping power in the Sultanate, after Britain. After lengthy deliberation, the German authorities decided to make a gesture of support for the Sultan. The Kaiser had planned to spend April 1905 at his private villa on Corfu and was persuaded against his better judgment by Chancellor Bülow to land briefly at Tangier. Bülow, however, had urged the Kaiser to be noncommittal, instead of which the latter, always impetuous when discretion should have formed the better part of valor, blurted out his support for Moroccan independence and insisted that an open door trading policy be maintained. A year and a half of stormy diplomacy followed before the matter was settled at the Algeciras Conference of January 1906. The United States had shown a limited degree of sympathy toward Germany, with President Roosevelt later speaking of that "unbelievable scamp" Delcassé,[48] and on June 6, 1905 the French Premier, Maurice Rouvier, responded to German pressure by removing Delcassé from the Foreign Ministry. However, the British authorities took exception to Germany's bluster, which was intended in part to destabilize the recently concluded Anglo-French Entente by exposing its ineffectiveness in time of crisis. Edward VII made a further visit to Paris in May 1905 to demonstrate his government's support and at Algeciras Britain was among the clear majority of powers that supported the French position. Germany had landed a few blows, but France, as Frederick Schuman once observed, had now indeed drawn Britain into continental politics and so "terminated the diplomatic hegemony of Germany and ... created a coalition which could defy the Triple Alliance."[49]

Matters took a further turn for the worse in April 1911 when Paris intervened directly in Moroccan disturbances by occupying the cities of Rabat and Fez and invoking the partition agreement with Spain. The German Foreign Minister, Alfred von Kiderlen-Wächter, responded in July 1911 by sending the ageing gunboat *Panther* to Agadir as a marker of Germany's interests in the region, only to trigger a major crisis between the European powers themselves. The British Chancellor of the Exchequer, David Lloyd George, warned Germany in his Mansion House speech of July 22 that Britain would stand by France, provoking a strident German press campaign against him. The Pan German League and, more significantly, the Chief of the German General Staff, Count Hellmuth von Moltke, were happy to contemplate war, but the Kaiser and Chancellor Bethmann-Hollweg were not. Nor were France's political leaders, who were advised by their military commander, General Joffre, that a war with Germany offered less than a 70 percent chance of success. In November 1911, therefore, Berlin accepted French and Spanish control of Morocco (formalized in 1912), but received in return 100,000 square miles of the French Congo, adjoining the existing German colony of Kamerun.

At first sight the Moroccan crises intimated a gathering storm in European diplomacy, for their eventual resolution had been reached at the price of deteriorating international relations, of aroused public opinion in France, Britain and Germany, and of an ongoing French mistrust over the unpredictability of German foreign policy. However, the French ambassador to Berlin, Jules Cambon, while personally offended by the precipitate nature of the *Panthersprung*, as the dispatch of the wooden-hulled *Panther* was colorfully dubbed, nonetheless enjoyed excellent personal relations with Kiderlen-Wächter which, ironically, had been forged during the resolution of the first Moroccan crisis. Now, as Cambon and Kiderlen turned their attention to the second confrontation, it quickly became clear that the German government had no territorial ambitions in Morocco and that it was prepared to accept a slice of the French Congo in lieu of gains in North Africa. Cambon was acting on instructions from his Prime Minister, Joseph Caillaux, who had proposed "a general discussion in order to eliminate the greatest possible number of difficulties that currently divide us and Germany on various parts of the globe."[50] The resulting deal, which confirmed French preeminence in Morocco and the extension of German territory in central Africa without war, indicated that Berlin and Paris had indeed resolved peacefully the most pressing issues that divided them well before the crisis of July 1914. Cambon and Kiderlen-Wächter evidently believed as much, exchanging inscribed personal photographs after the dust had settled, on which Kiderlen had inscribed: "Au terrible adversaire et charmant ami," provoking Cambon to respond with added finesse: "Au charmant adversaire et terrible ami."[51]

The ensuing pattern of developments in Africa lent substance to this spirit of guarded optimism. The transfer of the northeastern French Congo to German Kamerun affected many French trading companies, which now found their operations divided by the new frontier. However, an elegant compromise was reached in September 1912, by which firms retained their (French) integrity, but established a

German-registered subsidiary to accommodate the new political circumstances. Further mutual trading companies were created and the joint construction of a central African railway was mooted as France afforded Germany further opportunities for colonial development without the need for war. Both countries also discussed the future of central Africa individually with Britain, believing that there were clearly ample resources and wealth in the region to go around. Berlin had willingly resolved outstanding differences with France, but regarded the Anglo-German talks more positively, even hoping they would lead to a general rapprochement with London. There were some grounds for hope for, as the British Foreign Secretary, Sir Edward Grey, commented in 1911, it did not "matter very much whether we ha[d] Germany or France as a neighbour in Africa," declaring himself keen to partition the Portuguese empire "in a pro-German spirit."[52] The other potential loser in this economic and civilizatory project (as it was perceived) was little Belgium, whose vast colonial territories in the Congo basin constituted an inconvenient obstacle to the full realization of Franco-German and German-British ambitions.

Private and quasi-official financial and commercial cooperation developed between the great imperial powers beyond Africa. Even in the Balkans, where foreign policy rivalry restricted international financial collaboration, private Franco-German initiatives raised loans for various governments, including that of Serbia. In China an international consortium of the major European powers, Japan and the USA emerged following the 1911–12 Revolution, despite France's problems in reconciling close financial cooperation with Germany in the Far East with its political obligations to its alliance partner Russia. The community of European financial interests was particularly pronounced in the Ottoman Empire, whose public debt was administered by a consortium of Turkish, French, British, German, Italian and Austro-Hungarian representatives. Almost half of the debt itself was in French, and a fifth in German hands. When Russia tried to join the consortium in 1912, France opposed the move, for while Russian involvement might have served to contain German political influence in the Ottoman Empire, Paris regarded the existing, congruent French and German commercial interests as more significant. Similarly, Austrian, German, French and British banks cooperated in administering the Turkish state tobacco monopoly, despite periodic political and military tensions between the Triple Entente and the Triple Alliance.

Public debt aside, the "Berlin to Baghdad" railway came to symbolize Berlin's ambitions in the Near and Middle East, but in reality German financiers, with much of their money tied up domestically, could not or would not put up the necessary capital to monopolize this vast and complex project. In 1899, for example, the Deutsche Bank had won the concession to build the Anatolian section of the railway from the Ottoman government, but offered the Franco-British Banque Ottomane a 40 percent interest in the project, which was followed in 1903 by Swiss, Italian, and Austrian involvement. France and Germany quarreled briefly during mid-1913 over arrangements for a French-controlled spur running from the main line into Syria, but matters were quickly resolved, for Paris regarded the accommodation of German interests in Turkey as a means of diverting Berlin's ambitions away from Europe itself. There were striking parallels with the successful Kamerun-Congo negotiations, prompting the French press to interpret the Syrian railway agreement as evidence of a wider improvement in Franco-German relations. In June 1914 a comparable deal was struck between Berlin and London which provided for an extension of the railway from Baghdad to the Gulf port of Basra, under British control. All in all, the Turkish railways project had ultimately served to reconcile the imperial ambitions of Europe's major powers, for Germany had secured a significant outlet for its global political ambitions (*Weltpolitik*), France was assured a major role in Syria, and British interests in the Persian Gulf had been accommodated. When the German military stressed the strategic dimension of the Baghdad railway, the German ambassador to Constantinople countered that its rationale was economic and its function to promote great-power détente.[53] Further initiatives during 1914 included the founding of the Constantinople Consortium in June to finance Constantinople's new metro with French, German, Belgian and Swiss participation.

Until 1914, therefore, each European crisis was resolved in turn. Conscious efforts were made both to remove any grounds for confrontation and, more positively, to promote long-term cooperative ventures in their place. Franco-German relations were at their poorest during the Second Moroccan Crisis, but, as with all imperial disputes, were resolved through a combination of territorial demarcation and commercial accommodation. By 1913 Anglo-German relations were similarly on the mend, prompting the *Frankfurter Zeitung* to write in October of "a better understanding between the governing minds in both countries … [an] end to the sterile years of mutual distrust."[54] Similarly, on July 23, 1914, Lloyd George was able to welcome the considerable improvement in relations between the two countries, concluding that "the points of cooperation are greater and more numerous and more important than the points of possible controversy."[55] Yet, leaving aside the wisdom of hindsight, France, Britain, and also Russia were at war with Germany barely a fortnight later.

2.3 Why the War Spread

Photographs show enthusiastic urban crowds cheering their soldiers off to war, but a relatively small proportion of any city's population will make a good show for the cameras. In fact, most city-dwellers were at work or at home, while in the smaller towns and countryside that defined so much of Europe's social landscape mobilization may have proceeded smoothly enough, but also resignedly. Half a million people participated in antiwar demonstrations across Germany, while "stupefaction" and "surprise" typified the response in provincial France, where recorded instances of "weeping" and "desolation" outnumbered "enthusiasm" by a factor of three to one.[56] The (French) masses, Richard Cobb observes, accepted "if reluctantly the inevitability of war,"[57] but of widespread war fever there was little sign. Ordinary Russians, General Brusilov believed, knew and cared even less what the war was about: "Why any German should want to make war on us because of these Serbians, no one could say ... They had never heard of the ambitions of Germany; they did not even know that such a country existed."[58] None of this impeded the process of mobilization which, in Britain's case, saw the eventual recruitment of a volunteer army 2.5 million strong, but ultimately Europe's leaders had made their decisions for war without troubling to consult their people, and had thereafter sought their retrospective approval at best.

As if in anticipation of the carnage to come, accusation and counteraccusation flew almost immediately over "war guilt." Each power published sets of selected diplomatic documents during the opening months of the war, designed to vindicate its own conduct and condemn the enemy's. Not surprisingly, this dialogue of the deaf intensified further after the war, for the victors based important elements of the peace settlement on the assertion of German responsibility, while the Germans themselves strove to dispute this verdict and thereby undermine the legitimacy of the imposed peace settlement. We shall return to this interwar debate in due course, for its evolution helped among other things to create the moral basis for the appeasement during the 1930s of Hitler's government, but more recent research has done much to explain the genesis of the catastrophe of 1914. In this regard the contours of German foreign policy in the decades before 1914, and Germany's particular role during the July crisis are usually regarded as critical.

The German Empire was proclaimed in January 1871, ending centuries of acute political fragmentation in central Europe that had left the German-speaking lands prey to repeated foreign invasion and to French encroachment on their western frontier. German unification, driven by the Prussian Minister President, Otto von Bismarck, had come at an astonishingly small price, through relatively brief wars in which Prussian (and wider German) casualties were modest by earlier and later standards. The third and final war, sought by both sides, saw Germany triumph over France and impose a punitive peace on the defeated power, which included the enforced return of Alsace and northeastern Lorraine (the Moselle) to German rule. The unbridled joy of the liberal historian Heinrich von Sybel typified the mood in Germany as he wrote to his colleague Hermann Baumgarten in January 1871: "How have we so earned God's grace, enabling us to experience such great and powerful events? ... The substance of every hope and effort of the past twenty years has now been realized in such an immortally marvelous way!"[59] However, Bismarck for one realized that any potential reckoning may have been delayed, but not necessarily averted. Observers such as Benjamin Disraeli appreciated that a powerful Germany threatened to destabilize the continent, and fears of this sort demanded that Berlin reassure its various neighbors and neutralize potential French revanchism through a particularly skillful and circumspect foreign policy.

While Bismarck remained Chancellor (Prime Minister) of the new Germany and Wilhelm I became and remained Emperor this balancing act was, more or less, achieved. Berlin acquired a modest haul of African colonies during the mid-1880s, but scarcely challenged British and French preeminence in this department. On the continent itself tensions flared up intermittently between Berlin and Paris, while in southeastern Europe Austria-Hungary and Russia began to vie for preeminence as Turkish power waned. Since Vienna and St Petersburg were both allied to Berlin, Bismarck became engaged in some fancy footwork that enabled him to retain Austria-Hungary as Germany's premier ally (within the framework of the German–Austro-Hungarian–Italian Triple Alliance), yet reassure Russia that Germany entertained no aggressive designs in eastern Europe and would not support any war started there by Vienna. Historians agree that the death of Wilhelm I, and the accession to the throne of Wilhelm II, after a brief reign by his dying father, Friedrich III, marked a decisive turning point in German foreign policy. The younger, erratic Wilhelm was determined to establish a "personal government," independent of the hitherto dominant Chancellor. In March 1890 Bismarck was dismissed from office, receiving an honorary dukedom in return.

The pilot, as a cartoon in the British satirical magazine *Punch* observed, was leaving the ship and what followed drew savage criticism from Bismarck himself, first in the press and then in his memoirs. Germany's new leaders, Caprivi and Marschall, swiftly dispensed of Russia's friendship to promote their alliance with Austria-Hungary, thus contributing to the conclusion of the 1984 Franco-Russian military accord as effectively as anything Paris could offer St Petersburg. The German ambassador to Russia had feared as much, but his warnings fell on deaf ears in Berlin. Then, in 1897, the German Naval Minister, Admiral Alfred von Tirpitz, began work on a German battle fleet of 60 capital ships. At the outset Tirpitz intended his powerful navy to rally society behind the Emperor and the national flag and also, as Volker Berghahn observes, to lay "the foundation of an expansionist German foreign policy."[60] However, by 1905 this imperial strategy had assumed an explicitly anti-British flavor as the burgeoning German Navy sought to match the Royal Navy's home waters fleet and thereby dissuade Britain from obstructing Berlin's colonial ambitions. Beyond the obvious strategic implications, any such challenge touched on a British raw nerve, for many regarded the high seas themselves as a British imperial possession. The mood had been epitomized in an earlier painting (1880) by the artist John Brett which depicted the ocean, stretching serenely to a distant horizon, entitled *Britannia's Realm*.[61] London responded in 1906 with a naval program of its own, and thanks to Britain's centralized taxation system found it far easier to fund the resulting naval arms race than Berlin. In Germany the federal states, and not the central government, raised most of the taxes. Yet it was the German central government that had to pay for the ships and by 1912 Tirpitz had effectively lost the naval arms race at the cost of a marked deterioration in German–British relations and something of a crisis in German domestic and budgetary politics. Periodic efforts by both sides to call a formal halt to this arms race failed to secure any agreement, but in February 1913 Tirpitz accepted earlier British proposals for a 16:10 (British:German) ratio in battleships (Dreadnoughts). By January 1914 Winston Churchill felt confident that the naval race was over and believed that relations with Germany were on the mend. Just as Anglo-German colonial rivalry itself had largely fizzled out by 1914, so is it impossible to trace a red thread leading directly from the associated naval arms race to war.

That said, the naval race had proven anything but harmless, for it contributed (alongside the Moroccan adventures) to the emergence of the Triple Entente between France, Russia and Britain and then to its rapid transformation from a series of agreements over colonies into a de facto Franco-British defensive military alliance. From 1906 it was anticipated by an inner circle of the Prime Minister Herbert Asquith, Foreign Secretary Sir Edward Grey, and senior figures in the General Staff that the British army would fight alongside France in a future conti-nental war. By the autumn of 1911 plans had been elaborated and discussed with the French General Staff to the point where almost anyone in the know appreci-ated that in any future Franco-German war Britain was committed to intervene. This, however, remained something apart from any wish by London actually to start such a war, or from any expectation that France would attack Germany. On the contrary, it was consistently anticipated that any war in western Europe would result from a German assault on France.

This takes us back to the character of the 1894 Franco-Russian military agree-ment, whose existence (the details remained secret) did much to influence subse-quent German military planning and thus create in turn the preconditions for the conflagration of August 1914. Relations between Berlin and St Petersburg were already deteriorating during the later 1880s, with commercial tension, hostile press comment, and a major arms deal between France and Russia serving as straws in the wind. Poor personal relations between Tsar Alexander III and Wilhelm II did little to help, but the lapsing of the Russo-German Reinsurance Treaty in June 1890 and improving German–British relations marked the tipping point. The Russians in particular feared that Britain might at any moment join the German-dominated Triple Alliance. In May 1890 the Grand Duke Nicholas, Commander in Chief of the Russian army, initiated a regular exchange of military missions with France after successful talks in Paris with the French Minister of War, Charles de Freycinet. Thereafter, in August 1891, the two powers agreed to consult during any future European crisis and relentless French pressure contributed to the formal military agreement of 4 January 1894, despite the persistence of mutual suspicions up to the very last moment. This military accord committed Russia and France to joint mobilization should any member of the Triple Alliance mobilize for any reason, a supplementary agreement reached in 1899 provided for common action in the Balkans should Austria-Hungary break up, while in March 1902 provision was made for military cooperation in the Far East.

The ailing Russian Foreign Minister, Nikolai Karlovich Giers, had resisted the 1894 accord to the best of his ability, seeing in France's insistence on "immediate and simultaneous mobilization" the creation of a military alliance which promised to split the European community into hostile camps and so increase the likelihood of a major war.[62] However his master, Tsar Alexander, insisted that Russia had to "correct the mistakes of the past and destroy Germany at the first possible moment." When Giers asked what might be gained from such a strategy the Tsar replied "that Germany as such would disappear. It would break up into a number of small weak states, the way it used to be."[63] General Obruchev, the Russian military commander, concurred, and turning his thoughts to the practicalities of a future conflict concluded that in the modern technological age mobilization meant war. It was, therefore, crucial to mobilize first in order to strike the initial blow, and to do so without undue political interference at the moment of crisis, for, as Obruchev observed:

> At the outset of every European war there is always a great temptation for the diplomats to localize the conflict and limit its effects as far as possible. But in the present armed and agitated condition of continental Europe, Russia must regard any such localization of the war with particular skepticism.[64]

The proposed Franco-Russian military accord appeared to deliver precisely what Obruchev desired, for beyond a speedy mobilization the Russian commander was particularly concerned to prevent Germany remaining neutral in any Austro-Russian war. He noted that in 1878, after an earlier Balkans war, Bismarck was able to dictate terms at the Congress of Berlin, playing the neutral "honest broker" to Russia's disadvantage. Obruchev shuddered at the thought of a neutral Germany, backed by its 2 million bayonets, dictating terms after any future Austro-Russian conflict and in 1914 his successors were indeed rewarded with German involvement in a major European war.

Secrecy was built into the very terms of the Franco-Russian military convention. French negotiators had initially assumed that the agreement would be made public, but the Tsar feared that this could provoke a preemptive German attack. Knowledge of the convention was thus restricted on the French side to the Prime Minister, War Minister and President, with the Tsar warning that if the terms of the convention became public knowledge, then Russia would consider it annulled. Within absolutist Russia such secrecy was not a great problem, but even in republican, parliamentarian France these terms were observed to the letter. Whatever French public opinion might have made of all this, and the official Russian military visits to France at the time were extremely well received, France's elected representatives were never informed of the convention, nor offered the chance to debate its terms at any point before the outbreak of war in 1914.

If the details of the military convention remained secret, the wider Franco-Russian entente was general knowledge and no one seriously doubted the existence of some sort of military arrangement between Paris and St Petersburg. From the mid 1890s therefore, German military planning needed to factor in the probability that any French war of revenge for 1870 would bring with it a Russian attack on Germany. Thereafter, while the politicians, businessmen and diplomats of Europe proved capable of defusing a series of international quarrels and felt able in early 1914 to look to the future with guarded optimism, their military commanders eyed up enemy military capacity with a growing anxiety that periodically verged on paranoia. They refined their own plans, demanded ever greater resources of their governments, and came eventually to conclude that a war unleashed on their own terms would certainly be preferable to a war unleashed by their enemies.

Germany's military commanders understood very well the enormity of any future European war. Count Helmuth von Moltke (The Elder), who served as Chief of the Prussian General Staff from 1857 to 1891, had pioneered and institutionalized the concept of future-orientated war planning, based on the use of modern communications (railways) to mobilize and deploy armies of up to a million men. The 1864 war against Denmark and the 1866 war against Austria could be characterized as "industrialized cabinet war," based on "conscription and the skilful use of modern technology,"[65] but the 1870–1 Franco-Prussian War saw French republican leaders react to the defeat of Napoleon III's imperial army at Sedan with a *levée en masse* and a six months' "people's war" against the invading German armies. Charles de Freycinet, architect of the 1894 Franco-Russian military accord, played a prominent role in organizing this resistance. Prussia and its German allies prevailed, but only after a struggle that required 100,000 troops to protect lines of communication against guerrilla forces (*francs tireurs*), which in turn provoked German atrocities against French civilians. As Stig Förster observes, "the demon of an industrialised people's war began to raise its head," posing sociopolitical as well as military dangers for monarchist Germany in any future major conflict.[66] Even during the 1860s, Prussia's monarchy had balked at the prospect of its army coming under parliamentary control.[67] Few German military experts now had any illusion that a European war would be short. A war of annihilation, demanding the full mobilization of each side's resources, had replaced the chimera of rapid and decisive victory.

Moltke contemplated preemptive strikes against France (1875–6) and Russia (1887), but these proposals brought warnings from Britain and in 1875 Russia, and thus received short shrift from Bismarck. Thereafter Germany's Chief of Staff turned his thoughts to deterrence, with a country's armaments policy serving to avoid war altogether rather than to provoke it. If it were to come to war with France and Russia, Moltke favored a defensive strategy through which the German army would absorb any Franco-Russian offensive and then counterattack, against Russia, at an opportune moment. Such a strategy would have rendered the Franco-Russian alliance far less dangerous in 1914, for neither ally planned a first strike against Germany while the German army would have remained dug in along its lines of defense. Under such circumstances, with French (and also Belgian) territory inviolate, Britain would have remained neutral in the shorter term and the prospects for containing the crisis in the Balkans would have been altogether more favorable.

However, Moltke's successor, Alfred von Schlieffen, while agreeing with key parts of his predecessor's diagnosis, offered a very different prescription to resolve the challenges confronting Germany's military.

The prospect of a drawn-out war was unthinkable to Schlieffen, for it promised the ruin of the commerce and industry upon which Germany's future depended. Such ruin threatened to bring severe social and political dislocation in its wake, leading the new Chief of Staff to conclude that either a war had to be short, or it was futile, regardless of who eventually triumphed on the battlefield. Any campaign against Russia was unlikely to be brief, given the vast scale of the country, its poor transport infrastructure, and its increased expenditure on armaments. A direct attack on France appeared almost as problematic, in this case because of the great fortresses built to block any invasion from the northeast, but that apart, an invasion of France appeared the better option. To avoid the fortresses Schlieffen proposed that the German forces sweep through the Low Countries, across the lightly defended Franco-Belgian frontier, envelope Paris, and then march east to pin the main French armies on the German frontier, or to destroy them in southwestern Germany. As the historian Gerhard Ritter observed, this was an extremely audacious plan "that depended on many coincidences of luck,"[68] and others have commented that the German military never disposed of the necessary resources to ensure success. It also remained unclear why a German military victory in northern France need have halted French resistance in the center and south of the country (it had not in 1871), particularly since this time, Russia and possibly Britain would also have been committed to the battle against Germany.

Schlieffen was succeeded as Chief of Staff by Helmuth von Moltke (The Younger) on New Year's Day 1906. The younger Moltke was nephew to his elder namesake, but lacked his uncle's strategic and organizational brilliance. However, if Schlieffen had managed to persuade himself that a short, sharp war was possible, Moltke had no such illusions and his pessimism grew as war approached. On July 28, 1914, for example, he wrote to the Chancellor, Bethmann-Hollweg, warning of an imminent global war "that will destroy civilisation in almost all of Europe for decades to come."[69] Resigned to fighting a grim war of attrition, Moltke and his staff modified, without altogether abandoning, Schlieffen's operational plan. Alsace and German Lorraine would be adequately defended, thus depleting the main offensive through the Low Countries, and the Netherlands' neutrality would now be respected for it was perceived as a vital trading partner in any extended war. Moltke's plan no longer envisaged a lightning victory against France, instead aiming to secure for the German armies an optimal strategic advantage, on French territory, in preparation for the grim, lengthy struggle that lay ahead. With Schlieffen's planned sweep through the southern Netherlands now removed from the equation, the heavily fortified Belgian city of Liège became the key to success or failure in Moltke's eyes. The German armies would have no choice but to secure Liège if they were to avoid the wooded, broken hill country of the Ardennes which stretched southwards from there into northeastern France. Resupply through the

Ardennes was deemed impossible and, if properly defended, Liège could have held up fatally the German advance. An immediate strike against its fortresses before they could be fully garrisoned was, therefore, deemed essential the moment hostilities began in the west. Residual staff planning for an offensive against Russia alone had been formally abandoned in April 1913. This would leave little or no time for political mediation or second thoughts once the Austro-Serbian crisis suddenly gathered momentum in late July 1914, and in any case the General Staff had not seen fit to trouble Germany's political leaders with the details of its operational planning. It was only on July 31 that Bethmann-Hollweg was informed that the speedy seizure of Liège and a rapid advance through Belgium were imminent, regardless of the political consequences.

Few today would question the centrality of German decision making to the subsequent pattern of events and it is telling that even during the war itself different parts of the imperial establishment sought to shuffle off the blame for what had happened onto each other. Thus the former Chancellor Prince von Bülow raged against his successor, Bethmann-Hollweg, and senior members of the German Foreign Office for blundering into a war that, he claimed, the military or the crown had not sought. However, Bethmann-Hollweg's adviser, Kurt Riezler, stressed the part played by the military, and Germany's senior generals certainly feared Russia's growing military strength. When the Kaiser summoned a meeting of his military seniors on December 8, 1912, for example, to discuss the appropriate reaction to a British pledge of support for France in any future Franco-German war, Moltke had urged an immediate preemptive strike against France. His request may have been unsuccessful at the time, but the German Army Bill of 1913 and fresh demands for war by Moltke in May 1914 set down further markers that were called in during the July 1914 crisis. By this time France had introduced a three-year period of military service, strengthening the German military's determination that it was now or never. Even in 1914 the French and Russian armies combined were 1 million stronger than those of Germany and Austria-Hungary, and by 1917, according to Strachan, Russia would have possessed an army three times the size of Germany's.[70]

However, recriminations aside, few voices in Berlin had spoken out against war, the only meaningful difference being between the moderates and pessimists on the one hand and the hard-liners on the other. The former favored a localized Austro-Serbian war, fought in defiance of Russian pressure and with German blessing, but they were prepared for and even pushed for a wider war. Among them was Chancellor Bethmann-Hollweg who on July 14 confided to Riezler that German policy was a "leap in the dark," but for all that "our highest duty."[71] The hard-liners sought a wider war from the outset, as much to suppress domestic political reform as to confirm the verdict of the Bismarckian wars of unification and then further enhance German global power not through commerce and technical-industrial muscle, but with the sword. The likelihood of Russian mobilization in support of Serbia was welcomed rather than feared in such circles. As Admiral von Müller, Chief of the Naval Cabinet, confided to his diary on July 27, Germany had "to keep quiet, letting

Russia put itself in the wrong, but then not shying away from war."[72] Serbia's conciliatory, if equivocal, reply was sufficient to persuade Wilhelm II, who had previously characterized the Belgrade government as royal murderers, that war was no longer necessary. However, Austria's decisive, negative response to Belgrade's offer and a hopelessly dilatory effort by Bethmann-Hollweg to persuade Vienna consider a British offer of mediation sufficed to keep the wheels of war turning. That Moltke simultaneously urged his Austrian counterpart, Conrad von Hötzendorf, to take speedy military action betrayed the gulf between civilian and military planning in Germany at this critical juncture, which hardly helped and provoked a degree of wry amusement in Vienna. Who, the Austrians asked, really controlled affairs in Berlin? The answer should have been the Kaiser, but Wilhelm II, for all his vaunted claims to personal rule, was unable or unwilling to master the crisis.

On July 29 Russia announced that it was mobilizing against Austria-Hungary, and on the following day declared a general mobilization. German leaders were now confronted with the relatively straightforward task of rallying their public opinion against Russian aggression rather than having to justify a German assault upon the Triple Entente. On August 1, Germany responded to the Russian mobilization with an ultimatum to St Petersburg, and when this was ignored declared war.

Why, then, had Russia declared general mobilization, thereby wittingly or unwittingly intensifying the crisis? A combination of historic weakness and growing contemporary strength served to ensure that, this time, Russia would do something. Russia remained an autocracy, but the 1905 Revolution had precipitated limited constitutional reform in the form of a representative parliament, or Duma. Although the Duma was relatively weak, its powers included the approval or rejection of the Foreign Ministry's annual budget, which meant in effect that public opinion had come to count for something in Russian politics. Foreign Minister Sergei Dmitriyevich Sazonov's "discussions over cups of tea with press editors and Duma representatives: all reflect[ed] the changed context of the making of Russia's foreign policy,"[73] and on July 30, 1914 Sazonov warned the Tsar that the popular mood demanded action in support of Serbia. Sazonov's own instincts were less bellicose. Appointed Foreign Minister in 1910, he sought to steer a middle course between Germany and Russia's Entente partners, which, given Russia's military weakness at that point, was only wise. Although higher military spending had begun to address the devastating outcome of the Russo-Japanese War (1904–5), Sazonov nonetheless insisted in 1912 that Russia was in no position to intervene militarily during the Balkans crisis. When Russian public opinion responded during April 1913 to the government's continuing inaction with a series of banquets and 50,000-strong demonstrations in support of Serbia's demands for an Adriatic port, Sazonov ordered their suppression.

This played badly with Russia's military leaders and also with the Moscow and St Petersburg press which lamented a century of defeats and betrayals, real or alleged. During the early twentieth century this culture of victimhood focused on Germany's growing economic might and Russia's increasing dependence on its wealthy western neighbor. The Russo-German commercial treaty of 1904, which had been concluded very much on Berlin's terms, came due for renewal in 1914. A fierce press campaign bemoaned Russia's relative commercial backwardness and growing reliance on German markets, for by 1913 45 percent of Russia's exports were to, and 50 percent of her imports were from Germany. In relative terms Germany was far less dependent on these Russian markets, with its trade largely oriented to the west. Furthermore, German economic power threatened to undermine Russian influence in the Near East and even to exert an alarming gravitational pull on the Tsar's non-Russian western provinces, such as Poland and the Baltic states. The appointment of the German General Liman von Sanders to a commanding position in the Turkish army in October 1913 did little to help, even though he was hastily downgraded to "Inspector General" in the face of Russian protests. Russia's financial dependence upon its ally France for inward investment was much less controversial. However, this perception of failure and backwardness coexisted uneasily with a record of rapid domestic economic expansion and modernization and an ongoing military reform program, which by 1914 was delivering results. The army's command structure, artillery capacities, and munitions supplies were all in markedly better shape than during the aftermath of the Russo-Japanese War. The army was also expanding rapidly, with military expenditure in 1913 some 50 percent higher than in 1908, meaning in Keith Neilson's estimation that by 1914 "the use of force to support Russian diplomacy was no longer precluded by military weakness,"[74] or as Strachan observes, war was now "fully permissible."[75]

Nonetheless, on July 24 the Council of Ministers advised Serbia to be as conciliatory as possible toward Austria-Hungary without compromising its sovereignty, but the composition of the Council had changed since the earlier Balkans crises. It was no longer prepared to tolerate Russian passivity come what may, added to which Russian military intelligence had believed since 1912 that Germany was planning a preemptive strike against Russia at the earliest opportunity. Sazonov now linked the 1914 Balkans crisis to this received view, seeing in Austria-Hungary's actions a foil for German ambitions. Responding to past "failures" of Russian foreign policy, the dynamic Agricultural Minister A. V. Krirovshein typified the mood, arguing that the time had come to set a limit to "retreat, humiliation and withdrawal."[76] Sazonov began to lay the ground for a partial mobilization on July 24 and 25, even before the Austro-Hungarian ultimatum to Belgrade had expired. Thereafter, once Vienna had declared war on Serbia, the Tsar came under extreme pressure from his General Staff and from Sazonov to sanction this mobilization, which, as noted, occurred against the Habsburg Empire on July 29. This initial step may have been intended to lend weight to Russian diplomatic pressure, but the announcement of general mobilization on the following day swiftly provoked a German response. In 1894, of course, General Obruchev had anticipated, indeed planned for, such a sequence of events, but in 1914 the Tsar apparently hoped to the very end that peace might be preserved. Germany, he believed, was bluffing and would respect Russian firmness, but Berlin regarded Nicholas II's mobilization order as a green light for war.

The Franco-Russian military agreement had been designed to ensure that neither of the signatories would have to face Germany alone in any future conflict. Caillaux's administration fell in 1912 precisely because of its willingness to accommodate Germany, and thereafter vocal support from the French President, Raymond Poincaré, for Russia's Balkan policy served to raise the stakes further. In September 1912 the French General Staff had even welcomed the prospect of war in the Balkans "as likely to weaken Austria-Hungary, so freeing Russia to take on Germany."[77] "Under these conditions," David Hermann observes, "the Triple Entente … could achieve a victory permitting it to remake the map of Europe."[78] With Russia and Germany at war on August 1, therefore, and with German operational planning envisaging a first strike in the west rather than against Russia, it is less than surprising that war engulfed the west of the continent within days. But the determination in Paris to sustain the alliance with Russia at any cost, and the presence of the French President and Prime Minister in St Petersburg midway through the July crisis, invite further examination of France's role in the crisis.

Poincaré and Prime Minister René Viviani began a prearranged visit to Russia on July 20. Its original purpose had been to strengthen the Triple Entente by brokering better Russo-British relations, but now the ensuing series of diplomatic receptions marked the only substantive multilateral exchange of views during the weeks preceding the outbreak of war. The contours of French policy were confirmed during a formal diplomatic reception at the Winter Palace on July 21, by which time it was common knowledge that Austria-Hungary would take a hard line against Serbia. Poincaré was careful to avoid any diplomatic entanglements with the German ambassador, instead confining himself to social small talk, but then adopted a very different tack when asking of the Austro-Hungarian ambassador, Count Szapany, whether there was news of Serbia. Szapany avoided detail, but concluded, "Monsieur le Président, we cannot suffer a foreign government to allow plots against our sovereignty to be hatched on its territory," provoking from Poincaré the reply: "Serbia has some very warm friends in the Russian people. And Russia has an ally France. There are plenty of complications to be feared!"[79] By July 22 members of the Russian court were increasingly exercised by the crisis, with the Grand Duchess Anastasia, a Montenegrin by birth, anticipating a great European war with undisguised enthusiasm. Her father had already telegraphed her from Montenegro, predicting war by the end of the month, and during dinner at Krasnoïe-Selo the Grand Duchess found herself seated next to the French ambassador, Maurice Paléologue. Waving a tiny casket filled with soil from German Lorraine, Anastasia declared to all and sundry: "There's going to be a war! …There'll be nothing left of Austria … You're going to get back Alsace and Lorraine … Our armies will meet in Berlin … Germany will be destroyed!"[80] A hard look from the Tsar saw her lapse into silence, but it was in this atmosphere that extended and unminuted discussions took place between the Tsar and the French President. There is nothing to suggest that either side proposed war, but the solidarity of the alliance and the determination of France to stand squarely behind Russia were made abundantly clear in a series of speeches and press releases.

In other words, no one in Vienna or Berlin had reason to doubt that Russian involvement in the crisis would almost certainly entail French involvement. The tone of the visit also left Paléologue convinced that he had carte blanche to encourage and support the Russian authorities in whatever course of action they deemed appropriate. As his record of a meeting with his British counterpart Sir George Buchanan and Sazonov on July 24 relates: "Taking my stand on the toasts exchanged between the Tsar and the President, the declarations of the two Foreign Ministers and the communiqué to the Havas Agency yesterday, I had no hesitation in advocating a policy of firmness."[81] Somewhat alarmed, Sazonov had responded: "But suppose that policy is bound to lead to war?" to which Paléologue replied that war could still be averted if the "Germanic powers" were "prepared to negotiate and compromise."[82] Sazonov met with the German ambassador, Count von Pourtalès, that evening to be told that Germany stood fully behind Austria-Hungary; Sazonov replied that Russia would not leave Serbia to face Austria-Hungary alone. In other words, the Austro-Hungarian rejection of Belgrade's reply to its ultimatum left war inevitable, despite eleventh hour efforts by Britain to mediate in the Austro-Serbian dispute.

It remained to be seen whether Britain would be drawn into the escalating crisis. The Triple Entente, it should be remembered, had emerged in response to colonial tensions between Britain on the one hand and France and Russia on the other. Thereafter the Entente served in part to keep the country's potential enemies close and this closeness demanded a degree of coolness toward Germany. As Foreign Secretary Sir Edward Grey had commented in 1905: "Nothing we do in our relations with Germany is in any way to impair our existing good relations with France,"[83] or as Ambassador Buchanan reported to London on July 25, 1914 from St Petersburg: "For ourselves position is a most serious one, and we shall have to choose between giving Russia our active support or renouncing her friendship."[84]

However, beyond fear of their own allies, British statesmen were unsettled by the growing might of Germany, and in particular by its increasingly radical and erratic foreign policy during the reign of Wilhelm II. The Victorian statesman Lord Palmerston had observed that Britain had "permanent interests but not permanent allies,"[85] and among these was the preservation of a balance of power on the neighboring continent. This equilibrium would have been shattered by a German triumph over France, leading Grey to observe in 1906 that Britain would have no choice but to intervene in any Franco-German war. On July 29, 1914 he learned from the French ambassador, Raymond Cambon, that France would not stay neutral during a Russo-German war, after which the Foreign Secretary, true to his longstanding policy, warned the German ambassador, Prince Lichnowsky, that Britain would be unable "to stand aside and wait for any length of time."[86] Lichnowsky informed Berlin accordingly, but the British Cabinet remained largely opposed to war, and Grey took care not to inform his Cabinet colleagues of a suggestion from Lichnowsky (on August 1) that if France stayed neutral, then Germany would not attack France.

One might therefore presume that Britain would have joined the war in any event, but at what political price (perhaps the rupturing of the Liberal Party and the involvement of the prowar Conservatives in government) and after how long must remain conjecture. The Belgian question, while not the fundamental reason for Britain's speedy intervention, was undoubtedly the issue that made it possible. This crisis followed immediately on the failure of frenetic, last minute diplomatic maneuvering in Paris and it is to there that we must first turn.

During the days and hours preceding the German attack on Liège, the German ambassador to Paris, Baron von Schoen, persevered in his efforts to localize the conflict to southeastern Europe and his task may not have appeared entirely hopeless. Poincaré and Viviani were still returning from their Russian visit aboard the battle cruiser *France* during the early days of the crisis, leaving the Minister of Justice, Jean Baptiste Bienvenu-Martin, and his adviser Philippe Berthelot temporarily in charge. Bienvenu-Martin was initially receptive to von Schoen's localization proposals, but not at the cost of Entente solidarity. On July 27 the Russian ambassador, Izvolsky, arrived back in Paris and immediately demanded of the French government unqualified support for Russia's position. A further conversation on July 28 between von Schoen and Bienvenu-Martin demonstrated that the options for peace were evaporating as the German ambassador refused to put pressure on Vienna, while the French Justice Minister refused to put pressure on St Petersburg. On July 30 Paris sent a qualified warning to Russia to avoid giving Germany a pretext for war, but continued that: "France is resolved to fulfil all the obligations of the alliance."[87] This was good enough for the war party in the Russian capital and full mobilization followed on the same day.

On July 31 Paléologue wired the French Foreign Ministry on the Quai d'Orsay, 16 hours after the event and by a circuitous route to circumvent German jamming of telecommunications traffic, that: "The mobilisation of the Russian army has been ordered," but his brief telegram then tarried several hours longer at the Quai d'Orsay as officials lengthened it to 97 words. Their falsification justified the Russian mobilization as a response to Austro-Hungarian and German mobilization, although in reality Vienna ordered full mobilization on August 5 and Germany had mobilized in response to Russia's move. Such was the delay in finally communicating news of Russia's action to the French Cabinet (now presided over by Poincaré) that von Moltke had managed by then to have the contents of a publicly displayed Russian mobilization notice from across the Polish border read to him over the telephone. Thereafter he demanded mobilization of the Kaiser even as the French Cabinet remained ignorant of the situation. When von Schoen met with Viviani at 7 pm on July 31 to deliver an ultimatum demanding French neutrality in the burgeoning conflict, the French Prime Minister still remained unaware of the situation in Russia. French mobilization was, therefore, ordered in response to what appeared to be a unilateral German measure. The permanent secretary at the Quai d'Orsay, Pierre de Margerie, whose officials were even then busily embellishing Paléologue's telegram, was present at this meeting, but chose to say nothing.

When at 9 pm Poincaré convened the French Cabinet, the German ultimatum, rather than any news from Russia, formed the basis of a discussion which concluded at 1 am on August 1 with a decision for war. Falsified telegram or not, neutrality in any Russo-German war was never an option for Poincaré, added to which the French General Staff believed that 1914 represented the most favorable moment for hostilities. The new three-year military draft had swollen the French army, but elections in the spring of 1914 had returned a more left-inclined Chamber that threatened to revoke the extended conscription law.

Von Schoen had requested this neutrality, no more, no less, and would only have made the (now infamous) request that France surrender the fortresses of Verdun and Toul as a guarantee of good faith had Paris first agreed to remain neutral. To that extent German diplomacy was ostensibly less provocative than some histories would have it, but with the decisions for war now effectively made in the key continental capitals, Poincaré was able to play a longer game than his German counterparts and thus secure immediate British participation in a conflict to which France was already committed. The French mobilization order was issued at 3.40 pm on August 1, despite residual misgivings on Viviani's part. The French army planned to invade Germany at the outset of hostilities, but Poincaré insisted that for the moment all French forces remain at least 10 kilometers from the Belgian frontier, "with a view to assuring for ourselves the collaboration of our English neighbors."[88] Any French declaration of war against Germany would have required a debate and vote in parliament, and although the Cabinet decided on August 2 to convene parliament in 10 days, after the completion of mobilization, Poincaré very much hoped that Germany would start the war for him before then. A parliamentary debate would have revealed the existence of the 1894 Franco-Russian military agreement, the terms of which had, as long as Russia's actions could be construed as "provoked," effectively committed France to war against Germany from the moment on August 1 that Germany had declared war against Russia.

Had the German military stuck with the operational plans devised by the elder Moltke, dug in along the French frontier without any formal declaration of war, and offered Austria-Hungary whatever support proved necessary in the face of a Russian invasion, Poincaré would have been hard pressed to convince his parliament to declare war on and invade Germany. Furthermore, such a scenario would have made immediate British intervention unlikely in the extreme. Schlieffen's strategy, however, particularly as modified by the younger Moltke, left Germany in no position to await developments. To Admiral von Tirpitz's angry question, "Why did we not wait?" the "answer consisted of one word: Liège."[89] Late on August 1 German troops began occupying Luxembourg, and on August 2 Berlin delivered an ultimatum to Brussels demanding unimpeded passage for the German army through Belgium. The Belgian government and king were not prepared to concur. The British Cabinet hoped almost to the last that German forces would remain south of the rivers Sambre and Meuse and thus confined to the southwestern corner of Belgium. This should have provoked a protest, perhaps a few Belgian mortar shells directed at the passing Germans, but little more. Britain would have had the time and leisure to ponder its options, but on the same evening Berlin declared war on France before launching an onslaught against Liège on August 4. Poincaré, the *faux* Lorrainer,[90] had his war without the need for parliamentary scrutiny or approval. For his part Belgium's King Albert genuinely felt that he and his country had been cornered into a battle for their honor, and the Liberal Cabinet in London agreed under these circumstances to follow the bidding of Prime Minister Asquith and Foreign Secretary Grey. On August 4 Britain declared war on Germany and resolved to send an expeditionary force to France to confront the invading German armies.

There is little to suggest that a wider conflict could have been averted once Austria-Hungary and Serbia had made their decisions for war at a relatively early stage. The Russians and Germans were determined this time to support their respective allies in this Third Balkan War and France was determined to support its Russian ally. As Jules Cambon, French ambassador to Berlin, predicted on July 25: "France, the victim of her alliance, will follow the destiny of her ally on the battlefields."[91] The younger Moltke's strategic planning would not have spared France in any case, but it also saw the outrageous violation of a small, potentially friendly, neutral neighbor, and ensured that centuries of friendship and cooperation between England/Britain and Prussia/Germany were replaced by an uneasy but indispensable de facto alliance between Britain and France during the coming half century or more.

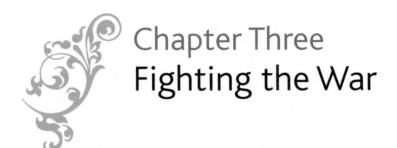

Chapter Three
Fighting the War

3.1 The Opening Gambits: 1914

By August 18, 2 million French troops faced 1.7 million German as the early border skirmishing gave way to a series of major battles. In essence the French armies were committed by their operational Plan XVII to frontal attacks on Alsace and Lothringen as Russian forces attacked Germany from the east. The German armies sought through a modified "Schlieffen Plan" to win a sufficiently decisive (if not outright) victory against France to allow them swiftly to shift their focus of operations eastward. Here they would parry the anticipated onslaught by a numerically superior Russian army in conjunction with their Austro-Hungarian allies.

The German breakthrough at Liège took eleven rather than the two days anticipated, while French forces seized the Alsatian city of Mülhausen twice during August before finally being driven back toward the frontier at Altkirch. A further French offensive toward the Alsatian capital of Strassburg also foundered and by August 20 defeated French troops were falling back on Nancy in French Lorraine. The French doctrine of all-out attack, *offensive à l'outrance*, had shattered in the face of decimating German firepower from prepared lines of defense, followed by counterattack. As a young French officer, Charles de Gaulle, recounted:

> Those who survived lay flat on the ground, amid the screaming wounded and the humble corpses. With affected calm, the officers let themselves be killed standing upright, some obstinate platoons stuck their bayonets in their rifles, bugles sounded the charge … but all to no purpose. In an instant it had become clear that not all the courage in the world could withstand this fire.[1]

Meanwhile the Belgium army to the north was in full retreat, back toward the great fortress of Antwerp, prompting the French commander, General Joseph

Joffre, to attack northeastwards into the Ardennes. Success here, where the Belgian, French, German and Luxembourg borders converged, promised to split the German armies facing France from those advancing through Belgium, but by August 24 the French forces here were also defeated and Germany had effectively won the so-called Battle of the Frontiers.

This, however, was a purely defensive victory by an army conducting an essentially offensive strategy. Although the Allied forces were in retreat along a front extending from Belgium to the Swiss border during the final days of August, Joffre had committed fewer troops to the battle than Moltke. A purge of incompetent French senior officers, exemplary if harsh discipline within the ranks, and the increasingly effective use of artillery as a defensive weapon meant that all in all Joffre's army had suffered a series of tactical defeats, rather than a decisive strategic defeat.

German commanders saw things otherwise at this stage, and convinced themselves that the war in the west was effectively won. Their forces, however, may have been advancing, but were extended across a huge front with logistical support close to breaking point. Only through a process of "furious improvisation," living off the land and somehow managing to keep the armies supplied with ammunition, had the advance been sustained so far.[2] To compound these problems communications between each army and between the armies and headquarters were hopelessly inadequate. The ceaseless marching and fighting was also exacting its remorseless toll. By September 6 Germany's field strength had declined by 265,000, and as Hew Strachan observes: "A stage would be reached when the Germans had too few men."[3] Yet, despite the increasingly marginal situation, Moltke had removed two entire army corps from the western front on August 25 after the fall of the Belgian fortress at Namur in order to address a deteriorating situation on the eastern front.

During the closing days of August the French army held onto the key northeastern fortresses at Verdun and Nancy, effectively stabilizing the line from the Belgian to the Swiss border. Joffre was now able to concentrate his forces away from the central Lorraine front and toward Amiens, a vital communications center in northwestern France from where he could parry the Germans' southward advance from Belgium and toward Paris. Some 700,000 terrified Parisians had already fled their city, no doubt fearing that 1914 would bring a repeat of the siege of 1870–1 and its attendant horrors. The British War Minister, Lord Kitchener, intervened personally at this critical juncture to rally the exhausted British Expeditionary Force (BEF), and keep it in the battle as Joffre prepared to counterattack in Picardy on the River Marne. On September 6 the Allied armies began moving forward. Joffre hoped to exploit the gaps between the advancing German columns, isolating them from one another before surrounding and destroying them. This, however, was not to be. Even if the German armies had decided to stand and fight, and had won, they no longer had the resources to push on to Paris. As Martin van Creveld concludes:

> There is every reason to believe the advance would have petered out. The prime
> factors would have been the inability of the railheads to keep up with the advance,
> the lack of fodder, and sheer exhaustion. In this sense … it is true to say that the
> Schlieffen Plan was logistically impracticable.[4]

With victory promising so little and defeat inviting catastrophe, the German High
Command authorized a limited but timely retreat on September 8 from the Marne
back to the River Aisne, so extricating its exposed armies from the Allied trap. Here the
front eventually stabilized after a series of localized attacks and counterattacks, with
heavy British losses made good by reinforcements from the colonial, Indian Army.

The German advance into northeastern France and in particular Belgium
brought with it a wave of atrocities during August against the civilian population,
which inflamed Allied popular opinion at the time and informed anti-German
propaganda thereafter. The war came to be portrayed and even understood as a
struggle between western civilization and Teutonic barbarity, leaving the Germans
struggling to make their views heard in key neutral countries such as the United
States. The Bishop of London, A. F. Winnington-Ingram, doubtless had the Belgian
atrocities in mind when preaching his Advent sermon of 1915, declaring the war "a
great crusade – we cannot deny it – to kill Germans: to kill them, not for the sake
of killing but to save the world; to kill the good as well as the bad, to kill the young
men as well as the old …"[5]

What, then, had happened and why? John Horne and Alan Kramer have established that almost 4,500 Belgian and some 750 French civilians – men, women and
children – died in an orgy of reprisals against resistance which was more imagined
than real. The executions, deportations, looting and burning began around Liège
and thereafter swept through the Belgian towns of Aarschot, Andenne-Seilles,
Tamines, Leuven, Dinant and Arlon. Border villages in northeastern France suffered similarly. The German military was haunted by memories of the prolonged
guerrilla war of 1870–1, fought across northern France against *francs tireurs* (un-
uniformed civilian snipers), even after the decisive defeat of Louis Napoleon's army
at Sedan should (in German eyes) have been the end of the matter. German commanders remained fixated during the early twentieth century by the specter of the
French "nation in arms," and memories of 1870 filtered down to the 1914 generation of young German conscripts who were gripped by a fear of covert, civilian
treachery as they themselves poured uninvited across the French and Belgian borders. "We were told not to expect to meet the enemy in honest battle," as a soldier
from Hamburg recounted, "the enemy hides behind the hedges in the clothes of
the peaceful civilian. Horror stories and rumours are being told."[6] The fact that one
Bavarian regiment was supplied before it left Germany with "highly sought-after"
nooses for hanging partisans doubtless contributed to this paranoia.[7] Isolated acts
of civilian resistance, instances of "friendly" fire, rearguard actions by pockets of
retreating French and Belgian troops, and large amounts of alcohol did the rest.
Any church bell, any unexplained action by (for example) the village priest or mayor,

any sudden noise, unnerved the increasingly exhausted German troops, preyed on their fear of *francs tireurs* and triggered bloody countermeasures. The outrages were initially perpetrated by ordinary soldiers and the junior officers commanding them in the field rather than forming part of any predetermined plan. Some senior officers tried to halt the violence; the military commandant of Brussels, General von Lüttwitz, belatedly put a stop to the pillage and burning of nearby Leuven, while in Namur Major-General von Below nipped any atrocities in the bud. More often, however, senior commanders either turned a blind eye (maybe believing that a brief but intense display of preemptive terror would deter any genuine guerrilla campaign), or they sought to justify their armies' actions. To this end, official protests against the purported deployment of civilian combatants were lodged with the Belgian and French governments. By late August, however, the atrocities had died down almost completely and did not recur. They were replaced by the more mundane but sufficiently grim realities of foreign military occupation in wartime, although as Thomas Weber observes: "Maybe surprisingly, over time the treatment of the local population by ordinary soldiers became less, not more, severe."[8]

During the remainder of the autumn the fighting shifted steadily northwestwards from Picardy into Flanders, where in November the futile slaughter of the first Battle of Ieper (Ypres) confirmed that an effective stalemate had been reached along the entire western front. During the fighting in Flanders German commanders had sought to break and turn the western flank of the Allied forces, cutting them off from the English Channel and rolling them up from west to east. This had signally failed. The German forces had conquered Luxembourg, the key industrial northern départements of France, and virtually the whole of Belgium, but France remained undefeated and the French and Belgian armies very much in the field. Meanwhile time had been bought for Britain to recruit, train and equip an expeditionary force vastly superior in numbers than the original four divisions that had joined battle in August 1914. In terms of available manpower the balance would tip inexorably in the Allies' favor. The Prussian War Minister, Erich von Falkenhayn, had already replaced an ailing and disillusioned Moltke as Chief of the General Staff in mid-September and on November 25 he conceded that the war of movement and the resulting great encounter battles of August to November were over. The German army was ordered to take up defensive positions all along the front, even if commanders on both sides continued to imagine that the spring of 1915 would see a resumption of mobile warfare.

If the war in the west would henceforth be a story of bloody stalemate, sustained by the economic and scientific might of the world's most advanced industrial nations, the equally bloody war in the east remained more mobile as armies attacked, retreated, and counterattacked across the vast spaces between the Carpathian Mountains and the Baltic Sea. The initial shape of this war was determined by German and Austro-Hungarian efforts to engage immediately in battle, before Russia's cumbersome process of mobilization could commit numerically overwhelming forces to the conflict.

Austria-Hungary was in many respects the least militarized of the Great Powers, training the smallest proportion of its male population and with an army half the size of that of Germany or France. Its officer corps was relatively small and its forces had little in the way of modern artillery. In spite of this, the Austro-Hungarian commander, Conrad von Hötzendorf, was committed before 1914 to an offensive strategy, but against Serbia or possibly Italy, not Russia. When the likelihood of war with Russia increased, Conrad developed plans for an attack northwards from Austrian Poland (Galicia) into Russian Poland, on the wholly false assumption that a powerful German army would simultaneously strike southwards from East Prussia into Poland. In Conrad's imagination this pincer movement would cut off and destroy the Russian forces around and to the west of Warsaw in a massive battle of annihilation.

But however serious the Russian threat might have been, the politics of the war demanded an immediate and exemplary Austro-Hungarian attack into Serbia. The Dual Monarchy's operations in the Balkans seemed ill-starred from the outset, plagued by personal rivalry between Conrad and his regional commander, General Oskar Potiorek, and compromised by the relative inexperience of his troops. The battle-hardened Serbian army actually outnumbered the Austro-Hungarian forces deployed against it, and despite the nagging fear that Bulgaria might intervene on Vienna's side, it was well placed to pursue its strategy of "offensive defence,"[9] meaning swift counterattacks. By mid-August the Austro-Hungarian offensive from Bosnia into western Serbia had been repulsed and the Habsburg monarchy had to suffer the indignity of a short-lived Serbian incursion into southern Hungary. The humiliated Habsburg army responded with a savage wave of atrocities and reprisals against Serb civilians both in Serbia proper and within Bosnia. Austria-Hungary had failed dismally to secure the strategic and political victory in the Balkans that had driven it to war in the first place. Now it faced the strategic uncertainties of a two-front war, in the Balkans and Galicia respectively.

Although the Russian army had been reorganized and strengthened since the Russo-Japanese War, it still suffered from a shortage of competent officers and NCOs and was wracked by personal rivalry between its senior commanders. Operational strategy was usually decided piecemeal at regional level, although in 1913 Russian planners yielded to French pressure for a rapid strike against East Prussia to divert as many German troops as possible from the western front. In August 1914, therefore, Russia set out to defeat the Germans in East Prussia, turn on the Austro-Hungarian armies in Galicia, and then overrun the German provinces of Silesia and Posen before launching a frontal attack on Berlin. This, Strachan observes, required the formation of three separate army groups and led to a fatal dissipation of manpower.[10]

Thirty-eight Russian divisions, each of sixteen battalions and organized into two armies, invaded an East Prussia defended by eleven German divisions, each of twelve battalions. The First Russian Army commanded by General Paul Rennenkampf attacked westward toward the East Prussian capital, Königsberg, but was checked on August 20 at the Battle of Gumbinnen. However the commander of the Second Russian Army, General Alexander Samsonov, believed the First Army had carried the day and that the Germans were evacuating East Prussia. He attacked hastily from the south to cut off this apparent retreat, but despite initial thoughts of abandoning East Prussia, the German army had resolved to stand and fight. Brilliant operational planning by Colonel Max Hoffmann was complemented by the strategic capabilities of General Ludendorff and also the talents of a swash-buckling field commander, General Hermann von François, to inflict a crushing defeat on Samsonov at the Battle of Tannenberg between August 23 and 31. The Second Russian Army was surrounded and destroyed as 50,000 soldiers were killed, 92,000 taken prisoner and 400 guns captured, leaving Russia's anti-German strat-egy in tatters. Samsonov chose suicide over the disgrace of abject defeat. The Germans had known from intercepted uncoded Russian telegraph messages that Rennenkampf's forces would not intervene in this decisive battle, added to which Hoffmann knew that Samsonov and Rennenkampf had been mortal enemies since the days of the Russo-Japanese War. Neither had ever been likely to help the other and now each saw his army perish separately. Between September 8 and 10 Rennenkampf's army was expelled from East Prussia at the Battle of the Masurian Lakes, and Russia had lost in total 310,000 men.

Such were the victories Schlieffen had dreamed of in the west, but which had eluded his successor almost entirely. However, Hoffmann's decisive role in the East Prussian campaign was, to his personal irritation, largely overlooked. Instead the titular and essentially passive commander of the eastern armies, General Paul von Hindenburg, emerged from Tannenberg with a towering reputation which he con-tinued to foster through press contacts and a vigorous media campaign. This "Hindenburg myth" would soon enough prove immensely important to German wartime politics and thereafter to the fate of the postwar Weimar Republic. But more immediately Tannenberg saw Hindenburg appointed Commander in Chief of the Eastern Front (Oberost) in early November, with Ludendorff his Chief of Staff and Hoffmann his Chief of Operations. The battle also seemed to confirm the superiority of the German army over the Russian, and as Strachan observes: "Never, throughout the war, would the Russians acquire the conviction that they could beat the Germans."[11] The fact that many of the German soldiers on the east-ern front were reservists added to this impression which, it might be claimed, exposed as chimerical in the extreme the fear of Russia, verging on paranoia, that had done so much to influence German military thinking on the road to war. The French, regarded by the Germans as beatable in a matter of weeks, had proven to be no such thing.

Meanwhile Russian and Austro-Hungarian strategic planning had proceeded vir-tually on opposite premises, with the Russian command (Stavka) under the Grand Duke Nicholas preparing its main offensive from the east against the Bukovina and Galicia, while the Austrians as we noted resolved to strike north into Russian Poland and (so they hoped) link up with the Germans to the east of Warsaw. The Russian attack on Austria-Hungary's thinly defended eastern flank was overwhelmingly successful, taking the Galician capital of Lemberg (Lvov) on September 2 and sweeping westwards toward Cracow. The Austro-Hungarians' main strike into Poland did achieve temporary successes (with the bulk of the Russian army deployed further east), but the absence of any German support and the collapse of the eastern front forced Conrad's forces into a general retreat by mid-September with the loss of 350,000 men. He was able to salvage something from the wreckage by holding the fortified Galician city of Przemysl against Russian sieges during September–October and then through the 1914–15 winter, by purging his command of less competent officers and fighting a successful if costly defense along the northern foothills of the Carpathians.

German tactical offensives from Silesia into Russian Poland were more successful and finally relieved some of the pressure on the beleaguered Austro-Hungarians. German forces eventually took the city of Łódź on December 6 after protracted and confused fighting. Thereafter a combination of exhaustion and winter conditions forced a pause in active campaigning in the east, although the scale of operations across this vast landscape precluded any resort to the entrenched stalemate that was already developing by default on the more constricted western front.

Elsewhere, early naval engagements saw the Royal Navy pick off German cruisers that had briefly preyed on Allied merchant shipping across the globe and assert effective control over the North Sea. Admiral Lord Fisher and the commander of the fleet at Scapa Flow, Admiral Sir John Jellicoe, shared an essentially cautious and defensive temperament, settling eventually on a "distant blockade" of Germany by sealing the northern and southern exits from the North Sea. They hoped that the German fleet might be lured out to battle, but no such encounter occurred. Instead a string of smaller scale engagements saw German U-boats sink several British warships during the mid-autumn and German battle cruisers bombard a succession of English east coast ports, against which the Royal Navy sank several German ships during a skirmish in the Heligoland Bight on August 28. The successful *flight* of Admiral von Hipper's battle cruisers at the indecisive Battle of the Dogger Bank on January 24, 1915 set the tone for the remainder of the war. On February 2 Admiral Friedrich von Ingenohl was replaced as naval commander in chief by the more defensively inclined Hugo von Pohl, who was determined that the German fleet would survive intact to serve as a bargaining chip in eventual peace negotiations.

Finally, the Central Powers of Germany and Austria-Hungary were joined by the Ottoman Empire in November, tying down a Russian army on the Caucasus front and briefly offering Berlin the tantalizing possibility that Germany, through the Ottomans, might foster an Islamic rising against the established European colonial powers in North Africa and Western and Central Asia. The Turkish forces repulsed a Russian offensive during November, went onto the attack over Christmas, but were decisively repulsed by a Russian counterattack over the New Year as temperatures in the border mountain ranges plunged to minus 36 degrees centigrade.

The Ottomans, Strachan concludes, were "a worthy ally of the Central Powers," capable of major defensive victories,[12] but this particular defeat effectively stifled any prospect of a wider Islamic insurgency in the Russian Caucasus. Ottoman military power was a necessary adjunct to such a rising, but the Russian victory of early 1915 seemed to confirm the image of Ottoman decline, already established by the earlier Balkan and Libyan wars.

3.2 The Elusive Victory: 1915

If the great powers had gone to war in 1914 with largely negative and reactive aims, the increasingly costly and murderous struggle soon enough demanded a greater purpose. During the early autumn of 1914 Germany's leaders secretly compiled an ambitious shopping list of objectives, dubbed the September Memorandum, which envisaged Belgium becoming a German protectorate, the annexation from France of the iron ore fields at Longwy and Briey (just beyond the prewar German frontier), and German protectorates in Russian Poland and the Baltic lands. France, now that it was fighting, swiftly declared that victory would allow the reannexation of Alsace and German Lorraine, while British officials began to mull over their colonial maps with an eye to territories in the Middle East and beyond. Russia could hope, at last, to seize control of Constantinople and also extend its Caucasian and central Asian dominions further into Turkish Anatolia and Persia (present-day Iran). The Ottoman Empire dreamed of establishing a pan-Turkish, or Turanian, empire extending through the Caucasus region and deep into central Asia, thus giving the disintegrating multinational state fresh focus and purpose as a preeminently Turkish dominion. The Habsburgs sought finally to put an end to south Slav separatism by asserting domination of the Balkans. For their part the Italians were to be lured into the war in May under the secret terms of the Treaty of London (April 26) which promised Rome Austria-Hungary's remaining Italian territories, but also Slovenia, Dalmatia (the present-day Croatian coast) and a decent chunk of western Anatolia. These mutually irreconcilable aims demanded outright victory for either the Allied or the Central Powers, not to mention a good measure of back-stabbing thereafter, but such a victory eluded both sides during 1915.

The British authorities had become sucked into the bloody stalemate on the western front somewhat against their better judgment and were, therefore, receptive to Russian appeals for an attack on Constantinople. This, it was hoped, would relieve pressure on other fronts and also reopen Russia's key trade route from the Black Sea into the Mediterranean. In March 1915 the Royal Navy began a bombardment of the Gallipoli peninsula at the entrance of the Straits leading on to Constantinople, but the ships hit minefields and were forced into an ignominious withdrawal. Troops were then landed piecemeal onto the peninsula, only to be pinned down by dogged Turkish defense on the landing beaches. A more concerted offensive in August at Suvla Bay was repulsed with horrific casualties, and in October the surviving Allied troops, many of them Australians and New Zealanders (Anzacs), were plucked from the beaches.

A further Allied landing took place at the northeastern Greek port of Salonica with a view to opening a way to Serbia, but Greece was neutral and, in the wake of Gallipoli and a change of government in Athens, Paris and London were bombarded with furious Greek protests against this flagrant violation of a small neutral power. In any case, the landing at Salonica was reduced to irrelevance when, in October 1915, Bulgaria joined the Central Powers, itching for revenge after its defeat in the Second Balkan War. During the following month a combined Austro-Hungarian, German, and Bulgarian offensive overwhelmed Serbia and Montenegro and confirmed the Central Powers' domination of the Balkans for the duration of the war. The French and British naval blockade of the Ottoman Empire was now effectively broken as the railway route from Europe into Turkey (which ran through Serbia) was reopened.

To the north, however, the Central Powers were faring less well. The Austro-Hungarian forces facing the Russians appeared near to collapse as losses reached 1.25 million by the New Year. In March 1915 the dismal tally had increased by a further 800,000 and included ominous mass desertions by Czech, Romanian-speaking and Ruthenian (Ukrainian) units. When on March 22 the great fortress of Przemysl finally fell to the Russians, Conrad even began to contemplate a separate peace with St Petersburg. To the north, however, Hindenburg and Ludendorff were pressing Berlin for the resources to build on their earlier victories by launching an annihilating offensive against the Russians. The Austrians' plight added fuel to their case for a transfer of manpower from the western front to the east. In May a German-Austrian army group commanded by General August von Mackensen smashed through the Russian lines between Gorlice and Tarnow in Galicia, recaptured Przemysl and took 100,000 prisoners during an advance of 80 miles.

The German Commander in Chief, Falkenhayn, remained cautious, refusing to believe that the vast Russian Empire could ever be beaten in a single, decisive battle. He opted instead for a version of attrition, compelling his opponents "to exhaust their resources while committing as few as possible of [his] own."[13] However, Hindenburg and Ludendorff still hankered after a decisive strategic victory and eventually, in August, were authorized to eliminate Russian forces in Poland. Warsaw swiftly fell and in the headlong Russian flight German forces also retook Lemberg in Galicia and pressed on to the Lithuanian capital of Vilnius. By the end of the year the Central Powers had advanced some 430 kilometers, taken 1.5 million prisoners and 2,600 guns, and achieved the greatest single victory of the war.

This campaign created its share of civilian misery, with vast columns of refugees (estimates vary from 3 to 5 million) taking to the roads. This time the atrocities were Russian instigated, with their fury directed against the subject peoples of their western borderlands: Poles, Lithuanians, Latvians, and especially Jews, who were regarded as pro-German fifth columnists. "The Jews," the Russian authorities raged, "are sending their gold to the Germans; this tainted gold has been found in aeroplanes, coffins, barrels of vodka and breasts of duck and mutton!"[14] By early 1915 the French ambassador to St Petersburg was deeply uneasy about the likely fate of Russia's Jews, but also noted that Russian Poles were greeting the Germans as liberators. On February 15 he tried to reason with an unnamed Russian grandee: "'You must admit,' I said, 'that the Poles have some ground for not loving Russia.' 'That's true enough [the Russian replied]; we've sometimes been pretty hard on Poland. But Poland has fairly paid us back.' 'In what way?' 'By giving us the Jews.'"[15] In March the ambassador recorded in his diary that the wholesale deportation of Jews from western Poland had begun:

> Everywhere the process of departure has been marked by scenes of violence and pillage under the complacent eyes of the authorities. Hundreds of thousands of these poor people have been seen wandering over the snows, driven like cattle by platoons of Cossacks, abandoned in the greatest distress at the stations, camping in the open round the towns, and dying of hunger, weariness and cold.[16]

By July, he noted, the Jews of Lithuania and Latvia had met the same fate, bringing the global total of Jewish expellees to 600,000, and by early August 800,000. To these were added 300,000 Lithuanians, 250,000 Latvians and 743,000 Poles. Small wonder, therefore, that Ludendorff could record that in the west of Russian Poland the inhabitants "gave us no trouble."[17] On the contrary, the German army received a warm welcome as it entered Warsaw on August 6, 1915, not least from the surviving Jewish population, and the same welcome was proffered elsewhere in Poland. "It is no irony to say," Jay Winter observes, "that the advancing German army units were seen as liberators of some Jewish communities, reduced by [Russian] fire and slaughter to a miserable state."[18]

The subsequent years of German occupation saw the ruthless requisitioning of foodstuffs and other strategic materials from the occupied eastern territories and some east Europeans conscripted as forced laborers, but the mass murders and deportation of entire communities had stopped with the departure of the Russians. The encounters of German and Austrian soldiers with backward, rural communities, whether Christian or Jewish, Winter speculates, may have fueled a sense of superiority and ultimately xenophobic prejudice that informed and mobilized later, Nazi policy,[19] but the immediate contrast with the experiences of the Second World War could not have been greater. Von Hindenburg was happy to flirt with Byelorussian nationalism, granting the language official status in January 1916 and allowing considerable cultural and political freedom, which culminated in the proclamation of the Byelorussian National Republic in March 1918. Ukrainian nationalists similarly saw in Germany a potential ally in their struggle against Russian domination.[20]

On the western front, meanwhile, 1915 witnessed a series of Allied attacks which consumed vast quantities of high explosive, and human life. British commanders were convinced that preparatory bombardment held the key to success. As Sir John French noted in January:

> Breaking through the enemy's lines is largely a question of expenditure of high explosive ammunition. If sufficient ammunition is forthcoming, a way out can be blasted through the line. If the attempt fails, it shows, provided that the work of the infantry and artillery has been properly coordinated, that insufficient ammunition has been expended ... [21]

Sir Douglas Haig was equally bullish, claiming in a newspaper interview that with sufficient preparatory shelling "we could walk through the German lines at several places."[22] It turned out to be less easy and initial Allied attacks during March were shattered by German defenders who were well dug in along the chalk upslopes of northern France. A British offensive at Festubert in May also failed, triggering the "shells scandal" as British military commanders lambasted the War Office for allegedly failing to provide the BEF with adequate equipment. Thereafter, a new business-oriented Ministry of Munitions under Lloyd George presided over a vast increase in armaments production, but victory on the battlefield remained elusive.

A French offensive in Artois had also collapsed during May, betraying the huge difficulties underlying effective coordination of infantry action and artillery support as an attack became enmeshed in the deep belt of German defensive positions. Overall command and control were hopelessly compromised, and of the belligerent armies only the German had been trained to improvise in the immediate chaos of battle. Joffre's strategy during 1915 has been dismissed as "trying to bite through a steel door with badly-fitting false teeth,"[23] and the failure of the Allies' September offensive in the Champagne provided bloody confirmation of this verdict. Designed to relieve pressure on the Russians, French and British losses totaled 242,000 to the Germans' 141,000, all, it has been claimed, for the conquest of a cemetery by Pétain's troops. Indeed, as the front line shifted a mile here, or there, cemeteries came to be used alternately by both sides, with their dead sharing burial grounds while those yet to fall occupied separate trenches divided by the mud and wire of no-man's-land.

By the end of 1915 half of France's regular officers were dead or crippled, but Allied commanders continued to insist, as the German defenders dug ever deeper into the chalk hills, that "more guns, longer preliminary barrages, better communications, and better staff work" would bring victory during the following year.[24] Thus plans were laid on December 6 at French Headquarters in Chantilly for a combined great offensive on the western and eastern fronts during 1916. Yet of all the western offensives during 1915 only a German thrust at Ieper in April had enjoyed any measure of success. This had been staged to test chlorine gas, a significantly cheaper and arguably more terrifying weapon than high explosive:

Figure 3.1 The Western Front, 1915.
Source: Ullstein Bild.

The complicit wind pushed the green mist towards the French lines. It clung to the ground, hugging every rise and fall in the terrain, plunging into hollows, swallowing hillocks and barbed wire entanglements, an engulfing tide ... [that] occupies space so methodically that frantic pain-racked men search vainly for a breath of air ... the intolerable burning in the eyes, nose and throat, the suffocating pain in the chest, the violent cough that tears the lungs ... and brings bloody froth to the lips.[25]

But if this innovation brought an initial breakthrough, it was subsequently contained by adding gas masks to the standard equipment required by both sides.

3.3   The High Noon of Attrition: 1916

By 1916 the home fronts in Austria-Hungary and Russia were already creaking at the seams, but in general civilians remained willing to tolerate the carnage on the battlefields They were also willing to sacrifice a fair deal of their own personal freedom as the war effort demanded growing state intervention and control in almost every facet of the economy and society. Fiscal and monetary management, the direction of production and labor and the suspension of domestic political conflict all served to squeeze out higher war production from increasingly exhausted and indebted economies. In May Britain finally introduced conscription for 18 to 41 year olds, although this measure also served more systematically to retain essential workers in their jobs. Unfortunately, this residual political optimism, enhanced economic planning and also military innovation served to facilitate and prolong the unprecedented slaughter.

Having dealt with the Russians during 1915, von Falkenhayn could now return to his main preoccupation and attempt to force a decision on the western front. If Haig (who had replaced French as British commander) and Joffre still imagined that a breakthrough would lead on to a resumption of open warfare in the old style, von Falkenhayn harbored no such illusions, or ambition. Perceiving the French army as near exhausted, he resolved to draw it into a futile and ruinously expensive defense of a site whose symbolic importance precluded its surrender. Belfort was considered for this purpose and rejected before the German command settled on the northeastern town of Verdun and its complex of surrounding fortresses. There is scarcely space in a general history such as this to do justice to the static battles and resulting carnage that typified the Great War, but a more detailed consideration of the Battle of Verdun provides the supreme example of such warfare.

The character of the fighting that unfolded around Verdun owed at least something to Falkenhayn's less decisive, even timid, side. "The French General Staff," he argued, "would be compelled to throw in every man they have. If they do so the forces of France will bleed to death – as there is no question of a voluntary withdrawal – whether we reach our goal or not."[26] In other words, the actual capture of Verdun was of secondary importance, with success to be measured in terms of a ruinous French casualty rate as against a modest German one. However, he neglected to contradict the conflicting impression within his forces facing Verdun that it was to be taken by storm. Operational planning within this Fifth Army, commanded by no less a person than the Crown Prince of Prussia, was therefore fatally at odds with von Falkenhayn's inherent conservatism. The Fifth Army seized one strongpoint after the other, only to be deprived of the necessary reserves finally to carry the day at critical moments during its advance. As Alistair Horne acidly observes of von Falkenhayn's strategy: "Once France had lost Verdun, the carrot to lure the French army into the abattoir would have been removed; the deadly salient itself where the actual bleeding was to take place would have been excised by the Fifth Army's advance."[27]

This is not to deny the fury of the German offensive. Over 1,220 German artillery pieces of every size and purpose supplied with 2.5 million shells were in place along an eight-mile front facing Verdun by February 1. The contest threatened to be one-sided, for the French command had come to regard fortresses as white elephants and even as potential traps. During the Franco-Prussian War of 1870 one French army after another had been bottled up inside fortresses such as Metz and Belfort as the German field armies overran northern France and laid siege to Paris. Then, during 1914, Liège and France's most modern fortress at Manonviller had fallen relatively easily to the advancing Germans. During the autumn of 1915, therefore, Verdun's fortresses had been stripped of over 50 artillery batteries and 128,000 heavy shells for use elsewhere, while the troops left to defend the salient were among the less enthusiastic at France's disposal. They also shared their commanders' complacency, one "*poilu*" (ordinary soldier) excusing the absence of a vital communications trench with the words: "It doesn't matter. One can pass very easily, the Germans don't shoot."[28] Such sentiments were in truth less banal than first impressions might allow, for soldiers on the front line had trouble enough coping with mud, lice, rats, and even their own excrement before confronting the enemy's shells and bullets. Although matters improved as the war progressed, the French army was also notorious for its lamentable medical care, which resulted in a catastrophic death rate among soldiers with inherently treatable wounds. It was equally notorious for its savage and arbitrary discipline. A lackluster unit, for example, could see every tenth man summarily tried and shot after a poor showing in battle. All of this did as much to encourage the avoidance of trouble in any shape or form as to terrorize men into battle. Tacit ceasefires could and did develop along quieter sections of the front, such as at Verdun during 1915 and early 1916, even allowing peasants-turned-soldiers to tend vegetable plots and replace cumbersome items of military uniform with more comfortable civilian clothing.

When the hailstorm of German shells began to pulverize the French positions early on February 21, soldiers a hundred miles distant on the Vosges front could hear a steady rumbling beyond the horizon to the northwest. An aggressive German reconnaisance that same afternoon into a raggedly defended moonscape was followed on February 22 by a full-scale offensive during which the flame thrower, first blooded at Hooge in July 1915, was used to devastating effect. French resistance in the Bois des Caures was eventually overwhelmed by equally determined, numerically superior German assaults, but at the end of the day the Fifth Army had not achieved its stated objectives. Despite the increasingly chaotic torrent of dysfunctional orders emanating from the French command at the rear, a desperate resistance by outnumbered French units continued to slow the German advance at key strongpoints during February 23. The village of Samogneux only finally fell when the French defenders were decimated by devastating fire from their own artillery, but the grim mathematics of the wider battle appeared very much in von Falkenhayn's favor. Ten thousand French prisoners, tens of thousands of dead and wounded and a growing tally of captured guns gave the Germans grounds for optimism. The Kaiser himself came to the front to witness the fall of Verdun.

On February 24 the German offensive finally broke through the prepared field defenses to the north of Verdun, strongpoints fell, Fort Douaumont appeared threatened, and French machine gunners were ordered to fire onto the backs of their fleeing compatriots. Many of these unfortunates were from colonial units, unceremoniously scythed down by their metropolitan comrades, to disappear both from the battle and the subsequent French official history. With communications shattered, the wounded trapped, and reinforcements lacking, the battle was effectively lost. "On the dark evening of 24 February," it has been claimed, "the way to Verdun was open to the enemy."[29]

The disasters of February 24 were succeeded on 25 February by scenes of near farce when the greatest fortress in the complex surrounding Verdun, held by a few dozen men, was captured almost inadvertently by equally few Germans. Defending French machine gunners had been half blinded by the driving snow and so mistook approaching German helmets for the headdress of North African Zouaves. The fall of Fort Douaumont triggered panic. French forces mingled with terrified civilians as they streamed southwards from the front, while in Verdun itself the bridges across the Meuse were prepared for demolition. With all seemingly lost, barrels of red wine were brought up from the town's cellars and smashed to avoid them falling into enemy hands.

However, as the military rout reached its climax, a new general, Edouard de Castelnau, arrived to rally the French command and organize a defense of Verdun. He did so at the very moment when Joffre had settled on a withdrawal to lines behind the town on the southwest side of the River Meuse. However great the moral impact abandoning Verdun might have had, this strategic retreat would have served French military purposes well enough. The broken landscape would have soaked up the fury of the German offensive at a far lighter cost to the defending forces, but it was not to be. General Philippe Pétain was appointed de Castelnau's field commander, reestablished an effective chain of command and organized logistical support for the continued defense of the town. The line stabilized on February 27 after the wreckage of the *village* of Douaumont finally fell to the Germans at the cost of thousands of dead on each side. The tone had been set for the months ahead, during which the deadly arithmetic of von Falkenhayn's battle of attrition saw meters of ground lost or won for thousands of lives.

The prospect of a bloody stalemate was reinforced as von Falkenhayn denied the Crown Prince's army the fresh divisions vital to a final breakthrough. The German superiority in artillery was also compromised, for a vast morass of shelled and churned mud prevented the movement of heavy guns forward to the new front, while the defending French artillery was rapidly strengthened. Von Falkenhayn eventually released the necessary reinforcements during March, but the German troops struggled to seize strategic objectives on the west bank of the Meuse, as a prelude to their main offensive on the east bank. German losses approached 82,000, those of the French almost 90,000 by the end of March alone, but the preparatory offensive on the west bank only finally attained its objectives at the end of May, with the fall of the aptly named Mort Homme ridge. Summer may have brought warmer weather, but it also heightened the stench of decomposing bodies, whether human or of slaughtered draft horses. The battlefield had become an "open cemetery in which every square foot contained some decomposed piece of flesh."[30] One soldier recounted: "You found the dead embedded in the walls of the trenches, heads, legs, and half-bodies, just as they had been shovelled out of the way by the picks and shovels of the working party."[31] The German artist Otto Dix was haunted and "inspired by the ethics of mass death and destruction"[32] in equal measure, but finally found it in himself to produce his War Series of etchings in 1924. These included cratered landscapes stretching beyond the horizon, and victims of gas attacks, black-faced and lifeless, stacked against the trench parapets.[33] A brutal indifference to the wounded and dying of one's own side, let alone the enemy, became the norm.

During the course of this battle von Falkenhayn began to doubt the possibility of a victory at any "acceptable" cost in lives and matériel and by late April the Crown Prince and senior field commanders had come to the same conclusion. The German army was being bled white every bit as much as the French, but the Prince's chief of staff, the hard-bitten General Schmidt von Knobelsdorf, remained an isolated optimist. Unfortunately for the soldiers of both armies, he had the ear of the Kaiser and direct access to von Falkenhayn. In spite of the bloody evidence to the contrary, he was able to win approval over the head of the Crown Prince for persevering with the attack on the east bank. A few miles to the south, Pétain had come to the same conclusion as the Crown Prince. He had always been a hands-on officer, close to the ordinary soldiers, and Verdun was asking too much of his army. As survivors shuffled back from the cauldron of the battle, Pétain observed: "Their expressions, indescribably, seemed frozen by a vision of terror; their gait and their postures betrayed a total dejection; they sagged beneath the weight of horrifying memories; when I spoke to them, they could hardly reply, and even the jocular words of the old soldiers awoke no echo from their troubled minds."[34] Left to his own devices, Pétain would have ordered a fighting withdrawal across the broken country southwest of Verdun, where, as noted previously, enormous casualties could have been inflicted on the advancing Germans for a far smaller loss, material and psychological, to the French army. Joffre had, as noted, proposed a similar strategy some weeks earlier, but now he changed his mind and resolved to finish off the engagement at Verdun at a single, victorious stroke. This would release the main French army for the great joint Franco-British offensive on the Somme that had been planned the previous December. On May 1 Pétain was promoted upstairs to command Army Group Center and replaced at Verdun itself by the bullish General Robert Nivelle who promised to land the decisive blow. Von Knobelsdorf had been delivered a French counterpart whose presence was vital to the continuation of the slaughter.

Skirmishes and increasingly intense artillery duals culminated in a French counterattack against Fort Douaumont, which had been reduced above ground to a tangle of steel, loose brick, and concrete. French casualties piled up against the parapets of Douaumont's improvised fortifications, but the German defense held. Pétain was left to take the rap for Nivelle's futile bloodbath, which also provoked the first cases of serious indiscipline within the hitherto stoical French army. The planned German offensive followed on June 1 and made rapid progress toward Fort Vaux, some 3 kilometers southeast of Douaumont. On June 2 German forces secured Vaux's superstructure, but remnants of the French garrison held out in its underground galleries and passageways for five more days. Nightmarish machine gun and grenade battles ensued in the subterranean blackness before thirst forced the French garrison to surrender. Its losses stood at some 100 as against over 2,700 German attackers, but Nivelle swiftly evened up the odds by ordering a series of near suicidal and futile counterattacks.

By June 12 Nivelle had exhausted his reserves, lost a significant part of his artillery, and saw discipline continue to deteriorate by the day. The very man who had coined the immortal phrase "ils ne passerons pas" now talked of withdrawal, although Pétain reluctantly concluded that the sacrifice had now become so huge that Verdun would, after all, have to be held. In the event, the town was saved by a pause in the German offensive. Von Falkenhayn was unnerved by the onset of a new Russian attack in Galicia, earmarked three divisions for transfer from France to the eastern front, and postponed major operations around Verdun until the situation had become clearer. Von Knobelsdorf was only able to resume his now depleted attack (against Fort Souville) on June 23. A bombardment of phosgene gas preceded the assault which rapidly brought the streets of Verdun itself under fire from German machine guns. But here the French held. The transfer eastward of the three German divisions prevented a final breakthrough and the offensive stalled. The battle continued to rage into the autumn, during which time the French army retook forts Vaux and Douaumont, but to no particular purpose beyond the incessant killing. Estimates of the final losses vary, but with over 377,000 French and 373,000 German dead judged realistic.

In August von Falkenhayn paid personally for this futile slaughter through his dismissal as Chief of the General Staff. The entry of Romania on the Allied side, far earlier than von Falkenhayn had predicted, undermined the last shreds of his credibility. The heroes of Germany's eastern front, von Hindenburg and Ludendorff, were now granted overall control of the war effort, by which time a catastrophe of the Allies' making was unfolding on the Somme. As at Verdun the watchword was attrition, with Brigadier General Sir John Charteris claiming: "We are fighting primarily to wear down the German armies and the German nation."[35] British and French forces attacked east of Amiens on July 1 and if the French commanders had learned sufficient from Verdun to avoid heavy casualties, the same could not be said for their British counterparts, who advanced into the teeth of the German machine guns and close range artillery fire. These guns, General Haig had assumed, had been destroyed by his preliminary bombardment and in any case were "much overrated,"[36] but by the end of the day his losses exceeded 60,000 killed, wounded

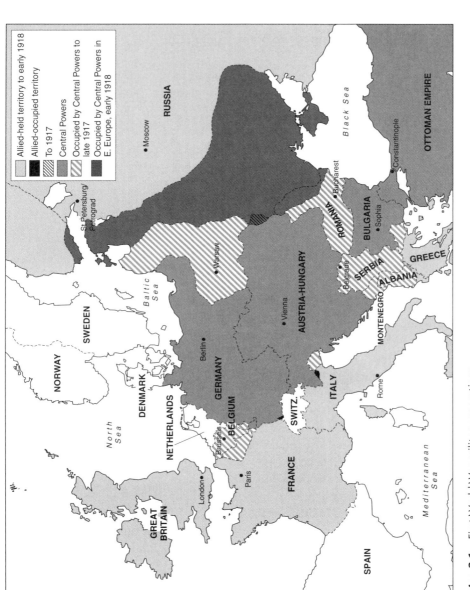

Map 3.1 First World War military operations.

Legend:
- Allied-held territory to early 1918
- Allied-occupied territory
- To 1917
- Central Powers
- Occupied by Central Powers to late 1917
- Occupied by Central Powers in E. Europe, early 1918

or missing. In fairness to the British command, the haunting image of soldiers trudging across no-man's-land in straight lines, spaced at 100-yard intervals, weighed down by 66 pound packs, may be misleading. Robin Prior and Trevor Wilson note that the only troop movements really visible to observers were not attacks across no-man's-land into the teeth of the German machine guns, but the view of soldiers marching up to the British front itself.

> Of all the observers [they write] watching the deployment of the infantry on 1 July, probably only one group actually had a view of the advance not obscured by smoke and dust. This group was in Albert, and what they were observing was the Tyneside Irish marching towards their own front line in close formation and then being cut down in large numbers.[37]

In other words the German gunners, dug in on the heights overlooking the battlefield, were sometimes able to make short work of the enemy even before they had reached their own front line and then entered the battle proper. Historians, Prior and Wilson observe, have been reluctant to relativize "the foot-soldiers' equivalent of the charge of the Light Brigade,"[38] but the outcome of the Battle of the Somme, like Verdun, was decided by heavy weapons and ordinance in another utterly dehumanizing encounter, something neither contemporary observers nor later memory were prepared to accept. Over the course of the entire war some 5 million soldiers were killed by artillery against 3 million by small arms fire.[39]

That said the dehumanized reality of this industrialized warfare did find expression at the time. The words of Siegfried Sassoon's 1916 poem "At Carnoy": "To-morrow we must go/ To take some cursèd Wood ... O world God made!" were committed to paper in 1918 by the artist Christopher R. W. Nevinson in a lithograph entitled *That Cursed Wood*. The picture is totally devoid of any human form, consisting of a low, grey horizon along which are ranged a line of shattered, skeletal tree trunks bereft of branches, leaves or any other sign of life. Several diminutive biplanes are dotted across a dirty, pale yellow-grey sky, hovering vulture-like above the sterile desolation.[40] Meanwhile Sassoon, a decorated war hero, had written to *The Times* in 1917, denouncing British war aims as aggressive and imperialistic, only to be declared insane by an embarrassed military establishment.

The initial French attack achieved some tactical gains, but the offensive was finally abandoned four months later without significant territorial advantage. Allied losses stood at 600,000 and the German toll was only slightly lower. Allied commanders comforted themselves that attrition of this sort would do for the German army and its home front before it did for their own, although at a meeting of the British War Committee on November 3 the Chief of the Imperial General Staff, General Sir William Robertson, was unable to hazard a guess as to how long the war might yet last. For his part Lloyd George openly doubted that attrition was working in the Allies' favor (and in fact the Germans were doing far more killing than dying as the wider war progressed), although no one at the meeting ventured any alternative strategy. However, the grim lesson for von Hindenburg was that despite Verdun the Allies had been able to mount such an attack at all. Although it was premature to admit as much, ultimate German failure was becoming increasingly conceivable.

On the eastern front the battles proved more decisive and ultimately went well for the Central Powers. A Russian attack on the Lithuanian capital, Vilnius, was repulsed in March with heavy losses, but in June General Alexei Brusilov launched a devastating offensive against the Austrians in Galicia, advancing 60 miles and taking 500,000 prisoners. This attack, it should be remembered, had precipitated the transfer eastward of three German divisions from Verdun at the height of that battle. However a German-led counterattack drove back the Russians at a ruinous price to the latter. Brusilov's own casualties approached a million and the Russian army was to all intents and purposes broken. Moreover, the Russians' initial successes delivered the Central Powers an unexpected bonus when Romania seized the moment to join the Allied cause. An Austro-German-Bulgarian army group made short work of the Romanian forces and secured the country's oilfields and grain reserves to provide something of an antidote to the British blockade.

There seemed little prospect of breaking the blockade itself. On May 31 a new German naval commander, Admiral Reinhard Scheer, finally committed his High Seas Fleet to combat against the Royal Navy's Grand Fleet. The resulting Battle of Jutland marked the only encounter between the great capital ships of these opposing navies and may have represented a German tactical victory: 14 British ships totaling 110,000 tons were sunk, against 11 German ships totaling 62,000 tons. However, the strategic situation remained unchanged, for the Royal Navy still dominated the high seas while the German surface fleet returned to port and remained pretty much at anchor for the remainder of the war.

3.4 The Tipping Point: 1917

The winter of 1916–17 revealed another side to the war of attrition as the civilian populations of central and eastern Europe slowly, but surely, began to starve. This battle of endurance between industrial societies was always stacked in the Allies' favor as long as the British blockade remained in place. German U-boats had struggled to impose a counterblockade on British ports, but this involved the sinking of ships rather than their seizure – the latter hardly a practical option for a submarine. Furthermore, in order to comply with the laws of "cruiser warfare," the U-boats had to surface, halt civilian vessels, and allow time for their evacuation, all of which left the submarines themselves extremely vulnerable to concealed guns on seemingly innocent freighters, or to the sudden appearance of British destroyers. In February 1915, therefore, U-boat commanders were authorized to remain submerged and attack merchant shipping on sight, but the sinking of the liners *Lusitania* on May 6 and *Arabic* in August exacted a heavy toll in civilian lives, neutral Americans among them. The British naval blockade of continental Europe had certainly triggered massive protests in the United States, but, as Michael Howard observes: "It was now clear that, in the battle for American public opinion, Germany was at a major disadvantage: whereas the British blockade cost the Americans only money, the German cost them lives."[41] U-boat captains were hastily instructed to surface and once again give due warning before attacking merchantmen.

By the end of 1915 the U-boats had sunk 885,471 tons of Allied shipping, and a further 1.23 million tons during 1916. However, German naval planners estimated that in order to cripple Britain's maritime trade, and with it the British war economy, 600,000 tons would need to be sunk monthly. Admiral Holtzendorff was confident that this target was attainable and concluded: "I can say now without hesitation that, as circumstances are now, we can force Britain to her knees within five months by means of unrestricted submarine warfare."[42] To this end the German military joined with the political right to demand a resumption of unrestricted submarine warfare, but Chancellor Bethmann-Hollweg knew that this would bring the United States into the war and so guarantee Germany's ultimate defeat. The industrial magnate Walther Rathenau shared Bethmann-Hollweg's pessimism and also questioned the economic logic of unrestricted submarine warfare. The value of a neutral United States to Germany, he asserted, far outweighed the economic benefits of an all-out U-boat campaign. Germany's parliamentarians were divided on the matter, but in any case ultimate power lay elsewhere – with the Kaiser and his military chiefs. On January 9, 1917 Germany decided in principle to resume unrestricted sinkings, warned the United States of this decision on January 31, and resumed an unlimited U-boat campaign on the following day. Until July the U-boats met their grim target, sinking 600,000 tons or more monthly and prompting the British Foreign Secretary, Arthur Balfour to fret: "It is very tiresome. These Germans are intolerable,"[43] and another British commentator to observe that: "The question is, whether the British army can win the war before the navy loses it."[44] With one out of four vessels leaving British ports falling victim to the U-boats the submarines were doing all that was asked of them, and more, but British economic and maritime power eventually prevailed in this new form of warfare. The British domestic economy was more robust than German planners had imagined and a successful restructuring of the agricultural economy combined with an efficient rationing system to enhance the country's grain reserves. While the cities of Germany and Austria suffered near starvation during the winter of 1916–17, British (as well as French and Italian) town-dwellers experienced no such thing. Furthermore, despite British naval chiefs' misgivings, a convoy system was introduced in April, reducing losses to 500,000 tons by August and just 300,000 tons by December. Despite its continuing and undoubted terrors, the U-boat campaign had been contained at "an economically acceptable level."[45]

If the U-boat campaign proved an economic and strategic failure, it represented a still greater political catastrophe from Berlin's point of view. Woodrow Wilson had been reelected President of the United States in November 1916 on a neutrality ticket. However, in December he attempted to play the honest broker in the war that raged across the Atlantic. What, he asked the two sides, were their peace terms? The Allies, not unreasonably, demanded the restoration of Belgian and Serbian independence, but then went on to demand the reannexation by France of Alsace-Lorraine without a plebiscite, although in the aftermath of the Somme Paris was secretly sounding out Berlin over a compromise deal here. Further east they sought the effective dismemberment of the Habsburg and Ottoman empires, their territories either to be shared between the Allied victors or to emerge as new states, as demanded in the Habsburg case by Czech or Slovak nationalists. The aged Habsburg Emperor, Franz Joseph, had died in November 1916 and his successor, Karl I, struggled in vain to save something from the wreckage by means of a separate peace with France.

Less, oddly enough, was said by the Allies about Germany, whose own demands vacillated wildly between notions of a compromise peace (as favored by the Chancellor, Bethmann-Hollweg) and the extreme demands of the military command. Bethmann-Hollweg had dared hope that Hindenburg might underwrite moderate peace aims and had even supported his appointment as army commander in place of Falkenhayn with this in mind. However the defeat of Romania stiffened Hindenburg's instinctive resolve to fight on to total victory, a sentiment that found ample support in intellectual circles as "German culture and German militarism became intertwined."[46] The prominent economist Werner Sombart, for example, characterized the Anglo-German conflict (in perhaps unwitting reflection of Napoleon) as a struggle between "shopkeepers and heroes," while the author Thomas Mann may have regarded Germany's democratization as inevitable, but nonetheless lauded the struggle of Germany, the land of "music, poetry and philosophy" against a superficial western view of "civilization."[47] The memory of Beethoven, Goethe and Kant was evoked, bizarrely, to serve as a posthumous alibi for the Belgian atrocities. Max Planck and Albert Einstein were among the hundreds of men of learning who supported, at the very least, extensive German colonization of Eastern Europe.

Much of this belligerence may have been "defensive," designed to shield intellectuals from accusations that they were insufficiently patriotic, even prepared to flirt with pacifist pressure groups.[48] "Their over-the-top rhetoric often compensated for deep-seated insecurity," as Peter Hoeres concluded,[49] and in any case this mood was not universal. The painter Max Beckmann, for example, chose to serve as a medical orderly rather than as a soldier, declaring: "I won't shoot Frenchmen, I owe too much to Cézanne,"[50] but his was a relatively lonely voice. The government itself also foresaw colonial concessions in Africa, Austrian domination of the Balkans, a German protectorate over Belgium, and limited gains along the Franco-German border, where the iron ore fields of Longwy and Briey would be annexed; supporters of these aims included the prominent National Liberal politician and future Weimar Foreign Minister Gustav Stresemann. In the event, Bethmann-Hollweg transmitted the tone of these demands to Woodrow Wilson, but thought better of releasing the detail. But even the tone sufficed to antagonize the United States and also the Allies, who rejected the German note on December 12.

Even the German hawks had now accepted that unrestricted submarine warfare would bring the United States into the war. In an effort at least to disrupt any active American contribution to the fighting, the Foreign Secretary, Arthur Zimmermann, telegraphed the Mexican government, which was involved at the time in low-level border skirmishing with the United States. He proposed a full alliance between Mexico and Germany, after whose victory Texas, New Mexico and Arizona would revert to Mexican control. The Mexican government wisely declined such an alliance, but a British intercept of the telegram was passed on to the United States in February, and thereafter, with the U-boat campaign in full cry, Woodrow Wilson took personal responsibility for the declaration of war against Germany on April 6. Declaring that the war represented a crusade for democracy, he could now look forward to playing a major part in framing a future peace settlement, assuming the Allies emerged victorious. Meanwhile the German and Austro-Hungarian governments struggled to secure a victorious future for the Hohenzollern and (with diminishing conviction) Habsburg dynasties.

In fact, Germany's rulers had unnecessarily overplayed their hand. Although Ludendorff had doubted his army's capacity for further resistance immediately after the Battle of the Somme, the western front remained secure enough for the time being, while in the east an outright victory for the Central Powers became increasingly thinkable. Ukrainian grain and Caucasian oil and minerals offered at some not too distant point to render the British blockade increasingly irrelevant but, by the same token, would have left the disastrous U-boat campaign largely superfluous. The 1917 Russian revolutions will receive fuller attention in due course, but during late February and early March 1917 a wave of desertions and mutinies within the army combined with urban strikes and demonstrations to topple the Romanov dynasty. Following the unilateral formation of a new, provisional government and the declaration of a Petrograd Soviet (Council) of Workers' and Soldiers' Deputies, Tsar Nicholas II abdicated. Imperial rule was replaced by a makeshift dual system of governmental and Soviet authority, which did little for administrative or executive coherence within the embattled multinational Russian empire. Matters were further complicated as the Petrograd Soviet cloned itself within individual army units, thereby undermining the role and authority of the officer corps even as the Provisional Government resolved to stay in the war.

While the western Allies comforted themselves that a semblance of democratic government was at last emerging in Russia, the German army seized the moment. In July 1917 a last Russian offensive against the Austrians in Galicia collapsed as the Germans broke through to the north and finally destroyed the Russian army's capacity for meaningful resistance. The wartime casualty ratio of seven Russians to one German had taken its toll and logistical problems rather than residual fighting henceforth determined the pace of the Central Powers' advance along a front stretching from the Baltic to the Black Sea. In September German troops entered the Latvian capital of Riga, pushed on northwards into Estonia and eastwards through Belarus. As a second, Bolshevik, revolution swept Petrograd and Moscow, its leader, Vladimir Ilyich Lenin, determined to end hostilities with the Central Powers as civil war loomed within Russia itself. An armistice followed on December 5 and peace negotiations opened on December 22 in the Belorussian-Polish border town of Brest-Litovsk. A final battle erupted between the German High Command and the civilian authorities over the desired terms of peace. The Foreign Office, the Kaiser, and even the commander of Germany's eastern forces, Max Hoffmann (now a general), advocated a moderate settlement as the forerunner to a compromise peace on the western front. However the High Command and Hindenburg personally urged a "victorious peace," which would see Russia lose Finland, the Baltic States and Poland, but also the Ukraine, Belarus, and the Transcaucasian lands. The moderate option was offered to the Soviet negotiator, Leon Trotsky, but even this seemed too much for him and he walked away from the negotiations declaring there would be neither war nor peace. For good measure Trotsky also appealed to the ordinary German soldiers to rise up and overthrow their class enemies. However, the German army thereafter simply swept eastwards and on February 9, 1918 the Central Powers recognized an independent Ukraine with its capital in Kiev. As German forces approached the Caspian Sea and their Turkish allies overran Russian territories south of the Caucasus, Trotsky had little choice but to bow to the Central Powers' demands. Hindenburg now got his victorious peace and on March 3, 1918 the Treaty of Brest-Litovsk saw Germany (briefly) supplant Russia as the hegemonic power in Eastern Europe.

Matters appeared almost as grim for the Allies on the western front. After viewing the human and material wreckage of the Somme battlefield in early 1917 an appalled Ludendorff had ordered the construction of a new line of purpose-built fortifications well behind the existing, improvised front line. Dubbed the Hindenburg Line by the British, the new positions were designed to maximize any advantages the terrain might offer and deliver a flexible strategy of defense in depth. Here the German armies bunkered down, and waited, while the U-boats went about their work and the war in the east swung finally in their favor.

The Allied commanders could not afford to be so passive, and in any case Nivelle had never been predisposed to inaction. Despite widespread doubts within senior military and political circles, he was determined to reenact the tactics of a series of successful counterattacks at Verdun during the autumn of 1916: saturation bombardment, creeping barrage, and ground attack in strength, – "violence, brutality, and rapidity" as he put it.[51] However, Nivelle's latest plans and exhortations became known to his German counterparts well in advance and on April 16, 1917 a preliminary French bombardment simply thundered down onto empty trenches.

When the French infantry finally reached the new German front further to the rear it was mown down wholesale, suffering 120,000 casualties within 24 hours.

Even before the offensive, the historian Élie Halévy (who was working in a field hospital) remarked to a friend: "I don't know what soldiers you have come across, weakened perhaps by loss of blood. I myself have seen only the rebelliously inclined who constantly seek some way of finishing this massacre and who, finding none, brood on vengeance."[52] Now, in the aftermath of Nivelle's bloodbath, sporadic indiscipline finally erupted into open mutiny on May 3 and 4 and within days half the French army was refusing to obey orders. Battles erupted between deserting soldiers and the gendarmerie. One regiment even attempted to capture and destroy the Schneider-Creusot munitions works, vital to the French war effort, while in the capital and in provincial industrial centers deserting soldiers mingled in the streets with striking workers. Years of privation in the trenches was exacerbated by a growing estrangement between life in the embattled army and civilian life, so adding fuel to the mutiny. Industrial workers were well paid and women enjoyed an unprecedented degree of financial and social independence, leaving the soldiers to reflect that the France they had gone to war to defend no longer existed. The execution of Margaretha Zelle (Mata Hari) by the French authorities represented a more exotic dimension of this (male) fear of the morally subversive power of unfettered female sexuality. Zelle had arrived in Paris from the Netherlands in 1903 to take up a career as a showgirl on the Paris stage, but numerous love affairs with prominent military and diplomatic figures had landed her in trouble by 1917. Her personal adventures were subsumed by the political right within a frenzied campaign against left-wing defeatism and even treason. Accused of using her romantic liaisons to spy for the Germans, Zelle was granted the semblance of a trial and shot on October 13.

At this critical juncture German military intelligence appeared remarkably poorly informed, or possibly concluded that any effort to profit from the troubles could backfire by galvanizing the French army into one final effort to resist. The Germans, therefore, sat tight in their dugouts as Pétain struggled to pull Nivelle's chestnuts from the fire. Pétain favored the carrot over the stick, offering an improved leave system and granting widespread amnesties to the mutineers. Just 20 deserters were actually executed as the army was promised that there would be no more major offensives for the foreseeable future. An irreversible collapse, comparable to that in Russia, had been averted.

To the north, the British army attacked at Arras in early April, but fruitlessly, suffering 130,000 casualties before the battle was abandoned at the end of May. Further British offensives continued through the summer and into the autumn, at a terrible price in life and for modest territorial gains. After a successful tactical assault on the Messines Ridge in June the main battle of Passchendaele (Third Ypres) erupted during late July and raged on until November, by which time British gains amounted to some 4½ miles – all to be lost again in three days of fighting during early 1918. On November 20 a British tank attack at Cambrai enjoyed initial success, but was reversed by a German counterattack. When the fighting for this patch of Flemish countryside finally subsided, the British army had suffered 240,000 casualties (70,000 dead) against German losses of 200,000. It was, Michael Howard observes, an open question as to whether attrition was actually working,[53] even if some senior German commanders began to doubt whether their exhausted and outgunned troops could continue to withstand the seemingly remorseless Allied pummeling.

The war between Italy and Austria-Hungary also took a distinct turn for the worse from an Allied perspective. The Austrians had achieved a tactical victory in the Trentino during May 1916, but thereafter the course of this campaign had been determined by repeated Italian attacks across the exposed limestone plateau to the north of Trieste. General Luigi Cadorna's troops inched forward at a heavy cost and by the autumn of 1917 both sides appeared close to breaking point. At this critical moment, however, Ludendorff was able to transfer seven divisions from his victorious army in Russia to Italy and launch an offensive on October 25 at Caporetto on the Isonzo River. The Italians were routed, with 500,000 deserting and over 275,000 surrendering before a new front was established on the River Piave just short of Venice. Five British and six French divisions had been rushed across the Alps to stabilize the line as the Germans and Austro-Hungarians helped themselves to huge quantities of stores and seized 2,500 abandoned artillery pieces. The sheer volume of wine appropriated and consumed by the victorious German and Austrian troops, it has been suggested, did something to compromise their advance.

Turning to the Near and Middle East, the Ottoman armies had suffered badly at the hands of the Russian General Nikolai Yudenich in eastern Anatolia during 1915 and 1916, triggering a savage backlash within Turkey against the Christian Armenians, who were particularly numerous in the northeast of the country. These Armenians were regarded as sympathetic to the Russian invaders and, despite vehement protests from appalled German railway officials and business-men stationed in Turkey, were deported to Syria or Palestine with extreme brutal-ity, or simply killed, leaving a million dead in an act of genocide for which any adequate act of contrition still remains outstanding.

German agents had enjoyed some success in fomenting insurrections in Persia (Iran) and across Muslim North Africa, added to which a British military thrust northwards from Basra toward Baghdad ended in disaster when the Indian Army forces involved were surrounded in April 1916 at Kut-el-Armera and forced to sur-render. Thereafter, however, the Ottomans' military hold over their Arab domin-ions began to disintegrate, partly through the successful efforts of a British Colonel, T. E. Lawrence, to stir up an Arab insurrection. A second British assault took Baghdad in March 1917, while in Palestine General Sir Edmund Allenby captured Gaza in October after an earlier failed attack, thereafter taking Jerusalem on December 11. The British Foreign Secretary, Arthur Balfour, had already informed Lord Rothschild on November 2 that Britain was favorably disposed toward the creation of a Jewish national home on Palestinian soil, without prejudice to the region's Christian and Muslim communities, but the devil, as history has since shown, would be in the detail.

3.5   Defeat and Victory: 1918

Despite the string of military setbacks during 1917, the Allied armies remained amply supplied at the turn of the year, life on the home front was tolerable, and the political situation appeared reasonably stable. The seemingly limitless resources and bottomless purse of the United States promised to sustain the Allied war effort almost indefinitely, added to which 1 million American troops were due to arrive on the western front by the summer. It was anticipated that these reinforcements would, finally, allow the Allies to launch a decisive offensive in 1919.

Despite their string of military successes during 1917, the Central Powers' prospects were less rosy. Germany was confronted by growing socioeconomic dislocation and deepening political polarization between left and right as the former explored the possibility of a compromise peace coupled with domestic political reform, while the latter rallied in September 1917 around a new annexationist and monarchist mass party, the Fatherland Party. The depth of material suffering in the Austrian half of the Habsburg Empire was, if anything, still greater, while the empire's nationalities increasingly looked toward political independence at the war's end. Victory in the east, it is true, did promise to improve the Central Powers' economic position, through treaties with the Ukraine (February) and Romania (May) that demanded massive deliveries of grain and oil, but the rulers in Berlin knew that time would, ultimately, work against them.

The victory in the east, therefore, seemed at best to offer Ludendorff a final window of military opportunity as he transferred 44 divisions from there to the western front, where 199 German divisions now faced 100 French and 58 British. On March 21 Ludendorff opened his final campaign against the British forces east of Amiens, seeking to drive a wedge between the British and French armies and pin the former in the Channel ports as the French fell back to defend Paris. Initial results exceeded even Ludendorff's expectations, with his forces covering 40 miles during the first four days of the offensive. The British and French armies were still fighting under separate commands and when the hard-pressed British commander, Sir Douglas Haig, appealed to Pétain for reinforcements the latter refused for fear of weakening the French section of the front. The politicians intervened and on March 26 banged military heads together to create a single Allied command under the French Field Marshal Ferdinand Foch. He successfully coordinated the fragmenting Allied resistance and by April 5 the first German attack had petered out, but only to be followed by a renewed offensive on April 9. This second attack, again against the British, was delivered south of Ieper and within three weeks had overrun all the land so bloodily gained by the Allies during 1917 and left Haig staring at outright defeat. His desperate plea: "With our backs to the wall, and believing in the justice of our cause, each one must fight on to the end"[54] was received by his soldiers with mixed feelings, but the line held. Ludendorff was able to deliver a final devastating blow on May 27 (this time against the French army) and push forward to Soissons, within artillery range of Paris, but the Allied line had buckled rather than broken. Foch was willing to yield ground to buy time and the promised Americans were at last beginning to arrive.

On July 16 a final German attack, this time toward Reims, collapsed within two days and the numerical superiority that Ludendorff had enjoyed just months earlier was no more. On August 8 a British counterattack east of Amiens made liberal use of tanks, with aerial support, against the overextended German front and broke it irrevocably. This "Black Day of the German Army," as Ludendorff described it, initiated three months of continuous Allied advance and a German fighting retreat which continued to inflict very heavy casualties indeed on the Allies. If 900,000 Frenchmen had died in 1916, the year of Verdun, and 546,000 in 1917, the year of the Nivelle mutiny, a further 1,095,000 fell during 1918, the year of victory. However, German soldiers became uncharacteristically willing to surrender or desert, despite the very real risk of being killed rather than being taken prisoner at the moment of surrender and despite the known mistreatment of prisoners, in breach of the Hague Convention, by both sides. Among other things, details of prisoners were deployed in dangerous work building fortifications and digging trenches within range of their own artillery.[55] Finally, after the Allies breached the Hindenburg Line in late September, Ludendorff advised the imperial government to seek an armistice as swiftly as possible. It was not just the ordinary soldiers who had had enough. The collapse had reduced Ludendorff himself to a nervous wreck, needing medical care and scarcely in a position to sustain his command

Germany's allies were also collapsing in short order. A final Austro-Hungarian offensive against Italy failed in mid-June, and as desertions and insubordination within the multinational army reached unprecedented levels Vienna appealed publicly on September 16 to Woodrow Wilson for peace terms. Bulgaria capitulated at the end of the month and the Ottoman Empire at the end of October, but Vienna discovered that actually ending the fighting would not necessarily prove straightforward. A final Italian offensive was launched at Vittorio Veneto on October 24, putting the Habsburg forces to flight. By the time an armistice was finally agreed on November 4 the Habsburg Empire itself had effectively ceased to exist.

Powerful voices in the Allied coalition insisted that Germany be laid low, visibly and irrevocably, and perhaps even returned to its fragmented, pre-1871 existence as a collection of small and medium-sized states before an armistice be granted. The United States military commander, General John Pershing, was adamant that Germany should be invaded and occupied during 1919, and the French President, Raymond Poincaré, favored invasion followed by unconditional surrender. For

Britain, however, the prospect of a power vacuum in central Europe, with a potentially hegemonic France to the west and the incalculable threat posed by the emerging Soviet Union to the east, precluded so draconian a policy. Furthermore, German resistance stiffened notably during October, forcing Haig to the bleak conclusion that the German army was "capable of retiring to its own frontiers and holding that line."[56] The views of Marshal Foch and the French Prime Minister, Georges Clemenceau, proved equally decisive. Both men felt that enough blood had been shed and when Woodrow Wilson's representative, Colonel House, intimated that, perhaps, it might prove advantageous to continue fighting, Foch retorted that the terms of the armistice made any further bloodshed indefensible.[57] The armistice conditions certainly stripped Germany of any capacity to contest the eventual settlement, added to which Woodrow Wilson had made it plain from the outset that any peace would have to be reached with a democratic, representative German government and not the imperial authorities. A German revolution would in effect form part of the wider peace settlement.

We shall turn shortly to the issues of revolution and peacemaking, but on November 11 a ceasefire came into effect on the western front. The fighting elsewhere in Europe was, however, far from over. A series of vicious border wars coupled with bouts of "ethnic cleansing" flared up across Eastern Europe, the German army continued to engage the Red Army in the Baltic with Allied approval, and revolutionary upheaval and civil war swept Europe, even as an influenza pandemic now killed as many Europeans as had the fighting itself. Burdened with debt and hostage to the hugely unrealistic expectations of populations that had been nourished since 1914 by increasingly dubious propaganda campaigns, it remained to be seen whether the increasingly fractious Allies could return Pandora to her box – or (to do violence to classical mythology) merely succeed in releasing her malevolent twin sister.

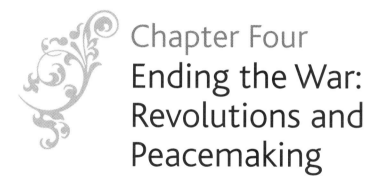

Chapter Four
Ending the War: Revolutions and Peacemaking

4.1 The Home Front in Wartime

August 1914 marked the end of a golden economic age, a time, in Gerd Hardach's words, of "substantial economic growth … unhampered movement between nations of goods and capital [and] unrestricted travel."[1] Certainly it would be remembered as such, for since the 1870s world trade had expanded steadily, assisted by the almost universal adoption of the gold standard, through which (to simplify somewhat) nations with a trading deficit transferred gold to their creditors. This provided a transparent and trustworthy basis for commercial activities in an era of steadily growing prosperity. The City of London remained the nerve center of this global trading system, and so compensated for a relative decline in Britain's wider economic standing and particularly its industrial competitiveness. The activities of the City balanced the national books and its bankers and brokers could see little but harm in any major war. With a view to steadying the City's nerves, therefore, the British Chancellor of the Exchequer, David Lloyd George, reassured a nervous business community on August 4, 1914 that despite the outbreak of war, it would be "business as usual."

This was soon revealed to be wishful thinking at best. It needed speedy government regulation of credit, currency and trade to calm the City's nerves, added to which it quickly became apparent that the traditional reliance on gold to settle trade imbalances would no longer do. The warring powers were, quite simply, importing too much and exporting too little as they subordinated their economies to the insatiable demands of arms production. Expediency took the place of prudence, and since tax revenues could never hope to cover this vast expenditure, money was printed in excessive quantities and governments amassed a nightmarish mountain of domestic or international debt. Britain would later struggle to honor this huge burden of obligations, but on the continent government borrowings could not realistically be honored on any terms. As we shall see, the resulting social and political price would prove very high indeed.

The resulting traumas of inflation were largely put off until after the war, but the military's limitless appetite for munitions and manpower posed an immediate and elemental challenge. Europe's material and human capital, the wealth of a continent at the height of its powers and accumulated over a century or more, was ruthlessly mobilized and squandered in a sustained orgy of mutual self-destruction. The demands of the French army were typical enough. There were 1,400 shells for each heavy gun at mobilization, of which only 400 per gun remained by mid-September 1914. By then, daily production stood at 8,000 to 10,000 shells against an average daily consumption of 300,000. The French state had, traditionally, equipped the army, but clearly lacked the productive capacity to meet its wartime needs. To make matters worse, the advancing Germans had seized key industrial areas on France's northern and northeastern borders, and the country only managed to sustain its war effort by mobilizing its remaining private industrial and manufacturing capacity. A partnership was formed between this private sector and the state, through which government ministries identified priorities and issued instructions, while business leaders were entrusted with carrying out these objectives on a day-to-day basis. Quite apart from ammunition, vast quantities of other equipment needed to be produced: if the army started the war with 3,000 machine guns it eventually possessed 300,000; its stock of 2,000 telephones grew to over 350,000; its 136 aircraft were supplemented by a further 35,000, and so on.

Sustained fighting and sustained military production each demanded growing direction and control of the labor force. In common with its allies and enemies alike, France had to square the circle as millions of young, economically active men were conscripted into the army only to be killed, wounded or captured in their hundreds of thousands, year in year out. A quarter of all male workers were called up by the army at the outset, but it soon became apparent that skilled operatives could not be spared indiscriminately for the remorseless carnage at the front. During 1915 some 500,000 conscripts with key skills were returned to arms production, yet relentless military losses of around 1 million each year equally demanded that conscripts had to be found from somewhere. Accordingly the male peasantry (whose families could take their places in the fields) formed the backbone of the wartime army, while growing numbers of women, juveniles and prisoners of war struggled to sustain military and agricultural production.

The British government had possessed almost unlimited statutory economic powers from the outset, but its commitment to economic liberalism left it reluctant to invoke them. Instead the authorities simply placed orders for munitions with private firms in Britain, Canada and the neutral United States, offering generous prices to spur on delivery. However, the results were disappointing, and only 500,000 of the 10 million artillery shells ordered by the government were actually delivered by the end of 1914. North American companies all too often lacked the necessary know-how and experience, while in Britain itself production was disrupted, ironically, by the absence of conscription as tens of thousands of workers essential to the domestic war effort volunteered to fight, and were accepted by the army. Eventually, employers and trade unions collaborated with the authorities to reclaim essential workers from the trenches.

It took Britain several years finally to resolve these problems, but the tipping point came in May 1915 when an offensive at Festhubert in northern France failed abjectly. The military commanders placed the blame on the shortage of heavy munitions, and this "shells scandal" was enough to precipitate the fall of the first Asquith government. Lloyd George was appointed Minister of Munitions in Asquith's second administration, which included the Conservative politician Andrew Bonar Law and Arthur Henderson, the first Labour politician to enter a British government. This "national coalition" rapidly established a close working partnership between the government and the business community, not too dissimilar to that in France. Businessmen-turned-civil-servants set very high production targets which were met through increasing standardization, the forcing down of production prices, and also a protracted guerrilla war against the trade unions. Before the war the trade union movement had established restrictive craft practices across much of industry, which militated against technological innovation or the standardization of production methods. It also closed off key elements of the production process to all but members of a particular union, a process known as demarcation. Even before Festubert, the unions had grudgingly abandoned their defense of restrictive practices and accepted "dilution" of established trades for the duration of the war. This permitted the recruitment of semiskilled and unskilled labor, which as often as not was female. If 28 percent of Britain's labor force had been female in 1914, the proportion reached 35 percent by July 1918, a trend that was marked by the official propaganda of the day. In 1917 the Ministry of Information commissioned the making of 66 prints entitled "The Great War: Britain's Efforts and Ideals," which were exhibited in London during July 1917. These were completed by 18 different artists, each of whom received the handsome fee of 200 guineas (£210) for their set of six works. A. S. Hartrick's set included a print entitled *Women's Work: On Munitions – Heavy Work, Drilling and Casting*, which showed an impressively sturdy, Britannia-like figure laboring at her work bench in a scene that would previously have evoked universal incredulity.[2]

Following the death of Lord Kitchener in a German U-boat attack during June 1916, Lloyd George replaced him as War Minister. His energetic record was vindicated during the Battle of the Somme where the British forces enjoyed a clear advantage over the Germans in terms of matériel, but the economy still suffered from scarcities and bottlenecks. In December 1916, Lloyd George replaced Asquith as Prime Minister and further tightened the government's grip on economic life.

A new Ministry of Food succeeded in expanding domestic agricultural production by prioritizing grain and potato production over livestock rearing. Rationing was introduced, and extended from June 1917 onwards, but the situation in Britain (and France), although difficult during the 1917–18 winter,[3] remained benign in comparison with the crisis confronting the Central Powers. Of the western Allies, only Italy experienced severe urban food shortages, after a poor harvest in 1917. The ration cards introduced at that point were finally withdrawn in 1921. The British and French experiences in particular contrasted starkly with the growing famine that afflicted Germany and much of Eastern Europe. The British naval blockade of Germany restricted the latter to supplementing its diminishing domestic supplies with whatever food it could buy from neighboring neutrals, whereas Britain, the U-boats notwithstanding, imported substantial quantities of foodstuffs, paid for though US credits.

The new coalition also moved, finally, to challenge Britain's traditional aversion to military conscription. The relentless losses at the front meant that a reliance on volunteers no longer sufficed, while the needs of the domestic war economy continued to demand that key male workers be exempted from military service. Selective conscription provided an orderly response to this double challenge and with time the net was cast ever wider. During 1918, for example, the army had to call up an additional 900,000 men to withstand and subsequently repel the German spring offensive.

If France and Britain managed to cope with the growing challenges of war production, their major ally, Russia, was less successful. Munitions output did soar from 43,000 tons in 1913 to 397,000 tons in 1916, but production for the civilian market collapsed and labor relations deteriorated as the industrial proletariat grew by a third to meet the demands of the war economy. Accident rates soared in Russia's hard-pressed factories. The virtual collapse of Russia's external trade and the loss of key industrial regions to the Central Powers further undercut the war effort, and the territorial losses also triggered a refugee crisis which brought with it urban overcrowding and disease. Furthermore, although wartime harvests were just 10 percent lower than in peacetime and the curtailing of exports left ample supplies in the countryside, too little of this was reaching the towns. The peasantry preferred to consume or hoard food rather than exchange it for a currency which bought fewer and fewer scarce consumer goods. And even when the peasants were ready or able to sell, the Russian railways were struggling to meet the demands of the military, leaving too little capacity to transport food to the towns and cities. In an ominous portent of what lay ahead, the first food strikes broke out in 1915. Thus, if the other European allies coped with the immediate challenges of the war, the impact on the Russian monarchy was soon enough to be fatal. By late 1916 the British authorities had gloomily written Russia off as a spent force.

The contrast with the experience of the United States of America could hardly have been greater. US manufacturers turned their hand to arms production from 1914 to meet Allied demand and made good money in the process. After the USA's entry into the war its industries focused on the production of ammunition, explosives and transport, and government regulation proved sufficiently generous to allow even the most marginal companies to turn over a tidy profit. By 1917 the United States had also become the Allies' primary financier, providing credits that benefited its own exporters and consolidated its dominance of the global economy, which was to be sustained for the remainder of the twentieth century. Food was also shipped in growing quantities across the North Atlantic, and the European Allies substituted American and Canadian supplies for those from more distant producers in Australasia and South America. A single ship, after all, could cross the Atlantic in less than half the time it required to make a single voyage to and from Australia or New Zealand.

The Allies, therefore, enjoyed a global economic reach even in wartime that was denied to Germany and its partners. Alongside the European Allies stood the USA, Japan and, of course, Europe's overseas empires, which supplied raw materials and also soldiers. All in all the Allies were able to dedicate more than double the amount to the war effort than could Germany and its allies: $57.7 billion to $24.7 billion. The naval blockade of Germany added to this miserable situation, but was not its root cause. The Triple Entente always disposed of greater economic power than did the Central Powers, and with the United States' entry into the war Germany's position had become next to hopeless in any protracted struggle. Furthermore, German counterefforts to cut the sea lanes between the Americas and Europe through U-boat warfare were economically unsuccessful and (by bringing the USA into the war) politically and militarily disastrous. In addition, unrestricted submarine warfare added to the growing Allied conviction that Germany was fighting an immoral war, a feeling which had initially been triggered by the German atrocities in Belgium and France. Germany itself came to be seen by Allied citizens as a profoundly immoral society, something Allied propaganda enhanced through its repeated and effective depictions of German bestiality. The subsequent public clamor after the war for retribution against Germany was due in no little part to this abhorrence of "Teutonic" *Schrecklichkeit*.

For all that, as Niall Ferguson observes, the German economy displayed remarkable staying power under the circumstances[4] and if one measures total war expenditure against total enemy deaths, then the German-dominated Central Powers were over three times more effective than the Allies. The death of each Allied soldier effectively cost the exchequers of Berlin, Vienna and Constantinople $11,344.77, while their Allied counterparts had to fork out $36,485.48 for each enemy kill.[5] And Germany certainly displayed great ingenuity when it came to meeting practical economic challenges. The country's premier armaments manufacturer, Krupp, had possessed considerable surplus capacity in peacetime and so was able to expand massively its weapons production once hostilities began. Krupp had also been a major exporter of weapons before the war and this capacity, too, was now switched to the home market, although some foreign companies continued to manufacture Krupp armaments under license. Among them was the British armaments company Vickers, which paid royalties for Krupp grenade fuses throughout the war and beyond.

German scientists also made a substantial contribution to the war effort as they succeeded in creating substitutes (*ersatz* products) for unobtainable strategic imports, of which synthetic ammonia was possibly the most crucial. The chemicals giant BASF had pioneered the process in 1913 and rapidly expanded production during the war itself, to provide Germany with a nitrate-based feedstock for explosives and for agricultural fertilizers. Work also began on the production from coal of synthetic petrol, but the capture of the Romanian oilfields in 1916 saw this project put on the back burner until it was revived a generation later by the Nazis. Meanwhile the economy increased its trade with neutral neighbors and diverted the capacity of its export trade to war production, while the military simply requisitioned goods and even forced labor from conquered territories. However, for all this the increasingly unequal economic struggle against the Allies reduced the Central Powers' economies to near breaking point as the war progressed and ever more was demanded of their factories, farms and, of course, people.

At the outset the demands of war in Germany had resembled those in Britain and France. Stocks of munitions were exhausted by October 1914, prompting the mobilization and increasing direction of economic life through a series of Wartime Raw Materials Agencies. The new agencies were manned and operated by private businessmen and industrialists with considerable initial success, but by mid-1916 the economic balance had tipped towards the Allies. Germany's army chiefs, von Hindenburg and Ludendorff, decided to take a direct hand in matters and enjoyed sufficient political power within the imperial order to stamp their mark on the wartime economy.

On 31 August the "Hindenburg Program" sought to compensate for Germany's growing inferiority in terms of manpower and resources by intensifying production to an unprecedented degree. In November the army command took the various government agencies directly under its wing, and in December 1916 decreed the total mobilization of labor. This Patriotic Auxiliary Service Law called up all men aged between 18 and 60 for war production, diverted all remaining civilian production to the war effort and even attempted briefly to conscript Belgian labor. However, furious protests from the neutral Netherlands (a vital German trading partner) brought this particular practice to a speedy end. At the same time the army itself released 1.2 million skilled workers in September 1916 and a further 1.9 million in July 1917, but for all this the economy could scarcely meet the increasingly utopian demands of the military planners.

Alongside bottlenecks in the supply of labor, transport and raw materials, Germany was swept by an urban famine, which peaked during the winter of 1916–17. Labor shortages, the requisitioning of farm horses for the war effort, and a lack of fertilizers reduced the harvest by a fifth, and despite being renowned for its administrative efficiency, Germany botched both its agricultural policy and its rationing policy. Efforts to hold down prices by statute and operate an orderly rationing system failed and the authorities themselves, Ute Daniel observes, were forced to accept "that a great part of the foodstuffs which … they needed to run their rationing policies simply vanished …"[6] Up to 50 percent of produce was allegedly finding its way onto the black market, or was passed on illicitly by country dwellers to their kith and kin in the famine ravaged cities. Things reached the point in the winter of 1916–17 where the authorities were reduced to laying on so-called "hamster trains"[7] to transport and deposit townsfolk in the countryside, where they might scavenge, beg for, or steal food. Unless an urban family remained wealthy enough to buy on the black market there were precious few alternatives. The ration book entitled a German citizen, dressed increasingly shabbily in worn or patched clothes, to a third of the meat normally consumed before the war, half the fish, a fraction of the fats or eggs, half the sugar and only half the flour. Even when it came to potatoes, only three-quarters of the peacetime diet remained legally available.[8]

Key groups were favored in order to keep Germany in the war. Soldiers received better rations, the arms industry circumvented the rations system, while those in the countryside simply held onto the food they grew. April 1917 witnessed the first bread strikes, just a couple of months after they had broken out in Russia. A better harvest in 1917 and thereafter the requisitioning of food first from occupied Romania and then in 1918 the Ukraine allowed a gradual improvement in rationing allowances and so averted outright collapse, but an air of misery and exhaustion continued to hang over the German home front and fuel an increasing clamor for an end to the war and even for political reform.

If the situation in Germany was bad, in Austria it was worse. After a poor harvest in 1914, Hungary, the breadbasket of the Habsburg Empire, resolved to favor its own population at the expense of the Austrian. Hungarian pigs, or so it was said wryly in Austria, meant more to [the Hungarians] than Austrian human beings. During the autumn of 1918 the situation in Vienna had deteriorated to the point where the city's military commandant was reduced to piracy. Heavily laden barges heading up the River Danube for Germany with requisitioned Romanian wheat were seized and their contents distributed to bakeries in the Austrian capital. A furious Ludendorff threatened military reprisals, but by the autumn of 1918, of course, the German military confronted more pressing problems elsewhere.

All in all, the continent of Europe was sufficiently populous and wealthy to sustain total war for more than four years, but only through a ruthless cannibalization of its potential, and at a high, indeed sometimes fatal, price to the constitutional status quo. From the disintegration of the British-Irish union in the west, to the emergence of the Soviet Union in the east, the map and political landscape of Europe was to change profoundly and irrevocably. Talk of a "return to normalcy," or of a lasting peace, was to prove illusory. And in the center of Europe, where defeat or (in Italy's case) "mutilated" victory was all this suffering had brought, a new mass politics was swift to emerge and ensure that the bloodshed and trauma of the "Great War" would soon enough be overshadowed by its successor.

4.2   Revolution in Russia

The Russian revolutions of 1917 culminated in the formation of the world's first avowedly Marxist state, but in the former Romanov Empire both the theory and practice of Marxism assumed peculiarly Russian forms. If the empire's literature, art, industries and science had been based on western models since the time of

Peter the Great, its politics owed a great deal to a Byzantine and Mongol-Tatar past. The checks and balances, the reciprocal social arrangements that existed in the west between civil society and the state/crown, were largely lacking in Russia. During the Middle Ages the country's Mongol overlords had insisted on the dissolution of traditional urban assemblies, and when the Russian monarchy shook itself free from the Golden Horde in 1480 it took upon itself absolute patrimonial powers, leaving no notion of a society independent of the state. Such a mentality, Richard Pipes argues, was to survive from the imperial into the Soviet era.[9]

Defeat in the Crimean War (1854–6) at the hands of Britain and France triggered efforts to reform and revive the empire. Parallels were drawn with the sweeping domestic reforms initiated in Prussia following its defeat at Napoleon's hands in 1806, which had brought about its military revival and subsequent emergence as a major European power. However, the reform movement soon found itself engaged in a two-front struggle, against defenders of the traditional absolutist order, but also against sections of educated society who deplored the rigidity of the tsarist order and so declared war on authority as such. These nihilists, as they were called, attracted strong support from Russia's university students, among whom Dimitry Pisarev's writings became highly influential. "What can be broken needs to be broken, what survives the blow that is fit,"[10] Pisarev proclaimed, but efforts in 1874 to foment a mass peasant rising failed, leading the nihilist movement, People's Will, to launch a campaign of political terror to subvert the monarchist order.

Tsar Alexander II, who came to the throne in 1855, was receptive to the pressure for reform. In 1861 the privately owned serfs gained their legal freedom, followed in 1863 and 1866 by crown and state peasants. They did not, however, gain title to the land they farmed, with control instead passing to the local commune. Furthermore, the state indemnified the nobility against their loss of property and demanded that the newly freed serfs now pay off this indemnity over 49 years. Not surprisingly, social discontent continued to bubble under the surface in rural Russia, intensified by rapid population growth and growing pressure on available land. Rural unrest and even land seizures became increasingly common.

Alexander never conceded the principle of absolute patrimonial rule, brusquely rejecting a petition from the Moscow gentry to convene a representative assembly with the words: "No one is entitled to present me with petitions concerning the common benefits and needs of the government."[11] The government, Pipes observes, feared that it was so unpopular that any constitutional concessions would unleash chaos.[12] Nonetheless, the Tsar undertook a further range of civic and governmental reforms, which at the very least transferred a degree of functional power from the crown to society at large. In 1881, however, Alexander II was assassinated by People's Will and his son, Alexander III, reasserted the principle of political autocracy, which was confirmed in turn by Nicholas II when he came to the throne in 1894.

The emancipation of the serfs had at least facilitated economic growth as huge numbers of peasants took seasonal jobs away from their villages and outwith agriculture in order to raise cash for taxes and redemption payments. Nicholas II was happy to embrace this accelerating social and economic change as long as his autocratic political inheritance went unchallenged, but economic modernization created political pressures of its own as an urban middle class developed and began to demand the creation of a constitutional order based on a universal, direct franchise. The growing, increasingly well-educated bourgeoisie participated in and was informed in turn by the expansion of publishing and journalism. New businesses were founded, as were new associations to promote the interests of this emergent middle class. This growing economy also created an expanding industrial working class, which, if relatively small by western standards, nonetheless became concentrated and politically significant in urban centers such as St Petersburg, Moscow, Odessa, and Rostov-on-Don. Sheila Fitzpatrick observes that the majority of these industrial workers maintained very close ties to the land, often working in the factories on a seasonal basis or even commuting from their villages. Western-style trade unionism, which came to serve as a mediatory, stabilizing force within developed capitalist economies, was absent and instead, Fitzpatrick continues, the peasants-turned-workers brought their rural revolutionary heritage into the factories.[13] Strikes became more common and since they often reflected political as much as economic objectives, the state was quick to crush them with force, as it did all oppositional groups. Those leading opponents of the regime who escaped being exiled to Siberia could find that sanctuary in Switzerland, on the lakeside shores of the Ticino or in Zurich, offered a (more pleasant) alternative.

In Russia itself things came to a head in 1905. In January 1904 it had gone to war against Japan over conflicting territorial claims in the Far East, but this conflict proved unpopular from the outset and a series of setbacks culminated in outright defeat by August 1905. During late 1904 liberal opposition to the war and the government waging it had become intense and on January 9, 1905 popular discontent triggered a peaceful protest in St Petersburg against the Tsar's domestic and foreign policy. The demonstrators were put to the sword by mounted troops in the so-called "bloody Sunday" massacre; unprovoked carnage that was neither forgiven nor forgotten for the remainder of Nicholas II's rule. However, the government remained unrepentant and refused to address the concerns of either the workers' organizations or the peasantry until, finally, defeat at the hands of Japan triggered a new wave of social and political protest. As strikes swept the country during September, sometimes with the connivance of liberal employers, the government caved in. The Manifesto of October 17 promised full civil liberties and conceded a parliament, or Duma, elected by a broad franchise.

These concessions were met by a mixed response. The Liberals and more enlightened elements of the gentry and big business were ready to collaborate with a repentant tsarist order, but other parts of the establishment deplored the Tsar's readiness to compromise with the reformists. However the tsarist order had little time left for maneuver, as the popular mood had become alarmingly rebellious. The empire's Polish and Baltic populations vented their longstanding resentment against repression and "Russification," mutinies swept the army and navy from October to December, peasant unrest and land seizures peaked despite thirteenth-hour pledges to phase out the hated redemption dues, and on October 17 (on the day the Tsar published his reformist Manifesto) the workers of St Petersburg proclaimed a Soviet, or council, with quasi-governmental pretensions. Strikes swept the Russian capital and were only finally suppressed with the arrest of the Soviet's leaders on December 3. The concessions contained within the October Manifesto were complemented by military force as the government gradually reimposed control over the empire, but few believed that a durable settlement had been reached, and subsequent events within the Duma added to the sense of stasis.

The four Dumas that sat between 1906 and 1917 were hamstrung as the Tsar clawed back many of the concessions promised in October 1905, while within the parliament itself there was near deadlock between reformers, reactionaries, and revolutionaries. The Liberals formed the Kadet, or constitutionalist, party and made common cause with the peasants' Trudovik group in the First Duma (April 1906). The Kadets were dismayed that the Tsar had, after all, kept a firm grip on the political process by appointing his own ministers, only conceding a limited, property-based franchise, and creating an upper house, or State Council, where half the members were directly nominated by himself. The Kadets demanded a government answerable to the Duma rather than the Tsar, and also joined the Trudoviks in demanding the redistribution of private land directly to the peasants. The Tsar remained unmoved, dissolving the Duma after just two months and facing down efforts by the Kadets and other radicals to organize a new wave of civil resistance (the Vyborg Manifesto).

Nicholas appointed a new Prime Minister, Peter Stolypin, who tried to square the circle by addressing the land question constructively while cracking down on civil disorder. He offered additional credits for peasants actually to buy land, sought to break up the communes and consolidate individual private holdings, and offered vacant Siberian land to those who wished to start afresh in Russia's east, all in an effort to create a politically conservative, landowning peasantry. However, the Second Duma (February 1907) proved unsympathetic. The socialist parties had boycotted the 1906 elections, but in 1907 attracted sufficient support to create a blocking majority along with the conservative right. The liberal Kadets were squeezed, the parliament hamstrung, and in June once again dissolved. The Third Duma (1907–12) saw the Octobrists – landed gentry and businessmen who supported the Tsar's October Manifesto – emerge as the strongest group. However, Stolypin now discovered that it was not only the radical extremes that opposed his reformist proposals. The more conservative wing of the Octobrists shared the Tsar's personal doubts and the Prime Minister's plans were run into the sand. In September 1911, with little to show for his efforts, Stolypin was assassinated and the prospect of measured reform receded still further.

During the period of the Fourth Duma (1912–17) reformist and revolutionary politicians lambasted the tsarist administration, which responded by bypassing parliament as far as possible. Individual ministers reported directly to the Tsar, who withdrew alongside his family into increasing isolation. To make matters worse, the Tsar's eldest son and heir to the throne was a hemophiliac, leaving the royal family vulnerable to a self-styled cleric, Grigoriy Rasputin, who claimed to be able to control the disease through hypnosis. However, Rasputin quickly became notorious for his bouts of drunken debauchery and sexual license, which the Tsar and Tsarina continued to tolerate for the sake, so they believed, of their son. Society at large was less forgiving and as Edward Acton observes: "No amount of censorship could quell public animosity and disapproval."[14] This hostility to Rasputin's presence and growing influence at the heart of the Russian state was to become critical during the course of the war.

With or without Rasputin, working-class and peasant radicalism flourished. Marxism became influential as a force for modernization and change from the 1890s, going through various organizational transmogrifications and participating in several strike campaigns before the Russian Social Democratic Workers' Party (RSDWP) was launched in 1898 and refounded in 1903. Among the leading members of this new party was Vladimir Ilyich Lenin, whose political vision owed something to the writings of the nineteenth-century revolutionary thinker P. N. Tkachev. Tkachev spurned any notion of gradualism – of a patient education of the masses as part of a more peaceful road to socialism – instead declaiming: "The question 'What should be done?' should no longer concern us. It has long since been resolved. Make the revolution!"[15] Lenin appreciated that radical elements of the peasantry supported the non-Marxist Social Revolutionaries and that even agitation among the working class, which constituted just 5 percent or so of Russia's population, was fraught with difficulty. However, he was convinced that any revolutionary movement had to focus on the urban working class.

During a congress of exiles, held in London in 1903, Lenin split the RSDWP. His own Bolshevik (literally "majority," but in reality a minority) faction advocated a top-down revolution to be imposed by a disciplined, ideologically unified cadre onto an unwilling or unwitting society.[16] Lenin was anxious to preempt the growth of western-style trade unionism or of the gradualist political reformism which was being adopted increasingly by the socialist parties of Western Europe. The opposing Mensheviks subscribed to a more orthodox version of Marxism, advocating parliamentary work and cooperation with liberal or peasant parties to advance the immediate cause of reform and so create a bourgeois-liberal order which, Marx had taught, was the necessary precursor of the socialist revolution.

The two socialist factions grew apart, especially after the 1905 Revolution, and in 1913 Lenin established the Bolsheviks as an independent party. He was no doubt emboldened after his faction won six of the nine seats reserved for workers in the 1912 Duma elections. By 1914, as labor unrest swelled alarmingly, the Bolsheviks also dominated the trade union movement in St Petersburg and Moscow. The Mensheviks, meanwhile, continued to collaborate patiently with the Liberals and peasant parties.

The war quickly brought matters to a head. As we have already seen, the economy faced growing problems, while the army suffered a succession of military disasters at the hands of the Germans. Patriotic fervor had greeted the coming of war, but popular opinion quickly turned against the regime, creating a climate of "social criticism, fear, and escapist tendencies."[17] The Tsar was blamed for the military defeats (he had assumed direct command of the army in 1915) and the War Ministry for shortages of weapons, munitions and military equipment of almost every description. People spoke darkly of the Tsarina Alexandra's German origins, and Rasputin's continued presence and nefarious activities at court inflamed opinion even further. Rasputin was eventually murdered in 1916 by members of the royal court itself, but this proved too little and too late to improve the public mood. The government reacted in the manner it knew best, through arrests and oppression, but nothing could still the demands for a representative government that enjoyed public confidence, or address the growing anger in business circles regarding the government's handling of the war effort. From 1915, as a young, volatile, rural labor force was drafted into the munitions factories, the number and intensity of strikes began to rise. And the conscription of peasants into the army had unwittingly created a mass of armed malcontents who were no longer scattered across the empire in their isolated villages.

In early 1917 the popular mood boiled over as one revolutionary anniversary or cause for protest followed hard on the heels of another. The Bloody Sunday massacre of 1905 was commemorated on January 9 by demonstrations in Petrograd (St Petersburg) and on February 14 further demonstrations accompanied the reconvening of the Duma. Thereafter, on February 23, the celebration of International Women's Day (by radicalized female factory workers among others) coincided with rumors of bread rationing, which in turn triggered panic buying and a strike by 80,000 metal and textile workers. The strikes spread and on February 26 soldiers from the 160,000-strong Petrograd garrison fired on demonstrators. However, that was the extent of the tsarist regime's resistance as a succession of regiments mutinied and joined the people in the streets.

Now the politicians made their move as members of the Duma formed a Temporary Committee (of government) and Menshevik leaders announced the formation of a Provisional Executive Committee of a new Workers' Soviet, based on the 1905 model. The Mensheviks called for the election of deputies to this self-proclaimed body, which the depleted garrison appeared powerless to suppress. Soldiers continued to desert in droves and on March 2 a shaken military command recommended that Nicholas abdicate. In everybody's eyes the Tsar had become the personification of the problem. Nicholas II complied and also abdicated for his sickly son. With discretion the better part of valor, his brother Mikhail refused the throne and the Romanov dynasty came to an end. The Tsar and his family were placed under house arrest.

Russia was left with two potential sources of authority, the Petrograd Soviet, which enjoyed widespread backing from workers and soldiers, and the Duma, where the leader of the Kadets, Pavel Nikolaevich Miliukov, set about forming a Cabinet. The Soviet gave him its immediate blessing and on March 3 Miliukov was able to announce a government headed by Prince Lvov, with himself as Foreign Minister and with one Socialist member, Alexander Kerensky (also a member of the Soviet), as Justice Minister. Giorgiy Yevgenievich Lvov, an ennobled civil servant, had joined the Duma as an independent liberal deputy and may have appeared destined to bestow on Russia the form of constitutional government already familiar across much of Europe. The Duma moved swiftly to establish by decree the full trappings of a liberal democracy and declared that a Constituent Assembly would be elected in due course to formalize and legitimize Russia's democratic transformation. The Russian Army Command (Stavka), civil service, and the Allied governments were quick to recognize Lvov's administration as Russia's legitimate government.

However, the problem of dual Soviet/parliamentary authority, and with it the problem of where ultimate power resided, remained unresolved. War Minister Aleksandr Guchkov lamented that the Soviet enjoyed "all the essential elements of real power," including popular legitimacy,[18] and Lvov and Miliukov added to their difficulties by upholding the alliance with their Western allies and so refusing to end the increasingly unpopular war. Meanwhile the Soviet was replicating itself across the regions and cities of Russia, and also in the army. On March 1 the Petrograd Soviet had issued its Order Number 1, which was intended to provide for the election of a soviet within the Petrograd garrison. But as Jahn observes, the Order "was mistaken as valid for the rest of the country"[19] and enacted by each and every military unit. A situation had been created where "the enlisted men ... recognized only the authority of the Petrograd Soviet, while the officer corps recognized only the authority of the Provisional Government."[20] The French military mission in Petrograd observed with horror the resulting chaos within the postimperial army, where every last order could now be questioned by those it affected and, given a genuine choice, fewer and fewer soldiers were keen to risk death or capture at the hands of the advancing Germans. The military mission's reports back to Paris were to color their superiors' view of the mutinies that swept the French army in May 1917. Left-wing politics, as it now appeared to France's officer corps, threatened the very integrity of the army and so served to stab the embattled nation in the back.

Meanwhile antiwar demonstrations broke out in Russia during mid-April as the government held to the annexationist agenda of its tsarist predecessor. Eventually a new coalition government was formed on May 5, again under Prince Lvov, but with greater participation by members of the Soviet Executive Committee. This, however, served increasingly to alienate the "'responsible' Socialists [of the Soviet] ... from the irresponsible popular revolution,"[21] especially since Lvov still refused to quit the war. His coalition tried to square the circle under the watchword of "revolutionary defensism," to defend of Russia what could still be held, rather than succumb to the Bolshevik doctrine of "revolutionary defeatism," to which we shall return.

Lvov had aligned his government with international socialist calls for a peace without annexations or indemnities, but efforts to bring Russia's allies around to a similar view proved fruitless. In any case, the Kadets still hankered after Constantinople and felt morally bound by the Tsar's earlier alliance commitments. They also feared that if a Russian surrender resulted in outright German victory across the continent, then Russia's role in this German-dominated Europe would be much reduced. Accordingly Kerensky, now War Minister, authorized a new offensive against Germany's Austro-Hungarian allies in Galicia. The assault was launched on June 18, but proved deeply unpopular with the ordinary soldiers and had collapsed by early July. Behind the lines, meanwhile, the economy deteriorated further and an exasperated peasantry set about the satisfying task of seizing all the land it could lay its hands on. Peasants serving at the front became increasingly keen to desert, return to their home village and get a piece of the action.

Although the German High Command had ignored the 1917 French mutiny, it was far keener to accelerate the process of internal collapse in Russia. The Bolsheviks had already demanded an immediate end to the war, but their leader, Lenin, was living in exile in Switzerland. Here he had participated in the international socialist movement's conferences at Zimmerwald (September 1915) and Kienthal (April 1916), during which the Bolsheviks espoused the doctrine of "revolutionary defeatism." Most European labor organizations hoped for a speedy and equitable peace settlement, but not at the cost of their own national interests. The Bolsheviks, however, argued that the war was a capitalist, imperial conflict between national bourgeoisies and so did not concern the working classes and the labor movement at all. Victory or defeat for these capitalists, it made little difference in Bolshevik eyes, and in the Russian context defeat was clearly the easiest and most practical exit route from the war and then on to socialist revolution. Lenin and his colleagues now turned their backs on the Second International, accusing its members of failing to prevent the outbreak of hostilities in 1914 and thereafter of actually supporting the war effort in collaboration with their capitalist class enemies. In place of the Second International Lenin and his supporters proposed a new International, dedicated to revolutionary purism and an immediate end to hostilities.

Whatever the German authorities' views on socialist revolution, they could heartily endorse the notion of revolutionary defeatism, so long as it was confined to Russia. On April 3, 1917, Berlin granted a special train (dubbed the "sealed train") diplomatic immunity in order to carry Lenin from exile in Switzerland across Germany, through Sweden, and so into Russia. Upon his arrival Lenin immediately denounced the government's "revolutionary defensism" as nothing but a fig leaf for a "predatory imperialist war."[22] He then called in his "April Theses" for a revolutionary government based on the Soviets and for the collectivization (state control) of the economy. As the weeks passed the Bolsheviks gained strength at grass-roots level, particularly within the factories and the army, but more moderate elements appeared to control the machinery of government and decision making both centrally and locally. Furthermore, the Mensheviks controlled the trade unions, and when the Soviets themselves convened an All-Russian Congress in June the Mensheviks and the rural Social Revolutionaries dominated, not the Bolsheviks.

However, radicals established factory committees in Petrograd which by May were under Bolshevik control, and in the country itself the passage of events was soon to change everything. During July the governing coalition fractured as Socialist ministers unilaterally offered immediate concessions to the peasantry on the land question and also moved to honor earlier promises of home rule made to minority nationalities such as the Ukrainians. The Kadets resigned from the government in protest on July 2, only to trigger mass demonstrations and calls for a purely Socialist regime. Against Lenin's better judgment, the Bolsheviks became embroiled in these protests, which were spearheaded by 20,000 sailors from the naval garrison stationed on the island of Kronstadt just to the west of Petrograd. Troops loyal to the Provisional Government were able to put down the unrest, partly by dint of branding Lenin a German agent (the Bolsheviks did receive funding from Berlin) and so turning the masses against him. Leading Bolsheviks were arrested, although Lenin himself managed to flee to Finland after a good shave and sporting a blond wig, where he was forced to lie low for several months.

A second coalition government was formed on July 25, this time led by Kerensky, but within a month relations between the new government and the army command of General Lavr Kornilov had collapsed. The General deplored the incessant disorder that was plaguing Russia and, with Kerensky's blessing, prepared to march on Petrograd with combat troops to disarm the crowds and dissolve the Soviet. However, with an eye to the febrile popular mood Kerensky subsequently denounced the General, whose plans were in any case completely undermined by desertions, a rail strike and opposition both from garrison troops and the various militias that had sprung up since the February Revolution. Kornilov was arrested and the government itself was reduced to an increasingly incoherent shambles. Far from abolishing the Soviet and reestablishing his government's authority, Kerensky had been forced to arm the former to defend the capital against Kornilov, with weapons which were not returned for safe keeping once the immediate crisis had passed. Furthermore, despite playing a minimal part in the resistance against Kornilov, the Bolsheviks gained much of the credit at grass-roots level. As Fitzpatrick observes: "The Bolsheviks' strength was that they were the only party uncompromised by association with the bourgeoisie and the February regime, and the party most firmly identified with ideas of workers' power and armed uprising."[23]

Lenin returned from Finland and on October 10, after some internal debate, the Bolsheviks' Central Committee agreed that the time had come to seize power. The Petrograd and Moscow Soviets had already fallen under Bolshevik control following elections in late August and early September, while the army was in no condition to offer serious resistance in the aftermath of the Kornilov Affair. The Provisional Government took half-hearted and ineffective steps to preempt a

Bolshevik rising, but on October 25 the Bolshevik militias, commanded by Leon (Lev) Trotsky, seized key points in the capital as government ministers either surrendered or fled. It was a low key affair. The "storming" of the government-held Winter Palace by the Bolsheviks, immortalized melodramatically by the Russian film director Sergey Eisenstein, in reality only claimed six lives and, as Hubertus Jahn notes: "Hardly anyone in Petrograd noticed what was going on. The theatres were playing as usual, restaurants were as busy as ever, and public transport continued uninterrupted."[24]

On October 26 Lenin announced decrees to the newly convened Second Congress of the Soviets of Workers' and Soldiers' Deputies which proclaimed an end to the war, the abolition of the private landed estates in accordance with the wishes of the Social Revolutionaries, and the creation of a Council of People's Commissars to act as a provisional Soviet government until the Constituent Assembly had been elected into office. At this stage, Martin McCauley observes, Lenin imagined that Russia stood at the beginning of an extended road to socialism, during which the country would undergo a sweeping program of economic modernization under the benign guidance of German comrades whose own revolution would make Berlin the socialist capital of Europe.[25] However, events were to move faster and more decisively in Russia than Lenin could have imagined, while the German comrades were to ensure that their revolution did not follow Russia's example, so leaving the Soviet Union a vast yet isolated revolutionary state.

Having secured Petrograd, the Bolsheviks seized control of Moscow after five days of stiff resistance and also the main industrial centers of Russia's European heartland. Any opposition was labeled "counterrevolutionary," but although the Bolsheviks had welcomed the departure of their Menshevik rivals and the more moderate Social Revolutionaries from the Second Congress of the Soviets – in protest against the violence of the October Revolution – elections to the Constituent Assembly were allowed to proceed on November 25. Lenin might have gone along with the peasants' hunger for land, but this had not converted them to the Bolshevik cause and the Social Revolutionaries under Victor Chernev emerged victorious with 370 seats to the Bolsheviks' 175.

However, the Assembly was not due to meet until January 18, which allowed Lenin time to exploit tensions between the left and right of the Social Revolutionary party and form a coalition government with the former. This, he claimed, negated the validity of the Social Revolutionaries' election victory, and even called into question the legitimacy of the Assembly. When it convened on January 18 it refused to approve Lenin's provisional government and so sealed its own fate. During the early hours of January 19, 1918 a meeting of the Assembly was interrupted by the commandant of the Bolshevik Guard. Tapping Chernev on the shoulder he declared that: "I have been instructed to inform you that all those present should leave the Assembly Hall because the guard is tired."[26] With that the Assembly was peremptorily and permanently dispersed and the Bolsheviks' claim to monopoly power definitively asserted. Any further opposition by Russia's anti-Bolshevik majority would, and did, mean civil war and the scene was set for a sustained orgy of bloodletting. Trotsky's Red Army, founded in February 1918 around a nucleus of factory Red Guards and demilitarized soldiers and sailors, reintroduced a tight command structure before conscripting some 5 million workers and peasants who subsequently provided the Bolshevik Party with its mass membership and an enduring militarist legacy. As Fitzpatrick observes, the army tunic and boots were worn even by civilian party members and the coercion and summary justice of martial law continued into peacetime. The Red Army engaged 50,000 former tsarist officers as field commanders – each watched over by a political commissar and with each officer's family held hostage to ensure their functional loyalty.[27] This force, a tenth of whom were combat troops, was eventually to defeat a series of opponents across the vastness of the former Russian Empire, but at a terrible price in human life: 1.2 million soldiers and 8 million civilians who died through violence, famine or disease.[28]

The Russian civil war has been aptly described by Norman Davies as "a multi-sided free-for-all."[29] The Ukrainian capital of Kiev, for example, changed hands 15 times as "Reds," "Whites," the Poles, and Ukrainian nationalists and anarchists of various hues fought to secure the bread basket of Eastern Europe. Czech and Slovak prisoners of war and deserters, formed into the Czechoslovak Legion, struggled to extricate themselves from the Soviet Union and return home, in the process seizing stretches of the Trans-Siberian Railway. The German army had also been slow to depart at the end of the war, only evacuating the Ukraine in February 1919 and remaining in the Baltic lands with Allied approval to stave off any assault there by the Red Army.

In early 1918 Allied forces had also arrived on the scene, disembarking on the peripheries of the former Russian Empire in a half-hearted attempt to offer support to the indigenous anti-Bolshevik (White) forces and so keep Russia in the war. The West's leaders had little clear idea of what Bolshevism represented or where it might lead, knowing, Margaret Macmillan observes, "as much about Russia as they did about the far side of the moon."[30] Woodrow Wilson dared hope that beyond an aversion to big business the Bolsheviks were about providing greater freedom for the individual citizen, while as Lloyd George remarked: "Don't you think Bolshevism will die out of itself? Europe is very strong. It can resist it."[31] The French Premier, Clemenceau, was less sure, but the British and Americans quickly concluded that active intervention against the Bolsheviks per se would prove ruinously expensive and only serve to fan the flames of revolution – rather than extinguish them. The fear was prescient, for as Allied troops remained encamped ineffectually around the fringes of Russia, their presence did indeed lend the Bolshevik cause the appearance of a revolutionary war of defense. The Soviet Union's rulers were quick to play this card on a number of occasions and thereafter Soviet historians were to depict the civil war as a (failed) intervention by the forces of international capitalism against those of the international

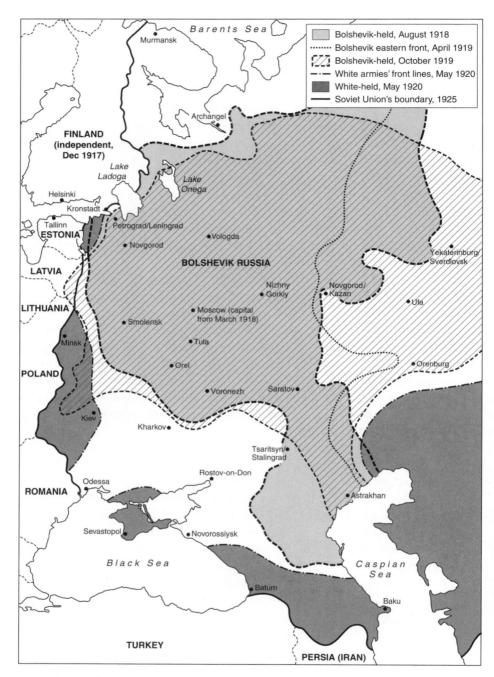

Map 4.1   The Russian Revolution and Civil War 1917–1921.

proletariat. Eventually the Allies evacuated their troops in January 1921 before Britain and then France established full diplomatic relations with the Soviet Union in 1924.

Outsiders apart, the ill-coordinated Whites arguably lost their best chance of victory in November 1919 when General Anton Deniken's army reached Tula, just 100 miles south of Moscow. Advancing independently of Deniken, the Polish army had reached Smolensk, a similar distance west of the Soviet capital and well placed to offer the Whites decisive tactical support. However, at this critical juncture Polish emissaries sought but failed to gain reassurance from Deniken that he would respect their country's new-found independence. With this the Whites squandered any chance of Polish support and also the confidence to maintain their own advance on Moscow. As Deniken's forces prevaricated they were overwhelmed by the Red Cavalry, already flushed by its earlier victories against other White opponents. Thereafter the Red Army picked off a series of poorly coordinated White armies before proceeding to crush national uprisings in the Ukraine, the Caucasus, and Central Asia. By 1921 the Bolsheviks had to all intents and purposes consolidated their grip on the territory of the defunct Russian Empire, albeit at a price in lives equal that of the Great War itself. Famine and disease accounted for more of these fatalities than the fighting itself. Only in the extreme west did Finland and the Baltic States, as well as Poland, succeed in clinging on to an independence that they had first achieved as an indirect consequence of Germany's wartime victories on the Eastern Front.

Unlike People's Will, the Bolsheviks were neither anarchists nor nihilists. However, they did share the "all-or-nothing" iconoclasm of the Russian revolutionary tradition, which translated into an intolerance for opposition and a crypto-religious, millenarian vision of the future. The fusion of Marxist positivism, which asserted that the socialist road represented the inevitable, scientifically determined route to history's final destination, with the legacy of Russia's distinctive historical experience only served to intensify the Bolsheviks' determination to eliminate whatever stood in their way – whether institutions, people, or ideas. The Bolsheviks did not hesitate during the civil war to eradicate under the watchword of "War Communism" the freedoms and representative institutions that had been grudgingly conceded by the Tsars over the previous half century or more.

Lenin had consistently stressed the need for party unity and conformity, so when a ragbag of revolutionary dissidents kicked over the traces during mid-1918, assassinating the German ambassador in July and wounding Lenin himself on August 30, reprisals and counterreprisals followed. The revolution's police force, the Cheká, struck down any dissent with gratuitous torture and deadly force, and as McCauley observes:

Each provincial section of the Cheká developed its own favourite methods of torture. In Kharkov Chekists scalped their prisoners and took the skin, like "gloves" off their hands. In Voronezh they placed the naked prisoner in a barrel punctured with nails and then set it in motion. They burnt a five-pointed star into the forehead and placed a crown of barbed wire around the neck of priests. In Tsaritsyn and Kamyshin they severed bones with a saw. In Poltava they impaled eighteen monks and burnt at the stake peasants who had rebelled ...[32]

By mid-1919, the Cheká had shot at least 8,389 people without trial and arrested a further 87,000 as the Bolsheviks equated their "revolutionary terror" to the situation pertaining in France in 1794.[33]

Striking workers or peasants hoarding scarce food fell victim to this revolutionary terror every bit as much as the guardians of the old order. Among the latter, the imprisoned Tsar and his family were the most prominent victims, shot in cold blood and without any semblance of a trial in January 1918. In March 1921 the sailors of the Baltic fleet, stationed at Kronstadt in the Gulf of Finland, mutinied in protest against the excesses of War Communism, demanding a more libertarian form of soviet rule and economic reforms to address the increasingly dire plight of the population. They had a point, for the peasants had responded to requisitioning by ceasing production, the towns emptied as their inhabitants sought to scratch out an existence in the countryside, and starving factory workers resorted to protest strike action. Bands of homeless children were reduced to roaming the country, a situation even welcomed by the Bolsheviks as a blessing in disguise: "The state could give the children a true collectivist upbringing (in orphanages) and they would not be exposed to the bourgeois influence of the old family."[34] After savage fighting the sailors were crushed by 50,000 troops of the Red Army.

With this the initial, most radical phase of Bolshevik rule had run its course. At the Tenth Communist Party Congress, held immediately after the Kronstadt Rising, Lenin announced the introduction of the New Economic Policy (NEP) to retrieve something from the wreckage. In 1920 Russian manufacturing output stood at just 12.8 percent of 1913 levels,[35] with the 64 largest factories in Petrograd closed. Two-thirds of the city's population had either left or died.[36] Now, in an effort to breathe some life into the economy, small businesses and some peasant farms were privatized, the state sector was decentralized, and foreign investment was encouraged as part of a strategy that was to survive until 1928.

Lenin, however, did not. In January 1924 the second of two strokes killed him and a leadership struggle followed, primarily between the General-Secretary of the Central Committee, Joseph Stalin, and the founder of the Red Army, Leon Trotsky. Stalin advocated a continuation of the New Economic Policy and a circumspect foreign policy, "Socialism in One Country," whereas Trotsky remained committed to world revolution and to the rapid collectivization of economy and society. Stalin, who was quick to claim Lenin's mantle in January 1924, was able to push through his agenda and in 1927 ousted Trotsky from the Communist Party. The disgraced revolutionary was sent into exile in Siberia before being expelled from the Soviet Union in 1929.

On balance the NEP was successful. A level of prosperity was restored and traditional and "bourgeois" entertainments tolerated alongside Communist experimentation. The cinema boomed in a country where the new rulers understood how to use film as a potent propaganda tool, even if the public preferred Hollywood-produced movies to the home-grown masterpieces of Eisenstein, and also found the lure of American jazz irresistible. However, the Bolsheviks themselves baulked at the support offered to the revolution by Futurist artistic circles, and older communists looked askance at elements of the social and moral revolution that followed in the wake of their political coup. The Bolsheviks may have expressed doubts about the function of the traditional family, which was dismissed as an instrument of (male) bourgeois repression (of women). Women had achieved full legal emancipation by the end of the civil war, but the country's new leaders were less certain when it came to notions of free love, promoted by the cultural avant-garde. Children were organized and encouraged to "reeducate" and generally spy on their parents, but this undermining of the traditional family soon enough saw youth criminality and hooliganism swell to dangerously disruptive levels. Moral retrenchment was to follow during the 1930s.[37]

There had already been a crackdown on the bolder adherents of cultural innovation and experimentation. Some artists who had initially identified with the revolution now fled, Marc Chagall among them. Arriving in Paris via Berlin, and followed by some of his greatest works smuggled through Lithuania in a diplomatic bag, his wife Bella provided the living connection with his Russian homeland that enabled him to continue painting. Other Russian exiles, Jackie Wullschlager observes, often found it difficult to remain creative once exiled from the homeland that had provided their inspiration. His fellow artist, the composer Sergei Rachmaninov lamented: "When I left Russia, I left behind the desire to compose; losing my country, I lost myself also."[38]

The New Economic Policy and the sidelining of Trotsky notwithstanding, the October Revolution had created a state that was fundamentally opposed to the Western liberal capitalist order and which presented itself as the legitimate, indeed historically inevitable, successor to that same capitalist order. The Third International (Comintern) which was founded in Moscow in March 1919 claimed to represent the aspirations of the whole of mankind, but equally served to hamper the more conventional diplomacy of Stalin's foreign ministers, Georgy Chicherin and (from 1930) Maxim Litvinov. John Maynard Keynes was among the many Westerners who took the Bolshevik challenge very seriously indeed, not least because the Great War had impoverished and destabilized the capitalist order, perhaps beyond the point of material or moral recovery. If in the past society had been prepared to forgo immediate consumption so as to accumulate wealth and allow future generations to consume more freely, the war had destroyed any such certainties. The accumulated wealth of a century or more had been dissipated in an orgy of destruction and killing: "Thus the bluff is discovered;" Keynes wrote, "the labouring classes may no longer be willing to forgo so largely, and the capitalist classes, no longer confident of the future, may seek to enjoy more fully their liberties of consumption so long as they last, and thus precipitate the hour of their confiscation."[39] The European labor movement began to split into factions – the radicals looking to the Third International in Moscow, the moderates to the Second (Amsterdam) International which continued to pursue their interests within the liberal-capitalist order – so presenting the delegates at the Paris Peace Conference (1919–20) with a range of new and unforeseen challenges. Revolution greatly complicated the task of concluding a satisfactory peace with Germany and its defeated allies.

4.3   Revolution in Germany

The complexity of the challenges that confronted the peacemakers was confirmed as revolution broke out in Germany during the closing days of the war. Germany was not the first Western state to experience significant upheaval for, as we have seen, an army mutiny and socialist-inspired strikes had swept France during May 1917. However, the French authorities succeeded in containing this unrest after several nervous weeks, which in any case had constituted an antiwar protest rather than a direct challenge to France's political and social order. Britain had also experienced rebellion, during April 1916, as Irish nationalists launched a short-lived armed insurrection in Dublin against British rule. The rising was quickly crushed and its leaders, Patrick Pearse and James Connolly, were among those shot by the army. That was not to be the end of the matter, but the political and social order of Britain itself remained largely unaffected by these events. In Germany's case, however, the revolution had comprehensive and profound consequences, as the monarchy was swept aside and a new, republican order struggled to cope with domestic upheaval and the traumas of defeat.

The political landscape of prewar Germany had been defined by the Bismarckian constitutional settlement of 1871. During the 1860s Germany, then a loose confederation of small and medium-sized states, witnessed an upsurge in liberal-nationalist sentiment. The liberal-dominated Prussian parliament demanded constitutional reform, to create in effect a constitutional Prussian monarchy, only to be rebuffed by the Minister President, Otto von Bismarck. Influential liberal voices also demanded the reconvening of a German national parliament, such as had briefly existed during the 1848 Revolution. Bismarck was a loyal monarchist and staunchly Prussian, but he was prepared to promote German unification as long as it occurred on Prussian terms and guaranteed the privileges of the Prussian monarchy and aristocracy.

Short, sharp and victorious wars followed against the perceived enemies of a unified Germany: Denmark (1864), Austria (1866), and France (1870–1), which did indeed serve to reconcile Prussia's liberals to the "half-loaf" of national unity at the expense of a Western-style constitutional monarchy. The victory against Austria had excluded that country from the old, German Confederation and simultaneously brought most of northern Germany under Prussian domination. The victory over France served to lure the still-independent southern states into a new, federated, German Empire. Bismarck also conceded a little to the liberals' domestic agenda. The lower house (Reichstag) of the new national parliament was elected by universal male adult suffrage (of those aged 25 and upwards). The national government answered to the Emperor, Wilhelm I of Prussia, rather than to this parliament, but the Reichstag could and did debate legislation and had the power to approve or reject civil and military budgets. A potentially volatile settlement had been reached through which the Emperor (Kaiser) and his ministers were confirmed as the architects of government policy, but their budgets were dependent on approval by a popularly elected Reichstag.

The longer term historical consequences of this settlement have been fiercely debated. During the 1960s the historian Fritz Fischer argued that the survival of monarchist rule created tension and instability within Germany's rapidly industrializing society. For one thing successive German governments struggled to reconcile industrialists' demands for access to foreign markets in a globalizing world economy (a presumption toward free trade) with the politically powerful agrarians' demands for high import tariffs to protect the domestic market for their grain. This in itself reduced domestic government during the early twentieth century to "a politics of muddling through,"[40] but the effects of this tension on foreign policy proper were much more destructive. Here, Fischer argued, the increasingly radical foreign and armaments policy pursued by Germany during the early twentieth century amounted to an effort by its rulers to divert the ambitions of this modernizing society away from further constitutional reform. However, quite apart from international tensions, this "global policy" or *Weltpolitik* created difficulties closer to home. It may have been welcomed, indeed demanded, by Germany's influential patriotic and military leagues, but a hugely ambitious battleship building program had not come cheap. The national taxation system struggled to cope as various new tax options were rejected in turn by the Reichstag. When Germany provoked the 1911 Moroccan crisis, but failed to benefit decisively from the confrontation with France and its allies, parliamentary critics assailed the government from all sides. Conservative newspapers concurred, asserting that only through war could Germany break free from the shackles that bound it domestically and internationally. "A major conflict," wrote the *Deutsche Armeezeitung*, "would play positively in domestic affairs, even if it brought tears and grief to individual families," while the *Post* argued: "It is widely believed that a war can only be of advantage, in clarifying our precarious political situation and healing a range of socio-political [disorders]."[41] Hemmed in on the domestic and foreign policy fronts, so Fischer argues, Germany's conservative and monarchist rulers risked war in 1914 to restore the country's international fortunes, reforge a spirit of domestic unity and so regain the political credit they had squandered over the past decade or more.[42]

However, without neglecting Germany's major contribution to the outbreak of war, more recent work has questioned this essentially negative image of imperial Germany in a number of important respects. Despite the constitutional stasis at the heart of national government, liberalism flourished within the southwestern states of the federation and in the city states of Hamburg, Bremen and Lübeck. The 1871 constitutional settlement permitted these liberal states a degree of influence at the center, for the upper house of the German parliament, the Bundesrat, was filled by nominees of the state governments, even if Conservative Prussia, containing two-thirds of the German population and with a property-weighted franchise, predominated. When Alsace-Lorraine was granted a constitution in 1911 and with it three seats in the Bundesrat, liberal influence increased just that little bit further. All in all the 1871 federal settlement served to reconcile conservatives and liberals alike to the new national state, and as Winkler concludes, "a unitary state would undoubtedly have instigated a far smaller degree of national integration than did the federal state created by Bismarck."[43]

Conservative–liberal tensions apart, there had been a ferocious anti-Catholic campaign by Protestant liberals (the *Kulturkampf*) shortly after unification, as the Catholic Church was accused of harboring unpatriotic attitudes. However, this conflict fizzled out during the 1880s and by 1900 the Catholic Center Party had become well integrated within the national political process, despite residual religious bigotry in society at large. Bismarck and his allies particularly feared Germany's socialist movement, introducing repressive antisocialist laws in 1878, which were only finally rescinded in 1890. Thereafter antisocialist prejudice remained strong in governing circles. Despite this, however, influential voices in the Social Democratic Party of Germany (SPD) came to see participation in parliamentary politics as a practical road to political power and advocated a reformist future for German socialism. The contrast with the revolutionary-catastrophalism of their Russian counterparts could not have been greater, as the leading SPD theoretician Eduard Bernstein wrote:

> In every advanced society we can see the class struggle assuming milder forms and, looking to the future, things would scarcely be hopeful were it otherwise. … Today we are pushing through reforms by way of the ballot slip, demonstrations and similar means that would have demanded bloody revolution a century ago.[44]

Bernstein's views attracted fierce criticism from radical firebrands such as Rosa Luxemburg (who had cut her political teeth in Russian Poland rather than Germany) and most Social Democrats remained closer to the orthodox Marxist vision of class struggle for the time being. However in 1908 laws governing the freedom of association in Germany were significantly liberalized, reducing police powers of dispersal and opening membership of political associations to women and youths of 18 years or more. The Social Democrats continued to agonize over how far, if at all, they might participate in the process of government, but in 1909 the SPD in Baden, which was effectively a constitutional monarchy, crossed the Rubicon as it formed a governing "bloc" with the liberal parties in the state parliament.

Whatever the SPD's views, most other Reichstag deputies continued to oppose the "parliamentarization" of the national government, and in any event would have been hard put to force through the necessary constitutional changes. Reform would have demanded approval in the Bundesrat, but monarchist Prussia had sufficient votes there to block the enabling legislation. That said, both the Reichstag and the Prussian parliament embraced a reforming agenda which saw the introduction of a new national legal code in 1900, improvements to welfare provision, workplace regulation, trade policy and even (in Prussia) the introduction of a progressive income tax. All of this reinforced a growing willingness by the country's labor movement to exploit the reformist potential of the existing order rather than to plan its complete overthrow, with the trade unions especially hostile to any notions of political adventurism. The extension of workplace consultation in the decade before the war encouraged the trade unions further to maximize benefits for their members within the existing liberal-capitalist order.

And from 1909 German liberalism began to rediscover its taste for reform. Liberal industrialists wondered aloud whether the National Liberals' alliance with the agrarian Conservatives was in their own best interests, for the tariffs demanded by the agrarians clashed with liberal industrialists' preference for open international markets. For their part the Progressive Liberals began to contemplate political cooperation with the Social Democrats in the Reichstag; the Liberal–Socialist coalition in Baden had, after all, shown such an alliance to be possible. An electoral pact between the Progressive Liberals and the Social Democrats contributed to an SPD triumph in the 1912 Reichstag elections, with the latter now the strongest single party in parliament. Even the liberal parliamentary fractions found this hard to accept, for many had no particular wish to emulate Britain and place government firmly within parliament. "For many German observers," Frank Müller observes, "the British constitutional crisis [of 1911] highlighted the relative independence of the Reichstag from the government, the balanced distribution of power within the Reich, and a sense of the state's social responsibility."[45] Meanwhile, outside the Reichstag, the conservative response was particularly virulent. Heinrich Claß, leader of the Pan-German League, published under a pseudonym a rabble-rousing tract, *Wenn ich der Kaiser wär* (If I were the Kaiser), in which he demanded the suspension of a wide range of democratic rights, and particularly repressive measures against Germany's small Jewish minority. Such anti-Semitic rantings could even evoke a degree of sympathy from the Kaiser himself, who bemoaned the striking Jewish presence in the media, commerce, and the financial sector. Much of German society shared a certain aversion to its Jewish conationals, but the popularity of the overtly anti-Semitic political groupings waned from election to election and, as Winkler observes, "for the overwhelming majority of German Jews, Germany was an enlightened land, founded on justice and cultural progress – their Fatherland."[46]

The Germany of Wilhelm II, then, was something of a curate's egg, deeply reactionary in some regards, but a country capable of social and also erratic political reform. This ambivalence was demonstrated with the coming of war, as the Pan Germans anticipated a victory that would see off Social Democracy once and for all, whereas the Chancellor, Bethmann-Hollweg, understood that the labor movement would play a central part in the war effort and thereafter demand its price. As for the Social Democrats themselves, despite sustained criticism of their own government's foreign policy, Russia's apparent responsibility for the actual outbreak of hostilities convinced them to support an ostensibly defensive war. For German socialists the prospect of a tsarist Russian invasion was shocking enough, but there was more to their stance than this. During the Reichstag debate of August 4, 1914 the SPD chairman, Hugo Haase, spoke of the "threatening horror of a foreign invasion" and concluded: "So we will do what we have always promised, we will not leave our Fatherland in the lurch during its hour of need."[47] In other words, isolated radicals apart, there was no realistic prospect of the SPD adopting anything resembling Lenin's doctrine of "revolutionary defeatism." Notions of class war had been subordinated in August 1914 to the national interest, and far more bound the SPD to the rest of German society than distinguished it by way of particular class interests. The SPD, therefore, subscribed to a domestic wartime political truce, the *Burgfrieden*, along with its erstwhile political enemies to the right.

During the initial stages of the war radicals within the SPD conceded the point, without being particularly happy about it. Henriette Roland-Holst understood patriotic loyalty to represent "feelings, moods, tendencies and passions which burst out from the subconscious with irrepressible force,"[48] but her fellow radical Robert Michels characterized the reasoning of leading Social Democrats (from whom he personally distanced himself) more accurately: "In the event of a defeat of the state to which they belonged, the proletarians would necessarily suffer greatly from unemployment and poverty, consequently it was their supreme interest and must be the supreme interest of their representatives to avoid this eventuality."[49] Trade union chiefs agreed with the SPD's leaders, arguing that: "The concept of thinking socialistically involved an awareness that it was not the private gain and advantage of the individual which guarantees victory, but rather the sacrifices of the individual to the common weal of the nation."[50]

For all that, nothing could gloss over the growing suffering on the home front for, as we have already seen, famine and deteriorating working conditions took their toll from 1916 onwards. April 1917 saw wildcat strikes sweep Germany's great industrial centers as half-starved workers demanded better rations, while in June the sailors of the German navy demanded the same. The government's foreign policy hardly inspired confidence either, for its increasingly strident annexationist program appeared to bar any route to an early peace and rested uneasily with socialist demands for a negotiated international settlement. By 1916 a growing minority of Social Democrats refused any longer to vote the annual war budgets through parliament. Having fallen out with the patriotic majority within their own party, this peace faction formed the USPD (Independent Social Democratic Party of Germany) on April 6, 1917. If their mass following was radical, the leaders themselves came from every side of the socialist labor movement, including fire-brand revolutionaries such as Karl Liebknecht, leading orthodox Marxists such as Karl Kautsky, but also the prominent revisionist theorist Eduard Bernstein. As a result the USPD lacked any coherent program, and while it served as a barometer of radical ambition and frustration during the revolutionary years, it was never able to formulate a convincing revolutionary strategy of its own.

Leadership of the revolution, then, would fall to the patriotic, Majority Socialists and their allies in the trade union movement. Even before the revolution began, their contribution to the war effort had brought about some notable concessions from the imperial government, including greater workplace consultation and a promise of postwar electoral reform in Prussia – potentially ending the political domination of Germany's largest constituent state by its agrarian gentry. However, such developments also served to widen the schism between these labor leaders, who saw every advantage in further compromise and collaboration, and working-class radicals who began to lose faith in the very process of government itself. The radicals' thoughts turned increasingly to direct control of day-to-day affairs in their individual workplaces – a form of anarcho-syndicalism – rather than to any agenda for central government.

Meanwhile, during 1917, the Majority Social Democrats began to forge wider political alliances in parliament. On June 26 they demanded of Chancellor Bethmann-Hollweg a clear statement of war aims and plans for domestic constitutional reform, without which they threatened to withdraw support in parliament for war credits. On July 2 Bethmann-Hollweg refused, only to spur growing cooperation between the Center Party, Social Democrats, Progressive Liberals and National Liberals on the constitutional question and efforts to secure a speedy peace. Several days of chaotic political intrigue followed as Bethmann-Hollweg persuaded the Kaiser, after all, to concede universal male suffrage for the Prussian parliament, only to provoke outrage in army circles and on the political right. Under attack from all sides the Chancellor resigned his office on July 12, to be replaced by a Prussian civil servant, Georg Michaelis, who enjoyed the confidence of the army high command rather than the Reichstag. After four undistinguished months in office he was succeeded in turn by the arch-conservative Bavarian Catholic politician, Count Georg von Hertling.

In the midst of this upheaval the Center Party, SPD, and Progressives – henceforth dubbed the majority parties – formulated and gained Reichstag approval for a peace resolution that demanded a negotiated settlement "based on a durable reconciliation between nations" and ruled out "the forcible seizure of territory and political, economic or financial repression."[51] However, Michaelis still answered to the Kaiser and the peace resolution had no immediate prospect of becoming official policy. Pressure groups were formed to oppose or support the resolution:

the powerful Fatherland Party on the right, which demanded a victorious, "Hindenburg" peace, and the smaller People's League (Volksbund) on the center left, which united liberal intellectuals with both Catholic and Social Democratic labor leaders. Although the Volksbund failed either to recruit a mass following or to impact on government policy, its formation indicated that the political middle and left would work together to overhaul German political and social life when the moment came.

And the moment was not long in coming. By September 29, 1918 it was plain to Ludendorff that Germany would lose the war and that speedy armistice negotiations were imperative. Continuing pressure from the Reichstag majority parties for constitutional reform and a negotiated peace was reinforced when the United States intimated that it would only deal with a representative German government. In any case Ludendorff and his colleagues had no wish to cope with the traumas of impending defeat, while Chancellor Hertling was equally appalled at the prospect of defeat and constitutional reform. Thus, on October 3, Ludendorff engineered the appointment as Chancellor of the liberally minded Prince Max von Baden and so initiated the so-called "revolution from above." Von Baden formed a Cabinet recruited from and answerable to the majority parties, which included a trade union leader (Gustav Bauer) and a Social Democrat (Philipp Scheidemann), although it is telling that no politician from the democratic majority itself had thought to offer their services as Chancellor. Nonetheless, on October 28 new legislation formalized this de facto parliamentarization of Germany which, in effect, transformed the country into a constitutional monarchy. In future both the government and the military would answer to the Reichstag.

Meanwhile armistice negotiations with United States officials (of which more later) were progressing and it appeared conceivable that a defeated Germany would escape the traumas that were devastating Russia. On October 29, however, Wilhelm II abruptly left Berlin and his newly democratized parliament for military headquarters in the Belgian town of Spa, while Ludendorff was sacked by the newly empowered parliament for appearing to question the peace talks and new constitutional arrangements. Almost simultaneously the naval chiefs ordered the fleet to engage the Royal Navy on the high seas, which threatened to derail the armistice negotiations. The stench of counterrevolution hung in the air. The sailors of the high seas fleet would have none of it, mutinied, and soon enough took control of the naval ports themselves. This "revolution from below" quickly swept across the length and breadth of Germany; after years of fighting, starvation and grueling working conditions the soldiers and workers had quite simply had enough of the empire and its war. From Flensburg to Munich and from Strassburg to Königsberg self-appointed workers' and soldiers' councils sprang up, convincing the army command and then the Kaiser that the monarchy was a dead letter.

The Kaiser had, in any case, not had a good war, shying away from the military limelight and evoking unfavorable comparisons with Germany's greatest war hero, Paul von Hindenburg. By 1916 Wilhelm was fretting over his military commander's popularity and Bethmann-Hollweg was among the bourgeois politicians who began to contemplate a postwar Germany without the Hohenzollerns as heads of state. Now, with capitulation imminent, Wilhelm II abdicated on November 9 and accepted political asylum in the Netherlands, but not even the Social Democrats had reckoned with the complete disappearance of the monarchy. As crowds of workers streamed into the center of Berlin a meeting was hastily convened between Max von Baden and a deputation of senior Social Democrats, led by the parliamentarian Friedrich Ebert. The Chancellor conceded that the Kaiser's abdication had stripped him of any authority and suggested to a nonplussed Ebert that he succeed him. The Social Democratic leader doubted the very legality of such a step, but his colleague Philipp Scheidemann whispered: "For heaven's sake, just say 'yes' "[52] and the imperial government followed its emperor into oblivion with barely a whimper. On the following day Scheidemann proclaimed the republic to an expectant crowd from a Reichstag balcony. The monarchies in the smaller German states disappeared with equal rapidity.

The workers' and soldiers' councils soon came to be dominated by the Majority Social Democrats and they quickly made themselves useful in sustaining and legitimizing the task of local administration alongside the existing professional civil service. They also lent political weight to the SPD's national leaders as they proclaimed the immediate democratization of all state governments and the extension of the franchise to include women. On November 10 Ebert announced the formation of a provisional government consisting of three Majority socialists and three Independents, which would secure the election of a constituent assembly as swiftly as possible. This, the SPD understood, would establish a pluralistic republican order within which socialists, liberals and political Catholicism would collaborate to secure a tolerable peace and advance domestic reform. Of any proletarian dictatorship there was not a word and "for Friedrich Ebert and his comrades," as Hagen Schulze observes, "the revolution was already over."[53] On the same day Ebert and the army's Quartermaster General, General Wilhelm Groener, agreed to work together to expedite the process of military demobilization and uphold domestic order. Equally crucially, von Hindenburg agreed to stay on as Commander in Chief and so smooth the way from the monarchy into the republic, earning plaudits even from Social Democratic circles. He finally stepped down after the signing of the Versailles peace settlement and thereafter his replacement, Walther Reinhardt, worked closely with Social Democratic leaders, seeing in the Republic "the best hope for a recovery of German power."[54] However, the military's loyalty to the new political order was contingent. With the benefit of hindsight, it is now generally agreed that the initial compact between the army chiefs and the revolution carried an unforeseen price. Lacking any emotional or ethical commitment to the Republic, Reinhardt's successors were, a decade later, to become involved in plans to undermine and ultimately destroy Weimar.

Some Independent Socialists certainly doubted the wisdom of sharing power with non-Socialists, at least before the revolution had been consolidated, and were even less enamored with any deal involving the imperial army. However, events in the former Russian empire provided ample warning of where the imposition of one-party rule might lead and the USPD's leaders shared their majority colleagues' horror of violent revolution. Karl Kautsky for one declared civil war to be the ultimate social catastrophe, invariably ending in dictatorship rather than democracy, added to which the USPD understood perfectly well that serious insurgency would trigger an Allied intervention and thus a renewal of hostilities. Despite his reformist credentials, Eduard Bernstein had come to oppose the war and so had also ended up in the USPD. Now, with the war over, he defended the emerging compromise settlement between the labor movement and the institutions of the defunct empire. Radical revolutions, he observed, tended to occur in agrarian societies where the state was less developed, and the population consequently less dependent on the state and so prone to see radical strategies as less destructive. Germany, he continued, was by contrast a sophisticated and functionally interdependent society in which risk taking would prove highly problematic. Given the degree of reformist potential that had already been apparent in imperial society, Bernstein concluded, radical adventurism was not called for.[55]

Trade union leaders were of the same opinion. Industry and labor had been locked in discussions well before the fall of the monarchy as both lost confidence in the imperial authorities' ability either to prosecute the war effort or manage the domestic economy. Both sides shared an interest in ending the war before economy and society collapsed in chaos or, worse, before fighting enveloped Germany's western industrial regions. Now, the revolutionary events of October and November lent these discussions a new urgency and on November 15 industry and labor concluded a wide-ranging settlement of differences, dubbed the Stinnes-Legien agreement after the industrialists' leader Hugo Stinnes and the convener of the majority unions (ADGB), Carl Legien. Shareholders' rights and managerial authority were recognized by the unions, in return for which they secured a universal system of collective pay bargaining, an eight-hour, six-day week, and enhanced workplace consultation. During 1920 and 1921 parliament accorded the deal legislative substance. Although a negotiated compromise, the Stinnes-Legien agreement was no less revolutionary for that; as Gerald Feldman once remarked: "The industrialists were, in effect, abandoning their long-standing alliance with the Junkers and the authoritarian state for an alliance with organized labor."[56] That in effect committed industry to working within the parameters of the new republic. Beyond this the two sides agreed to collaborate in demobilizing the exhausted war economy, a role they fulfilled in conjunction with the civil service.

The wider compromise agreement between the monarchists and republicans had built on the Bismarckian settlement of 1871 by further democratizing German politics and society, and elections to the constituent assembly duly followed on January 19 (with the blessing of the workers' and soldiers' councils). The results confirmed what the Social Democrats had always known: there was no popular majority for proletarian rule in Germany. Instead the cross-party consensus that had articulated the 1917 peace resolution – between Majority Socialists, left liberals and the Catholic Center Party – received an overwhelming mandate which also enjoyed qualified parliamentary support from the Independent Socialists and the right-liberal German People's Party (DVP).[57] The resulting Weimar constitution formalized this settlement, which sought to accommodate many of the key institutions and interests of imperial society. Senior civil servants remained in post, as did judges and educationalists in a sometimes uneasy accommodation with their new political masters.

That, however, is to forget why the constituent assembly found it necessary to convene in the provincial city of Weimar at all, rather than remain in Berlin. This accommodation between the old and the new was not to everyone's liking, for extremists on the left and the right had little time for compromise. Within the USPD was a radical splinter group known as the Spartacus League, whose leaders, Karl Liebknecht and Rosa Luxemburg, deplored the very notion of a multi-party democracy. They were willing to participate in any parliament *faute de mieux*, but stood in principle for some ill-defined form of pluralistic proletarian rule. Bolsheviks they were not, but, as Luxemburg fumed, pursuing socialism through parliament was a "risible petty bourgeois illusion," against which civil war represented merely "the class struggle by another name."[58] At the turn of the year the Spartacists joined with anarcho-syndicalist activists to form the Communist Party of Germany (KPD).

The left radicals had something of a constituency among the immediate victims of the war – half-starved and exhausted workers and disillusioned soldiers for whom the moderation of the SPD and the trade unions verged on the meaningless. Demonstrations boiled over into riots and insurrection during December 1918, and in January culminated in a short-lived rising in the capital. This was crushed by a scratch force of Social Democratic militia, newly formed volunteer units (Freikorps) of a decidedly nationalist and antiparliamentarian bent, and also regular army volunteers. On January 15 army officers seized and murdered Luxemburg and Liebknecht. The revolutionary left now had its martyrs and during 1919 this sense of victimhood was intensified as a series of wildcat strikes in industry and a left-radical rising in Munich during early April were crushed by the Freikorps with considerable brutality. The KPD attached itself to events such as these but, unlike the Russian Bolsheviks, failed consistently to plan and carry through any major rising on its own account.

The final phase of this incoherent but intense radical insurrection was played out in March 1920. Freikorps and certain army units moved to topple the legitimate republican government rather than disarm under the terms of the peace treaty. Dubbed the Kapp Putsch after their figurehead leader, a civil servant named Wolfgang Kapp who had a track record in far-right politics, these plotters seized the government quarter of Berlin, but were toppled within days as the civil service and army command refused to recognize their authority. The legitimate government had fled to Stuttgart, but even as the Kapp Putsch crumbled it proclaimed a general strike for good measure. With the benefit of hindsight this was less than wise for, as Hagen Schulze observes, the government "placed itself in the role of the sorcerer's apprentice"[59] as the strike wave radicalized and turned against the authorities themselves. The Cabinet's collaboration with the former imperial order was perceived by socialist activists as increasingly flawed and in Germany's heavy industrial heartland, the Ruhr District, the strike boiled over spontaneously into a localized civil war. Fifty thousand armed workers battled with government forces, which only prevailed at the cost of thousands of lives on both sides.

There were also longer term political costs. The badly shaken Social Democrats were henceforward unwilling to work closely with the army command, for military leaders had equivocated during the Kapp Putsch. For their part the army chiefs despaired at the Social Democrats' calling of an (unnecessary) general strike, which, they observed, had only served to inflame the situation. The Social Democratic Army Minister, Gustav Noske, resigned and with this, Schulze concludes, "the chance was lost to reshape the Reichswehr [army] as a reliable democratic instrument; a fateful decision for the Republic's future and one of German Social Democracy's gravest errors."[60]

In fairness to the SPD, historians enjoy the wisdom of hindsight and during the early 1920s the Republic faced greater immediate challenges from beyond its borders in the form of a peace settlement that did not seem to offer the young German Republic real peace and a fresh start. Dismissed by the French Socialist Albert Thomas as "a sum total of insufficiency,"[61] yet condemned by many of his fellow socialists as vindictive and self-defeating, the postwar peace accords fell far short of the ideals expressed by Woodrow Wilson in his Fourteen Points. Quite simply, the statesmen of the day found it infinitely harder to extricate their countries from the entanglements of war than it had been to unleash hostilities in the first place.

4.4   The Legacy of War and the Treaty of Versailles

The Paris peace settlement, and particularly the Treaty of Versailles between Germany and the Allied powers, has wanted neither for detractors or apologists. At the time John Maynard Keynes commented witheringly that: "It is an extraordinary fact that the fundamental economic problem of a Europe starving and disintegrating before their eyes, was the one question in which it was impossible to arouse the interest of the Four [Allied leaders],"[62] whereas for Woodrow Wilson, the German treaty, "completed in the least time possible," represented "the greatest work that four men have ever done."[63] His Secretary of State, Robert Lansing, was less sure, concluding: "The terms of the peace appear immeasurably harsh and humiliating, while many of them are incapable of performance," and the British diplomat Harold Nicolson observed bleakly that: "We arrived as fervent apprentices in the school of President Wilson; we left as renegades."[64]

In fairness to the peacemakers, the rebuilding of Europe demanded far more than any official delegation or treaty could have offered. Text on the page, signatures at its foot, could never repair what was permanently broken, still less restore the world of 1914 that in vital respects was lost beyond recall. As Paul-Marie de la Gorce wrote of the wartime French army: "The combatants already sensed that, at the war's end, they would not again discover the world they had known," even becoming "strangers in their own land."[65] The same might be said of all major wars. In *Suite Française*, the Jewish novelist Irène Némirovsky (who subsequently died at Auschwitz) recounted the defeat of France in 1940 and then the early stages of the German occupation in a small country town. At one point her unlikely German hero, Lieutenant Bruno von Falk, is found deep in conversation with his platonic, just still platonic, French love, Lucille Angellier, whose husband is languishing in a German prisoner of war camp. Home leave beckons for the lieutenant, prompting Lucille to ask nervously of his wife. "My wife," he replies, "is waiting for me, or rather, she's waiting for someone who went away four years ago and who will never return. ... Absence is a very strange thing." Lucille then reflects in silence that "there are some women who expect to welcome back the same man, and some who expect a different man. [...] Both are disappointed."[66]

If war changed men the same could be said of women, as some became alien, even threatening beings in the eyes of male society. Women did often further the war effort in what were considered traditional feminine roles. Thus the Voluntary Aid Detachment of the British Red Cross called for nurses, cooks and kitchen-maids, but also for "motor-drivers" in a society that had only recently come to terms with women riding bicycles in public. The volunteers were to expect deployment in any theater of war, whether France or Mesopotamia (Iraq), Italy or Russia. The Scottish doctor Elsie Inglis went one better, independently setting up a network of field hospitals run and staffed by women – in the face of initial (male) advice to go home and concentrate on her knitting. In January 1917 a fortnightly women's magazine, *Vogue*, appeared for the first time in Britain, priced at a shilling. Its content was a far cry from earlier Victorian domesticity, the early January issue advertising itself as a lingerie number and a subsequent issue featuring a woman spearing a polar bear.[67] The British journalist Charles à Court Repington observed at the time that "the ladies liked being without their husbands, and all dreaded the settlement afterwards ..."[68] And as already seen, the relative freedom afforded to many women in wartime France helped to fuel the 1917 army mutiny. Soldiers had gone to war in 1914 to defend a (male-dominated) society which had seemingly disappeared by default, regardless of the army's heroism and sacrifice.[69]

As revolutionary Germany subsequently adjusted to defeat the vote was conceded to women readily enough, but fears persisted of female sexual licentiousness and, it was alleged, the resulting threat of sexually transmitted disease. Even the work of radical artists sometimes depicted a society in which casual and organized prostitution abounded, often juxtaposed grotesquely against hideously disfigured war veterans or against the spivs and speculators feeding on a world of scarcity and inflation. Indeed, female pleasure-seeking was reaching such extreme lengths, some claimed, as to intensify the inflationary spiral which was undermining personal wealth at an alarming rate. Cabaret songs, such as *Wenn die beste Freundin*, (When the best girlfriend) spoke of reckless, female shopping sprees, pet-like men, and of the traditional male family friend (of the husband) displaced by a female family friend (of the wife), so parodying the repeated subversion of personal and social expectation during the war and its aftermath. It was not as if pre-war society had been static, but the customary pace of change and adaptation had been dramatically disrupted, so evoking strong reactions and thoughts of returning somehow to a mythical, lost golden age.

There were also the more immediate and tangible legacies of the war. Millions of soldiers were demobilized and prisoners of war were released sooner or later, at best into a changed world where most, Richard Bessel observes, "managed somehow to pick up the pieces of their civilian lives."[70] For others it was less easy as they returned from the conflict physically crippled or mentally damaged, sometimes to be greeted as heroes, but at others to be rejected as misfits or cowards and uncomfortable reminders of a past best forgotten. The physically and all too often the facially disfigured were ubiquitous across postwar Europe, commemorated in Max Beckmann's lithograph *The Way Home*. In this picture the artist himself confronts a hideously disfigured war veteran with half his face destroyed, still in uniform, on a streetscape dotted by distant figures on crutches and by a prostitute, perhaps offering the only female company still available to the disabled veterans.[71] The mentally damaged were little better off. Dozens of victims of shell shock had been executed by the British army during the war itself, as it periodically refused to recognize the symptoms of mental breakdown for what they were. The recuperating officers at the Craiglockhart hospital in Edinburgh, portrayed in Pat Barker's novel and the subsequent film *Regeneration*, were arguably among the more fortunate. The ordinary shell-shocked British soldiers' German counterparts were to suffer a less extreme indignity when stripped of their pensions in 1926 for alleged wartime cowardice.

Political changes could complicate matters further, as veterans of the defeated armies all too often returned to countries which had not existed in 1914; or, as borders changed, to find their home town transferred to "enemy" control. As Carolyn Grohmann reminds us, the male populations of Alsace and of the Moselle (German Lorraine) who "in no small measure had fought in the war as German soldiers ... [were] treated with great suspicion by the French authorities upon their return to the region"[72] and could scarcely be accorded the welcome customarily reserved for homecoming soldiers. For the demobilized soldiers of the Habsburg armies, past sacrifices must have appeared particularly futile as the order they had fought – willingly or unwillingly – to defend evaporated during the autumn of 1918. And for a postwar Alsatian widow or bereaved mother whose husband or son had died for Germany, grief under French rule was necessarily a very private thing, or at best something shared within the confines of the immediate and trusted community. Many in postwar Ireland no doubt encountered similar problems as the British army was turned against their country during its struggle for independence – yet so many male Irish had fought and sometimes died for Britain between 1914 and 1918.

For most of Europe's bereaved, however, remembrance and grief could be and were publicly expressed. Imposing war memorials mourned the fighting dead on the former battlefields and also in the great cities of Europe, often "grandiose, self-serving tributes," in Jay Winter's words,[73] which were no doubt intended in part to legitimize the wartime carnage or at least assuage the guilt of the rulers who had unleashed it in the first place. Some memorials, such as the Cenotaph in London, did provide a genuine (and unanticipated) popular focus and the sacrifice was, of course, marked in stone more modestly in countless towns and villages across Europe. These memorials often included the names of those who had migrated from that place well before the war (or even their children), so reuniting families fractured by the forces of economic modernization and migration in an unwanted and unexpected way. In other cases the commemoration of the war dead has been redefined generations later as a result of cultural and political changes far removed from the conflict itself. In 2007, for example, the Scottish victims of Passchendaele received their own battlefield memorial, the word "Scotland" chiseled into its base. It was not lost on the Flemish authorities (who sponsored the monument) that the exact location of the memorial would determine which particular local town benefited the most from the resulting tourism. On other occasions inscriptions could be enigmatic, such as the memorial in the picturesque Breton town of Pont Aven (now subsumed within a car park favored by tourists) which reads approximately – in French and Breton – "Sons of Brittany who died for France." For their part the war cemeteries, some vast, some very small, remain deeply evocative to this day, even if the simple passage of years has erased the immediacy of the sacrifice. "The collective remembrance of old soldiers ..." Winter reflects, "is ... a quixotic act ... an effort which is bound to fade over time,"[74] although surprisingly slowly for all that. As late as 2004 a new memorial was unveiled in the Somme village of Contalmaison to commemorate the near total loss there of the 16th Battalion of the Royal Scots during the 1916 offensive.[75]

Rather more curious was the fate of Ieper (Ypres), scene of three great battles which had utterly devastated the beautiful and ancient Flemish town. While the Belgian authorities struggled to bring ruined agricultural land back into production and restore the wrecked towns and villages of southwest Flanders, others suggested that the ruins of Ieper might be preserved as a war memorial in their own right. First floated at the 1916 Paris "Exhibition of the Reconstructed City," but vehemently opposed by the city's mayor, René Colaert, the idea resurfaced after the war. In November 1919 the British journal *The Graphic* published an article entitled "Ypres as a British War Memorial," which advocated maintaining the desolate, "picturesque" ruins in their wartime state for that very purpose.[76] Debate raged in Belgium itself over the town's future, but Colaert and the burghers of Ieper themselves saw to it that their city was restored sensitively and painstakingly as a living entity. The restoration of its magnificent Cloth Hall was only finally completed in 1967.

As for a memorial to mark the carnage around Ieper, the city's eastern or Menin (Menen) Gate was remodeled on grandiose and controversial lines to serve the purpose. The names of over 50,000 men missing in action from the three battles of Ypres are inscribed on it. On Belgian prompting a moving acknowledgment of the sacrifice made by British and Empire troops still takes place there each evening around sunset, as the last post is sounded: "When the music of the bugles resounds, then all pomp and misplaced grandeur fade, then there is nothing but the Missing, somewhere deep in the clay of Ieper, who are embraced, comforted, cradled by the tones of that evensong."[77]

More immediately, however, there were the formalities of the peace settlement. One print in the British Ministry of Information series "The Great War: Britain's Efforts and Ideals," which was publicly exhibited in 1917, anticipated the mood accurately enough. Drawn by William Nicholson and entitled *The End of the War*, it depicted a British soldier hammering a massive steel spike into a tree trunk to wedge it against a now-closed door marked "WAR." In the background was a ruined town, the ground around the soldier was bloodsoaked (providing the only color in the print) and a broken military drum lay abandoned on the earth at his feet.[78] Against such idealism, however, were set unrealistic expectations, territorial and economic greed, a thirst for revenge, and fear – of national bankruptcy, of revolution, and of further war.

The victors, the Allied and Associated Powers, scarcely shared a common set of positive war aims and this was ultimately to prove fatal to the peace settlement. Aims and objectives frequently conflicted as promises made to lure one potential ally into the war violated undertakings to another, as the interests of a maritime power disregarded those of a continental state, or as those of a creditor state conflicted with those of its debtor allies. Even among the victors, the Paris Peace Conference was not a gathering of equals, with the Asiatic powers feeling slighted, even humiliated. Among the European powers only France and Britain were able forcefully to project their aspirations. The Soviet Union, heir to the defunct Russian Empire, was excluded from the conference altogether as the issue of Soviet representation became entangled with ill-informed Allied efforts to grapple with the challenges thrown up by the Bolshevik Revolution. Did it carry the threat of global revolutionary contagion, or was it little more than a transitory phase in the history of a profoundly unstable country? The presence of prerevolutionary Russian exiles in Paris, who claimed to speak for their homeland, complicated matters further, but in any case the French Premier Clemenceau remained bitterly opposed to any Soviet presence at the talks. Instead, he advocated the containment of the new Soviet state with the least possible effort and the minimum of expense.[79]

If the Russian Revolution was an unwelcome and vaguely threatening distraction, treatment of the defeated Germany was central to Allied discussion and, very often, disagreement. For the American President, Woodrow Wilson, the German question formed an indispensible part of a wider global agenda, and for the British delegation peace with Germany served as the means to other ends, including a revival in international commerce, but also colonial aggrandizement. For Clemenceau and his colleagues, however, the treatment of Germany was virtually their be all and end all, with other ambitions playing a decidedly subordinate role. Historians, including Pierre Renouvin, once characterized French wartime policy and thus the formulation of its war aims as relatively incoherent.[80] However, more recent interpretations have stressed the consistency and conviction behind plans for eastward expansion designed to tip the imbalance between German and French power in Paris's favor.

Beyond the reannexation of Alsace and the Moselle (German Lorraine) French leaders had formulated a range of more discrete economic, military and territorial objectives, which were reminiscent of France's glory days of the late eighteenth century under the First Republic, or thereafter during the early 1800s under Napoleon. This policy, David Stevenson concludes: "was not merely security-conscious and defensive, but included elements of anti-German imperialism fired by a conviction of cultural superiority and memories of historic greatness."[81] Thus the French philosopher of science, Pierre Duhem, had declared in 1915: "German science" possessed a "geometric spirit, which was hopelessly inferior to the French 'esprit de finesse.'"[82]

Returning from the esoteric to the world of power politics, French policy-makers were determined to cut down to size Germany's heavy industrial capacity and, as Jacques Bariéty has observed, "to facilitate on the contrary, the industrial expansion of France, of Belgium, of Italy and of Poland [in order to achieve] a profound change in the ratio of industrial forces on the European continent."[83] Georges-Henri Soutou takes the argument further, seeing the ultimate annexation of the Rhineland at the heart of French wartime policy, observing that: "The whole of the political, administrative and military class was in agreement from the autumn of 1914 that the simple return of Alsace-Lorraine would not suffice to modify fundamentally in Paris's favor the Franco-German imbalance,"[84] and, as Anna-Monika Lauter concludes, this meant securing the Rhine frontier as a minimum demand: "All in all French war aims regarding the Rhine frontier … led to the formulation by the country's most senior leaders of a detailed expansionist project."[85] Were annexation to prove impossible, Paris envisaged a Rhineland consisting of one or more nominally independent states, but bound to France through a monetary and customs union.

The British Prime Minister, David Lloyd George, was initially preoccupied with domestic political survival, it seems. During the early stages of the infamous "Khaki election" campaign of November–December 1918, he stressed the need for "a just and lasting peace" to secure Europe's future,[86] but public opinion demanded both retribution and German treasure and the Prime Minister had an election to win. By early December the talk was of hanging the Kaiser, and stripping Germany bare, even of personal holdings of gold and silver, all jewelry, and the contents of the country's picture galleries and libraries. The promise to "squeeze [Germany] until you can hear the pips squeak"[87] delivered Lloyd George's Liberal-Conservative coalition its election victory on December 15 and, as one of Keynes's Conservative friends remarked, filled the House of Commons with "a lot of hard-faced men who look as if they had done very well out of the war."[88] Thereafter the British Premier spent much of the peace conference scrambling to recover what he could of his original moderation, which created difficulties of another kind as he confronted French ambitions. During the war itself Paris had feared that the British presence in the north of France might become permanent, thus creating "a certain similarity from the French point of view between the British and the Germans."[89] With the war over the British military commander, Field Marshal Douglas Haig, did nothing to soothe French sensitivities when opining that in effect Britain had won the war since France "lacked both the moral qualities and the means for gaining the victory."[90] The French in turn noted their greater blood sacrifice, of 1.3 million soldiers against 723,000 British, all of this fueling "a feast of mutual recrimination."[91]

The United States President, Woodrow Wilson, arrived in France on December 13, 1918 to a hero's welcome, carrying an exceptional and unrealistic burden of expectation. In January 1918 he had enunciated his Fourteen Points in a speech to Congress, offering a vision of a postwar world where national self-determination, open diplomacy and a new moral order would secure lasting peace. The enemy powers would be treated firmly but fairly, offering them a place in this new compact from the outset. American military and especially economic power had done the rest and now victors and vanquished alike expected him to reconcile the irreconcilable. Whether Wilson himself appreciated the enormity of the task confronting the peace negotiators is open to doubt. Strong on principles and self-belief, weaker on detail and genuine consultation, the American leader believed that his country's financial strength would be decisive. His European allies owed $7 billion to the United States government and $3.5 billion to private American banks, so the USA "would get its way simply by applying financial pressure."[92] Altruism, then, had its limits even for the US President, and the Americans were very clear from the outset that their European allies would have to repay this staggering debt. Neither he nor his advisers anticipated that the Europeans would in turn seek to offload this burden onto the defeated Germany, thus compromising international relations for a decade or more.

More immediately, however, Wilson was convinced that a new world authority, the League of Nations, would hold the key to a lasting peace. Once this body had been established, he claimed, the rest "would sooner or later fall into place."[93] In the event, the Covenant of the League, which was approved on April 28, 1919, gave the new forum few teeth. French negotiators had struggled to create a League

Figure 4.1   Woodrow Wilson's triumphal arrival in Paris for the peace conference, 1918.
Source: Mary Evans Picture Library / Rue des Archives / Tallandier.

of Nations army as part of a genuinely supranational organization, no doubt the better to contain Germany, but the USA and Britain were not prepared to sacrifice national sovereignty in this way. The League emerged as a consultative body, lacking substantive powers and without the United States as a member, for in 1920 the US Congress refused to ratify the Versailles Treaty (of which the League Covenant formed a part).

Furthermore, Japan failed to persuade its British and American allies to include a racial equality clause in the Covenant, so eventually turning the Asiatic superpower against the West during the interwar period. That said, Japan did get compensation of a different kind. The League awarded it Germany's Pacific island colonies to the north of the Equator (those to the south went largely to Australia and New Zealand) and also temporarily, as it turned out, Germany's Chinese mainland colony, Shantung – much to China's consternation.[94] A furious Chinese government subsequently repudiated Versailles and, as repeated nationalist demonstrations swept Beijing, signed a separate peace with Germany in September 1919. Endemic civil war soon enough crystallized around a struggle between Bolsheviks and Chinese Nationalists, with the former ultimately victorious in 1949 – an outcome with far-reaching global consequences.

It is little wonder, then, that during the spring of 1919 the West's leaders struggled to agree among themselves on the text of a peace treaty with Germany. During the armistice negotiations of October and November 1918 German delegates believed that they had wrested several vital political and procedural commitments from their American counterparts. Woodrow Wilson's Fourteen Points lay at the heart of this, with their vision of open diplomacy and a restitutive and negotiated peace settlement rather than a punitive one. It was agreed from the outset that Germany would have to compensate the civilians of the war zones for their personal losses and compensate Belgium more fully for the violation of its neutrality; Article XIX of the Armistice agreement spoke of "réparation des dommages" or restitution of damage as it appeared within French civil law.[95] Even this prospect worried senior German government advisers, but compensation of this kind was a world apart from the reparations demands that subsequently took shape.

Similarly, Wilson's pronouncements appeared to offer Germany the chance to rebuild its international trading links and so restore its standing as an economic great power. The principle of national self determination also appeared benign, for Germany itself was overwhelmingly German-speaking and could even look across its borders to large Germanophone populations (mainly former Habsburg subjects) who might in time be integrated within an expanded German state. The 1918 German Revolution reinforced this optimism, for Woodrow Wilson had repeatedly stressed that the democratization of Europe, and particularly the overthrow of the German semi-absolutist monarchy, constituted a central US war aim. Revolution there had been, and Germany's provisional government was dominated by Social Democratic ministers, who could hardly be blamed and thus punished for the Kaiser's war – or so the argument ran. The new German authorities preferred to forget the immediate past (during which their country had formulated far-reaching reparations demands of its own against Russia and Romania) and instead looked forward to a peace of reconciliation. Despite the draconian military stipulations of the armistice, therefore, which demanded thoroughgoing disarmament, the demilitarization of large swathes of Germany itself, and also a partial Allied military occupation, Berlin briefly imagined that the eventual settlement might amount to a peace between equals.

Everything that evoked this misplaced optimism in Berlin was the very stuff of nightmares in Paris. During November and December it had become painfully clear to the French that the British and Americans were about to call in their wartime loans, whether private or public. In addition, US support for the French franc was terminated and the French Minister of Commerce, Étienne Clémentel, saw his proposals for a postwar inter-Allied trading bloc rebuffed. Despite the evocation of a glorious imperial past, the future appeared less rosy and Paris was haunted by deep-seated fears of decline, as a trading nation, as a financial center, and more elementally in terms of population. France would now be squeezed, Clémentel feared, between the "Anglo-Americans" and a resurgent central European economy dominated by Germany's great industrial combines. Furthermore, France's leaders were convinced that the German Revolution was mere window dressing and that their eastern neighbor remained "incorrigibly malevolent."[96] And whatever the shorter term fate of its military establishment,

German industry posed a more subtle, but no less terrible, threat. His Prime Minister, Georges Clemenceau, agreed, declaring that: "Industrially and commercially Germany had won the war; her factories were intact, her war debts were internal and could easily be liquidated through financial manipulation, and in a short time the German economy would be stronger and healthier than that of France."[97] Within weeks of the armistice, therefore, the reparations question had been revisited and demands radically revised.

Fear of Germany apart, the French Finance Minister, Louis Klotz, despaired of repaying the government's domestic wartime debt, let alone France's massive international obligations to Britain and the United States. Greatly exaggerated claims upon Germany for the actual loss and damage inflicted on France provided an imagined escape route – le Boche payera (the Hun will pay) – to soothe the nerves of the French state's creditors. Clémentel's successor, Louis Dubois, calculated French claims as equivalent to £2.6 billion, his colleague Louis Loucheur hazarded £3.0 billion, but Klotz trumped them with an estimate of French losses totaling £5.36 billion. Loucheur, to be fair, hoped that his own impossibly high sum (Keynes calculated legitimate French claims to be £800 million)[98] would shock the Allies into canceling inter-Allied debt after all and aiding French postwar recovery, but neither London nor Washington blinked.

Paris had one further card to play. In March 1919 Professor François-Émile Haguenin traveled secretly on behalf of the Quai d'Orsay to Berlin. Would the German Foreign Office, he enquired, consider pursuing a common European economic policy with France, rather than looking to the USA? Berlin rejected the professor's approach, suspecting that Paris was trying to drive a wedge between Germany and the USA. At the very least, he was told, France had to make a public offer on such terms, which of course it could not afford to do. Haguenin regretted the lack of interest shown in Berlin and "stressed again that Germany and France were economically interdependent; henceforth he would seek to establish private economic accords [between the two countries]."[99] As we shall see, similar initiatives resurfaced intermittently during the 1920s, without amounting to much at the time. However, Haguenin's allusion to the prewar era of private economic cooperation between France and Germany was unmistakable and if the war had left a legacy of mutual recrimination and paranoia, the conviction nonetheless grew in business and political circles that sooner or later Franco-German collaboration should, indeed would, occur.

That, however, was for the future and during early 1919 France's public stance remained very tough indeed. Coupled with the lurid promises made by government candidates during Britain's "Khaki election," the effect on German policymakers was dramatic. By this time Berlin had learned that the Allies meant to justify the eventual reparations bill on the basis of German "war guilt," and in December German diplomats were informed by US embassy officials in the Swiss capital, Bern, that a final levy of 200 billion gold marks was not unreasonable. The response was confused. Berlin began a protracted legal and political battle to refute the

notion of war guilt and so, it was hoped, destroy the moral basis for levying reparations altogether. However, German negotiators simultaneously pleaded national
destitution and asserted that a global reparations figure of 30 billion marks would
be more realistic, piously appealing to the victors to display a measure of mutually
beneficial altruism. All of this served to irritate Allied negotiators at best and enrage
them at worst. When on May 13, 1919 the German Foreign Minister, Count Ulrich
von Brockdorff-Rantzau, objected to Georges Clemenceau against the linking of
war guilt and reparations he received short shrift from the French Premier, who
protested that the change of regime in Germany did not exonerate the country.

Relations between the Allies themselves had by now deteriorated to the point
where any negotiated settlement with Germany became impossible. As we have
seen, the East Asian powers were alienated by the course and general tone of the
peace talks, and closer to home it became increasingly doubtful whether Italy
would agree to sign up to the emerging settlement. Allied soldiers were already
being demobilized, their war economies were already being scaled down or
switched back to peacetime activities, yet much of central and eastern Europe was
slipping into chaos, all of which made time of the essence.

The high noon of these inter-Allied altercations occurred between February and
April 1919 and, reparations apart, focused on the future status of the Rhineland.
French patriotic leagues continued to recall the glory days of Napoleon's empire,
when the Rhine had constituted France's natural frontier. To this were now added
bogus ethnographical claims that the Rhine marked the frontier between Europe's
"Greco-Latin" and "Germanic" populations. All of this, French nationalists
declared, left Berlin's claims to the Rhineland contrived and superficial. As the
Ligue des Patriots declared: "It has often been repeated that the Rhine is France's
natural frontier; we wish to demonstrate that it is also the legitimate frontier,"[100]
or as the nationalist politician and writer Maurice Barrès exclaimed: "As if the
recovery of the left bank were an annexation! ... It is the recovery of that which
belongs to us."[101] In other words, influential voices on the French right were con-
testing not merely the 1871 Treaty of Frankfurt, but also the Vienna settlement of
1814–15 which had returned France to its pre-1789 boundaries.

The government in Paris could not simply ignore these expectations and even
shared them to a degree, but the practicalities of inter-Allied negotiations demanded
a different outcome. France refused to countenance a plebiscite in Alsace-Lorraine,
being fearful that the population would opt for Germany in a free vote, and over
this the other allies raised no objections. However disagreements flared up during
early February 1919 as French negotiators proposed occupying Germany's Ruhr
District – the heart of its military-industrial complex – only to be angrily rebuffed
by Woodrow Wilson. Then, on February 28, Prime Minister Clemenceau's chief
aide, André Tardieu, proposed that French-influenced states be established along
the Rhine under League of Nations sovereignty, but this merely served to deepen
the crisis in inter-Allied relations before a compromise of sorts was stitched
together during March and April.

Clemenceau, still recuperating after a failed anarchist-inspired assassination attempt on February 19, was prepared ultimately to trade off claims to German territory for long-term security and on March 14 the British and American leaders offered France permanent military treaties of guarantee. The wartime alliance would now, apparently, continue into peacetime on condition that France accepted German sovereignty over the Rhineland. This was not the end of the matter, however. Building on these signs of compromise, on March 24 Britain publicly advocated the conclusion of a moderate and therefore durable peace, which was to include universal arms cuts and a strong League of Nations which Germany could join sooner rather than later. This went too far for Clemenceau, who hankered after a peacetime alliance directed against Germany. "The Germans," he raged "are a servile people who need force to support an argument,"[102] and days later Marshal Foch repeated his own demand for a Rhineland buffer state, or at the very least a permanent military frontier 50 kilometers to the east of the Rhine. Yet again ultimate German sovereignty over cities such as Trier, Speyer, Mainz, Koblenz, Cologne and Aachen was open to question and a series of rows followed between Clemenceau and Woodrow Wilson. The American President, already seriously ill, made ready as if to return home without a peace settlement. His brinkmanship paid off and by April 22 a deal was struck, which included high reparations (the exact sums yet to be determined), security pacts, and a temporary occupation of the Rhineland. Thereafter western Germany would remain permanently demilitarized, although the Saarland, a pocket of coalfields and heavy industry to the north of Lorraine, would fall under French economic control and League of Nations sovereignty. In 1935 the region's population would be allowed to choose between France, Germany, or the League of Nations in a plebiscite. When the time duly came the Saarlanders opted for the Third Reich rather than the French Third Republic by an overwhelming majority.

The French Cabinet accepted the deal as the best available on April 25, but Poincaré, President of France, warned of German defiance and the enduring threat of a future war of revenge. Marshal Foch predicted bleakly that the putative settlement would merely represent a ceasefire of 20 years. French public opinion also dismissed the inter-Allied compromise as inadequate, and even Clemenceau harbored serious personal doubts, consoling himself that under the terms of the draft settlement any future Allied evacuation of the Rhineland would be contingent on German good behavior. "Germany," he predicted to Barrès, "will not pay and we will remain," while assuring his Cabinet that: "Germany will default and we shall stay where we are, with the alliance."[103] In other words the reparations question had become a political and diplomatic tool in the hands of the French government, for, in the event of German noncompliance, the Treaty of Versailles appeared to legitimize whatever sanctions any Allied government deemed appropriate.[104] Clemenceau was resigned to playing a long game, confiding to the French Senate that: "In reality we shall occupy the country (Rhineland) until it is willing to unite itself to France."[105] France's leaders, it appears, were envisaging a major de facto revision of the peace accord from the very outset.

For its part the Italian delegation was even less happy as it became plain that promises made by London and Paris in 1915 to lure Italy into the war would not be honored in full. On April 24 the country's leading statesmen left for Italy after the Foreign Minister, Sidney Sonnino, openly expressed regret for having entered the war on the Allied side: "I have ruined my country whilst believing that I was doing my duty."[106] One sticking point came over conflicting Italian and Jugoslav claims to former Habsburg territories in Slovenia and on the eastern Adriatic coast, with Clemenceau in particular inclined to favor Jugoslavia. The other concerned southeastern Turkey, promised to Italy in 1917, but now regarded by France and Britain as within Greece's sphere of interest. Although the Italian delegates returned to Paris on May 5 they were now less inclined to support each and every claim on Germany. The myth of a "mutilated [Italian] victory" had been born and, as we shall see, this was to help direct Italian politics onto a radically new path that would add the word "fascism" to the vocabulary of government.

The Belgians were little happier at the cavalier treatment their delegates received, until eventually Brussels was mollified with a reasonable reparations settlement and the acquisition of a slice of German frontier territory (Eupen-Malmédy) and its 70,000 bemused inhabitants. Even after that, however, Belgian governments fretted over the perceived threats of both French and Dutch economic or territorial ambitions which appeared to threaten the country's integrity.[107]

If the key agreements had been reached between three main Allied leaders in closed session, much of the detail on frontiers, reparations, economic relations and the other myriad provisions of the Treaty of Versailles' 440 Articles had been thrashed out by subcommittees, resolved hastily in corridor meetings, or drafted by panels of experts, each working in relative isolation. No one, it seems, had had the opportunity to examine the complete draft, consider its cumulative tone and impact and make appropriate amendments before presenting it to the German delegates for written comment (but certainly not negotiation) on May 7.

When the terms were ceremonially handed over to the defeated enemy, Clemenceau spoke for the Allies and was unable to overcome his personal anger and hostility, leaving the unenviable task of reply to Germany's Foreign Minister, Count Brockdorff-Rantzau. He was a diplomat of the old school, a consummate professional who put public service above politics and thus had the trust of the Germany's new, socialist-dominated government. He cut an isolated figure during the ceremony and certainly knew well enough not to antagonize the victor powers at this critical moment. However, he either neglected or was unable to deliver his address in French. The content of his Germanophone reply was largely conciliatory, Margaret Macmillan observes, but the translators botched their task fatally. To compound the disaster his clipped aristocratic tone and terse demeanor made an awful impression.[108]

Although the German delegates had come to suspect that the terms of the treaty would be harsh, the text still provoked shock and outrage. The (Jewish) Hamburg banker Max Warburg, who had been included in the delegation as a financial expert, raged that it represented "The worst act of world piracy ever perpetrated under the flag of hypocrisy." Brockdorff-Rantzau felt the lengthy document might better be replaced by a single sentence: "L'Allemagne renonce à son existence."[109] German domestic reaction was equally negative as political parties of every persuasion condemned the draft treaty, and trade union and industrial leaders jointly denounced it as "a death sentence for German economic and national life."[110]

Events were to demonstrate that such pessimism was overdone, and historians have observed that the terms of the Versailles Treaty were relatively mild when compared to the exceptionally harsh settlement imposed by the German Empire on the Soviet Union at Brest-Litovsk. In 1919, however, debate essentially focused on whether it was appropriate or wise to punish the new German Republic for the transgressions of the defunct Empire. French leaders protested and probably believed that the revolution had changed little in Germany, but their domestic socialist opponents argued that the "other" and safer Germany, of republicans and liberals who now controlled politics in Berlin, should be given a fair break. The British and Americans also became increasingly uneasy during May and were reasonably sympathetic to the tone and content of the German written response of May 29. It had not been particularly difficult for the German lawyers, diplomats and other experts to expose the crass discrepancies between the Allied leaders' principled, even high-minded declarations on the one hand and the text of the draft treaty on the other. On June 2 Lloyd George warned the Council of Four that the terms of the treaty would have to be moderated before Britain signed. British doubts turned to anger when a senior French military commander in the Rhineland, with the connivance of Marshal Foch, tried to engineer indigenous but essentially synthetic "anti-German" risings in cities such as Mainz.[111] France appeared to be revising the treaty unilaterally even before it had been signed, but the offending general, Charles Mangin, was recalled to Paris and finally, on October 11, officially relieved of his command.

Ultimately, however, the US authorities feared that excessive revision of the draft could destroy what remained of Allied solidarity and with it any credible treaty and stood by France rather than Britain. The only major amendment concerned the future status of Upper Silesia, a German industrial region in the far southeast of the country, where Poland, Germany and the new Czechoslovak state met. The area was essentially bilingual (German/Polish) and had been awarded to Poland in the draft treaty, which in French eyes also served to deprive Germany of important industrial assets. For Lloyd George, however, a German-controlled Upper Silesia could provide reparations, whereas "he would sooner give a clock to a monkey" than hand the region to Poland.[112] Meanwhile, French Intelligence reports had led Clemenceau to believe (rightly or wrongly) that if push came to shove Berlin would prefer to retain all of Silesia over the Rhineland. Eventually it was agreed there would be a plebiscite in the region to determine its fate, and after voting of 60:40 for Germany in March 1921 it was partitioned, with most of the industry going to Poland, but most of the territory to Germany.

The rest of the new Polish-German frontier was no less controversial. The celebrated Polish pianist and longstanding patriot, Ignace Paderewski, had lobbied hard in the United States during 1916 and 1917 on behalf of his homeland and gained direct access to Woodrow Wilson. Believing "La Patrie avant tout; l'art ensuite [The Fatherland first; then art],"[113] Paderewski played no little part in ensuring that the thirteenth of Woodrow Wilson's Fourteen Points promised the restoration of an independent Poland with access to the sea.

In Paris itself, however, things were complicated by the absence of a single Polish voice and by the fact that Poland was still in the process of rebirth as an independent nation while the delegations went about their work. As founder of the Polish Legion, which had initially fought for the Central Powers against the Russians, Józef Piłsudski fell out with the Germans in 1916, was interned, but then released during the German Revolution. He made his way to Warsaw where he took control of the emerging government, but in Paris the Polish National Committee, led by Roman Dmowski, held sway and formulated a series of extreme territorial demands which delighted the French and dismayed the British in equal measure. Paris saw a strong Poland as indispensable to the future containment of Germany, while Lloyd George became increasingly convinced that for the peace terms to endure they would have to prove acceptable to Germany. Dmowski's rabid anti-Semitism, and anti-Jewish riots in Poland itself alienated British delegates (several of whom were Jewish) even further.

The main point of contention was the fate of the German-speaking port city of Danzig, possession of which Poland, with French support, regarded as indispensable. However, Britain felt that the principle of national self-determination demanded a different outcome and eventually the city was made a Free State under League of Nations protection with guaranteed Polish access to its port facilities. Beyond this, the German province of West Prussia (which now became known as the Polish Corridor) was handed over to Poland to provide it with direct territorial access to the sea to the west of Danzig. German opinion was outraged at the loss of this territory to a former subject people, but also because the Corridor now isolated the province of East Prussia from the rest of the country. It was also disputable whether West Prussia itself was indubitably Polish, for it contained a mixed population of Protestants and Catholics, Germans and Poles and also another Slavonic people, the Kashubes. The Protestant Kashubes favored Germany, the Catholic looked to Poland. Now many of the local Germans either chose to leave or were dragooned out of their homes and forced by Polish paramilitaries to flee westward across the new frontier, a process exacerbated by Poland's seizure and subsequent award of the province of Posen (Poznan) to the south of the Corridor. An appalled Jan Smuts, Prime Minister of South Africa, exclaimed: "Are we in our sober senses, or are we suffering from shell shock?"[114] Lloyd George predicted more somberly that the eastern German frontier settlement would "lead sooner or later to a war in the east of

Europe."[115] And indeed, the Soviet Union and postwar Germany did mull over the prospects of destroying a Poland both states abhorred, before eventually the Nazified Wehrmacht took on the same task in 1939 as "a sacred duty."[116]

On June 16 the final terms were handed to the German delegation and Marshal Foch busied himself with preparations to invade central Germany should Berlin refuse to sign. The territorial losses to Poland provoked outrage, those to France, Belgium and Denmark (Danish-speaking northern Schleswig) were met with resignation. The interim reparations transfers were burdensome, including the sequestration of virtually all German assets outwith the country, the confiscation of the merchant fleet, and the loss of lucrative patents and other intellectual property, but the "blank cheque" of a final reparations bill yet to be defined caused genuine alarm. On June 21 the Social Democrat Philipp Scheidemann, who months earlier had proclaimed the German Republic, angrily resigned as Chancellor rather than approve the treaty. Few in Germany questioned his condemnation of the settlement, but cooler heads argued that outright rejection would bring about even greater misery and the disintegration of the country itself. Gustav Bauer, another Social Democrat, was left to cobble together a coalition government willing to sign, and on June 23, 1919 persuaded a disconsolate German National Assembly to ratify the terms. The only outright act of defiance was the scuttling of Germany's high seas fleet at Scapa Flow in the Orkney Islands, where it had been interned after the Armistice.

The signing ceremony on June 28 was not a particularly happy occasion. Bauer declined to attend, instead dispatching his Foreign Minister, Hermann Müller, and the Transport Minister (!) Johannes Bell. Marshal Foch also refused to participate, remaining at his headquarters in the Rhineland, from where he lamented that "Wilhelm II lost the war … Clemenceau lost the peace."[117] The Chinese also stayed away, furious at the handover of the German colony of Shantung to Japan. The occasion hardly wanted for pomp and ceremony, prompting the veteran French diplomat Paul Cambon to fume that: "They only lack music and ballet girls, dancing in step, to offer the pen to the plenipotentiaries for signing."[118] The US Secretary of State, Robert Lansing, wondered at the crass lack of chivalry; Hermann Müller, a longstanding partisan for democracy and social progress in Germany, came close to vomiting once back at his hotel.

It is easy to criticize, and Keynes's *Economic Consequences of the Peace* did just that, but, the triumphalism of the signing apart, the profound disagreements between the Allies and the scale of the challenges confronting them arguably prevented anything better. As the anti-German coalition began to unravel during the spring of 1919, it had become doubtful whether a joint settlement with Germany would be possible at all. Strictly speaking it was not, for the US Congress subsequently refused to ratify the agreement. Since the American military guarantee to France was conditional on US ratification of the entire treaty, the former duly lapsed, and because Lloyd George had made the British military guarantee conditional on the American one, it too lapsed. The Italians felt shortchanged, the British, already embroiled in fresh imperial adventures and soon to face civil war in Ireland,

Figure 4.2   Watching the signing of the Treaty of Versailles, June 28, 1919.
Source: © Hulton-Deutsch Collection/CORBIS.

deplored the continuing instability on the European mainland as an unwelcome distraction, while the French, increasingly isolated and fearful, began to lash out against a truculent and despairing Germany. As the British Foreign Secretary, Arthur Balfour, mischievously observed, the French "were so dreadfully afraid of being swallowed up by the tiger, but would spend their time poking it."[119] It also became increasingly difficult for the new republican administration in Germany to justify the peace settlement to its own people. Old-style monarchists and a right-radical movement that eventually gelled around the National Socialist Party blamed the "dictated peace" for all Germany's woes and so condemned the revolutionaries of 1918 for the "betrayal" of the Armistice and Versailles.

4.5   Eastern Europe and the Mediterranean

The German settlement had been regarded as the main business of the peace conference from the outset. Once the German representatives had put ink on paper at Versailles, the US, British and Italian leaders left Paris, entrusting the business of the remaining peace treaties to their subordinates. This, however, was to underestimate the mare's nest of problems in eastern Europe, Turkey, and the Middle East, where a witches' brew of revolutionary and ethnic conflict flared up alongside economic collapse and famine. These events were often beyond the reach and control of the Allies, who were reduced to providing a measure of emergency food aid and granting retrospective approval to new borders, turning a blind eye to forced and frequently violent population transfers which gave birth to seething grievances that a Nazi Germany would later exploit with consummate ease.

Quite apart from the chaos triggered by the Russian revolutions, two great and ancient empires, both allies of Germany, had collapsed and disintegrated during the autumn of 1918: the Habsburg and Ottoman empires. The House of Habsburg had governed vast swathes of Europe over the centuries, from present-day Spain and Belgium to southern Poland and the western Ukraine. During the nineteenth century, however, the Habsburg Empire had become concentrated along the River Danube from the Bavarian border at Passau in the west, to the Iron Gates on the Romanian border in the east. The Habsburgs governed the Alpine lands of present-day Austria, Slovenia and also the Südtirol – a German-speaking province south of the Brenner Pass, which was annexed by Italy after the First World War. The Empire also extended south from the Danube basin to the Adriatic Sea and present-day Croatia, and north-eastward across the Carpathian and Tatra Mountains as far as the Polish city of Cracow and into the southwestern Ukraine at L'viv / Lvov (then Lemberg).

Large it may have been, but in an era of democratization and growing national consciousness the multinational Habsburg monarchy grew increasingly vulnerable. Until 1866 the western Habsburg lands had also formed part of the loosely constituted German Confederation, but defeat at the hands of Prussia saw the Habsburgs excluded from German affairs and the Kingdom of Hungary exploited the situation to wrest a substantial measure of autonomy within the Empire. Austria-Hungary, as it now became, contained a narrow majority of German and Magyar speakers combined, but was soon enough beset by a tide of Slavonic nationalism, centered on the Bohemian capital of Prague and also the northwestern Balkans. The Austrians granted cultural concessions to some minorities, oppressed others, and periodically played one group off against another, while the Hungarians strove simply to suppress the various minority languages and create a homogeneous, Magyar-speaking state. By the early twentieth century the heir to the throne, Franz Ferdinand, was among the minority who considered granting the Balkan Slavs far-reaching autonomy but, as we have already seen, he himself fell victim in 1914 to the very forces he sought to appease. Vienna went to war to crush Slavonic nationalism once and for all, and by 1918 had lost.

Little could be saved from the wreckage as German Austria fell out with Hungary over the fate of the Burgenland, a German-speaking frontier territory hitherto ruled by Budapest. A plebiscite organized by the Allies saw it opt narrowly for Austria, with the exception of the main town, Sopron. The Austrians had always considered themselves part of German Europe, and Vienna as a great, perhaps the greatest, German city. Any sense of Austrian nationhood was wholly lacking and as the monarchy collapsed and a republic was proclaimed by the local Social Democrats, union with the new German Republic was anticipated, particularly by the Social Democratic and urban population. The rural, Catholic party was more suspicious of largely Protestant Germany, but all agreed that to live in a small Austria surrounded by hostile neighbors would not be an enviable prospect.

Union with Germany, however, was expressly forbidden by the Treaty of Versailles and the peace accord of September 1919 between the Allies and rump Austria signed at St Germain. The Austrians were spared reparations, but this simply reflected the dire state of an economy devastated by war and by the disintegration of the Habsburg-governed Danubian commercial area. Austria was reduced to dependence on Allied food deliveries, and the former great imperial capital of Vienna struggled to define for itself any sort of sustainable role as its subject peoples and even its immediate hinterland to the north and east went their own ways.

All Austrians agreed that the terms of St Germain were unjust and the country went into three days of official mourning. In addition to the Burgenland, Austria had managed to ward off the Jugoslav army and retain southern Carinthia with its capital Klagenfurt in a plebiscite in which, Francis Carsten once estimated, some 10,000 Slovenes opted to remain in Austria rather than join Jugoslavia.[120] However, larger and more significant German-speaking territories were lost. The 250,000 South Tirolese were now ruled from Rome, and despite repeated pleas to the Allies from Vienna, as well as some resistance on the ground, some 3 million German speakers in Bohemia and Moravia found themselves in the new state of Czechoslovakia. The latter, despite its name, in fact contained significantly more Germans than Slovaks.

The country's Social Democrats formed a provisional government and tightened their grip on Vienna and other industrial towns, such as Graz and Linz. Communist radicals, inspired by short-lived Soviet risings in neighboring Bavaria and Hungary, were given short shrift by the Socialist majority, but relations between Vienna and the countryside were less easily resolved. As the famine intensified, an urban workers' militia, the Volkswehr, took to raiding the neighboring countryside for food, so deepening the prejudices of rural, Catholic Austria against Socialist and "cosmopolitan" Vienna. For those on the right of European politics the terms "cosmopolitan" and "Jewish" came to serve as interchangeable negatives, and in Austria existing anti-Semitism was further nourished by these tensions between Vienna and the provinces. It seemed to matter little that Austria's Jewish population had long since regarded themselves as among the most patriotic of German patriots, still less that Otto Bauer, Austria's Jewish postwar Foreign Minister, fought tenaciously for the South Tirol, German-speaking regions of Bohemia-Moravia, and for union, *Anschluß*, with Germany during the peace negotiations. When his Chancellor, Karl Renner, was unable to move the Allies on any of these points an outraged Bauer resigned.

If Austria struggled to come to terms with an unjust peace, Hungary's predicament rapidly eclipsed that of its western neighbor. As the war spluttered to a close during October the Magyars looked toward a future of independent nationhood. A National Council, which sought to establish a liberal democratic order, was formed on October 24 under the leadership of Count Mihály Károlyî and quickly gathered sufficient popular support to force the Emperor Karl's hand. Károlyî was appointed Prime Minister and legally at least Hungary remained a kingdom, under the House of Habsburg. As Francis Carsten observed, "The war was over, a new era was beginning, and there had been no bloodshed."[121] There things might have remained, but the Magyars' strong and unequivocal sense of nationhood, along with previous efforts to "Magyarize" their Slavonic and Romanian minorities, left them all the more dangerous in the eyes of neighboring states. As R. J. W. Evans notes, "the one fixation" of the Czechoslovak Foreign Minister, Edvard Beneš, "was the *bête noire* of the old Habsburg world and his consequential fears of a restoration in Austria and especially Hungary."[122] Claims by Czechoslovakia, Romania and Jugoslavia on Hungarian-speaking territory were repeatedly indulged by the Allies, who displayed little or no sympathy toward the protests emanating from Budapest. As a British official explained to Károlyî: "The Entente governments had many more important things to worry about than the fate of ten million people in Hungary,"[123] while Paris was keen to see its prospective allies in eastern Europe favored at the expense of a defeated enemy. In March 1919 an exasperated Károlyî handed power to a Communist-dominated leftist coalition, effectively led by Béla Kun (the new Foreign Minister), which combined a Bolshevik-style domestic agenda with a determination to resist with force Allied inroads into Hungarian territory.

The Allied Commander in Eastern Europe, Marshal Franchet d'Esperey, proposed nipping this second Bolshevik revolution in the bud through military intervention, but the Council of Four in Paris instead sent a fact-finding mission to Budapest. Comprising South African Premier Jan Smuts and the British diplomat Harold Nicolson, the initiative collapsed in a flurry of mutual and sometimes personal recrimination, with Nicolson later dismissing Kun as: "A little oily Jew – fur-coat rather moth-eaten – string green tie – dirty collar."[124] A reenergized Hungarian army fought off its would-be predators for several months, but as the domestic economy collapsed and grass literally grew in the streets of Budapest, Kun's Social Democratic coalition partners opened talks with the Allies and on August 1 secured his resignation.

On August 3 Romanian troops occupied the Hungarian capital and then, in a dramatic turn of events, the heir to the Habsburg throne, Archduke Joseph, arrived in Budapest and was declared Regent, pending the definitive restoration of Habsburg authority. Hungarian monarchists had managed to persuade Franchet d'Esperey to sanction this extraordinary move. They argued that a Habsburg revival not just in Budapest, but also Vienna, would recreate a Danubian Catholic monarchy capable of defusing Austrian demands for an *Anschluß* with Germany. Furthermore, they continued, Catholic, conservative Bavaria might be persuaded to join such a monarchy, in the aftermath of the Munich Soviet and the consolidation of Social Democratic power in the Protestant north of Germany.

This echoed earlier efforts by senior French military commanders to dismember Germany, whatever their political masters might or might not have promised at the Paris Peace Conference. However, the Czech authorities were alarmed, no doubt fearing that a revived Danubian monarchy would reclaim Magyar-speaking southern Slovakia and German-speaking southern Bohemia-Moravia, or even challenge Czech and Slovak statehood altogether. Since Paris regarded the nascent Czechoslovak state as the keystone of its anti-German and anti-Bolshevik strategy in east-central Europe, French commanders on the spot were ordered to withdraw their support for the Archduke Joseph. On August 26 he left Budapest, and the "Red Terror" of Béla Kun's regime was replaced by a "White Terror" which saw the landowning classes wreak revenge on Kun's supporters. In 1920 the former Habsburg Admiral Miklos Horthy was proclaimed Regent and was to remain in office for 24 years, presiding over what Evans has described as "a subversive but gentlemanly fascism located within the establishment."[125]

While the former heartlands of the Habsburg Empire struggled against the traumas of defeat and disintegration, new states were emerging or existing states expanding around its periphery. The Czechs of Bohemia and Moravia had experienced a cultural and socioeconomic renaissance since the mid-nineteenth century. Prague had been largely German speaking in 1848 and Czech had been the language of its rural hinterland. By 1914, however, Prague was largely Czech speaking with Germanophone communities to be found around the peripheries of Bohemia and Moravia, where the provinces bordered on Germany in the north and west, and on Austria proper in the south.

The celebrated artist Alphonse Mucha – perhaps better known in the West for his earlier posters of the Parisian actress Sarah Bernhardt – returned to his native Bohemia in 1910 and threw his energies into giving the Czechs' national aspirations artistic substance. Following independence he designed the first Czechoslovak postage stamps and banknotes, as well as the new state's police uniforms. The future Foreign Minister of Czechoslovakia, Edvard Beneš, had been Professor of Sociology at Prague University before the war, but like the country's future President, Tomáš Masaryk and the Slovak leader Milan Štefanik, he chose exile when war came. Czechoslovakia's future leaders lobbied particularly hard in Paris for their country's independence, but also in the United States and Russia. Štefanik served in the French air force, which strengthened the trust and even admiration felt in Paris for these leaders and their cause, which simultaneously furthered French strategic interests in central and eastern Europe. A deal was struck between Czech and Slovak leaders to form a postwar federation and create a Czechoslovak National Council, which seized power relatively bloodlessly in the Czech and Slovak lands at the war's end. The Austrians left Prague on October 28, 1918, and in January 1919 Masaryk became President of the new state.

Czechoslovakia was the child of its indigenous bourgeois elite, more particularly the Czech elite, which took the western liberal-democratic order as its role model, and a democratic system of government prevailed in Czechoslovakia until March 1939, far longer than in most of Eastern Europe. However, democracy proved a two-edged sword in a state where barely 50 percent of the population

Figure 4.3   Czechoslovak Independence Day, Prague, October 28, 1918.
Source: TopFoto.

were Czech. Even their Slovak confederates came increasingly to resent the union, which had been agreed upon in the distant US city of Pittsburgh during the heady months of 1917. Minor hostilities flared between Czech and Slovak forces in 1919, and between the wars the Slovak Populists led by Father Andrei Hlinka (originally a supporter of Czechoslovak union) campaigned against Czech domination and even looked toward a reconciliation with Hungary, declaring: "We have lived alongside the Magyars for a thousand years." Geographically, he continued, Slovakia was linked to Hungary rather than to the Czech lands,[126] and might have added that the Slovak capital, Bratislava (formerly Pressburg), was barely half an hour distant from Vienna by road or rail and that both cities stood on the River Danube. Clashes between Czechoslovakia and Poland over the fate of the border town of Teschen, with Hungary over the delineation of the southern Slovak border, and the nagging problem of the German minority were to provide ample fuel for the revisionist flames of the later 1930s.

The Polish settlement was arguably still more problematic. Quite apart from disputes over its German border the emergent Polish state, a parliamentary democracy, quickly found itself embroiled in a major domestic outbreak of anti-Jewish violence and also a series of conflicts with other successor nations and then with the Soviet Union. Poland's eastern territorial claims were complex, resting partly on language and partly on the country's history. Prior to its partition between Russia, Austria, and Prussia during the eighteenth century Poland was effectively the main power in east-central Europe. The union between Poland and Lithuania in 1386 initiated more than a century of territorial expansion until, by the early sixteenth century, the Kingdom of Poland extended from the Black Sea coast to the Baltic Sea and from the River Oder to the central Ukraine and present-day Belarus. Only the country's heartland was solidly Polish speaking, but following the eighteenth-century partition, pockets of Polish speakers remained well to the east of the basic linguistic frontier (which approximated to Poland's present-day eastern border). By the early twentieth century the Polish elite regarded its erstwhile Lithuanian confederates with some disdain and after the First World War Poland seized the Lithuanian capital of Vilnius – which has since been restored to Lithuania and again serves as that country's capital.

If British leaders continued to harbor doubts regarding Poland, France was sympathetic, partly through longstanding personal and cultural affinities between the two nations and partly because a strong Poland, like a strong Czechoslovakia, would serve to isolate the Soviet Union and thus the Bolshevik "contagion," and also help contain Germany. However, while the defeated Germans were no immediate threat, the Soviet Union was another matter. Fighting between Poland and the Soviet Union broke out in February 1919 as the German military evacuation of the Polish/Soviet borderlands brought the two sides into contact. At this stage the bulk of Soviet forces were still embroiled in the civil war, allowing Piłsudski's armies to take both Vilnius and Minsk by August. He also consolidated Latvia's independence during a confused period of civil war and external intervention in the Baltic lands, by both Germany and the Soviet Union, before the latter recognized the independence of Lithuania, Latvia and Estonia, as well as Finland, in 1920.

However that was not the end of the matter, for the Soviet Union harbored far-reaching revolutionary ambitions which overshadowed its territorial dispute with Poland. In March 1919 Moscow had created a Communist International, the Comintern, whose task was to coordinate global revolutionary activity, particularly by minority elements of prewar socialist parties which had now come out in support of the Bolshevik Revolution. At this stage Soviet foreign policy focused on the German situation, where the new republican administration was struggling to cope with domestic unrest and the harsh peace terms. If the Bolshevik revolution could be extended to Germany, Moscow reasoned, the rest of Europe would follow. Much of the German unrest was the work of the ultranationalist right, but for Soviet leaders that was all grist to the mill and the Red Army, encouraged by Lenin, began to contemplate intervening directly in Germany – no doubt attracted by the virtual military vacuum that Allied-imposed disarmament had created there.

When command of the growing Red Army forces opposite Poland was given to General Mikhail Tukhachevsky Soviet policy seemed clear, for he was a leading exponent of revolutionary warfare. Piłsudski decided to strike first, joining with Ukrainian partisans in the spring to seize Kiev, but the Red Cavalry soon drove

Figure 4.4 Lenin addressing troops heading for the front in the Russo-Polish War, May 1920, painted by Izaak Brodsky. Note the addition of banners and the removal of Trotsky and Kamenev from Brodsky's painting (seen in the original photograph, figure 4.5, on the podium steps to Lenin's left).
Source: Mary Evans Picture Library.

Figure 4.5 Lenin addressing troops heading for the front in the Russo-Polish War, May 1920, anonymous photograph.
Source: Mary Evans Picture Library.

the Polish forces back, its commander predicting it "would clatter through the streets of Paris before the summer is out."[127] Tukhachevsky launched his own offensive on July 4, exclaiming: "To the West! Over the corpse of White Poland lies the road to worldwide conflagration,"[128] and his advance was so rapid that soon enough he was offering Berlin possession of former German territory that had been ceded to Poland by the Versailles Treaty. An embarrassed German government refused to take the bait, but in East Prussia the population and authorities watched nervously as the Red Army swept through neighboring Poland and approached that country's northwestern border (with German Pomerania) well beyond Warsaw.

Just when the fall of the Polish capital seemed imminent, Piłsudski struck on August 15 at the Red Army's extended lines of communication from the south, isolating and then destroying Tukhachevsky's main forces in an engagement dubbed the "miracle of the Vistula." The rout of the Red Cavalry followed a fortnight later and on October 10 Lenin was forced to sue for an armistice. The Treaty of Riga followed on March 18, 1921. It awarded Poland much of western Belarus and also the northwestern Ukraine, but also effectively destroyed Soviet hopes of exporting the Bolshevik Revolution by force of arms. Lenin's thoughts turned to domestic stabilization and the adoption of the New Economic Policy with its concessions to capitalism. Under Lenin's successor, Joseph Stalin, the watchword "socialism in one country" was to displace any serious interwar commitment by the Soviet Union to world revolution.

In the Balkans, meanwhile, a furious struggle began to partition the spoils of war, but also to create states on terms acceptable to minority national communities. In neither respect did the portents look particularly hopeful. As a defeated power, Bulgaria could not expect much. The country had entered the war on the Central Powers' side hoping to make good the losses it had suffered in the 1913 Second Balkans War. However, with defeat in October 1918 and the Treaty of Neuilly on November 17, 1919, Bulgaria's Aegean coast in Western Thrace was ceded to Greece, while strips of territory were surrendered to Romania in the north and Jugoslavia in the west. Prime Minister Alexander Stamboliiski signed the treaty under duress and continued to contest the reparations settlement thereafter, but on other matters he cooperated with the Allies, and maintained correct relations with neighboring Jugoslavia.

Things changed following his death during a coup in June 1923. Stamboliiski's peasant party, the Bulgarian Agrarian National Union, had seen off a determined Communist electoral challenge in 1919 and thereafter pursued a radical domestic agenda which favored the small landholder and small urban property holder. The government became sufficiently repressive in pursuit of its goals to provoke its enemies in the old establishment – army, monarchy, church and traditional parties – to plan its overthrow. Their violent coup succeeded, but the new regime became embroiled in a battle with the Communists over the political spoils and the wider party political system became hopelessly fragmented. The country's Macedonian minority added to the chaos, launching raids on Greek and Jugoslav Macedonia and so triggering a Greek occupation of southwestern Bulgaria in 1925.

As an Allied state Romania fared better, seizing Transylvania from Hungary and the Bukovina from Austria before the peace conference retrospectively confirmed these gains. Bucharest also secured Romanian-speaking Bessarabia (present-day Moldova) from the wreckage of the Russian Empire and in addition a slice of northern Bulgaria (the southern Dobrogea/Dobrudja). A fierce dispute flared up between Bucharest and Belgrade at the peace conference over the fate of Hungary's southern, Banat province, before the great powers partitioned the territory between the two, all of this leaving the Kingdom of Romania with double the territory and population of 1914. However, while prewar Romania had been almost entirely Romanian it now contained sizeable minorities and confronted resentful neighbors.

This was one of the unresolved paradoxes of the wider Paris Peace Settlement. New states were formed, existing states expanded, all in the name of national self-determination, yet few were genuinely homogeneous national states. Most lacked a coherent economy, a common ethnicity, a unifying language, a single religion, or a sense of shared history – and the interwar period offered precious little time for any new-found sense of commonality to develop. This was not lost on the great powers which, R. J. Crampton notes, looked to minority protection treaties, goodwill and the League of Nations to sort things out.[129] Instead, domestic turmoil and, eventually, interference by Europe's great powers nurtured grievances and widened fractures across the checkered map of central and eastern Europe. Some of the Balkans' smaller national communities, such as the Macedonians, were variously informed by their neighbors that history and culture would justify their annexation – in their case by Greece, by Bulgaria, by Jugoslavia, or even by Albania. What no one seemed prepared to discuss was independent Macedonian statehood and even today post-Jugoslav Macedonia is required to describe itself as FYROM – an acronym for Former Yugoslav Republic of Macedonia – to demarcate itself from the northern Greek province of Macedonia; such are the sensitivities that remain very much alive in the Balkans.

Comparable issues lay at the heart of Jugoslav affairs from the outset. The 1915 Treaty of London had promised Italy western Slovenia and much of present-day Croatia's coastline, and whatever the various South Slav people disagreed on, they were united in their determination to resist Italian expansion along the eastern shoreline of the Adriatic Sea. There were also the Austrians and Hungarians to consider and in July 1918 the Serb leader Nicola Pašić agreed with his Croat counterpart, Ante Trumbić, that a federation was the only plausible way forward. This was a union born of necessity rather than brotherly solidarity. Different languages apart, the emerging Jugoslavia was sundered by two great cultural and religious fault lines, one within Christianity between its Roman Catholic and Orthodox denominations and the other between Christianity as a whole and Islam. The Jugoslav Muslims were a vulnerable minority, but the Catholic/Orthodox divide was synonymously the divide between (Catholic) Croats and Slovenes on the one hand and (Orthodox) Serbs on the other. The former group looked west toward Rome and beyond, the latter east to its historic protector, Russia, and also southeast toward the Greek Orthodox heritage of Constantinople.

Trumbić despised the Serbs, confiding to a French writer: "You are not going to compare, I hope, the Croats, the Slovenes, the Dalmatians whom centuries of artistic, moral and intellectual communion with Austria, Italy and Hungary have made pure occidentals, with these half-civilized Serbs, the Balkan hybrids of Slavs and Turks."[130] The Serbs for their part were conscious that they had wrested their hard-won independence from the Ottoman Empire to become a nation-state, while Slovenia remained an Austrian province, Croatia a Hungarian. They had expected from the outset that the Croats and Slovenes would have to unite with Serbia "on Serbian terms, under Serbian leadership,"[131] and in October 1918 Pašić announced that Serbia would, indeed, control the new state. This was in part a moral claim arising from the war, for if Serbia had been a victim of Habsburg aggression, many male Croats and Slovenes of military age were veterans of the Austro-Hungarian army for which they had fought loyally. On December 1 Prince Alexander of Serbia proclaimed the Kingdom of the Serbs, Croats and Slovenes, with its capital the Serbian capital of Belgrade and its army, banks and civil service effectively a carryover from their old Serb counterparts. When a new constitution was finally adopted on June 28, 1921 it confirmed that Jugoslavia would be a heredity parliamentary monarchy, but also that it would be a centralized state whose 33 departments would answer directly to Belgrade.

The Croats, not surprisingly, had second thoughts about union and on October 29, 1918 declared independence from Austria-Hungary without simultaneously opting for Jugoslavia. However, with Croatia itself in a state of chaos and under attack from both Italian and Serbian forces, it finally requested union with Serbia on November 25. The Serbs, meanwhile, had bullied the tiny, ancient state of Montenegro into joining the Jugoslav kingdom, which also contained significant Magyar, Romanian, Albanian, Bulgarian, and even Italian and German minorities. In Bosnia, cradle of the First World War, a Serb-speaking Muslim community coexisted uneasily alongside its Orthodox Serb and Catholic Croat neighbors. The new country, Margaret Macmillan observes, was "three times bigger than the old Serbia but with even more enemies."[132] In the event successive interwar Jugoslav governments struggled unsuccessfully to square the circle between Serb hegemonic ambition and Croatian nationalism, before the state faced invasion by the Germans, Italians and Bulgarians and fragmented into bloody chaos during the Second World War.

Bloody chaos erupted far more quickly in the Aegean lands, where the Turks and Greeks harbored irreconcilable claims. The charismatic Prime Minister of Greece, Eleutherios Venizelos, was a native of Crete who had lived through the 1898 War of Independence against the Ottomans and the return of the island to Greece in 1913. This marked another stage in a process of Greek self-determination that had begun in 1830, when the south of present-day Greece had wrested its

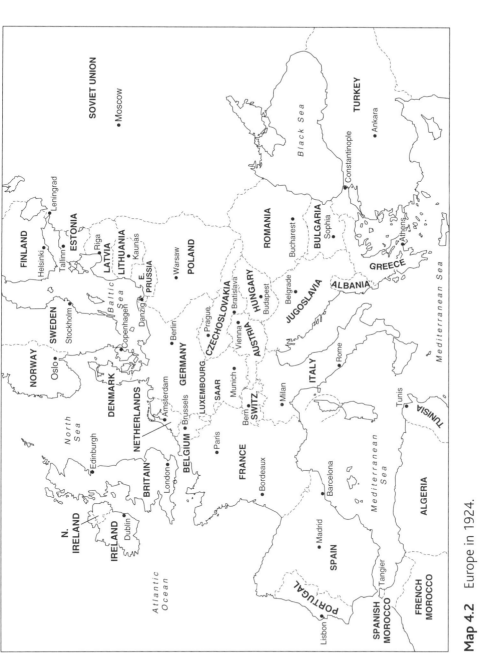

Map 4.2 Europe in 1924.

independence from the Ottoman Empire. During the late nineteenth and early twentieth centuries the Greeks were able to liberate their conationals in Thessaly, Epirus, southern Macedonia, and also on clusters of islands in the Aegean Sea, some literally in sight of the Turkish mainland.

Now Venizelos looked to the peace conference to make the Aegean a uniquely Greek sea, with the Turks pushed back from the western shoreline of Asia Minor. The greatest potential prize was Constantinople, which he planned to proclaim capital of a greater Greece in recollection of the glory days of the medieval, Greek-speaking Byzantine Empire. The "recovery" of Constantinople would also mark the endgame in a centuries-old battle between Christianity and Islam for control of southeastern Europe, and the eastern Mediterranean beyond. The city's Byzantine cathedral, Santa Sophia, which the Ottomans had converted into a mosque, would be redeemed for Christianity, an ambition that struck a chord across Europe. In Britain, for example, the Archbishop of Canterbury played a prominent role in the founding of the Santa Sophia Redemption Committee.

As we shall see, the Turks were to have the final say in all of this, but conflicting Greek and Italian claims were of more immediate significance. In 1912 Italy had seized the Dodecanese Islands off the southwestern coast of Turkey, Rhodes being the most important of the group. Rome had further ambitions in Asia Minor, where it had been promised territory by the 1915 Treaty of London and the 1917 St Jean de Maurienne agreement, and also hoped to acquire Albania, but both these objectives clashed with Greek claims. Eventually the Council of Four upheld Albanian independence, but in Asia Minor western meddling only served to exacerbate matters. In May 1919 Italian forces landed along Turkey's largely defenseless Aegean coast, provoking strong Greek protests, which led in turn to Greece occupying the port of Smyrna (present-day Izmir) and its hinterland on May 15. The Ottoman Sultan remained on his throne in Constantinople through all of this, although his writ barely ran in what remained of Turkey. However, the army, which perceived itself as the guardian of a modernizing national Turkish state, was not prepared simply to stand by and witness the fragmentation of its homeland. The country's greatest war hero, General Mustapha Kemal (Atatürk), was powerless to offer immediate resistance, but traveled deep into the Anatolian interior where he began to reorganize his forces far beyond the reach of Allied troops. In November 1919 he proclaimed Ankara the new Turkish capital.

In August 1920 the Allies presented the last Ottoman government, still in Constantinople, with their peace terms. They effectively compromised Turkish independence, for large parts of the country were to come under Greek, Italian or French occupation, and there was also talk of establishing autonomous Kurdish and Armenian states under Allied protection. In Ankara, however, Atatürk rejected the peace terms and quickly reached a separate agreement with the Soviet Union to carve up the southern Caucasus region. This placed the remnants of Armenia within the Soviet Union and thus secure from any renewed Turkish atrocities, but most crucially for Atatürk he was now able to stabilize

Turkey's northeastern frontier and turn his attention westwards. As clashes between Turkish and Allied troops intensified, the French and Italian governments decided at this stage to cut their losses. During 1921, to British fury, they unilaterally concluded their own agreements with Atatürk which ended French or Italian involvement on the Turkish mainland. The Entente Cordiale notwithstanding, the British Foreign Secretary, Lord Curzon, lamented that: "In every quarter of the globe the representatives of France are pursuing a policy ... unfriendly to British interests."[133]

A humanitarian catastrophe was to follow. In June 1920 the British Premier, Lloyd George, had authorized the Greeks to invade Anatolia from Smyrna, and Venizelos also lost no time in occupying Eastern Thrace – almost to the gates of Constantinople. The campaign went well initially, but the Greek advance into Anatolia was checked in 1921 and Atatürk launched a decisive counterattack in late August 1922. The Greek forces collapsed and on September 10 the Turks retook Smyrna, burned it to the ground, and killed many of its Greek inhabitants. As the resurgent Turkish army advanced on Constantinople during October the occupying British forces, already left in the lurch by their French allies, sought an armistice, following which a comprehensive settlement was agreed at Lausanne in July 1923. Three thousand years of Greek settlement in western Asia Minor effectively came to an end as the non-Muslim population was expelled to European Greece. In return the considerable Turkish population of Thrace was bundled over the border into Turkey, so destroying communities that had existed for many hundreds of years. Greece could barely afford to receive these Asian Greeks who, often as not, were strangers in their new homeland. Some owed their Greek nationality, it transpired, to religion rather than language and actually spoke Turkish. Similar problems of national identity were to afflict neighboring Bulgaria for generations to come; was a locally resident Turk a Bulgarian Muslim and not a real Turk? Would conversion to Christianity turn such a person into a Bulgarian proper?

Returning to the Greco-Turkish crisis, defeat brought recriminations within Greece itself. Venizelos had lost the elections of November 1920 to his royalist opponents, but army officers sympathetic to him seized power after the defeat at Smyrna. Several years of political turmoil followed before Venizelos introduced a republican constitution in 1927. Thereafter renewed political violence saw the monarchy restored in October 1933. As for Turkey, Atatürk saw himself as a modernizer and looked westward rather than to the Islamic East of which the Ottoman Sultan, the Caliph, had been guardian for generations. The Roman alphabet replaced the Arabic and Turkey declared itself a secular state. Constantinople became Istanbul, and to the west of the great city Turkey recovered Eastern Thrace and the city of Edirne (Adrianople), and with it a more substantial foothold in Europe. The Montreux Convention of 1936 restored the Bosphorus Straits and Dardanelles to full Turkish military control and placed major restrictions on the passage of foreign battleships through the Straits and on their presence in the Black Sea.

Finally, Turkey was to regain the Mediterranean port of Alexandretta on the Turkish-Syrian border in 1939. During the Second World War the country remained neutral and was thus spared the resulting traumas that scourged the wider Mediterranean region.

Space prevents our doing justice here to the wider history of the Middle East. During the war a British officer, Thomas Edward Lawrence "of Arabia," had encouraged the Ottoman Empire's Arab subjects to revolt against Turkish rule in order to secure their independence. The reality was to be otherwise, for Paris and London regarded the region as ripe for colonization and during the peace conference paid scant regard to the interests or ambitions of the indigenous population, largely Muslim, but sometimes Christian, largely Arab, but also Kurdish. Added to this was the running sore of Jewish settlement in British-controlled Palestine, which its native Arab population viewed with increasing alarm. Edwin Montagu, Secretary of State for India, was mindful that these developments were fueling Muslim unrest in the Raj and warned of the Pandora's Box European interference in the Middle East would open. He warned against telling "the Moslem what he ought to think, let us recognize what they do think," to which the British Foreign Secretary, Arthur Balfour, retorted bluntly: "I am quite unable to see why Heaven or any other Power should object to our telling the Moslem what he ought to think."[134]

4.6   Western Upheavals

Finally, we should remember that if the greatest postwar turmoil occurred in Eastern Europe and beyond, there were two notable upheavals in the west. One affected the Moselle (German Lorraine) and Alsace, the other Ireland. Alsace and the Moselle had formed the western borderlands of the (Germanic) Holy Roman Empire for generations before Louis XIV of France and his successors began annexing the patchwork of little city states and princely territories that extended across the two regions. Alsace was almost entirely German speaking at the time, the Moselle spoke German in the north, but from Metz southwards French was the language. This linguistic balance remained undisturbed until the French Revolutionary Terror when, suddenly, Alsace's Germanic culture became an issue. Proposals emerged "for using the guillotine on one-quarter of the inhabitants of Alsace" – no doubt to encourage the others to attend to their French lessons – or otherwise for deporting the whole Alsatian population to the Vendée on the Atlantic coast (a Royalist stronghold whose native population had been decimated by revolutionary forces) and peopling Alsace with Frenchmen from the interior.[135]

It did not come to that and during the more peaceful decades of the nineteenth century the middle classes began to use French, even if the vernacular remained *Elsässerditsch*, or Alsatian German. In 1871 the Treaty of Frankfurt saw both provinces returned to Germany, and French speakers, notably those civil servants who had originated from the interior of France, were obliged to leave unless they agreed to become German nationals. Some Francophone Alsatians joined them voluntarily in what promised to be permanent exile. By 1914 French was only widely understood in the Francophone south of the Moselle, where it did remain the language of education and where social links with French Lorraine remained very much alive. Much else changed between 1871 and 1914. Both the Moselle and Alsace experienced explosive economic development and attracted many tens of thousands of immigrants, very few of whom were French speakers. Metz became increasingly a German-speaking city, while throughout Alsace and the northern Moselle German was the language of education, administration and the media, and the spoken Germanic dialect was used almost universally.

However the new German rulers were often patronizing and prone to heavy-handedness as they fretted over where the region's loyalties ultimately lay. Consequently the native population, regardless of their mother tongue, came rather to resent the incomers, while the Mosellans also resented being governed from Strassburg (the capital of Elsaß-Lothringen) as they had little love for their Alsatian neighbors. Nonetheless, as we have already seen, everyone could agree by the early twentieth century that the region as a whole had no particular hankering for renewed French rule.[136] Accordingly, although the French wartime government was determined to reclaim the "lost provinces," it was equally anxious to avoid a plebiscite at all costs. Given the chance to vote freely on its future, Paris feared, the region's population would opt for Germany. Quite apart from the tens of thousands of German incomers and the indigenous Germanic culture, the region was largely Catholic and supported church involvement in education and many other aspects of daily life. This arrangement was secure as part of Germany, but France was an avowedly secular state with all that that entailed. The added presence of a significant Protestant minority in northern Alsace only served to set the provinces still further apart from France.

When the German Empire collapsed and the Armistice followed hard on its heels the German revolution swept the urban and industrial centers of both provinces, leading to the formation of workers' and soldiers' councils. In addition the Landtag (parliament) of Alsace-Lorraine, which had been granted enhanced powers in 1911, effectively declared independence. Alsace-Lorraine, so the Landtag argued, was attached to Germany through the person of the Kaiser, and since he had abdicated the link was severed. However, rather than simply await the arrival of French troops, scheduled for late November, the Landtag transformed itself into a Nationalrat, or National Council, and claimed far-reaching domestic autonomy, even if under French protection.

The Mosellans were less convinced than the Alsatians by all of this and in any case, when the French forces occupied the region on November 24, the Nationalrat was immediately closed down and a process of Francization initiated. It did not take long for a powerful Alsatian autonomist movement to develop in reaction to this and for eminent figures, such as the Mosellan and future French Premier, Robert Schuman, to protest in the French National Assembly against the attempted destruction of Alsatian and Mosellan culture. Such protests proved ineffective and, in any case, Paris had determined from the outset to create new ethnographical facts on the ground. Within weeks of the French occupation, the entire population of the two provinces had been registered on "racial" lines into four categories, with "A" including people who had held French citizenship before 1871, or whose two parents had done so, and then with gradations through "B," "C," and so to "D," which included people of entirely German or Austro-Hungarian descent, their locally born children included. In cases of mixed marriages, where one spouse was a native Alsace-Lorrainer the other an incomer, the father's origin determined the classification accorded to their children.

Thereafter a limited number of outright expulsions, dubbed *épuration* (ethnic cleansing), began, but very many tens of thousands of undesirables were persuaded that it would be in their best interests to leave voluntarily. The settling of private personal scores, denunciations of every sort, military occupation and official pressure combined to make life intolerable for those without the "A" card, decorated in the French national colors. Even native Alsatians or Mosellans were sometimes denounced by neighbors with a grudge or who may simply have wished to remove a business competitor. Strikers in the region's steel mills or coal mines could be told that industrial militancy was a German affliction, and accordingly bundled across the frontier. Stripped of virtually all their possessions, over a hundred thousand inhabitants of the Moselle and perhaps more from Alsace were, Carolyn Grohmann relates, deposited across the new border, often under degrading circumstances.[137] More generally, civil servants, war veterans and enthusiasts of Alsatian culture, such as René Schickele, were regarded with great suspicion by their new rulers and therefore sometimes opted to leave. The alternatives were hardly attractive, for as Grohmann observes: " 'Dangerous' Mosellans and Alsatians were normally sent to camps in the French interior ... whilst even those declared innocent, but who had worked as civil servants before 1918, were obliged to accept demotion, premature retirement, or transfers from their home towns."[138] Wiser heads feared at the time that this process of persecution and degradation would trigger a terrible reckoning at some point in the future, although no one could have anticipated the traumas of the Nazi occupation of 1940–4.

If France's reannexation of the Moselle and Alsace constituted a (highly unpleasant) storm in a teacup, the case of Ireland was to have far graver consequences, as a war of independence against British rule was followed immediately by domestic civil war. In 1914, at the outbreak of war, Irish nationalists could and did serve loyally in the British Army. The nationalist leader, John Redmond, appealed to Irishmen to serve "wherever the firing-line extends, in defence of right, of freedom and of religion in this war,"[139] Redmond being mindful that the Westminster Parliament had approved Irish Home Rule in September, alongside proposals for Scottish and Welsh autonomy. Thus, while the Protestants of the

North fought the war as Unionists and Ulstermen, whose loyalty to the crown was unbending, service for the Catholic nationalists was more of a contractual arrangement where military service was being traded implicitly for a degree of national independence.

However, Redmond's constitutional route to self-determination was not the only game in town. Insurgency had always been a potential option in the Irish nationalist armory and at Easter 1916 militants took advantage of Britain's entanglement in the Great War to mount an uprising in Dublin. It was crushed vigorously, with 16 rebel leaders executed and 3,500 of their supporters arrested. Thereafter British efforts to appease Irish opinion by breathing new life into the Home Rule project failed to deliver concrete results and, as counterinsurgency operations continued, Irish opinion moved rapidly away from constitutionalist politics and toward the main militant separatist party, Sinn Féin. In the December 1918 General Election, Alvin Jackson observes, Sinn Féin was able to attract 48 percent of the total poll in Ireland,[140] which, when leaving aside the unionist vote, represented a clear majority of nationalist opinion.

If the Great War had disrupted socioeconomic and personal relationships and so catalyzed the process of political upheaval, it also provided the two sides in the ensuing War of Independence with militarily experienced personnel. The pro-British forces in the army, the police and the paramilitary "Black and Tans" were often war veterans, but so were many in the Irish Republican Army (IRA). The 1920 Government of Ireland Act attempted to find a way out of the burgeoning crisis by partitioning the island between six largely Protestant counties in the northeast and the Catholic majority to the south and west and providing separate home rule administrations for each region. However, as Jackson observes, "the volunteers of the IRA were not fighting for Home Rule, still less for partition and Home Rule, and consequently the Act was a dead letter outside the Six Counties."[141]

By December 1921 a new settlement of sorts had been reached between the British authorities and Sinn Féin's leaders, Arthur Griffith and Michael Collins. The south of Ireland would be granted de facto independence, even if its leaders would still swear loyalty to the British crown and the new state would remain a Dominion within the British Empire. Northern Ireland was given the choice of joining this new Irish Free State or remaining self-governing within Britain proper; it opted for the latter. The whole settlement represented a classic case of the half full or half empty glass conundrum. IRA volunteers prolonged the war in Northern Ireland in a vain effort to reunite the island of Ireland, while in the South they turned on the men and the administration that had forged the 1921 compromise. The ensuing civil war (1922–3) left further scars on a tormented national history and tore republican families and communities apart, even if total casualties amounted to just 1,500 souls – or a bad half-hour of fighting on the wartime Western Front. As Anne Dolan remarks, estranged blood relatives were "forced to construct communities within community; to define themselves against each other; to take the grand opposition of great nations at war and inflict it on a small and particularly organic society."[142] Among the dead was Michael Collins himself, killed in an ambush by IRA hardliners.

Thereafter the new state struggled to address the challenges of a moribund economy, population loss and issues of identity which often saw traditionalist Catholic values prevail over those of secular modernity. Many of the South's Protestant minority elected to leave, their trauma adding to the determination of Protestants in the then more liberal North to remain outwith the new Irish state. Eamon De Valera, who had led the rejectionists during the civil war, served three separate terms as Prime Minister after 1932 and was President from 1959 to 1973. In 1937 he negotiated an end to Dominion status, before Ireland became a fully independent republic in 1949. De Valera has been associated with the inward and even backward-looking aspects of interwar Irish history, but he is also perceived as a reformer. Equally significantly, his service as Prime Minister within the constitutional parameters of the Collins/Griffith settlement began to heal the raw wounds left by the War of Independence and the civil war. All in all, as Jackson concludes, the Free State laid the foundations of a stable democracy[143] which today is regarded as an inherently prosperous and cosmopolitan society, able to embrace the contemporary European movement (the recent plebiscite notwithstanding) with fewer reservations than its more apprehensive British neighbor.

But what of Scottish and Welsh autonomy, which had also formed part of Westminster's 1914 home rule agenda? Scotland was a junior partner in the British imperial union and so perceived membership of the United Kingdom in fundamentally different terms from the Catholic Irish community. Scottish business and the country's elite (including the Calvinist Church of Scotland) had carved out a reasonably congenial niche for themselves within the multinational British state. Violent insurrection had been firmly off the agenda for a century or more and with bigger fish to fry in the aftermath of the Great War, the British state could comfortably afford to sideline residual demands for Scottish and Welsh home rule. Unlike Scotland, Wales had been fully integrated into the English legal and governmental system. When the Welsh nationalist party, Plaid Cymru, was founded in 1925 it therefore based its appeal around Wales's distinctive language and culture, whereas when the National Party of Scotland was formed in 1928 it could allude to the remnants of Scottish statehood (such as the separate, Roman legal system) and the country's historic nationhood. This party subsequently merged in 1934 with the Scottish Party (formed in 1929) to create the present-day Scottish National Party.

This was all very well, but much of Scottish opinion was either conservative or unionist and did not regard constitutional change as a priority. A domestic patriotic pride and an imperial footprint could be maintained within the Anglo-Scottish union. Labour politicians sometimes mooted home rule, or even "Red Flag Nationalism," but without this becoming a priority. Socialism was more important to the country's labor movement. The Second World War and the creation thereafter of the modern British welfare state and the formation of state-owned pan-British industrial corporations such as the National Coal Board and British Railways relegated political nationalism to the fringe of public life, despite efforts immediately after the Second World War to revive the constitutional question.

It was only during the later 1960s, as the British Empire disappeared, the welfare state slipped into disrepair, and the nationalized corporations became a byword for waste and inefficiency that political nationalism in both Scotland and Wales found space. A first upsurge in nationalism during the 1970s was followed by a second, more sustained growth in support from the later 1980s which, ironically, owed a lot to Prime Minister Margaret Thatcher's privatization of the state-owned British corporations and her assault on British public welfarism. In addition, Welsh language activists won important concessions from the authorities which first halted and then reversed the decline in the use of Welsh. The domestic substance of "Britishness" was being stripped away. Nationalist victories in key by-elections and a discernible growth in underlying support for a new constitutional settlement finally moved a skeptical Westminster Parliament in 1998 to cede limited powers to a new Welsh National Assembly and far more extensive, legislative and institutional powers to the reconstituted Scottish Parliament. Neither the Welsh nor the Scottish settlement have proven to be the final word, however. With Plaid Cymru at the time of writing a junior coalition partner in the Welsh government, and with the Scottish National Party currently running an effective minority government in Scotland, the only meaningful debate in Wales and Scotland is over how much more power to transfer from London to Cardiff and Edinburgh.

4.7 The Fascist Revolution in Italy

Fascism enjoyed a relatively brief pedigree as a system of rule, emerging explosively out of the febrile political landscape of postwar Italy, before disintegrating during the closing phase of the Second World War. Its German counterpart, National Socialism, enjoyed an even briefer tenure of rule and thereafter it was only in Spain and Portugal that echoes of Europe's fascist generation survived for several decades to come. This, however, is not to underestimate the devastating impact and profound legacy of the fascist interregnum, nor to forget, as Roger Eatwell and Roger Griffin have reminded us, that fascism in its day was an ideology of some substance[144] whose supporters were convinced that it, and not liberal democracy or Marxism-Leninism, represented the future.

Italy was at once a very young and a profoundly ancient country. Heir to classical Greece and heartland of the ancient Roman Empire, the Italian peninsula had thereafter been subjected to waves of invasion and settlement by external powers. The south evolved into a cosmopolitan mixture of Mediterranean cultures – Latin, Greek, Arab – onto which were grafted periods of Norman and Spanish rule. Naples ranked at the time as one of the Mediterranean's greatest and most prosperous cities, its charisma enhanced if anything by the proximity of Europe's most unpredictable and sporadically destructive volcano. In the center of Italy lay Rome, home to the western Catholic Church and ruled by the papacy, while to the north lay a cluster of prosperous city states, pocket-sized kingdoms, and principalities which periodically came under French or Austrian rule. It was in this northern region that an industrial revolution took hold during the nineteenth century, creating economic links with northwestern Europe to reinforce the preexisting political and cultural connections.

The European liberal-national revolutions of 1848 swept Italy, with the south rising against its Bourbon rulers and the north seeking to end Austrian dominance. The risings ultimately failed, but in 1859 an alliance between France and the northwestern Kingdom of Piedmont dislodged the Austrians from most of northern Italy, while a militia force commanded by the patriot Giuseppe Garibaldi overthrew the Bourbon rulers of Naples and Sicily. Rome remained under papal rule (and French protection), Venice remained within Austria, Nice and the Savoy were ceded to France as a price for the latter's support, but nonetheless Italy was again a country rather than simply a cultural or geographical expression. Piedmont assumed control of this new Italian kingdom, a constitutional monarchy with its capital in Turin. Venice was acquired in the wake of the 1866 Austro-Prussian War thanks to Italy joining in on the winning, Prussian side. Then in 1870 another Prussian victory, this time over France, had the unintended consequence of delivering up Rome to the resurgent Italian national state as the demise of Napoleon III's empire at the Battle of Sedan saw the French garrison withdrawn. Rome replaced Turin as the Italian capital.

Italy existed in law and in name, but it remained a deeply divided country. National policy was made by northerners in the interests (so the south would complain) of the industrialized north. The great landowners of the south reached an accommodation of sorts with the new state, but their fellow southerners were largely excluded from the franchise, which was based on a literacy qualification, and were equally excluded from property ownership due to the absence of any meaningful land reform after Garibaldi's military triumphs. The free trading policies of the northern-oriented government also militated against economic modernization in the underdeveloped south, which was scourged by poverty, corruption and gangsterism. The corrosive effect of the north–south divide was compounded nationally by a schism between devout Catholics and liberals, with the former refusing to accept the overthrow of papal power in the celestial city. This running sore in church–state relations was only finally resolved in 1929 when the Fascist leader, Mussolini, recognized papal sovereignty over the Vatican City and granted the church a greatly extended role in Italian civil society, of which more later. Meanwhile an emergent and increasingly militant urban working class and also the rural poor came to pose an increasingly concrete threat to the constitutional status quo even as a liberal political elite traded favors and high office, largely oblivious to the "barbarous" rural, peasant world beyond the provincial and national capitals.[145]

When war came in 1914 Italy opted for neutrality, despite being part of the Triple Alliance with Berlin and Vienna. The Alliance was defensive and since Germany and Austria-Hungary were the technical aggressors there was no obligation on Rome to join the fighting. Even so, the government sought to exploit the situation to its best advantage, while Italian industry did a lively trade supplying both sides in the conflict. More critically, the war offered an opportunity to acquire the remaining slices of Italian-speaking territory under foreign rule and so complete the nineteenth-century process of unification, the Risorgimento. The Triple Alliance in any case provided for automatic compensation of Italy were Austria to gain significant territory in the Balkans, leading Rome to demand the transfer of the Trentino (north of Lake Garda) and border territories around and including Trieste from Habsburg to Italian rule. Berlin encouraged Vienna to be forthcoming, but the Austrians, understandably, begrudged surrendering their own territory. Eventually, the Italian demands were more or less conceded in principle by the Austro-Hungarians, but sufficiently slowly for Rome to ponder whether the western Allies might not be more generous.

The Prime Minister of the day, Antonio Salandra, characterized Italian foreign policy, in self-explanatory terms, as "sacro egoismo" and, territory apart, it was not lost on Italy's leaders that it would be advantageous to be on the winning side when it eventually came to peace negotiations. There was also the issue of whether Italy wished to be associated with the liberal democracies of northwestern Europe or with the more autocratic Central Powers. He and his Foreign Minister, Sidney Sonnino, now took the crucial decision to align Italy with the Allies without consulting parliament and in defiance of public opinion, which was overwhelmingly for neutrality and peace. As Martin Clark commented of the age: "Kings, Prime Ministers and Foreign Ministers, not parliament, made policy; international treaties were, at best, ratified by parliament later."[146] The western Allies could afford to be extremely generous with Habsburg (and Ottoman) territory and so bought Italy's support. The Treaty of London (April 26, 1915) committed the country to opening hostilities against Austria-Hungary in May, despite fruitless efforts by the country's Liberal elder statesman, Giovanni Giolitti, to uphold Italy's neutral status at the eleventh hour.

The ensuing war went badly. The Austrians were well dug in along the southern upslopes of the Alps and on the stony Istrian border hills, and their Slav troops had little love for the Italians. If Czech soldiers were deserting in droves to the Russians on the eastern front, no such thing occurred in the west, where the Habsburg forces fought a genuinely popular defensive campaign. The Italians struggled at great human cost to capture a handful of border towns, before an Austro-German offensive at Caporetto swept the Italian armies aside in October 1917, taking 300,000 prisoners and advancing as far as the River Piave just short of Venice. The Italian army was not to attack again until the closing days of the war and only when the Habsburg Empire was literally falling apart at the seams.

The front-line soldiers themselves tended to be southern peasants, with northern industrial workers often spared military service. Northerners who did serve often found their way into the artillery, the engineers, or were afforded staff roles far from the actual fighting. The southerners resented dying for Alpine territory they regarded as alien, and equally resented the draconian military discipline which characterized the Italian army of the day. The church for its part saw the war at best as "a divine punishment to be borne as patiently as possible," but Pope Benedict XV was even less enthusiastic. In May 1915 he had refused to sanction Italy's entry into a war he condemned as "an appalling butchery" before calling in August 1917 for disarmament and a negotiated settlement of the wider conflict.[147] Italian military headquarters angrily demanded that Benedict be hanged, but it did not come to that and, as Clark concludes, "The Catholics took part in the war, but they kept their distance."[148] Rural skepticism and religious doubts were compounded by principled Socialist hostility to war in any shape or form. The labor movement did work in and even helped to administer the war economy, but its underlying antimilitarism was reinforced by the demands of the war itself as long hours and periodic food shortages exacted their price. Rioting broke out in Turin during August 1917, forcing the authorities to improve food supplies and working conditions, but a reckoning was to follow hard on the heels of the peace, not least due to the revolutionary example afforded by Russia.

Amid this flood tide of popular antipathy to war, however, one prominent Socialist leader argued stridently in favor of Italian participation on the Allied side. Benito Mussolini was editor of the main Socialist newspaper, *Avanti*, but since his party demanded that it oppose any involvement in the war he resigned his post on November 15, 1914. Thereafter he founded the prowar newspaper *Popolo d'Italia*, which began by demanding that Italy join the fighting and thereafter criticized parliament for its lukewarm prosecution of the war effort.

Mussolini claimed that he had forced the government's hand in 1915 in the face of parliamentary opposition and ensured Italy's entry into the war, but whatever the case prowar opinion remained in the minority. After the catastrophic defeat at Caporetto the various prowar factions determined to stiffen the nation's resolve by forming a League (*Fascio*) of National Defense. Democratic interventionalists, who identified with the parliamentary order of northwestern Europe, united with diehard nationalists and also with right-wing liberals in an alliance which soon enough became deeply critical of the liberal monarchy. Local leagues sprang up and as Clark observes:

> These local bodies, patriotic and paranoid, became centres in which landowners, eminent citizens, labour agitators and youthful careerists met to exchange ideas and to deplore government inertia. Many lasting friendships began there, and some of them were the nuclei of later Fascist organizations.[149]

The peace conference and its aftermath were to pose more immediate challenges, however.

"Italy," Clark concludes, "had won the war but she bungled the peace, and bungled it spectacularly and publicly."[150] Although Italy did acquire most of the territory promised by the Treaty of London, Foreign Minister Sonnino also coveted the Dalmatian (present-day Croatian) coastline. Since the city of Rijeka (Fiume) was the key to the northern Dalmatian coast Sonnino demanded its transfer to Italian control, only to be publicly repudiated by Woodrow Wilson. Orlando and Sonnino returned temporarily from the peace conference to Italy in protest, but this setback had effectively discredited the government's foreign policy. The celebrated writer and military adventurer Gabriele D'Annunzio condemned the emergent peace settlement as a "mutilated victory" and in September 1919 seized Fiume at the head of a volunteer force of some 2,000 men. Feted by Italian opinion and enjoying the tacit support of the army, D'Annunzio was finally expelled from the city in January 1921 by the Italian navy, shortly after Jugoslavia and Italy had resolved their territorial differences. Fiume was declared an independent statelet before Jugoslavia, after all, ceded it to Italy in 1924, by which time Mussolini was Prime Minister.

Postwar governments also struggled to contain a wave of domestic unrest as unemployment peaked at some 2 million in November 1919, inflation soared and a radicalized labor force unleashed a wave of strikes. High prices simultaneously triggered food riots which a rattled government bought off by imposing swinging price cuts – only to antagonize the country's shopkeepers and the wider middle classes. By September 1920 employer–employee relations in Italian industry had plumbed new depths, triggering a wave of factory occupations by their workforces. The government again resolved to buy off the troublemakers, this time by pledging a war profits tax and promising the trade unions effective control over the hiring and firing of labor. However, the enabling legislation failed to get through parliament and urban society remained deeply polarized between dissatisfied workers and a middle class appalled at the repeated appeasement of proletarian "troublemakers" under the menacing shadow of the Russian example.

Meanwhile, many peasants returning from the war either purchased or simply seized land, often with the help of the church. This might, in time, have created a conservative rural social order, for some 40 percent of country families came to own at least some land. However, the immediate effect was to alarm the traditional landowning classes and large tenant farmers, leaving rural society as deeply divided as urban Italy.

Postwar electoral reforms saw Liberal governments introduce universal male suffrage and also proportional representation in an effort to mobilize a moderate majority and contain political extremism. However, these reforms did nothing to calm Italian political life and in the 1919 elections the Socialists (by now openly revolutionary) made striking gains. So did a new, radical, peasant-oriented party, the Popular Party, leaving it and the Socialists with a majority of seats between them, but unable to form a coherent governing coalition. Liberal leaders continued to cobble together increasingly spatchcock coalitions before Prime Minister Giolitti called fresh elections in 1921. By this time the Socialists had nailed their colors to the revolutionary mast by joining the Moscow-based Communist International (Comintern), but the strike campaign had collapsed. Giolitti reckoned on Socialist losses and appreciated that they were internally divided between radicals and a more moderate, reformist minority. Socialist losses there were, but without the Liberals reasserting their prewar dominance. The government consisted of a shaky, unsustainable coalition which included Liberals, reformist Socialists, and also a new party: the Fascists.

As noted above, the Fascists owed their existence to the experience and immediate legacy of the war. Mussolini founded the Fasci di Combattimento in Milan on March 23, 1919 as a loose alliance of leagues which drew on former military personnel for most of their membership. During late 1920 these leagues mutated into armed squads which resolved to take on the forces which, they held, threatened Italy's internal cohesion and potential greatness. The Socialist Party with its anti-war record and espousal of class struggle was an obvious target, while the Popular Party was almost as unacceptable to the squads, given the threat it posed to rural social stability. As the struggle for land redistribution intensified across the central provinces of Emilia and Tuscany the squads intervened on the rural landlords' side against Socialist and Popular Party activists. In the cities too, the Fasci took on the Socialist trade unions, but simultaneously demanded that employees be given a role in the day-to-day management of the workplace. Sometimes described as anarcho-syndicalist, this demand complicates any effort to place workplace Fascism either on the right or on the left. In fact, as we shall see, neither the Italian Fascists nor their German Nazi cousins perceived themselves in left–right terms at all, instead claiming to offer society a resolution of the potentially destructive confrontation between labor and capital. "The Fascists," as Clark observes, "were 'bringing the workers into the system,' while making sure they did not dominate it. And who else could do that?"[151]

Mussolini took care to stand apart from the day-to-day violence unleashed by his squads and in October 1921 founded the National Fascist Party and also a Fascist trade union movement to serve as counterweights to the street violence. These organizations provided him with a route to power within the fracturing Liberal state, not least because this new-found respectability soothed the authorities. Compared to Bolshevism, militant Fascism certainly appeared the lesser evil, leaving the Italian left simultaneously confronting the old establishment and Mussolini's burgeoning patriotic movement. The Fascist Party's membership swelled from 200,000 in late 1921 to 500,000 by June 1922, making its exclusion from any non-Socialist parliamentary coalition virtually unthinkable. In late July the traditional trade unions again organized a strike, this time to launch an anti-Fascist government, but failed to garner much support in the face of strong-arm Fascist countermeasures.

On October 24, 1922 the Fascists held a mass rally in Naples, demanding they be given the reins of government. The last pre-Fascist Prime Minister of interwar Italy, Luigi Facta, halfheartedly recommended that the King, Victor Emmanuel III, declare martial law, but the army commander, Marshal Diaz, doubted the military's willingness to confront the Fascists and after some prevarication the King declined to act. A novel combination of paramilitary and conventional party politics, which combined violence with the offer of political and social stabilization, now super-seded the nineteenth-century Liberal order. Fascist mythology spoke of a "March on Rome" during October 27 and 28, but in reality Mussolini traveled from Milan to Rome by train on October 30 to accept the post of Prime Minister from the King.

Once in power Mussolini squared his diehard supporters by creating a Fascist Grand Council which appeared to link party and state, but the Cabinet continued to meet and it was there that most political decisions continued to be taken. More significant in the shorter term was another reform of the electoral system, which abolished proportional representation. Henceforward the party with the largest vote would take up two-thirds of the seats in parliament, provided it gained 25 percent or more of the votes cast. Leaving little to chance, Mussolini integrated non-Fascist sympathizers within a National Bloc which then contested the elec-tions of April 1924, but the Bloc would have triumphed whatever the electoral system, polling as it did over 66 percent of the votes cast. Almost two-thirds of National Bloc deputies were Fascists in any case, leaving the opposition forces hopelessly outnumbered and also badly fragmented.

There it might have remained, but on May 30 the Reformist Socialist leader, Giacomo Matteotti, denounced the conduct of the elections, protesting that they had been compromised by corruption and violence. On June 10 Matteotti was snatched away and murdered by Mussolini's bodyguards. Some press coverage was hostile and the opposition staged a walkout from parliament, but relatively little came of the crisis in the immediate term. Mussolini denied any personal involve-ment and managed to soothe public opinion by making the Fascist militia answer-able to the King and bringing more non-Fascist grandees into government.

However, Italy was not yet a Fascist state and on December 27 an independent official enquiry implicated Mussolini in Matteotti's death. It was the turn of the squads to feel threatened and as Fascist-inspired riots swept Florence, militia chiefs demanded of Mussolini the creation of a "real" Fascist regime in which party poli-tics would play no part (and the rule of law little more). Their leader, however, decided to play the injured party, maintaining his total innocence and denouncing the opposition parties for boycotting parliament. The Fascist squads were prom-ised a continued, if ill-defined role in the new Italy, but Mussolini simultaneously assured the conservative establishment that law and order would be upheld. This was good enough for the King, who persuaded the (non-Fascist) War and Navy ministers to remain in post and so underwrote the moral credibility of Mussolini's administration.

Mussolini and his followers had enjoyed their fair share of good luck along the road to power, but by early 1925, the Fascist takeover, part legal, often illegal, part revolutionary, yet appealing to the reactionary, had been consolidated. Mussolini's position as leader (Duce) of this new order was essentially to remain unchallenged until the Allied invasion of Italy in 1943.

Thus in less than a decade two radical ideologies, Bolshevism and Fascism, had seized power in the east and south of Europe respectively. Of the two Bolshevism was undoubtedly the more extreme, for despite its declared intention "to forge a totalitarian state and society"[152] Fascism accommodated significant elements of the existing domestic establishment (including the courts, the monarchy and the church), respected existing property relations, and initially at least, conducted its foreign policy within the framework laid down by the Paris Peace Settlement. The army officer corps also retained its integrity, remaining "more loyal to the monarchy than to the regime," as Bosworth observes.[153] Lenin, in contrast, was prepared to unleash a devastating civil war in order to press his *va banque* political agenda. Within weeks of seizing power by force he had effectively abolished any pretense at political pluralism and swept away the independent legal system and private property rights upon which liberal democracy is essentially based. Trotsky's Red Army was more a political, Bolshevik army than a national force. Mussolini moved more tentatively toward a system of one party rule and never claimed for his Fascist regime the absolute moral and political authority claimed by Lenin, by Stalin, or for that matter by Hitler. The Fascist order was far from benign and the admiration for this order displayed by a certain Miss Jean Brodie[154] (and other, less fictitious, characters) was at the very best misguided and mistaken. Nonetheless, avoiding the alternative armageddons of class or race war, Mussolini's regime was neither particularly feared nor abhorred until, during the 1930s, the Rome–Berlin axis drew Fascism into the Nazi orbit and ensured its ultimate destruction.

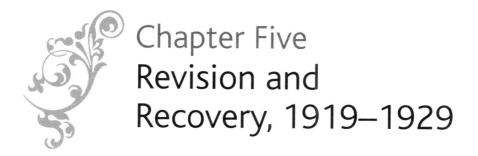

Chapter Five
Revision and Recovery, 1919–1929

5.1   From Versailles to the Dawes Plan

Had Woodrow Wilson's vision of the postwar world materialized, the League of Nations would have been central to international affairs, presiding over universal disarmament, adjudicating disputes between League members and bringing sanctions or even military force to bear against transgressors of the League's Covenant. Wilson had imagined that the League would, in due course, iron out the deficiencies and injustices of the hastily drafted peace treaties, but on French insistence its primary remit became instead to uphold the same Paris Treaties. Furthermore, once the United States Senate had refused to ratify the Versailles Treaty and with it the League's Covenant, the new organization began its life as "a very European institution,"[1] based in Geneva. It was certainly perceived as such by leading diplomats of the day[2] and if the adherence of Germany to the League in 1926 ended its role as a victors' club, it also reinforced this European-centeredness.

Historians have often been quick to dismiss the efficacy of the League, which of course failed to become the ultimate arbiter of international affairs. It did hold permanent or temporary sovereign rights over former German territories such as the Saarland, Danzig and, briefly, Memel, where outright transfer to any victor power was simply too controversial, and offered legal underpinning for the Allied occupation of German territory and supervision of the disarmament process. It also took on the colonial territories of Germany and Turkey and distributed these among the victors through a mandate system, but in the final analysis high politics were still dominated by the Great Powers. Membership of the League was understood to symbolize acceptance of the post-1918 peace settlement – and thus the importance of Germany's accession in 1926 – but this role quickly faded during the 1930s as Europe's dictators pursued revisionist foreign policies on their own account.

The League's longer term substantive achievements were altogether more subtle, extending the scope and refining the conduct of international relations, before ultimately laying the groundwork for today's United Nations. As Andrew Webster reminds us, its efforts to achieve disarmament did bring agreement in specific areas, such as the use of poison gas in warfare which was banned by the 1925 Geneva Protocol. This was breached by Italy during its invasion of Abyssinia, but upheld during the Second World War.[3] The greater goal of universal disarmament proved more elusive, however. After 10 years of preliminary negotiations, the World Disarmament Conference opened in Geneva in February 1932, but inconclusive discussions were torpedoed in October 1933 when Hitler withdrew from the Conference and the League itself. The Conference finally folded in June 1934, after which rearmament quickly became the new vogue.

Looking beyond disarmament, the League's Permanent Court of International Justice in the Hague had been involved in 600 international agreements by 1939 and was transferred to the United Nations in 1946. Similarly, the League's Economic and Financial Organisation (EFO) undertook important economic, social, and health initiatives during the 1930s which were designed to promote longer term political stability and peace. With United States involvement, its economic statistical series became the most comprehensive available, and its policy proposals radical and innovative. If it failed during the 1930s to solve the international economic crisis unleashed by the Great Depression, its ideas and personnel informed the 1944 Bretton Woods Agreement on the liberalization of world trade. Similarly its legacy could be seen in the signing of the General Agreement on Tariffs and Trade (GATT) in 1947, the creation of the European Coal and Steel Community (ECSC) in 1952, and in the framing of post-1945 relief policy in Europe, which found institutional form in the US-funded European Recovery Program (Marshall Aid) of 1947.

The League's immediate postwar relief program was dwarfed by the efforts of the American Relief Administration, but this is not to underestimate the significance and longer term impact of its welfare agenda. Its Health Organisation (LNHO) pioneered the generation of international health data, initiated the systematic reporting of outbreaks of deadly disease, and eventually transmogrified into the United Nations World Health Organization in 1948. The International Labour Organization (ILO) promoted the extension of the eight-hour day (with mixed success) and environmental health, particularly of women. Similarly, the Social Committee sought to promote women's and children's welfare, overseeing the creation of new statistical series and also the framing of the Human Rights Convention. As Patricia Clavin concludes: "The … League had come of age, reflecting a truly universal and genuinely global perspective,"[4] and so outgrowing its European roots.

In the immediate aftermath of the post-1918 peace settlements, however, the European powers were confronted by a tangle of territorial, military, and economic imperatives, for which watchwords such as "war guilt" and "security" came to serve as a shorthand. War guilt had provided the legal basis for a reparations settlement that extended far beyond the simple restitution of damages to civilian property, or beyond the payment of a loser's "indemnity," as had occurred after earlier wars. Thereafter the issue became central to a dialogue of the deaf between Paris and Berlin as French leaders insisted that Germany's guilt was a product of its deeper national character, which in turn justified their own hawkish postwar policy. The German authorities played on a profound and widespread sense of national outrage as they denounced the settlement and the associated concept of war guilt as little more than victors' justice, but their campaign to refute this guilt also had more concrete objectives. Considerable resources were expended by the German Foreign Office as it strove to convince neutral and increasingly sympathetic British and American opinion that Germany's role in the outbreak of war had been grossly exaggerated and that accordingly the reparations and wider peace settlement were founded on false premises. From there, Berlin hoped, it would be possible to negotiate the revision of key dimensions of Versailles, both territorial and economic.

The editing and publication of Germany's prewar diplomatic documents was central to this strategy. The Social Democratic elder statesman Karl Kautsky had begun this task in March 1919 with very different objectives in mind, but his conclusion that in 1914 Germany had acted "unspeakably carelessly and unthinkingly" found little favor with the Foreign Office at so delicate a stage in the Paris Peace Conference. Publication was suppressed and Kautsky integrated within an editorial collective whose *German Documents on the Outbreak of War (Die deutschen Dokumente zum Kriegsausbruch)*, published in December 1919, exonerated Germany.[5] Not everyone was convinced, especially since well-founded rumors circulated that Kautsky's own findings were altogether less positive,[6] but in 1922 the Foreign Office initiated a much more ambitious effort to demonstrate Germany's essential innocence. Historical research was engaged as a tool of political revision as 40 volumes of edited diplomatic papers appeared between 1922 and 1927 under the title *Die Grosse Politik der Europäischen Kabinette*.[7]

However, the collection was based on Foreign Office records only, neglecting military papers and those of the Chancellor's Office (*Reichskanzlei*). Marginal notes penciled onto the originals were often omitted, as were key German records of·the fateful meetings held in Berlin during early July 1914, leading Holger Herwig to conclude that this whole enterprise "polluted historical understanding at home and abroad well into the post-1945 period."[8] In this vein *Die Grosse Politik* contributed to the revisionist cause after Versailles, with the Weimar statesman Gustav Stresemann for one regarding its publication as an act of self-defense. Later and more fatefully this revisionist campaign helped prepare the ground for the Allied appeasement of Hitler during the mid and late 1930s.

In this regard Germany received unwitting help from elsewhere in Europe. In November 1917 the Bolsheviks wasted no time in opening the archives of the Tsarist and Provisional governments and publishing their contents in an effort to discredit Russia's participation in the Great War. This promotion of Russian war guilt pointed, inevitably, at the complicity of Russia's principal ally, France, but for its part Paris remained strangely silent. Finally, in 1926, French officials began to appreciate how damaging this silence appeared. In 1929 the first volume of *Documents diplomatiques français 1871–1914* was published, but it was only in 1953 that the exercise was concluded with the appearance of the thirty-second volume.[9] "Ironically," Anthony Adamthwaite observes, "the French made better progress translating *Die Grosse Politik*, so publicising the German case against war guilt."[10] The equivalent British effort (*British Documents on the Origins of the War*) appeared between 1926 and 1938,[11] but tensions arose between the historians involved and the British Foreign Office when the latter insisted on the omission of potentially damaging documents – not least those that compromised its wartime ally France. As the British Foreign Secretary Austen Chamberlain observed, his "first duty [is] to preserve peace now and in the future. I cannot sacrifice *that* even to historical accuracy."[12]

Whatever the extent of Germany's responsibility, therefore, it began increasingly to look, in Annika Mombauer's words, "as if Britain and France might have something to hide."[13] There was growing, if qualified, international sympathy for Germany's predicament and so for revision of the peace settlement, all of which was reinforced by the evolution of European and North Atlantic relations during the years 1919–1924. An erratic and mutually destructive decline in Franco-German relations, from the peace treaty, through a contested reparations schedule (1920–1) and on to the Franco-Belgian invasion of Germany's Ruhr District (1923) lay at the heart of this story. Finally Britain and the United States intervened in late 1923 as the very existence of a united Germany appeared threatened and with it the stability of Europe and the wider international order. From this emerged a revised reparations settlement in 1924 based on the report of a leading American banker, Charles G. Dawes, and then a wider diplomatic accord between the European powers at Locarno in 1925.

It was in this atmosphere that statesmen such as Lloyd George openly questioned the notion of German war guilt, preferring instead to conclude that Europe had slid into war during July and August 1914. From there it was a relatively short step to asserting, a generation later, that French intransigence during and after the Paris Peace Conference did much to foster the emergence of National Socialism. No one has seriously questioned Germany's responsibility for the outbreak of the 1939 war in Europe but, the argument ran, a more magnanimous post-1918 settlement could have averted the second great war of the twentieth century. However, when Fritz Fischer's work demonstrated, during the 1960s, the very substantive contribution of Germany to the crisis of 1914 and also the apparent continuities from Imperial foreign policy through that of the Weimar Republic and so into the Third Reich, the way was also opened for a reappraisal of France's post-1918 foreign policy.

France, it seemed, had after all been justified in mistrusting Weimar Germany's bona fides. Rather than being too hard on Germany, it was the failure of Paris to impose its will on its recalcitrant neighbor, especially during the 1923 crisis, which appeared to open the road to German revisionism, Allied appeasement, and ultimately the Second World War. More generally, the argument ran, the problem with Versailles lay not in its terms and contents, but with the failure to enforce these terms adequately. From the 1970s this perception stimulated a series of revisionist studies of French policy which underlined the degree to which Paris felt betrayed and isolated by its wartime allies.[14] Inter-Allied economic cooperation was a thing of the past, leaving France weighed down by a massive burden of domestic and foreign wartime debt. Allied military guarantees offered to France during the peace conference, in return for continued German sovereignty over the Rhineland, lapsed when the United States Senate refused to ratify the Versailles Treaty. France, the argument continued, was in effect left to confront alone its vengeful and unrepent-ant German neighbor. The revisionists also stressed that France's postwar German policy only hardened as a last resort. Repeated efforts by Paris to resolve the conun-drum of inter-Allied war debts and reparations, preferably through cancellation of the former, were rebuffed. Efforts to offer Germany a (subordinate) place in a post-war continental European order were met with a combination of Allied indiffer-ence and German defiance, which by mid-1922 had brought both Franco-German and Franco-British relations close to breakdown. Finally, it is argued, the French Prime Minister of the day, Raymond Poincaré, resorted reluctantly to coercion in 1923 in an effort to force Berlin to comply with earlier reparations agreements and with the Versailles settlement more generally. French and Belgian troops occupied Germany's Ruhr District, the heartland of its military-industrial complex, without British participation or support. It is generally accepted that this French policy often lacked coherence and even wanted for legality, but nonetheless when all was said and done France appeared dedicated to upholding the Versailles Settlement, whereas Germany was bent on its overthrow.

However, the most recent French research, while not questioning Germany's revisionist strategy, effectively tars France with the same brush. We have already seen that France's leaders only accepted the Versailles Settlement after particu-larly hard-fought negotiations and that even then Clemenceau faced widespread domestic criticism over the treaty's perceived inadequacies. Military chiefs indulged in a series of adventures in the Rhineland and the Danube Basin designed to create new geopolitical realities on the ground even before the treaty had been signed and delivered. Politicians in Paris had to be more circumspect than their generals, but nonetheless appreciated that the terms of the peace settlement were malleable and open to varying interpretation. In particular, the treaty seemed to open the way for unilateral action by any individual Allied state should Germany default on reparations:

> The measures which the Allied and Associated Powers shall have the right to take, in case of voluntary default by Germany, and which Germany agrees not to regard as acts of war, may include economic and financial prohibitions and reprisals and in general such other measures as the respective Governments may determine neces-sary in the circumstances.[15]

Prime Minister Clemenceau and his successors took this to include the prolonging of the military occupation of western Germany beyond the periods of five, ten, and fifteen years specified for the three zones in the treaty, or even the extension of the occupation to further parts of Germany. Similarly, Paris believed, German noncompliance with the disarmament provisions of the treaty provided legitimate grounds for prolonging or widening the occupation of German territory. However, French leaders were conscious that Britain would not tolerate blatant French adventurism and they could not afford to exhaust the patience of their key wartime ally, which was already being stretched to the limit.

British attitudes aside, French resources were severely strained. Public finances had buckled under the crushing burden of wartime debt and the inflationary pressures that this debt had unleashed. France had been a net creditor before the war, with external assets amounting to over $8.5 billion in 1914, but these assets stood at less than $4 billion in 1919, against which was set $30 billion of war debt to Britain and the United States. France had become a net debtor, reduced to borrowing from Spain, Argentina, and even Uruguay to stave off financial collapse. The country remained the strongest military power in Europe, but the scale of wartime casualties and a low birth rate threatened to leave France permanently and dangerously overshadowed by its more populous German neighbor if the latter were ever to rearm. Added to this, domestic resistance to onerous periods of peacetime conscription combined with the need to maintain sizeable armies of occupation in Morocco and Syria to compromise matters further.

The residual triumphalism born of military victory appeared at best a wasting asset. In January 1920 Clemenceau declared in his final speech as Prime Minister that "[France] must take up the mentality and habits of a victorious people, which once more takes its place at the head of Europe,"[16] but in reality the country was gripped by a deep unease bordering on fatalistic pessimism when looking to the future. The French Governor of Morocco, Marshal Louis Lyautey, lamented: "Alone, exhausted, ruined, without government, without compass, living from day to day, haphazardly. The future is terrifying,"[17] while the writer Paul Valéry betrayed a profound existential angst: "We civilizations know that we are mortal."[18]

Accordingly, any revision of the Versailles Treaty would have to occur with great subtlety and almost by default. The Director of Economic Affairs in the Foreign Office, Jacques Seydoux, who represented France at a succession of major postwar international conferences, was particularly disturbed by the military potential of Germany's heavy industrial sector. Although they were banned from producing large-caliber weapons under the terms of Versailles, Seydoux understood all too well that Germany's former armorers, such as the mighty Krupp combine, would be able to revert to arms production when circumstances allowed, leading Klaus Tenfelde to observe:

> The company sought to preserve [armaments] construction expertise and experience, and await better political times. ... Arms control seriously hampered such

strategies, but in spite of these legal constraints Krupp resumed its activities step by step from around 1927, long before Hitler's rise to power.[19]

Furthermore, Seydoux was among French leaders who believed that Germany's industrial barons dominated the country's high politics and as such had been responsible for the outbreak of war in 1914. Now, it was feared, they were planning anew for a war of revenge, so forcing France to take preemptive countermeasures.

Initial efforts by Paris to strip Germany of its major industrial regions and so reverse the balance of heavy industrial power between France and Germany had largely failed. The Versailles Treaty handed France Germany's heavy industrial assets in the Moselle, but only to leave it with an overblown, underperforming metallurgical sector, which did nothing to stunt German potential. As before this centered on the Ruhr District whose industrial barons were indemnified by the German government for their losses in the Moselle. They used this compensation to refurbish or renew plant exhausted by the demands of wartime production, and rather than sourcing iron ore from France (as they had done in large measure before 1914) they looked to Scandinavia and Spain. This had the twin benefit of freeing German heavy industry from dependency on its politically hostile French neighbor while cutting off the French iron ore fields from the vital German market and leaving them operating at 50 percent of capacity.

Secretly and in contravention of the 1919 peace settlement, Paris initiated a "battle for the Rhine." Autonomist movements in the region were encouraged to turn their backs on a Prussian-dominated Germany and look instead toward France and, Paris claimed, their common historic and cultural roots that dated back to the days of the Roman Empire. These alleged links were, Anna-Monika Lauter observes, reinforced by a mythologized memory of the Napoleonic Confederation of the Rhine which claimed that the Rhenish population desired a permanent attachment to the French state.[20] Only the award of the region to Prussia at the Congress of Vienna in 1814 and the presence of Prussian officialdom in the region were alleged to have thwarted its Francophile aspirations. Efforts were also made to isolate the Rhine and Ruhr economically from Germany and reorient business activities toward the west, so creating a heavy industrial common market presided over by the French state and even French big business.

Beyond the Rhineland, French policy encouraged various separatist and antirepublican movements across Germany in an effort to fragment the Bismarckian Reich into a collection of smaller independent or autonomous states "too much concerned with inner rivalry to become a danger for neighbouring countries."[21] France reopened its embassy in Munich in a clear effort to foster Bavaria's particular status, but some initiatives were conducted at one remove from the ministries in Paris. The French High Commissioner in the Rhineland, Paul Tirard, pursued a personal and often covert strategy to promote regional autonomism, while French public money found its way into the hands of German political adventurers, such as a certain Adolf Hitler, who promised to destabilize and even destroy the German Reich.

Subterfuge aside, a succession of international conferences formed the better known dimension of this complex story and France did not neglect conventional diplomacy. Reparations dominated the early discussions, for the Versailles Treaty had left the calculation of the final German reparations bill to be decided in 1921. The Allies themselves agreed during the summer of 1920 that France would receive the lion's share of the reparations receipts (52 percent), with Britain entitled to 22 percent, Italy 10 percent, and Belgium 8 percent. The remainder was allocated to wartime allies such as Serbia and Romania. However, it proved far more difficult to decide on the actual sum to be levied and on what terms. In June 1920, the Boulogne Conference proposed a total bill of 269 billion gold marks, to be collected over 42 years.

However, the administration of the interim schedule (which demanded payment of 20 billion gold marks by May 1921) had already come up against a succession of difficulties. Berlin demanded that property lost with the surrendered territories be credited to the account and did gain compensation of 8 billion marks for such losses to Poland. The delivery "in kind" of materials such as coal and timber dominated the agenda of the Spa Conference in July 1920, which immediately confronted some very inconvenient realities. The Allies had acknowledged from the outset that Germany's exhausted and malnourished workers would be hard put actually to mine the coal and produce the other goods demanded of their country in part settlement of the interim reparations account. The Versailles Treaty, therefore, provided for reparations payments to be diverted by the Reparations Commission to fund "such supplies of food and raw materials as may be judged by the Governments of the … Allied … Powers to be essential to enable Germany to meet her obligations for reparations."[22] This conundrum was revisited at Spa as the Ruhr District struggled to restore orderly production in the aftermath of the Ruhr workers' rising, which had flared up in response to the Kapp Putsch.[23] Among the German delegates was the postwar mine workers' leader and committed republican, Otto Hué, who spoke movingly of the chaos and hunger scourging the Ruhr, before concluding: "Gentlemen, you can pass whatever resolution you like, but in the final analysis the decision rests in the gnarled hands of the miners."[24] The Allied negotiators conceded the point, reducing monthly delivery quotas from 2.4 to 2 million tons, which remained more than Germany thought possible, but less than France had wanted.

Thereafter the final reparations bill was agreed in London between the Allies and Germany in May 1921. At 132 billion gold marks, reparations were to be covered through a phased German bond issue and paid in monthly installments of 50 million gold marks, but added to this were monthly "clearing payment" surcharges of 37 million gold marks to meet Germany's additional international obligations, a levy of 26 percent on German export earnings, and German liability for the costs of the Allied military occupation of the Rhineland. The settlement was less severe than Seydoux had proposed at Boulogne or even in January 1921, but German negotiators had insisted during the negotiations that it remained beyond their country's means. Their intransigence was only finally broken in March when three major industrial centers on the Rhine and Ruhr (Düsseldorf, Duisburg and Ruhrort) were occupied without time limit by French and Belgian forces and a temporary customs barrier was created between the occupied Rhineland and the rest of Germany. Whatever the rights and wrongs of the deal, it had been imposed under duress and triggered a political crisis in Germany, where Chancellor Fehrenbach's center-right coalition government resigned rather than recommend ratification. As with the ratification of Versailles it was left to the three "Weimar" parties (SPD, the Center Party, and the German Democratic Party (DDP)) to form a government that was willing to deliver approval by the Reichstag, only to trigger renewed charges of treason from the far right and the Communists. The new Chancellor, Joseph Wirth, made the best of a bad job, declaring that he would seek a further reduction of the London reparations schedule through a policy of short-term fulfillment (*Erfüllungspolitik*) and the Reichstag voted the deal through with some misgivings.

This grudging compliance did nothing to mollify French leaders, who accused the German government of deliberately fostering rampant domestic inflation and social chaos precisely to undermine the orderly payment of reparations. However, Germany lacked sufficient hard currency reserves both to meet the reparations bill and import the food its population needed. The taxation of a dwindling domestic base of real assets, declining profits, and falling real wages to meet the reparations schedule was equally problematic, leading Gerald Feldman to ask: "Could German leaders mediate a distributional conflict whose major function, no matter who won, appeared to be serving the well-being of Germany's enemies?"[25] The reparations schedule would only have been tenable, Feldman argued, in a "creditor's utopia," and certainly not in the febrile, disintegrating sociopolitical landscape of postwar Germany.[26] As he concluded: "The only people who really believe that Germany could fulfil their reparations obligations ... are some historians."[27]

The realities of life in postwar Germany certainly ruled out easy choices. High inflation allowed businesses to borrow heavily to invest and then pay off the depreciating loans and allowed landowners to pay off debts and mortgages. More generally the money printed allowed the country to maintain a reasonable level of economic activity and keep unemployment low. However, the retired, war wounded pensioners, and war widows found that the value of their state pensions fell from month to month. Salaried professionals and employees in the public and private sectors also saw their incomes fall in both absolute and relative terms, while many industrial workers fared equally poorly. Profitability in sectors such as coal mining was pared to the bone, leading real wages to fall inexorably. Before the war a Ruhr miner's real income was comparable with that of his British counterpart, but now it fell to less than a third even as food remained in desperately short supply. The German bread grain harvest had yielded over 14.6 million tons in 1913 (on post-1919 territory), but fell to 9.9 million tons in 1921 and just 7.3 million tons in 1922. Dairy cattle were inadequately fed and each cow yielded 1,500 liters of milk annually as against 2,200 liters before the war, while the lack of coal periodically kept the country's fishing fleet in port. The average daily calorie intake of a typical Ruhr mining family condemned it to creeping starvation even as the Ministry of Labor urged an intensification of output as "'an instrument of national liberation' under the democratic control of the new state."[28] Distraught parents watched as their malnourished children fell victim to rickets, to typhoid, or simply failed to cope with influenza or the common cold in underheated, increasingly damp homes. In September 1921, confronted with urban schools full of half-starved children, the National Ministry of Education warned that "the prevailing situation [in Berlin] has triggered widespread unrest within the urban population," but without being able to offer any solution to the problem.[29] In 1923, when high inflation flared up into hyperinflation and banknotes literally became worth less within hours than the paper and ink used to produce them, the situation was to become immeasurably worse.

Senior figures in the French and German governments tried to square the circle during the summer and autumn of 1921. Under the terms of the Wiesbaden Agreements, Louis Loucheur (French Minister for the Liberated Regions) and Walther Rathenau (German Minister for Reconstruction) agreed to substitute Germany's gold-based reparations liabilities to France for a program of deliveries in kind, such as coal, coke, timber and even labor, coupled with the creation of Franco-German joint ventures to rehabilitate the devastated towns and countryside of northern France. Both politicians had begun their careers as successful businessmen with a shared expertise in the electrics industry. Beyond the immediate problem of reparations, they acknowledged that the war had left the United States commercially and technologically preeminent and agreed that Franco-German economic collaboration might offset America's new-found strength. However, the agreement failed to stick. French industrialists had been happy to collaborate with their German counterparts before the Great War, but now they bridled against a second German economic penetration of their country, instead looking to opportunities for themselves east of the Rhine. More critically, fears of an emergent Franco-German economic bloc alarmed the British Prime Minister, David Lloyd-George, who proposed to his French counterpart Aristide Briand (the two sometimes conversing in Welsh and Breton respectively when confidentiality demanded) the launching of a multilateral European recovery program.

This informed the agenda of the Genoa Conference on security, economic reconstruction, and reparations in April 1922. By this time Briand had been replaced as Prime Minister by Raymond Poincaré. The new Prime Minister was more inclined to secure German compliance with the Versailles settlement before embarking on any fresh diplomacy and his mood was not lightened by growing difficulties with Germany during March over existing reparations commitments. Poincaré stayed away from Genoa, but any progress there was fatally derailed by a separate agreement between Germany and the Soviet Union. Soviet and German officials had been discussing commercial cooperation and diplomatic recognition since January and agreed a draft accord in Berlin shortly before the Genoa

Conference opened. Rathenau (now Foreign Minister of Germany) was unnerved by parallel talks in Genoa between the Allies and the Soviet Union which extended from trade to war debts and reparations, and especially by threats from the Soviet Foreign Minister Grigoriy Chicherin, to conclude such an agreement with the Allies if Germany declined to sign up to their own draft accord. With the full backing of President Ebert in Berlin, Rathenau resolved to preempt any Allied-Soviet rapprochement. The Soviet-German agreement was signed in the nearby town of Rapallo, only to be met with British irritation and French fury.

Poincaré and his military commanders feared that political and economic cooperation between Berlin and Moscow would be followed by a military alliance, so undermining entirely France's strategic position in Eastern Europe. These fears were exaggerated but no less real for that and reanimated French plans effectively to exclude Germany from the Rhineland and the Ruhr. The French military commander in the Rhineland, General Jean-Marie Degoutte, and High Commissioner Paul Tirard agreed that Germany was irreclaimably malign and militaristic, but while Degoutte advocated the fragmentation of Germany in the shortest possible time, Tirard was more cautious.

Building on his experience as a colonial administrator in Morocco and exploiting his role as president of the Inter-Allied Rhineland High Commission, Tirard progressively undermined the formal powers of the Prussian and Bavarian state civil services in the Rhineland without necessarily consulting Paris directly, and often through verbal rather than written orders. A policy of "peaceful penetration" was initiated to appeal to the hearts and minds of the Rhenish population through a lavishly funded cultural policy, and to the Rhenish pocket through the encouragement of commercial links between the Rhine and the French interior. In this regard Tirard drew parallels with the Francization policy in Alsace and the Moselle, but given the limitations imposed on it by the Versailles settlement, his Rhenish strategy was a policy that dared not speak its name. French domestic commerce was left angry and bewildered at his concessions to its "Boche" competitors, and newspapers in provincial France failed to understand why the "Boches" of western Germany should be treated any more favorably than their eastern brethren. However, Tirard also considered a more radical strategy should the German Republic collapse or should punitive sanctions be imposed. In such circumstances, Stanislas Jeannesson observes, the High Commissioner's agenda extended to total legislative control of the region, a Rhenish currency, a customs border between the Rhineland and Germany, and a program of ethnic cleansing (épuration) involving the expulsion of tens of thousands of Prussian and Bavarian[30] civil servants along with their families.[31]

Now, after Rapallo, Tirard's activities on the Rhine were complemented by increasingly concrete and coherent planning in the French capital. Almost immediately, Poincaré and his military commanders countenanced a unilateral French military occupation of the Ruhr District and the Premier's resolve was hardened when the Rapallo crisis was followed by the progressive disintegration of the reparations regime.

The Inter-Allied Loans Committee was convinced by American expert opinion that the May 1921 settlement was excessive and so proposed in June 1922 that Germany's overall reparations liability be reduced. Poincaré sought to tie such a reduction to a commensurate cut in France's debt to its wartime allies, but his appeal fell on deaf ears. A further inter-Allied conference was held in London during early August, but only served to exacerbate the situation. British opinion was increasingly inclined to disown the 1921 reparations agreement, with the influential *Economist* magazine condemning it as the main source of international tension. Feelings were heightened when the former Chief of the War Trade Intelligence Department, Sir Henry Penson, published the results of a fact-finding mission to Germany. He warned his readers that the German economy was chronically unstable, creating millionaires and mass poverty to the point where it could collapse without warning. It was time, he concluded, "for a complete reconsideration of the whole reparations question,"[32] a judgment retrospectively endorsed by Winston Churchill, who supported the wider peace settlement but condemned "the monstrous character of [the Treaty's] financial and economic clauses."[33]

Despite this hostility Poincaré, in some desperation, proposed combining enforcement of the reparations regime with France's strategic and geopolitical agenda on the Rhine and Ruhr. He advocated the seizure by France of German corporate assets on a grand scale, to serve as a "productive pledge," but all of this was vehemently rebuffed by British and Belgian negotiators. The Belgians suspected France of coveting its 1792 Rhine frontier which, they feared, would leave Belgium itself prey to absorption in a greater France. The British Foreign Secretary, Lord Curzon, accused Paris of harboring hegemonic ambitions in Europe, and warned that Britain could never accept the realization of these aims. The London talks collapsed, leaving the British Prime Minister, Lloyd George, to remark bleakly that "we agree that we disagree," while Poincaré declared that he was returning home "empty-handed, but with his hands free."[34]

Events in Germany hardened his resolve. Weimar's leaders felt increasingly helpless in the face of domestic chaos and foreign pressure as Cabinet committees devoted hours at a time to resolving matters as seemingly trivial as regional potato shortages and the use of scarce sugar by distilleries, or agonized over whether dwindling hard currency reserves should be paid into the Allied clearing account or used to import bread grain. Hoarding and racketeering were rife in a society where there was, quite simply, too little food to go around, prompting the authorities to issue over a hundred separate decrees and ordinances in a quixotic struggle piecemeal to contain the damage. In late 1921 the trade unions had acidly dismissed this torrent of legislation as incoherent to the point where "it left nothing more to desire in terms of its opacity,"[35] and meanwhile an international flight from the German mark was compounded by a domestic flight from the currency as businessmen did what they could to stay viable. Finally, Chancellor Wirth announced a unilateral suspension of reparations cash payments (but not deliveries in kind) on August 30, declaring to a somber Reichstag that: "The entire nation understands the slogan 'bread first, then reparations.'"[36]

France's residual confidence in the ethical and political bona fides of the German Republic had already suffered a major blow when the internationally respected German Foreign Minister, Walther Rathenau, was gunned down by right-wing extremists on June 24. In the eyes of these radicals his efforts to comply as best he could with the peace settlement were unacceptable, his Jewish origins unforgivable. Now, the intensifying reparations crisis reinforced Poincaré's fears as Paris continued to insist that it was essentially synthetic, engineered by a government determined to evade its obligations. However, as Georges-Henri Soutou observes, French policy sought ultimately to secure political control of the Rhineland and the Ruhr, rather than merely seeking reparations from these regions.[37] Thus the French Finance Minister, Charles de Lasteyrie, doubted if an occupation of the Ruhr would benefit the French Treasury, but was happy to support the strategy for political reasons. As he stressed in August: "From a financial point of view, the occupation of the Ruhr can in no way be justified. Its sole interest is political."[38] Tirard agreed, speaking of a Rhineland occupation "sustained for several generations,"[39] which was of course something very different from the time-limited occupation specified in the Treaty of Versailles. Such an extended French presence, Tirard calculated, would bring the region permanently under the suzerainty of Paris.

Plans for an invasion of the Ruhr were finally sanctioned in November 1922 and refined during December. At this critical point the political character of the projected occupation was made absolutely clear. Poincaré dared hope that "by March or April Germany will fall to pieces,"[40] and went on to "stress explicitly that [they] were no longer discussing payments; France had to develop a 'political plan.'"[41] Seydoux did remain more moderate, suggesting that the Ruhr operation should aim to secure German compliance with the Versailles settlement and beyond that to reach agreement with Germany on long-term economic cooperation. However, while Poincaré never entirely ruled out this more circumspect strategy, his clear preference was for a new peace treaty that established Allied protectorates over the Rhineland and Ruhr and, as noted, even countenanced the breakup of Germany itself.

Poincaré was by now actively promoting the Bavarian separatist cause, deploying secret agents and supporting various under-the-counter initiatives to this end.[42] He personally endorsed discussions with extremist groupings in Bavaria and knew of proposals to use the French army to screen a Bavarian separatist rising against "Prussian" military intervention. Matters took a particularly bizarre turn when a Bavarian intermediary opened discussions with Adolf Hitler. Hitler emphasized that his priority was to destroy the "November criminals" in Berlin and that he wished to avoid direct confrontation with France on the Rhine and Ruhr. Since Paris also wished to weaken the government in Berlin there was a spurious community of interests which, Soutou concludes, made "the affair ... a matter for serious consideration."[43] Not everyone was so convinced. French military intelligence noted the pan-Germanist leanings of Hitler and his confederates and French diplomats in Munich agreed. Paris was advised by these cooler heads to seek a reasonable agreement with the responsible authorities in Berlin rather than flirt with the witches' brew of antirepublican sentiment that had assembled in the Bavarian capital. However, it was only after Hitler's failed Munich Putsch in November 1923 that Poincaré himself dropped the matter.[44] He also regarded the separatist movement in the former Kingdom of Hanover, which had been conquered and annexed by Prussia in 1866, as worthy of support. On July 18, 1922 he passed on a plan from the army's Political Section to Tirard to extend any future Ruhr occupation eastwards to support a rising in Hanover, but without this strategy ever being put into effect.

For all of this, Poincaré was at pains to stress in public that the invasion of the Ruhr represented nothing more than a limited police action to enforce the reparations clauses of the Treaty of Versailles. In the weeks leading up to the occupation, France had established through the Reparations Commission two German technical defaults on reparations deliveries in kind – of coal and timber respectively. London was skeptical, but rather than openly break with France, Britain simply abstained when the matter came to a vote on the Commission. Last minute and hurried diplomatic efforts by Britain and the United States to mediate were rebuffed by Paris, further enraged when Whitehall announced that in order to meet its debt obligations to the United States it was freezing French and Italian gold reserves held in London. For its part Berlin seemed quite unable to respond coherently or effectively at all. On January 7 the German ambassador to Washington warned that the United States would not intervene and the German Chancellor, businessman Wilhelm Cuno, who had replaced Wirth in November 1922, was reduced to talking of "moral resistance" of a completely passive nature designed to bring around world opinion.[45]

This stress by Paris on reparations, which historians have tended to accept at face value until recently, served two distinct purposes. Firstly it disguised the enormity of French objectives which, as Jeannesson observes, "ignored the most elementary realities of the international situation, let alone the very existence of Great Britain."[46] At least the fig leaf of a (minor) reparations default served to avoid openly challenging or provoking London at a time when Lloyd George's coalition had been replaced by a new Conservative government led by Andrew Bonar Law, which was prepared to give France the benefit of the doubt. Lord Curzon remained Foreign Secretary and continued to be deeply suspicious of Poincaré's motives, but during early 1923 his priority was to secure a peace settlement in the Near and Middle East (in the aftermath of Atatürk's victories) that served British imperial interests. Germany would have to wait.

Secondly, the invasion of the Ruhr threatened to create profound difficulties for Poincaré in France itself. There was little enthusiasm for the Ruhr adventure among French industrialists, with one senior figure complaining that efforts to dissuade the government had proven a hopeless task, tantamount to "tossing grain into the wind."[47] The myth of a German-induced coal shortage in France was precisely that – a myth. Retreating German forces had destroyed many coal mines in northern France during 1918, but by 1922 domestically produced coal and output from the French-controlled mines in the Saarland were amply supplemented by German reparations deliveries. The supply of coke was, potentially, a more critical issue, for French metallurgy was almost entirely dependent on deliveries from the Ruhr District. However, during the latter part of 1922 this metallurgical grade coke was readily available and its price on the open market remained stable. Not surprisingly, officials in the French Finance Ministry continued to warn that the invasion of the Ruhr would cause more budgetary problems than it solved.

However, Poincaré's repeated assurances that all he sought was punctilious German compliance with the reparations regime ("we are fetching coal, that's all") were also intended to reassure a potentially hostile French public. During the reparations crisis of spring 1921 Briand had recalled the 1919 cohort of conscripts to the colors in order to force Germany to the negotiating table, only to trigger massive opposition from the French left. When the unwilling conscripts themselves were sent to occupy further slices of German territory, worrying reports landed on official desks in Paris. Indiscipline, fights with civilians and even the singing en masse of the Communist anthem, the "Internationale," were widespread. The French public, Lauter concludes, may have wanted Germany to honor its reparations pledges, but was strongly opposed to any disruption of postwar normalcy in France itself, including that caused by additional periods of military service.[48]

Throughout 1922 left-inclined newspapers cautioned against any new adventures by Poincaré in Germany, but his stage management of the German deliveries defaults late in the year – turning a technical breach of the reparations regime into an elemental crisis – persuaded a reluctant press. The Prime Minister personally urged metropolitan newspapers to play down the occupation as a "straightforward police operation" which was vital to the "national interest,"[49] and on the whole the Ruhr adventure was initially accepted by the media as an unavoidable, necessary evil which represented little more than a technical extension of the legal Rhineland occupation.

The ensuing Ruhr Crisis was in the event far more than a "technical" matter, instead representing a defining episode in the history of interwar Europe. It certainly paved the way toward a decided improvement in international relations during 1924 and 1925, but only after delivering a body blow to the longer term prospects for democracy in Germany and significantly compromising Franco-British relations. On January 9, 1923 French and Belgian troops crossed the demarcation line into unoccupied Germany at points all along the River Rhine. Key port installations, railway junctions, chemical works and other strategic points were seized, but the main thrust of this invasion focused on the Ruhr District and its heavy industrial assets. Within a fortnight the region and its rural surroundings were heavily garrisoned by more than 100,000 troops, with a Belgian military government established in the northwestern Ruhr and a French military government in the remaining, larger part of the region. Alongside these military regimes a French-dominated economic directorate, the Micum or Interallied Mission for Factories and Mines (Mission Interalliée des Usines et des Mines), was charged with securing reparations deliveries and also devising a longer term strategy to exploit the region.

The French invaders were hopeful that the people of the Ruhr would be inclined to collaborate, proclaiming that the French army had come as a liberator, to free the region from the Prussian yoke and to free the workers from their domineering employers. In part the French were victims of their own Rhenish propaganda, which portrayed French rule during the Napoleonic era in glowing terms, while vilifying post-1814 Prussian rule as relentlessly oppressive. However, Paris had more substantive grounds for optimism. While Prussia as a whole was strongly Protestant, the Rhine Province (which included the western half of the Ruhr) was largely Roman Catholic and some leading Rhenish Catholic politicians, such as Konrad Adenauer, did seek greater autonomy for the region, albeit within Germany. The Ruhr District also contained a substantial Polish-speaking minority, which had migrated to the region a generation or so earlier to work in the steel mills and mines. These Poles, the French reasoned, would surely prefer Gallic to Prussian control given that Poland itself was a close ally of France. Then there was the Ruhr's organized working class which, in March 1920, had risen in protest against the Kapp Putsch, only for events to take so radical a turn that Berlin used military force to crush the insurgents, and with great brutality. Poincaré for one was confident that these workers would now welcome the French into the region. Trouble, such as it was, was feared from the industrialists and from Prussian and German civil servants.

In the event neither Paris nor Berlin had anticipated the drastic reaction to the invasion. During the initial days of the occupation the Ruhr's industrial barons, led by Fritz Thyssen, offered to collaborate with the Micum in order to maintain reparations deliveries in disguised form, for reparations (hitherto paid for by the German taxpayer) constituted a major part of their business. The response from Berlin, however, was sufficiently drastic to kill off any such notions. The Ruhr's magnates were threatened with imprisonment unless they eschewed any form of cooperation with the invaders and within days they transmogrified from would-be fifth columnists into heroes of the resistance. Their sudden refusal to cooperate with the Micum or the military authorities triggered a wave of arrests and courts martial of leading Ruhr businessmen at French army headquarters in Mainz. This, however, provoked an intense reaction among the people of the Ruhr (and Rhineland) which soon enough took the form of a grass-roots "passive resistance" campaign against the invaders.

The German and Prussian governments had not entertained the notion of mass civil disobedience and the official trade unions were also initially skeptical. France, the government feared, would exploit disruption by the region's public servants (including railwaymen) to replace the German and Prussian administrations with a creation of its own. And indeed, passive resistance on the railways saw the establishment in March of a new Franco-Belgian railway company, the Régie, to operate the track in the Rhineland and the Ruhr. The unions were unsure if their members had the stomach for any sustained struggle after the relentless trauma of the war and postwar years, and were possibly even more afraid that Communist activists would profit from the ensuing mayhem. Such had been the case during the 1920 Ruhr rising.

However, an undercurrent of workplace anger was apparent even before the invasion, and the Mainz courts martial triggered spontaneous protest strikes and mass demonstrations which extended from the mainstream official and Catholic-organized workforces to the Polish trade union (which had organized many of the Polish migrants living in Germany), and even the Communists. When the French military court acquitted the industrialists of all major charges they returned as heroes to a Ruhr District in uproar but without effective leadership. Fearing bloodshed, government ministers in Berlin now took a series of improvised measures designed to get a grip on the situation and then, with trade union and Social Democratic cooperation, they underwrote and instrumentalized the grass-roots passive resistance campaign to serve Germany's foreign policy objectives.

Passive resistance proved highly effective as labor, management and the authorities collaborated to thwart the French operation. The railways ground to a halt, canal installations were destroyed, the coal mines began to shut down and sometimes to flood, and the strategically vital coke ovens, after some weeks of hesitation, were allowed to go cold – so destroying their ceramic linings and rendering them useless. By the end of March 1923 the Micum had managed to seize an estimated 238,000 tons of stockpiled coal and coke compared with the 4.2 million tons of scheduled reparations deliveries. French business opinion was not impressed. The industrial journal *L'Usine* complained in late March that the country's metal industry had already been set back four months by the crisis, and in early April *L'Echo National* reported that just 77 of France's 219 blast furnaces remained operative.[50] When passive resistance was finally abandoned on September 26, France, Belgium and Luxembourg had only received some 25 to 30 percent of their scheduled reparations deliveries and the French public finances and currency were in increasing difficulty.

Politically and strategically, however, the French Premier had triumphed, for he retained the confidence of parliament and of his army throughout, whereas the German government was forced to abandon the passive resistance campaign unconditionally. Poincaré anticipated that, at last, Germany "would be overwhelmed by domestic crisis and ... become prey to the forces of disintegration."[51] Accordingly, Pierre de Margerie, now French ambassador to Berlin, was ordered to refrain from substantive discussions with a collapsing government and state, for any further diplomacy would only serve to lend it unwelcome credibility.[52]

Why, then, had German policy collapsed so abjectly? Three factors combined to undermine passive resistance: the financial and human price of the campaign, the draconian countermeasures of the French and Belgian occupiers, and the Cuno government's failure to articulate a foreign policy capable of exploiting the possibilities offered by passive resistance.

While some historians write of a general strike in the Ruhr, no such thing occurred. Indeed the government, employers and unions were agreed from the outset that people would turn up for work as far as possible and continue to receive a regular wage or salary. Only when Micum officials or their imported laborers tried directly to exploit factories or mines did the German employees refuse to collaborate in any way. Given the degree of disruption to the Ruhr's economy it was appreciated that many employees would often be unable to work productively, leading the state to underwrite the payment of "unproductive wages." This placed a huge and growing burden on the public exchequer which was worsened by massive compensation payments to companies which suffered loss or damage at the hands of the occupiers and to civil servants who were expelled from the Rhineland and Ruhr in their tens of thousands, along with their families.

As expenditure increased tax receipts fell, for the French choked off all revenues to Berlin from the occupied western territories and for good measure themselves tried to raise certain taxes in the region. A currency crisis of astronomical proportions followed as the national bank, the Reichsbank, furiously printed money to cover the spiraling cost of resistance. Until April 1923 the bank had covered its money issue by selling off Germany's remaining gold reserves and so kept the mark relatively stable, but thereafter domestic and international confidence in the currency collapsed completely. Soon enough, billions of marks were needed to buy a single US dollar and Germany's printing presses were no longer able to churn out sufficient volumes of new banknotes. Czechoslovakia did brisk business printing money for Berlin. To make matters worse, the French authorities confiscated banknote printing plates in the occupied territories and seized supplies of currency entering the region. With yesterday's currency already worthless, a desperate population besieged company pay offices or looted the few food outlets that remained open. Major industrial enterprises were reduced to printing their own company-backed banknotes, which dubious market traders could only hope would somehow be redeemed by an already bankrupt national exchequer. Many town councils resorted to the same expedient. By August Cuno's government had collapsed and the Liberal politician Gustav Stresemann agreed to form a national government dedicated to resolving the all-consuming hyperinflationary crisis. This, his new Cabinet understood, demanded a rapid end to passive resistance.

Quite apart from the currency and budgetary crisis, life in the Ruhr and much of the Rhineland had become intolerable for other reasons. Passive resistance reflected a profound conviction among the people of the Ruhr that they personally had done everything possible to deliver reparations at an appalling cost to themselves. As one group of miners' delegates declared to the French military: "The German working class had starved, frozen, and toiled to meet the obligations of France as far as possible. In particular they as miners knew that the German people had done its duty."[53]

Trade union leaders and ordinary workers repeatedly emphasized the substantial benefits the German revolution had delivered them and compared the political economy of the German Republic with the very different situation in France. There, wartime concessions to the labor movement had been largely rescinded and replaced in the heavy industrial and mining sectors by a climate of fear and repression. Statutory workplace consultation and the extensive welfare and social insurance provision to be found in Germany had no direct French counterpart.

The suppression of the labor movement in former German territory such as the Moselle or the Saarland had become common knowledge as German delegates met their counterparts (and former compatriots) from French-controlled German-speaking territory at international socialist or trade union conferences. In the minds of the Ruhr's labor force, therefore, the occupation of their region combined straightforward imperialist adventurism with a direct attack on the German revolution by a right-wing, militaristic French government. As one miners' leader wrote in the Social Democratic daily newspaper *Vorwärts*:

> We must finally be absolutely clear about this, that the realisation of Poincaré's plans would mean the economic and political collapse of the German working class's trade-union and political organisations. The struggle must be sustained until France realises that economic disagreements cannot be settled by the use of force, that agreement will only be possible when we sit around the table and negotiate.[54]

The workers, unionized blue-collar civil servants (such as railwaymen and forestry workers) and their families were, therefore, prepared to make almost any sacrifice to thwart this perceived agenda, after which they planned to return to the more mundane task of fighting their own corner within Weimar Germany. Thousands were arrested or injured and hundreds were to die in the process.

The French response became increasingly oppressive as they confronted a hostile population. No military occupation of a densely populated industrial region can be trouble free and random indiscipline by soldiers, including theft, violence, rape and the occasional murder, scarred everyday experience in the Ruhr. The billeting of the army of occupation in private homes and school buildings and of its thousands of horses on outlying underresourced farmsteads added to the misery. The situation was exacerbated by the occasional German terrorist outrage, which prompted draconian curfews, the collective punishment of entire communities, the taking of civilian hostages, and some loss of life, but especially by the intensification of a food blockade which had very different origins.

This blockade began as a proxy struggle as the French military strove to assert de facto sovereignty over the Ruhr and encountered resistance from Prussian officials. The French Chief of Civil Administration, General Denvignes, reacted by introducing a range of formalities to be met by food importers, while demanding the right to exercise existing controls such as the presentation of ships' manifests (on the River Rhine) or environmental health checks, which under the terms of Versailles were the proper province of the German or Prussian authorities. With neither Prussian officials nor private importers willing to comply with this trespass on German sovereignty, the Belgian and French military simply sealed the demarcation line between the Ruhr and unoccupied Germany and waited for their opponents to back down. Declaring that he gave the orders now, and that French military decrees "define[d] the current legislative framework"[55] Denvignes forced the Prussian authorities to give way. However, the French military resolved thereafter to use the food blockade as a weapon against any sporadic outbreaks of violent resistance, but more generally against the defiant if nonviolent local population.

As food supplies ran short and famine-related illnesses scourged the children of the Ruhr, local medical officers and education authorities feared that many would literally die. During the war urban children had been evacuated to farms in the countryside to spare them the worst effects of the famine, and postwar food short-ages meant that the program had never been entirely abandoned. During early 1923, therefore, official and voluntary agencies were able quickly to initiate a full-scale evacuation of children from the Ruhr. Distraught parents volunteered 300,000 ragged and starving children for transfer to farmsteads in unoccupied Germany far beyond their families' reach, yet remained determined to bear whatever costs resistance demanded.

By August, however, the whole of Germany was paying a disproportionate price for a campaign whose outcome was increasingly doubtful and which was, in any case, economically unsustainable. Whatever their personal feelings, busi-nessmen were forced to collaborate with the invaders simply to survive. And as the Convener of the Free Trade Unions, Theodor Leipart, warned in August, the prolongation of passive resistance was now serving Poincaré's objective; the sep-aration of the Ruhr from Germany. Social Democratic Prussian ministers warned the national government that time was their enemy and that speedy action was essential to save the country from disintegration. The people had done their utmost, but the time had come for effective diplomacy from the center.

In fact the Cuno government had long since been fatally compromised by the deeper ambivalence in German foreign policy objectives. On March 27, 1923 the Social Democratic parliamentarian Hermann Müller stressed that "the resist-ance is only possible because the workers, particularly the Socialist workers have risen up to a man,"[56] but went on to demand that the government open negotiations from a position of strength. Theodor Leipart agreed, warning Chancellor Cuno's Secretary of State[57] on behalf of the trade unions "that now is the time to negotiate … before our strength wanes visibly, rather than after this decline is apparent to our enemy."[58] The German ambassador to London, Friedrich Sthamer, was equally con-cerned by Berlin's diplomatic passivity, advising that Britain, too, was awaiting a German initiative "that the British could find their way to support, or to recommend to an international conference."[59] On April 20 this British pressure became irresisti-ble after Lord Curzon demanded that Berlin put a figure on reparations.

However, while the German Cabinet agreed that respond it must, it was fatally split between those bent on soothing Social Democratic and British opinion while simultaneously attempting to ridicule the French, such as Foreign Minister von Rosenberg, and those seeking a genuine settlement, such as Labor Minister Brauns who demanded that: "Our note must include everything we perceive as tolerable and in such a form that the will to negotiate is unmistakable."[60] Unfortunately for Brauns's faction, and for Germany, von Rosenberg eventually persuaded the Cabinet to make a hopelessly inadequate offer on May 2 of 30 billion gold marks (as against the 1921 figure of 132 billion). Even this sum was not backed by any realistic guarantees, not least because German industry refused to underwrite it in any form. Paris and Brussels immediately rejected the German Note; London and Rome made clear their profound disappointment, but at least suggested Berlin reconsider its position. A more constructive German offer followed on June 7, which Britain and Italy accepted as the basis for further negotiation. However Poincaré remained "determined to force the Germans to capitulate uncondition-ally,"[61] demanding the complete abandonment of passive resistance and the resumption of reparations deliveries in full before any talks could begin. As the German Chargé d'Affaires in Paris, Leopold von Hoesch, concluded bleakly:

> We would henceforth not merely tolerate, but actively assist France in the exploita-tion of the occupied territories with a customs frontier, import and export con-trols, collection of coal production tax, and coal and coke distribution. To its great satisfaction this would achieve everything that our passive resistance has so suc-cessfully prevented. I would not give any credit to French guarantees of a step-by-step evacuation.[62]

In other words, tardy and half-hearted German concessions had combined with French intransigence to leave any efforts at a compromise settlement doomed to failure.

In any case, the chaos that followed across the occupied territories convinced the French military commandant, General Jean-Marie Degoutte, and his Prime Minister that outright victory was within their grasp. A further deterioration in Franco-British relations did little to help. In June 1923 Britain began to repay its war debt to the United States at the rate of £33 million per annum, but the repayment of France's debt to Britain, which was scheduled to begin in August, failed to mate-rialize and so aligned the British Treasury alongside the Francophobe Foreign Office. Curzon, who had already condemned French behavior in the Ruhr as "absolutely barbarous,"[63] responded on August 11 by questioning the very legality of the Ruhr occupation and warning that: "Things might finally go so far as to force Great Britain to separate action in the interest of an early settlement of repa-ration."[64] British public opinion had come to sympathize with Germany, but the government remained deeply divided on the matter, with the War Minister, Lord Derby, adamant that Britain stand by its wartime ally, and most Conservative back-benchers staunchly Francophile. On August 20 Poincaré called London's bluff by way of a diplomatic Note to Curzon 79 pages long which refuted the Foreign Secretary's speech of August 11 in painstaking detail and reiterated the French Premier's earlier demands at great length.

By this stage Cuno's government had collapsed, leading President Ebert to invite the leader of the right-liberal German People's Party (DVP), Gustav Stresemann, to form a new administration. By August 14 a coalition extending from the DVP to include the three Weimar parties[65] had been formed and, whatever divided them with regard to domestic policy, all were agreed that hyperinflation had to be cured and passive resistance brought to an end. Equally, they understood that the democratic order itself was in mortal danger as the far right accused Stresemann's administration of being infested with Jews and Socialists determined to repeat the "treason" of 1918, while military leaders began to consider the merits of a coup d'état as a way out of the mounting chaos. The Social Democratic parliamentarian Otto Wels spoke for many when warning wavering colleagues that the coalition represented "the last possible constitutional government."[66]

It remained to be seen whether Stresemann could reach agreement with Poincaré and so bring the confrontation in the Ruhr to a close. His preference was for a multilateral international solution to the overall reparations question, but equally he understood that any immediate resolution of the Ruhr crisis itself demanded contact with Paris and wide-ranging concessions on his own part. These included notions of long-term French participation in German heavy industry, so rebuilding the pre-1914 relationship on terms decidedly favorable to France. There was significant support for a negotiated settlement on these lines in France itself. The French Radicals, who formed part of Poincaré's coalition, were concerned at the country's increasing international isolation and their consciences troubled by the brutality of the Ruhr occupation. Even some staunch supporters of the Ruhr adventure, including President Millerand, believed the moment ripe for a favorable Franco-German agreement. The alternatives were fraught with danger. As the veteran diplomat Paul Cambon observed: "All of public opinion is convinced that sooner or later the current conflict between France and Germany will have to end; it is vital that France is not held responsible should these hopes not be realized,"[67] while the Socialists (who maintained close contacts with their German counterparts) warned more starkly that Poincaré was simply destroying German democracy and thereby strengthening those same reactionary forces he affected to detest.[68]

However, Poincaré remained fixated on the imminent breakup of Germany and was unwilling to negotiate with Berlin on any terms. On September 19 he met the British Premier, Stanley Baldwin, in Paris and although these talks produced little new, the French communiqué claimed that Britain had agreed to tow the French line. Von Hoesch reassured Berlin otherwise, but whatever the case the meeting had clearly failed to engage with Stresemann's efforts to open immediate negotiations. The German Cabinet now agreed to abandon the passive resistance campaign, which ended unconditionally on September 26. As von Hoesch reported from Paris: "France knows it has won the game, and that this is not the moment to moderate a naked *force majeure*."[69]

During the autumn of 1923 the situation in occupied western Germany plumbed new depths as unemployment engulfed its industrial centers, while the French authorities tightened their grip on the regional administration and economy, and even lent support to short-lived separatist risings. All of this brought Berlin in October to the brink of ceding the occupied territories. Elsewhere in Germany the legitimate government's authority was threatened by Bavarian separatism, which mutated in November into Hitler's Beer Hall Putsch, Communist insurgency, and most seriously by ongoing plans for a military coup d'état. The survival of Stresemann's coalition government (which resigned then immediately reformed in late September) during these critical months was in itself remarkable, its ability to negotiate the minefields of international diplomacy and also to stabilize the currency in October even more so.

The heavy industrialists of the Ruhr found themselves at the epicenter of this crisis, for the Micum and French military insisted that with passive resistance over, reparations deliveries of coal and industrial goods recommence almost immediately. In addition the coal mining companies were presented by France with a bill for coal production tax backdated to January 1923. With many mines left inoperable after months of passive resistance, coke ovens requiring complicated and expensive reinstatement and the metallurgical industry equally disrupted, the Ruhr barons looked to Berlin for help. The response was not encouraging, for as part of the currency reform Stresemann's government had agreed massive cuts in public spending to balance the budget and squeeze out inflation. The Ruhr was given notice that the special payments that had underwritten the passive resistance campaign would shortly cease, so depriving the region's economy of the life support that had kept businesses operating and the population fed at all. The businessmen feared for more than their balance sheets as the smell of social revolution hung in the air. The abandonment of passive resistance had triggered angry demonstrations and even riots across the region, leading Edward Thornton, British Consul General in Cologne, to warn: "The measure of impending disaster is so stupendous that it would be idle for me to mince my words or attempt to gloss over facts."[70] As unemployment climbed beyond 80 percent and starving townspeople literally fought gun battles with farmers in a despairing attempt to loot what food they could from the countryside, the Social Democratic Lord Mayor of Bochum reflected that although he had seen "everything conceivable" during the passive resistance campaign, he had "never seen such hordes of people, starving and roaming around, in my entire life."[71] The French military fired on the looters and demonstrators and assured panicky local officials and businessmen that order would be maintained, but insisted that in return Allied ordinances be followed to the letter. The Ruhr's industrialists were left in no doubt that their mines and factories would simply be confiscated and operated directly by the Micum if they failed to deliver reparations or refused to comply with other Allied demands.

Stresemann was forced to leave the industrialists to seek the best deal available from the Micum and also reimpose labor discipline, without being able to offer any further support beyond certain tax exemptions. The reparations bill would have to be footed by the industrialists themselves, with compensation to follow from Berlin if and when a degree of normality was finally restored. Even before the Ruhr crisis some leading industrialists had been heard to complain that the Weimar settlement had imposed excessive burdens on German business, particularly in the form of the eight-hour day. Social Democratic members of Stresemann's Cabinet conceded that the original settlement was something of a luxury in the dire circumstances of autumn 1923, and even the trade unions were prepared to give ground. On October 2, however, declining faith in the capacity of the Weimar Republic to function at all prompted the Ruhr's mining chiefs to announce a unilateral increase in the length of the working day and the abandonment of collective wage bargaining. Political uproar followed as republicans condemned this direct attack on the revolutionary settlement, and even middle management in the mining industry itself questioned the wisdom of their bosses' *démarche*. The employers were forced to back down and a compromise deal was eventually hammered out in parliament, but the partnership forged between Carl Legien (unions) and Hugo Stinnes (employers) in November 1918 to underwrite the postwar socioeconomic order was dead in spirit, even if the legal niceties continued to be upheld for a little longer. State arbitration rather than free collective bargaining came increasingly to define the landscape of industrial relations, with the resulting compromise settlements often leaving neither side satisfied and the employers prone to blame the Republic itself for deals they could sometimes barely afford. Weimar had been gravely weakened by the events of 1923 and would be ill-placed to cope with the challenges of the Great Depression less than a decade later.

As autumn slipped toward winter the bilateral Franco-German confrontation was increasingly complemented by wider international mediation, driven by Britain and the United States. France's involvement in the Rhenish separatist cause accelerated this process. The separatists never enjoyed much popular backing, but between October 21 and 24 French and Belgian military and logistical support emboldened them to launch a series of risings, against which the Prussian authorities could only deploy the remnants of their uniformed police force in the occupied territories. Even these policemen were giving the separatists a run for their money, but it was British intervention that proved fatal to the insurrection.

Britain occupied a small, but strategically vital part of the Rhineland consisting of Cologne and its hinterland east and west of the River Rhine and so had a voice on the Allied Rhineland Commission. German sovereignty was respected in Cologne and Britain planned to evacuate its zone in 1925 in accordance with the Versailles Treaty. All of this greatly complicated French efforts unilaterally to circumvent the peace settlement in western Germany and while the Belgians had participated in the Ruhr adventure, Brussels was now inclined to extricate itself from the affair and so looked toward London. On October 23 British Foreign Office seniors decided to back Berlin against any French attempt to detach the Rhineland from Germany. Two days later the British Prime Minister publicly condemned France's role in the Rhineland risings and a string of warnings from London subsequently landed on French and Belgian ministerial desks. The Belgian authorities were quick to disown separatist insurgents in and around Aachen on November 2 and to restore order across the entire Belgian zone. Poincaré dissembled, passing off the entire affair as a misunderstanding, but his military was slower to abandon the insurgency, and to Britain's fury even backed an abortive rising in the Bavarian Palatinate on December 27.

London simultaneously engaged French policy on several other fronts. Paris hoped to advance its Rhenish agenda by launching a separate currency for the occupied territories, but lacked the financial muscle to underwrite the issue unilaterally. British support was indispensable, but the Governor of the Bank of England, Montagu Norman, declared that he had no wish to entangle Britain "in the policy which is now being pursued by France in the Rhineland, and towards the economic separation of the Rhineland"[72] and refused to provide the necessary capital. Instead, the Bank of England backed the Reichsbank as it replaced the discredited mark with a new provisional currency, the Rentenmark. The Rentenmark was able to hold its value and so undermined the attraction of any separate currency in the occupied west. Similarly, when France proposed that the Franco-Belgian Régie (railway) should permanently replace the Reichsbahn (German Railways) in all the occupied territories, London continued to recognize the Reichsbahn in Cologne and insisted that the Régie could only remain temporarily in existence elsewhere pending a final settlement of the Ruhr crisis.

Against this series of setbacks, France was able to notch up two significant successes in the form of the Micum Framework Agreements of November 23 and the establishment of economic councils in the occupied territories, which appeared to institutionalize French and Belgian involvement in the public affairs of the region. The Micum Framework Agreements bound the Ruhr industrialists to deliver reparations from the region on a scale and to a timetable that was subject to periodic reassessment by the Micum rather than the Reparations Commission. The agreement also empowered France to levy certain taxes and issue import and export licenses in the Ruhr District. The economic councils on the Rhine and Ruhr were welcomed by local business as an indispensable means of stabilizing the region, but of course they simultaneously duplicated much of the Prussian and German administration. An uneasy standoff followed between the indigenous local authorities and the Allies. As late as April 1924 the president of the Micum, Paul Frantzen, still felt able to dictate terms to Ruhr industrialists, to the consternation of Gustav Stresemann, who had resigned as Chancellor in November 1923 but continued to serve as Germany's Foreign Minister.

However, Britain and the United States looked beyond the specifics of the Ruhr crisis toward a review of the wider reparations question. The United States President, Calvin Coolidge, had close links to American business, which was

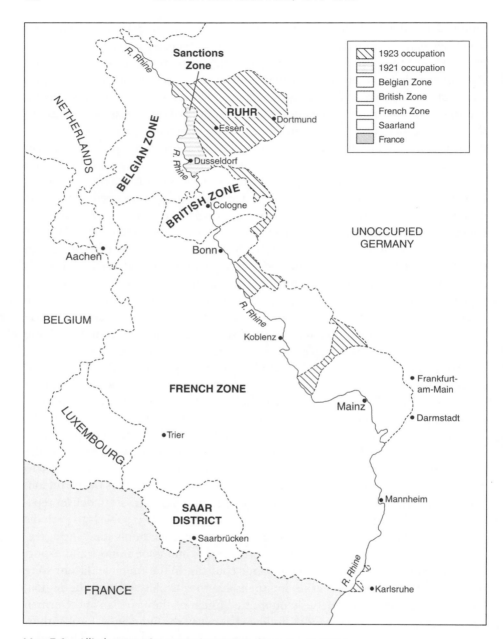

Map 5.1   Allied occupation zones in western Germany ca. 1924.

alarmed by the chaotic state of Germany and the wider dislocation of the
European economy. On October 9 Coolidge announced that the United States
still stood by the New Haven Declaration of December 1922, which had proposed
the reexamination of the reparations question by an international committee of
experts. After weeks of hard bargaining Paris accepted the proposal on condition

that the committee fall within the remit of the Reparations Commission, be purely consultative in nature, and include no German delegates. Britain was prepared to accept the deal if United States participation was secured and on December 26 the Dawes and McKenna committees were established. The former was to examine Germany's budgetary and currency problems, the latter to establish ways of repatriating exported German capital, all with a view to reestablishing orderly reparations payments.

Stresemann greeted the work of the Dawes Committee as "a gleam of light on the otherwise dark horizon,"[73] but none of this need have undermined France's Ruhr and Rhineland policy. However on December 6 Baldwin had lost a general election and the Conservatives left office, to be replaced by a Labour–Liberal coalition led by Britain's first Labour Prime Minister, James Ramsay MacDonald. The new government was more united in its determination to resolve the crisis in western Germany and if French security concerns were still regarded as legitimate, London, the French ambassador warned, was not prepared to sacrifice British interests to that end. On March 13, 1924 Poincaré reassured the French parliament that regardless of the Experts' Reports, France would not evacuate the Ruhr until reparations were paid in full, only to trigger a stiff response from the British Foreign Office. As Sterndale Bennett fumed: "He has pushed the same aims consistently for six years and has really gone a long way towards their attainment. He is also a master of the art of finding another road to the same destination if he finds the direct road blocked."[74] However, by this time France's own budgetary misery was such that a loan of $100 million was drawn from the US bank of J. P. Morgan, whose nearness to the State Department served to compromise French diplomatic independence. Meanwhile Wilhelm Marx's government had steered Germany's finances off the rocks, chalking up a budget surplus in March and securing a £5 million loan from Britain to tie the new German currency to gold. Suddenly French soldiers and officials in occupied Germany were heard to complain that their devaluing francs bought less and less from week to week in a remarkable reversal of fortunes.

The Experts' Reports were published on April 4. McKenna concluded that the export of capital had been triggered by the progressive collapse of the mark and that with currency stabilization much of the money would return to Germany. Poincaré's claim that capital export had been designed to undermine the reparations regime was regarded as a secondary factor. Dawes found that Germany was inherently capable of paying reparations and proposed negotiating a five-year deal pending a final settlement. However, his report continued that payments would only be possible "when Germany's economic sovereignty is restored. Its operation will be proportionately postponed if there is a delay in effecting that restoration."[75] In other words, France would need to return the Ruhr to German control and accept that the Rhineland was an integral part of Germany under temporary Allied military occupation. Whatever his views on Dawes' assessment of the German economy (and he had doubts) Stresemann agreed with his Cabinet colleagues that the political implications of the Dawes report were exceptionally positive. On April 16 the German Foreign Office assured the Reparations Commission that Berlin would accept both reports unreservedly.

As if to confirm all of this, Poincaré equivocated. German poverty, he repeated, was self-inflicted; France would stay in the Ruhr until reparations had been paid in full, and also reserve the right to amend the Experts' Reports through the Reparations Commission. However on May 11 the French electorate voted Poincaré out of office, to be replaced on June 13 by a center-left coalition led by the Radical politician Édouard Herriot. Regarded by contemporaries and historians as inherently more accommodating than Poincaré, Herriot was nonetheless anxious to retain something of his predecessor's strategy. He was prepared to enact the Dawes Report, but sought to retain France's right to impose unilateral sanctions on Germany and certainly wished to maintain a military and economic presence in the Ruhr, which extended to control of its railways.

The new reparations conference opened in London on July 16. The United States President and Secretary of State stayed away, but the United States ambassador to London, Frank Kellogg, and of course the American financial community played an intimate role in the proceedings. Seydoux and the Permanent Secretary at the Quai d'Orsay, Philippe Berthelot, accompanied Herriot to London and, if the French Premier achieved a certain notoriety for his failure to prepare thoroughly for negotiating sessions and also his penchant for tearful outbursts – "some sessions were more opera than conference"[76] – Berthelot and Seydoux were from a different mold. France's own financial problems during early 1924 had convinced Seydoux in particular that an acceptable reparations agreement had to take precedence over any Rhenish ambitions and that a United States role in European affairs was to be welcomed. British and American pressure on Herriot did the rest. By the time the Germans joined the talks on August 6 it was clear that the eventual settlement would attempt to accommodate both Allied and German interests, although inter-Allied and thus French war debts remained stubbornly off the agenda. The presence of Germany as an equal negotiating partner was a bitter pill for the French delegation, Herriot looking "as though he were having a tooth drawn."[77] However on August 11 the French Premier conceded a full evacuation of the Ruhr within a year and an immediate withdrawal from Dortmund and various points along the Rhine. German negotiators prevaricated briefly over the year's delay, but Kellogg and Ramsay MacDonald warned Stresemann that Herriot's offer was personal and secret and that failure to seize the moment risked the collapse of the entire conference. On August 16 Marx and Stresemann accepted the terms and secured ratification by the Reichstag on August 29. Even the conservative and monarchist German National People's Party (DNVP), which consistently refused to accept the Versailles settlement or the verdict of the German Revolution, split down the middle between realists and die-hards, so delivering the necessary two-thirds majority to convert the national railways into a security against future reparations payments. The London Agreement was formally concluded on the following day, allowing for the resumption of reparations payments backed by an American loan to Germany of 800 million gold marks (!), but also for the gradual normalization of life in western Germany. On August 25, 1925 the last French troops duly marched out of Düsseldorf and across the Rhine silently, without ceremony. "There are recollections," the former French Premier Georges Clemenceau reflected grimly "it is better to leave unevoked."[78]

5.2   From Locarno to the Young Plan

If the Dawes Agreement had defused the immediate Franco-German crisis it did nothing to address France's deep-seated security fears or to secure the long-term diplomatic rehabilitation of Germany. In November 1924 Ramsay MacDonald's coalition collapsed and fresh British elections brought Baldwin and the Conservatives back to power. Paris now proposed a multilateral security scheme operated by the League of Nations in place of any bilateral Franco-British security pact, and also the use of collective sanctions through the League should Germany breach the disarmament provisions of the peace settlement. The British Foreign Secretary, Austen Chamberlain, was potentially sympathetic to France's predicament, but less keen on the notion of collective sanctions, preferring instead to depoliticize both the reparations and disarmament questions by handing them over to committees of experts. Winston Churchill was blunter in his rejection of the alliance option, declaring that France should be left "to stew in her own juice."[79] Stresemann, however, still feared that a possible bilateral Franco-British security agreement could block any speedy diplomatic rehabilitation of Germany. His concerns were nourished when the Allies delayed their scheduled evacuation of the northern Rhineland after Germany breached its disarmament obligations. Berlin now seized the initiative, proposing during January and February 1925 that the European powers, Germany included, negotiate a Rhineland security pact designed to resolve outstanding national concerns in Western Europe.

Both Britain and France reacted positively, the former in an effort to reconcile its obligations to Paris with its desire for a stable continent, which demanded in turn the rehabilitation of Germany. In other words London was anxious to act as honest broker in any future settlement of Franco-German differences. For Paris the change in strategy toward Germany was altogether more dramatic and complex. Aristide Briand, who had now begun his tenure as France's outstanding interwar Foreign Minister, appreciated that collective security could no longer be directed against Germany. Instead any agreement needed to engage Berlin and preferably on terms favorable to Paris before the passage of time eroded France's position further. The country's army chiefs understood that a low French birth rate coupled with a widespread dislike of military service demanded a more defensive military posture. In 1929 this was to culminate in the commissioning of the Maginot Line, a network of fortifications behind the Franco-German frontier designed to shelter France's diminishing army from any future German attack. France's postwar alliances in Eastern Europe promised little and the territory its army occupied in the west of Germany was scheduled for step-by-step evacuation over the coming decade. The domestic financial and currency crisis also continued to compromise France's diplomatic potential, while business leaders understood that the restoration of German customs sovereignty in 1925 would end the artificial advantage France had enjoyed in trade between the two countries. Franco-German business cartels offered a way to regulate future relations on terms acceptable to French commerce, and even provided a route toward a European economic union, with Germany and France at its core, to resist the imagined nightmare of global competition, American or Soviet. Thus strategic and economic factors had combined to demand a political deal between Paris and Berlin.

Events in Germany briefly threatened progress. Stresemann's foreign policy attracted fierce criticism from the monarchist DNVP which had made notable gains in the 1924 Reichstag elections as disenchantment with Weimar and its foreign policy grew. The country's Social Democratic President, Friedrich Ebert, met an untimely death in early 1925 after contracting appendicitis. The resulting presidential election became a struggle between Germany's republicans, who supported the Center Party's Wilhelm Marx, and monarchists who rallied behind the former war hero and retired military commander, Field Marshal Paul von Hindenburg. When Hindenburg won, Stresemann's foreign policy was threatened on two fronts. He struggled constantly to rally sufficient domestic support for a cautious, negotiated revision of Versailles, and simultaneously battled to reassure international opinion that Germany remained a trustworthy partner. Each concession to the German right alarmed the Allies, every concession to the Allies enraged the right (and also the Communists on the radical left!) still further.

All of this became apparent when Briand responded positively on June 16 to Stresemann's original proposals, but added a few suggestions of his own. He insisted that as part of the accord Germany should join the League of Nations and so be bound by its statutes, and insisted that the security pact should extend beyond the Rhineland to provide for the arbitration of all European frontier disputes. This might have reassured Briand's East European allies that their borders with Germany were secure, but Berlin hankered after a revision of the German-Polish frontier. Stresemann and the Foreign Office were sufficiently realistic to view this as a long-term aspiration, but the monarchists saw revision and even the complete destruction of Poland as an immediate imperative. The DNVP attacked Stresemann for selling Germany short and President Hindenburg distanced himself from the Foreign Minister. Chancellor Hans Luther, who had previously masterminded the currency stabilization under Stresemann's chancellorship in 1923, also evaded responsibility for the security pact initiative. Only when an exasperated Stresemann threatened to resign did the Cabinet support a qualified acceptance of Briand's terms.

The Locarno Conference subsequently opened on October 2. The ambiguity of Stresemann's position informed France's understanding of Locarno and its aftermath. Seydoux spoke for most when claiming that while Briand and France sought peace as an end – the means to which would vary – Stresemann and Germany were using peace as a means to a different end – German continental supremacy. Berlin, Seydoux warned, would revert to other (military) means if peaceful methods disappointed, concluding that: "An abyss separates the two conceptions."[80] Seydoux remained equally convinced that German industry still fostered hegemonial ambitions: "It has not changed its views and continues to organise so as to become mistress of Europe."[81] French industry however was less skeptical as the pre-1914 West European business networks were reconstructed after Locarno and it became possible in the company boardrooms to regard the Great War as a ruinously destructive interruption to normality, whose effects were finally being overcome.

Stresemann's foreign policy nonetheless remained ambivalent and historians have disagreed over his ultimate aims as much as did his contemporaries. For Fritz Fischer and his followers there existed an underlying continuity of foreign policy objectives from the Wilhelmine Empire, through Weimar and so into the Third Reich.[82] Others are less sure. Thus Jonathan Wright asks in his essentially sympathetic biography of the Weimar statesman: "Had Stresemann developed from the feverish advocate for victory and annexation during the First World War to a position where he saw German and European interests as contingent?"[83] Stresemann's pre-1914 career could be seen as impeccably liberal as he gave Saxony's industrialists an effective political voice while lending personal support to further electoral reform and to an accommodation between employers and organized labour. His wife, Käte, was of Jewish origin, even if her father had converted to Protestantism, and this created an unbridgeable chasm between Stresemann and the radical right. As Wright concludes, "There is a persuasive argument that in his first political career in Saxony, Stresemann showed many of the qualities which later made him a pragmatic Republican."[84] Similarly, Stresemann's (Alsatian) French biographer, Christian Baechler, portrays his career as a genuine journey "from imperialism to collective security."[85]

However, if liberal principles could make of Stresemann a "pragmatic Republican," he was equally a principled nationalist, determined before 1914 that Germany should acquire further colonies; if needs be in conflict with Britain. During the war he became a fierce supporter of the Imperial government's annexationist agenda even as he still advocated domestic constitutional reform and a role for the SPD in postwar government. This balancing act between reaction and reform left him "stranded in a political no-man's land"[86] and so excluded from government as the German Empire gave way to the new, republican order. His annexationist record compromised efforts to forge a single liberal party in Weimar Germany, with the anti-annexationists tending toward the DDP and annexationists toward the DVP, which elected Stresemann as party leader. He was to seek vainly to create a mass, Protestant liberal party composed of his own followers and converts from the DDP and also the DNVP, but his personal commitment to the

Republic was sealed by the murder of Rathenau in 1922. Other influential DVP members, such as the Ruhr industrialist Hugo Stinnes, agreed. "The Rathenau murderers have," Stinnes declared, "in my view shot the monarchy. Stresemann shares this opinion."[87] In fact Stresemann went further, persuading the DVP's National Committee to declare that German recovery was only possible on the basis of the republican constitution.

For all this, Stresemann continued to court the monarchist right. On October 23, 1923 his own Cabinet had sanctioned the return of the Crown Prince to Germany from exile in the Netherlands and thereafter Stresemann kept the Prince informed on German foreign policy. On September 7, 1925, weeks before the Locarno Conference opened, he reassured the would-be heir to the German throne that his foreign policy masked essentially expansionist goals behind a facade of moderation. It was also an open secret that Stresemann was turning a blind eye to clandestine German military cooperation with the Soviet Union, which included the production of advanced weapons and the conduct of training programs, both illegal under the terms of Versailles. Moscow enjoyed in return technology transfers from Germany which were ultimately to serve the Red Army well during Hitler's invasion of the Soviet Union. Wright, however, concludes that the appeasement of the Crown Prince served the wider purpose of reconciling the DNVP and President Hindenburg to a foreign policy which sought ultimately to embed Germany within the post-Versailles international order on terms more acceptable than those set down in 1919. This, Stresemann believed, would in turn impact favorably on the domestic political scene and serve to "help to ensure consensus at home and stabilize the Republic."[88]

However, the deal struck at Locarno enraged the right. Stresemann had signed away any claim to Alsace and the Moselle and committed Germany to membership of the League of Nations, which implied a fundamental acceptance of the post-1919 international order. The DNVP had been lured into government by Stresemann and Luther after the December 1924 Reichstag elections, but now it stormed out and launched a ferocious opposition which was echoed by newspapers belonging to the conservative press magnate Alfred Hugenberg. Yet again, Stresemann was branded a traitor who was allowing France to play the great power at Germany's direct expense. Accepting Dawes, the conservatives raged, had conceded the principle of reparations payments; now Locarno conceded on the equally vital questions of territory and military potential.

The German monarchists lacked the necessary parliamentary strength to derail Stresemann's policy, but senior Foreign Office officials were uncomfortably aware that the German nationalist press was also read in France. The French National Assembly doubted German good faith and eventually approved the Locarno settlement with great reserve and skepticism. French parliamentarians appreciated that Germany was hardly in a position to recover Alsace or the Moselle and so had lost nothing substantive, but in guaranteeing the 1919 Franco-German frontier Locarno protected Germany from France as much as France from Germany. This effectively undermined France's remaining influence in the Rhineland, a process reinforced in December 1925 when the Allied armies evacuated the northern Rhineland and the Rhineland Commission's powers in the remaining occupied territories were scaled down. Equally crucial were the guarantee mechanisms for the Locarno accord, which saw Britain and Italy underwrite the territorial status quo. For sure this reassured Belgium and France, but also meant that any future unilateral French action against Germany threatened British and Italian intervention on Berlin's side. This situation was to contribute to French inaction in the face of Hitler's opening foreign policy gambits a decade later.

As Briand had wished, Locarno also discussed east European frontiers, but Stresemann succeeded in securing separate and nonbinding arbitration accords for Germany's eastern borders without British or Italian guarantees attached. Furthermore, Berlin was able to maintain its special relationship with the Soviet Union by obtaining an opt-out from Article 16 of the League of Nations Covenant (the sanctions clause), which Moscow feared could be used against it. In April 1926 Germany and the Soviet Union signed the Treaty of Berlin which effectively reaffirmed the 1922 German-Soviet Rapallo agreement. Germany reassured Moscow that it would boycott any unprovoked League attack or League sanctions against the Soviet Union.

However, an attack on the Soviet Union by League members was as unlikely as any German invasion of Alsace or Lorraine. Immediate changes to the Polish frontier were also unlikely. In 1926 the leader of the Polish Socialist Party, Józef Piłsudski, overthrew the democratically elected government in Warsaw and established a nationalist dictatorship with army backing. Since Piłsudski was resolutely opposed to any frontier concessions and since some 35 percent of the Polish budget was devoted to military spending against a background of relative economic and social stability, the prospects for German revisionism were not good. The lightly armed German forces, after all, numbered 100,000 and could not threaten any of Berlin's neighbors. In any case, most of the Germans living in territories surrendered to Poland had either left or been driven out, so weakening any German ethnographical case for border revision. Berlin was reduced to seeking a seat on the League of Nations Minorities Committee to provide whatever protection it could for the Germans still remaining in Poland. All in all, as Stresemann's Permanent Secretary, Carl von Schubert, put it, German reassurances to Moscow served to achieve equilibrium and stability rather than to initiate any radical revision of the 1919 settlement. Possible frontier changes were consigned to an indefinite future, after the whole of the Rhineland had been evacuated by the Allies and the Saarland (it was hoped) restored to Germany by plebiscite in 1935 if not sooner.

In fact, Stresemann's achievement was altogether more subtle, restoring Germany's bona fides as a member of the international community and parity for Berlin in international diplomacy. He stressed the need for "a peaceful Germany at the centre of a peaceful Europe"[89] and alluded to the economic dimension of Locarno, which secured further United States loans for Paris and Berlin, but also opened the way toward the creation of a new Europe where "it might ... be possible to solve political problems by economic means."[90] Not for the first time, intimations of post-1949 Franco-German economic cooperation within the cadre of an emergent European Union had come to the surface. In 1926 the International Steel Cartel linked the metallurgical industries of Germany and France, and in August 1927 a Franco-German trade treaty opened Germany to French agricultural products and wine, and France to German industrial products. Jean Monnet, the father of the post-1945 European Union, was among French officials who formulated the deal.

On September 10, 1926 Germany was admitted to the League of Nations, initiating a brief Franco-German rapprochement which rested on a highly personal diplomacy between Briand and Stresemann. The two foreign ministers met in the French town of Thoiry just a week after Germany joined the League. Briand was exceptionally forthcoming, proposing an early evacuation of the Rhineland, the speedy return of the Saarland to Germany, and even suggesting that Germany should be allowed to buy back Eupen-Malmédy from Belgium. In return Germany was to float a bond issue of 1 billion gold marks in order to accelerate reparations transfers to France. This would provide Paris with the necessary collateral to stabilize the franc, which was rapidly devaluing on the international currency exchanges.

The two statesmen were pleased with their work, but the agreement foundered on a series of mishaps and obstacles. A delighted Stresemann boasted in public about the scale of his achievement, which triggered an angry reception abroad and especially in France. Poincaré had resumed office as Prime Minister and although he sanctioned Briand's diplomatic initiatives, that did not prevent him or other French leaders from questioning their results. An anxious Poincaré asked of Philippe Berthelot, Permanent Secretary at the Quai d'Orsay, whether German efforts at rapprochement were sincere. The Germans, replied Berthelot enigmatically, were "probably sincere, and also insincere like all other nations whose vital interests were at stake."[91] Meanwhile the French army continued to fret over the laggardly pace of German disarmament and the clandestine military links between Berlin and Moscow. The negative attitude of the global creditor nations was also vital. Britain still opposed the emergence of a Franco-German economic bloc and so hesitated to support the proposed German bond issue. The United States also refused to participate until France honored its war debts obligations to Washington, which Poincaré would not. Finally, as the practicality of the bond issue became increasingly doubtful, the French authorities succeeded in stabilizing the franc by other means. A heavily discounted currency exchange value was set which promised to open up international markets to French products, while making imports of foreign goods into France much more expensive. A healthy trade surplus beckoned and with it an inflow of foreign currency and gold into the Bank of France's depleted coffers. Suddenly the franc was a good bet for investors and the embattled Thoiry agreement was surplus to requirements.

Nonetheless, the process of rapprochement spluttered on and in January 1927 the Inter-Allied Military Control Commission wound up its activities in Germany. Thereafter, convoluted international disarmament and security talks culminated in the Kellogg-Briand Pact of August 1928 which declared war illegal. Britain and the United States had been pressing France to scale down its armed forces and so remove any justification for German rearmament, but Briand insisted in return on further collective security guarantees to reinforce Locarno and the international status quo. As these talks threatened to produce significantly more disagreement than agreement, Briand proposed that France and the United States should agree a bilateral pact to outlaw war. This would have committed neutral America to upholding France's position in the world, implicitly at least, but Washington evaded the snare by proposing and obtaining an antiwar agreement open to all. When the Kellogg-Briand Pact (Pact of Paris) was concluded on August 27 Germany was among the signatories.

However, the accord was essentially cosmetic and despite the conclusion of further agreements the international climate worsened during 1929. If Dawes and Locarno had been framed against a backdrop of economic stabilization and recovery, diplomacy now confronted an ominous deterioration in the global economic climate which asked uncomfortable questions of the war debts and reparations regimes. Germany's public indebtedness had become a matter of international concern during 1927 as the national government introduced ambitious but expensive welfare and unemployment insurance initiatives and the regional governments spent heavily on schools, housing and healthcare. American private investors continued to lend to the country, but only on a short-term basis and in return for very high interest payments; as Patricia Clavin observes, "the Weimar Republic was running out of cash and out of time."[92] The crisis was not confined to Germany, for there were unmistakable intimations of economic decline within Europe and globally. Agriculture and mining had been struggling since 1926 as world prices for primary products fell, and this trend also impacted on European heavy industry. Manufacturers now struggled to sell in foreign markets whose purchasing power derived from agriculture or mining, leading American investors to see their own capital and stock markets as a safer bet than overseas. With fresh funds from the USA drying up, the volume of foreign capital entering Europe fell from $1.7 billion in 1928 to $1 billion in 1929.

Owen D. Young, chairman of the US industrial giant General Electric, had played an influential part in the formulation of the Dawes Plan and in 1928 became chairman of the Second Expert Committee on Reparations. In June 1929 it tabled proposals which were quickly dubbed the Young Plan. This reduced Germany's overall liability to a third of the original, 1921 total, scheduled the final payment for 1988, and offered deep cuts in annual transfers to allow for Berlin's growing budgetary crisis. Young also effectively freed Germany from foreign financial supervision; a Bank for International Settlement was established in Basel in neutral Switzerland (where it remains located to this day) to administer reparations and other international financial transfers.

The Young Plan dominated the agenda at the Hague Conference which opened on August 5, but the negotiations were anything but plain sailing. By August 31 agreement had been reached on reparations and Allied debt, and Stresemann secured the prize of a complete Allied military evacuation of the Rhineland by June 1930, after which only the fate of the Saarland remained to be settled in 1935. However, on the way there had been damaging disputes between the British and French governments, rows over the servicing and repayment of European Allied debt to the USA, contentious proposals for a Franco-German economic axis, and some hard bargaining before Germany secured an Allied withdrawal from the Rhineland.

The Franco-British dispute followed the familiar postwar fault lines that periodically divided the entente. In May 1929 Ramsay MacDonald returned to power in Britain at the head of a Labour minority government which displayed little sympathy toward Paris. French and British ministers rowed in public and descended to personal insult as Joan of Arc's memory was dragged into an altercation between the British Chancellor of the Exchequer, Philip Snowden, and his French counterpart, Henri Chéron, over the two countries' respective shares of the much reduced reparations cake. The British Foreign Office accused France of sabotaging the prospects for disarmament by maintaining an excessively strong army despite the guarantees offered by the earlier Locarno agreement. The Governor of the Bank of England, Montagu Norman, lambasted Paris for using its growing financial strength to pursue overtly political aims in central and eastern Europe, to which his French counterpart Émile Moreau riposted that the Bank of England had not shied from efforts to put "Europe under a veritable financial hegemony" just years earlier.[93]

Despite continuing tensions over disarmament, the prospects for Franco-German relations in the form of bilateral economic collaboration appeared somewhat more promising. The recovery of the French franc was complemented by rapid growth in the output of motor cars, electrical goods and chemicals, modern economic sectors which promised to compensate for France's endemic inferiority in the traditional and less dynamic heavy industrial sector. This recovery engendered a renewed sense of national self-confidence, and offered France the means once again to seize the initiative in European affairs. In June 1929 Briand proposed to Stresemann the creation of a European economic and political union in order to offset the economic might of the United States and achieve "a kind of liquidation of the war."[94] Berlin was not attracted by political union and could not afford to antagonize the United States or forgo the benefits of global trade, but during a Reichstag debate on the Young proposals Stresemann rounded on his conservative critics and the nationalist press for their sterile opposition to any kind of international reconciliation. He then took up Briand's proposal for an economic union, looking to a future "when from economic necessity French, German and perhaps other European economies must seek a common way to maintain themselves in the face of a competition to which they are not equal."[95]

In September Briand repeated his call for a European Union in public, and presented the League of Nations with detailed proposals in May 1930. However, a
combination of factors ensured that his efforts would be stillborn. The British government had been alarmed in 1928 when Louis Loucheur, the French Labor
Minister and joint architect with Walther Rathenau of the 1921 Franco-German
Wiesbaden Agreements,[96] pressed Briand to promote the concept of a federal
Europe. This, Whitehall warned, was envisaged "on the economic basis of the
organisation of production, rationalisation etc … they were ready with Germany
to organise Europe without us."[97] London warned Berlin to steer clear of any continental trading bloc, but in any case Briand needed Stresemann and Stresemann
did not survive the relentless stress of political leadership in a country increasingly
divided over foreign and domestic policy. Exhausted and ill, he struggled to patch
together a Reichstag majority to approve the Hague Agreement and Young Plan,
but on October 3 died of a stroke. The Reichstag did go on to give its approval after
a nationalist-inspired referendum to block the Young Plan failed, but in March 1930
the SPD-led coalition collapsed.

It was replaced by a center-right coalition under the Chancellorship of Heinrich
Brüning which complicated relations with Paris through plans for an Austro-
German customs union. Nonetheless, high-level German and French municipal
and ministerial delegations, the latter including the German Chancellor Heinrich
Brüning and Foreign Minister Julius Curtius and French Prime Minister Pierre
Laval and Foreign Minister Briand, exchanged official visits to Paris and Berlin
respectively during 1931. These promised to keep the French Foreign Minister's
European agenda in being, and even led to the establishment of joint Franco-
German commissions to pursue common economic and political objectives and
set the process of integration in train. However, a collapse in French exports combined with a surge of German exports to France put the newly fledged commissions under enormous strain. The publication during 1932 of the second volume
of Stresemann's personal papers, including his controversial letter to the Crown
Prince at the time of Locarno, delivered the coup de grâce to these efforts at rapprochement and, ultimately, a European union.[98] The French right had never
believed in German good will and had consistently doubted the wisdom of Briand's
strategy. Now the letter to the Crown Prince was taken by these circles and by the
right-wing press as proof positive of German duplicity. An appalled German
Foreign Office was left a helpless bystander as the 1932 French election campaign
was poisoned by the Stresemann memoirs. Although the center-left won, Briand
had died in March after a protracted illness and his Prime Minister, Laval, was
removed from office. Within months Adolf Hitler's government in Germany was
to brush aside any further efforts to revive the process of reconciliation between,
as Briand had put it, the two great peoples of Europe.

European relations had been dominated during the 1920s by efforts to construct
a stable postwar order acceptable to the victors and, latterly, to the vanquished.
When in 1927 Briand, Chamberlain and Stresemann jointly received the Nobel

Peace Prize for their efforts at Locarno it must have seemed that Europe had left the worst behind it. However, the process of negotiation and revision was clearly not over and by the time the Young Plan had been ratified an economic blizzard of unprecedented severity was howling across the continent. To a degree this storm had originated in America and it was not simply the child of the reparations settlement, despite the claims of the German right and Nazis to that effect. Nonetheless Keynes's proposal in 1919 that inter-Allied war debt be canceled, so allowing reparations to be set at a lower, more politically acceptable level, would, if adopted, have greatly eased the process of postwar stabilization and allowed the European powers to move beyond the improvisation, repair and damage limitation that defined so much of their activity in the decade after Versailles.

5.3   Economy and Society: A Faltering Recovery

Although the First World War had delivered a hammer blow to the European economy, most of the continent's leaders believed, or at least persuaded themselves, that a return to the belle époque of the Edwardian era, a "return to normalcy," would be possible. This was taken to be synonymous with a return to the prewar gold standard under which all currencies had been freely exchangeable for gold at a fixed rate and gold coinage had circulated domestically alongside paper currency. People could have complete confidence in the value of any gold standard currency and in the fixed rates of exchange between such currencies. World trade had prospered, finance and investment had flowed freely between countries, and national economies had grown steadily. It was the gold standard, postwar governments believed, that had fueled this prewar prosperity, but economic historians now agree that they had confused cause and effect. Instead, the similar rates of development in advanced economies, and also the dominant and benevolent role of the City of London as financial hub of the international economy, had underpinned the successful operation of the gold standard. Thus Derek Aldcroft concludes: "it can be argued that the gold standard worked, at least for the major industrial economies, largely because it was never subject to serious strain."[99]

In 1919, however, the European economy was anything but stable. Eighty percent of war expenditure had been financed by massive domestic and international loans. Europe's governments borrowed $260 billion between 1914 and 1918, which was some six and a half times the entire global national debt taken on between the 1789 French Revolution and 1914. In addition, governments had exported gold, sold off domestic and lucrative foreign assets built up over generations, created easy credit and simply printed money, all to fund the war, only to trigger alarming levels of inflation and currency depreciation. Both sides in the war had comforted themselves that the loser would pay all through indemnities or reparations, but without daring to question the practicality of such a notion.

Patterns of international trade had also changed to Europe's disadvantage. The world as a whole was poorer in 1919 than it had been before the war, but this reflected economic decline in Europe itself. The United States and Japan had become significantly wealthier as their agricultural, industrial and manufacturing sectors met Allied orders or captured markets elsewhere in the world from the warring Europeans. Other countries on the periphery of the global economy, such as Brazil or Australia, also experienced accelerated economic development as their raw materials fetched high prices on world markets and their own industry met orders previously placed in Europe. If European powers had conducted almost 60 percent of world trade in 1913, their share was less than half in 1920. The United States's share had risen from over a fifth to just under a third.

The east of the continent had witnessed the most extreme decline. The Bolshevik Revolution and ensuing civil war had reduced Russia to famine and chaos, while across much of central and southeastern Europe territorial and social upheaval pitched previously poor regions into utter destitution. Writing of the situation in war-ravaged Poland, the British Director of Relief observed:

> The population here was living upon roots, grass, acorns and heather. The only bread available was composed of these ingredients, with perhaps about 5 per cent of rye flour. Their clothes were in the last stages of dilapidation; the majority were without boots and shoes and had reached the lowest depths of misery and degradation.[100]

Aid on a massive scale was needed across Eastern Europe to address this immediate crisis and the American Relief Administration did provide $1.25 billion of food, but from mid-1919 the burden was taken on by private organizations and the volume of assistance fell sharply. All in all, total food aid was barely sufficient to feed each child in central and eastern Europe for a month, and even in relatively prosperous Czechoslovakia the League of Nations found that 60 percent of children were malnourished in March 1921.[101]

Food apart, the capital goods, raw materials and consumer goods famine in these regions was not addressed at all, leaving governments struggling to meet even the most basic of needs. "The whole economic and social organisation of many countries was allowed to rot away,"[102] as Derek Aldcroft noted, thus condemning millions to eke out the barest of existences on the breadline or worse. Unable to compete effectively on the international market and facing oblivion at home, one government after another resorted to protecting its struggling agricultural and industrial sectors through the imposition of tariffs or import quotas. The strategy was perfectly understandable, but the inevitable result was a further decline in world trade and continued stagnation within the protected economies themselves.

In Western Europe the situation was considerably better, but far from ideal. The neutral states (Scandinavia, the Netherlands, Switzerland and Spain) had done well from the war, and by 1920 output in Britain and Italy had already recovered to 1913 levels. France and Belgium, which had been most directly affected by the physical devastation of the war, saw output in 1920 lagging 30 percent below prewar levels, but everywhere there were structural problems that could not be wished away, added to which failures of policy exacerbated the degree of economic destabilization.

Looking first at structural problems, it was becoming apparent even before 1914 that heavy industry was no longer the growth sector it had once been, as a wave of technological and scientific innovation and the beginnings of the modern consumer economy attracted the smart money elsewhere. The war, however, seriously disrupted the process of economic modernization through its insatiable demand for the arms, shipping and equipment that only the heavy industrial sector could provide. Science mattered increasingly in modern warfare, but in 1918 the emaciated belligerent economies each played host to an overblown heavy industrial, war goods sector whose shareholders and workforces were not going to accept contraction and decline without a struggle. They had friends in government, where planners equated military strength with a large and growing population, but also with possession of a military-industrial complex. As a result, significant new investment was poured into Europe's heavy industrial sector, so compromising the continent's longer term economic potential.

Turning to policy, any pretense at international cooperation had been abandoned even before the peace conference opened. The postwar City of London lacked the financial muscle and credibility any longer to coordinate international financial affairs in conjunction with the major continental central banks, while the financial community in New York was partly unable, partly unwilling, to assume such a role. National governments had to seek their own road back to the perceived "normalcy" of 1913, which had not only been a gold standard era, but one of laissez-faire economic liberalism. Wartime, by contrast, had been an age of increasing regulation and control and had also seen significant social and political concessions made to organized labor to boost the war effort. As Keynes had observed, these changes were not entirely reversible, but most people nonetheless resented the ubiquitous presence of the state in their daily lives and governments caught the popular mood when they swiftly abandoned the bulk of wartime economic regulation.

This economic liberalization unleashed a tidal wave of demand as consumers cashed in the savings they had accumulated during the war and scrambled to obtain scarce consumer goods. Industry, meanwhile, hurried to repair or replace exhausted factory equipment, all of which rapidly soaked up unemployment, but also triggered roaring inflation as too much money chased far too few goods. The boom ended in Western Europe and the United States during the summer of 1920 when the authorities tightened monetary and fiscal policies and consumers began to baulk at the rocketing prices of many goods and services. The crisis then intensified as the United States market for European exports evaporated, capital flows from the USA to Europe dried up, and cash-strapped European economies were forced to export gold to pay for their foreign purchases. The year 1921 witnessed a devastating crash, with huge volumes of capital destroyed on tumbling stock markets and with high unemployment levels that persisted in Britain throughout the interwar period.

Recovery followed relatively swiftly in the west during 1922, but this is to ignore the very different story in central and eastern Europe where governments had evaded the 1921 slump by offering cheap credit and printing ever larger volumes of new currency. The region's fragile new democracies (Czechoslovakia apart) baulked at the immediate pain of rigorous deflation, preferring to avert a revolutionary social conflict by sanctioning a fool's paradise of unrestricted credit. The authorities in Berlin and Budapest were particularly reluctant to undergo a deflationary cold cure which would merely serve to facilitate the orderly payment of reparations to their former enemies. The ultimate result was devastating inflation across the region which, Aldcroft notes, "checked economic activity more sharply than in countries which had adopted deflationary policies."[103] Central and East European industry remained moribund well into the 1920s, and stripped of its savings and investment capital the region found itself particularly dependent on foreign loans and dangerously vulnerable to shocks in the international economy. Some 40 percent of Eastern Europe's foreign borrowing merely served to meet interest payments on earlier loans and most of the remaining borrowed money financed day-to-day consumption and welfare services. A fifth at best could be invested in the productive economy and so provide income to service and, eventually, repay the burgeoning debt mountain. United States investors did provide Europe with massive credits during the mid and later 1920s, but as Aldcroft concludes: "Even before the disastrous events of the early 1930s the debt burden of some of the peripheral countries was becoming untenable."[104]

In the meantime, the individual European economies began to readopt the gold standard. Any serious debate, Patricia Clavin notes, was restricted to how rather than whether to go down this road.[105] In Britain, for example, the Cunliffe Committee's recommendation in 1918 to return to gold was accepted without question. However, if the prewar gold standard had operated in the interests of the wider international economy, it was impossible after the war to reach any international consensus on how to proceed. The restoration of the gold standard occurred piecemeal, country by country, in accordance with perceived national interests.

Germany was the first major European economy to move, and despite the hyperinflationary traumas of 1923, Berlin returned to gold at the prewar parity rate of 4.20 marks to the US dollar. The new currency was backed by United States and British official loans, but the gold-based Reichsmark was seriously overvalued, given the relative decline in German economic strength since 1914. German goods intended for export were left artificially dear, imported goods were artificially cheap, so creating a stubborn German trade deficit and an outflow of capital (over and above reparations payments of 10.3 billion marks) to cover this deficit. The

Weimar coalition governments baulked at imposing additional taxes on Germany's struggling economy to cover these capital outflows, instead borrowing heavily on the international markets. With domestic investment capital scarce after the hyper-inflation, the private sector, including traditional heavy industry, also borrowed from abroad and foreign lenders became increasingly nervous about Germany's creditworthiness. Unwilling to commit their funds long-term, they expected ever higher rates of interest on short-term loans. All in all, Aldcroft observes, this flood of loans (28 billion marks by 1930) only served to exacerbate the situation as it increased Germany's capacity to import and simultaneously decreased the lending countries' ability to buy German exports.[106] By the late 1920s Berlin was reduced to borrowing money even to meet interest charges on previous loans and the situation across most of Eastern Europe was equally precarious. A succession of countries had accumulated international debts which were not "self-liquidating," that is not serviced and paid off by the economic activity they were funding.

While Germany struggled to control its finances, Britain stabilized its domestic budget and returned to gold in 1925 at the prewar parity rate of \$4.86 to £1. As noted, the British financial and political world regarded a return to gold as self-evident, and even though prewar parity overvalued the postwar pound by 10 percent, London's continued significance as an international financial center appeared to demand such a step. Berlin had already set an example and if sterling was to compete with the gold-backed dollar, then the stronger and more stable it was the better. The impact on British industry was less positive, however, as overpriced British exports struggled and the Bank of England kept interest rates high to dampen domestic demand for artificially cheap imports. Employers squeezed wage and cost levels downwards in a battle to remain competitive, but in doing so inflicted real pain on their employees. In May 1926, a miners' strike exploded into a nine-day general strike, but even the unions supported the return to gold, the authorities held firm, and the general and miners' strikes collapsed in turn. The negative impact of an overvalued currency was, arguably, less debilitating than Britain's overreliance on traditional heavy industry, but Keynes nonetheless protested that Britain was being crucified "on a cross of gold,"[107] and the general strike left a legacy of bitterness which continued to poison British industrial relations well into the post–Second World War era.

That said, the restored British gold standard set a precedent and Mussolini returned Italy to the gold standard in 1927 at a rate of 90 lira to the pound. This was around 25 percent of the prewar value, but still well above the 1926 exchange rate which had seen a pound buy 150 lira. Accordingly Italy, like Britain, was condemned to pursue a deflationary economic policy, but for Mussolini a strong lira symbolized national prestige and with it the prestige of his Fascist regime. As he vowed to "defend the lira to the last breath, to the last drop of blood,"[108] the authorities moved to squeeze down wages by some 10 to 20 percent and cut the price of staple foods by way of compensation. This very process enhanced the role of the Fascist Party in Italian society, but at a price to the government's popularity. Big business, which had chalked up impressive rates of growth since 1913, calculated that it was better placed to weather the deflationary storm than its smaller rivals, but the wider economy struggled. Living standards stagnated, unemployment tripled by 1929, and agriculture was hit by falling prices and a series of poor harvests.

The situation in Eastern Europe was equally problematic. Here postwar democratization had brought widespread land reform as large estates were parceled out between a new generation of small landholders, but relatively few of these new farms were genuinely competitive. Just 17 percent of landholdings in Poland and 33 percent in Jugoslavia were capable of producing a living wage. Only Czechoslovakia and the Baltic lands fared better by emulating the Scandinavian example of specialist stock rearing and concentration on higher value dairy products. Farming apart, raging postwar inflation did nothing to enhance the credibility of already fragile political systems. Poland saw 14 changes of government between 1919 and May 1926, before Piłsudski seized power with army backing. Harsh deflationary measures followed here to restore economic confidence, but many other countries, such as Romania, depended on League of Nations loans to provide a fig leaf of economic credibility and so allow a return to the gold standard. The price was high, with domestic interest rates often at 25 percent or more, economies underperforming and the downward pressure on prices hitting the struggling East European agricultural sector disproportionately hard.

France was the main exception to this deflationary tale, but its experience created problems of another sort for the interwar gold standard. Initially at least, the prospects for France had seemed less rosy as the economy struggled to recover from the war and the value of the franc fell precipitately between 1919 and 1925. Rumors flew that the struggling center-left coalition that succeeded Poincaré in 1924 had been sabotaged by a "mur d'argent" (wall of money) as the wealthy shareholders in the Bank of France blocked all efforts to control their excesses. However, the reality was otherwise for the French political and tax systems were quite unable to deliver a balanced budget and with it impose the necessary deflationary pain.

Poincaré returned to power in 1926 at the head of a center-right coalition, and in December pegged the currency to gold at 25.51 francs to the dollar or 124 francs to the pound sterling. However, in stark contrast to either Britain or Germany, Paris did not return to gold at prewar parity, instead setting the franc at 80 percent below its 1913 value. This rate significantly undervalued the franc, given the much higher price it was fetching on the foreign exchange market in late 1926; an undervaluation, Clavin remarks, that "was as good for France, at least until around 1932, as it was bad for the future health of the gold standard system."[109] The cheap currency made French goods extremely competitive on world markets, and simultaneously left imports into France artificially dear. With its export industries booming and its home industries largely sheltered from foreign competition, the economy prospered and Paris quickly chalked up a sizeable trade surplus. The strong trading account triggered a massive and sustained flow of gold and gold-backed foreign currencies into the coffers of the Bank of France, but at the direct expense of reserves held by Britain, Germany, or Italy. For France's main European competitors the only realistic choice appeared to be between unsustainable borrowing (Germany) or remorseless deflation (Britain and Italy).

This disorganized return to gold was all the more unstable thanks to crucial differences between the pre- and postwar gold standards. Before 1914 European central banks had held sufficient stocks of gold to cover their immediate liabilities and gold coinage had circulated freely, but after the war no major European economy was in a position to return to this full, or "specie" gold standard. Instead the stronger economies introduced a "bullion" standard, where gold no longer circulated freely, but could be used to settle major private and public international contracts. The smaller countries of central and eastern Europe lacked the wherewithal even to introduce a "bullion" standard, instead fixing their currencies at a set rate against "bullion" standard currencies and holding stocks of these currencies in place of gold itself. As often as not sterling was chosen and these reserves were held on deposit in London, but "exchange" standard countries could choose to liquidate these holdings or convert them to gold at any time. London, however, lacked the necessary reserves to honor these international obligations and needed to preempt an international run on sterling at almost any cost to the national economy. Accordingly, the Bank of England kept interest rates high to depress domestic economic activity and so squeeze down Britain's inflation rate and trade deficit.

By 1929 the Banque de France and the US Federal Reserve had accumulated 50 percent of the world's gold supply, but neither country played by the prewar "rules of the game." These had seen creditor countries cut interest rates to boost their domestic economies, attract imports, initiate an outflow of gold and so keep the international system in balance. Now, however, most central banks remained more concerned with their domestic political economy and only cooperated internationally to protect their own interests; the smooth operation of the international gold standard took a back seat.

Until the Great Depression began in 1929, however, it was not all doom and gloom. Although the Great War had set the European economy back by some eight years, agriculture continued to struggle, and heavy industry to underperform, Europe was still a significantly wealthier continent by the later 1920s than it had been in 1913. The average European growth rate over the period 1913 to 1929 (and this average smoothes out dramatic variations and fluctuations) was 2 percent, with the West doing better than the East, and neutrals better than former belligerents.

Of the individual economies France and Belgium fared particularly well during the later 1920s thanks to their undervalued currencies, and (French) expansion centered on modern sectors such as chemicals, artificial fibers, electrics and motor cars. If French recovery had lagged behind Britain's during the early 1920s, things were very different by 1929. France's industrial production was up 40 percent on 1913, income per head was up 25 percent and exports had risen by 50 percent. As we have seen, things were less rosy in central and eastern Europe. Italian growth faltered after Mussolini's overpriced return to gold, while Germany only finally made up the ground lost after 1913 at the peak of its postwar recovery in 1928. It remained a compromised recovery as German agriculture stagnated, unemployment remained stubbornly high, and export levels stayed too low to cover the import of foreign goods, let alone service the burgeoning levels of international borrowing or the reparations account. Eastern Europe also experienced something of a boom during the later 1920s, but per capita incomes still lagged significantly behind those in the West. The Baltic states of Estonia, Latvia and Lithuania were, alongside Czechoslovakia, the most prosperous, whereas, despite a fitful recovery, Poland and Bulgaria remained poorer than in 1913.

The crucial question, however, was how well the European economy would cope when the next natural downturn in the trade cycle occurred. Such a downturn was due by the end of the 1920s and, as we shall see,[110] the deep-seated structural weaknesses in the primary products and heavy industrial sectors combined with the dysfunctional gold standard and in particular with the alarmingly unstable edifice of international credit and debt to turn a recession into a full-blown "Great Depression."

5.4   A Contested Modernity

Bare economic statistics measure output and patterns of economic activity but leave much unsaid about the pace and character of change in interwar Europe. In many countries output struggled to regain prewar levels, yet social and cultural change continued apace during the 1920s, leaving interwar Europe feeling very different from the Europe of the prewar belle époque. This "modernity," described by Peter Demetz as "above all, a modernization that thrives in the industrial world of the new metropolis, an emancipatory nationalism, and a democratization based on widening suffrage to include women and working people,"[111] was embraced by some, but repelled others. However, advocates and opponents of modernity shared to a greater or lesser extent in the fruits of scientific and technological progress, and cultural innovation became the common property of most occidental societies. Film, the musical, jazz, modern architecture and design, art and literature consistently transcended national boundaries and created a new breed of international celebrity, often film stars or performance artists who were featured in glossy magazines, themselves produced by international teams and enjoying an international readership.

Even Hitler and Mussolini admitted that old-style nationalism had had its day, despite their vehement espousal of national greatness. Their domestic and foreign policies transcended the confines of the traditional nation-state, whether by design or default. The "Jewish-Bolshevik conspiracy" of Hitler's imagination was perceived as a global force which recognized no frontiers, no limitations, in its pursuit of world domination. Similarly, the 1937 Munich exhibition of

Figure 5.1   The new consumerism: a German newspaper stand, 1929, photograph by Willy Pragher.
Source: Landesarchiv Baden-Württemberg, Staatsarchiv Freiburg, W134 Nr. 863B.

"corrupt art" targeted modernist internationalism rather than confining its disapproval to German art alone. The Austrian expressionist painter Oskar Kokoschka pilloried the exhibition in his 1937 work *Self-Portrait as Degenerate Artist*,[112] but in any case even Nazi art found itself reprising (international) classical and romantic forms, or sometimes echoing the poster art, painting and portraiture of Stalinist Socialist Realism.[113] Beyond that, Goebbels, as Elke Fröhlich observed, "retained a certain feeling for modern trends, for example for expressionist art, and knew too what a damaging effect the negative selection process was having on cultural life."[114]

For Mussolini fascism was a universal creed that promised to succeed the liberal-democratic order across Europe, although the regime veered uncomfortably between a glorification of Rome's past greatness and an embrace of the modern and contemporary – whether in the shape of futurist art or in a vast program of urban redevelopment in the Italian capital. A new square, the Piazza Augusto Imperatore, for example, integrated contemporary (and arguably inferior) fascist architecture with excavated treasures from the imperial Roman past. "The whole square," Carolyn Lyons remarks, "was pure propaganda, a piece of political art that brought together the Three Romes (Roman, papal/Christian, and fascist) and presented the Duce as the new Augustus."[115] It was left to General Francisco Franco in Spain and António de Oliveira Salazar in Portugal to establish during the 1930s dictatorships that rested on more traditional and circumspect national interests.

To return, however, to the liberal-democratic order, it was agrarian societies that remained the least changed. Even in highly urbanized societies such as England it was still possible to regard rural parts of Wessex in terms familiar to the nineteenth-century novelist Thomas Hardy. In the countryside of southern and eastern Europe, characterized by Derek Aldcroft as "Europe's Third World," the sense of timeless backwardness was much stronger.[116] But even here, great metropolitan centers, such as Kraków, Prague or Budapest, had left their hinterlands behind and in the northwestern half of Europe urban life already dominated many societies. The radical nineteenth-century German philosopher Karl Marx had predicted that this new urban landscape would become dominated by an impoverished, factory-employed working class which would eventually rise up against its masters, but by the 1920s the working class (itself by no means universally impoverished) was already in relative or absolute numerical decline as a new, postindustrial mass class began to emerge.

The members of this new middle class worked in the professions, in banks, offices, science-based industries, retailing, schools and hospitals, in the cultural or leisure sectors, or for government departments. They earned salaries, could often look forward to a retirement pension, and in normal times could aspire to a decent apartment, or in England pursue the dream of a life in suburbia. Despite the traumatic financial losses of the war and its aftermath, consumption was a possibility for many. Electrification had brought into being a new generation of household goods such as the domestic telephone, vacuum cleaner or washing machine, radios, and gramophones and the records to play on them. The motor car offered a revolutionary and accessible form of independent personal transport in the incarnation of the Model T Ford, inconceivable a generation earlier. Air travel promised eventually to displace the ocean liner and bring continents closer together. As Christopher Hitchens remarks of the era: "Travel becomes a theme, even a need. The concept of speed becomes pervasive, as perhaps is the awareness of time being short."[117] Beyond consumer durables and travel, money was being spent on fashion and accessories such as commercial brands of perfume, and on a widening variety of mass entertainment.

Much of the cultural world embraced modernism, envisaging a future founded on innovation, rather than the nostalgic, sometimes invented, retrieval of a lost past. To the horror of the conservative-minded, the enduring symbols of the past were progressively undermined as religious observance declined, individualism flourished, sexual values became increasingly liberal, and youth was celebrated in its own right rather than being regarded as nothing more than a stage on the path to adulthood. The past could be put aside, the present and future celebrated. The German communist playwright Bertolt Brecht was essentially a part of this occidental modernity even as his plays attacked capitalist society, and the songs written and composed by Kurt Weill for Brecht drew massively on modern American music in particular.

In 1933 Weill, who was of Jewish descent, fled Germany for New York where, declaring himself sick of setting Marx to music, he pursued a successful career composing for Broadway. As for Brecht, he too left Germany in 1933, moving first to Scandinavia, then to Santa Monica in California, where he continued to write plays attacking fascism, and capitalism. His classic work *Mother Courage* was among the latter. In 1947, as the Cold War intensified, Brecht was hauled up before the Un-American Activities Committee in Washington, and consequently took the opportunity to return to Germany and work with the Berliner Ensemble theater in East Berlin.

Paris, London, Rome and Berlin were central to cultural modernism, but now as part of a two-way exchange of goods, ideas and taste across the Atlantic. The New York magazine *Vanity Fair* provides a telling example of this process. Founded in 1913 by publishers Condé Nast, *Vanity Fair* was, in Sandy Nairne's words: "a new incarnation for a new century. It positioned fashion and society alongside current debates within literature and the arts and translated the portrayal of outstanding individuals from drawing or caricature into the most appropriate medium for the modern age – photography."[118] Or as the current editor of *Vanity Fair*, Graydon Carter, puts it, the founding editor, Frank Crowninshield, was "conscripted … to edit a journal that would slip off the dusty velvet cloak of the Edwardian era and escort its readers into the fizzy, raffish affair that came to be known as the Jazz Age."[119] The launching of the new magazine coincided with the first major exhibition in the United States of European avant-garde art, and *Vanity Fair* itself became renowned for its pathbreaking photography and art work. Edward Steichen was preeminent among the photographers, but international artistic celebrities such as Man Ray and Cecil Beaton were also involved. It attracted the best in new writing, publishing essays by Gertrude Stein, Aldous Huxley, D. H. Lawrence and Noel Coward, among others, while P. G. Woodhouse served as its drama critic. Later, during the 1930s, the magazine gave greater prominence to international affairs and politics, profiling Roosevelt and Hitler among other world leaders.

With London, Paris and (briefly) Berlin editions launched during the 1920s, *Vanity Fair* served to engage American high society with the European modernist movement, while presenting the United States's own cultural achievement to a global audience. The very term "Jazz Age" spoke volumes in this regard. Britain, for example, abandoned the naming of historical eras after domestic monarchs – Georgian, Regency, Victorian, and finally Edwardian – before the Edwards were succeeded by the global "Jazz Age" that originated, of course, from the African-American musical tradition. America became a magnet for the ambitious and the already famous. New York and Hollywood drew in artistic and literary celebrities from Europe and elsewhere, and they contributed in turn to America's cultural identity. Many sought refuge from Europe's Bolshevik or, more often, fascist regimes, with the loss felt most dramatically by Germany and the lands to its east, where cultural and intellectual life was impoverished for several generations thereafter. They were joined by scientists and prominent academics, among them Albert Einstein, who had featured in a 1923 edition of *Vanity Fair* as Germany's greatest living scientist. Fear for the future had already deprived Germany of many of its most gifted Jewish citizens, such as Einstein, long before Himmler and the SS went about their murderous work.

By 1936, however, with America still licking its wounds in the wake of the Wall Street Crash and the Great Depression, *Vanity Fair* ceased publication. The mood had changed as societies turned in on themselves and the very concept of a globalized modernism came under attack, in the fascist societies for sure, but also within the remaining democratic polities.

The interwar experience of the now-celebrated English painter Ben Nicholson serves as an example of this process. During the 1930s Nicholson produced a series of "white reliefs," flattened geometric forms that were pure white and eschewed any attempt at literal depiction or representation of animate life or landscape. Owing much to the French-inspired theory of "significant form" and to revolutionary Russian "constructivism,"[120] the reliefs were received skeptically by the English artistic establishment as the "product of a foreign ideology, the epitome of continental audacity."[121] Nicholson's supporters, however, praised the "architectural" quality of the white reliefs, which would surely find their place in the clean white rooms and spaces of modernist architecture and design. The German Bauhaus movement, founded by Walter Gropius in Weimar in 1919, but from 1925 based in the industrial city of Dessau, came increasingly to advocate a practical collaboration between modern art, architecture, and design and this argument was readily adopted by English modernists. In 1933 the English furnishers Heal's stocked an iconic Bauhaus steel chair designed by Mies van der Rohe and retailing at £2 9s 6d, while customers could also visit the store's Mansard Gallery and pick up works by Picasso, Matisse or Modigliani.[122]

The Swiss architect Le Corbusier (Charles-Edouard Jeanneret) was among the most celebrated advocates of this modernist architecture, abandoning decoration and reference to past architectural style for the clean, disciplined and frugal world of the engineer: "We no longer have the money to erect historical souvenirs. At the same time, everyone needs to wash! Our engineers will provide for these things and so they will be our builders."[123] The house of the future would, therefore, be a functional building, providing shelter, admitting light, and with rooms for cooking, work, and "personal life."[124] "Modernism," Alain de Botton observes, "claimed to have supplied a definitive answer to the question of beauty in architecture: the point of a house was not to be beautiful but to function well."[125] Functionalist modernity, influenced by Le Corbusier and the Bauhaus, came to characterize Scandinavian urban planning in particular, but modernist buildings did more than simply function. In Sweden, Mary Hilson argues, they incorporated "a modern aesthetic underpinned by democratic values,"[126] and in general they "spoke" of a future that embraced "speed and technology, democracy and science."[127] It was no accident that a 1927 advertisement for Mercedes-Benz depicted a "new woman," right foot on the car's dashboard, against the backdrop of a sculpted, gleaming white Le Corbusier building in the Weissenhofsiedlung in Stuttgart.[128] Clean-lined art deco roadhouses sprang up to provide food and accommodation for a new generation of motorists, notable examples surviving at Maybury and Fairmilehead on the outskirts of Edinburgh, while art deco hotels graced aspiring or chic resorts from the Terra Nostra on the Azores island of São Miguel to the Monte Carlo Beach outside Monaco. However, in creating this vision, modernists were in reality prepared to sacrifice utility or practicality. Le Corbusier's celebrated, pristine white Villa Savoye, built for the family of that name at Poissy outside Paris, was graced with a flat roof that leaked persistently and disastrously. Only the flight of the Savoye family from Paris in 1940, as the German armies approached, saved Le Corbusier from a potentially ruinous court case.

Certainly Nicholson was delighted to see his work appear in modern architectural settings, but as Victoria Button observes, a growing "little England" mentality promoted nationalist thinking in the cultural sphere. Years before Hitler and Goebbels took it on themselves to pillory modernist art, the English art journal *The Studio* attacked the internationalism of modern painting, concluding that: "Painters would be better advised to stay at home. ... Britain is looking for British pictures of British people, of British landscapes ... a thoroughgoing nationalism."[129] As for Nicholson, he rebuilt his career on the Penwith Peninsula of west Cornwall, the rugged and austere landscape of which inspired him to reintroduce a naturalist element into his abstract painting and so reclaim a market for his work.

Central European photography, a bulwark of interwar modernism, also had to make its peace eventually with a resurgent nationalism. Immediately after the First World War and in the wake of the Bolshevik Revolution, Vienna, Prague, Kraków and notably Berlin attracted intellectuals from the East, in the same way as New York would later give refuge to Europeans fleeing the world Hitler was creating in their homelands. A decade of intense, cosmopolitan cultural ferment, based around photography and film, left few questions unasked, few facets of society unobserved. The Czech photographer Jiří Jeníček claimed primacy for Central Europe in the art of "new photography," a "crystal core" that embraced

Czechoslovakia, Hungary, Austria and Germany.[130] One might add Poland, but (Germany apart) this modernist ferment remained confined to the region's main urban centers. Given the fragmentary nature of socioeconomic advance in Eastern Europe, cultural modernism developed in "a notably restricted climate,"[131] creating a hothouse atmosphere, but appalling the representatives of the traditional, rural majority. As Iván Berend observes, the region experienced a "semifailure" as fragmentary advances in infrastructure triggered a "modernization crisis," even before the First World War, and the interwar cultural revolution intensified this process.[132]

Modernist photography exploited traditional art forms, such as cut-and-paste, now called into service to excise and reassemble photographic images or to combine them with nonphotographic material to create an almost infinite range of works of the imagination, sometimes disturbing, often iconoclastic, dubbed "photomontage." The very nature of the photograph itself was also subjected to scrutiny and experimentation. The American photographer Man Ray had worked in prewar France on photographic "production" through which manipulation of photographic negatives in the darkroom displaced the "reproductive" imagery of the photograph taken, developed, and printed.[133] The technique was seized upon in interwar central Europe to create a range of ethereal, otherworldly works.

The subject matter of photographers reflected its age: mechanization, social and political upheaval, and challenges to conventional sexual roles and relationships. The French *femme nouvelle* (new woman) of the prewar era, Matthew Witkovsky remarks, "had seemed to be wearing the carpeted salon interior, her 'natural' environment, out on the boulevards," but the *neue Frau* (new woman) of Weimar Berlin "looked shockingly at home on the street – or in the workplace."[134] Young employed women helped fuel a consumer boom in things like clothing, cosmetics and women's magazines, but the image of women "stealing" jobs during the Great Depression from unemployed male heads of German households fueled Nazi promises to return women to the hearth and home while their men were guaranteed work in a revitalized economy. But meanwhile the photographer Else Neuländer-Simon could celebrate the seemingly unlimited horizons of the new woman. *Ramona in der kleinsten Flugmaschine* (Ramona in the littlest airplane) depicts a young woman, wearing a modish hat, eyes heavily made up, lipstick applied, a gleaming smile, leaning out from the cockpit of an airplane.[135] Neuländer-Simon's Hungarian contemporary Jószef Pécsi celebrated the female revolution in wardrobe and manners in his photograph *Fashion*, which shows a slim young woman sitting in a Bauhaus-style chair, wearing a sleeveless dress, low cut, smiling and relaxed as she holds a lighted cigarette in her right hand and an ashtray on her lap with her left. Behind her, two naked female shopfront models stand regarding each other inanimately.[136]

At least, the outraged could comfort themselves, these new women were relatively small in number, unmarried and young and from well-to-do families.[137]

Figure 5.2   New technology, new woman: *Ramona in the Littlest Flying Machine*, photograph by Yva (Else Neuländer-Simon).
Source: Ullstein Bild – Yva.

Women on the whole had to settle for the less glamorous jobs, as shop assistants, secretaries or servants, or worked in male-led family firms or on male-owned farms. And married women often settled, or had to settle, for a domestic life, the more affluent surrounded and abetted by the growing array of electrical gadgets that expedited the range of household chores. In Brecht and Weill's *Threepenny Opera (Dreigroschenoper)* it was left to Jenny, kitchen maid in a dockside inn, to fantasize about her rescue by marauding pirates from a life of grinding drudgery. Even Socialist and Communist women, it seems, usually held remarkably traditionalist views on gender roles and the family.[138]

Figure 5.3   Advertisement for Electrolux vacuum cleaner.
Source: Good Housekeeping Archives.

However, German modernist photography went further in investigating the very essence of sexuality, espousing images of gender reversal, androgyny and homosexuality – dimensions that Parisian counterparts hesitated to countenance. Lotte Jacob, who left West Prussia (the Polish Corridor) for America after the Great War, explored these issues in her portrait of Klaus and Erika Mann, both short haired, both wearing men's shirts and ties, both with cigarettes as Erika sits behind Klaus, chin on his shoulder, her left hand clutching her cigarette as she rests it on Klaus's arm. The photograph serves as a double take of sorts, for a casual glance reveals two young men in the beginnings of an embrace, except that one of the men turns out, at second glance, to be a woman.[139]

For all the outrage this modernist art generated, a significant body of work remained connected to the land and rurality that were so pivotal to central European identity and existence. "Country life and landscape," Witkovsky observes, "formed the very basis of national identity in modern central Europe,"[140] and before 1914 Czech and Polish modernism had formed part of the nationalist assault on the multinational Habsburg and Romanov empires. Russian art and music was, as often as not, equally rooted in its homeland. During the 1920s, and more particularly the 1930s, the rise of fascism added a new dimension to this elemental identity, particularly within the Nazi advocacy of a nationhood ultimately founded on "blood and soil" (*Blut und Boden*).

However, even the Nazis were prone to neglect such ideology as Hitler and his lieutenants embraced technology and technological progress, whether as part of their domestic agenda or in tandem with rearmament. "National Socialism," it is observed, "above all represented not the rejection of modernism, but rather state control of its most perverse aspects – primarily using film and photography."[141] The photographer Paul Wolff had always combined an unbridled enthusiasm for the latest photographic technology with nostalgic depiction of the German homeland. He could also celebrate the modern, with Hitler's new motorways (*Autobahnen*) an appealing choice. Fritz Todt was appointed by Hitler in July 1933 to direct the motorway building program, which promised to project Germany into the age of the motor car, but would also, Todt believed, serve to display the country's natural beauty to best effect. Landscape architects were commissioned to offer advice on alignment and planting, so as "not only to preserve the countryside but to enhance its effect through road building."[142] Wolff, therefore could embrace enduring tradition and progress in one, as in his 1936 photograph *Reichsautobahn*, which shows a single car powering along a brand new motorway that snakes gracefully across a flat, vast landscape.[143] Little matter that in reality motorway construction proceeded fitfully and that by 1938 there was just 1 car for every 44 Germans, compared with 1 for 27 British and 1 for 5 Americans.[144] The Nazis' "people's car" (*Volkswagen*), the iconic beetle-like design of Ferdinand Porsche, was only finally to dominate Germany's highways in the postwar Federal Republic (West Germany).

A similar ambivalence characterized public buildings in the Third Reich. Pre-Nazi and Nazi ideologues fretted over Berlin, a relatively new creation that lacked the "rootedness" of a Vienna or a Paris, even suggesting that a new, "Germanic" capital be built "somewhere in the heart of Germany, in a forest, on a heath … in which a better national leadership will dwell …"[145] Hitler, however, settled for Albert Speer's grandiose and ultimately abortive plan to redevelop Berlin's official architecture as a succession of quasi-neoclassical granite and marble megaliths ranged along two great boulevards that cut north to south and east to west through the city. As Friedrich Tamms, who designed sections of the Autobahn network, declared, these buildings "must contain something unapproachable that would fill people with wonder, but also with awe."[146] That said, the boulevards were intended to link with an orbital motorway system, with new railway stations that would form the very hub of the European transport system and with an airport at Tempelhof, located to the south of the city center. Modernity and an evocation of past empires were to coexist uneasily in Hitler's capital and even he (unwittingly echoing Le Corbusier) equated functionality with beauty. The final measure of beauty, he declared, was "a crystal-clear accomplished functionality."[147]

The ambivalence went further. Leading modernists, such as the last director of the Bauhaus, Mies van der Rohe, sought to make their peace with the new political order and although van der Rohe's design for a new Reichsbank headquarters was rejected, there were other outlets for modernist architects. As Gerdy Troost declared at the time in *Das Bauen im Dritten Reich* (Building in the Third Reich), Nazism could and should embrace the modern technological era:

> Buildings are created that express measure and wonder, working through clear, economical lines to symbolize precise, exact work carried out within. With their freely expressed concrete, steel and glass they make a striking impression. How light, inventive and ambitious these technical buildings are! Here the artistic will to form has triumphed over matter.[148]

Hitler Youth centers sprang up across the country, designed by the prominent modernist architect Hans Dustmann, and new factories, such as the Heinkel aircraft works to the north of Berlin, served as a striking legacy of the 1920s modernist movement. Nazi architecture drew strongly on the garden city concept, which also influenced development in democratic Britain, but industrial modernity demanded larger urban units. New cities were planned and built: Wolfsburg to house the Volkswagen workforce and Peine-Salzgitter to accommodate the employees of the huge Hermann-Goering Steelworks. "The layout of these new towns," Jeffry Diefendorf notes, "accorded with modern planning concepts. Industry was located downwind of the rest of the city, housing was set in greenery, a rational street grid facilitated transportation flow, and so forth."[149]

This tension between modern technique, metropolitan art and a subject matter in which "rural life served as an antidote to metropolitan living, marked by alienated labor and political radicalization" was particularly pronounced in Austria.[150] It ran from depictions of rural landforms and rural life unsullied by the discordant modern to the overtly political, such as the cover of a 1932 edition of the Austrian Nazi journal *Der Notschrei* (Cry for help). The issue in question shows a young woman set against an alpine backdrop, ski poles resting over her shoulders, with the words "Ski heil!" superimposed across the image.[151] The pun on the Nazi greeting "Sieg heil!" is perfectly obvious, but in its subject matter the image is also reminiscent (probably unintentionally) of a "new woman" style German photograph of Leni Riefenstahl, taken in 1931, ski poles over her right shoulder, her face and body glistening with sweat.[152]

Riefenstahl had turned from dancing, after a knee injury, to film acting, before in 1932 making her debut as a director with *Das blaue Licht* (The blue light). Even at this stage her subject matter contained intimations of Nazi ideology and soon enough she was to use the technical virtuosity of modernist cinematography to laud the Nazi regime with her artistically stunning film *Triumph of the Will*.[153] This transformed events at the 1934 Nuremberg Rally "into a compelling visual fantasy in which the spectator, the masses, and Adolf Hitler are conjoined in narcissistic oneness constitutive of national identity."[154] In 1938 *Olympia* followed, a two-part spectacle in which Riefenstahl chronicled the 1936 Berlin Olympics, while simultaneously celebrating the identity and history of the "Aryan" race, posited in Nazi ideology as the foundation of the contemporary German "master race." Her recognition of the record-breaking black American sprinter Jesse Owen coexisted uneasily with her central message.

Interwar modernist cosmopolitanism had had its day and it was only in 1983 that the mood of the times finally favored the relaunching of Vanity Fair. The world had once again engaged massively with American culture, but Frank Crowninshield appreciated that if Vanity Fair was to project "the progress and promise of American life," it would equally need to engage with the world beyond America.[155] The founding editor of the relaunched magazine was English (Tina Brown) and her successor, Graydon Carter, Canadian, as the magazine celebrated the renaissance of a self-confident global culture; a confidence that arguably reached its zenith in the wake of the collapse of Marxist-Leninist regimes across Europe and Asia, or in China's case its embrace of capitalism, before 9/11 and the events that followed dealt it a heavy blow.

Chapter Six
The High Noon of the Dictators

6.1 Economic Armageddon: The Great Depression in Europe

In April 1927 the Wall Street financier Bernard Baruch had celebrated an end to boom and bust, "a new era without depressions," and in the early autumn of 1929 the celebrated Yale economist Irving Fisher reassured the public that: "Stock prices have reached what looks like a permanently high plateau." The sentiment was nothing new. In 1825 the British Conservative politician Benjamin Disraeli had similarly proclaimed an end to boom and bust, given the superior commercial knowledge of the age.[1] The same could be said of interwar investors who were prepared to take a punt on what shares might yield several years down the line, rather than simply paying fair current value. Certain retail bankers even encouraged their customers to speculate in junk or subprime stocks using borrowed money, among them Charles E. Mitchell of the National City Bank. A former electrical goods salesman, Mitchell marketed high-risk stocks "like so many pounds of coffee," paying his salesmen by results.[2] However United States consumers, whose appetite underpinned American economic growth, were only able to continue spending by taking on a $6 billion mountain of "installment purchase" debt and thanks to the easy credit policies of President Coolidge's administration. Edward Chancellor concludes: "Put another way, in their appetite for immediate gratification, the consumers of the 1920s were devouring their future."[3]

The collapse on the Wall Street stock exchange of October 24, 1929 is often taken to symbolize the start of the global Great Depression, or even (erroneously) to have been its cause. The former British Chancellor of the Exchequer Winston Churchill happened to be visiting the United States on a lecture tour at the time and had taken the opportunity to snap up £20,000 of shares. Days later, on October 24, as he walked along Wall Street, a stranger invited him into the visitors' gallery of the stock exchange, where he witnessed the spectacle of "Black Thursday."[4] Decorum was maintained on the trading floor and the Dow Jones index only fell six points to 299, but by October 29 it had crashed to 230, the so-called "day of the millionaires' slaughter" when fighting broke out on the floor of the dealing room. Groucho Marx and Irving Berlin had lost fortunes, whereas Charles Chaplin had heeded the isolated Cassandras and sold his stocks for cash near the top of the market in 1928.

For all the hyperbole, the Wall Street Collapse itself was not necessarily under-stood by contemporaries in apocalyptic terms. A million or so Americans had lost money but, as the events of 1921–2 had demonstrated, recovery from stock mar-ket crashes and wider slumps could prove relatively rapid. It appeared for a while that history would repeat itself. The New York stock exchange had staged a decent recovery by early 1930, leading the new US President, Herbert Hoover, to predict in March that "the worst effects of the crash upon employment will have passed during the next sixty days."[5] By April the Dow Jones index was up 50 percent from its low of 198, and the New York property tycoons J. J. Raskob and Walter Chrysler sought to outdo each other with plans for huge skyscrapers – the Empire State and Chrysler buildings respectively.

The greater disaster unfolded in slow motion. The Dow Jones crashed anew during late April, finally bottoming out at 42 points in the summer of 1932 as the wider economy went into deep recession. The USA's gross national product had fallen 60 percent and a third of the industrial workforce was registered as unem-ployed. The number of bank failures in the United States also continued to rise at a dizzying rate; from 659 (small, local affairs in the main) in 1929, to 1,352 in 1930, 2,294 in 1931, and 4,004 in 1933.

A terror gripped wholesale and retail, national and international banking as investors and depositors pulled their money out of allegedly insecure institu-tions – and countries. Central European banks began to fail during 1931 and lenders started a run on the Bank of England, forcing Britain to abandon the gold standard and renege on a host of international financial obligations. Disbelief and shell shock held sway. As the German Chancellor, Heinrich Brüning, put it: "The realisation slowly dawned that the world [was] facing a situation without parallel in history."[6] Output fell further, only finally bottom-ing out in the United States, Britain and Germany during the autumn of 1932, but at this bleakest moment the potential for recovery was already apparent, to the experts at least. Even the political fallout of the slump, most notably the dramatic upsurge in support for Hitler's Nazis, appeared by the autumn of 1932 to have been a passing phase.

Until very recently historians have tended to judge the actions of the key deci-sion makers from the lofty heights of our own allegedly sophisticated economic age. Elementary blunders during the interwar depression (or so they were judged) made a serious situation very much worse than it should have been. However, from the perspective of today, and writing in Edinburgh[7] of all places, profound economic and financial crisis no longer appears the exclusive domain of a strange and distant past, but instead a condition doomed to repeat itself. As the *Financial Times* commented recently:

We have been here before. F. Scott Fitzgerald described the 1929 crash as "the most expensive orgy in history." Yet, two years later, his belt pulled tight, Mr Fitzgerald felt nostalgic for the Jazz Age when people lived with the "insouciance of Grand Dukes and the morality of call girls." It was 50 years before financial capitalism fully returned. The doctrine of laissez faire has survived worse and will again.[8]

Left sadder and wiser by the current implosion of the latest in a long history of speculative bubbles, we might wish to treat interwar policy makers a little more kindly than was once customary.

We should also remember that even slumps have their winners, or at least those who get through relatively unscathed. For such people the purgative experience of a major crash might seem a price worth paying, lending support to politicians prepared to rebuild economic and financial stability from the baseline of any slump. The nostalgic optimism displayed by F. Scott Fitzgerald during 1931 could be shared by many less illustrious American and European citizens. In Germany, for example, most employees did not lose their jobs and hourly real wage rates actually rose during the depression. A starkly polarized social landscape resulted as millions of unemployed or bankrupt Germans faced utter ruin and destitution while others prudently deposited their swelling earnings in savings accounts. In Britain, the contrast between abject poverty and relative prosperity could be geographically defined. South Wales, northern England and the Scottish Central Belt, the cradles of the first industrial revolution and under the cosh of chronic structural unemployment since 1921, suffered appallingly, while new wave industries, such as car manufacture in and around Birmingham and Coventry, provided for relative prosperity in central and southern England, outwith the agricultural sector at least.[9] This in turn generated political support for a Conservative-dominated National Government, led initially by the former Labour leader Ramsay MacDonald. Finally, the chronology of the slump varied. While Germany and the English-speaking world struggled through the early 1930s, France, with its massive gold reserves and sound budget, rode out the storm for several years, before slipping into recession during 1932 and remaining in difficulty during the 1930s as the earlier victims of the slump saw their economies recover.

Meanwhile, to the east, the Soviet Union witnessed rapid industrial growth during the depression years, leading some in the west to conclude that whatever its human rights record, Stalin's regime represented the future ordering of economy and society. After 1928 the Soviet Union underwent a cultural, social and economic sea change as freedom of expression was severely curtailed and journalists and social scientists were pressed into service to laud agrarian reforms and a simultaneous drive to industrialize the Communist state. However, the Soviet story was Janus-faced, as the agricultural sector was used and abused to provide the necessary resources for forced industrialization and urbanization.

During mid-1929 a drive began to wind up Lenin's New Economic Policy in the countryside, which had fostered the emergence of a million or more independent family farmers, the kulaks. A confused process of forced collectivization followed, which gained momentum from late 1929 onwards as landholdings were integrated into large state-owned productive units. This campaign, so Stalin decreed, demanded the "liquidation as a class" of the entire kulak community,[10] which soon enough involved their expropriation, exclusion from the new collectives, and thereafter the chaotic deportation of some 4.5 million people to Siberia. They were joined by other rural opponents of the collectivization process, "sent on journeys with little food or water to Siberia in railway wagons," as party activists heeded warnings against "rotten liberalism" and so ensured that deportation often amounted to a death sentence.[11] After a brief pause during 1930, almost 90 percent of peasant households were eventually collectivized by 1936. Many slaughtered their stock in protest, gorging themselves on mountains of meat and thereafter paying scant attention to any remaining livestock or to their crops. As food production plummeted and famine swept rural Russia during 1933, party cadres continued to requisition what they could, thus ensuring that the industrializing cities at least had adequate supplies of bread and potatoes.

Against this lamentable tale was set the "pathos of construction," idealized in official Soviet accounts of the first five-year plan.[12] The plan was launched in 1929 with the declared aim "decisively to free industry and the national economy from dependence on foreign countries,"[13] who wished the Soviet Union anything but well. Despite vainglorious and ultimately fantastical attempts to ratchet up production targets and telescope the five-year schedule into four, the results were impressive enough. Coal output almost doubled between 1927 and 1932, as did oil, iron ore and pig iron production, so contributing to a near doubling in national income. The state intervened systematically to accord key schemes priority, some using forced or prison labor, but others were built by members of a younger generation that identified positively with this program of breakneck modernization. The workers and technicians who flung up the giant new metallurgical complex of Magnitogorsk in the wilderness of the southern Ural Mountains "seemed," Alec Nove observes, "to have been fired by a real faith in the future and in their own and their children's part in it."[14] The internationally renowned designer and poster artist Gustave Klucis celebrated some of the greatest projects of the Stalinist era, such as the building of the Moscow metro and the completion of the Dnepostroi Dam. His posters depicted resolute workers, their gaze fixed into a socialist future, a modern world inhabited by the new socialist masses.[15] Art and literature were also pressed into service, as the doctrine of "Socialist Realism" demanded the production of work that promoted and idealized the imagined socialist future. The celebrated author Maxim Gorky, whose 1907 novel *Mother* was seen as a precursor of Socialist Realism, was invited back to the Soviet Union from Italy to launch the new genre. Klucis was later to fall victim to the Stalinist terror, but engineering workers in far-off, depression-ravaged capitalist countries could sense the emergence of this socialist behemoth when their own companies were kept viable by Soviet orders for producer goods and other heavy equipment.

This process of rapid industrialization occurred not just at the cost of agriculture, but of smaller private firms, which tended to disappear or be merged into collectives, and of consumer goods production, which was neglected. Industrialization itself outpaced the time-consuming and expensive business of properly training the burgeoning industrial workforce, leading to poor productivity and labor discipline as demoralized rural recruits drifted from one job to another, or simply upped and returned to their families in the countryside. There were also insufficient resources to match urban population growth with housing needs, leading to dire conditions. As Nove concludes: "No Soviet citizen [was] likely to deny that lack of space, shared kitchens, the crowding of several families per apartment, often divided rooms, were the lot of the majority of the urban population for over a generation, and that this was a source of a great deal of human misery."[16]

Alongside this, the feminization of whole branches of the economy and the drafting of former country women into the unskilled labor force did little for family life, and in particular the lives of the women themselves. The "new man" was a rarity in the interwar Soviet Union, leaving women to struggle with their household and child-rearing duties alongside their work, while their men found solace, or oblivion, in vodka. Foodstuffs and textiles were rationed, if cheap, but there was too little to be had at these low, "official" prices. A network of outlets selling food and other consumer goods at "commercial" prices was tolerated and became a source of tax revenue for the state, but the soaring prices fetched on the open market were followed soon enough by increases in the price of rationed goods. People were compelled to accept whatever they were offered – "do not prevaricate or fuss" typified the attitude of sales staff as real wages fell by some 11 percent according to confidential official statistics, but in reality by rather more.

However, for all the suffering and a residual bitterness that was to see some communities (briefly) greet the Germans as liberators in 1941, the fact remained that during the depression years "Russia was growing, the western capitalist system was apparently collapsing."[17] It was, or so it seemed, as Karl Marx had predicted almost a century earlier. A crisis-prone capitalist order was in its death throes, whereas the Soviet Union was suffering the growing pains of a youthful, self-confident future. Ironically, as Hartmut Pogge von Strandmann relates, it was only orders from the Soviet Union for heavy producer goods – heavy machinery and industrial machine tools – that kept many firms in Germany's Ruhr District afloat.[18] In 1937 George D. H. Cole concluded that of the major world economies only the Soviet Union had the ability to ensure full employment,[19] and not a few well-placed socialites in Britain and elsewhere were willing adherents to the Soviet dream, some further motivated to espouse Bolshevism by the increasingly barbaric alternative of Nazism.

Returning to the mainstream European economy, why had the slump plumbed such depths? A seven- to ten-year trade cycle had been observable since the nineteenth century, leaving a downturn due around 1929. However, the severity and duration of the slump, Derek Aldcroft concludes, stemmed from events in the

United States. The speculative and credit-driven boom prompted efforts by the US Federal Reserve to cool the economy through interest rate hikes. Despite this, intense stock market speculation continued beyond an initial economic downturn, so triggering the October crash as investors finally confronted reality. Higher US interest rates had already slowed the flow of capital from America to Europe before the crash and now the deepening economic slump brought these capital exports to an abrupt halt. America also reduced its import of goods from elsewhere, so intensifying the growing crisis. In Peter Fearon's words, "When the US boom broke, the general collapse was inevitable."[20] Most central and eastern European economies were left dangerously exposed, since they had covered their trade deficits with borrowed foreign capital, much of it from the United States. Governments struggled to eliminate potentially ruinous trade deficits through domestic deflation (so cutting the demand for imported goods) and by imposing high tariffs on remaining imports. These measures, of course, also served to intensify further the scale and duration of the slump.

The 1929–30 economic downturn then triggered the financial crisis of 1931 as nervous investors from the main creditor nations, France and the United States, tried to recover their outstanding foreign loans. The repatriation of loans to the United States and then France swelled to a torrent, forcing the original borrowers to realize what assets they could at whatever price they might fetch. Debtors began to default, blaming greedy bankers for their woes, but in eastern and central Europe the banks themselves now faced imminent collapse. The war and its inflationary aftermath had destroyed much of the region's domestic capital, leaving its banks dependent on foreign deposits and loans to operate at all. Much of this imported money had been lent or invested long term by these local banks in industrial and agricultural ventures that were in increasing difficulty as the slump deepened. Now the banks had to pay back nervous depositors and so called in the loans from their business and agricultural borrowers, but many of these firms simply collapsed so triggering a run on the banks themselves.

The first major bank to fall was the Austrian behemoth Creditanstalt. It traced its origins back to the days of the Habsburg Empire, when it had operated on a grand scale, and after the war it engaged in a series of mergers with weaker, failing banks until, as Clavin notes, a huge volume of toxic debt had accumulated on its balance sheet.[21] The run on the bank began on May 8, 1931, and after a delay of several weeks the Austrian government intervened and effectively nationalized the crippled giant. Since the bank controlled 64 companies representing 65 percent of the nominal capital of Austrian businesses, the prospects for the wider economy were open to question. Currency traders were spooked and rushed to sell the Austrian schilling, forcing Vienna to introduce tight exchange controls. Austria had morphed into a state-directed economy which would prove relatively easy to absorb into the Third Reich's own state-regulated economy following the 1938 Anschluss.

The crisis spilled over into Hungary, which had been heavily dependent on the Austrian financial system for capital, and once again elemental crisis forced the state to intervene in the country's banking system and impose controls on foreign exchange movements. Comparable events swept Bulgaria, Jugoslavia, Czechoslovakia and Romania, with only Poland avoiding the need for exchange controls until 1936. Italy also faced a banking crisis, but the Fascist regime kept the scale of the problem under wraps as a totally secret state bailout and a consolidation of the banking sector from 457 firms in 1931 to 266 in 1933 stabilized the situation. Spain, with a silver- rather than gold-based currency, escaped the worst effects of the Great Depression, but was, of course, shortly to experience upheaval of a very different kind when civil war broke out in 1936.

The unfolding banking crisis was particularly devastating for Germany, which had been living on borrowed capital and borrowed time for a decade or more. The immediate trigger for the crisis might have proven inconsequential in more stable times. A textiles company, Nordwolle (Northern Wool), used a sizeable bank loan to buy up a year's supply of wool in early 1931, only to see commodity prices collapse. The overstretched company was unable to repay the Darmstädter und Nationalbank, whose own depositors began to fear for the bank's stability, especially in the wake of the Creditanstalt disaster. Concern turned to panic during June as the Darmstädter lost 40 percent of its deposits and other major German banks also came under pressure. As the commercial banks hiked their interest rates and struggled to recall what loans they could, the state Reichsbank was left with insufficient funds to underwrite the growing mountain of public and private debt. International investors had long doubted the fundamental stability of Germany's finances and now began to offload their remaining Reichsmark holdings, forcing the Reichsbank to sell off its gold reserves to prop up the beleaguered currency.

Finally, on July 13, Germany's financial institutions closed their doors, and when normal business eventually resumed during early August the country's financial landscape had changed profoundly. A new government-owned bank underwrote the operations of the private banks, currency controls had been enforced, and the remaining 6.3 billion Reichsmark balances held by foreign depositors were frozen. Among these were £62 million of British deposits, added to which the Austrians held a further £27 million of British funds. As elsewhere in central and eastern Europe, the German state tightened its grip on the financial sector and so on industry, which had always fostered close links with the country's banking system. This increase in the state's economic power during the twilight years of Weimar would subsequently assist the National Socialists in their efforts to harness Germany's economy for rearmament and war. Among other things, Britain was encouraged to trade heavily with Nazi Germany for only through such trade could the blocked British balances held in Germany be utilized.

Britain itself was not spared by the 1931 financial crisis. As Germany's banks closed their doors, foreign depositors began to sell off their UK sterling balances in order to repatriate their assets. Public opinion singled out "greedy irresponsible French bankers" for driving down the British currency in this way,[22] but it was domestic economic weakness that proved critical. Both Britain's balance of payments account and the national budget were deep in the red, with forecasts of worse to come. The minority Labour government identified a program of spending cuts, but the profound divisions these cuts provoked left it unable to overcome the consequences of the economic crisis. If this reflected the experience of its counterparts elsewhere in Europe, in Britain at least the political consequences were modest. The Labour administration collapsed, but Prime Minister Ramsay MacDonald and his Labour Chancellor Philip Snowden remained in office within a Conservative-dominated National government. MacDonald was vilified thereafter by the British left for his alleged betrayal of socialism, but the complete departure from government of Social Democracy in Germany soon brought far greater disaster in its wake.

Britain left the gold standard on September 21, cut interest rates and allowed sterling to devalue by 30 percent against the remaining gold-backed currencies. Thereafter, and in contrast to Germany and the east of Europe, the private sector rapidly picked up the slack as a cheaper pound stimulated exports and a major domestic housing and consumer durables boom saw output recover to 1929 levels as early as 1934. France and Belgium, which had until then avoided the worst of the economic crisis, remained on gold, but struggled to compete in world markets as the United States followed Britain and devalued the dollar in 1933. Paris also suffered the indignity of seeing its sterling deposits held in London devalued, so souring Franco-British relations in an increasingly uncertain world.

In 1932 France finally slipped into recession, not to recover convincingly before the outbreak of the Second World War as the contrast with its German neighbor became stark and debilitating. The French authorities stuck by the 1928 exchange rate until 1936 and struggled (eventually in vain) to bring in budget surpluses with virtually unanimous support across the political spectrum. As Tom Kemp observes: "The experience of the inflation and depreciation of the twenties had a traumatic effect on the French rentier who saw devaluation as a step little better than expropriation."[23] Even the Communist Party, looking for allies on the left of bourgeois politics, agreed.

Meanwhile, the authorities in Berlin began to fund infrastructural work during the latter half of 1932, a policy adopted and expanded by the new National Socialist government in 1933 as it poured money into construction and heavy industrial projects. The state presided over an ever larger share of economic activity as consumer-led expansion was accorded low priority and foreign trade was limited. These government-led projects served first to soak up the oceans of unemployment that were scourging Germany, and then from 1935 to 1936 to rearm the country. The German recovery, Richard Overy concludes, was centered upon "a wide range of increasingly coercive economic policies,"[24] but economic growth and full employment on any terms could appear attractive enough to many in Germany and elsewhere.

Returning to the international scene, the faltering attempt to recreate the pre-1914 global, gold-backed financial system was dealt a final blow as currency and trading blocs emerged to defend national or regional interests. Britain dominated the sterling bloc, an informal trading association based around the Empire and

Dominions, but also including much of Scandinavia, Portugal and a diverse collection of countries extending from Jugoslavia and Greece, to Egypt, Iraq and Iran, Japan and also Argentina and Uruguay. Britain, therefore, retained something of a global financial footprint. At the same time, London imposed a General Tariff on imports, with only the Empire spared, following the establishment of an "Imperial Preference" system after the Imperial Economic Conference, held in Ottawa during the summer of 1932. This effective abandonment of a century-old commitment to free trade was, along with going off gold, a major revolution in Britain's financial position, but it did suffice to underpin relative prosperity and rising living standards for those in work.

France, meanwhile, stuck to the gold standard, and alongside Switzerland, the Netherlands and Belgium, Italy and Poland, created the "Gold Bloc" for the settlement of accounts between themselves. Germany scrapped its most-favored-nation agreements, replacing them with a series of bilateral trading deals which eventually saw particularly close economic ties, based on barter-style trade, between Nazi Germany and southeastern Europe. Hungary and Bulgaria became heavily dependent on this arrangement and so open to German political influence. More generally, the end of the international gold standard, the series of disorganized devaluations, and tit-for-tat tariff increases destabilized the international economy and heightened uncertainty, leaving individual countries with little alternative but to find their own road to recovery.

A series of international conferences failed to offer any convincing alternative. At the height of the banking crisis, on June 21, 1931, the United States President, Herbert Hoover, had announced a moratorium on all payments of war debts and reparations. The United States had previously written off 65 percent of French and Belgian debts owed to it and 35 percent of British debts, while, as we have seen, Germany had seen its reparations bill cut in 1924 and again in 1929. The financial legacy of the war had nonetheless remained a major international political irritant, but Hoover's gesture failed to resolve the fundamentals of the wider global crisis. In July 1932 the Lausanne Conference saw Britain and France agree to cancel Germany's outstanding reparations debt after a final payment and once Allied war debt to the United States was effectively written off by Washington. The United States baulked at this European impudence and reacted furiously when France then defaulted on payments and Britain scaled down its own repayments. The new US President, Franklin D Roosevelt, unilaterally left the gold standard in April 1933 and allowed the dollar to devalue by 40 percent to boost the domestic economy. Appeals from Herbert Feis, economic adviser to the State Department, to coordinate an international devaluation off gold fell on deaf ears, and in 1934 the Californian senator Hiram Johnson pushed an Act through Congress which barred any further American loans to foreign governments already in default on earlier US credits. Quite apart from reinforcing isolationist sentiment in the United States, the war debts fiasco and Johnson Act left President Roosevelt greatly constrained in 1939 when France and Britain went to war with Germany and were once again in desperate need of international financial backing.

Meanwhile for the German authorities a nod was as good as a wink and no further reparations payments were made on any terms until after the Second World War. Some payments were made during the early 1950s, but then suspended pending German reunification. On October 3, 1990 the remaining debt went into effect again, due finally to be paid off in October 2010.

The Lausanne Conference had also discussed the chronic indebtedness of Eastern Europe whose national economies were struggling to cope with falling commodity prices and growing protectionism, but failed to resolve these problems. A World Economic Conference was scheduled for June and July 1933 in London, but collapsed on July 3 as United States–European relations plumbed new depths over protectionism and exchange rate regulation. An embittered Roosevelt lamented: "I am in an awful mess with Europe … European statesmen are a bunch of bastards,"[25] as Britain and Nazi Germany used the conference to strike a bilateral deal regulating trade and credit transfers between the two countries. All in all, Clavin observes, as national economic economic interests became paramount after the 1931 financial crisis they "reinforced and justified the recourse to nationalism that had dominated European economic and political life since 1931."[26] Put slightly differently, governmental intervention in national economies, often unavoidable under the circumstances of the time, served to undermine the internationalism of the global economy. Governments are by their nature national, and politicians, whether democratic or fascist, felt beholden to national opinion.

6.2   The Rise of the Nazis, 1919–1933

There are times when the writing of history demands perspectives and a depiction of the past that would not necessarily have been shared by the contemporaries of that age. Such is arguably the case with the rise of the Nazis, for the enormity of the Nazi regime's deeds demands big explanations of how and why such a government could ever have come to power in one of the heartlands of post-Enlightenment Europe. It is easy to assume that everyday politics in late Weimar Germany and perceptions of the near future already factored in the imminence of a Hitler chancellorship and with it the establishment of some form of Nazi dictatorship. For sure the country's political police forces monitored the Nazi movement, and political rivals were alarmed or overawed by its spectacular growth, but that was something apart from believing that a "Third Reich" was imminent. Ernst Feder served as editor of the left-liberal *Berliner Tageblatt* from 1919 until 1931 and was intimately involved with public affairs in Weimar. He belonged to the smallest of the three "Weimar" parties, the liberal DDP (in 1930 renamed the German State Party – Deutsche Staatspartei), and had Jewish ancestry. His political diaries, which covered the period 1929–32, have since been published[27] and, as Volker Berghahn recently observed: "What is so interesting about his diaries is that he, a Jewish editor of *BT* and at the center of political life in Weimar Germany, had few premonitions, even in the early 1930s, of what was going to come."[28]

Cabaret artists in Berlin freely ridiculed Hitler, the would-be dictator, although it was left to Charles Chaplin to offer up the most memorable caricature after Hitler had come to power. During the autumn of 1932 the Nazi movement seemed to have peaked as its electoral support began to decline and its formidable paramilitary arm, the Sturmabteilung (SA) or Storm Troopers, teetered on the brink of insurrection or open mutiny. The money had run out, Goebbels's diary bemoaned the shambolic state of the National Socialist German Workers' Party, and the republican Social Democrats, bruised and battered by years of economic mayhem, looked forward to more prosperous times and a recovery in their own fortunes. The same, after all, had happened once the economic crisis of 1923–4 had been resolved.

For all that, Hitler was appointed Chancellor in January 1933 and quickly succeeded in suspending the republican constitution and replacing it with an improvised political structure which took on the grandiose title of the "Third Reich."[29] Books bearing titles such as *From Bismarck to Hitler*[30] or *Kaiserreich to Third Reich* investigate the longer term, structural forces in German history that smoothed the way to Hitler's dictatorship.[31] However, the accidents of history, contingent factors, or moments when Hitler could have all too easily been tripped and left as little more than a historical curiosity also deserve attention. Structure and contingency aside, the criminal enormity of the Third Reich raises particular explanatory challenges. Was Nazism a grotesque historical freak show, pure and simple, brought into being by a deviant and morally compromised society; or did it establish and then exercise power, at least in part, through normalizing the abnormal, that is through using an ostensibly reasonable, even moderate, political vocabulary to describe and justify its increasingly extreme and abnormal agenda?[32]

Despite its potential and its undoubted resilience in moments of crisis during the 1920s, the young republic confronted significant and growing challenges. Elements of Germany's establishment were, initially, prepared to cooperate with the new republican order, but many influential figures and institutions were ambivalent or openly hostile from the outset. The judiciary, schools and universities, much of the Protestant clergy, and a struggling farming community were prone to lament the stability and prosperity of the bygone Imperial age, sometimes through rose-tinted spectacles. As time passed, long-suffering businessmen and influential military leaders joined the dissenters, asking whether the constitutional settlement might be revised to provide Germany with stronger, perhaps authoritarian, leadership in an increasingly troubled age. Some intellectuals questioned the multilateralism of the modern world, looking instead to an imperialist future in which Germany would break free from the shackles allegedly binding it. Nineteenth-century Social Darwinist theories regained impetus, portraying domestic society and international relations as a struggle in which the fittest would triumph, the weak go under. Some influential academics looked to the east, underpinning potential German territorial claims there with seeming academic respectability. Racial or geopolitical theories dressed up these prejudices in new trappings, espousing eugenics, or regarding the grizzly consequences of elemental struggle as a moral imperative.

Such prejudices could find expression in anti-Semitism. The eminent scientist Johannes Stark, who won the Nobel Prize in 1919 for his seminal contribution to early twentieth-century physics, was then quick to support National Socialism and rail against "Jewish" modern physics. He was prepared to exclude himself from mainstream natural science and a public academic post out of racial prejudice alone, before taking up a leading position in Berlin and also the presidency of the German Research Council once Hitler became Chancellor. The German student body was also drawn to Nazi-inspired, racialist anti-Semitism. In 1926, for example, the student corporations of Munich University proposed expelling their Jewish members, so incurring the wrath of the university's Rector, Karl Voßler. A distinguished scholar of the Romance languages and committed democrat, Voßler was noted as a particularly fierce critic of National Socialism, eventually losing his job in 1937. He denounced any thought of excluding "Jewish fellow students, who regard themselves as German Jews, who aspire to the way of life of German students, bearing the flag, the sword, and uniform."[33] The Rector dismissed racial theory as a zoological rather than humanistic argument, before observing that even if Jewish students were somehow not German, they still deserved the particular hospitality due to any guest.[34] Such principled defense of civilized norms, however, could not prevent the student body at one university after another falling under the control of the National Socialists, often years before Hitler's government enforced so-called racial standards and hounded Jewish students and academics from Germany's seats of learning.

Intellectual prejudice is one thing, but the creation of a political mass movement capable of taking power quite another. Among the radical grouplets that emerged from defeat and revolution was the German Workers' Party, or DAP, founded in Munich in 1919. Anti-Semitic and anticapitalist, it attracted a young Austrian-born soldier Adolf Hitler as an early member. He was soon noticed by the party's leader, Anton Drexler, as an accomplished public speaker and quickly rose to prominence in the fledgling organization. Renamed the National Socialist German Workers' Party (NSDAP) in February 1920, it depended heavily on Hitler's oratorical abilities, allowing him to demand and gain effective leadership of the party in July 1921.

The NSDAP formed part of a radical nationalist milieu in which paramilitary organizations predominated. It created a paramilitary arm of its own, the SA, in 1921 to protect meetings against violent opponents, but when a Bavarian army captain, Ernst Röhm, took control of these storm troopers its ambitions grew rapidly. Individual SA units were led by former junior army officers or Freikorps commanders, who maintained close links with other paramilitaries and also with elements of the Bavarian army. Thoughts turned to mounting some kind of coup, or *Putsch*, against the Weimar Republic, and while the conservative politicians who controlled Bavaria would not countenance so radical a step, they were keen to gain greater autonomy for Bavaria, or even secede from the Republic altogether. Left severely compromised, these politicians effectively lost control of the Bavarian military who, Ian Kershaw observes, "were playing their own game."[35] A marriage of convenience developed between the army and the paramilitary would-be putschists, giving the latter access to weapons and training.

Röhm stood at the center of this process. Resigning his commission in the Bavarian army, he played a leading role in a new paramilitary alliance, the Kampfbund, which included the SA. Hitler was left as a gifted propagandist for this broader-based, essentially paramilitary movement. Furthermore, many radical nationalists looked to the former war hero Ludendorff for leadership following his return to Germany from exile in Sweden, thereby marginalizing Hitler all the more.

Hitler, however, remained determined to exploit the growing crisis that swept Germany during 1923. An abortive attempt by the Communists to launch a national coup from their strongholds in Saxony and Thuringia during October provided him with a pretext for action. Even before the Saxon and Thuringian crisis, prominent nationalists, including Ludendorff, had been plotting in secret against the Republic and the Bavarian authorities were now ready to join such a coup provided it attracted support from key pillars of the state, such as the army command. Hitler had to act quickly, before events passed him by. On November 7 he and his storm troops burst in on a meeting in a Munich beer cellar, held by the Bavarian Premier, Gustav Kahr. Hitler leapt onto a chair, fired a pistol shot into the ceiling and declared that the "national revolution" had begun and a march on Berlin was imminent, but that was as good as things got for the would-be German Mussolini.

Hitler extracted declarations of support from Kahr, from the Bavarian military commander, General Lossow, and from a surprised Ludendorff, but thereafter Lossow was quick to order loyal troops into Munich as the putschists failed to exploit militarily their initial advantage of surprise. Lacking clear orders, rebel troops began to drift away from their posts, forcing Hitler and Ludendorff to organize a mass demonstration in Munich in order to regain the initiative. A column some 2,000 strong marched through the city at noon on November 8 with a view to seizing the War Ministry, but without any clear strategy beyond that. "The participants on the march," Kershaw observes, "knew the cause was lost. One of them remarked it was like a funeral procession."[36] Armed policemen soon put a stop to the business, killing 14 of the demonstrators in a short, sharp firefight. Hitler narrowly escaped a bullet which felled one of his leading lieutenants, Erwin von Scheubner-Richter. "Had the bullet which killed Scheubner-Richter been a foot to the right," Kershaw reflects, "history would have taken a different course."[37] As it was, the poet Stefan Zweig later reflected that Nazism and its leader did appear finished: "In this year 1923, the swastikas and stormtroops disappeared, and the name of Adolf Hitler fell back almost into oblivion. No one thought of him any longer as a possible in terms of power."[38]

The Bavarian authorities' own loyalty to the Republic had, however, been severely compromised by the maneuvering of the preceding months and the courts in Munich were reluctant to punish Hitler and his associates too severely. During the ensuing trial in early 1924 Hitler was given ample opportunity to lash out against the Republic and promote his own prejudices. Rather than remaining one among various radical nationalist spokesmen, he had effectively staked his claim as the supreme leader of the far right and within a couple of years this claim had become reality. At the end of the trial, Ludendorff was acquitted of treason and although Hitler was found guilty, he received a derisory sentence of five years' internment and the prospect of early parole. The whole process was greeted with outrage, even in Bavarian conservative circles, while in Berlin the Permanent Secretary at the Foreign Office, Ago von Maltzan, spoke for many when condemning the whole business as a fiasco, "a trial in name only ... a catastrophe for the cause of justice."[39] Hitler, meanwhile, was confined to comfortable quarters in the fortress of Landsberg, a pretty provincial Bavarian town. Here he played host to a steady trickle of visitors until his release by the courts, in the face of widespread official objections, on December 20, 1924. Plans to deport him to Austria had foundered first on Bavarian indecision and then on Vienna's objections to taking back its errant son.

The story of Hitler's rise to power now followed two distinct but related strands. On the one hand the astonishing growth of the NSDAP from a fringe party with a handful of seats in the 1928 Reichstag to the most popular party in Germany by 1932 demands an explanation. On the other, prior to his appointment as Chancellor, Hitler never gained the absolute parliamentary majority he sought to govern on his own terms. The Nazis were not "voted" into office, leaving open the question of why an adventurer whose past behavior and policy pronouncements were erratic at best was appointed Chancellor at all.

One might begin with the fragmented nature of Weimar's party political landscape which had its origins in the Imperial era. Bismarck's 1871 constitution had given the Emperor the power to appoint and dismiss governments, regardless of parliamentary arithmetic. For sure any Chancellor needed to get his civil and military budgets through the Reichstag, but this simply encouraged individual parties to strike the best bargain possible for their constituents in return for supporting the budget. No party had to trouble itself with responsibility for the actual conduct of government and under these circumstances Germany's political parties each represented and became ever more beholden to a particular social "clientele." The big landowners dominated the Conservative Party, industry the National Liberals, the professions the Progressive Liberals, devout Catholics the Center Party, Protestant skilled workers the Social Democratic Party and so on. There were also a number of small regional parties representing Germany's Polish, Danish, and other minorities. This setup continued into Weimar, but with the business of government now rooted more firmly in parliament it proved very difficult to construct stable governing coalitions, and critics of Weimar could claim that everyone was looking to satisfy and retain their own following rather than seeking to govern in the wider national interest.

The situation was not hopeless and, after all, the French Third Republic functioned for several generations with a similarly fragmented party political system. The British two-party system was more the exception than the rule. As the largest single party, the SPD was indeed resigned to its minority status and prepared to make the best of things within governing coalitions at national and state level, or otherwise serve as a constructive opposition. The Catholic Center Party was similarly pragmatic and provided more of Weimar's chancellors than did the Social Democrats, but there was no third mass party to set against organized labor or political Catholicism and so balance the system. The leader of the right-liberal German People's Party (DVP), Gustav Stresemann, also worked constructively within the Weimar system, but hankered after the creation of a mass middle-class party that could match or even overshadow the Social Democrats. In this regard he spoke for many who remained true to their tribalistic instincts throughout the 1920s, yet professed to hope for something very different.

This search for an elusive national unity found concrete expression in 1925 when Friedrich Ebert's death triggered presidential elections. An inconclusive first round of voting persuaded the parties of the center-right and right to put up a unity candidate against the center-left republican candidate for the ensuing run-off vote. Conservatives and Liberals had already toyed with the idea of approaching Field Marshal Paul von Hindenburg to stand for President immediately after the Revolution. His towering wartime reputation and his consistently professed belief in statesmanship above party politics appeared in many voters' eyes to place him on a higher moral plane than any party politician.[40] The Marshal was accordingly presented in 1925 as the national candidate, pitted against the Center Party politician, the *Parteimann* Wilhelm Marx, who sought to rally the republican vote.[41]

Hindenburg won and, as we shall see, so provided the essential preconditions for Hitler's political triumph in 1933. For one thing, Hindenburg demonstrated that it was, indeed, possible to straddle the social milieus around which Weimar politics was organized, even if it had taken a man above parties rather than a party leader to achieve this. For another, as Wolfram Pyta observes, when the Great Depression came "the Weimar Republic lacked a strong, reliable presidential backbone during its battle for survival."[42] Hindenburg was punctilious in his observance of constitutional propriety (to the outright frustration of many of his would-be right-wing allies), but he did seek to replace the parliamentary, party-political landscape of Weimar with a *Volksgemeinschaft* – a more organic national political and ethical community based upon a stronger, authoritarian presidency as and when circumstances allowed. For the moment, however, the prospects for such a change appeared minimal and in the 1928 Reichstag elections the republican parties did reasonably well.

Hitler, meanwhile, had wasted little time in relaunching the NSDAP following his release from Landsberg. He used his spell in custody to dictate *Mein Kampf*, a trenchant if somewhat disorganized combination of political agenda and part-re-invented personal history, but he also drew tactical lessons from the 1923 fiasco. It was clear that the German establishment would never brook violent assaults on the constitution. Instead, he resolved to destroy Weimar by exploiting the very constitutional freedoms it guaranteed. The NSDAP would pursue a so-called "legality policy," to contest elections, win an outright majority, and then legislate the Republic out of existence. The paramilitaries, which had held sway on the radical right until 1923 were to be granted a strictly auxiliary role as strong-arm protection and uniformed propagandists, but always to facilitate an electoral vic-tory rather than to plot further coups d'état.

Hitler delegated the day-to-day management of the legality policy to loyal and capable subordinates, among whom the National Organizer, Gregor Strasser, stood out, in Ian Kershaw's estimation, as "one of his more inspired appointments."[43] Strasser molded the NSDAP into a formidable organization that eventually deployed some 300,000 activists to outmatch its major rivals both during election campaigns and also, crucially, during the lulls between them. Strasser was also an accomplished parliamentarian who, unusually for a Nazi, built bridges to rival parties and particu-larly to the trade union movement. Equally significant was the appointment of Joseph Goebbels as party chief in Berlin, where he created a formidable Nazi move-ment out of nothing and rapidly distinguished himself as a consummate propagan-dist. His newspaper, Der Angriff, combined the style of left-wing papers with the substance of the radical right to provide a devastatingly effective propaganda vehi-cle. Goebbels never missed an opportunity to make the wider headlines. When Ernst Maria Remarque's pacifist novel All Quiet on the Western Front came out as a film in 1930, Goebbels organized a "spontaneous" display of public anger (by dis-guised SA and party members) that saw the film withdrawn. "National Socialism on the streets," he gloated, "dictates the government's actions."[44]

In early 1930 he was made National Propaganda Director and saw to it that Nazi election campaigns assaulted the senses and played on people's emotions through a combination of noise, color, light, music, and pageantry. The uniformed Nazi paramilitaries projected a sense of power and purpose, and the use of aircraft to transport Hitler from rally to rally helped evoke the modern, even as the NSDAP appealed to a range of traditional values. Goebbels also played to Hitler's excep-tional abilities as a public orator, able to engage and inspire his audiences even when his speeches stretched to two hours or more. Most Germans, of course, never actually heard or set eyes on Hitler in the flesh, but his legend proved potent in its own right.

The 1928 Reichstag elections saw the NSDAP poll a modest 2.6 percent, but its right-radical rivals had at least disappeared from the scene and in 1929 the repara-tions question provided Hitler with an important break. The 1924 London Reparations Agreement ("Dawes Plan") had provided for a reassessment of Germany's liabilities after five years, and in the darkening economic climate of 1929 Stresemann was able to persuade the Allies to cut the annual payments under the terms of the "Young Plan." Although the final payment would not be made until 1988, virtually all responsible political and economic figures supported the deal. Most understood that Germany's total liability and the modalities of payment would be looked at again before too long and for the moment the reduced annual levy offered the hard-pressed German budget breathing space. Furthermore, Stresemann had also secured the military evacuation of the southern Rhineland by the French five years ahead of schedule, so leaving the eventual fate of the Saarland as the one unresolved issue on Germany's western frontier.

Hindenburg concurred, but the conservative German National People's Party, which had traditionally spoken for agriculture and particularly for the great landed estates of northern and eastern Germany, disagreed. Some DNVP parliamentarians had voted for the Dawes Plan in 1924 and thereafter for Locarno, but the party's hardline majority always baulked at any conciliation of the victor powers. In 1928 these hardliners elected a radical right-wing media mogul, Alfred Hugenberg, as party leader. More moderate, traditional agrarians, such as Count von Westarp, left the party, but this merely gave the xenophobic Hugenberg free rein. In 1929 he appealed directly to public opinion through a referendum campaign against the Young Plan. He brought together the largest war veterans' association, the Stahlhelm, and also the Nazis to support his campaign, but the referendum flopped and the Reichstag ratified the Young Plan by a large majority.

If the DNVP was duly humiliated, Hugenberg's newspapers and the cinema newsreels produced by his Ufa film studios had provided the NSDAP with invaluable, free publicity during the campaign. Many individual states had only grudgingly and recently allowed Hitler to appear and speak in public at all and the respectability lent to the Austrian-born provincial and his political movement through Hugenberg's endorsement was equally critical. As the Great Depression tightened its grip on Germany, voting Nazi became thinkable to many citizens for the first time.

During 1929 the Nazis began to perform strongly in state elections, and in September 1930 early Reichstag elections were called after the governing coalition failed to agree on budgetary savings. In 1928 Nazi strategists had targeted the urban working-class vote, but now a deepening crisis in the farming sector and the growing difficulties facing small businesses persuaded the party to cast its net wider. This "catch-all" strategy was not without its risks, leaving the NSDAP as a dangerously disjointed and diverse social coalition which always threatened to fly apart. However, the Nazis' espousal of the myth of the *Volksgemeinschaft* simultaneously created a strong cement that held together potentially antagonistic elements of their constituency.

The September 1930 Reichstag elections saw the Nazi vote surge to 18.3 percent, leaving it the second-largest party in parliament. The authoritarian character of the *Volksgemeinschaft* was exploited very effectively by Hitler, who insisted that he was not just another party leader, but instead intended to reflect the popular will as a plebiscitary dictator. Most German voters could remember Hindenburg's wartime role as "Übervater der Nation" (High father of the nation), as Jesko von

Hoegen puts it,[45] and authoritarianism was also lent intellectual respectability by important contemporary political theorists. Carl Schmitt, for example, doubted the efficacy of a pluralistic political system during times of emergency, concluding that such times demanded a strong leader enjoying popular confidence. Schmitt was initially opposed to the NSDAP, but in 1933 came to see it "as guaranteeing a unified state, which alone could ensure a stable system of law."[46]

Beyond delivering strong government, the concept of *Volksgemeinschaft*, as we noted, addressed a relatively widespread desire in Germany for moral and social cohesion. Even thinkers on the right of the SPD contemplated, in Gunther Mai's words, "a solidarism based on sacrifice, duty and obligation,"[47] but the National Socialists radicalized this concept in crucial ways. The *Volksgemeinschaft* became the socialism of a thwarted ruling people (*Herrenvolk*) and if some earlier versions of the ideology had rested on a Christian sense of solidarity, the Nazis transformed it into an explicitly racialist creed, both anti-Semitic and anti-Slavonic.

For the moment, though, domestic solidarity took center stage as the Nazis addressed the misery of the Great Depression. By 1932 German output had almost halved and registered unemployment rose remorselessly toward 33 percent. Other Germans had simply withdrawn from the labor market or faced ruin as their farms and businesses went under. It was less than a decade since malnutrition had wrecked the health of a generation of urban children and now the scourges of childhood rickets, pneumonia and mental illness were inflicted in turn on the offspring of these earlier victims. Crime soared and the social rhythm of life was severely disrupted. Men, and particularly young men, hung around the streets and tenement courtyards during their long days of idleness, so imposing on time and space that normally belonged to their women and children. In such circumstances the Nazi policy of providing work for every adult male while ascribing women a domestic role in society could appear almost utopian, and as Helen Boak writes: "Members of the working class were not even convinced that women should be employed at all."[48] The Nazis' ability to act as well as talk was equally important. Self-funded soup kitchens, used clothing stores, and other support groups engaged and motivated Nazi activists themselves and impressed a public that despaired of the state's increasingly parsimonious and sclerotic welfare efforts.

No "racial" German was to be excluded. As Hitler declared: "It is madness to believe that a single occupational group can exclude itself from the German community which shares in the same fate; it is a crime to set farmers and city dwellers against one another, for they are bound together for better or for worse."[49] In May 1932 Gregor Strasser in effect guaranteed German jobs for German workers in a keynote speech to parliament. He went on to criticize the government for squandering public money on "the stabilisation of the … banks"[50] and lamented that honest toil had allegedly served to enrich greedy cosmopolitan bankers, "to fatten the coffers of the money-lender so that he need not work."[51]

Many supporters of the smaller parties that had represented farmers, small businesses or pensioners in parliament concluded that the NSDAP now offered them a more credible future. Liberal voters, many Conservatives, and also an ominous number of Social Democrats switched to the Nazis for similar reasons; only the Catholic parties withstood the onslaught, at least until 1933. In the July 1932 elections the NSDAP attracted 37.3 percent of the vote, leaving it the strongest single party in parliament. The KPD (Communists) also gained, but only sufficiently to lend credibility to the Nazis' anti-Bolshevik scaremongering, for which there was a large and ready audience.

Their politics apart, who were these Nazis? Before and after the Second World War international scholarship agreed that Germany's sorely tried middle classes had gravitated toward the NSDAP, both as voters and activists. Some observers noted that the Catholic middle classes stuck by the Center Party and the Bavarian People's Party, so leading to the characterization of the typical Nazi supporter as a middle-class Protestant from a small town or rural background. As Karl-Dietrich Bracher concluded, the NSDAP's "essential base [was] among the petty-bourgeois, middle-class and small landholding groups which had been hardest hit by the outcome of the war, the economic crisis, and the structural changes of modern society."[52] Bracher's characterization of Nazism as a backward-looking movement, opposed to the realities of modern life, was common to post-1945 liberal thought. As the American sociologist Seymour Martin Lipset observed, Nazism's small town or rural supporters were strongly opposed to "big business and big labor," key pillars of modern, capitalist society.[53]

There was telling circumstantial evidence to underpin this line of thinking. While the largely middle-class political right and center collapsed during the depression years the Social Democratic vote (strongly working class) declined less sharply and the Communist vote, which was largely working class, actually rose. The Nazis' strongly professed hatred of the political left could plausibly be seen as middle-class hostility toward organized labor, and the Nazis were vocal in their support of small retailers against modern department stores and of small farmers ruined by the collapse in global farm prices. The depression years, observers concluded, had seen a marked polarization of German politics on class lines, with the middle classes tending toward "fascism" and the working classes toward communism.

No one has since questioned the importance of the middle-class vote and of middle-class activists to Nazism. However, during the 1980s historians and social scientists began to ask whether class interests had really been central to the Nazi breakthrough. For one thing the Nazis opposed class politics, instead invoking the vision of a solidarist *Volksgemeinschaft*. Even this, scholars once claimed, involved the integration of middle-class groupings alone, but it is now accepted that the NSDAP's appeals to the "national community" resonated across class boundaries. The change in emphasis is discernible in the work of individual historians, such as Peter Fritzsche, who in 1990 described Nazism as an "antisocialist bourgeois union of impressive proportions,"[54] but thereafter emphasized the capacity of Nazi ideology to transcend class barriers altogether.[55]

Perceptions were influenced by the end of the Cold War and the collapse of a series of socialist regimes, but empirical breakthroughs were at least as important and in any case preceded the fall of the Berlin Wall. The advent of the computer allowed new, highly sophisticated analyses of the National Socialist electorate, with the work of Jürgen Falter and Dirk Hänisch among the most important.[56] It confirmed that many middle-class Germans supported the Nazis, but also established that some 40 percent of Nazi voters were working class. This was only slightly below the proportion of workers in the electorate as a whole (45 percent) leading Falter to conclude that "with reference to the social origins of its voters, it possessed the character of a people's or national party more than any other large Weimar party."[57]

Meanwhile membership rolls and records also came to light and revealed that at least 40 percent of party members were workers and that the majority of the paramilitary storm troopers (SA) were young, male blue-collar workers, many of whom were unemployed. Smaller organizations, such as the trade union cells (NSBO) and youth group (HJ), also attracted workers more readily than other social groups during the early 1930s. In terms of its constituency, therefore, the Nazi movement could indeed claim with some justification to be the social embodiment of the *Volksgemeinschaft*, gaining support from most sections of German society. As Detlef Mühlberger concluded: "On the eve of its acquisition of power, the Nazi Party represented a microcosm of German society in terms of the social make-up of its membership."[58] This achievement was not to be lost on Hindenburg when he came to make fateful decisions on Germany's constitutional future during early 1933.

However, despite their spectacular success the Nazis remained a (large) political minority and were excluded from power during 1932. The durability of the Nazis' appeal was also open to question as long as they were denied the levers of power; indeed a further round of Reichstag elections on November 6 saw them lose 34 seats. Hitler's party faced financial ruin during the late autumn and the SA teetered on the brink of open mutiny, leaving the NSDAP's prospects far from assured. The international economy was showing the first signs of recovery and the German government was finally prioritizing economic expansion and job creation over strict budgetary discipline. The material suffering, fear and resentment that had catapulted the NSDAP to political prominence looked set to soften during 1933.

The President's constitutional plans had not directly involved Hitler at the beginning of the Great Depression. Instead his hopes rested on Chancellor Brüning whose Cabinet came increasingly to reflect the presidential will rather than the balance of forces within parliament. Most legislation was now enacted through emergency decree under Article 48 of the constitution rather than through the Reichstag, but the power to use Article 48 did require parliamentary approval. It was here that the realities of political life became particularly frustrating for the aged President. The nationalist forces in parliament, including the DNVP and the NSDAP, remained too weak to provide the necessary votes on their own, forcing the government to look elsewhere. So it was that the politically moderate parties, including the SPD, agreed to provide Brüning and Hindenburg with the necessary parliamentary votes to invoke Article 48. However they did so to close the door to Hitler and buy time for the Republic until economic recovery underpinned its future. As the Social Democrats put it, they had decided to support the lesser evil of Brüning (himself a mild-mannered and decent man) to ward off the greater evil of Hitler.

The nationalist right certainly had little time for Brüning and soon enough their frustration turned on the President himself. In 1932 Hindenburg's first term of office expired, and while he hoped to retain power without a contest, the national-ist camp insisted on elections. Hindenburg eventually emerged victorious over Hitler, but he had faced a virulent smear campaign at the hands of the monarchists and the Nazis who (with some justification) accused him of having betrayed his Emperor in November 1918. Yet again, it was the parliamentary parties that had come to his aid – this time by persuading their electors to back the incumbent President and so block Hitler's ambitions.

Among Hindenburg's confidants General Kurt von Schleicher was particularly influential. He now proposed creating a nationalist majority government, dominated by traditional conservatives, by harnessing Nazi and also Catholic Center Party sup-port. During talks with Schleicher, Hitler declared himself amenable to such a solu-tion as long as fresh elections were called, while the conservative clericist wing of the Center Party had become more influential than hitherto. Although the Center Party had been a mainstay of the Republic, it now offered the nationalist bloc the potential at last to transform Germany into an authoritarian state by constitutional means.

Brüning was forced out of office on May 30 and elections followed on July 31. Hitler triumphed, but still fell well short of the absolute majority he needed to impose one-party rule on Germany. Hindenburg was prepared to offer him a share of power, as Vice Chancellor, and was more than a little exasperated when Hitler turned him down. However the Nazi leader had consistently aimed to sweep aside the party political horse trading of coalition government, not to participate in the very same process. Hindenburg could at least agree with Hitler on this point, but with the Nazis out of the equation and now deeply uncooperative, the President and his new Chancellor, Franz von Papen, were unable to assemble a majority in parliament to sanction the further use of Article 48 powers. After several weeks of stalemate the President dissolved parliament and called fresh elections for November 6. The Nazis, as noted, suffered a sharp setback as their program and behavior came under increasing scrutiny. Nazi propaganda had denigrated Papen and his followers as reactionary conservatives, so leaving the NSDAP looking dan-gerously left-wing to erstwhile middle-class supporters. Others simply began to doubt Hitler's judgment as he brusquely rejected offers of a share in power: "a party whose leader does not know what he wants and has no programme."[59]

However, the NSDAP remained the largest single party in the Reichstag and the parliamentary arithmetic still blocked any prospect of a stable governing majority or even the use of Article 48. Between them the Nazis and Communists could block any such move and were willing to do so. After several weeks of hectic bargaining, which extended to thoughts of suspending the constitution, the President was forced, very reluctantly, to abandon his friend von Papen and appoint General von Schleicher as Chancellor in his stead on December 2. Schleicher and his army colleagues had impressed on the President the danger of civil war if Papen simply went on governing extraconstitutionally, but since Article 48 was also no longer a realistic option Schleicher himself had to turn back to parliament. He set about trying to put together a national government with the broadest possible appeal, focused on economic recovery and with a working majority in the Reichstag. This required support from at least a minority of Nazi parliamentarians, and a growing tactical rift between Hitler and his National Organizer, Gregor Strasser, appeared to offer Schleicher a way forward. Strasser never questioned Hitler's authority or the fundamentals of Nazism's racialist and imperialist ideology, despite his own noteworthy contacts with the official trade union movement. However, he believed that tactical compromise offered the Nazis the surest route to power and the events of 1932 had reinforced this view.

A tearful Goering had already begged Schleicher for some kind of post in his Cabinet so as to salvage "a scrap of power from the abyss,"[60] but Strasser was offered the vice chancellorship and on December 8 appeared ready to accept. Kershaw doubts whether he ever had the necessary support within the NSDAP to deliver Schleicher the 60 or so Reichstag votes he was counting on,[61] but Hagen Schulze writes more dramatically of a personal failure of nerve on Strasser's part: "The course of world history hung at this critical moment on Strasser's nerve. Strasser bottled it. His advisers begged and cajoled him, as one would a sick dog, but he was unable to take the final step, publicly to revolt against Hitler."[62] Strasser did pull himself together in January 1933 and was, briefly, again considered for the vice chancellorship. However, he had resigned his party offices in December and it quickly became apparent that his earlier influence within the NSDAP had completely evaporated. "His shares are no longer in demand," a delighted Goebbels gloated.[63] Strasser walked away from politics, to be murdered in June 1934 on Hitler's orders.

Schleicher's days were now effectively numbered. He made concessions to the Social Democrats and trade unions in a final attempt to broaden his political base, but this served to horrify the business and agricultural communities who condemned the general as "a Socialist in uniform."[64] Papen had been biding his time since December, cultivating his excellent personal relations with Hindenburg and even maintaining his official apartment within the Reich Chancellery. Now he acted as middleman between the conservative politicians who wished to see an end to Schleicher, the President, and the National Socialists whose parliamentary strength remained indispensable to any viable "national" coalition.

If everyone understood that this coalition had to include the Nazis, the notion of Hitler as Chancellor continued to create problems. Hindenburg, the former

Prussian Field Marshal, doubted whether an Austrian-born ex-corporal could serve as Chancellor of Germany. Cooler heads within the DNVP feared Hitler's lack of scruples and the Nazis' capacity for terror – as Reinhold Quaatz warned: "If we go with Hitler we'll have to keep him on a tight leash, otherwise we're finished."[65] The DNVP's leader, Hugenberg, reacted with consternation when he learned at the eleventh hour that the deal finally struck between Hitler and Hindenburg not only granted the Nazi leader the chancellorship, but also the prospect of fresh Reichstag elections. Hugenberg appreciated that this was tantamount to letting Hitler off the leash, for any electoral campaign held under these circumstances promised a Nazi triumph. The deal brokered by Papen had restricted the Nazi presence in the Cabinet to Hitler and two further colleagues, but it seemed inevitable that the Nazis would demand a majority of government ministries after any such election. A furious row broke out between Hugenberg and Hitler, which delayed the swearing in of the Cabinet by 15 minutes. It took a plea from the Cabinet Secretary, Otto Meissner, not to keep the President waiting any longer finally to bring the DNVP's leader back into line.[66] On January 30, 1933 Hitler became Chancellor of Germany and although his first Cabinet was indeed packed with conservative politicians, and with von Papen as Vice Chancellor, they were outmaneuvered within a matter of weeks.

6.3   Hitler in Power, 1933–1939

First impressions after January 30 were deceptive. The theologian Karl Barth, who belonged to the SPD, spoke for many when writing that: "The German body politic is too inert, both in domestic and foreign affairs. [It] has too little of that *élan vital* and dynamism that is required to establish a either a regime like Mussolini's or engage in a counterrevolution."[67] The political scientist to be, Theodor Eschenburg, concurred, noting that "at most people shook their heads over the seemingly inane exultation of the Nazis,"[68] but on January 31 fresh elections were set for March 5, and on February 1 the Reichstag was dissolved. The whole Cabinet understood that these elections were designed to destroy parliamentary democracy altogether; Papen was duly assured "that the coming election to the Reichstag would be the last one and a return to the parliamentary system would be avoided forever."[69] Hindenburg, too, regarded the elections as a democratic route to an authoritarian order. A nationalist triumph would provide the required two-thirds parliamentary majority for an Enabling Act designed to leave the government constitutionally independent of the Reichstag.

Hitler's popularity and the upsurge in support for the NSDAP immediately it took power were vital in this regard. A torchlit parade through Berlin by the SA and Stahlhelm was hastily laid on to celebrate Hitler's appointment as Chancellor, and Hindenburg was delighted when the march was joined spontaneously by huge numbers of civilians in a city known for its left-wing sympathies. With some 1 million people on the streets of the capital it seemed that Germany's national unity had been reborn and Marxism's days were numbered. More fatefully, perhaps, Hindenburg came increasingly to regard Hitler as the charismatic embodiment of the *Volksgemeinschaft* that he had long desired. Hitler thus became the guarantor of Hindenburg's historical legacy and a worthy successor to the 86-year-old head of state. Hindenburg was content to withdraw from day-to-day politics, only retaining firm control of army affairs, where Hitler was careful to let him be.

The election campaign saw the government forces turn on the left and against the Communists with particular fury. The Nazis did not stop at verbal aggression. Hermann Goering, who now controlled law and order in Prussia, granted auxiliary police powers to the SA, Schutzstaffel (SS), and Stahlhelm, and ordered the uniformed police to stand aside as the SA paramilitaries unleashed a wave of political, and downright criminal violence. Numerous personal scores were settled in the name of the new order; "an early indicator of the 'breach of civilization,'" Kershaw observes, "that would give the Third Reich its historical character."[70]

The National Socialists' anti-Communist paranoia was lent unexpected credibility when a young, Dutch, ex-Communist loner, Marinus van der Lubbe, set fire to the Reichstag on February 27. With Hitler literally raving and demanding the immediate lynching of all Communist leaders, a series of confused orders and hastily improvised meetings culminated on February 28 with the proclamation of an emergency decree: "For the Protection of People and State." It vested plenipotentiary powers in the hands of the government, sidelined the army and President, and effectively stripped the people of their civil liberties. It also swept away the sovereign rights of the individual German states and so paved the way to direct Nazi rule in each of them within a matter of weeks. SA units took to the streets of one state capital after another to express "public outrage" at any resistance to Berlin, so providing a pretext for the Nazi Interior Minister, Wilhelm Frick, to dispatch National Commissioners with emergency powers to "restore order" and depose the legally constituted state governments.

The Nazis polled 43.9 percent on March 5, while their DNVP allies picked up a further 8 percent. The "national coalition" had a simple majority, but not the two-thirds needed to pass the Enabling Act. The opening of the new Reichstag in Potsdam on March 21 provided the opportunity for political theater and national pageantry on a grand scale. The Nazis played ruthlessly on the enduring strength of the "Hindenburg myth," while the President personally endorsed the new government and urged all political parties to support the proposed Enabling Act. The black, red and gold horizontal tricolor of the Weimar Republic had already been replaced by the National Socialist banner, red with a black swastika on a circle of white in the center of the flag. The horizontally striped black, white and red imperial flag was accorded equal status with the Nazi emblem and both were draped from Potsdam's buildings and lampposts. In an elaborate ceremony, the traditional pillars of the nation, including the army, the land and the churches, reaffirmed their alliance with the National Socialists, who represented the new. Hindenburg welcomed the reincarnation of the great patriotic union of August 1914 and declared that with the future of Germany in Hitler's safe hands, he could finally withdraw from active political life. Hitler paid homage to the Field Marshal and assured him that he would lead Germany in the spirit Hindenburg desired. A symbolic handshake between the elderly President in his military uniform and a deferential, frock-coated Chancellor sealed the country's political future.

On March 23 the Reichstag debated the Enabling Act. The Communist deputies had been barred from parliament, so skewing the voting arithmetic in Hitler's favor, but despite the intimidating presence of armed SA men around the building his tone was conciliatory as he sought the widest possible support in the chamber. The Center Party's approval was critical. Hitler promised the churches a secure future, but Pyta suggests that the Center Party deputies voted for the act *faute de mieux*, partly out of a sense of abandonment in an increasingly Nazified Germany.[71] Only the Social Democrats opposed and were verbally savaged by Hitler for their efforts. On March 24 the Act became law. It finally dawned on a horrified Hugenberg and Papen that it had not only freed Hitler from parliamentary control, but also from the President. They had always seen Hindenburg as an indispensable counterweight to Hitler, but had failed to anticipate the rapprochement between the two men and Hindenburg's subsequent indifference to the business of government. Virtually all of Weimar's parties now voluntarily dissolved themselves and on July 14, 1933 Germany became a one-party state. Only remnants of the SPD and KPD struggled to maintain a tenuous existence underground or in exile abroad.

The Reichstag did not disappear altogether. The new order and its most prominent supporters agreed that the authoritarian state would require some form of popular legitimation. Elections to the Reichstag were duly held in November 1933, in 1936 and 1938 with an all-NSDAP slate. The parliament met once or twice a year until 1942, and as Hans-Christof Kraus notes, was envisaged as a counterweight to the regional party chiefs, the Gauleiter, if and when the Third Reich received a formal constitution.[72] As it stood, the Reichstag provided a forum for major domestic and foreign policy announcements by Hitler, so providing a quasi-legitimizing process that disguised the reality of power within an essentially totalitarian system, before it formally granted him untrammeled power as supreme judiciary lord or *Oberster Gerichtsherr* in 1942. In addition to this sham parliament, referendums were called from time to time to provide retrospective public approval for key foreign policy or domestic events.

Alongside this constitutional and legalistic maneuvering, a Nazi insurrection from below had also occurred during 1933. The SA unleashed a reign of terror that ebbed and flowed into 1934, before the murder of its senior commanders finally brought the violence to a halt. The SA had proven useful to Hitler in the shorter term as it bludgeoned the most obdurate political enemies into submission and circumvented tedious legal obstacles that stood in the way of Nazism's totalitarian ambitions. The Nazi paramilitaries also set up ad hoc internment camps where their enemies could be held, sometimes beaten, and even murdered without due legal process. A more formal initiative followed on March 22 when a concentration camp was opened outside the pretty Bavarian town of Dachau to great fanfare in the media. As Robert Gellately writes, newspapers reassured law-abiding citizens that the authorities had rounded up dangerous and work-shy Communist conspirators who, in an act of public magnanimity, were now being offered the chance of rehabilitation through hard work in the open air. Thus the editor of the Bavarian newspaper *Bayerischer Heimgarten* reported of Dachau: "[prisoners] work cheerfully and willingly and, probably, most of them are happy that they now have a regular life, good food and a roof over their heads."[73] Rumors of brutality and death nonetheless did the rounds, explained away by the media as the inevitable consequence of rounding up and confining Communist diehards. When such desperadoes attempted escape, so readers were reassured, they were shot to protect the public.

Once Hitler was firmly in power, the SA's violence and lawlessness had served its purpose and needed to end. However the SA's Chief of Staff, Ernst Röhm, also harbored political ambitions that Hitler could never accommodate. The decorated war veteran, badly wounded in 1916 at Verdun, had always retained a deep contempt for bourgeois, civilian society, including the Nazi Party's own functionaries. He complained in a series of newspaper interviews and speeches that 1933 had failed genuinely to revolutionize German society, and in private the SA chief expressed his growing contempt for Hitler. He demanded a "Second Revolution," through which a greatly expanded and strengthened SA, a "people's militia," would dominate German society. The professional army would go. To make matters worse, a Hohenzollern prince, August Wilhelm, had joined the SA and been given the rank of general; Röhm now toyed with the idea of installing him as Regent once the elderly Hindenburg died and also with restoring the Bavarian royal house to its throne.

The army chiefs were incensed by Röhm's presumptuousness, which flew in the face of Hitler's repeated guarantees that the NSDAP would respect the army's position in the state. Senior party chiefs, including Goering and the commander of the SS, Heinrich Himmler, were fearful for the stability of the new regime and also denounced the SA's rowdiness, which Röhm seemed unable or unwilling to control. By 1934 the SA had become a byword for protection rackets, the settling of personal scores, drunken brawls, intimidation, and straightforward robbery. Employers and managers were openly threatened by storm troopers on their payrolls, and beyond this it was well known that Röhm and several of his senior commanders were homosexual. Wild rumors circulated of orgies, the kidnapping of male teenagers, and worse. Röhm was among Hitler's few personal friends, but by June 1934 the latter knew that action was required against the SA and its Chief of Staff.

The SA's volunteers were part-timers, poorly armed, poorly trained, and no match for the forces at the state's disposal. Furthermore they were sent on leave in mid-June, defusing any prospect even of a botched uprising. In fact the army had no need to intervene. It merely stood aside on June 30 as Himmler's SS rounded up Röhm and dozens of his senior commanders and shot them without any semblance of a trial. Röhm contemptuously refused the offer of a pistol and suicide, defying Hitler to shoot him personally, before his jailers gunned him down. A cowed SA became increasingly marginalized within the Third Reich. Heinrich Himmler's remit expanded rapidly from command of the SS to embrace the police and security and also the growing network of concentration camps, all of which were integral to the state apparatus, rather than posing any threat to Hitler's authority as Röhm's SA had done. For Himmler the camps offered various opportunities: preemptive incarceration of people deemed likely to commit crimes, a vehicle for enforcing racial policy (of which more later), and a source of free labor which allowed the SS to develop a business empire based around quarrying and other heavy work.

The SA command was not the only victim of the purge. General von Schleicher and his wife were murdered in their home, and Schleicher's close associate General von Bredow met the same fate. The net then spread wider as various scores were settled and former political opponents murdered. Franz von Papen and the Stahlhelm's joint commander Theodor Duesterberg probably owed their lives to Hindenburg's personal intervention. Unlike his coleader Franz Seldte, Duesterberg (who had some Jewish ancestry) had never been enthusiastic about the Nazis, but Papen posed a more substantial challenge. As Kershaw observes, many leading nationalists were dismayed "about the Pandora's box they themselves had helped prise open,"[74] and Papen was no different. Hindenburg fell mortally ill during the spring of 1934 and most nationalists aspired to replace him by a Hohenzollern Regent, to contain and eventually displace Hitler.

The activities of Röhm and the SA provided Papen with a pretext for action. On June 17 he spoke at Marburg University, criticizing the "false personality cult" surrounding Hitler and the "selfishness, lack of character, insincerity, lack of chivalry, and arrogance" that typified his regime.[75] The speech caused uproar and had reinforced Hitler's determination to dispatch his enemies, whether in the SA or the traditional nationalist camp. President Hindenburg was extraordinarily relaxed about the resulting bloodshed, including the death of Schleicher, happy to buy the rumor that he had been plotting treason in league with the French ambassador to Berlin. He had even fewer scruples when it came to Röhm and his associates: "It's all well and good," he told Hitler, "it couldn't have happened without shedding blood."[76] The same could be said of wider opinion in the country, relieved to be spared further SA rowdiness. Röhm's death was presented as the inevitable consequence of his corrupt high living, homosexual depravity and, finally, disloyalty to the regime itself.

Weeks later, on August 2, Hindenburg died. There was to be no royal succession, dashing the hopes of most nationalists. Hindenburg had always favored a durable *Volksgemeinschaft* over monarchist rule and remained convinced that

National Socialism had delivered on this count. The concluding section of his final, published testament (drafted, ironically, by Papen) endorsed Hitler and the NSDAP as the encapsulation of all he had sought since 1919. In a private letter to Hitler, which remained unpublished, Hindenburg left it to his Chancellor to decide the fate of the monarchy, so effectively endorsing him as the next head of state.

Hitler assumed Hindenburg's roles as President and Commander in Chief of the army without taking on the title of "President." It sounded too parliamentarian and instead he called himself Leader (*Führer*) and National Chancellor (*Reichskanzler*). A referendum was announced to legitimize this process and Hindenburg's son, Oskar, reassured voters in a radio broadcast that Hitler was acting fully in accordance with his father's last wishes. On August 19 almost 90 percent of the electorate turned out to vote, and of these over 95 percent approved Hitler's elevation to head of state. The army commander, General Werner von Blomberg, hastily organized ceremonies on August 2 at which Germany's soldiers swore personal loyalty to Hitler. He might, Kershaw believes, have hoped to bind Hitler more closely to the army, but General Ludwig Beck spoke for other officers, some skeptical, some dubious, when describing the occasion as "the darkest day of my life."[77]

However, the general public thought differently. Norbert Frei observes that: "In the following years the power of the 'Führer' myth as a force for social integration grew to fantastic proportions. Germany looked to a future with Hitler."[78] This "Hitler myth" appeared indispensable to the National Socialist regime. Citizens, Kershaw argued, habitually complained about this or that policy, or the conduct of particular Nazi grandees, but regarded the charismatic Hitler as above the everyday inadequacies of the Third Reich.[79] Equally, the conduct of policy in the Third Reich was pursued by a series of official and semi-official agencies in a disorganized and increasingly radical manner – with reference to the will of Hitler (real or imagined) providing a spurious reference and unifying point. Other historians, including Martin Broszat and Hans Mommsen, have stressed that in reality much policy developed with little or no input from Hitler. His role was essentially symbolic and when it came to the nuts and bolts of government his personality and inclination left him a "weak dictator."[80] Such claims challenged a longstanding view of Hitler as a "strong leader," driving forward a coherent agenda which focused on foreign and racial policy, and we shall return to this debate in a later chapter.[81]

Beyond Hitler's personal role, Frei regards the integrating power of Nazi ideology as indispensable to the Third Reich: "All in all, the results of the newest research indicate that any satisfactory explanation for the operation of the NS-regime is completely impossible without taking on board its considerable unifying power, with the *Volksgemeinschaft* factor incontrovertibly taking center stage."[82] The Nazi state was never egalitarian in a material sense, but the feeling of social equality, of a national community of experience and fate, became widespread and strong.[83] In Gunther Mai's words: "Social protest, the Nazis perhaps rightly believed, derived more from a demand for sociomoral justice and esteem than for material equality."[84] Much of this was at least partly symbolic. Rich and poor alike were expected once a week to take a simple meal of traditional thick stew-like soup (*Eintopf*), maybe of ham and split peas, maybe based on potatoes, as an act of communal solidarity and frugality. Management had to share canteens with their workforce (although the food on offer did then improve dramatically) and the *Kraft durch Freude* (*KdF*, or Strength through Joy) campaign did have an impact. The workplace environment was improved, cultural events were laid on, and paid holiday entitlement was doubled or quadrupled as a system of state-sponsored tourism evolved. The Norwegian fjords or Madeira beckoned for the well connected, the Black Forest or Baltic Sea coast for the majority. "Mass tourism," Michael Burleigh and Wolfgang Wippermann remark, "was part of a wider attempt to give the worker the feeling that no doors were barred to him. ... Workers gained the impression that in theory they could visit any theatre, dance hall, tennis or riding club."[85] Certainly, a combination of opportunism and positive enthusiasm saw membership of the NSDAP soar, from 850,000 in January 1933 to 5.3 million by 1939. Membership eventually reached a nominal 8.5 million during the twilight months of the Third Reich in 1945, although by this stage local party chiefs were doctoring the figures to create a fiction of Nazi-national solidarity and determination as a counter to the reality of imminent defeat.

Even the millions of workers who had belonged to Weimar's trade unions came increasingly to accept the changed environment. The Nazis' German Labor Front (DAF), which claimed to speak for employees and management across all trades and professions, replaced the traditional unions to promote social unity rather than the mediation of distinct class interests. "Trustees" replaced the former shop stewards to represent workplace interests, elected through a one-party, unified slate. If many workers were initially skeptical, abstention or ballot spoiling declined quite swiftly after 1934. The rapid fall in unemployment and a consummate rise in household incomes (even if hourly wage rates were held down) all contributed to a stability of expectations and ordered daily life which contrasted favorably with the chaotic misery of the Great Depression era. "The *Volksgemeinschaft*," Gunther Mai concludes, "seemed to offer a more effective solution to the protracted social and economic crisis than Weimar's liberal-capitalist corporatism – or at least an acceptable alternative."[86] As for the (diminishing) millions who remained unemployed during the early years of the Third Reich, the SA's welfare camps and the National Labor Service (Reichsarbeitsdienst) provided a Nazi version of workfare and even vocational retraining, before racialist indoctrination became part and parcel of the Labor Service's remit.

Although it enjoyed considerable popular support, the Nazi state steadily extended the coercive, often extralegal, powers at its disposal. Civil bodies, such as the churches and women's, youth, and veterans' organizations, and also economic life enjoyed progressively less room for any kind of independent existence, or any existence at all – a process the Nazis dubbed *Gleichschaltung* (coordination). Goebbels stressed that *Gleichschaltung* was not confined to institutional life. On becoming Propaganda Minister in March 1933 he defined his task as the "national

Figure 6.1   Burning "non Aryan" books, Berlin, May 10, 1933.
Source: akg-images.

education" of the German people and "the total standardisation of thought and feeling in the population."[87] On May 10, 1933 books that offended the Nazi creed, many authored by Jews, were stripped from university and library shelves and publicly burned. The spot in Berlin, opposite the city's Humboldt University on today's Bebelplatz, is commemorated by a vast empty glass cube, sunk into the stones of the square so that its upper face forms part of the pavement, although in Berlin at least this outrage was as much the result of spontaneous action by politically unaffiliated students as it was a Nazi initiative. In autumn 1933 Goebbels established the National Chamber for Culture which, "with its sub-departments for creative art, music, theatre, film, radio, writing and the press decided who was in future to be permitted to practise their profession in the field of culture."[88] "Non-Aryans," political critics and habitual nonconformists were barred, leaving them to choose between emigration and the loss of their vocation.

The churches were divided on how to respond. The Protestant church split, with Nazi sympathizers forming the German Christian movement and (with Hitler's support) securing the appointment of one of their number, Ludwig Müller, as National Bishop in September 1933. About a third of the church protested by forming the Pastors' Emergency League in the same month, before the Barmen Confessing Synod openly broke with the majority leadership in May 1934.

Thereafter a grim war of attrition between this anti-Nazi minority and the authorities saw arrests and even murders gradually wear down these lonely advocates of a genuinely Christian civilization. Their position was already tenuous when the National Church Minister, Hanns Hierrl, gained full legal authority over the Protestant churches in September 1935, and became almost impossible when wartime demanded loyalty to the nation and its armed forces. Nonetheless, isolated churchmen felt driven to preach against a criminal, genocidal war.

The Catholic Church remained essentially united and in July 1933 imagined it had secured its independence through an accord, or Concordat, with the Nazi state in which it agreed to withdraw from all political activity. However, the Catholics, like many before and after them, quickly discovered that Hitler's word was not his bond. Catholic involvement in the education system came under attack from 1935 and Catholic youth groups were harassed and marginalized before being abolished in February 1939. Membership of the Hitler Youth, long since encouraged, became mandatory for young Germans in the following month, confining nonconformity to underground movements. From the late 1930s the working-class "Edelweiss Pirates" met up at weekends to walk or camp in the countryside, free from the demands of the Hitler Youth. Young middle-class rebels, the swing movement, met in the privacy of parental homes to foster an appreciation for American swing and jazz music from the early war years onward. None of this posed a major threat to the Third Reich, but the authorities could not even contemplate the tolerance of difference or youthful rebellion. The Hitler Youth took on the Pirates, some of whose leaders were publicly hanged toward the end of the war, and Himmler ranted that the leaders of the swing movement should "be put into concentration camps for at least two or three years of beatings, punitive drill and forced labour."[89]

Returning to religion, the Church began to protest publicly at its treatment as members of the Catholic religious orders were put on trial in May 1935 and matters came to a head in March 1937. The Vatican issued a Papal Encyclical, "With Burning Sorrow," which denounced Nazi treatment of the Church and was read from pulpits across Germany as the state struggled to suppress its propagation through censorship and arrests. Most Catholic protests represented a form of institutional self-defense, but the withering denunciation in September 1941 by Bishop Galen of the state's euthanasia policy was of a different quality. Galen already had form in Nazi eyes, with his Lenten pastoral of 1934 showing "hatred of National Socialism in every sentence."[90] He was only restrained from denouncing the persecution of the Jews by the community's leaders in his bishopric of Münster (Westphalia), who feared an official backlash. Galen expected to die for his efforts, but the authorities decided to delay his arrest and hanging until after the final victory. Arrests of other outspoken churchman did continue through the war, although within limits until the expected victory rendered religion's contribution to national morale superfluous. The prominent Protestant theologian Dietrich Bonhoeffer, who was executed in Flossenburg concentration camp in 1945, owed his fate primarily to his close involvement in the political and military resistance to Hitler rather than for his outspoken moral denunciation of Nazism.

Much of this process of *Gleichschaltung* violated the spirit and substance of the law, and the destruction of a sovereign legal system was central to the history of the Third Reich. When it came to policing society, the Gestapo (Secret State Police) became feared for its untrammeled use and abuse of power. Seemingly ubiquitous, the relatively few secret policemen in fact relied heavily on voluntary denunciations by citizens on each other to identify their targets. People's Courts came to mete out punishments free from customary safeguards, and the concentration camps always operated outwith the parameters of the law. Isolated attempts by the regular courts to punish camp personnel for murderous acts were finally halted in 1936. Used initially to house political internees, the camps came increasingly to serve as forced labor camps for so-called "asocials": "workshy," "petty criminal," or even "feeble-minded" internees who were far more likely to die there than the political prisoners. As a "racial state" the Third Reich might reclaim political renegades, but not the people it dismissed as genetic outcasts.

Support for the regime extended to its increasingly radical anti-Jewish policies. If Daniel Goldhagen's controversial work *Hitler's Willing Executioners* exaggerates when portraying the German people as committed and longstanding advocates of annihilationist anti-Semitism,[91] this cannot, in Frei's words, wish away the central question of what "ordinary Germans wanted to do to their Jewish neighbors, with whom they no longer wished to live."[92] The 520,000 Jews of Germany became the primary domestic victims of the Third Reich, prompting over half of them to migrate before the outbreak of war in 1939 ended any realistic prospect of escape.

Anti-Jewish terror mirrored much of Nazi practice, combining a succession of rowdy, populist outrages "from below" with a more clinical, quasi-judicial approach by the authorities. The SA and other Nazi activists began a spate of random anti-Jewish attacks immediately after the March 1933 elections and again following the 1938 Anschluss with Austria, which witnessed open terror against the Jews of Vienna. However, the forced acquisition of Jewish businesses, and the boycott of Jewish shops on April 1, 1933 combined state sponsorship with local thuggery, as did the notorious pogrom (the *Reichskristallnacht*) whipped up by Goebbels, with Hitler's approval, against the Jews between November 8 and 13, 1938. Goebbels had been inciting mob violence against Berlin's Jewish community for some months, but the murder of a junior German diplomat in Paris at the hands of a Polish Jew provided the pretext for the pogrom itself. Synagogues were burned, thousands of homes and businesses wrecked, cemeteries desecrated and 30,000 Jews sent to concentration camps. Hundreds of Jewish citizens were killed or injured in a wave of outrages that went unpunished and attracted only isolated protests. Others chose suicide. As Burleigh and Wippermann conclude:

> This posture showed the regime that while the majority of "national comrades" were not fanatic anti-Semites ... the majority of the German people were neither willing nor able to oppose Nazi policy towards the Jews, which here for the first time both planned and took into account murderous violence against the Jewish minority.'[93]

However, some ordinary Germans were appalled at these events and sheltered and succored their Jewish fellow-countrymen, while a number of senior Nazis wondered at the wider impression this barbarity would leave. Goebbels, however, concluded that little now stood in the way of intensified persecution and ultimately the destruction of the terrorized remnants of the Jewish community.

A series of legislative measures and decrees had already excluded the Jews from mainstream society. The "Aryan Paragraph" was invoked to exclude them from public employment, the military and a growing range of professions, and the so-called Nuremberg Laws of September 1935 outlawed most cohabitation between Germany's Christians and Jews. These laws were partly occasioned by the wish to replace spontaneous attacks on Jews by more a controllable and internationally palatable form of persecution, but equally confirmed that the regime would not leave them in peace. Sexual relations between Jews and Christians were banned as "race defilement," although officials struggled to agree precisely on who was a Jew and how to treat the offspring of generations of intermarriage. Integration had resulted in the proportion and absolute numbers of Germans classified by the census as Jews to decline inexorably, decade after decade, but this left significant numbers of Germans – aristocrats, bourgeois, and ordinary folk alike – with some Jewish ancestry. In the event the Nuremberg Laws tolerated existing mixed marriages, allowed most half-Jewish citizens some civil rights and turned a blind eye to Germans with a single Jewish grandparent. "Full Jews," however (those with three or more Jewish grandparents), fell foul of the legislation, as did half Jewish citizens who attended the synagogue or had married a Jew. Most Jews who had earlier married Christians and whose marriages remained intact were to be spared the Holocaust, among them the celebrated philologist Victor Klemperer. Wearing the mandatory (from September 1941) Star of David badge and working as a forced laborer, his diary recorded life and events during the war years from the extraordinary perspective of a distinguished and upstanding German citizen who, within the space of a few short years, had become a pariah. For Klemperer and those like him divorce or bereavement would, quite literally, have been a death sentence.

Hitler declared the Nuremberg Laws the final word on the Jewish question, which temporarily evoked some relief in the fearful remnants of the Jewish community. However, after the *Kristallnacht*, the confiscation of Jewish businesses – so-called Aryanization – was stepped up and finally excluded the Jews from economic life. As Kershaw records: "Giant concerns like Mannesmann, Krupp, Thyssen, Flick, and IG-Farben, and leading banks such as the Deutsche Bank and the Dresdner Bank, were the major beneficiaries, while a variety of business consortia, corrupt Party functionaries, and untold numbers of small commercial enterprises grabbed what they could."[94] For good measure a fine of a billion Reichsmarks was levied on the community for its imagined misdemeanors. Jews were excluded from public leisure facilities and even designated park benches, their children barred from state schools and the possession of jewelry forbidden. Even emigrants were required, perversely, to pay a statutory emigration tax. Classic novels had Jewish names expunged from title and text, Jewish scientists, including Albert Einstein, were no longer mentioned in academic lectures, and the music of composers such as Felix Mendelssohn was no longer heard. By the outbreak of war slightly fewer than 200,000 Jews remained within Germany proper (excluding Austria and the Czech lands), before many successful emigrants were again caught up in the Nazi web as the Wehrmacht swept across Europe.

Nazi racialism extended beyond the Jews or ethnic minorities such as the Roma and Sinti traveling people. Using dubious science and a great measure of ignorant prejudice, the Nazis held that "race" defined human behavior. "Races," such as the Germanic, Latin, Slavonic, or Jewish, allegedly possessed biologically immutable personality and behavioral traits, but even the noble qualities of the Germanic master race were under constant threat from "racial" weaknesses. Eugenics, or the science of breeding an optimal society, was certainly not unique or original to National Socialism. As the English writer Julian Huxley lamented in 1930: "What are we going to do? Every defective is an extra body for the nation to feed and clothe, but produces little or nothing in return."[95] Medicine and social welfare were, Huxley warned in 1936, keeping alive the biologically incapacitated: "Humanity will gradually destroy itself from within, will decay in its very core and essence."[96] The possibility of using gas chambers to eradicate society's genetic misfits was aired publicly in Britain, although Marie Stopes, founder of the Society for Constructive Birth Control and Racial Progress, self-evidently envisaged resolving the "racial question" by less savage means. Efforts in Britain to give eugenics legislative force failed, but Sweden did introduce laws in 1934 that provided for the compulsory sterilization of citizens with congenital learning difficulties or mental illness, and for "sexual deviants," alcoholics, drug abusers, and epilepsy sufferers. That said, Mary Hilson notes that Swedish eugenic policy was overshadowed by better social and health care,[97] whereas in Nazi Germany eugenics became extreme and ultimately annihilationist.

People who were mentally ill or physically deformed or disabled, and those afflicted by debilitating injury or chronic and deadly illnesses were deemed "life unworthy of life" and accordingly faced sterilization or death. This demanded an element of passive support from the wider population. Mathematical school exercises engaged the minds of Germany's children in calculating the costs of sustaining unworthy life, and Goebbels promoted commercial feature films as instruments of indoctrination, appreciating that crudely overt state propaganda could alienate rather than persuade. "The Jew Süss" (*Der Jüd Süss*), a historical drama, promoted anti-Semitism through a tale of sexual license and corruption in which the depraved instigator, Süss, was arrested and publicly hanged by a wise prince. In 1941 euthanasia received similar treatment. "I accuse" (*Ich klage an*) was a contemporary drama based around the lives of a married couple, Thomas and Hanna Heyt, whose happiness was destroyed when Hanna contracted multiple sclerosis. A rapidly declining Hanna confided in her doctor that she would soon cease to be "a person any more – just a lump of flesh, torture for Thomas." She appealed to her husband to "deliver" her from impending deafness, blindness and idiocy and finally obtained from him the release into death that she yearned. A trial for murder duly followed, but the jury in its wisdom acquitted Thomas.[98]

The legal framework for sterilization of the "hereditarily ill" was laid down in 1933 and many thousands of women suffered the consequences. The semiclandestine euthanasia program followed in 1939, eventually dubbed "Aktion T-4" after the address of its headquarters on Tiergartenstrasse 4 in Berlin. Gassing vans, lethal injections and simple neglect of the vulnerable dispatched around 70,000 souls, their relatives bought off by letters of condolence that commonly blamed pneumonia for their demise. Many families suspected otherwise, some were happy enough to be relieved of the burden of visiting and caring for their unfortunate relatives or children, but the scale of the operation triggered growing public disquiet. In August 1941 Hitler called a halt to these killings in Germany proper, although in the occupied eastern territories quite the reverse occurred.

The "asocial" met comparable fates. Male criminals allegedly fathered on average 4.9 children, a family whose children went to basic school 3.5, the typical family 2.2, and an academic family just 1.9 children. Left unchecked, propaganda and educational leaflets warned, this trend would leave just 6 percent of the population fully responsible and productive within some three generations,[99] threatening the complete disintegration of German society. Again, women were frequently the victims of such policies, forced to endure sterilization in a drive to eradicate hereditary conditions, while the educationally weak were subjected to bizarre general knowledge and intelligence tests to determine their fate.

Such thinking combined with elements of traditional morality to define the place of women within the Third Reich. The message behind the slogan "Kinder, Küche, Kirche" (Children, Kitchen, Church) seemed clear enough, but did not quite explain that the essential destiny of the racially pure and morally upstanding women was biological. In reality more women were employed outside the home in 1939 than had been the case in Weimar, but they continued to fill roles deemed feminine, such as nursing, primary school teaching, retailing, or secretarial, leaving the professions and a range of industrial occupations to the men. Women were also encouraged to join a range of organizations and participate in voluntary welfare activities,[100] so providing a sense of purpose and engagement in the public sphere that must have contrasted with the bleakness of the depression years. However, a glance at the Nazi hierarchy – almost exclusively male – or the gender balance within the Nazi Party demonstrated unequivocally that women were deemed "nonpolitical." Indeed, the leader of the National Socialist Womanhood (NSF) organization, Gertrud Scholtz-Klink, was heard to complain as late as 1938 that she "had not yet once had the chance to discuss women's affairs with the Führer."[101]

The characterization of the Third Reich as a racial state subordinates the history of social class under Nazism. An "Aryan" industrial worker, after all, enjoyed immeasurably better prospects than a Jewish doctor or banker. Gender historians would add, perhaps with justification, that womanhood as a whole experienced a subordinate, instrumentalized role in National Socialist society predicated around maternity and nurture. Even so, there have been fierce debates over the significance of class struggle within Hitler's Germany. Tim Mason, for example, once argued that class tensions were such by 1938–9 as to drive Hitler into an early war as he struggled to rally as much of society as possible around the flag. This debate over class conflict under Nazism will, therefore, concern us when examining the origins of the Second World War.

All in all, however, few elsewhere in Europe anticipated the demise of the Third Reich during the prewar era. No society is stress-free and lacks resentful or disappointed groups; Hitler's state was no exception. The historian Hans-Ulrich Wehler once commented on British television that following the unification of Germany and Austria (the Anschluss) in March 1938 any League of Nations supervised plebiscite in Germany would easily have delivered Hitler 80 percent support. During the 1930s Nazi Germany was alternatively feared, loathed, or admired, but seldom ridiculed by its neighbors. Appeasement by Britain and France of Hitler's foreign policy ambitions was accordingly driven by a combination of last-gasp efforts at detente, pessimistic resignation, and a weary hope that war might ultimately be averted, or at least delayed sufficiently long to allow the Allies fully to rearm.

6.4   Dictatorship beyond Germany

The American President Woodrow Wilson would have been dismayed by the progressive disintegration of democratic government across Europe had he survived into the 1930s. Wilson had maintained in 1918 that national self-determination under a democratic form of government provided the surest prospects for peace, but interwar nationalism proved anything but peaceful and often served to undermine democracy. Across Eastern Europe, where new states had emerged from the wreckage of the Habsburg Empire and from the borderlands of the Russian and German empires, just Czechoslovakia remained a functioning parliamentary democracy. It was to fall victim to its neighbors during 1938 and 1939, with only a territorially reduced and authoritarian Slovakia maintaining a degree of independence. In Iberia, Portugal experienced a relatively benign form of authoritarian rule, but after a decade or more of revolutionary convulsions Spain was wracked by a civil war which saw the establishment of a military dictatorship. In central Europe Fascism and Nazism held sway in Italy and Germany respectively, and Nazism was infinitely more malign than the Kaiser's government, which Woodrow Wilson had so eloquently condemned. Just northwestern Europe, from Switzerland and France, through the Low Countries to Scandinavia and to offshore Britain and Ireland sustained parliamentary government, sometimes in the face of growing challenges. It is to these democracies that we shall first turn, some of which, France included, collapsed following military defeat in the Second World War.

6.4.1 Challenges in the surviving democracies

Britain and Ireland

Britain was among the more stable of Europe's democracies, enjoying an unusual degree of political consensus and material well-being during the 1930s. Pessimism and angst stalked intellectual circles,[102] and was also reflected in foreign and imperial policy. A more elemental fear gripped the unfortunate minority trapped in Britain's declining heavy industrial regions – South Wales, northern England and the Scottish Central Belt – but elsewhere a clear majority of the British population experienced a relatively short and mild recession during 1930–1 and was spared the domestic financial crisis that plagued many continental societies. When Britain left the Gold Standard in 1931 it effectively reneged on external creditors rather than its own citizens. "Much of the [growing] English middle class," Ross McKibbin observes, "and a part of the [shrinking] working class began to experience a standard of living which was not to become characteristic of the rest of Europe until after the Second World War."[103] The membership of building societies had exploded from 617,000 in 1913 to over 2 million by 1937, cash deposits surged from £82 million in 1920 to £717 million in 1938, and life insurance premiums almost trebled between 1913 and 1937.[104]

The 1931 and 1935 general elections accordingly delivered Conservative victories, and also the absorption of a significant part of the historic Liberal Party (the National Liberals) by the Tories. Conservatism thus came to represent the clear majority of society against a weakened Labour opposition, which itself supported democratic parliamentarianism. Around half of the working class voted Conservative during the 1930s. Among them were many Protestants in industrialized northwest England and industrial Scotland who were steered in that direction, McKibbin argues, by anti-Irish immigrant feeling, for the Irish vote was closely associated with the Labour Party.[105] Unpleasant as such sectarianism may have been it at least served to create a balance of political forces that the middle classes found reassuring. Nothing suggested that the working classes collectively posed any real threat to their interests – the British Communist Party, largely concentrated in London and the Scottish Central Belt, was only a few thousand strong at the height of the Great Depression[106] – so rendering the appeal to bourgeois Britain of fascism or any of its imitators very limited.

The British seemed to prefer to read about extremist solutions elsewhere from the armchaired safety of their living rooms, with Hitler's *Mein Kampf* selling over 89,000 copies in Britain by the end of 1938,[107] and with many Soviet-leaning publications emanating from the Left Book Club, founded by Victor Gollancz in 1936.

That said, fringe fascist movements had existed since the early 1920s and in 1932, during the Great Depression, a more significant fascist organization was founded. Led by a former Labour Member of Parliament, Sir Oswald Mosley, this British Union of Fascists (BUF) claimed that the national discipline and cultural dynamism of Italian-style fascism offered an escape from the alleged "decadence" of parliamentary democracy. Mosley was converted to fascism after a visit to Italy and offered supporters an eclectic mix of economic modernization (including equal pay for women), imperialism (which he saw as a force for global modernization), and political authoritarianism. British fascism adopted familiar facets of continental fascism. Mosley claimed the role of "Leader," the party used the stretched, raised arm salute, created a uniformed paramilitary wing, the Blackshirts, and took over the bundled twig emblem, the *fasces*, directly from Italy. The BUF's membership grew briefly to some 50,000.

In October 1934 Mosley also embraced anti-Semitism and began to identify with Hitler as the Blackshirts became embroiled in street brawls, notably in the East End of London, with left-wing groups. "The Jews as a whole," Mosley opined, "have chosen to organize themselves as a nation within the Nation and to set their interests before those of Great Britain." They were therefore to be excluded from public office, for "anyone in the service of the State under Fascism must be entirely British."[108] However, the apparent parallels with Hitler and Nazism (in early 1936 Mosley renamed the BUF the British Union of Fascists and National Socialists) served to repel public opinion and trigger official countermeasures. Following particularly violent street fighting during autumn 1936 parliament granted the police additional powers to deal with Blackshirt and other excesses in early 1937. Although the BUF managed to poll well in the East End in the March 1937 London County Council elections, its support in the rest of Britain was insignificant. "In England," Stanley Payne concludes, "it was not the Jews but the fascists who were destined for the ghetto, never escaping total insignificance."[109] A political and moral consensus founded on the legitimacy of parliamentary government characterized the British experience and in 1939, with the outbreak of war, the BUF was wound up. Mosley was interned despite his protestations of patriotic loyalty.

The Irish Republic saw the brief emergence in 1932–3 of a potentially fascist war veterans' grouping, the National Guard or Blue Shirts, led by the former police chief Eoin O'Duffy. However, the Blue Shirts were quickly absorbed by the Catholic, conservative and parliamentary Fine Gael Party and O'Duffy himself retired from politics in 1937. On the northwest of the continent, however, democracies faced more substantial challenges, the nature of which varied from country to country.

The Low Countries

In Belgium and the Netherlands, Martin Conway and Peter Romijn argue, it was not so much the absence of conflict that barred political extremism, but the way these societies mediated difference:

The relative absence of revolution, of mass movements of the extremes of left and right and of civil war was not the consequence of a failure of collective will or political imagination. It reflected the way that Belgium and the Netherlands developed political systems in which compromise rather than conflict was the defining characteristic.[110]

Belgian politics was fragmented into Catholic, Liberal and Socialist camps, each with its network of associations within which citizens organized significant elements of their daily lives, but none of these distinctive milieus sought to eradicate any other. Instead it was a question of securing one's own patch within a multifaceted society. Liberal/Catholic coalitions dominated government, with short-lived Socialist participation during the mid-1920s and 1930s.

A Communist oppositional movement was strengthened by the effects of the Great Depression, but the main challenges to established politics came from a growing Flemish nationalist movement in the north of the country and the advocates of a new Catholic social and political order, based in the Francophone south. The Vlaams National Verbond (VNV or Flemish National Federation) became a significant minority force, gaining over 15 percent of the Flemish vote by 1937; but it espoused conservative Catholic rather than fascist values. Its main objective was to secure greater rights for Belgium's (then narrow) Flemish majority in a society where French speakers dominated political and institutional life, making Francophobia rather than anti-Semitism its hallmark. As its newspaper, *Het Vlaamsche Volk*, declared in 1934: "As Germanics we Flemings belong to the spiritual Germanic front in the West. ... If we do not wish to be annihilated by the French robbers of land we must, in our centuries old struggle, more than ever seek the support of Germany.[111]

In the French-speaking south Léon Degrelle formed a radical nationalist force, Christus Rex, which launched its manifesto in February 1936. Catholicism and paternalism defined Degrelle's movement. As a student he had received a Jesuit education in Namur, which brought him into contact with the ideas of the French Catholic-monarchist organization Action Française and so the writing of its leader, Charles Maurras. After entering politics Degrelle rounded on Communism, but also on financial scandal within Belgium's francophone Catholic establishment. The banks were to be properly regulated and corrupt dealings in parliament quashed by transferring some of its powers to the King and using referendums to allow people a direct voice in government. After sweeping gains in French-speaking areas in the May 1936 elections Degrelle was received by King Leopold II, to whom he explained that he wanted "power, all power, and not a ministerial post ... either for himself or for some of his lieutenants."[112] Mass meetings followed in early 1937 at which Degrelle, perhaps fatefully, lauded Hitler: "He has remained thoroughly one of the 'people.' He lives more frugally than any workman: never any meat; vegetables and water. ... Simplicity and courage, that is what the people love."[113] However, his decline was as swift as his rise. In March 1937 he staged a parliamentary by-election contest against the incumbent Prime Minister, Paul van Zeeland, who defeated him roundly with strong support from the established church. Rex imploded before the German invasion of May 1940 offered Degrelle a second chance. He moved to remodel his movement on more fascist lines and later raised a Walloon (Belgian French) SS division to fight on the Eastern Front.

Politics in the Netherlands differed from the/politics of Belgium in some key regards. Belgium was linguistically divided, the Netherlands (*pace* the Frisians) was not. The Netherlands was divided between a Protestant majority and a large Catholic minority, Belgium was Catholic. Belgium had a sizeable heavy industrial working class, in the Sambre-Meuse Valley, but the more socially complex Netherlands did not. Dutch politics reflected the country's confessional divide, although the Socialists cut across this religious division. However, like Belgium, the Netherlands had developed a style of politics based around milieus and the respective tolerance of each such milieu for the others. Universal adult suffrage, male and female, was granted in 1919 and a proportional representation system introduced that underpinned the strength of the milieu-based parties. Characterized as "consensual rule" within "ideologically defined compartments," Dutch society was so constituted that: "At the level of daily life, belonging to a 'pillar' [or milieu] decided which baker and grocer a family would use, which school, trade union, or newspaper they would choose, or which party they would vote for."[114]

Such a system, bourgeois and founded on the rule of law, was infertile ground for political extremism. However, the Great Depression undermined income from international trade and further reduced agricultural earnings already compromised by falling international price levels. Italian-influenced right-radical parties emerged, as did a pro-Moscow Communist Party, but these extremists served to rally and unify the political mainstream rather than undermine it. The Dutch National Socialists (NSB), founded in 1931 by a civil servant, Anton Mussert, initially declared that "every good Dutch Jew is welcome in our party,"[115] but soon abandoned this tolerant stance. During the mid-1930s Mussert and his followers turned toward Nazi Germany for inspiration and so alienated the electorate. After peaking at 8 percent of the vote in the 1935 provincial elections, the NSB lost ground in 1937 and all but disappeared in 1939.

As in Belgium, it took the German invasion of 1940 to rekindle the fortunes of the radical right. Mussert was appointed titular "Leader of the Netherlands People" in December 1942 by the ruling German National Commissioner, Arthur Seyss-Inquart, but it was his radical deputy, Rost van Tonningen, and his followers who picked up the lion's share of the spoils. Van Tonningen advocated union with Germany and extreme racialist policies and by 1943 the NSB played a prominent part in local government. It presided over a society which came, in Stanley Payne's estimation, to display "a greater degree of collaboration, and even partial fascistization, than in the rest of Western Europe."[116] Ethnic, linguistic and cultural affinities with Germany had partially overridden traditional Dutch civic values and contributed, Payne concludes, to the relatively successful recruitment of

Dutch volunteers for the Waffen SS, some 17,000 in all. The reckoning for these National Socialists was harsh once the war ended; 120,000 were arrested and Mussert faced execution in a country where Germanophilia was henceforth in extremely short supply.

Scandinavia

Scandinavia had escaped involvement in the First World War, with the exception of Finland which entered the conflict as a Grand Duchy within the Russian Empire and emerged as a sovereign state after a short sharp involvement in the Russian Revolution. Even before the Revolution Finnish agents had enlisted Berlin's support for their country's independence and some 2,000 Finnish volunteers fought on the German side against Russia. This Finnish battalion later formed the nucleus of the Finnish national army, which consequently drew heavily on German military tradition. The Red forces within Finland were crushed by the arrival of German troops and by an indigenous White army led by Baron Carl Gustav Mannerheim, although communism did not disappear altogether. In late 1918 radicals broke away from the Socialists to form a new Communist Party which in 1920 gained control of the trade unions. Polling 14.8 percent in the 1922 elections, the Communists thereafter faced government repression and, eventually, prohibition.

The Treaty of Brest-Litovsk between Germany and the Soviet Union (March 1918) confirmed Finland's independence. It was subsequently upheld by the Allies at the Paris Peace Conference, and in 1920 a formal peace treaty was concluded with the Soviet Union. The language question might have proven fractious, given the existence of a Swedish-speaking minority settled along Finland's southern and southwestern coastline and on the Åland Islands (lying between southern Finland and Sweden), but on the whole was not. The Finnish constitution recognized the status of Swedish alongside the majority Finnish language and both groups identified themselves as Finnish nationals. The new political system was dominated by a strong presidency, but also possessed a parliament with blocking powers. Agrarian politics were powerful, as elsewhere around the Baltic, and in common with the rest of Scandinavia Finland possessed a strong Social Democratic Party.

However, there was also an influential paramilitary organization, which grew out of the White civil war units, named the Civil Guards. Strongly anti-Communist, these Guards were complemented in late 1929 by the civilian Lapua Movement and in 1930 this wider coalition pressurized parliament into banning the Communists altogether. Thereafter Lapua turned on parliamentarianism and social pluralism: "It's leaders," Francis Carsten once observed, "declared that no one would weep at the parties' grave; the power of the trade unions must be destroyed, the expenditure on social legislation and public education be reduced, and equal voting be abolished."[117]

However, while the far right could gain popular support on an anti-Communist ticket, it had less appeal as an antidemocratic movement. Its hostility to the Swedish language and its foreign policy agenda of conquering Estonia and the eastern,

Soviet part of the Karelian Peninsula alarmed the sober minded, and the Swedish Finns. As its support declined it resorted in 1932 to an antidemocratic coup, but this was botched and saw it marginalized. Although it reconstituted itself as the People's Patriotic Movement (IKL), the radical right was only able to win 8.3 percent of the vote in the 1936 elections and declined thereafter. Mainstream politics took a different path as, in 1937, the Socialists finally entered government in coalition with the agrarians. It was to be a united and patriotic democratic society that resisted and bloodied the invading Soviet army in 1940 before entering an alliance of convenience with the Third Reich in 1941, which saw dreams of a Greater Finland enjoy a brief revival.

The rest of mainland Scandinavia consisted of kingdoms which had experienced a convoluted relationship with one another over the centuries as boundaries changed and countries merged and separated periodically. Between the wars Iceland and the Faroes remained autonomous Danish dependencies, before Iceland took the chance during the Second World War to snatch its independence. If Scandinavia's identity was beyond question, the stability and effectiveness of its parliamentary democracies were not. The region's economies depended heavily on agriculture, but even before the Great Depression were suffering from the global fall in primary product prices. Prices fell further during the Depression and export volumes collapsed, leaving unstable minority governments exposed "to a number of voices calling for a more extreme response."[118]

In fact, each society responded during early 1933 in a manner diametrically opposed to contemporaneous events in Germany. Relations between the Agrarians and Social Democrats, the latter representing many workers in the towns and in agricultural processing industries, had long been fraught, but both camps prioritized the maintenance of parliamentary democracy over the promotion of conflicting social agendas. In January 1933 Denmark's Agrarians and Social Democrats forged a coalition, the Kanslergade Agreement, which included an interventionist social and economic program. The currency was devalued and agricultural prices underpinned to boost the farming sector, while the Social Democrats' constituents benefited from unemployment and social benefits as the first stage of an enduring commitment to universal public welfare. Swedish politicians struck a similar deal in May for similar reasons and with similar outcomes. Welfare reforms were universal rather than targeted specifically at the working class and served to underpin a reinvigorated democratic order, and reflationary economic policies, driven by the Social Democratic Finance Minister, Ernst Wigforss, also contributed to material and political recovery. Only Norway toyed briefly with a radically different solution, a National Bloc comprising the Agrarians and the fascist National Unity Party, before the Swedish example encouraged a "Red–Green" alliance comparable to that elsewhere on Scandinavia. These deals, and not the Second World War, have been seen as the watershed in twentieth-century Scandinavian history,[119] despite the varying and sometimes traumatic experiences of the region between 1940 and 1945.

Switzerland

Switzerland avoided both wars, even if it profited economically during each, providing its neighbors with food, armaments and banking services with few, if any, questions asked. Given its commitment to universal male military service and its exceptionally mountainous terrain, its usefulness as a neutral by far outweighed the problems of invasion and conquest. Unlike its larger French, Italian, and Nazi German neighbors, Switzerland was theoretically a confederation of autonomous statelets (cantons) bound together by voluntary oath (*Eidgenossenschaft*). In practice, however, the central government in Bern had become sufficiently powerful to leave the country a loose federation rather than a confederacy. Following a brief civil war in 1847 between Catholic particularists, stressing the rights of the Catholic cantons, and Protestant-led federalists, Switzerland was endowed in 1848 with a common citizenship, common civil liberties and a single tariff regime and currency. The federal parliament was elected by universal male suffrage and great issues of the day could also be resolved nationally by referendum. Nonetheless, each canton possessed an elected parliament and some practiced forms of direct democracy, whether by referendum or even a public show of hands in town squares.

Practically every Swiss citizen was clear that he (women did not have the vote) wished to be Swiss and not German, French or Italian, but that apart it was a country where extreme diversity held sway. During the First World War the Swiss Germans tended to sympathize with Germany itself, the Swiss French with France. However, the coming of Fascism in Italy and then Nazism in Germany reinforced the country's sense of common identity and ethos. Fascist Italy openly canvassed the notion of annexing the Italian-speaking Ticino to Italy proper, so alarming Italian-speaking Swiss, while the totalitarian, racialist values of the Third Reich alienated German speakers. As the prominent newspaper *Neue Zürcher Zeitung* remarked in December 1938:

> For the very reason that we reject the concept of race or common descent as the basis of a state and as the factor determining political frontiers, we gain the liberty and the strength to remain conscious of our cultural ties with the three great civilizations. The Swiss national idea is not based upon race or biological factors, it rests upon a spiritual decision.[120]

Only in the Schaffhausen district in the far north of the country did the proto-fascist National Front manage to gain significant support, peaking at 27 percent in 1933 elections.[121]

Most of the Swiss (almost 70 percent) spoke a variety of German dialects and used standard German in written communication, but a large minority around Geneva, Lausanne, in the western Valais, and the southern Jura spoke French (19 percent), and most of the remainder, living south of the Alpine watershed in Ticino, spoke Italian. A 40,000-strong minority in the southeastern Graubünden canton spoke a language descended from Latin, Romansch, which became the country's fourth official language in 1938. Apart from Biel/Bienne and Fribourg/Freiburg, few towns were bilingual. The change from one language to another was abrupt. Leaving the station platform in the Valais/Wallis town of Sierre/Siders a train travelling east was almost instantly in a German-speaking world. Leaving to the west the world was French-speaking. Religious communities were also sharply defined – Catholic and Protestant, and within the latter community Calvinist, Lutheran and Zwinglian – even if urbanization had blurred things somewhat. Some cantons were relatively liberal, others deeply traditional, all of this confirming the capacity of nationalism to gel around the concept of a "freedom from unfreedom" that celebrated diversity, rather than around the various homogenizing versions of nationhood to be found across much of Europe.

France

Before 1870 France had experienced two brief republican episodes, in the 1790s and during the 1848 Revolution, but monarchy and Bonapartist Empire had characterized its history. Received wisdom in Britain during the 1850s defined its neighbor as authoritarian by disposition, inclined toward despotism (benevolent or otherwise) rather than toward liberty. The second Bonapartist Empire, of Napoleon III, collapsed on the battlefields of the 1870 Franco-Prussian war, out of which defeat emerged the Third Republic. Like its later Weimar cousin it initially had something of a provisional air. Born of defeat, it was embroiled immediately in a bitter and bloody civil war as Paris rose in protest against the nation's military humiliation. The government, monarchist by inclination, fled to Versailles from where it assembled sufficient military forces to retake the capital from the "Commune" in a savage assault that saw prisoners executed in their thousands. However, unlike Weimar, the Third Republic survived. An initial standoff between supporters of the two royal houses, Orléanist and Bourbon, a botched monarchist-backed attempt at a coup d'état by a military strongman turned politician, Georges Boulanger, in 1889 and the long-running Dreyfus scandal punctuated the rocky road toward political and constitutional equilibrium of a sort.

   Alfred Dreyfus, a captain on the French General Staff, was accused in 1893 of betraying military secrets to the Germans, court-martialed, and sent to the South American penal colony of Devil's Island. There it might have rested, but Dreyfus was Jewish (and Alsatian born) and anti-Semitism had come to serve as a shorthand for antimodernism in France just as in neighboring Germany. As the influential leader of the monarchist movement Action Française, Charles Maurras, declared: "All that threaten[s] France … is 'Jewish.' 'Jewish' means rotten, foreign, democratic, libertarian, anti-clerical, anti-militarist, Marxist."[122] Catholic, monarchist opinion was happy to instrumentalize this anti-Semitism as a weapon against the Third Republic and in defense of the army, which was perceived as the true France's final hope. Most French voters, however, perceived France differently and if the army continued to be held in high esteem, post-1880 elections delivered republican and secularist parliamentary majorities. The clergy was excluded from state education and the wider civil administration became increasingly closed to aristocratic and high bourgeois Catholic-monarchist sympathizers, leaving an army career, de la Gorce observes, as their one remaining option for advancement in the public service.[123] Hence the sensitivity of the Dreyfus affair, which represented a final effort by the beleaguered monarchists to assert their values against those of the republicans.

Dreyfus's wife and brother were convinced of his innocence and fought for his release, and during 1897–8 it became clear that the evidence used to convict the Captain was doctored. As the scandal grew the republican majority resolved to wind up the "Dreyfus Affair" on its own terms, and despite further prevarication by the army Dreyfus was finally acquitted in 1906. The civil authorities moved to "republicanize" the officer corps as the monarchists were forced to concede their political impotence. Action Française, Charles Maurras acknowledged, "had ceased to be a political party," although he claimed for it a mission as bearer of "an all conquering idea."[124] So the schism remained and it took the Great War to persuade the monarchist minority and republican majority to set aside, but not fundamentally resolve, their differences.

The Third Republic had prevailed after several stormy decades, not least because French economy and society had been spared the strains and challenges of rapid industrialization and urbanization seen elsewhere in northwestern Europe. France experienced significant economic growth and modernization from 1906 until 1930, but half of the population remained located in villages and in the countryside, and around a third still worked the land. In the economy as a whole there were as many employers as employees, leaving the industrial working class a frustrated minority in a country slow to develop a modern welfare system or to tolerate trade union activity. French society was characterized, in Maurice Larkin's words, as: "A sullen consensus of land-holding peasants and self-employed members of the middle classes. … Both were determined that their hard-won prizes should not be put at risk by over-generous attempts to better the lot of other classes."[125] With inheritance divided by law equally between eligible heirs, farm holdings became ever smaller and more fragmented, leaving productivity significantly lower than in neighboring countries and a drag on overall French growth. Contrary to received myth, France was a major importer of foodstuffs and even wine during the interwar years. This situation was compounded by a stubbornly low birth rate which also threatened permanently to jeopardize France's underlying military potential vis-à-vis its populous German neighbor.

However, France was not a poor country by any means and there is nothing to suggest that most Frenchmen were particularly distressed by this state of affairs either before or after the Second World War. As Stanley Payne concludes: "Ultimately there was little need or room for new revolutionary nationalism,"[126] or as the Swiss journalist Herbert Lüthy remarked in 1953: "What do technical achievements and social progress, efficient plumbing and lifts that work amount to in comparison with the pleasure of being an unhampered individualist?"[127]

Women were less obviously blessed, becoming legal minors with regard to property ownership upon marriage and denied the vote until 1944. Male republicans noted that many more women than men attended church and feared that the clergy influenced their wider social and political attitudes. Once enfranchised, male politicians warned, women might elect a parliament ready to reverse the secularization of the later nineteenth century and so undermine republican liberties. The church and monarchism remained linked in most people's minds. Male progressives in the lower house, the Chamber of Deputies, squared their democratic consciences by voting through female enfranchisement, safe in the knowledge that the legislation would be blocked by the Senate which had a built-in secularist-Radical majority.

The deteriorating international climate seemed to demand a stronger military, and if German women were expected to create a racially superior society, their French sisters were at least expected to produce future soldiers. Natalist legislation, encapsulated in the Code de la Famille of 1938, promoted early marriage and a high birth rate through a system of generous allowances, but how far the sexual politics of the Third Republic offended women at the time is unclear. Churchgoing traditionalists arguably perceived the situation as God-given and emphasized women's duty as mothers over any political rights. More generally, as Huguette Bouchardeau observed a generation later: "Since society wants us to be wives, mothers, lovers, self-sacrificing, soothing, useful in the home, etc. we conform. In some periods all women conform; at other times only the majority of them."[128]

All in all, the French political system had avoided systemic crisis until the mid-1930s. For sure there were 44 governments during the interwar period, many lasting a matter of weeks or months, but this was little different from the pre-1914 pattern. Furthermore, Cabinets were formed from within a stable party system, overwhelmingly republican, consisting of the Socialists (SFIO), the Radicals, Democratic Alliance, and, on the right, the Republican Federation. Consequently, the same politicians rotated office and traded favors from one Cabinet to the next. The Communists (PCF) to the left and the monarchists to the right lacked the support necessary to mount any serious challenge to the Republic, with the PCF typically holding a dozen or so seats in parliament. A French fascist movement, Le Fasceau, founded in 1925 by Georges Valois, had spluttered out by 1928. Other right-wing movements, such as the Jeunesses Patriotes (Patriotic Youth) and the veterans' association founded by François de la Rocque, the Croix de Feu (Cross of Fire), advocated traditional national values rather than the radical upheaval of Italian Fascism or Nazism.

During and after the Great Depression, however, the republican order was subjected to a series of new challenges which included variants of fascism. As we saw earlier the slump came late to France, leaving open the hope that the country would be spared the global economic carnage. In 1931, as whole communities across the Rhine faced destitution, 8 million visitors took the opportunity to visit the Colonial Exposition in the Bois de Vincennes outside Paris. France appeared prosperous and secure with its massive gold reserves, strong budget, and an empire which, with its

54 million overseas inhabitants, offered a counterweight to Germany's population. Even when depression came in 1932 and lingered through the 1930s France was never ravaged by mass unemployment. Although industry was hit very hard, the countryside (previously a drag on economic progress) now served to soften the impact of the slump. For one thing the unemployed returned from the towns and cities to farming communities where they or their relatives held pockets of land, so disguising unemployment levels, and for another the agricultural sector itself continued to expand at the same plodding rate as during the 1920s.[129]

However, leftist advances in the 1932 elections prompted a minority of middle-class voters to fear for the existing social order. Constitutional change offered these bourgeois a possible defense of privilege, but nothing prepared the political mainstream for the right-wing riots that swept Paris during February 1934. Government ministers were rumored to have links with a shady financier, Alexandre Stavisky, who fled Paris to evade the growing scandal. The police caught up with him in a chalet outside the Alpine town of Chamonix and claimed to have found him dead, a victim of suicide. Maurras, however, insisted that the police had murdered him on government orders to save compromised Radical members of the Cabinet from financial and political disgrace. Accusations multiplied in Maurras's newspaper *Action Française* before 40,000 right-wing demonstrators (but not the Croix de Feu) massed in Paris on February 6 to protest against alleged government corruption. Some became violent and as shots were fired the authorities retaliated with deadly force. Fifteen people were killed, perhaps 1,500 injured in a shambles that persuaded the republican majority that France might not, after all, be immune to the fascist wave sweeping Europe. The right-wingers were in fact a mixture of monarchists, Catholics and other traditionalists, but the effect of the Stavisky riots was, Payne argues, "to magnify French antifascism, which had been vocal and organized ever since 1923, before any fascist or even any major right-wing authoritarian force existed."[130]

The Radicals, Socialists and, remarkably, the Communists resolved to settle their differences to see off the perceived fascist threat and in April–May 1936 this Popular Front won elections that saw Léon Blum become France's first Socialist Prime Minister. The various right-wing leagues were duly banned in June 1936. However, opposition to France's modest gaggle of antirepublican outfits was all the victorious coalition had in common at a time when, fascists apart, a crisis in the public finances and the challenge of Hitler's remilitarization of the Rhineland during March pressed in on the new administration. The Communists, who remained outside the government proper, demanded rearmament to withstand Hitler, the Socialists prioritized social reform and economic reflation, while the Radicals (already divided and weakened over whether to join the Popular Front at all) wished to defend republican liberties and institutions and were very doubtful about reflationary measures such as devaluation.

To complicate matters still further, many workers occupied their workplaces before Blum formally took office on June 4. The unions were not directly involved,

Figure 6.2 A rioter throws a missile from a burning street barricade in Paris during the Stavisky riots of February 6–8, 1934.
Source: The Granger Collection/TopFoto.

but the elemental emotion underpinning the occupations demanded an official response, which on June 7 took the shape of the Matignon Agreements. A 40-hour week, a fortnight's paid annual holiday, significant pay rises and statutory collective bargaining were conceded, and ultimately combined to trigger inflation, a drop in productivity, and so a situation where the initial beneficiaries often ended up losers. The reduced working week created a shortage of skilled labor in key industrial sectors, while the millions of small employers, who often voted Radical, were saddled with increased output costs which were almost impossible to absorb. Blum's government did extend government control over the strategically vital armaments industry and railways, and in September 1936 devalued the franc in an effort to boost exports and reflate the economy. However, the costs imposed on the economy by the Matignon Agreements negated the competitive advantage of this devaluation, and by the time Blum finally left office in April 1938 industrial production had fallen by 5 percent. Germany's rose by 17 percent over the same period. To make matters worse the monied bourgeoisie, already spooked by the June 1936 strikes with their anarchist-revolutionary flavor – "the most intense period of social unrest since the days of the Paris Commune"[131] – began to spirit their assets out of France and into neighboring Switzerland to evade the impact of rising inflation. Only the peasantry came out reasonably well, for many poorer families spent their wage hikes on food and pushed up agricultural prices.

In some desperation Blum first tried in February 1937 to placate the Radicals by announcing a pause in socioeconomic reform, and then in June sought vainly to obtain decree powers over the economy from the Senate. In the face of refusal he resigned, returned in March 1938 after an interregnum by the Radical Camille Chautemps (who devalued the franc yet again), but finally stood down in April. The Popular Front era was over, replaced by a Radical-led government under Édouard Daladier which set a more conservative tone, even if many of Blum's reforms remained in place. The Popular Front had failed to transform France fundamentally, but its supporters perceived its demise as a heroic defeat. "In the rich mythology of the French left," Julian Jackson writes, "nothing succeeds like failure."[132]

Meanwhile, new right-wing and nationalist groups sprang up after the banning in 1936 of the various leagues. François de la Rocque relaunched the Croix de Feu as a conventional party, the Parti Social Français, which signed up 1 million members and established a presence in local government. It continued to advocate traditional values rather than looking directly to fascism, and in 1940, after a brief flirtation with the Vichy state, de la Rocque joined the resistance. Of the other organizations, the Francistes were the most categorically fascist, but were numerically weak. Jacques Doriot's Parti Populaire Français (PPF), which recruited 100,000 members, embraced militaristic values, forged links with various fascist parties elsewhere in Europe and claimed a place for France in a new, fascist Europe. However, Doriot failed in his efforts to create a powerful right-wing coalition and indeed no single nationalist or fascist grouping came to dominate the antirepublican right. The PPF was in decline by the time war broke out in 1939 and it took the defeat of 1940 to revive its fortunes.

In more general terms, the outbreak of the Spanish Civil War did nothing to calm the political mood, even if the French state followed the British lead and remained a relatively passive bystander. The Popular Front parties inclined toward the republicans and the political right to Franco's nationalists as the Spanish civil war transmogrified into a proxy struggle between European socialism and fascism. The slogan "better Hitler than Blum" was already doing the rounds in right-wing circles and, as Joan Tumblety notes, this mentality informed even the republican right.[133]

Debate has raged between historians over whether the French Third Republic was already fatally compromised by its economic and political difficulties before the German attack in May 1940 delivered a military defeat. "It may be said ..." Tom Kemp concludes, "that the French economy suffered a continuous relative as well as absolute decline which further undermined confidence and prepared the way for the Armistice of 1940."[134] Tumblety notes that the fall of the Popular Front government in 1938 did defuse some of the angst of the republican right, but for many the Communists at home remained a more immediate enemy than Hitler across the Rhine, with whom a deal might always be possible. For some the 1938 Munich Agreement with Hitler, which saw the Sudetenland transferred peremptorily from Czechoslovakia to Germany, appeared to offer such a prospect.[135] However, as Peter Jackson reminds us, Daladier's government presided over something of a financial and economic recovery during late 1938 and early 1939, which greatly enhanced France's capacity to rearm and even contemplate a long war against Germany with growing confidence.[136] We shall return to the traumatic events of May–June 1940 in due course.

6.4.2   Nationalists, Fascists, and Bolsheviks

Iberia

Interwar Portugal displayed many of the characteristics of a Third World society. Some two-thirds of the population was illiterate and most scratched a living on tiny landholdings, often of a hectare or less. There was little industry beyond a rudimentary textiles sector and the country struggled to earn export revenues from agricultural products and fishing. Unlike Spain, Portugal fought in the First World War, on the Allied side, and ruined its public finances for its trouble. Inflation undermined living standards and triggered labor unrest.

Political life was predictably volatile. The monarchy had been toppled in 1910, to be replaced by a secular republican order in 1911, but the military and clergy had little time for the new republic. The army launched a series of coups which culminated in May 1926 with the seizure of power by General António Carmona, who was effectively the military dictator of Portugal until 1932. After this he continued to serve as a figurehead president, but real power lay with António de Oliveira Salazar. A trained economist, Salazar became Finance Minister in 1928 and Prime Minister in 1932, before pushing through major constitutional reforms in 1933. The New State (*Estado Novo*) was essentially corporatist and authoritarian, resting on military power and a security police force, the PIDE. However, alongside a corporative chamber to represent economic and social interests, a weak, directly elected National Assembly was retained and Salazar eschewed the cult of personality characteristic of fascist and Bolshevik regimes.

In fact, far from promoting fascism Salazar's regime arguably acted as a barrier against it. A National Syndicalist movement, which openly promoted fascist values, attracted some support from the working and lower middle classes (Salazar's supporters were more patrician), but was suppressed by the authorities in 1934 on the grounds of its fascistic "exploitation of youth, the cult of force through so-called direct action, the principle of the superiority of state political power in social life, the propensity for organizing masses behind a single leader."[137] Instead, Frances Lannon notes, Salazar sustained his rule through a precarious balancing of key interest groups within Portuguese society,[138] despite his regime's coercive traits and later promotion of a fascist-style militia.

As for its social impact, Derek Aldcroft observes that Salazar's economic policies were partially successful. Heavy-handed state regulation did the economy few favors, but Salazar maintained a balanced budget, achieved balance of payments surpluses and managed to foster modest industrial development through a policy of import substitution. All in all Portuguese growth outpaced that of its Spanish neighbor between 1913 and 1938, leaving it wealthier than Spain (which was scourged by civil war from 1936). However, Portugal remained poor by European standards and continued to be dogged by a chronically backward agricultural sector.[139]

Spain stayed out of the First World War, but was profoundly affected by it nonetheless. Its industrial sector, based largely in the north of the country, was boosted by orders from the Allied powers and also from countries formerly supplied by Britain, France and Germany. The coal mines of Asturias, the Basque metallurgical and engineering industries, and the Catalan textiles industry expanded and attracted labor from the countryside, so swelling the potential of the trade unions, both socialist (UGT) and anarcho-syndicalist (CGT). However, this hothouse-like wartime boom fueled inflation and so reduced real wages, which prompted the unions to stage a series of strikes. Some were suppressed with military force, setting a precedent for the postwar years when social and political tensions constantly threatened to boil over. There was also unrest in the south where agriculture was dominated by large estates, often with absentee landlords. Grindingly poor landless laborers toiled for a pittance or, frequently, found themselves unemployed. Despite profitable wartime trade with the Allies, the landlords rather than their laborers benefited, leaving the land question a running political sore. In northern Spain the peasantry owned their holdings, but struggled to make a living from tiny parcels of land.

In Joseph Harrison's estimation the state failed to address these challenges[140] and the same could be said of the country's industrial and agricultural magnates. Furthermore, in Catalonia and the Basque Country powerful nationalist movements flexed their muscles, but Madrid was unwilling to make cultural or political concessions. In this brooding standoff between stasis and change, Frances Lannon remarks, "the fundamental agenda … was social revolution and how to avoid it,"[141] which afforded the army a pivotal role in Spain's domestic affairs. The army had concerns of its own, demanding improved pay and more rapid promotion, which only strengthened its negative perception of civilian government. On September 13, 1923 a military coup established a dictatorship led by General Miguel Primo de Rivera.

The monarchy remained, as did many of the country's traditional institutions, and as Fontana and Nadel once observed: "The regime never attempted a mobilisation of the masses of a fascist type. It was a regime of landowners, of order-loving people and small gentry, which would follow a policy of pure conservatism, varied with flashes of enlightened paternalism."[142] Accordingly the government steered an "eclectic and pragmatic" course in an effort to uphold the existing social order.[143] Primo de Rivera's regime addressed domestic workplace tensions by introducing arbitration procedures in 1926 (the Labor Code) which recognized the Socialists as negotiating partners but cracked down on the anarchists. Public works and a generous welfare policy were promoted and efforts were made to develop tourism through converting historic buildings into reasonably priced hotels – the Paradors.

Soon enough, however, the dictatorship came up against its limitations. Primo de Rivera did finally win a drawn-out colonial struggle against partisan forces in

Spanish Morocco in 1925 and achieved rapid economic growth at home. However, there were no significant productivity gains, either in the expanding industrial sector or in the chronically backward agricultural sector, leaving people no wealthier at the end of the day. Trade policy vacillated inconclusively between efforts to protect home industries through import substitution and the promotion of export-led growth. The government was also living beyond its means, with tax receipts inadequate to prevent an ever worsening budget deficit.

There was also the question of Spain's constitutional future. By 1925 the worst of the postwar instability was over, offering Spain a priceless opportunity finally to establish a stable democratic order. Thus Stanley Payne argues: "Had Primo de Rivera stepped down in 1926 … a democratized constitutional monarchy could have maintained the continuity of institutions that was probably necessary for a new system of democracy to succeed."[144] However, rather than returning power to parliament under the monarchy, Primo de Rivera now sought to introduce a more authoritarian political order and remained in office until his erstwhile supporters in the army came to doubt the sustainability of his regime. In January 1930 he resigned.

King Alfonso XIII was already politically compromised by his tacit support for Primo de Rivera, and months of prevarication following the general's resignation only served to heighten tensions. The authorities hesitated to call a national election, but their decision to allow municipal elections in April 1931 proved every bit as fatal to the old order. A republican-socialist coalition triumphed, triggered the abdication of King Alfonso and thereafter the proclamation of the Second Spanish Republic. The Socialists and Radicals agreed a new constitution which reflected the more modern side of Spain's Janus-faced society. Although agriculture remained the largest single sector, the industrial and service sectors together employed some 55 percent of the population, female employment had increased significantly, and access to university education saw a growing minority of women enter the professions. The constitution granted employees a minimum wage and the eight-hour day and women were legally emancipated. The Republic also conceded a degree of autonomy to Catalonia and the Basque Country, although the resulting practicalities continued to be disputed until the Republic's defeat in the civil war reimposed central control.

However, these changes failed to reconcile the new Spain with the old and this deficiency was soon to prove fatal to the republican order. The Republic struggled to deliver meaningful land reform in the face of landowner hostility, while its assault on the entrenched powers of the church, which republicans perceived as a bulwark of traditional privilege, effectively discriminated against Spain's many practicing Catholics. The resulting battle between secularism and Catholicism assumed a religious and elemental intensity of its own as republicans, in Payne's words, displayed "extreme intolerance and a desire for domination, which might be expected to stimulate an equivalent response in Catholics."[145]

The Republic held its first parliamentary elections in November 1933. A coalition of left-wing Radicals and Socialists, led by Manuel Azaña, had governed the country since 1931, but by 1933 had made enemies on the political right in particular. The latter, strongly Catholic, had stood aside in 1931 as the Republic displaced the monarchy, but soon became alarmed by the secularist left's presumption that it alone possessed the moral right to govern. A wave of antireligious violence heightened these fears when, in May 1931, republican activists torched dozens of churches and other religious buildings in an orgy of material and cultural destruction. The right regrouped and formed a new political alliance, the explicitly Catholic CEDA (Spanish Confederation of Autonomous Rightist Groups).

A violent election campaign saw CEDA and the moderate republican Radicals triumph over the Socialists and a left republican rump. CEDA had narrowly outpolled the moderate Radicals, but the creation of a governing coalition was less straightforward. Many within CEDA made no secret of their monarchist sympathies and most hoped to reform the constitution on corporatist, Catholic lines. CEDA was prepared to play by the existing constitutional rules for the time being, but the republican left understandably regarded it as a threat to the Republic. The Spanish President, Alcalá Zamora, shared these doubts and blocked any participation by CEDA in government. An unstable, Radical-led minority government took office, but even this arrangement proved unacceptable to the political left.

Beyond its fears for the constitution the left had simply refused to come to terms with its defeat. Instead, even before the second round of voting was over, the left's leaders pressed unsuccessfully for an annulment of the election.

> This whole dismal maneuver [Payne concludes] revealed what had become the permanent position of the left under the Republic: they would accept only the permanent government of the left. ... From this time forward the left would flout legality ever more systematically, eventually reducing the legal order to shambles and setting the stage for civil war.[146]

In other words, the rightist rebellion of 1936 which triggered the civil war was far from unprovoked.

The first left-inspired violence came within days as the anarchist trade union, the CNT, staged an abortive rising against the new government during December 1933. More serious trouble followed in 1934. The Socialists had reacted to electoral defeat by adopting a revolutionary stance, which included the somewhat hysterical branding of CEDA as a proto-fascist party. Thus, when the President finally bowed to electoral logic in October by admitting three CEDA ministers to the governing coalition, the left rose in revolt. The authorities on the spot dealt with the trouble in most parts of Spain, but the revolutionaries did secure the coalfields of Asturias. The government deployed the army, including battle-hardened troops from Spanish Morocco under the command of General Francisco Franco, who crushed the rising with considerable brutality.

Franco was appointed Army Chief of Staff in the following year, while the main parties became increasingly estranged from one another even as they fragmented internally. A number of financial scandals rocked the Radicals, and President Zamora meddled in routine political procedure to the point, Payne concludes, where "his constant interference made normal parliamentary and constitutional functioning impossible."[147] Sorely provoked by the dysfunctionality of the Republic, CEDA finally broached the notion of a coup with Franco.

Zamora called fresh elections for February 1936, by which time the left had reorganized and regrouped. In partial reflection of events in France, the small Communist Party acted on Comintern instructions to form an antifascist Popular Front with the Socialists, the left Radicals and other leftist organizations. In Spain, however, Comintern sought to revolutionize politics and society rather than to uphold the existing order, as in France. The elections saw the Popular Front parties take over 47 percent of the vote, against almost 46 percent for the right, although the complex alliances that fought the election preclude any precise calculation.[148] Whatever the case, Spain was clearly split down the middle and the Popular Front had fallen short of an absolute majority of the votes cast. Nonetheless its supporters interpreted the result as "an absolute mandate to work their will on Spain,"[149] and took to the streets to press their claim. Franco urged the authorities to impose martial law, but instead the defeated center-right government hurriedly surrendered power to the left even before the election results had been validated.

The turmoil was trying the patience of army chiefs, but open rebellion was slow in coming. Republicans had been suspicious of the military from the outset, but Spain's soldiers lacked the will or unity of outlook to act on their own volition. Franco understood this, but by April 1936 a conspiracy of sorts began to gel around the person of Brigadier General Emilio Mola and the proto-fascist paramilitary Falange organization. The plotters still lacked real momentum and as late as June 23 Franco wrote to the Prime Minister, Casares Quiroga, from his new command in the Canaries, pledging the army's loyalty but urging the government to restore law and order and show the military due respect.

Meanwhile, the political mood became ever more inflamed. Armed clashes and tit-for-tat killings between Falangists and left-wing militia culminated in the murder by leftists on July 13 of the prominent monarchist politician Calvo Sotelo. The republican government appeared indifferent, more or less daring the right to do its worst while seeking to rally and strengthen the forces of the left. Finally, on July 17, 1936, Mola responded to this atmosphere of incipient civil war, giving the nod to the army in Morocco to launch a military coup. Rebellion followed on the mainland a day later. The rebels were only partially successful, but managed to secure the southwestern cities of Cadiz, Seville and Cordoba and much of northwestern Spain away from the industrialized coast. In September 1936 Franco was made Commander in Chief of these nationalist forces, set up a rebel government and declared himself head of state for good measure.

The republican response was initially confused. The socialist trade union, the UGT, proclaimed a general strike even as the government tried, too late, to conciliate the plotters. The Communist leader, José Diaz, appeared to inhabit a dream world, informing an increasingly incredulous Moscow that "the fascist insurrection is definitely crumbling," despite alarming evidence to the contrary.[150] However the Republic had retained control of Madrid, Barcelona and Valencia, leaving the two sides evenly matched at the outset. Around 12.3 million people, Derek Aldcroft estimates, supported the nationalists and 12.7 million the Republic. The republicans initially held the key industrial centers, but the nationalists controlled more of the productive land and food supplies.[151]

Both sides had foreign sponsors, the nationalists Italy and Germany, and the Republic the Soviet Union. Britain prevailed on France to opt for a policy of nonintervention which effectively deprived the moderate republicans of substantive international support. During the earlier stages of the war Soviet support for the Republic was decisive in halting the nationalist offensive on the outskirts of Madrid. Moscow delivered 52 shiploads of arms, including tanks and artillery, between September 1936 and September 1937, but in 1938 a mere 13 shiploads arrived. Similarly the number of Soviet military personnel in Spain dwindled from an initial 1,000 to 200 or so by January 1939.[152] The republicans could count themselves unlucky that Japan had attacked China in July 1937, for although Stalin was happy to meddle in Spanish politics Moscow accorded China higher strategic and military priority than Spain.

Hitler was less concerned about the political niceties of the Spanish civil war, instead regarding it as a welcome distraction for the international community from his own activities in central Europe.[153] From Germany's point of view the longer the struggle dragged on the better, but the rebels were nonetheless particularly fortunate that German transport planes ferried a powerful nationalist military contingent from North Africa to Seville at the beginning of the civil war. The navy remained loyal to the Republic and would have blocked any sea passage. That apart, over 5,000 German volunteers and an air squadron of 92 planes, the Condor Legion, represented Berlin's contribution to the war. Franco's request for an entire German army division was turned down.

Mussolini was more supportive of the rebels, for he regarded a nationalist victory as essential to his own strategic and political ambitions in the western Mediterranean. Seventy thousand Italian troops backed by artillery and air support bolstered the nationalist effort in a war which Rome hoped to conclude sooner rather than later. During the summer of 1937 Italian submarines attacked and sank Soviet and republican shipping, and if Franco's campaign proved more protracted than Mussolini had hoped, the nationalist victory was also his own.

Spain's outstanding cultural heritage and also its vibrant contemporary cultural life became entangled in the conflict, perceived as a struggle between tradition and modernity. Both sides in the civil war saw art "as an essential part of the larger battle" and the Republic's Director General of Fine Art, Josep Renau (himself the creator of a series of republican war posters), reflected that: "Since the first moments of the civil war, the fate of the historical and artistic heritage of Spain has had a profound effect on worldwide public opinion."[154] It was no coincidence that the 40,000 foreign volunteers who fought for the Republic included "more arty types than it knew what to do with."[155] Their output, literary and visual, mobilized widespread international sympathy for the republican cause both during and after the conflict.

Among the Republic's indigenous adherents was Luis Buñuel, whose first film, *Un Chien andalou* (An Andalusian dog), was made in collaboration with Salvador Dali and released in France in 1929. Sixteen minutes long, the film lacked a coherent plot, instead presenting a temporally disjointed and graphic depiction of marital violence and infidelity. This exercise in surrealism was followed in 1932 by a savage denunciation of poverty in the agrarian south of Spain, *Tierra sin pan* (Land without bread). The Catalan artists Joan Miró and Pablo Picasso, although (and perhaps tellingly) resident in Paris, also lent the Republic vociferous support, producing a series of paintings and posters during the war years and contributing to the Republic's pavilion at the 1937 Paris International Exhibition. The pavilion was, Marko Daniel notes, entirely devoted to propaganda of an artistic and cultural nature, beginning with the building itself. It was designed by Josep Lluis Sert, a follower of Le Corbusier: "a light, unostentatious, elegant exercise in Rationalist architecture ... in marked contrast to the attention-seeking German and Soviet Pavilions that glared at each other across the approach to the Pont d'Iéna."[156] Among the paintings was Picasso's celebrated work *Guernica*, which depicted the effect of the aerial bombing of the eponymous Basque town by volunteer German airmen of the Condor Legion. Its jumbled mélange of broken, tortured human and animal bodies continues to serve as a searing condemnation of the indiscriminate destruction of modern warfare. Photography also served the Republic, with one work of photomontage depicting an oppressed woman, silent, burdened by traditional dress and religious jewelry, but alongside her a new woman in overalls, shouting out with hope and determination. A caption reads: "Upon release from her shroud of superstition and the misery of timeless slavery is born THE WOMAN capable of taking an active part in planning the future."[157] The attack on the ancient values of the church and by extension the nationalists was plain enough.

Franco, too, understood that beyond the social and political, the civil war represented a cultural struggle between a modern and a traditional Spain. Thus Lannon argues: "When Franco took up arms against the Republic, he was also taking up arms against an intellectual and artistic golden age which he abhorred and which he repudiated as alien to Spanish tradition and identity."[158] As the nationalists slowly overran Spain, thousands of Spain's cultural elite went into exile, but as we have seen, the order they supported was equally intolerant – of traditional, Catholic culture. Churches continued to be desecrated and more than 6,000 priests were murdered in a wave of revolutionary upheaval which violated the rights and liberties promoted by the European Enlightenment, whatever the views of Spanish religion itself on such liberties.

Not surprisingly, Catholic opinion regarded Franco as the lesser of two evils from the outset and in July 1937 Spain's bishops sided publicly with the nationalists. Nationalist poster art was replete with religious imagery, angels and giant crosses shown accompanying Franco's armies as they battled to deliver Spain from the unspoken horrors of international communism. In its stead the nationalists

Figure 6.3   Guernica after the bombing raid by the German Condor Legion, April 26, 1937.
Source: Ullstein Bild – Imagno.

promised a world of social harmony. A 1939 poster entitled *Never Again* was typical enough, showing a nationalist soldier, bayonet fixed to rifle, protecting a family and peaceful village from a bestial red monster, rising up over a fiery horizon.[159] The nationalists also had their equivalent of the Guernica painting in the form of Ignacio Zuloaga's *Toledo in Flames*, which depicts the destruction of one of Spain's outstanding artistic and architectural treasures during the siege of the city by republican forces. Both paintings were exhibited in London during 1937, with Zuloaga's work receiving as much attention as Picasso's.

By early 1937 the nationalists in the north and south had linked up in the west of the country, reached the outskirts of Madrid, and begun to eliminate the

Map 6.1   The Spanish Civil War 1936–1939.

republican enclave on the north coast. Bilbao fell in June and Gijon in October. Soviet support proved a mixed blessing for the Republic. Although its tanks and munitions were vital for the defense of Madrid during the 1936–7 winter, Moscow demanded its price, literally in the form of Spain's reserves of precious metal, and also politically. The Communist-backed forces crushed anarchist supporters of the Republic in a civil war within the civil war in Barcelona, and the republican government itself became molded to Soviet requirements. The more moderate (bourgeois) wing of the Popular Front coalition began to doubt the republican cause. By December 1938 the nationalists reached the Mediterranean coast between Valencia and Barcelona, so isolating Catalonia from the rest of republican Spain. In January 1939 Barcelona fell to the nationalists, followed by the remaining large cities during March. On April 1 Franco declared the war over. Around 500,000 people had died, but only 200,000 in the fighting. Murder, executions and famine had killed the majority.

At the end of the day it had proven impossible for the Spanish Republic to reconcile the seething resentment of impoverished rural society and the almost millenarian utopianism of the labor movement with an ancient moral and social order which still commanded widespread support. Franco's monument to the conflict, a huge cross erected in the Valley of the Fallen, portrayed his victory in terms of a religious redemption, nothing more, nothing less.

That said, the brutality of Franco's war and of the peace settlement that followed, his intolerance of values associated with the Republic and his sympathy for the fascist powers left his regime deeply unattractive to liberal opinion. By 1942 around 2 million people had passed through or died in the nationalist government's concentration camps, the labor movement had been suppressed, women's rights curtailed, and Catalonia and the Basque Country stripped of their autonomy. Church and property rights were restored and a policy of economic autarky initiated, which arguably compromised the country's future material development. Already severely damaged by the fighting, the economy only recovered to 1929 levels during the early 1950s. However, Franco's regime survived well beyond the Second World War. It was above all thanks to the outbreak of the Cold War that his government was able to reach an understanding with the United States during the 1950s and carry on until 1975 when, following the dictator's death, King Alfonso's grandson, Juan Carlos, took the vacant Spanish throne as head of state of a constitutional, parliamentary monarchy.

Italy

By the 1930s Italy had left the constitutional turmoil of the postwar years behind it. The Fascist state was organized on hierarchical lines, with the slogan "Mussolini ha sempre ragione" (Mussolini is always right)[160] literally chiseled onto monumental stone as an assertion of the moral claim of the Leader (*Duce*) to leadership. Success evidently got the better of him during the 1930s, as he became increasingly detached from the real world and megalomanic,[161] but his public image remained essentially positive. Even Winston Churchill lauded him in 1933 as "the greatest living legislator," and in 1934 the Broadway composer Cole Porter praised the Italian dictator in the tune "You're the Top":

> You're the top!
> You're the great Houdini!
> You're the top!
> You are Mussolini![162]

No one thought of doing the same for Hitler.

Beyond Mussolini's personal role in government, the King remained head of state and the army ultimately owed its loyalty to him rather than to the *Duce*. Fascism itself began to settle into a bureaucratic routine. The once powerful provincial party bosses, the *Ras*, had their wings clipped and the wholesale co-option of the civil service into the Fascist Party in 1935 served further to dilute the revolutionary zeal of the latter. For all his egotism, Mussolini tended to accommodate key groups in society, rather than to suppress them or shoehorn them into a Fascist mould – in sharp contrast to practice in Nazi Germany. "Consent," Mussolini acknowledged, "is as unstable as the sand formations on the edge of the sea."[163]

The Catholic Church and the state appeared to settle their longstanding differences with the signing of the Lateran Pacts in February 1929, but the honeymoon turned out to be brief. The Pacts did restore the sovereignty of the Vatican and paid compensation for the Papacy's other territorial losses during the Risorgimento – the nineteenth-century wars of Italian unification. The Church also secured a continuing role in education, which resulted in many young Italians receiving more of a Christian than a Fascist schooling. However, each side continued to pursue its own discrete interests. Fascism claimed to be a moral rather than a theological force, but moral grounds alone led to assertions of superiority over the Church. Roman Catholicism, Fascist ideologues maintained, derived its authority from its place in Italian society and the timeless values of the Roman metropolis. "The goal," Payne concludes, "clearly was to incorporate Catholicism within and under Fascism as part of a general 'religion of Italy,' in which Fascism would predominate."[164] However, the government, in Victoria de Grazia's words, was "not inclined to expend excessive energy regulating groups that posed no obvious threat to [its] rule."[165] By 1932 the Church and state had reached a second, implicit accommodation which certainly clipped the wings of the Catholic youth organization, but otherwise left the clergy free to pursue unhindered the Church's religious objectives. Catholicism played a long game, aiming at the eventual "Christian reconquest" of the Italian people from "fundamentally pagan" Fascism. The clergy was expanded and efforts made to ensure that young Italians became the next Christian rather than a Fascist generation.[166] Meanwhile, during the later 1930s, the Church became concerned by Mussolini's links with Hitler. Assets were quietly shifted abroad as the Vatican began to countenance a post-Fascist and post-Nazi world order with the United States of America at its hub.

As for the Fascist youth organizations, they eventually signed up 90 percent of male children and adolescents, but only 30 percent of their female counterparts. Even the male groups were forced to tolerate discussion critical of Fascism, which sometimes boiled over into open dissent. The Fascists may have organized most Italians in one way or another, but general Fascistization, Payne concludes, was always more appearance than reality[167] and certainly never as all-pervasive as the Nazification of German society.

The Fascist regime was able to ride out the Great Depression even if a deliberately overvalued currency and efforts to secure self-sufficiency in grain added to the severity of the slump, which saw 1 million Italians unemployed in 1933. Public finances were reasonably strong before the economic crisis, which allowed the state to underwrite the recovery. Public works were promoted and the state bought heavily into failing banks and businesses, so leaving Italy with the highest proportion of public ownership outwith the Soviet Union. Expanded armaments production boosted national output beyond pre-Depression levels by 1937 at the latest and it rose a further 20 percent by 1939, which compared favorably with the country's western, democratic neighbors. The economy also achieved striking productivity gains between 1922 and 1939, with growth at double the pace of population increase, even if wage rates were held down and welfare provision expanded relatively slowly. Italy became more urban as industrial production overtook agricultural output in 1937, the service sector expanded, and people left the countryside for the towns and cities. This migration contributed to a decline in the proportion of landless laborers in farming from 44 to 27 percent between 1921 and 1936, which was also partly the result of improved access for these laborers to land, as tenants or sharecroppers.

Fascist ideology sought to defuse the class conflict that had characterized post-1918 Italy by organizing politics and society within corporations. These associations purportedly bound the employees, managers and owners of each economic sector together in the pursuit of agreed goals and claimed to represent their interests at national level. While serving as Minister of Corporations between 1929 and 1932, Giuseppe Bottai spoke of labor and capital as "the two (reconciled) halves of a 'living organism,'"[168] but as with so much else in Fascist Italy, reality fell short of ambition or expectation. In fact the regime's new Labor and Civil Codes, which eschewed any overt Fascist agenda, proved even-handed enough to survive into the post–Second World War era, rather than its corporations.

Culture and propaganda were central to Fascist Italy. They were mobilized for party political purposes, and to instill a sense of national unity and common imperial destiny in a highly variegated society. Fascism claimed to represent a new, conformist civilization, *Romanità*, which combined the greatness and values of ancient Rome with Mussolini's new Rome, under the watchword "Believe, Obey, Fight."[169] Architectural monumentalism and large-scale murals were the most obvious artistic expression of *Romanità*. "Eternal Rome," now modern, saw its mission as the "revolutionary reformulation of western Catholic civilization,"[170] to which Moscow provided the only (undesirable) alternative.

Even so, the Fascists were prepared to tolerate a Soviet regime which, under Stalin, prioritized the building of "Socialism in One Country" rather than world revolution. Rome recognized the USSR in 1924 and Fascism was quick to borrow propaganda motifs from Soviet pageantry and art forms. The New World was equally a source of inspiration when it came to the dissemination of the political. In 1927 a team from the Fox-Movietone newsreel in the US had interviewed Mussolini and so introduced him to sound film. He was impressed: "Your talking newsreel has tremendous possibilities. Let me speak through it in twenty cities in Italy once a week and I need no other power."[171] The press and radio were heavily regulated by the Fascist state but cinema enjoyed a freer existence, in part because a relatively independent film industry was perceived as a more effective tool of propaganda and education. The film school Centro Sperimentale di Cinematografia in Rome provided innovative theoretical and practical training of the highest quality, and Luigi Freddi, head of the General Directorate for Cinematography, was personally more interested in artistic integrity and box office success than political content. Many feature films conveyed a regime-supporting subliminal message of carefree modernity, serving as a dream factory comparable to Hollywood's role in American culture, and others evoked Italy's past and allegedly restored imperial greatness, but overt propaganda was the province of the state-controlled and highly polished newsreel *Cinegiornale*. As Lutz Becker concludes, the post-1945 Italian film industry could undoubtedly trace its roots back to the Fascist era. While most German directors were compromised by Nazism and "arrived at the end of the war burnt out and deeply disoriented ... their Italian counterparts had maintained their critical discourse ... and had preserved their integrity, their energy and the creative urge to look beyond [Fascism]."[172]

Other parts of the cultural world also maintained a degree of independence. The Milan-based Novocentro Italiano tried during the 1920s independently to create a style expressive of the new Fascist order, but its efforts fell out of official favor during the 1930s. The Futurists continued to produce modernist work influenced by a "machine aesthetic,"[173] which began with the motor car before focusing on air travel. Abstract artists attached to the Paris-based movement Abstraction-Création continued to paint and to exhibit at the Quadriennale exhibitions in Rome, but the state tended to tolerate this cultural pluralism, somewhat grudgingly, as a necessary evil. As Bottai (now Minister for Culture) reflected in 1940: "Art which is directly controlled by the State ... owing to its lack of expression, loses all its efficacy as propaganda."[174]

If cultural life enjoyed a degree of freedom, political dissidence was persecuted. Some 14,000 opponents of the regime (a low figure in comparison with the Soviet Union or Nazi Germany) were either exiled to remote corners of the country or to the islands, or imprisoned for varying lengths of time. Among them was the Marxist politician and thinker Antonio Gramsci, who died while serving a 20-year sentence, but not before penning his *Prison Notebooks* which were published posthumously and influenced postwar Socialist thinking. All in all, however, the restrained harshness of Fascism, at least within Italy's borders, pales into near insignificance when compared with the behavior of the Nazi or Soviet regimes.

Mussolini and his government were racialist from the beginning, although their primary victims were beyond metropolitan Italy's shores and borders – Jugoslavs living in territory claimed by Rome, and the native peoples of Italy's African Empire who were treated with considerable brutality. Mussolini also shared a north Italian prejudice against the "backward" south of the country – variously written off as "Arab" or "African." Naples, he complained, was "feckless and unmodern" and perhaps deserving of some kind of purge,[175] but barbarity of this sort never transpired in reality. Anti-Semitism came later as Italy fell increasingly within Germany's orbit during the late 1930s and a minority of intellectuals embraced Nazi notions of biological racism. Efforts were made to characterize Italians as the original master race, leaving the country's well-integrated, 47,000-strong Jewish minority increasingly vulnerable. Many Italian Jews had been tolerant or even supportive of Fascism, but a purge of Jewish public servants began in September 1938 and racial legislation, reminiscent of the Nuremberg Laws, followed.

However, this law's bark was much worse than its bite. An acid test of Italian attitudes to annihilationist anti-Semitism came in early 1943 as the German and Vichy authorities stepped up efforts across France to transport Jews – refugees and French nationals alike – to the gas chambers. The Italian Foreign Ministry received a harrowing report from its embassy in Berlin containing photographs of concentration camp massacres and evidence that the Jews were being gassed en masse. "Details in this document were such," the Foreign Ministry concluded, "that they could not fail to arouse a feeling of horror, even among the most cynical."[176] A note attached to the report for Mussolini's attention asserted that: "No country, even allied to Germany, can ask Italy, the cradle of Christianity and law, to be associated with these acts for which the Italian people may one day be accountable."[177] Since Italy controlled the southeastern corner of France it was in a position to help Jewish refugees and did so energetically. Mussolini seemed to concur, being singularly reluctant to halt the armed protection of Jewish communities in Italian-occupied France and the provision of sanctuary for thousands of Jewish French residents in Italy itself. A similar initiative gave shelter in Italy to 17,000 Jews from the Croatian province of Dalmatia. However, when the Allies invaded Italy in 1943 the Jews' fate worsened. Mussolini's regime collapsed in July, to be replaced in unliberated Italy by German military occupation and the SS. Although Mussolini continued as head of a shrinking puppet republic until the final weeks of the war, the German authorities now dispatched 7,000 of Italy's Jews to the death camps, while a further 200 died in Italy itself.

It was foreign policy that ultimately proved Fascism's undoing. Until the early 1930s Mussolini left its conduct largely in the hands of professional diplomats, even if he nudged it in a revisionist direction. Rome maintained cordial relations with its former wartime allies and cosignatories of the Paris Peace Settlement, France and Britain, but prodded and probed at the territorial status quo in southeastern Europe. By 1926 Albania was closely tied to Italy, and during the later 1920s links were developed with Hungary and Austria, neither of which regarded the post-1918 peace settlement as the last word in European relations and both of which (like Italy) harbored territorial grievances against Jugoslavia. The Fascist regime did toy briefly with notions of exporting Fascism (as the Comintern sought to promote world Communism) but at this stage Mussolini himself dismissed the idea, concluding: "Fascism is not goods for export."[178]

From 1932, however, Mussolini pursued more radical goals. The completion of the Fascist revolution at home, it was held, demanded an overseas empire worthy of ancient Rome's memory and also the promotion of Fascist-style movements elsewhere in Europe. Mussolini claimed spiritual and moral patronage over such movements, which, some Fascist ideologues claimed, even included Russian Bolshevism. Italy and the Soviet Union continued in any case to maintain cordial relations and expand trading links, and during the Ethiopian War Moscow actually increased oil shipments to Italy rather than join a blockade ordered by the League of Nations. These Russian efforts to maintain a positive relationship with Rome possibly encouraged the prominent Fascist ideologue Sergio Panunzio to hope in 1939 that Moscow and Stalin had been drawn into Rome's moral orbit: "Moscow bows before the light radiating from Rome. The Communist International no longer speaks to the spirit; it is dead."[179]

In the event, the nemesis of Fascism was to lie further west. During the Weimar era Hitler had been an admirer of Mussolini's regime and Nazism in opposition had drawn heavily from the Fascist lexicon. Once Hitler became Chancellor of Germany, however, relations deteriorated. The Nazi leader had his doubts about the racial pedigree of Mediterranean peoples and made these known to an unappreciative Mussolini. The Nazis' thuggish behavior after the establishment of the Third Reich began to appall leading Fascists, some of whom decried its "parochial and exclusivist" racialism. The leading Fascist journal *Gerarchia* concluded in 1935 that the real differences between Nazism and Fascism were "profound and unambiguous,"[180] and Mussolini himself denounced National Socialism as a threat to world civilization. An abortive Nazi coup in Austria in August 1934 also played badly in Rome, which regarded its little neighbor as a client state and territorial buffer against Germany. Following Hitler's declaration of German rearmament in March 1935 Italy joined with France and Britain in condemning the move. The Stresa Front, named after the Italian town in which the three Allied powers conferred during April, seemed to reaffirm the geopolitical constellation of the post–First World War era, which was underpinned by detailed Franco-Italian military and strategic joint planning to see off any future Nazi threat.

The Front did not survive for long. The Anglo-German Naval Agreement of June 1935 gave Germany the green light to create a high seas fleet, and although the Agreement appeared to enshrine the principle of British naval superiority, it nonetheless breached the Versailles Treaty. Mussolini's regime had long since hankered after Ethiopia (Abyssinia) and in January 1935 it appeared that France had granted Italy a "free hand" in this independent African state in return for Italian support against any Austro-German Anschluss or the militarization of the Rhineland.[181] The Italian dictator concluded that the time had come for this military adventure of his own and in October 1935, after some months of perfunctory diplomacy, attacked Ethiopia from the East-African Italian colonies of Eritrea and Somaliland. The League of Nations (and in particular Britain) condemned the attack and imposed sanctions on Italy, but could not reverse it. By May 1936 the war was essentially won to widespread domestic acclaim, which boosted the standing of the Fascist Party within Italian society. Weeks later the Spanish Civil War broke out and, as already seen, Mussolini intervened on the winning, nationalist side.

All of this brought Italy and Germany closer together. MacGregor Knox maintains that Italian leaders had perceived an inherent community of interests between Italy and Germany from the early days of Mussolini's regime, for Italian dominance of the Mediterranean implied, sooner or later, a confrontation with France. However, the disarmed Weimar Republic lacked any useful military capacity and Knox agrees that Hitler's adventures in Austria during 1934 repelled the Italians: "It was thus German pigheadedness, not predilection for France, that at last opened Mussolini to French advances ... that the dictator had resolutely ignored in 1931–2."[182] The collapse of the Stresa Front and the outbreak of the civil war in Spain finally brought Rome and Berlin together. In January 1936 Mussolini let Germany know that his interest in Austrian independence had lapsed, and in October Rome and Berlin concluded an agreement (the Axis) to coordinate their activities in Spain. Despite sustained British efforts to woo Mussolini back into the Western fold, in November 1937 Italy joined the German-Japanese Anti-Comintern Pact (1936), which was directed against the Soviet Union, before concluding a formal alliance with Germany in May 1939 (the Pact of Steel).

Italy was not committed to join Germany in any war and at the time of the Munich crisis, despite earlier vocal support for military intervention on Berlin's side, Mussolini's initiative as honest broker arguably dissuaded Hitler from attacking Czechoslovakia outright. It remains open to debate whether Mussolini wished to continue playing a mediocre diplomatic and military hand with some finesse and so achieve incremental gains at a relatively low risk and cost, or whether he saw general war as his ultimate goal. Knox asserts the latter, noting Mussolini's claim that: "The clash with the Western powers is ever more inevitable,"[183] and Mussolini certainly upped the ante by claiming Nice, Corsica and swathes of French North Africa, but during 1939, when all was said and done, Italy continued to play for small prizes and to hedge its bets. Rome seized Albania (where it already enjoyed influence) outright in March 1939 without eliciting any strong response from the League of Nations powers. London attempted to draw a line in the sand by offering security guarantees (against Italy) to Greece and Turkey, but given the fraught state of relations with Nazi Germany the French and British also sought to patch up post-Ethiopia relations with Italy and avert an arms race in the Mediterranean. By this time Mussolini's ambitions extended beyond the Mediterranean, by way of Gibraltar or the Suez Canal to the oceans, but the outbreak of general war in September 1939 came earlier than Italy desired. Mussolini hesitated and only finally joined the war with a spatchcock attack on the French Mediterranean border town of Menton as German forces swept south through France during June 1940.

Eastern Europe

Democracy did not fare well in interwar Eastern Europe. The First World War triggered an initial wave of hyper-inflation and famine that the victor powers were unable or unwilling to remedy, so bringing the region's social and economic system close to collapse. The prospects for free-minded democratic tolerance were undermined further by the seething resentment of national minorities trapped behind borders they abhorred and by majorities who sought to extend their power, whether at the expense of their domestic minorities or through territorial expansion. Despite a short-lived economic recovery during the later 1920s, low levels of productivity, economic underdevelopment and a reliance on foreign capital all contributed to the devastating impact of the Great Depression on Eastern Europe, which was, in R. J. W. Evans's words, "spiritual as well as material."[184]

Fascist or fascist-inspired movements proliferated across interwar Europe, but they struggled to make headway before the Second World War. The East European regimes that displaced the post-1918 democracies tended to emerge from within the existing establishment and sought to defend it from radical challengers, whether right-wing (fascist) or left-wing (socialist or Bolshevik). In the north of the region parliamentary republics tottered and fell, in the south monarchies largely survived but presided over increasingly authoritarian forms of government. All the post-democratic regimes were nationalist, most identified closely with the local church, whether Roman Catholic, Orthodox or Lutheran, and several were strongly anti-Semitic. Beyond these general tendencies, however, the individual post-democratic regimes varied quite significantly, with some showing greater tolerance towards political opposition and religious and national minorities than others.

Of the larger East European states, Poland's regime was among the less oppressive. The military strongman Jósef Piłsudski displaced the democratic system in 1926, but he was not a racialist and sought a degree of consensus and popular legitimation for his government. Poland's large Jewish minority was tolerated, to the point where several Jewish organizations were included in a political front designed to deliver a parliament supportive of the regime in controlled elections. During the early 1930s, as Piłsudski's health deteriorated, the military played an increasing role in government and shortly before his death in 1935 a new constitution strengthened the powers of the President over Parliament.

To the right of the regime, the extreme nationalist, Catholic, and virulently anti-Jewish National Democrat Party functioned as a form of anti-regime opposition, looking towards Fascist Italy for inspiration. It was dissolved twice by the authorities during the early 1930s, but the government itself eventually bent to the authoritarian wind sweeping the continent. After Piłsudski's death, Poland's military leaders bolstered state involvement in economic life and toyed briefly with notions of a one-party state, but confronted by a growing threat from Nazi Germany and the Soviet Union eventually concentrated on rallying the nation for a future war.

A military ruler, Admiral Miklos Horthy, also took power in Hungary. His regime still regarded the Habsburgs as the country's legitimate rulers, but they were barred from the throne by the Paris Peace Settlement. From 1919, therefore, Horthy served *faute de mieux* as Regent and Head of State, presiding over a system which retained as much as possible of the pre-1918 constitutional order. This provided for a strong executive and weak, elitist parliament and if the regime tolerated opposition parties, they were barred from power by the constitution. The Socialists remained weak in any case, but the constitution did keep a variety of more powerful, populist, right-wing movements at bay.

During the economic turmoil of the 1930s a fascist-style league, the Arrow Cross, proposed far-reaching agrarian and labor reform and the restoration, more or less, of Hungary's pre–First World War boundaries. Its membership exceeded 200,000, but despite its considerable popularity it was unable to assume office through the electoral process. As Payne observes: "[This path] was effectively blocked by a semiauthoritarian government. In Hungary, as in Austria, Romania, and elsewhere, the lack of political democracy would be decisive in blocking the political success of a large, broad-based, and popular fascist movement."[185] Nor did it have the wherewithal to seize power illegally. Instead it watched as Horthy's Prime Ministers flirted with corporatist political reform on their own terms and cultivated links with Fascist Italy and Nazi Germany. During the later 1930s the authorities used a combination of social reform and political repression to keep the Arrow Cross in check. Although Horthy supported the Germans during World War Two, he retained domestic political autonomy until the Nazis overran Hungary during the closing months of the conflict and imprisoned the country's veteran leader. Released by the Allies, he eventually died in exile in Portugal in 1957.

A similar pattern emerged in Romania, a monarchy proper, where a "genteel semi-fascist" elite[186] slugged it out with the hypernationalist, anti-Semitic and swastika-sporting Legion of the Archangel Michael led by Corneliu Codreanu. Rigged elections in 1933 and the mass arrest of Legion members provoked it to assassinate the Prime Minister, Ion Duca, on December 29. The government responded by banning the Legion's paramilitary league, but could not prevent it concluding an electoral alliance with the National Peasant Party in 1937. The Legion attracted some 25 percent of the vote and its Peasant Party allies a further 20 per cent in the December elections, but the authorities simply redrafted the constitution to bolster the power of the crown. With the electoral road to power blocked, the Legion attempted a coup d'état in January 1939, but failed to gain army support. Romania's strong-arm rulers had curtailed the democratic process to the point where the Legion was unable to utilize a critical mass of popular support, demonstrating once again that the most propitious environment for fascism remained a failing liberal democracy, such as had existed in Italy or Germany.

To the south of Hungary and Romania, the Balkan states also experienced a variety of strong-arm governments, where the real contest was between monarchists and the military. In Bulgaria efforts by a coalition administration of the professions and military modernizers (Zveno) in 1934 to clean up corruption in government and contain the radical left and right quickly came up against royal opposition. Zveno was ousted from power by King Boris III after which a royalist government staggered through until 1941, when Bulgaria finally joined the war on Germany's side.

In Greece the monarchy had been toppled in 1927, but after a honeymoon period of several years the new republican order became chronically unstable. In October 1935 a new king, George II, took back the throne, but this did nothing to heal the rift between equally matched monarchist and republican camps. In 1936 George exploited an outbreak of Communist workplace militancy to establish a dictatorship under the soldier-turned-politician, General Ion Metaxas, who banned political parties and cracked down on civil liberties, but kept Greece aligned with Britain. Greece was drawn into the Second World War in October 1940 when Italy attacked the country from its Balkan protectorate, Albania. Although the Greeks repelled the Italians, Germany intervened, overran the country and occupied it until September 1944.

Turning to Jugoslavia, national tensions continued to bubble and threaten the country's stability. In 1934, during a visit to Marseilles, King Alexander was assassinated by a Macedonian nationalist and succeeded by his under-age son, Peter, with his cousin, Prince Paul, serving as Regent. A succession of governments struggled to address domestic economic concerns and, less successfully, to defuse Croatian resentment against the Serb-dominated Jugoslav state. By the time Croatia was granted far-reaching autonomy in August 1939 events elsewhere offered an alternative solution. Following the German occupation of the Czech lands in March 1939, Slovakia had been granted independence under Berlin's protection, albeit with some loss of territory to Hungary. Belgrade's Serbian élite feared that the Croats might hanker after a comparable outcome and following the German invasion of 1941 Jugoslavia was recast as a complex patchwork of Axis-annexed territories (such as Slovenia), occupied regions (such as Serbia), and autonomous statelets (notably Croatia).

Nazism was largely confined in Eastern Europe to German-speaking minorities, most notably along Czechoslovakia's German and Austrian borders, and to Austria. The Austrian Nazis were by no means the only challengers to the country's republican order. Even the two main parties in the Republic's parliament, the Social Democrats and the clericist Christian Social Party aimed ultimately to amend the constitution. The Social Democrats hankered after a purely socialist state, the Christian Socials a corporative regime with anti-Jewish overtones. To the right of the Christian Socials were several paramilitary and anti-parliamentary leagues, among which the Heimwehr (Home Guard) was the most significant. Originally formed to protect Austria's southern border from Jugoslav incursions, the Heimwehr thereafter clashed periodically with Socialist militants in a struggle that simultaneously pitched rural and small-town Austria against the left-leaning Viennese metropolis and other industrial centers.

Eventually, in March 1933, the Heimwehr joined forces with the Christian Socials to overthrow the Republic. A Socialist counter-coup was crushed in February 1934 and Austria became another member of Europe's growing collection of Catholic, conservative, and corporatist states. The Christian Socials and Heimwehr created the Fatherland Front, which became the sole legal political organisation in Austria and boasted a paper membership of several millions in a country of six million inhabitants. The prospects of any Nazi takeover appeared blocked. Nazi anti-Semitism and its plans to merge Austria within a greater Germany did have a certain resonance in the country, but Chancellor Engelbert Dollfuss had no time for the Nazis and renounced any thoughts of an Anschluss (union) with Germany as long as Hitler ruled in Berlin. He dismissed the Third Reich as "pagan and racist," and claimed that Austria was now the "true repository of German culture."[187] The Austrian Nazis tried to overthrow the government in August 1934 and although they succeeded in killing Dollfuss, were crushed without too much difficulty. The new Chancellor, Kurt von Schuschnigg, was equally firm in his rejection of Nazism. The full weight of the state bore down on the Austrian Nazis, many of whom were arrested or fled into exile in Germany.

Schuschnigg softened the government's anti-Jewish line as he strove to build a degree of social and political consensus, but broke with the more radical Heimwehr in the process. It was banned as the Austrian polity appeared to be stabilizing under Italian military protection. Mussolini hoped (in vain) that Austria might become a fully-fledged Fascist state, beyond which (as noted) the Alpine republic formed a barrier to possible German southward expansion. At the close of the Great War Italy had seized the German-speaking South Tirol and many German nationalists sought its liberation. However, the creation of the Rome-Berlin Axis in 1936 (and Hitler's renunciation of any claim on the South Tirol) deprived Austria of Italian protection and allowed Berlin to apply growing pressure on Vienna. In 1936 the Austrian Nazis were legalized, in return for a promise from Hitler of "normal" relations between the two countries. Barely two years later the Austrian state was swept aside when in March 1938 German forces invaded the country unopposed and to a generally enthusiastic welcome.

The Soviet Union

As we saw earlier, the Soviet Union was spared the ravages of the Great Depression, but experienced its own distinctive brand of dislocation and misery thanks to the effects of forced industrialization and a botched process of agricultural collectivization.[188] However by the mid-1930s day-to-day life for the ordinary Soviet citizen was showing unmistakable signs of improvement. The worst effects of collectivization were in the past, with the abolition of food rationing in 1935 promising better times to come within a sustainable socialist society. Food apart, the very serious social dislocation triggered by the linked processes of forced industrialization and collectivization – drunkenness, hooliganism, and petty delinquency – demanded that the regime take steps to restore order. The traditional family and the concept of paternal authority were rehabilitated in order to fill the moral vacuum. Divorce laws were tightened up and women urged to attend to their duties as wives and mothers, whatever additional burdens their daily working lives might impose. Stalin himself presided over this conservative cultural turn, a father figure and "mentor to whom everyone is grateful,"[189] in witting or unwitting reflection of the paternalistic status of the Tsar in pre-revolutionary times.

Social peace, the authorities reasoned, also demanded cultural peace. A new, proletarian Soviet-educated elite now espoused, in Hubertus Jahn's words, traditional Russian values, "petit-bourgeois taste and the style of socialist realism."[190] Art and culture embraced this Socialist Realism, an "iconography of happiness" which depicted life as it should be rather than as it was. As the official Soviet newspaper *Pravda* claimed in 1936: "Healthy people have a 'biological need' for harmonious forms; they 'love melodically organized sounds and bright colours' and they 'want to make their life happier and more beautiful, not complex and depressing.'"[191] The cultural innovators and artistic avant-garde of the revolutionary era had been tolerated as critics of the prerevolutionary order, but clearly had no place in the postrevolutionary scheme of things. Soviet leaders were as ready as Hitler and Goebbels to denounce much of cultural modernity as decadent. Equally the professional classes of the late Tsarist era, the doctors, teachers and engineers who had often been fierce political and cultural critics of the Romanov dynasty, were now being displaced or simply replaced as the simple passage of time put them into retirement.

Society apart, inter-war Soviet Russia experienced periods of powerful, personal dictatorship, firstly by Lenin and then, after a relatively brief power struggle, by Stalin. Stalin's initial claim to power rested on his self-proclaimed status as Lenin's nominated heir. Thereafter he supported a relatively measured domestic policy, which espoused Lenin's New Economic Policy (NEP) and thus a role for the private sector in Soviet economic life, and a foreign policy based on the principle of Socialism in One Country. This abandoned initial efforts to spread the Bolshevik revolution across the globe and instead cultivated diplomatic relations with "bourgeois" powers as the Soviet Union gained time to establish a socialist order within its borders.

The policies of forced industrialization and agricultural collectivization soon enough turned his domestic policy on its head – once he had outmaneuvered left-wing rivals such as Leon Trotsky who had always been critics of the NEP. However, his tenure as Soviet dictator was ultimately characterized by a murderous onslaught on what remained of civil liberties and the rule of law, dubbed the Stalinist "Great Terror." He had constantly feared denunciation and arrest as a political opponent of the previous Tsarist regime and this early experience combined with a paranoid personality to create a man who "had developed a keen sense for loyalty … extremely distrustful and suspect[ing] conspiracies everywhere."[192] Paranoia came virtually to serve as the guiding principle of Stalinist government.

The catalyst for the terror was, historians agree, the murder in 1934 of the popular Communist Party chief in Leningrad (St Petersburg), Sergey Kirov. There is less agreement over Stalin's role, if any, in the murder, but his exploitation of the event triggered a purge of his potential rivals which quickly enveloped the Soviet system. The veteran revolutionaries Grigory Zinoviev and Lev Kamenev were among the Terror's initial victims. Both had clashed previously with Stalin and faced periods of temporary expulsion from the Communist Party as a result. In 1935 they were charged with Kirov's murder and of plotting to kill Stalin, tortured to extract the desired confessions and put on trial in 1936. The verdict at these show trials was predetermined and execution was the inevitable outcome. Nikolai Bukharin and Aleksey Rykov, pillars of the Soviet political establishment and critics of Stalin's economic policies, met identical fates in 1938. The exiled Leon Trotsky was assassinated on Stalin's orders in 1940, despite having found sanctuary in Mexico.

The summary elimination of Communist grandees served to intimidate the wider Communist Party as much as to remove Stalin's rivals, real or imagined, and triggered an orgy of popular denunciation. Implicit guilt, a slippery concept which included being related to or simply friendly with earlier denuncees, became a sufficient basis for one's own incarceration or death. It became imperative to preempt personal catastrophe by beating potential denunciators to the punch. Within this desolate world of fear and mistrust, around 700,000 people were executed and a further two million dispatched to the prison camps of the Gulag. Many died of hunger, cold or savage mistreatment in a hell-on-earth later immortalized by the novelist Alexander Solzhenitsyn in a series of works including *One Day in the Life of Ivan Denisovich* and culminating in *The Gulag Archipelago*, for which he was arrested and exiled from the Soviet Union in 1974.[193] Stalin's victims included 110 of the 139 members of the Central Committee and 1,108 of the 1,996 delegates who had attended the Seventeenth Party Congress in 1934. Beginning in 1937 a swingeing purge of the army officer corps saw 30,000 officers arrested and the majority of senior commanders killed: 2 out of 5 marshals, 13 out of 15 generals, and 62 out of 85 corps commanders. The Soviet Union was to pay dearly for this bloodletting, for as Jahn concludes: "The army was thus effectively in a state of paralysis when the German Wehrmacht started operation Barbarossa and invaded the USSR in the dawn of 22 June 1941."[194]

A significant number of recent and contemporary scholars[195] have come to regard fascism as an ideology of some substance, combining traditional, restorationalist values with "a new spirit of quasi-egalitarianism"[196] and technocratic efficiency. Zeev Sternhell goes further, describing fascism an attempt "to adapt socialism to modern conditions on both the ideological and tactical planes."[197] This, he argues, included efforts to address the growing importance of the nation and national solidarity in the twentieth century. However, if parliamentary democracy largely collapsed across Southern, Central, and Eastern Europe, the regimes that followed adopted various forms. These owed as much to individual state histories than to any set of universal ideological principles. Many such regimes were indeed sympathetic to Fascist Italy or later to Nazi Germany and Roger Griffin for one stresses the breadth of fascist influence,[198] but their style and method of government was seldom if ever a carbon copy of Mussolini's, still less of Hitler's. There is even disagreement over whether one can define Italian Fascism and German National Socialism as two parts of a generic fascist whole, for Nazi biological racialism and its philosophy and method of rule set it apart from Mussolini's regime.[199]

Marxism, which offered an older alternative to bourgeois liberalism, had become the system of rule in adapted, Marxist-Leninist, form in the Soviet Union. All Marxists, Social Democrat or Bolshevik, perceived their ideology as the antithesis of fascism, including Nazism. Both fascism and Nazism sought to reconcile class differences within an organic national community, whereas Socialists sought to resolve or at least influence the "class struggle" in the proletariat's favor. The fascists, Soviet ideologists argued, were merely trying to avert the final disintegration of bourgeois capitalism by novel and more radical means, which included the "fiction" of national solidarity.

That said the similarities between the Soviet and Nazi methods of government and also between their respective dictators, Stalin and Hitler, may have outweighed the differences. Richard Overy, for example, argues that the Nazi economic New Order was increasingly "controlled by the party through a bureaucratic apparatus staffed by technical experts and run through arbitrary political intervention, not unlike the system that had already been built up in the Soviet Union."[200] This echoes Hannah Arendt's earlier proposition that both polities shared characteristics she defined as totalitarian,[201] and among Hitler's biographers, Alan Bullock was also struck by similarities between the two dictators' systems of rule.[202] Arendt's exploration of totalitarianism owed much to her efforts to understand the rise of political anti-Semitism,[203] but critics of the totalitarian model noted its exploitation during the post-1945 Cold War to mobilize western opinion against the Soviet Union. The equation of Soviet government with the Nazi system was, they argued, flawed and offensive given the scale and nature of the Holocaust which had no direct Russian equivalent. Whatever the case, Hitler's racially predicated onslaught against the Soviet Union in 1941 rendered such considerations irrelevant in practical terms; it temporarily saw the Soviet Union, terror and Gulag notwithstanding, serve as a valued ally of the western powers.

We must now turn our attention to the origins and course of the 1939–45 war, which pitted a tangle of competing national interests, socioeconomic systems and ideologies against one another. The Allied victory of 1945 was to remove the immediate and manifest threat posed by the Axis powers, but without immediately resolving the future of either Europe or the wider world on universally acceptable terms. The Cold War defined new fault lines which were only finally resolved when the collapse of the Soviet Union during the early 1990s brought this latent conflict to an end.

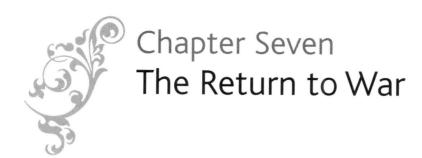

Chapter Seven
The Return to War

7.1　From Global Disarmament to War: 1932–1939

The Paris Peace Settlement of 1919–20 was already severely compromised by 1933. As we noted, the United States President, Woodrow Wilson, had perceived democratic government as a prerequisite for peaceful international relations, but democracy had either vanished or come under attack across much of Europe. Wilson had advocated free trade backed by a restored gold standard as the basis of world prosperity (and political stability), but the Great Depression had swept aside the uncoordinated efforts to restore this pre-1914 trading system. Wilson had also proposed the creation of a strong League of Nations with the capacity to resolve international disputes, but the League had lacked the necessary clout to act as a global enforcer from the outset. The refusal of the US Congress to ratify and so participate in the Wilsonian postwar settlement did nothing to help.

European society had not stagnated. A dynamic and often controversial cultural landscape accompanied remarkable technological and scientific innovation, and if culture divided opinion, there was near consensus that science and technology offered Europe a potentially glittering future. Europe was, therefore, by no means in a blind alley and if the Wilsonian vision had been severely compromised, peace had been more or less maintained and remained the clear official and popular preference. From 1933 onward international diplomacy remained focused on the maintenance of peace despite the increasingly radical and belligerent foreign policy pursued by Germany's National Socialist government. The Franco-British strategy of accommodating Hitler's ambitions perhaps beyond the limits of reason (dubbed appeasement) was controversial at the time and has since triggered fierce historical debate. Was Hitler set on war from the outset, and if so was the policy of appeasement fatally flawed?

The simple passage of events imposes an apparent pattern and logic on Hitler's foreign policy. Relatively cautious, preparatory steps were followed by increasingly radical and adventurous initiatives that eventually tipped Europe into war.

Figure 7.1   Hitler on his way to address the Reichstag on rearmament, January 1935.
Source: Ullstein Bild – Imagno.

The League of Nations had sponsored international disarmament talks in 1932, and they spluttered on into 1933 without reaching a conclusion. Hitler repeatedly stressed his commitment to peace, but suddenly withdrew from the talks and also from the League of Nations in October 1933, claiming that Britain and France remained determined to frustrate Germany's right to military parity with the other great powers. The Nazis had already begun to rearm covertly (although it was an open secret), but in January 1934 Germany signed a nonaggression pact with Poland which seemingly reinforced Hitler's peaceful credentials. In January 1935 the Saarland voted, as scheduled, on its future international status and opted overwhelmingly to return to Germany. The last direct Allied leverage on German foreign policy had evaporated and a significant heavy industrial region was again at Berlin's disposal.

After the Saarland had been formally returned to Germany in March, Berlin admitted the existence of the German air force and days later reintroduced conscription to create a peacetime army of 550,000 men. Although the Allied powers responded in April by jointly reaffirming their commitment to the Locarno Treaty at Stresa[1] neither Britain nor Italy appeared overly concerned in reality. In June 1935 London signed a Naval Agreement with Hitler's personal emissary, Joachim von Ribbentrop, which limited future German naval strength to 35 percent of the British. This revision of the Versailles Treaty said little for Allied solidarity and

Mussolini's opportunistic attack on Ethiopia in October compounded the damage. The League of Nations imposed sanctions on Italy and so brought Mussolini to mend his fences with Berlin.

Until 1936 Hitler had respected the demilitarized status of the Rhineland, which left this economically and strategically important region of Germany potentially vulnerable to French military intervention. He had originally planned to remilitarize the area in early 1937, but the distraction of the Ethiopian crisis provided an opportunity to move early. German operational planning for the action was another poorly kept secret, yet international reaction was muted, even resigned. Although both Hitler and his military commanders remained extremely jittery, the entry of the first troops into Germany's western borderlands on March 7 passed without incident. It now remained to be seen whether Hitler's government would be satisfied with a rearmed, fully sovereign Germany whose military and economic potential was little different from the Kaiser's empire or whether it harbored more radical objectives.

Hitler continued to reassure the European powers and German domestic opinion that he was a man of peace, but his government's economic policy suggested otherwise. By early 1936 the strains of rapid rearmament on the economy and balance of trade were beginning to tell, prompting the President of the Reichsbank and Economics Minister, Hjalmar Schacht, to advise scaling back the rearmament program. Hitler, however, took the opposite course. Goering was put in charge of foreign currency dealings and raw materials and then, in August, of a Four-Year Plan designed to prepare the economy for war. Goering's agency had teeth, absorbing half of Germany's total industrial investment between 1936 and 1942, and exploiting the Nazi security apparatus to cow any opponents in industry and commerce. And in any case, Richard Overy observes, the burgeoning importance of the new industries – chemicals, aviation, electrical engineering – offered "greater prominence to professional managers, chemists and engineers, many of whom were attracted to Nazism not because of its radicalism, but because it offered opportunities through massive state projects to master technical problems without financial constraint."[2] Yet again the Nazi regime was able to operate every bit as much through the mobilization of support as through repression.

Hitler justified rapid rearmament by stressing his determination to seize, settle and exploit vast territories in Eastern Europe, which made conflict between Germany and the Soviet Union inevitable. In November 1937, during a meeting with his military commanders, he identified Czechoslovakia as his first objective on the road to the east, but the Foreign Office and his army chiefs counseled caution. Hitler, however, was unappreciative of such advice and within weeks had dismissed the Army Commander, Werner von Fritsch, the War Minister, Werner von Blomberg, and the Foreign Minister, Constantin von Neurath, so strengthening his personal grip on the military and on foreign policy.

In the New Year Hitler embarked on his first foreign adventure, with his Austrian homeland, and not Czechoslovakia, the target. Goering, as head of the Four-Year

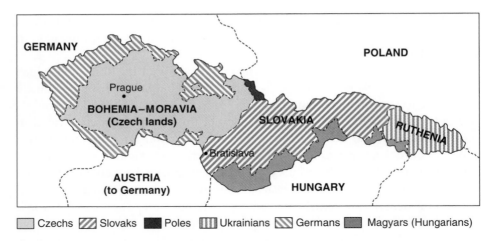

Czechs ▨ Slovaks ■ Poles ▥ Ukrainians ◩ Germans ■ Magyars (Hungarians)

Map 7.1   The peoples of Czechoslovakia 1938.

Plan, was particularly attracted by the iron ore deposits and other resources that Austria could contribute to German rearmament and pushed for an Austro-German currency union as the first step on the road to annexation. A meeting followed between the Austrian Chancellor, Schuschnigg, and Hitler on February 12, 1938 at which the latter, during a threatening interview, demanded that Schuschnigg include local Nazis in his Cabinet. The cowed Austrian leader agreed, but on March 9, safely back in Vienna, suddenly announced a referendum to reaffirm Austrian independence. After confused, increasingly hysterical discussions within Hitler's inner circle, an improvised German invasion followed on March 12. There was no resistance, the troops were greeted as heroes and international reaction was, again, muted. Berlin announced the union, or Anschluss, of Germany and Austria on March 13, and organized elections in both countries on April 10 to approve the union. If the 99 percent vote in favor appeared suspiciously high, the strongly positive response was nonetheless undeniable.

Within weeks Hitler had identified Czechoslovakia as his next goal. He initially proposed exploiting tensions between Czechoslovakia's various nationalities at an indeterminate point, but when Prague responded to routine German troop movements in May by mobilizing its own army, he resolved to expedite matters. Great play was made of the alleged Czech oppression of its German (Sudeten) minority, although Goering again stressed that the resources and defense industries of the Czech lands would be invaluable to the Four-Year Plan. The Sudeten Germans certainly harbored longstanding grievances, real and imagined, against the Czechoslovak state. Czech-medium schools were allegedly favored over German ones and public servants (police, railways, post office) in the German-speaking areas were predominantly Czech speakers, but Sudeten politicians had participated in government until the Great Depression devastated the region's economy. Amid complaints that public contracts went disproportionately to Czech firms and that welfare relief favored Czechs over Germans,[3] voters turned to the Sudeten German Party (SdP), led by Konrad Henlein. The SdP eschewed any role in government and sought the greatest possible autonomy for the Sudeten Germans, even persuading the British Foreign Office that Prague needed "to give these fellows a straighter deal."[4] However as National Socialist influence grew within the SdP Henlein became more strident, claiming in 1937 that "he could not restrain his followers' desire to join Germany for much longer."[5]

In March 1938 Hitler encouraged Henlein "to demand so much that we can never be satisfied,"[6] and on April 24 at a rally in Carlsbad the SdP leader demanded absolute equality between Czechs and Germans and full self-government for the Sudeten territories. Prague refused. Soon enough Sudeten radicalism boiled over into deadly clashes with the Czech authorities, so providing Hitler with a pretext for intervention on humanitarian grounds, but his underlying objective was the complete eradication of Czechoslovakia. The German army and Foreign Office officials feared that such an attack on Czechoslovakia could provoke British intervention, prompting the resignation of General Ludwig Beck as Chief of Staff, but Beck's colleagues doubted the wisdom of lobbying Hitler directly and the latter pressed ahead with his plans regardless. Work on Germany's western border fortifications was stepped up dramatically to forestall any rapid French intervention when the attack on Czechoslovakia finally came. As Kershaw observes:

> There could be no doubt that the crisis that brought Europe to the very brink of war in the summer of 1938 was instigated and directed by Hitler himself. And unlike the rapid improvisation and breakneck speed which had characterized previous crises, this one was consciously designed to escalate over a period of months.[7]

In the event British and Italian diplomacy averted war. The British Cabinet had decided in late August that the crisis could best be addressed by Czech concessions to the Sudeten Germans, but Viscount Runciman, sent on a fact-finding mission to Czechoslovakia, had advised senior members of the Cabinet on September 16 that any negotiated settlement between the Czechs and Germans was beyond reach, concluding that he "did not see how anything could now be achieved except by force in one form or another."[8] Runciman published his full report on September 21, recommending the transfer of German-speaking frontier districts from Czechoslovakia to Germany, but also that Prague should "remodel" its foreign relations with Berlin, entering the German sphere of influence and concluding a commercial treaty.[9] Since the British ambassador to Prague had already argued in March that "Czechoslovakia's present position is not permanently tenable,"[10] Chamberlain was prepared to endorse Runciman's recommendations while underwriting the nominal independence of the remainder of the country. Prague had also concluded a military agreement with the Soviet Union in 1935, but Moscow now looked increasingly toward reconciliation with Berlin. Reliable sources informed the Czechoslovak government "that there was no hope whatsoever for the Soviet Union to come to Czechoslovakia's assistance."[11] Tortuous, sometimes stormy meetings with Hitler followed during September at Berchtesgaden (September 15–16), Godesberg (September 22–3), and finally at Munich (September 29–30) as Chamberlain struggled to persuade the German leader to acquire the Sudeten territories in a measured, nonviolent manner.

Although Hitler had made great play of the Sudeten Germans' plight, any such resolution of the crisis threatened to box him in and deny him the ultimate prize of Prague. Despite protestations to Chamberlain at Berchtesgaden that "he … did not want a lot of Czechs,"[12] he remained determined to attack anyway, initially against the Sudetenland, until the eve of the Munich Conference. Chamberlain's diplomacy and Mussolini's declared readiness to mediate finally boxed in the German leader, who in any case was under intense pressure from Goering and his entourage to settle peacefully. On September 28 Mussolini's ambassador to Berlin finally persuaded Hitler to return to the negotiating table and on September 29 and 30 at Munich, trapped by his own rhetoric, he settled grudgingly on Mussolini's and Chamberlain's terms. Little matter that the "Italian" proposals had been drafted and transmitted to Rome for use at Munich by Goering and the German Foreign Office to avert war;[13] between October 1 and 10 the Sudeten territories and a sizeable Czech-speaking minority passed under German control without the Czechoslovak government having any direct say in the matter.

Chamberlain had always regarded settlement of the Sudeten issue as the key to a wider European peace and at Munich persuaded Hitler to agree that any future Anglo-German disputes would be settled by diplomatic rather than military means. However, the signed document to this effect, drafted by Chamberlain and brandished on his return home to a hero's welcome as a guarantee of "peace for our time," vouchsafed no such thing. Longstanding tensions between the Slovaks and Czechs came to a head in early 1939, prompting Hitler to intervene in this purely domestic dispute. In March the Slovaks accepted German military protection from their Czech confederates, which came in the form of a German invasion of the Czech lands and their absorption into the Third Reich as a protectorate. Slovakia gained its independence at a price. Its southern Magyar-speaking borderlands and its easternmost Ukrainian-speaking province of Ruthenia were ceded to Hungary, and the northern border town of Teschen was transferred to Poland. Days later, on March 21, Germany seized the Lithuanian Baltic port of Memel, which had been lost in the 1919 peace settlement. The Italian seizure of Albania on April 2 added to the febrile atmosphere.

There was no direct British or French military response to Hitler's post-Munich initiatives, but deteriorating German-Polish relations changed things. Hitler had opened talks with Poland in late 1938 with a view to returning Danzig to Germany and securing a route for a sovereign German motorway between East Prussia and the rest of the country through the Polish Corridor. Poland was offered closer economic cooperation and an anti-Soviet alliance in return, but its military government was as much opposed to Nazi Germany as to Soviet Russia. As Norman Davies observes:

The colonels were not going to bow and scrape to an ex-Austrian ex-corporal. Their instinct was to fight and to go down fighting. Every single Polish official who had to deal with Nazi and Soviet threats in 1939 had been reared on [Marshal Piłsudski's] moral testament: "To be defeated, but not to surrender, that is victory."[14]

The Polish Foreign Minister, Jozef Beck, turned down an invitation for direct talks in Berlin, instead passing on his views in writing through the Polish ambassador to Berlin. Hitler responded to this snub on March 28, 1939 by renouncing the 1934 German-Polish nonaggression pact and ordering urgent military planning for war against Poland. If the generals had harbored serious doubts about the Czechoslovak adventure, Kershaw observes, they had no such reservations this time.[15]

Hitler's aggressive posture, however, also triggered intense discussions between Warsaw and London, culminating on March 31 with a British offer of a military guarantee. This supplemented France's longstanding alliance with Poland and was formalised on April 6. The French military commander, General Gamelin, promised that within 15 days of any German attack on Poland a full-scale French invasion of Germany would follow, although Beck doubted whether France, still less Britain, would actually fight for Poland. Indeed, weeks later London warned Warsaw that in the event of war priority would be given to the defense of the Empire and Britain itself.[16] A Polish military mission to Paris during May also met with an equivocal response. Meanwhile, on April 17, the Soviet Union proposed a military alliance with France and Britain against any future German aggression. London's response was barely lukewarm, however, and when an Allied military mission finally set sail for Leningrad (today's St Petersburg) on August 5, the British emissaries, in Zachary Shore's words, "included not a single diplomat or soldier of influence," making "clear to the Soviets that their alliance was not desired."[17] This message was not lost on Moscow, which concluded that the prospects for an anti-German alliance including Britain were negligible.

However, while talks between the Soviet Union and the Western powers dragged on through the spring and summer, the German Foreign Minister, Ribbentrop, had in May persuaded Rome to conclude the Pact of Steel (falsely claiming that Berlin envisaged five more years of peace). More significantly, parallel negotiations between Berlin and Moscow made rapid progress. The long-serving Soviet Foreign Minister, Maxim Litvinov, was dismissed by Stalin in May. Jewish and married to an Englishwoman, Litvinov had been a committed advocate of collective security through cooperation with the Western powers. Even Litvinov, however, had kept open the door for rapprochement with Germany, commenting in 1935 that "our relations with her are determined not by her domestic but by her foreign policy."[18] Now his successor, Vyacheslav Molotov, was charged unequivocally with restoring relations with Germany, and Ribbentrop proved receptive.[19] An agreement on trade was concluded in June, and followed on August 23 by a secret understanding to create German and Soviet spheres of influence in Eastern Europe, continuing:

The question of whether the interests of both parties make desirable the maintenance of an independent Polish state, and how such a state should be bounded, can
be definitely determined in the course of further political developments. In any event,
both Governments will resolve this question by means of a friendly agreement.[20]

Poland's White Russian and Ukrainian eastern provinces would fall under Soviet
control and the remainder of the country be subordinated to Germany. To the
north Estonia and Latvia would fall under the Soviet sway, Lithuania go to
Germany, and on the Black Sea coast the Romanian province of Bessarabia (today's
Moldova) would be transferred to the Soviet Union. The rest of east-central and
southeastern Europe was left open to German ambitions.

The existence of the pact was made public knowledge, reinforcing Hitler's conviction that Britain and France now had little choice but to remain neutral in any impending Polish war. Goebbels hoped that war would now prove unnecessary: "We are on
top again. Now we can sleep more easily."[21] German public opinion also remained
relatively unconcerned; given the West's accommodating stance during the Sudeten
crisis, but Hitler remained determined actually to fight. Although a week of intense,
sometimes chaotic, diplomatic activity followed, during which Rome warned Berlin
it could not join any war, and which briefly offered the prospect of a Munich-style
compromise agreement involving the transfer of Danzig from League of Nations to
German rule, the British and Polish line also hardened. In any case, the contents of
the Russo-German pact and Hitler's continuing preparations for conflict suggested
that diplomatic mediation could only have delayed the inevitable, even if he struggled
to keep Britain neutral to the very end. On September 1 Germany invaded Poland.
Britain and France responded on September 3 by declaring war on Germany, but
thereafter failed to deliver the promised attack on Germany's western frontier, so
contributing indirectly to the the ease of the German-Soviet victory.

7.2   The Reasons for War

Few dispute that Germany precipitated the Second World War and if the debate
after 1914 was over "war guilt," two very different questions are asked of 1939.
The first is why Germany drove Europe into a second major war, which in 1941
became subsumed within a wider global conflict, and the second is why Britain
and France pursued a policy of appeasement that allowed Hitler to rearm and
consolidate his hold over central Europe before 1939 in breach of the Versailles
and Locarno treaties. Timely intervention, critics of appeasement maintain, could
have nipped the Nazi threat in the bud and spared Europe the horrors of total war
and genocide.

Disagreement over Hitler's personal role in the process is central to the first line
of enquiry. Did he act according to a predetermined strategy or did he simply react

to a fortuitous succession of events, leaving any sense of purpose or intention illusory? The former option was advocated by historians known, in self-explanatory fashion, as "intentionalists," the latter most notably by the late English historian A. J. P. Taylor.[22] However, if Taylor questioned the coherence of Hitler's foreign policy, Hitler's personal role in events was relativized further by historians labeled as "functionalists" or "structuralists." Hans Mommsen and Martin Broszat were prominent among them, doubting whether the Nazi dictator really had the capacity or will to shape or execute a coherent foreign policy.[23] Instead, they suggested, he served essentially as a figurehead within a dysfunctional political system whose various grandees jostled for power and influence. Invoking the supposed will of their *Führer* each sought to outbid the other by adopting increasingly radical policies which ultimately drove the Third Reich into war.

Adopting a somewhat different line, Tim Mason once argued that while Hitler sought war, his timetable was derailed by a deepening domestic crisis as economic difficulties inflamed latent working-class opposition to the regime. Faced by a crisis of major proportions, Mason argued, Hitler sought to cut through the Gordian knot by initiating hostilities several years earlier than planned.[24] Richard Overy, however, questioned both the true extent of economic (and resulting social) stresses in the Germany of 1939 – "an economy remarkably resurgent"[25] – and the degree to which working-class unrest troubled Hitler unduly. Furthermore, he argued, it was precisely the drive to prepare the economy and military for war at a breakneck pace that created problems, such as they were, and not these problems that led to war, as the functionalists in general would have it.[26] Even the stresses induced by rearmament left Germany, in Overy's view, "on as sound a footing in terms of finance, employment, output and balance of trade as the two Western powers." "To claim," he concludes, "that political conflicts and administrative discordance of themselves were a determinant of economic and social instability is greatly to distort the reality of economic policy-making and to underplay the powerful coercive effects of economic intervention in a one-party state."[27]

If an eventual consensus favored Overy's line of argument, the steam has in any case largely gone out of these debates. They never influenced international relations in a manner comparable with the post-1914 war guilt issue, even if they reflected and informed deep-seated ideological and political disputes within post-1949 West Germany. However, that is a story for another time and place. Historians have come to agree that although Hitler was far from all-powerful and did not shape events at will, he nonetheless played a decisive role in the formulation of Germany's foreign and military policy.[28]

Leaving aside the tendentious and self-serving ramblings of his autobiography, *Mein Kampf*, Hitler's untitled and unpublished second book (*Zweites Buch*), completed in 1928, provides a rather more convincing exposition of his aims and objectives and remained off the bookshelves precisely for that reason.[29] His racialism and anti-Semitism undoubtedly served to legitimize his program of territorial conquest and later underpinned an orgy of genocidal slaughter, but his foreign policy was informed more directly by an unqualified advocacy of war as the normal arbiter of international relations and by a view of the international economy that reduced trade relations to a zero sum game.

Hitler understood that domestic and international opinion remained strongly committed to peace during the 1930s and until 1938 tailored his public pronouncements accordingly, but this did nothing to modify his belief that war represented "part of a natural, indeed self-evident pattern of thorough, self-sustained national development."[30] Mussolini had pronounced similarly, and in public, on a number of occasions, but did seem able until 1940 to blend a muscular foreign policy and timely diplomacy with some skill. For Hitler, however, diplomacy ultimately served to enhance Germany's military options in an inevitable war, a vision totally at odds with the strategy pursued by his British and French counterparts, Chamberlain and Daladier, during the final years of peace.

Hitler also rejected international trade and a globalized economy as vehicles for national prosperity, instead taking an essentially Malthusian view of the future. Export markets, he held, were limited and shrinking as ever more countries industrialized and became self-sufficient in manufactured goods – the United States and Japan being recent examples – and as European manufacturers established subsidiary enterprises overseas.[31] The acquisition of *Lebensraum*, or living space, therefore aimed to secure direct German control over sufficient territory to provide for the country's present and future needs, providing access to food and raw materials and to land for extensive settlement. Since Britain and France had already secured the pick of overseas colonies, Germany's opportunity was held to lie in the vast, fertile and mineral-rich spaces of Eastern Europe. The menacing "Jewish-Bolshevik" Soviet Union would be eradicated in the process, as Germany secured hegemony over a continental landmass comparable in scale, if not method of rule, to that of the United States in North America. Intentionalists once debated whether Hitler's ultimate ambitions rested at that, or whether he sought global hegemony, but whatever the case, efforts by Western statesmen to dissuade Germany from war at the eleventh hour by offering economic concessions within the existing geopolitical framework, leaving it in Chamberlain's words "quieter and less interested in political adventures," were hopelessly wide of the mark.[32]

Given the apocalyptic cost of its ultimate failure, the Allied policy of appeasement, through which Paris and London attempted until March 1939 to pacify Berlin by accommodating or tolerating each of Hitler's initiatives or demands in turn, divided contemporaries and continues to provoke intense historical debate. The most celebrated contemporary denunciation came after the precipitate military collapse of France during May and June 1940. Under the pseudonym "Cato," three London *Evening Standard* journalists, including the future Labour leader of the early 1980s, Michael Foot, accused Chamberlain and his colleagues of failing to anticipate and arm expeditiously for an inevitable war. Dunkirk was "the story of an Army doomed before they took to the field" and Britain a country rendered virtually defenseless by Chamberlain's key appointees, notably Sir Thomas Inskip who served as his Minister for Defence Coordination. Entitled *Guilty Men*, "Cato's" savage denunciation continued:

> Here is an epitaph which should be placed on the grave of every British airman killed in this war, every civilian killed by Nazi bombers, every little child in this kingdom who may be robbed of life and happiness by high explosive or splintering metal rained down on this island by Marshal Goering's air force.[33]

However, leaving aside the fact that it was Britain, and not Nazi Germany, that in 1936 had planned a four-engined heavy bomber capable of pulverizing enemy cities into oblivion, "Cato" had less to say about France, yet London and Paris pursued their own interests and the French role was more complex and less subordinate to Britain's than its then leaders preferred to admit and historians have sometimes assumed.

French policy was partly informed by a desire to sustain the positive Franco-German relationship of the post-Locarno era, which had built détente around reciprocal security guarantees and the prospect of mutually beneficial economic collaboration between the two countries. Neither Paris or Berlin had, of course, ever committed most of their diplomatic eggs to this one basket, but the option of building a Franco-German axis was aired periodically and during the turn of 1931–2 even began to assume institutional form, whether to counterbalance American economic preeminence or to pave the way toward the creation of a wider European Union.[34]

The French diplomats and statesmen who had previously been involved in this process before 1933 preferred to hope that the glaring ideological divide between the French Third Republic and the Third Reich could be bridged. Deeper affinities between France and Germany, they argued, might yet prevail, particularly if the Nazi regime, or Hitler's role in it, proved to be short-lived. The ensuing French approaches to Berlin were always kept secret and when the Popular Front Premier, Leon Blum, and his Foreign Minister, Yvon Delbos, sought to strengthen the influence of "moderates" in Hitler's government by offering to initiate collaborative economic projects in Africa, even the French Cabinet was kept in the dark.[35] The Radical politician Edouard Daladier, who served as War Minister or Prime Minister in a succession of 1930s governments, and then as Prime Minister from 1938 until 1940, shared the view that a Franco-German settlement was desirable and tenable. Even after the 1938 Munich Conference Daladier, a war veteran, reflected that: "When at Munich I heard the heart of the German people beating, I could not prevent myself thinking, as I had done at Verdun, that between the French and German people there are strong ties of mutual respect which should lead to loyal collaboration."[36]

Daladier may have been trying, after Munich, to make the best of a bad job, but pacifist sentiment in France and Britain was reinforced by the feared human and material costs of another war. The French film-maker Jean Renoir had produced

Figure 7.2   After the Munich Agreement: French Premier Daladier returns home to a hero's welcome.
Source: Roger-Viollet/TopFoto.

his acclaimed antiwar masterpiece, *La Grande Illusion*, just a year earlier. The title was borrowed from Norman Angell's pre-1914 denunciation of war, *The Great Illusion*,[37] and the film's plot involved the relationship between French and German aviators during the First World War. Leaving aside the intricacies of the film's narrative, Renoir stressed the similarities between the aristocratic French and German airmen, who mourned the passing of their social world in the cauldron of war, and the love that blossomed between a working-class French aviator and a simple German war widow who sheltered him during his successful escape attempt from captivity as a prisoner of war. In 1939, with the coming of war, the French government banned the hugely popular film.

Sentiment apart, economic pressures also served to delay rearmament, with unavoidable consequences for French diplomacy. The Great Depression undermined the country's public finances, prompting cuts in military spending which soon enough compromised the army's role as an arbiter in European affairs. General Weygand, Vice President of the Army Council, warned the government in 1934 that the army was now barely strong enough to guarantee France's security in an increasingly unstable Europe,[38] and continued that German rearmament could negate even this defensive posture. Weygand also feared for the effectiveness of France's colonial army, hitherto regarded as compensation for Germany's greater population, noting that the Muslim soldier in particular had become "more quarrelsome and less devoted to his leaders. He is more sensitive to external influences; he mixes with the civilian population, a thing that formerly did not occur. Behind the appearances of discipline his mind tends to elude us."[39] Thereafter, during the Popular Front era, Blum's Minister for National Economy, Charles Spinasse, repeated that rearmament brought "a serious danger of financial and economic collapse,"[40] leaving conciliation of Germany indispensable if the Popular Front was to save its costly social program. Meanwhile, any thought of intervening in the Spanish civil war was dismissed as potentially ruinous, requiring, it was claimed, a million soldiers, and tantamount to initiating a wider European war. One could add that the divisions between the French political right and the Popular Front parties mirrored the split between nationalists and republicans in Spain.

Daladier had already tried in 1934 to square the circle between passivity and national security by contrasting "the offensive as it was applied in 1914 … which, alas! almost wrecked our liberties once and for all," with "defensive strategy." Referring to the fortifications of the Maginot Line, he continued that its impregnability was France's surest guarantee.[41]

It was against this background that Hitler remilitarized the Rhineland in March 1936. Winston Churchill later identified the lack of any French military response as a decisive moment on the road to war. France, he claimed, had 100 divisions available to reoccupy the Rhineland and had it done so "a check would have been given to [Hitler's] pretensions which might have proved fatal to his rule."[42] However, the collapse of the Stresa Front, and with it Franco-Italian military collaboration, had also left France diplomatically isolated. This weighed on the minds of French politicians and military commanders as the Rhineland crisis unfolded, for while sufficient forces were available for a swift riposte involving the occupation of the Saarland, it was less clear what would ensue were this demonstrative action to lead to all-out war. London had already warned Paris that it would not regard the remilitarization of the Rhineland as a casus belli and in a drawn out Franco-German war the balance of advantage would tip inexorably toward Germany. As the Mosellan industrialist and Senator François de Wendel bleakly concluded: "Locarno, the League, and all the crack-brained notions of these past years are over and done with."[43]

Even Colonel de Gaulle, the outstanding advocate of tank warfare and a mobile offensive military strategy, conceded in his seminal book *Vers l'armée de métier*, loosely translated as *The Professional Army of the Future*,[44] that Germany had twice as many men of military age and a military-industrial complex that eclipsed that of France. In all fairness, the Allied governments of the later 1930s did begin rearmament in earnest, so ensuring, contrary to "Cato's" claims, that when it came to the Battle of France in 1940, their forces were at least as well equipped as the Germans'. Similarly, when André François-Poncet stood down as French ambassador to Berlin in October 1938, his final meeting with Hitler left him distinctly in two minds regarding the future. Certainly, he wrote, Hitler's protestations of peace needed to be taken seriously, but only alongside "a moral renewal and the rapid and rigorous perfecting of [France's] military forces."[45]

Anthony Adamthwaite's claim that appeasement was conducted "with conviction and determination" might appear slightly harsh under the circumstances,[46] but during the Sudeten crisis France did play a double game, assuring London that it was exerting strong pressure on Prague to compromise, while in Prague essentially blaming Britain for the Munich deal. As Gerhard Weinberg concludes: "The publicly advanced argument that France could not commit itself in the absence of a British promise to help was a sham." Indeed, Weinberg continues, when Britain did, briefly, look like fighting after all, the mood in the French capital bordered on panic.[47] Thereafter, France stepped up the process of disengagement from eastern Europe under a smokescreen of reassurances to traditional allies in the region, even while making a renewed effort to reach an economic accord with Berlin. "Germany," Adamthwaite observes, "drew her own conclusions."[48]

Returning to Britain, the considerations driving the policy of appeasement were not vastly different from those in Paris (French notions of some form of Carolingian union aside[49]). Chamberlain had lost a cousin in the trenches of the Great War and shared Daladier's abhorrence of conflict. British public opinion tended to agree. And if successive French governments baulked at the likely economic and sociopolitical price of a major war, British governments concluded that in order to sustain domestic economic equilibrium and maintain the necessary material and military resources to hold "a very rich and very vulnerable" empire,[50] war in Europe had to be averted. Even as things stood the main Indian nationalist party, the Indian National Congress led by Mahatma Gandhi, had run civil disobedience campaigns, unsuccessfully during the 1920s, but with greater effect during the depression-scourged 1930s. In 1935 the Government of India Act provided for direct Indian participation in government, particularly at provincial level, even if British sovereignty in this keystone of the overseas empire was sustained until 1947.

The substance of British rearmament was set out by Sir Thomas Inskip and approved in Cabinet in December 1937. Focusing on air defense, naval strength to protect maritime trade and defend the Empire and, finally, the provision of limited army support to Britain's continental allies, it was presumed that the French forces would hold the Maginot Line in a "war of attrition in which the greater Anglo-French naval and economic power would prevail."[51] The reluctance to create and equip a large continental army at the outset was strikingly reminiscent of British thinking before the First World War and was further evidenced by the very limited conscription introduced after the German seizure of Prague.

Although later savaged by "Cato" for its relative neglect of land-based forces, this program was adapted to create approximate parity between German and Allied forces by 1940 and also developed the technologically superior Spitfire fighter aircraft, which was to outperform Germany's Messerschmidt 109 fighters during the Battle of Britain.[52] However, whether rearmament was intended to lend

British diplomacy genuine steel, not least by actively countenancing war, is less clear. Once appointed Prime Minister in 1937, Chamberlain quickly tightened his grip on foreign policy. He had previously criticized the "drift without a policy" that characterized foreign affairs and set in its place a "double policy of rearmament and better relations with Italy and Germany."[53] The conciliation of both dictators raised eyebrows at the Foreign Office, but Chamberlain eliminated serious criticism by replacing Sir Robert Vansittart as Permanent Under Secretary by Sir Alex Cadogan, and Anthony Eden as Foreign Secretary by Edward Halifax. Thereafter, Keith Feiling argued: "to gain time to arm against an inevitable war … was never his first motive, which was plain enough, simply the rightness of peace and the wrongness of war."[54] As a close confidant of Chamberlain betrayed, "Our policy was never designed just to postpone war, or enable us to enter war more united. The aim of appeasement was to avoid war altogether, for all time."[55] Against this background, Sidney Aster argues, rearmament, especially after Munich, can be seen essentially as an effort to buy domestic consensus between doves and hawks, rather than as a considered preparation for war.[56]

In fairness to Chamberlain, confronting Hitler was never going to be straightforward. The Saarland plebiscite, German rearmament, and the remilitarization of the Rhineland were water under the bridge when he became Prime Minister and neither Paris nor London retained any serious attachment to the Versailles Treaty. Following the Anschluss, and as the Sudeten crisis gathered momentum, the British dominions of Australia, Canada and South Africa made it plain that they would not join a war over Czechoslovakia. With Canada neutral the attitude of the United States would be open to question, and following the debt and trade standoffs of the 1930s, Chamberlain was perhaps wise to conclude that it was "safer to count on nothing from the Americans except words."[57]

Neither Chamberlain nor Halifax nurtured any illusions regarding Hitler. "Is it not positively horrible," the Prime Minister exclaimed, "to think that the fate of hundreds of millions depends on one man and he is half mad?"[58] Halifax agreed, regarding "Hitler possibly or even probably mad"; but warning that "any prospect of bringing him back to a sane outlook would be lost if the British involved him in a public humiliation."[59] However, as noted, hopes of salvaging the peace rested on the understanding that Hitler's ultimate objective was a greater Germany and on overblown expectations that domestic economic crisis would finally bring the German dictator to heel or precipitate his overthrow by more moderate elements. Chamberlain claimed that the Munich agreement had stymied Hitler's ambitions, but the belated efforts after Prague to patch together some sort of anti-German alliance on the continent and the half-hearted guarantee offered to Poland in February (of its independence rather than its existing frontiers) were not taken seriously by Hitler. His contempt was understandable and when Germany attacked Poland on September 1, 1939 Chamberlain hesitated to declare war immediately. Eventually, with the words: "Everything that I have worked for, everything I have hoped for, everything that I have believed in during my public life had crashed into ruins,"[60] he declared war on

Germany on September 3, followed hours later by France. A thirteenth-hour attempt by Hitler to salvage the situation, by offering to fly Goering to London for talks, was deemed "unworthy of relating" by a senior Foreign Office official and reached neither the Foreign Minister, Halifax, still less Chamberlain.[61]

7.3   From Poland to the Fall of France: September 1939–June 1940

If the Western declaration of war on Germany took Hitler by surprise, the diplomatic and military ground for his war in the east against Poland had been thoroughly prepared. Despite the discouraging noises from London and Paris earlier in the year, Poland's military and political leaders persuaded themselves at the eleventh hour that if they could resist the initial German attack the French and British might, after all, come to their rescue by attacking Germany in the west.[62] The French declaration of war seemed to confirm Polish hopes: "They left flowers and letters at the [French] embassy gates and sang verses of the Marseillaise,"[63] Richard Overy relates, but the attack promised by the French military commander, General Gamelin, did not materialize. Instead, Britain and France had resolved from the outset to play a long game, subjecting Germany to economic blockade and building up their own military strength before finally going on the offensive in 1941 or 1942. Only then, Gamelin maintained, would he dispose of the necessary equipment for a major offensive into western Germany[64] although he had always been confident that his army could repulse any German thrust westwards in the meantime.

German mechanized columns struck at Poland from East Prussia in the north, Silesia in the south, and across the western frontier. The open spaces of the North European Plain allowed for rapid progress against the relatively ill-equipped Polish armies, whose frontier garrisons were swiftly cut off and eliminated from the battle. Within eight days German forces had surrounded the Polish capital, Warsaw. The German air force achieved almost total air superiority from the outset, and thereafter its Stuka dive bombers smashed enemy communications, destroyed desperately vulnerable Polish military convoys and shot up fleeing groups of civilian refugees. Night-time German air reconnaissance film showed straggling enemy columns immobilized and blazing in the blackness, so providing devastating footage for subsequent propaganda films. Among these, *Feuertaufe* (Baptism of Fire), which chronicled the Polish campaign, made particular play of the destructiveness of German air power, both on the battlefield and against Warsaw, with the city shown enveloped by huge storm clouds created by the heat and smoke of indiscriminate bombing. Triumphalist and intimidating in equal measure, the film invited audiences in neutral states to draw their own conclusions.

The Polish army held on grimly in the ruins of Warsaw, fell back southeastward on Lvov and launched determined if limited counterattacks, but Soviet intervention on Germany's side hastened its demise. Since 1935 the Soviet Union had been supporting China against an expanding and aggressive Japanese Empire, still smarting at its cavalier treatment during the Paris Peace Conference. The Japanese had seized Korea in 1930, declared a protectorate over the northeastern Chinese province of Manchuria in 1933, and invaded China proper in 1937. Russian forces clashed with the Japanese along the northern Manchurian frontier before a little-known Russian general, Georgi Zhukov, won a decisive victory on August 28, 1939. A ceasefire was then agreed on September 15. With its own eastern front secured, the Red Army was free to attack westwards, across the Polish border, on September 17. The Warsaw garrison fought on against the Germans for another fortnight, and the government along with significant elements of the armed forces managed to escape to Western Europe, but on October 4 Poland capitulated. Almost a million Polish soldiers had been killed, wounded, or captured, while German losses were fewer than 50,000.

The German and Soviet forces had already held a joint victory parade in Brest-Litovsk and on September 28 agreed a new Treaty of Friendship, Cooperation and Demarcation, which laid the basis for collaboration between the SS and NKVD (Russian secret police) in occupied Poland and redrew the demarcation line, from the Baltic to the Black Sea, between the two powers. Lithuania now came within the Soviet sphere of influence, while central Poland was reassigned to Germany. The German-occupied territory was subdivided between a western zone annexed outright to the Reich and a Generalgouvernement, envisaged initially as a protectorate, but later earmarked for German settlement.

Both zones of Poland suffered appallingly. Hitler had stated repeatedly that an annihilationist form of racialism informed his plans for Eastern Europe and it was in Poland that these prejudices first found substance. His views on the Poles were clear enough: "More like animals than human beings, completely primitive and amorphous. … Now we know the laws of racial heredity and can handle things accordingly,"[65] or more succinctly that: "Asia begins already in Poland."[66] Academic historians, especially in the eastern universities of Germany, were able and willing to provide pseudo-scientific legitimation for the imminent mayhem, among them the young Theodor Schieder, later doyen of the postwar West German historical profession. Resettlement, he argued, was "restitution for the blatant Polish injustices of 1919" and demanded "population transfers on a grand scale," perhaps to the point of shipping Poles overseas,[67] to clear the land for German incomers. As Jonathan Wright observes, the ideological momentum behind the Polish atrocities saw conventional German racial and cultural prejudices (which in themselves need not have been deadly) merge "all too easily with Nazi racial imperialism."[68]

Heinrich Himmler's SS operatives, organized in *Einsatzgruppen* (task forces), were directed to carry out the wholesale removal of western Poland's indigenous communities, aided and abetted by the resident German minority, in a premonition of what awaited the conquered Slavonic nationalities within the Soviet Union from mid-1941. The respective conduct of the German forces in the First and

Second World Wars was oceans apart in this regard, for "the war against Poland," as Heinrich-August Winkler observes, "was no longer a 'normal European war,' but instead the first '*völkisch*' war in Europe."[69] There were few legal impediments standing in Himmler's way, unlike in Germany proper where the pre-Nazi legal code still offered victims of the Third Reich some meager shreds of protection. In former Polish territory German law did not apply, Polish law ceased to have effect and the German authorities equally refused to recognize the application of The Hague and Geneva Conventions. As Hitler put it, "We don't want to do anything there that we do in the Reich."[70] Although regular army units were most certainly involved in these atrocities, German-occupied Poland passed from military rule under SS control in late October 1939 with all the consequences that entailed.

The *Einsatzgruppen* set to work even before Poland had surrendered, murdering Jews and also the pillars of Polish civil society – priests, teachers, lawyers, doctors and landowners – among their 60,000 early victims. As the initial dust settled, surviving members of the professions were consigned to concentration camps opened at Auschwitz and Majdanek, which also served to deal with members of the Polish resistance, and the remaining Jews were herded into urban ghettos in the Generalgouvernement to be systematically sealed off from the outside world. Of the German-annexed territories' population, 88,000 were bundled into the Generalgouvernement by the end of 1939, and 365,000 by March 1941. Isolated protests were made by army commanders of the old school, including Colonel-General Johannes Blaskowitz, who condemned "the animal and pathological instincts" of the SS operatives in reports to his superiors, but to no effect.[71] Doubts expressed by Goering among others over the economic and logistical costs of the whole process also fell on deaf ears. Doctors screened the most vulnerable elements before killing those deemed "unworthy of life." The frail, the mentally, chronically and hereditarily ill were eliminated in short order, while orphaned children considered Aryan racials were removed on Himmler's instructions for adoption into German families. The ultimate wartime death toll in German-occupied Poland reached 6 million, or 18 percent of the population, half of these victims being Jewish. Against this, around 4,000 resident ethnic Germans had fallen victim to Polish brutality during the opening days of the war.

The fate of the populations under Soviet occupation was hauntingly similar. Whether Polish, Byelorussian or Ukrainian, community leaders such as policemen, village teachers and foresters were earmarked for deportation to the arctic camps of the Gulag or to the remote fastnesses of Soviet Central Asia. By June 1941 between 1 and 2 million inhabitants of eastern Poland had been transported east, while 26,000 Polish prisoners of war, reserve officers and thus members of the Polish professions in the main, were shot in batches during 1940 in the forests around Katyn. The Katyn massacre came to symbolize Soviet conduct in a pitiless wider war, which from 1940 also engulfed Estonia, Latvia and Lithuania before the German invasion of the Baltic lands during 1941 brought its own brand of terror.

The victims of Nazi and Stalinist terror sometimes imagined that one of the two dictatorships offered a less terrible alternative, opting for the frying pan to escape the fire. As Norman Davies relates: "On the frontier bridge over the Bug at Brest, people entering the USSR met others, including Jews, who were seeking haven in the Reich. 'Where on earth are you going?' exclaimed an SS officer on one occasion: 'we are going to kill you.'"[72] This serves as a reminder, were it needed, that for East European Jews the Third Reich was to prove immeasurably the worse option. However, while the Western powers were always refreshingly clear when it came to condemning Nazi barbarity, their view of the Soviet record was to become more complicated. On June 22, 1941 the German onslaught against the Soviet Union (Operation Barbarossa) created unlikely bedfellows of Churchill, Stalin, and soon enough the US President Roosevelt, and atrocities such as the Katyn massacre were played down or credited (wrongly) to the Third Reich. This particular pain has not healed: the Nazi-Soviet Pact of 1939 and all that followed remains a bone of contention between the current Russian Federation and its former subject peoples in eastern Europe, with the latter accusing the Russians of lacking an adequate degree of contrition for their earlier war crimes.

While Germany and the Soviet Union organized their conquests in Eastern Europe, and Soviet supplies of oil and raw materials began to boost significantly Germany's military and industrial potential, the Western Allies struggled to settle on a common strategy for the prosecution of the war. France also had a domestic political conflict to resolve. Many senior army officers, no doubt with a mind back to the events of the Russian Revolution and more particularly the French army mutinies of spring 1917,[73] had little time for communism, or the Soviet Union, and the Nazi-Soviet Pact fed their prejudices. The political establishment concurred and on September 26, despite protestations of patriotic loyalty from its leaders, banned the French Communist Party and its affiliates. The conservative newspaper *Gringoire* reflected majority opinion when insisting upon harsh action against the Communists, whose links to Moscow and by extension Berlin demanded the trial and execution of its leaders.[74] Military action against the Soviet Union now threatened to take precedence over any direct attack on Germany.

Having mobilised 2.7 million increasingly bored soldiers, France's leaders were certainly keen to do something to lend the war momentum and proposed in September 1939 that Allied troops land in northern Greece or even Istanbul to rally the Balkan states against Hitler. However the British Foreign Office feared an adverse Italian response and harbored painful memories of the 1915–16 Gallipoli campaign, so dismissing the proposal as "moonshine."[75] Thereafter Paris turned its attention to Scandinavia. There were strategic issues at stake, but the Soviet invasion of Finland on November 30, 1939 provided the emotional steam and evoked a powerful response in the French press. "Public opinion was immediately inflamed," General Gamelin recorded. "The natural reaction that condemned this new act of aggression, and the resentment aroused by the Soviets reaching an agreement with Germany to crush Poland, were bolstered by the more or less overt campaign attacking the ideas for which Bolshevism stood."[76]

The Soviet authorities had expected the Finns to cave in without a fight, failed to mobilize adequately, and therefore came off worst as Finnish troops, highly motivated and well dug in, repulsed clumsy frontal assaults. Stalin's purge of the Red Army's officer corps had also exacted its price and French and British observers were struck by this seeming "Russian impotence" which, an authoritative report to Gamelin concluded, left Stalin with little or nothing to offer the Allies.[77] Although Soviet diplomats hinted to their French counterparts that the alliance with Hitler would be temporary, Paris appeared set on a collision course with the Soviet Union.

The Allies envisaged landing an expeditionary force at the northern Norwegian port of Narvik and crossing through arctic Sweden to reach Finnish territory, but Norway and Sweden, both neutral, wanted nothing to do with the idea. Although Britain assumed this to be the end of the matter, the French Premier, Daladier, insisted that the scheme should proceed and eventually got his way. By March 13, 1940 the Franco-British task force had been assembled, supported by hundreds of aircraft, artillery pieces and machine guns, but on the same day, following a Soviet military breakthrough, a ceasefire was agreed between Helsinki and Moscow. The rug had been pulled from under Daladier's feet and the resulting political fallout removed him from office, but his successor, Paul Reynaud, maintained the anti-Soviet line and retained Daladier as his War, then Foreign Minister. The Baku oilfields in Soviet Azerbaijan offered an alternative target, added to which France countenanced naval attacks on Soviet shipping in the Black Sea, so provoking all-out war.

Chamberlain's negative reaction to this latter scheme verged on the hysterical and it was dropped, but all these anti-Soviet initiatives included an anti-German dimension. The Baku oilfields supplied Germany, and Swedish iron ore was similarly vital to the German war economy. During the summer months this ore could be shipped south through the Baltic Sea, but during winter when the northern Baltic froze it was taken by train to the Norwegian port of Narvik and then shipped through neutral Norwegian and Danish waters to Germany. While the Baku scheme promised war with the Soviet Union, the violation of Norwegian neutrality to choke off these iron ore shipments threatened no such thing and was therefore more attractive to Britain. After further ill-tempered haggling between the British and French over the finer points of strategy, it was agreed to mine the waters off Narvik. The operation was set for April 8, but a preemptive German strike had been some weeks in the planning and at dawn the next day its forces entered Denmark, followed by landings along the Norwegian coast.

The Danes did not resist and although there was some fighting in Norway, German forces quickly secured the south of the country. The Allies responded with counter-landings at Narvik and Trondheim, but the British-led expedition was ill-suited for the arctic weather or terrain (unlike their German counterparts) and suffered heavy losses. Although the German navy also paid a heavy price,

evacuation became the only option, but Reynaud had staked his political reputation on the success of the Norwegian campaign. He raged against the "old men"
leading Britain "who do not know how to take a risk,"[78] while Daladier demanded
of the French Cabinet on May 4: "We should ask the British what they want to do:
they pushed us into this war, and they wriggle out as soon as it is a matter of taking
measures which could directly affect them."[79] British officials riposted that they
had committed the lion's share of troops and equipment. The French, they continued, had "done absolutely nil" and Reynaud was denounced for strutting the political stage like a "pocket Napoleon."[80]

The Allied troops hung on in Narvik until early June, but meanwhile the
Germans had established a protectorate over Denmark, whose government
remained in office and King in residence, while a Norwegian pro-Nazi sympa-
thizer, Vidkun Quisling, was handed control of his country. The Norwegian King
and his legitimate government sought sanctuary in Britain. For all the ensuing
rigors of German occupation, the two Scandinavian countries were deemed
racially worthy and thus spared the barbarity meted out in the Slavonic east.
Sweden was allowed to remain neutral and unoccupied in return for its iron ore.
In 1941 Finland joined the German assault on the Soviet Union and temporarily
retook its eastern borderlands ceded to Moscow following the Russo-Finnish War
of 1939–40.

Norway apart, the British war effort during the 1939–40 winter focused on
naval operations, to safeguard overseas trade and maintain its maritime empire.
A German pocket battleship, the *Admiral Graf Spee*, achieved short-lived notoriety
as a commerce raider, sinking nine merchant ships before a fierce engagement
with the Royal Navy off Uruguay forced it into the port of Montevideo to carry
out major repairs. Indefinite sanctuary in a neutral port was not an option, forcing the *Graf Spee*'s captain to choose between fleeing to Argentina (which had
offered the battleship a "change of flag" agreement), renewed battle with the Royal
Navy, or simply scuttling his ship to evade capture and spare life. He chose the final
option. Other German battleships, such as the *Bismarck*, sunk in May 1941, were
equally unable to sustain operations on the high seas in the face of British naval
and air superiority, so confirming that the pattern of hostilities in the Atlantic during the Second World War would resemble that during the First.

Germany again attempted to blockade Britain and France by means of a U-boat
campaign, but here too initial German strength was pitifully low, just 18 U-boats to
take on well-protected British convoys. The German naval commander, Admiral
Erich Raeder, could only hope "that his forces would know 'how to die gallantly'
when the time came."[81] However, the fall of France in June 1940 and the entry of
Italy into the war tipped the balance more in Germany's favor. With the French
fleet neutralized and the large and modern Italian fleet, 100 submarines included,
now allied to Germany, the Royal Navy found itself "fighting with shrinking
resources in waters from the North Sea to Egypt, from the Arctic to the far reaches
of the South Atlantic."[82] The small German submarine force broke British naval

codes, so enabling it to locate and destroy convoys with devastating effect. A quarter of Britain's merchant fleet was sunk during 1940 alone. The U-boat campaign was extended to the western Atlantic and Caribbean once the United States joined the war in December 1941, and there the submarines exacted a heavy toll on an ill-prepared American merchant fleet. As Overy remarks:

> When the submarines surfaced near the coast they met an extraordinary sight. The seaboard cities were a blaze of light, illuminating the silhouettes of slow-moving ships passing along the familiar peacetime routes, their own lights still shining. … In four months 1.2 million tons of shipping was sunk off the American coast alone. U-Boat losses in January were only three, in February only two.[83]

During 1942 Germany enjoyed superior naval intelligence, sinking 1,662 Allied ships and reducing British imports to one-third of peacetime levels, but during 1943 improved Allied naval intelligence and the stepping up of antisubmarine air patrols using new, long-range aircraft turned the tide. By September 1943 the Battle of the Atlantic had effectively been won by the Allied air forces and navies. The German submarines remained a deadly nuisance, but were no longer a strategic threat to the Allied war effort, for the United States shipyards could easily outbuild the continuing modest losses.

On land, meanwhile, German attention switched to Western Europe. The prospects of a decisive victory against the French and British armies appeared tenuous, for the latter were as numerous and as well equipped as their German counterparts. Yet the German offensive, which began with attacks on the Low Countries on May 10, 1940 and ended with the capitulation of France on June 22, had devastated the French forces and virtually excluded Britain from the European mainland. If Paris could claim that the victory of 1918 had redeemed the defeat of 1871 and restored France as Europe's premier military power, the German victory of 1940 redeemed 1918 in turn and confirmed the verdict of 1871. Big questions were asked of these events from the outset. Had France suffered a military defeat pure and simple, or did its collapse betray the inner "decadence" of the aged Third Republic? At the time not a few seasoned French leaders wearily conceded the latter, contrasting their homeland's torpor with the virility of the youthful Third Reich. Berlin, in alliance with the Soviet Union and Italy, was seemingly free to reorganize the European political and economic landscape at will. As the prominent historian Friedrich Meinecke, by no means a supporter of National Socialism, celebrated in July 1940:

> Feelings of joy, admiration and pride in our army must dominate even for me personally. And the recovery of Strassburg! How could one's heart not skip a beat? This has been astonishing, surely the greatest positive achievement of the Third Reich, to rebuild an army millions strong from scratch within four years capable of such achievements.[84]

French military leaders were forced to agree, with Weygand and Pétain among the many who believed Germany had already won the war.[85]

Yet French military planning had been anything but irrational and by no means entirely defective. After evacuating the southern Rhineland in 1930 Paris settled on a defensive strategy, building a network of state-of-the-art fortifications, the Maginot Line, along the entire length of the Franco-German frontier. Completed in 1937, the emplacements were set into the eastern up-slopes of the Vosges Mountains in Alsace and through the hill country of the Moselle, dominating the crossings over the Rhine and lines of approach from the Saarland. Secondary emplacements, designed to exact a heavy toll on any invader before the battle proper began, lay between the Maginot Line and the actual frontier. The Line stopped at Luxembourg, so leaving the Franco-Belgian border largely unfortified. Since any German attack was expected to come through Belgium this may have appeared negligent, but Brussels was allied to Paris. With the Maginot Line secure it was planned to commit the bulk of the French army to defending Belgium on Belgian soil. Following the German remilitarization of the Rhineland in 1936, Belgium declared neutrality, but French military commanders maintained informal links with their Belgian counterparts with a view still to meet any German attack in Belgium.

In essence France's generals were planning to refight the First World War on more favorable terms. The Maginot Line was a world apart from the muddy and lethally dangerous trenches of 1914–18 and in the coming engagement the French army would bring the German army to a standstill in central Belgium. France's generals were loath to risk all in a fluid, "encounter" battle. Thus the War Minister, General Maurin, exclaimed in 1935 with reference to the Maginot Line: "Would we be mad enough to advance beyond this barrier to undertake some adventure?"[86] Similar sentiments applied to wider strategy; there was no question of risking everything on a single throw of the dice.

The army was taking delivery of modern and powerful tanks immediately before the war, well able to match those of the Germans, but refused to let these tanks dominate their wider strategy. General Brecart, Inspector General of Cavalry, had dismissed in 1933 plans to mechanize two cavalry divisions as "dangerous utopias … we have no idea what this can yield,"[87] and Colonel Charles de Gaulle remained a relatively lonely voice in advocating the creation of an armored corps. Tanks, his numerous critics countered, were ill suited for any assault on the hilly, wooded Rhineland. Armored divisions would, they continued, undermine the essential unity of the army: "It is difficult to treat with all the courtesy one would wish ideas that verge on delirium."[88] So as the tanks appeared, *La Revue d'Infanterie* insisted in December 1938 that their role would be confined to supporting infantry attacks over distances of 1,200 meters. As the influential journal concluded, "This obsession with tanks must cease."[89] But whatever the future deployment of tanks, the French command remained optimistic and Gamelin greeted news of the German attack on May 10 with singular assuredness.

German commanders, however, were relatively pessimistic and during late 1939 lobbied Hitler to reach a diplomatic settlement with the West. Some even considered deposing him to arrest Germany's "unstoppable journey into the abyss."[90] Hitler, however, hinted to a terrified General von Brauchitsch that he knew of these plans, junior army officers in any case warmed to Nazism, public opinion was behind the government after the Polish campaign, and none of the would-be plotters were clear what would replace the Third Reich. An unconnected, lone attempt by a certain George Elser to kill Hitler on November 8 through a bomb attack in Munich narrowly failed. And Hitler had in fact publicly offered France and Britain a comprehensive peace settlement on October 6. This initiative was rejected, although London persevered with a subterranean diplomatic effort during late 1939 to persuade Goering to overthrow Hitler, establish a conservative, free-trading Germany and restore a degree of sovereignty to Poland and the Czech lands.[91] This harebrained strategy also came to nothing.

German invasion plans were, therefore, drawn up during the autumn of 1939 in an unpropitious climate of conspiracy and diplomatic subterfuge. They were relatively conservative, and as it happened accorded with French expectations. Attacks on Belgium and the Netherlands were designed to screen the Ruhr District from Allied interference and exploit the resources of the Low Countries to enhance Germany's economic base during a protracted war with Britain and France. However on January 10 a German aircraft with details of these plans on board crashed near the Belgian town of Mechelen, forcing a review of options. A senior commander, General Erich von Manstein, seized the opportunity to lobby Hitler to adopt a more daring strategy.

Hitler in fact needed little persuading and the new plan was formalized on February 24. Germany would invade the Netherlands and Belgium as before and draw the French and British armies northward into the Low Countries. Another army would attack the Maginot Line to pin down the French garrisons there. However, the main thrust would see the bulk of German armor drive through Luxembourg, the southwestern corner of Belgium, and cross the River Meuse at Sedan before striking westwards across the open fields of northern France toward the English Channel. The main Allied forces would be cut off to the north, pinned against the secondary German attack into the Low Countries.

This involved moving huge volumes of men and material along minor roads through the broken hill country of the Ardennes, but Manstein had been persuaded by a tank expert, General Heinz Guderian, that the strategy was viable. Although other senior colleagues harbored doubts, few wished to reprise the futile attrition of the Great War, with the Chief of the General Staff, General Franz Halder, concluding: "Even if the operation were to have only a 10 per cent chance of success, I would stick with it. For only this can lead to the defeat of the enemy."[92]

On the eve of the battle 136 Allied divisions faced 135 German, and 2,900 German tanks faced an equal number of French tanks. However, while the German tanks were organized in armored divisions, most of the French were, as intended, deployed as infantry support. Equally significantly, with the cream of the French army, including most of its armor, committed to central Belgium, the German attack through the Ardennes encountered French reservist infantrymen ill-suited to resist such overwhelming force.

Belgium and the Netherlands were invaded on May 10, and on May 14, following the intensive bombing of Rotterdam, the Dutch capitulated. Belgian resistance rapidly disintegrated in the east of the country, allowing German units to engage the Allies' main line of defense through central Belgium, where French and German forces clashed without either gaining a decisive advantage. Meanwhile the Germans launched their main thrust into the Ardennes and initially created the "greatest traffic jam known to that date in Europe."[93] However, the chaos was resolved before the Allied air forces (engaged further north) thought to intervene. On May 12 German armored spearheads reached the next and final obstacle in their path, the River Meuse. Within a day they established bridgeheads west of the river with the help of massive air support and successfully repulsed French counterattacks. On May 16 the armor broke through the crumbling French lines and, as traumatized French soldiers fled the onslaught, German tank commanders ignored orders to await the arrival of supporting infantry forces and instead began their drive toward the English Channel. Counterattacks against these columns' northern and southern flanks failed to dam their progress and on May 20 the Second Panzer Division reached the mouth of the River Somme.

Allied efforts to salvage the situation were confused and ill-coordinated. On May 20 Weygand was recalled from the eastern Mediterranean to replace Gamelin, but this cost vital time as he held a series of meetings with field commanders to take stock of the situation. German infantry and artillery units meanwhile began to consolidate the northern and southern flanks of the corridor the armor had cut through northern France, allowing the tanks themselves to swing northwards up the Channel coast and toward the Allied forces retreating out of Belgium. On May 22 Weygand finalized plans for a counterattack, but his strategy rested on an exaggerated view of the forces available to him. Field commanders who were locked in desperate fighting knew better, but when his strategy came to nothing Weygand found a scapegoat in the small British Expeditionary Force and its commander, John Viscount Gort.

The trauma of defeat now left already prickly Franco-British relations near to breaking point. Gort had moved his army from Belgium into northwest France and staged a daring attack on the northern German flank at Arras on May 21, but thereafter his situation deteriorated. He abandoned any thoughts of further offensive action on May 25 and initially retreated northeastwards before turning west toward the port at Dunkirk. His French counterparts were no better placed and the Belgian government capitulated on May 28, but accusations that "perfidious Albion" had undermined Weygand's counterattack were reinforced by the confused events at Dunkirk. The British forces intended from the outset to evacuate from the port, but French commanders imagined a bridgehead around Dunkirk would be secured and held. This misconception delayed the evacuation of French troops for several days, although of the 338,226 Allied troops ferried to England under German aerial bombardment in a fleet of 700 British and 160 French ships, large and small, almost 140,000 were French. Some 30,000 or more French troops remained to be taken prisoner when the Germans entered Dunkirk on June 4, betrayed, it was alleged, by their British fair-weather allies.

Quite why the German armor had allowed the British the luxury of an improvised evacuation long remained the stuff of conjecture. At the time Hitler tried to pass it off as a peace overture to a beaten enemy, but in reality the evacuees owed their good fortune to German prevarication on May 24. Hitler and his generals swithered over whether to rush tanks northwards to Dunkirk or spare their armor for the imminent southward push through France. On May 26 the tanks did finally roll north, but the Allies had gained invaluable time to improvise a temporary defense of the Dunkirk perimeter and the new British Prime Minister, Winston Churchill, who had replaced Chamberlain on May 10, was provided with a mobilizing myth and an army with which to see off powerful domestic advocates of a compromise peace with Hitler.

During early June, as recriminations continued to fly between London and Paris, the German offensive southward through France began. French resistance stiffened. The headlong panic and flight of French reservists that had greatly eased the Germans' passage across and beyond the Meuse was briefly in the past. However by June 8 distant gunfire could be heard in Paris. On the following day German forces, with powerful air support, broke through the French lines north of the city, prompting the French government to leave the city on June 10 for the south. Churchill's exhortation to his allies to fight for their capital street by street was extremely poorly received and in the event Paris was declared an "open" (undefended) city. The apparent lack of British air cover was the next bone of contention. Weygand appealed personally to Churchill to commit the Royal Air Force (the RAF) to this final Battle of France: "Here is the decisive point ... this is the decisive moment," but this was tantamount to sacrificing British air power and thus the security of Britain itself. "This is not the decisive point, this is not the decisive moment," as Churchill riposted.[94] A fresh British contingent was landed in western France on June 13, some to face futile slaughter, the more fortunate 136,000 hasty reevacuation. Some 24,000 Polish troops were also shipped from France to Britain in the final days of the battle. On the following day the German army entered Paris.

The French government agonized over whether to fight on from North Africa, perhaps after consummating an offer from Churchill of a full Franco-British political union, or to seek an armistice. Almost to a man French military commanders in the colonies favored sustaining the war and transferring as many troops, aircraft and ships as possible to French North Africa. The Prime Minister, Paul Reynaud, was for fighting on, but much of his Cabinet, including his Deputy Prime Minister, Marshal Pétain, disagreed. General Weygand was also keen to conclude an

Figure 7.3 The Franco-German ceasefire is announced in Paris, June 22, 1940.
Source: Ullstein Bild.

armistice as soon as possible. Weygand and many of his senior colleagues blamed the civilian institutions of the Third Republic for the debacle and it was not lost on him that a request by the civilian government for an armistice (Pétain's role notwithstanding) would pull the army's chestnuts from the fire. Similar considerations had motivated the German Quartermaster General, Erich Ludendorff, in September 1918. Politics apart, it seems unlikely that Weygand, who had already proposed armistice talks on May 24, could conceive intellectually of a war fought from French colonies across three continents. As Paul-Marie de la Gorce observes, he was convinced that 1918 had confirmed the French army as the world's finest. Only the German army enjoyed a comparable stature and now, he believed, its crushing victory over France left it unassailable.[95] Reynaud resigned as Prime Minister on June 16, to be replaced by Pétain. He resolved speedily to conclude an armistice and so save what could be preserved of the "eternal France."

The elderly Marshal broadcast to the nation late on June 17 and approached the Germans on June 18, by which time their forces had reached Rennes, Tours, Dijon and Pontarlier. The resulting armistice took effect during the night of June 24–5. Loudspeakers broadcast the news on June 22 across the French capital, where German soldiers (we are led to believe) were already mingling freely and chatting with civilians, the troops in soft caps and often unarmed.[96] To the south, during the final, chaotic days of fighting to no good purpose German motorized units, often small in number and lightly armed, rounded up the demoralized French army and raced southward to Bordeaux, where the last government of the Third Republic had sought refuge. Lyons had also fallen and the Swiss citizens of Geneva could watch the German army moving through the French villages a short distance south of the city.

The Battle of France had cost 90,000 French lives and 30,000 German – significant totals, but modest compared with the set-piece carnage of the First World War. Almost 2 million French soldiers were taken prisoner, emphasizing the scale of the German victory. As Kershaw remarks: "A generation earlier, the fathers and uncles of these soldiers had fought for four years and not reached Paris. Now, the German troops had achieved it in little over four weeks."[97] German domestic opinion was at once relieved and elated. A delighted city chief reported: "One can safely say that the whole nation is possessed by an unprecedented and unbridled confidence in the Führer," while other officials took care in their reports to praise Hitler's "superhuman" stature and achievements.[98] Self-serving this may have been, but during the summer of 1940 Hitler undoubtedly basked in the high noon of his and his regime's popularity. "For perhaps the only time during the Third Reich," Kershaw observes, "there was genuine war-fever among the population."[99] Hitler's return to Berlin from the war, on July 6, was a staggering triumph as hundreds of thousands of citizens wildly lauded "the greatest warlord of all time."[100]

Paris had already suffered the humiliation of a massive German military parade through the heart of the city. For the Germans it further expunged bitter memories of 1918–19 as the columns of soldiers, bands playing and cavalry clattering along the Champs Elysées, retraced the route of the Allied victory parade at the signing of the Versailles Treaty. France was divided into occupied and unoccupied zones, the former encompassing the north and the Atlantic coastal strip, the latter the center of the country and its Mediterranean coast. Alsace and the Moselle were returned to German administration pending reannexation and, as after the First World War, these provinces saw the removal of those deemed unwelcome by the new rulers. A hundred thousand Mosellans and 4,000 Alsatian residents were bundled into France. Small border enclaves along the Alpine chain initially served as Mussolini's modest reward for joining the war during the closing phase of the French campaign. Rome also acquired certain transit and supervisory rights in French North Africa and the Horn of Africa and in November 1942, when the Axis powers overran the unoccupied zone, was allocated much of southeastern France and also Corsica. Occupied and unoccupied France remained a single administrative unit, although German and Italian military ordinances took precedence in the occupied zones.

The armistice itself was a theatrical event, signed at Rethondes in the Compiègne Forest using the same railway carriage and on the same spot where Marshal Foch had presented terms to Germany in November 1918. The French metropolitan army was restricted to 100,000 lightly armed troops and the air force virtually disbanded, but the French navy was maintained intact on condition it remained in port. The costs of the German occupation would be borne by France (as Germany had borne the cost of the post-1918 Allied occupation) and French prisoners of war would remain interned until a final peace settlement. A commission was established in the city of Wiesbaden to supervise the armistice. However, unlike the Germany of 1918, France had retained its colonies and although colonial officials had initially favored fighting on, most now fell behind Vichy. Significant armed forces were retained in this empire, largely beyond Germany's reach, troops that would be used for the Allied cause during the closing stages of the war.

Hitler himself seems to have struggled to come to terms with the apparent totality and immensity of his victory. On June 28 he visited Paris briefly and secretly in the post-dawn light, on an architectural reconnaisance. The visit, he confided to Albert Speer, "had been the dream of his life," but to Goebbels he suggested that much of the city was second rate. He had seen enough, he continued churlishly, to know that Speer's remodeled Berlin would be vastly superior,[101] but it is less clear what ultimate fate he envisaged for France itself. Goebbels's diaries claim that Hitler talked of reversing the verdict of the Peace of Westphalia, concluded in 1648, which had stripped the Germanic Holy Roman Empire of its French-speaking western provinces. He also contemplated resettling Burgundy with German speakers, perhaps from the Italian-governed South Tirol,[102] but such plans remained completely unfulfilled. The immediate priority was to conclude peace with France and Britain and excessively severe demands on France could only complicate this strategy. Thereafter the German military government strove to exploit France's industrial resources, the SS pursued racially predicated goals and the German Foreign Office sought a diplomatic rapprochement with the defeated enemy. Each was at cross-purposes with the other and the Foreign Office was further thwarted by Hitler's refusal to make the necessary concessions to rekindle serious thoughts of a Franco-German alliance.[103]

7.4 From Vichy to Pearl Harbor: June 1940–December 1941

With the armistice behind it, France's government had to come to terms with the defeat and its consequences. Few had a good word to spare for the Third Republic. Pétain's Deputy Premier, Pierre Laval, persuaded parliament on July 10 to grant the Marshal power to amend the constitution at will, arguing that "a great disaster like this cannot leave intact the institutions which brought it about."[104] On the following day Pétain duly declared the Republic at an end and set in its place the French State or État Français. He invested an exceptional degree of power in himself as Head of State and parliament was suspended indefinitely. The Marshal also nominated Laval as his political heir, a sort of ersatz Dauphin. This new government settled into the hotels of the spa town of Vichy in the unoccupied zone, rather than return to German-occupied Paris.

The republican watchwords of "equality, liberty and brotherhood (fraternity)" were replaced by the more conservative motto "work, family, fatherland." One Vichy propaganda poster depicted these three values as the foundation stones of a new France on which rested "discipline, order, thrift and courage" and above them the columns of "school, the artisan class, the peasantry, and the military." An orderly, solid house, "France" stood on these sturdy columns, while to the left a crumbling and tilting French edifice destabilized by internationalism, avarice, the Jews, parliament, communism and a host of other afflictions told the story of the defunct Third Republic.[105] The anti-Semitism was meant seriously and from 1941 a series of laws excluded France's hitherto integrated and emancipated Jewish minority from citizenship rights. Thereafter France participated willingly, even proactively, in the rounding up and expulsion of Jews – refugees and French-born alike – via the notorious French internment camp at Drancy to the death camps in Poland.

In 1940, however, Pétain's initial choice of ministers lent the Vichy regime some credibility as a national government, including as it did former republican politicians as well as figures from the antirepublican right for whom the "nightmare" of the Popular Front era had been banished and the Dreyfus Affair avenged. Vichy operated within the framework of French law and maintained diplomatic relations with foreign powers, including the United States of America. General de Gaulle, who had fled to London during the collapse, cut something of a lonely figure at this stage. Pétain maintained that by working with the Germans – a process he dubbed, immemorably, "collaboration" – France could find a place in Hitler's new European order and escape the fate meted out to Poland. "It is with honour," the Marshal declared, " and to maintain French unity – a unity of ten centuries – in the framework of constructive activity in the new European order that … I enter into the way of collaboration."[106]

Some politicians, including Laval, preferred to believe that collaboration continued down the long-established and honorable road of Franco-German reconciliation with its many eminent protagonists, his mentor Aristide Briand among them. Others comforted themselves that the armistice had bought France time. Parallels were drawn with Weimar's experience, where a 100,000 strong army and a host of restrictions on the fledgling republic's freedom of action did nothing in the longer run to prevent Germany's revival. Weygand may have been antirepublican and even the architect of the armistice, but he was not a collaborationist at heart, hoping that "France's internal reforms would one day allow her to avenge her defeat like Prussia after Jena" (during the Napoleonic era).[107] Weapons were squirreled away in remote corners of the countryside: 65,000 rifles, 9,000 machine guns, 3,500 lorries, and modest numbers of artillery pieces.[108] Vichy, however, was denied the luxury of a formal peace as Germany's war against Britain dragged on. From 1941 France was subjected to ever harsher requisitioning of resources and manpower as Germany's war with the Soviet Union demanded more of the Reich and its subject states than could humanly be delivered. By this time, with an Allied victory increasingly likely, German repression nourished an increasingly powerful resistance movement. Vichy's militia or Milice fought the resistance up to and beyond the

June 1944 Normandy landings in bloody and pitiless encounters, while real power passed to the Germans. German troops themselves were subjected to increasingly numerous attacks and their lines of communication repeatedly sabotaged, so triggering savage collective reprisals on communities known or suspected to harbor members of the resistance.

During the summer of 1940 Hitler sought to finish the war with Britain, either through a negotiated peace or through invasion. On July 19 he addressed the Reichstag, to celebrate the victory over France and offer London an olive branch. The speech as a whole impressed the prominent American journalist William Shirer, who remarked that "his oratorical form was at its best" and went on to praise his body language, particularly the use of his "feminine and quite artistic" hands.[109] However, a perfunctory appeal to Britain was squeezed into the final minutes of the speech, and beyond lambasting Churchill and threatening to destroy the British Empire, Hitler merely appealed "to reason, also in England."[110] The British response was immediate and negative, reiterated at length by Halifax on 22 July. On August 1, after a week or more of prevarication, Hitler settled on attack and the invasion of Britain. The first stage would involve a battle for air supremacy over the Channel and southern England to secure the sea passage, landing and resupply of the German forces.

With Britain's sea approaches well defended by the Royal Navy, official thinking had long since focused on the danger posed to cities by German air power. At the time of Munich Britain had just one fighter squadron equipped with modern Spitfire aircraft, and five in the process of being equipped with Hurricanes. A year later the Royal Air Force had 26 squadrons of these modern eight-gun fighters, and by the time of the Battle of Britain (August–September 1940) 47 squadrons were in service. Annual aircraft production had swollen from 240 to 660 during the final year of peace and was stepped up further once war broke out. German aircraft output was comparable, but the British fighters were technologically superior and their production once described as "the most important achievement of rearmament between Munich and the outbreak of war."[111]

Britain was also committed to building heavy bombers which were also superior to their German counterparts, but the devastation these Lancaster bombers and the American Flying Fortresses wrought on urban Germany lay in the future. For the moment a fear pervaded official circles that London and other British cities would prove defenseless in the face of German aerial attack and the Civil Defence organization began evacuating women and children from the cities on the first day of hostilities. The operation did not run particularly smoothly, with fewer than 50 percent of potential Scottish evacuees reporting to centers in Edinburgh, Glasgow, Dundee, Clydebank, and Rosyth. Many wives had no wish to leave their husbands, who had to remain behind to work in the war industries, and mothers of large families were unwilling to see their children scattered over several rural homes and beyond their care. Nonetheless, the Regional Commissioner for the Scottish Civil Defence Region concluded that the process of evacuation had "swept away more class and caste barriers … than at any time during the past 100 years."[112] Looking at Britain as whole, this sense of solidarity is possibly overstated and some working-class mothers were held personally responsible for the sorry physical state of their evacuated children, but the social polarization of the 1930s was undermined and the ethical and political basis created for the Labour electoral victory of 1945.

Meanwhile Chamberlain struggled to control the politics of a war he had striven to avoid. The Labour and Liberal parties refused to form a new national coalition as long as Chamberlain led the Conservatives, who themselves were split between a pro-Chamberlain majority and an anti-Munich, anti-Chamberlain minority. Divisions came to a head during early May 1940 when a two-day debate in the House of Commons over the conduct of the Norwegian campaign transmogrified into a vote of censure against the government. The government survived, but with its majority cut from 200 to 81. There was little personal animosity shown against Chamberlain, but he felt obliged to reopen talks with the Labour opposition over the creation of a National coalition. The Labour leaders, Clement Attlee and Arthur Greenwood, initially favored a coalition led by Halifax, but since he sat in the House of Lords and doubted his own ability to lead the country from outside the Commons, Churchill emerged as the preferred option. On May 10 Chamberlain resigned as Prime Minister but remained in the Cabinet as Lord President of the Council, only to be struck down by personal catastrophe weeks later. On July 24 he was diagnosed with bowel cancer and died of the illness on November 9, with his nemesis, Hitler, at the height of his military power. Churchill was eloquently generous. In his vale-dictory speech to the Commons he characterized Chamberlain's qualities as "surely among the most noble and benevolent instincts of the human heart – the love of peace, the toil for peace, the strife for peace, the pursuit of peace, even at great peril and certainly to the utter disdain of popularity or clamour."[113]

Churchill, however, was destined to be a warrior in the most unpropitious cir-cumstances imaginable. He struggled to salvage what he could from the fall of France and thereafter faced the might of the German armed forces. On July 13 the air offensive against Britain saw German fighters and bombers attack the military airfields and radar stations of southern and eastern England in the face of desper-ate resistance from the Royal Air Force, whose pilots included many Poles, Czechs, Free French and Canadians. Matters hung in the balance until an unauthorized German bombing raid on London's East End on August 24. A revenge strike by the RAF on Berlin goaded Hitler into ordering an all-out attack on London, which began on September 7. However, at this critical point German strategy had fallen between two stools. The bombing of London spared the airfields and the RAF's infrastructure the worst, while equally failing to deliver a knockout blow against the British will to remain in the war. By mid-September German losses had become unsustainable. Goering's air force continued to mount devastating raids on Britain's ports and industrial cities and the civilian death toll climbed inexorably, but the strategic imperative for invasion, air superiority, had proven unattainable. On September 17 Hitler postponed this invasion indefinitely.

By this time the United States President, Franklin D Roosevelt, had begun supplying Britain with surplus warships and other military equipment, despite the counterarguments of the isolationists and a widespread conviction in American political circles that Britain was destined to defeat. This American involvement was all the more ominous for Germany since Hitler proved unable to consummate his series of victories by bringing the war to any sort of conclusion at this optimal moment. During the summer of 1940 the Vichy government debated its foreign policy options: alliance with Germany (and thus war against Britain) or tenuous neutrality during which conflict with Britain would be kept to a minimum. A third option, to prepare for a new war against Germany, could scarcely be discussed openly. A British attack on the French fleet at Mers-el-Kébir in Algeria on July 3, designed to prevent it complying with the armistice terms and sailing to a port in metropolitan France, destroyed a number of ships and cost over 1,000 French lives. This stiffened the mood of the anti-British camp in Vichy, but it was only in mid-autumn, after the failure to knock Britain out of the war, that Hitler explored his options in the Mediterranean basin more fully.

On October 22 he held a short meeting with Laval at Montoire outside Lyons. The Frenchman openly countenanced joining the war against Britain, encouraged by Hitler's observation that this would leave Britain rather than France to reimburse Berlin's war expenses.[114] A further meeting was arranged for October 24, this time between Hitler and Pétain. In the meantime, the German leader traveled south to the Spanish border at Hendaye for discussions on October 23 with General Franco. German military chiefs had already expressed doubts over the potential usefulness of Spain to the war effort and the German Foreign Office felt similarly. Hitler was keen to secure cooperation for an attack on Gibraltar, which would then be transferred to Spain if Madrid joined the war in January 1941, but had little more to offer Franco. The Spanish dictator, however, sought control of French Morocco and western Algeria, which Hitler could not possibly grant without completely alienating France, potentially a much more valuable ally than Madrid. The meeting ended inconclusively and Hitler returned to Montoire for his promised discussions with Pétain, but these were no more fruitful. Hitler pressed the Marshal to join the struggle against Britain, whereas Pétain urged the swift release of French prisoners of war, clarification on the future status of Départements on France's northern border which, ominously, had been attached to the German military government in Brussels, and an early peace settlement. All Hitler obtained was a joint affirmation of the principle of Franco-German collaboration and a public, photographed handshake between the two leaders. Equally significant was a memorandum sent by Pétain's government to London on December 10 via the Canadian chargé d'affaires at Vichy. Clearly intent on playing a double game, Pétain offered Britain a maintenance of the status quo of "artificial chilliness";[115] London acknowledged receipt of the Note, no more. A meeting between Hitler and Mussolini on October 28 had also yielded little beyond the unwelcome news that Italy, against strong German advice, had decided to invade Greece during the coming Balkan winter.

The Italian army struggled against the Greeks, who also received significant British military support, and matters were complicated further when a pro-German Jugoslav government was overthrown during March 1941. Hitler was forced to intervene in the Balkans. Both Jugoslavia and Greece were rapidly crushed during April by the German army for the loss of 251 lives, and a more costly paratroop assault secured Crete from British and Dominion forces in May. Greece suffered the rigors of military occupation, Croatia gained its independence, but the Serbs of Jugoslavia were branded as racial enemies and experienced a fate comparable to that inflicted on the Poles: "Emigrants, Saboteurs, Terrorists, Communists and Jews" – a deliberately elastic listing – were to be eliminated by SS units.[116] A Croat militia, the Ustaši, joined in the hunt, wreaking death and havoc on the Serb population and slugging it out with two resistance movements, the royalist Chetniks and a communist partisan army under Jozef Broz (Tito).

With the northern Mediterranean coast entirely secure, Berlin made further efforts during May and June 1941 finally to agree Franco-German military collaboration and complete the conquest of the Mediterranean basin, but these initiatives were stymied by French prevarication. Threats by Marshal Keitel that France "would be treated like Jugoslavia"[117] should she refuse failed to impress. In the event Free French and British forces overran the French colony of Syria during June 1941 and also expelled the Italians from Somalia, Eritrea and Ethiopia. Finally, as the Italian garrison in Libya teetered on the brink of collapse, Berlin was forced to dispatch a German expeditionary force under General Rommel to North Africa to stiffen Italian resistance against British and Dominion forces. Maintaining this Afrika Korps turned into a logistical nightmare when, during 1942, a headstrong Rommel pushed many hundreds of miles beyond the main Libyan ports and into northern Egypt. Despite Herculean efforts by the Italians, supplies struggled to reach the front line along single-track Italian railways, through underdeveloped North African ports and along desert trails over almost impossible distances. Rommel's adventure became an increasingly wasteful diversion from the ferocious war that had broken out between Germany and the Soviet Union in June 1941, and on November 4, 1942 his Italian and German forces were defeated at El Alamein by the British Eighth Army commanded by General Bernard Montgomery. Other, American-led units landed far to the west in Morocco and Algeria and after short-lived Vichy resistance secured northwest Africa. For Pétain these Allied landings were a moment of truth, providing an opportunity to transfer his government to Algiers and so rejoin the struggle against Germany, but in the event he remained in Vichy as the German army overran the Free Zone to secure France's Mediterranean coast against Allied invasion. Thereafter a headlong retreat by Rommel westward into Tunisia was followed by the Axis powers' final evacuation of Africa in May 1943, leaving 250,000 troops to fall into Allied captivity.

Relations between Germany and the Soviet Union had deteriorated ominously during the autumn of 1940. The German Foreign Minister, Ribbentrop, hoped to divert Soviet attention toward southwestern Asia and invited his Soviet counterpart, Molotov, to talks in Berlin. Ribbentrop, however, displayed his customary arrogance and gaucheness, while Molotov, Norman Davies observes, "behaved with excruciating crudity, emitting a torrent of tactless demands."[118] Their substantive negotiations on November 12 and 13 confirmed that the ambitions of two great dictatorships were irreconcilable. Ribbentrop pressed for a Soviet thrust against India, the Persian Gulf and the Middle East, but Molotov demanded changes to the 1939 German-Soviet eastern European settlement to Moscow's advantage. Finland, Romania, the Balkans (especially Bulgaria), and Turkey were named and Molotov made it disconcertingly clear that Moscow had wider ambitions in the Mediterranean basin. He refused to countenance joining the German-Japanese-Italian Tripartite Pact on Berlin's terms and discussions on future economic cooperation also proved difficult.

Hitler had never warmed to Ribbentrop's strategy and now declared the "marriage of convenience"[119] with Stalin over. In December 1940 detailed preparations began for the invasion of the Soviet Union. On one level Hitler's reasoning was straightforward and conventional enough. Surely, he reasoned, an obstinate Britain would make peace if Germany eliminated the Soviet Union and removed Churchill's last potential continental ally from the equation: "The possibility of a Russian intervention in the war was sustaining the English. ... They would only give up the contest if this last continental hope were demolished."[120] However, a breathtakingly savage racialist agenda underpinned wider German objectives. The entire Bolshevik political class, often described as "Jewish-Bolshevik," was to be murdered out of hand, and on March 30, 1941 Hitler made plain in a speech to senior army officers that the coming war would be one of racial annihilation. Few senior German commanders displayed any qualms as a series of decrees exempted troops from disciplinary action, whatever steps they might take against enemy civilians or Soviet functionaries. The collective punishment of entire communities for partisan activities was envisaged and quickly became the norm as repression and resistance fed remorselessly on one another. As during the Polish campaign, units (*Einsatzgruppen*) were created to carry out "special tasks" or, more bluntly, state-sanctioned murder; most notoriously mass shootings of the region's Jewish citizens. Hitler and Himmler planned to deport most of the Baltic and Slavonic majority to Siberia, the "racially worthy" remainder to lead a serf-like existence at the beck and call of German incomers. As Himmler commented in August 1942, "We can only resolve the social question by killing the others and seizing their land."[121] In the event many were transported to Germany itself as slave laborers.

The invasion had originally been scheduled for May 15, 1941, to take optimal advantage of the summer weather, but the Balkans campaign forced a delay to June 22 – by coincidence the very same day that Napoleon had attacked Russia in 1812. On June 21 Hitler thought to inform Mussolini that the attack on the Soviet Union was imminent and on the following day a 3 million strong German and allied army was hurled against an equal number of well-equipped Soviet troops. In a "Proclamation to the German People" Hitler accused the Soviet Union of concluding a secret deal with Britain and staging frontier violations, but whether Stalin had been secretly preparing for his own attack on Germany and was simply beaten to the punch remains the stuff of debate. His military commanders had argued in May for a preventive war against Germany (and thus long after German preparations for Barbarossa had begun), but Stalin settled for a middle way. Soviet troops were grouped ready for a massive counterblow against any German attack rather than for defense in depth. The Soviet dictator chose to ignore British warnings during early June of an imminent German offensive. The Germans won stunning victories as their columns swept past and surrounded the Soviet armies, advanced hundreds of miles in weeks and soon enough seemed to have little more than space between themselves and complete victory. General Halder declared on July 7: "The Russian campaign has been won in the space of two weeks,"[122] and by December 1941 Leningrad was under siege, German units had reached the western outskirts of Moscow and had overrun the Ukraine.

However, the easy victories of the summer were overshadowed during the autumn by mounting logistical problems as German lines of communication snaked across a vast landscape. The retreating Soviet armies sabotaged the transport infrastructure, the Russian gauge railways took time to convert for German usage, while the roads became reduced to quagmires by the incessant autumn rain. The delay to the offensive brought about by Mussolini's Balkan adventure was exacting its price. When the frost finally came during early November and hardened the ground, many bogged-down vehicles remained immobilized in frozen, concrete-like mud. As temperatures dropped to minus 20 degrees centigrade ignition systems, oil, and radiators froze, as did the water pipes on German railway locomotives. Although the German High Command had (contrary to received wisdom) addressed the problem of equipping armies for the eastern winter, they were left without the transport capacity to deliver vital winter supplies to the front line. As Martin van Crefeld concludes:

> It is certain that the railroads, hopelessly inadequate to prepare the offensive on Moscow and to sustain it after it had started, were in no state to tackle the additional job of bringing up winter equipment. Therefore the question as to whether or not such equipment was in fact available is perhaps of secondary relevance.[123]

Even during August it had dawned on Hitler and his generals that they might have bitten off more than they could chew as disagreements surfaced over strategic priorities. Soviet engineers, already accustomed to the strains and challenges of forced industrialization and collectivization, dismantled and removed vital armaments factories to the east, where workforces "made up of women, old men and teenagers"[124] struggled in grueling arctic conditions and on meager rations to reassemble equipment and so create the economic preconditions for military survival.

Life on the Soviet collective farms became equally grueling as half-starved workers were occasionally forced bodily to pull the ploughs themselves for want of service-able tractors or oxen. Meanwhile the Germans were confronted by winter-hard-ened Siberian divisions rushed to the defense of Moscow. A desperate struggle began to survive the climate and stave off counterattacks by an increasingly deter-mined and well-organized Soviet army. And if Soviet losses had reached 3.3 million by January 1942, the German tally of 900,000 was on a completely different scale to the casualties suffered during earlier campaigns.

There were also intimations of a growing American political commitment to the Allied cause. The November 1940 presidential election saw Roosevelt returned to office as "the leader who could keep America out of the war without allowing the war to be lost," and a majority of Americans already believed that only their direct intervention would permit the defeat of Nazi Germany.[125] In August Churchill had sailed across the Atlantic by battleship to meet secretly with US President Roosevelt off the Newfoundland coast. On August 12, 1941 the two lead-ers agreed a declaration (published two days later) which reiterated the principles contained in Woodrow Wilson's Fourteen Points of January 1918. Dubbed the "Atlantic Charter" it committed Britain and the United States to a more equitable world economy, the abandonment of force in international affairs, and the crea-tion of a supranational system of global security (to replace the League of Nations). The Charter fell well short of a formal US-British alliance, but provided the basis for the postwar "special relationship" between the United States and Britain. More immediately it informed the Declaration of the United Nations, signed by the USA, Britain, the Soviet Union, and China on January 1, 1942 and provided an ideological blueprint for the post-Nazi world. Not surprisingly, the Atlantic Charter called for the "total eradication of Nazi tyranny."[126]

Hitler's expectation that a German victory over the Soviet Union would bring Britain to the negotiating table had been dealt a mortal blow; events in the Pacific Ocean compounded the damage. Until December Roosevelt was content to sup-ply and support Britain and (from mid-1941) the Soviet Union, sustaining their struggle against Hitler and so providing the American President with time to pon-der his longer-term strategy. However, Washington perceived in Japan an immedi-ate ideological and strategic threat, but assumed that military strength and economic sanctions would suffice to contain the Asian great power. However, in response to increasingly strident American warnings to end its military aggression in East Asia, Japan attacked and devastated the United States naval base at Pearl Harbor on the Hawaiian island of Oahu on December 7, 1941 using carrier-borne aircraft. There were almost simultaneous attacks on the British colonies of Hong Kong and Malaya. Hitler responded by declaring war on the United States on December 11, fearing that inaction would be tantamount to "letting [the members of the Tripartite Pact] be defeated singly."[127] Barbarossa had already made unlikely allies of Britain and the Soviet Union and London now lost no time in declaring war on Japan, so sealing a priceless alliance with the United States. "It was not part of the Japanese plan;" Davies remarks, "but they had unwittingly unlocked the doors of the Grand Alliance. 'The Big Three' – the war-winning trio of Churchill, Stalin, and Roosevelt – were in business.'[128] Put differently, two regional wars – essentially between Japan and China and between Germany and its neighbors – had exploded into a truly global conflict which was to end Europe's control over its own destiny for two generations or more.

Chapter Eight
Europe Eclipsed

8.1 Competing Caesuras: 1940–1 or 1945?

When the United States of America entered the First World War in 1917 it effectively decided the outcome of a conflict between two European coalitions. Victors and losers were, to varying degrees, left financially dependent on the United States, whose growing technological and productive might was also unmistakable. However, when postwar America adopted an isolationist foreign policy and turned its back on the peace settlement and League of Nations, it restored to European diplomacy a disproportionate weight and influence. It was Europe's statesmen, Allied and German, who in 1925 revisited the terms of the 1919 peace accord and reached a negotiated settlement of differences. The League itself also functioned essentially as a European body, based in the Swiss city of Geneva, from where it coexisted uneasily with the continent's great powers themselves. The victors had even exploited the collapse of the Ottoman Empire and the defeat of Germany to extend their colonial empires behind the fig leaf of League of Nations mandates.

Foreign policy apart, postwar European governments contemplated a return to financial "normalcy," which was understood to mean a return to the gold-backed economic world of 1914. The Soviet Union posed an ill-defined and unsettling challenge to the European capitalist order, but a resumption of the organic process of incremental adjustment and change that had characterized most dimensions of the European experience, private and collective, before 1914 appeared eminently attainable by the mid-1920s. Despite the devastating impact of the Great War, Europe was picking up the pieces and carrying on.

The Great Depression certainly struck a blow at Europe's economy and self-confidence, but no more spared the countries of the New World. A number of democratic political orders had already collapsed in southern and eastern Europe during the 1920s and the Depression accelerated this process. However, in democracy's historic, northwest European stronghold parliamentary government remained largely inviolate. Indeed, Scandinavia responded to the challenges of the Great Depression by strengthening parliamentary liberties under Social Democratic leadership, so establishing the basis for post-1945 public life in the region. It is impossible to predict what would have come of the fascists and military strong-men who held sway in much of eastern and southern Europe had peace prevailed. Apart from Mussolini, few entertained radical foreign policy ambitions and, as the post-1945 era has demonstrated, authoritarian regimes are inherently fragile affairs, prone to collapse under the weight of their internal contradictions.

Adolf Hitler's National Socialist order, however, displayed a unique and destruc-tive dynamic that fleetingly threatened to reorganize the continent in its own image, before its implosion brought an end to European self-determination. Hitler's drive to forge a German racial state of transcontinental proportions ultimately demanded either the subjugation or eradication of entire peoples, or the destruction of Germany in the attempt. There were moments before the war when this *va banque* strategy could conceivably have been stopped in its tracks. Winston Churchill was a particularly trenchant critic of the Franco-British appeasement strategy that facil-itated Hitler's increasingly blatant preparations for war. Even when this war came, Germany won the Battle of France as much by luck as by judgment, but thereafter Hitler was free to devour mainland Europe, strike out eastward toward Asia and in the process initiate a process of genocidal mass murder.

There was no credible European counterweight remaining to Hitler's Germany and it took the globalization of the war to destroy his formidable armies, a heroic British resilience notwithstanding. President Roosevelt hoped for a Wilsonian-style European settlement, allowing Washington and Moscow to preside benevolently over the restoration of democratically governed nation-states, sheltering under a sturdy United Nations umbrella. However, Western Europe had been left prostrate by Hitler's war and Stalin made it clear that he planned to impose Soviet control on a devastated Eastern Europe. When Churchill visited Moscow in October 1944 he acknowledged that Soviet military victories had dealt Stalin a strong hand in the east and only ventured to claim Greece for the western Allies. Moscow was ceded control of Romania and Bulgaria and significant influence in Hungary and Jugoslavia, but disagreements over Poland's future had already surfaced at the inter-Allied Teheran Conference of November–December 1943 and could not be recon-ciled at later meetings. The first intimations of the "Cold War" – a geopolitical power struggle which became dressed up in the language of ideological and moral confrontation – appeared while Hitler still ruled in Berlin. Roosevelt died three weeks before the war in Europe ended, leaving his successor, Harry S. Truman, to deal with these deteriorating Soviet-American relations and address the European power vacuum created in 1945 by Hitler's defeat. The Soviet Union, he declared, would be contained, and the two nuclear armed superpowers thereafter faced each other across a demarcation line dubbed the Iron Curtain. To its east, Europe's nations were ranked as clients of Moscow, to its west of Washington, even if a few smaller states were allowed the luxury of (often supervised) neutrality.

In many senses, therefore, time was called on our story during 1940 or 1941. Historians of the Second World War and historians of Germany, quite naturally, regard 1945 as the compelling historical caesura of mid twentieth-century Europe. However, from a European perspective the fall of France, Barbarossa and Pearl Harbor confirmed that the European global age had indeed ended. The collapse of the European world empires after the war served as retrospective confirmation of this sea change. In place of a Europe-centered world dawned a bipolar global order, with the Cold War at its heart, that was sustained until the fall of the Berlin Wall in 1989 and the subsequent collapse of the Soviet Union. But this Cold War was not simply about the control and ultimate destiny of Europe, involving a series of confrontations in east Asia, Africa, and also Latin America. Thereafter, far from "ending history" the post-Soviet age has witnessed the emergence of an increasingly multilateral world order, centered on the Pacific rather than the Atlantic Ocean, as witnessed by the inexorable shift in the balance of global economic power toward eastern Asia. A restored European community of nations, the European Union, collectively plays a major role in this new world, but without any prospect of the old continent, still less its former "great powers," reasserting the degree of power and influence it enjoyed prior to Hitler's victories of 1939–41. Seen in this light, 1945 marked a major episode of the emergent post-European age rather than its beginning.

8.2 Hitler's War – from Triumph to Oblivion, 1941–1945

However, the defeat of Nazi Germany and the denouement of its murderous potential still lay in the immediate future and demands attention. In early 1941 the material power underpinning this potential was arguably at its peak; Germany's industrial output was enhanced by that of Western Europe and Scandinavia, and Berlin could draw on the agricultural resources of virtually the entire continent. Raw materials, including oil, were delivered by the Soviet Union. German political influence was also unprecedented, with Italy, Croatia, Slovakia, Hungary, Romania, Bulgaria and Finland allied, Norway, Denmark and the Netherlands protectorates, much of France, as well as Belgium, Serbia, Montenegro and Greece occupied, and the remaining continental neutral states largely sympathetic to Berlin. The position of Sweden and Switzerland, as the remaining functioning continental democracies, rested uneasily on economic cooperation with the Reich. Aid from the United States was keeping Britain in the war, but little more. The German attack on the Soviet Union therefore represented an extraordinary gamble, as Hitler's racially predicated agenda sacrificed the half-loaf of Soviet raw materials deliveries in a bid to secure outright control over its productive capacity and secure indefinite German control of the entire European landmass.

During 1941 and 1942 the German armies overran the Soviet Union's economic heartland and, as we saw, only the extraordinary efforts of a workforce inured to

suffering by years of upheaval managed to sustain the Soviet economy and enhance
war production. The economic tide began to turn inexorably in the Allies' favor.
By 1943 Soviet output of heavy guns and tanks had, Richard Overy notes, out-
stripped Germany's by a significant margin,[1] by which time the United States's war
economy was single-handedly outproducing Japan, Germany and Italy combined.
So huge was the United States's potential that the country experienced boom conditions and its armies a standard of supplies that contrasted starkly with either its
allies or Germany. For despite the ruthless regimentation of its labor force, the
conscription of forced laborers from its neighbors, the pitiless and ultimately
deadly exploitation of Soviet prisoners, and a ferocious program of requisitioning
from its defeated enemies, Germany failed to realize the full capacity of its powerful military-industrial complex.

The armed forces dominated war production and prioritized technical sophisti-
cation over standardized mass output. The generals displayed little understanding
of the realities of large-scale production, instead demanding that German industry
deliver, often in small batches, 425 different aircraft types and models, 151 different
makes of lorry, and even 150 different motor cycles. Appeals from Hitler himself
to achieve "more primitive, robust construction" through "crude mass-produc-
tion" (the Soviet and to a degree the American method) fell on deaf ears.[2] After
Albert Speer was appointed Armaments Minister in 1942 a serious effort was made
to override the generals and reap the dividends of greater rationalization and
standardization. However, 1943 also witnessed the beginning of massive Allied
bombing raids on German industry which quickly disrupted many of Speer's hard-
won gains. German air defenses exacted a huge toll in Allied lives and aircraft during 1943, but by 1944 the German air force, increasingly short of fuel, was ground
down remorselessly and the American Flying Fortress bombers gained the freedom to range in their hundreds or even thousands above Germany, vapor trails
streaming through the thinly defended skies, raining unprecedented destruction
on Germany's great cities. Berlin, Hamburg, Cologne, Frankfurt, and later Dresden,
ended up as smoldering rubble. Production was dispersed to small factories scattered across Germany, or sheltered underground, where slave laborers toiled in a
Dali-esque nightmare of brutality and death. The Third Reich's war economy had
addressed the challenges of global, great power warfare far too late in the day and,
as Overy concludes: "Factory for factory, the Allies made better use of their industry than their enemy."[3] The increasingly desperate attempts by Germany to dra-
goon millions of prisoners and slave laborers into maintaining production levels
exacted a shocking price in human life for diminishing returns.

The military tide also turned during 1942 and 1943. Japan had eclipsed American
and British naval power in the Pacific and Indian Oceans in December 1941. The
destruction of Pearl Harbor was followed, days later, by the sinking of the British
battleships *Prince of Wales* and *Repulse* as they steamed to intercept Japanese landings on the east coast of Malaya. Little stood in the way as a handful of Japanese
army divisions swept aside the British strongpoints of Hong Kong and Singapore,

overran the oil-rich Dutch East Indies (today's Indonesia), captured the US-controlled Philippines, and pushed westward into Burma, the gateway to the British Raj. Even the island of Madagascar, off the southeastern African coast, appeared vulnerable to Japanese attack and with it the sea lanes around the Cape of Good Hope.

However, the United States mustered its remaining naval resources in May 1942 to block a Japanese invasion fleet heading for Port Moresby in Papua New Guinea and the islands of the Coral Sea to the northeast of Australia. A Japanese ground attack on Port Moresby was also repulsed during September, thus securing Australia from the threat of invasion. Meanwhile, on June 3, 1942, a massive Japanese naval assault on the US-controlled island of Midway, which guarded the approaches to Hawaii and the eastern Pacific, collapsed when three aircraft carriers were lost to American aerial attack. The heart had been ripped out of the Japanese navy and the country thereafter lacked the necessary industrial muscle to make good losses, still less to match the scale of American shipbuilding. As the Japanese Navy Minister conceded: "After Midway, I was certain there was no chance of success."[4] Not only would Japan's overextended maritime dominions be worn down by remorseless Allied counterattacks, which by April 1945 included air raids on Japan itself and culminated in the dropping of atomic bombs on Hiroshima on August 6 and Nagasaki on August 9, but from mid-1942 the United States could afford to turn its attention to the German war in Europe and the Mediterranean.

Following the expulsion in May 1943 of Axis forces from North Africa, American and British troops invaded and quickly conquered Sicily during July. On July 25, the Italian King bowed to army pressure and dismissed Mussolini, so breaking Italy's alliance with Germany and securing an armistice with the Allies on September 8. Mussolini was sprung from confinement by German paratroopers and German forces succeeded in occupying the Italian mainland, but in September the Allies crossed the straits of Messina and began a fitful, heavily contested advance up the Italian peninsula, reaching Rome in June 1944.

The decisive land battles, however, occurred in the Soviet Union where, after surviving the 1941–2 winter, German military leaders advocated a renewed attack on Moscow. Stalin had anticipated such an assault and concentrated his forces in front of the Soviet capital, but Hitler looked to the resources of the eastern Ukraine and beyond, including the oilfields at Maikop, the industrial cities of the Don and Volga basins, and the agricultural riches of the entire region. One German army would strike at Stalingrad and then push down the River Volga to the Caspian Sea at Astrakhan, another would head for the Caucasus Mountains. The German Chief of Staff, Franz Halder, fretted over Hitler's increasing interference in strategic planning, convinced that his armies were overextending themselves. Hitler's strategy, he complained, was unacceptably risky, continuing: "This so-called leadership is characterized by a pathological reacting to the impressions of the moment and a total lack of any understanding of the command machinery …"[5] Hitler wrote off Halder's warnings as pusillanimous, and with the main Soviet forces covering Moscow, the German offensive swept all before it. Armored columns crossed the

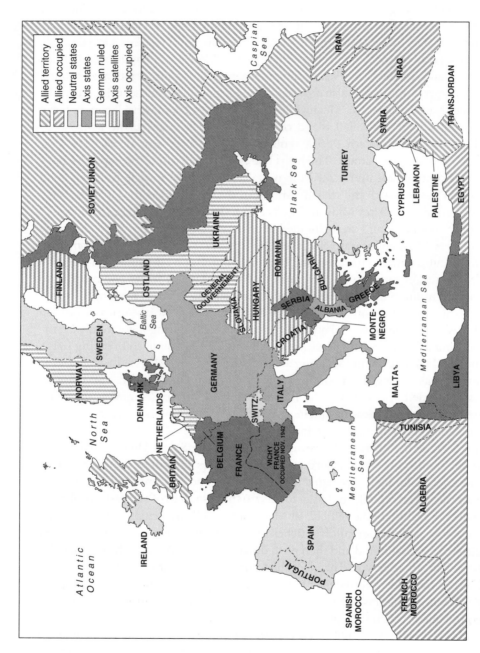

Map 8.1 Europe ca. November 1942.

Legend:
- Allied territory
- Allied occupied
- Neutral states
- Axis states
- German ruled
- Axis satellites
- Axis occupied

Figure 8.1   The Battle of Stalingrad: Soviet soldiers advancing against the encircled German Sixth Army, November 1942.
Source: Ullstein Bild.

River Don, which flowed from south of Moscow toward the Black Sea, approached the River Volga at Stalingrad (today's Volgograd) and drove southeastward to reach the Caucasus Mountains, which formed the boundary between Europe and Asia. On August 23 German forward patrols reached the outskirts of Stalingrad and Soviet morale teetered on the verge of collapse.

Stalin's regime responded with a judicious combination of carrot and stick. Desertion or defeatism was punished with the utmost savagery, but the memory and imagery of imperial Russia were also pressed into service. Past wars and triumphs were evoked and the Orthodox Church revived to lend moral succor to the "Great Patriotic War" against the Nazi invaders. German brutality did the rest, creating a mood where resistance to the bitter end appeared a more attractive option than the mass executions and slave camps of the SS. As the autumn dragged by, the German armies struggled to capture Stalingrad, now a grimly defended, war-ravaged wasteland stretched out along the west bank of the Volga. Unlike Hitler, Stalin became increasingly willing to listen to his best generals and during September Georgi Zhukov persuaded him that, given careful preparation, the Battle of Stalingrad could be turned into a graveyard for Hitler's ambitions. Zhukov ferried just sufficient forces across the Volga to hold and retake small groups of shattered buildings among the ruins at Stalingrad, whatever the cost, as he concentrated the mass of his armies on the northern and southern flanks of the Stalingrad salient.

Hitler repeatedly and publicly declared Stalingrad all but taken, but Zhukov's strategy denied the German field commander, General Friedrich Paulus, a final victory. Then, on November 19, the Russian commander hurled the bulk of his forces against the northern and southern flanks of the Stalingrad salient. The Romanian divisions holding these positions crumpled and by November 22 the Soviet armies had closed the ring to Paulus's rear and cut him off from the main German lines. Hitler forbade any break out, an attempt to relieve Paulus during December also failed, and efforts to supply his frozen and outnumbered army by air proved hopelessly inadequate. By February 2, 1943 the last surviving German units had surrendered and destroyed any remaining illusions within the Nazi hierarchy that the Soviet Union, allegedly a nation of racial and moral degenerates, could be swept aside.

Paulus had been captured days earlier and the prospect of ultimate defeat began to permeate the German public consciousness. Whispered conversations between ordinary Germans admitted as much, and in Paris a female secretary at Gestapo headquarters, while drinking coffee with a Viennese lady visiting the French capital, warned that defeat loomed and that the German atrocities in the east would bring the world to take its revenge on Germany in turn. Soviet prisoners, detailed to German farms and businesses, reassured (better) German employers that they would put in a good word for them when the Soviet armies arrived. One of Germany's outstanding anti-Nazi resistance groups, the White Rose, was spurred on by the defeat to call for the overthrow of Hitler's regime and a return to Christian moral principles, including an end to the wall of silence surrounding the fate of the Jews. Grouped around Kurt Huber, Professor of Philosophy at Munich University, and the siblings Hans and Sophie Scholl, the White Rose had distributed anti-Nazi leaflets across southern Germany from late 1942, but in February 1943 the authorities arrested the courageous activists and executed the Scholls within days. Huber died in July. At her trial Sophie claimed to stand for Germany's Christian conscience, values, she continued, that were shared, silently, by many: "Somebody, after all, had to make a start. What we wrote and said is also believed by many others. They just don't dare to express themselves as we did."[6] Meanwhile, in the aftermath of Stalingrad Soviet forces surged westwards, until their own overextended supply lines allowed the German armies to retake the city of Kharkov on the River Donets during March.

If Stalingrad had stemmed the German advance, it was the Battle of Kursk that determined the ultimate outcome of Barbarossa and opened the way to a Soviet invasion of Germany itself. On July 5 the cream of Germany's armored divisions attacked a large, Soviet-held salient around the city of Kursk, seeking to inflict a Stalingrad in reverse. However, the laborious preparations for this offensive had squandered the advantage of surprise, allowing Zhukov sufficient time to fortify and garrison the salient. The teeth of the offensive shattered on the granite of Soviet resistance after a week of bitter fighting, and a carefully prepared counteroffensive quickly threw the German armies into headlong retreat. Soviet forces reached the Ukrainian capital of Kiev on November 6 and were now poised to strike westward toward the German and Polish borders and southwestwards toward the Balkans. With the Battle of the Atlantic also lost and the Mediterranean slipping from Hitler's grasp the only question remaining was how soon and on what terms Germany would lose the war.

In addition to the growing pressure exerted by the advancing Allied regular armies, German lines of communication and garrisons to the rear of the front lines were harried by increasingly confident and effective partisan forces, many supplied by Allied air drops. The Nazis' brutality created a steady stream of partisan volunteers, some joining the Communist-leaning forces that dominated in Jugoslavia and Italy, others the forces loyal to democratic governments in exile, who coexisted uneasily with a strong Communist resistance in much of Western Europe. In Eastern Europe partisan activity was a predictable by-product of Germany's racial, annihilationist war. German reservists who were entrusted with maintaining security behind the front lines made little distinction between the hounding and murder of ethnic "undesirables" and operations against genuine partisans, so driving more and more of the local population to active resistance, however poor the odds of survival. Soviet soldiers who became trapped behind the German lines were also increasingly unwilling to surrender, for Stalin had declared surrender to be treason and the treatment meted out by the Germans to prisoners of war made joining the partisans a preferable option for most. This grim struggle was compounded by the simple desperation of these German troops, increasingly vulnerable in a vast landscape of steppe, marsh and forest, lashing out and so nourishing a savagery of its own.[7]

The Western Allies' efforts during 1944 culminated in the liberation of France. The scheme was not to Britain's liking. Churchill and his generals favored committing their limited land forces and more powerful navy to the Mediterranean war, wearing down the Germans in a process of "calculated attrition."[8] The Italian campaign, Churchill suggested, could be supplemented by landings in the Balkans. The United States, however, sought to engage and destroy the main German armies, which demanded a full-scale invasion of France. An effort by Canadian forces to seize the Channel port of Dieppe in 1942 had failed disastrously, ruling out any further direct assaults on the heavily fortified ports themselves. Beach landings offered an alternative and at the Quebec Conference of August 1943 the British side grudgingly agreed in principle to support American plans for such an assault, code-named Overlord. Stalin had long since demanded a full-scale invasion of Western Europe to relieve the pressure on his armies, and during the Allies' Teheran Conference of November 1943 joined with the Americans to prioritize Overlord over any British-inspired alternatives. The date (later delayed) for the cross-Channel assault on France, D-Day, was set for May 1, 1944.

The US General Dwight D. Eisenhower was placed in overall command, with the British victor of El Alamein, General Bernard Montgomery, in charge of the invasion bridgehead. Allied aircraft began systematically to destroy the communications network of northwestern France and disrupt German troop movements as a protracted campaign of misinformation did enough to leave Hitler and his generals guessing exactly where the assault might come. The Straits of Dover offered the narrowest and most plausible crossing point and German commanders committed the bulk and pick of their forces to defend the beaches around Calais. Disagreements between Rommel, now commander of the Channel front, and his superior, Field Marshal Gerd von Rundstedt, over whether to break any invasion on the beaches themselves or to launch a massive armored strike against the attackers as they began their advance inland were never adequately resolved. Rommel was left with insufficient forces to defend all the possible invasion points, while von Rundstedt's mobile armored reserve was too weak to respond decisively to any landing. As Overy concludes, "The Allies could not have disposed the German forces more favourably if they had done it themselves."[9]

When the invasion, briefly delayed by unseasonably stormy weather, finally came on June 6 it took the longer sea route to the Normandy beaches rather than the short crossing to Calais and caught the defenders of this "secondary" front off guard. A maelstrom of Allied firepower overwhelmed the coastal fortifications, while Allied air supremacy prevented the effective deployment of reinforcements. A further spell of unseasonable weather during early July disrupted the shipment of Allied supplies and grounded the fighter-bombers, so allowing Rommel to stabilize his defenses, but the relief was short-lived. Montgomery conducted a grim and costly battle for the strategic city of Caen which lay at the eastern end of the Allied bridgehead. This fighting sucked in the bulk of the German armor, leaving a far weaker contingent to face General Bradley's US forces when they broke out from the western end of the beachhead on July 25. Overriding his commanders' protests, Hitler ordered a suicidal counterattack which culminated in the envelopment and virtual destruction of the main German armies in France. On August 15 a second Allied army landed in southern France and raced northwards up the Rhone valley. The remaining German units bolted toward the German frontier.

On August 25, with resistance forces already on its streets, a Free French armored division led the Allied armies into Paris. Pierre Laval had sought to move from Vichy to Paris during the Normandy battle, but his German protectors would have none of it and secreted him and Marshal Pétain across the Rhine to temporary refuge in Baden. In 1945 both returned to France to face trial and both were sentenced to death for treason, although Pétain's sentence was commuted to life imprisonment. It was the Free French leader, Charles de Gaulle, oblivious to intermittent sniper fire, who arrived in Paris on August 26 and declared the French Republic reinstated.

During the lifetime of the Third Reich as many as 42 attempts were planned on Hitler's life.[10] The best known was in July 1944, when an influential group of military leaders tried to kill Hitler and bring a hopeless war to an end. Many officers who were not directly involved in the plot chose to turn a deaf ear to these conspiratorial discussions, before Colonel Claus Count von Stauffenberg planted a bomb in Hitler's eastern headquarters near Rastenburg (East Prussia) on July 20. He narrowly failed to kill the dictator. A furious Hitler had over 5,000 suspects and their families – military and civilian – arrested, among them Rommel who was allowed the option of suicide followed by the charade of a state funeral. Others were shot out of hand or placed before show trials conducted without a semblance of propriety by the notorious Nazi judge Roland Freisler. The condemned defendants were hanged from meat hooks using piano wire. Some 200 suspects in all died one way or another. This July Bomb Plot had finally ripped the heart out of the aristocratic Prussian officer corps and did nothing for the coherence and esprit de corps of the army command. Terrified survivors were left to obey Hitler's increasingly irrational orders as he steered Germany into the abyss.

By late August, American units commanded by General George Patton were approaching the German border on the Moselle with little organized resistance in front of them. A total German collapse was only averted when Patton out-ran his supply chain. His pleas for fresh gasoline and munitions went unheeded, for, as van Creveld remarks, the logistical planners "who considered the advance to the Seine impracticable even while it was being carried out [were never likely] to take the risk of supporting an 'unscheduled' operation across the German border."[11] Montgomery's army surged through Belgium during early September and set its sights on Germany's heavy industrial Ruhr District just 100 miles to the northeast. However, as the first German V2 rockets began to fall on London, Montgomery was ordered north to capture their launching sites in the Netherlands. An airborne assault, aimed at the Dutch Rhine crossing at Arnhem, failed in the face of stiffening German resistance and the momentum gained after the Normandy breakout had temporarily been lost.

The Soviet offensive resumed in January 1944, striking westward toward the Baltic and Poland. The siege of Leningrad was broken and by August Soviet troops were on the eastern bank of the River Vistula in central Poland. To the north, Finland signed an armistice with the Soviet Union in September and paid an immediate price as the retreating German army burned the wood-built towns of Lapland to the ground. In October Soviet forces briefly entered East Prussia before a German counterattack retook the lost ground. Another Soviet army struck southwestwards during August and September, forcing Romania and Bulgaria out of the war, and then linking up with Tito's Jugoslav partisans during October to liberate Belgrade.

The Hungarians had considered capitulating as early as March 1944, but Hitler had browbeaten the Head of State, Admiral Horthy, to sanction a pro-German puppet regime in Budapest and allow German troops to occupy the country. This delayed the final German collapse on the Danube front, but also exposed Hungary's 750,000-strong Jewish community to the furies of the Holocaust. By July almost 450,000 had been dispatched to the gas chambers of Auschwitz. Horthy tried again to negotiate an armistice with Moscow during October, but was taken into custody by the Germans who installed the Hungarian-fascist Arrow Cross in government. The Russians eventually captured Budapest on February 11, 1945, by which time the city's remaining Jews had been murdered or sent as slave laborers to Germany.

A tragedy of a different sort unfolded in Poland. Poland's Jews had made a last stand in the Warsaw Ghetto during April and May 1943, battling the Germans for

three weeks against hopeless odds rather than passively accepting death in the extermination camps. In 1944 their Christian fellow countrymen suffered a bitter fate of
their own. The Polish underground army, the Armia Krajowa, answered to the gov-
ernment-in-exile in London. It created a shadow state within Poland which the
Germans never managed to suppress, but also slugged it out with Ukrainian and
Soviet partisans whose territorial ambitions overlapped with its own. Stalin's territorial objectives, not surprisingly, accorded with those of the Soviet fighters. During
1943 he broke off relations with the London Polish government and at the Teheran
Conference demanded the Polish territories granted to the Soviet Union by the 1939
German-Soviet Pact. Despite furious British objections the Americans acquiesced,
for the survival of the Soviet-Western wartime alliance was of paramount importance. As Roosevelt stressed to Churchill, "he was unwilling to take any action that
might upset Stalin."[12] Poland would be "compensated" with a swathe of territory in
the east of historic Prussia, but Stalin had also created a puppet Polish government-
in-exile of his own which looked set to take control of Poland itself in the wake of
the Soviet advance. Soviet forces were already rounding up and deporting members
of the Armia Krajowa to Siberia and, as Peter Stachura remarks:

> As such, the Rising was not only anti-German but also anti-Soviet. With the Red
> Army ... reaching the environs of the Polish capital by July 1944, it was finally con-
> sidered by both the Polish Government in London and the AK High Command that
> Warsaw had to be brought under Polish control ahead of the inevitable advance of
> the Red Army into the city.[13]

The uprising began on August 1, only for its leaders to be denounced by Moscow
as "a gang of criminals."[14] The Western Allies mooted dropping supplies to the city
by air, but would have needed to refuel at Soviet airfields. Permission was denied.
The battle for Warsaw raged until October 2, by which time 250,000 Polish insurgents and civilians had perished at the hands of SS units. Himmler believed that the
annihilation of Warsaw offered a final chance to eradicate the Polish nation once
and for all: "Then the Polish problem will historically no longer be a big problem
for our children and for all those who come after us ..."[15] Once the fighting was
over the Germans evacuated survivors and systematically demolished the remnants of the city. When the Soviet army finally entered Warsaw on January 17,
1945 it was into a devastated ghost town. The last wartime meeting of the three
Allied leaders, held at Yalta in the Crimea during February 1945, agreed in effect to
partition Europe between the superpowers and assign Poland to the Soviet sphere.
A coalition government consisting of the Communist ("Lublin") Poles and the
London exiles was to be established in Warsaw, chosen by free and unfettered elections, but few doubted that the postwar reality would be very different. Even during the course of the Rising, Joanna Hanson concludes, pro-Soviet and Communist
opinions had gained ground in Warsaw itself as the incapacity of the Polish government in London to influence events became clear.[16]

Hitler launched his last major offensive during December 1944. He planned to strike westwards out of the Ardennes and capture the port of Antwerp some 125 miles distant. The Allied forces to the north, he hoped, would be eliminated and the Western Allies brought to the negotiating table. When the attack began on December 16 it achieved initial surprise and German armor advanced 65 miles as low cloud hindered Allied air operations. However on December 24 the weather cleared and 5,000 aircraft decimated the German armor, ending the offensive and reducing short-lived German counterattacks elsewhere on the western front to little more than pinpricks. The Allied advance resumed. On March 2 the first American troops reached the River Rhine and five days later crossed it at Remagen. German military discipline in the west collapsed and Nazi efforts to stem "defeatism" through the terror of summary executions exacted a savage price to little effect. British forces raced northwestwards to reach the Baltic Sea at Lübeck, while the Americans drove through the heart of Germany and on April 23 met up with Soviet forces at Torgau on the River Elbe. Other American units liberated the west of Czechoslovakia and captured the Bavarian capital of Munich. The German forces in northern Italy capitulated on May 5 and fears of a final stand by Nazi stalwarts within an "Alpine redoubt" turned out to be chimerical. The German army in Austria surrendered on May 7.

By this stage the German retreat from Eastern Europe had culminated in the flight of the entire population of eastern Germany.[17] Civilians joined soldiers in a stream of humanity, trekking westward through icy winter storms, although some became hopelessly trapped in fortress cities such as Breslau and Königsberg. The oncoming Soviet forces had fought their way toward Germany through a world of unparalleled death and devastation and now began to repay the Third Reich's barbarity in some measure. Uniformed male Germans (many of them teenagers and old men drafted into the Volkssturm militia) were shot out of hand, and their wives, daughters and sisters raped and often murdered. Such mayhem tended to last several days in any one place before Soviet officers brought matters under control, but the German fear of "Bolshevism," long since stoked up by Goebbels's propaganda, had been substantiated. Hopelessly outnumbered German army units fought on desperately, not in any expectation of turning the military tide, but to cover the flight and evacuation of their countrymen and countrywomen. German naval and merchant ships, their decks crammed with humanity, evacuated as many as possible from the port cities of the eastern Baltic. Some, including the *Wilhelm Gustloff*, were sunk with thousands of refugees on board. Then, during the final days of fighting, German army units tried to flee westwards toward the lesser evil of British or American captivity. Alongside these German troops were foreign volunteers, often organized into Waffen-SS units, for whom there were few realistic options left beyond dying fighting, so moving them to offer desperate if futile resistance.

One Soviet army had captured Vienna on April 13, while to the north Zhukov's forces on the River Oder launched their final assault on Berlin on April 16. Hitler ignored pleas to leave the capital for Berchtesgaden and spare it utter destruction, instead hatching fantastical plans to hurl his remaining, crumbling armies against the enveloping tide of 2.5 million Soviet soldiers. By April 25 Berlin was surrounded, and although the garrison defended each street and building ferociously, inflicting heavier casualties on Zhukov's forces than the American army suffered in the entire war, the Soviet advance could not be stemmed. On May 1, with the fighting a hundred or so meters distant, Hitler and his partner-become-wife, Eva née Braun, committed suicide. Goebbels and his wife chose the same fate for themselves and their unwitting children. Most of the remaining grandees of the Third Reich were picked up later, to stand trial at Nuremberg for war crimes and crimes against humanity. The fighting finally ended on May 9.

8.3   Holocaust

During the closing weeks of the war the Western Allies came upon the network of concentration camps that stretched across Germany. Their existence was hardly a secret, for the establishment of Dachau and other camps by the SS had been given generous and favourable coverage in the German press. By 1945, however, these extralegal institutions – brutal places from their inception – had descended into the nethermost pits of inhumanity. Slave laborers were herded together, wretchedly clothed and starving, to sustain what could be sustained of Germany's collapsing war production, guarded by a combination of atrocity-hardened guards and a motley crew of freshly enlisted, untrained SS conscripts, teenage women among them.

Shortly before the end, the internees were joined by a new tide of unfortunates. As the Soviet armies pressed into Poland the SS hurriedly closed down and demolished its web of extermination camps and drove the remaining prisoners – clothed in prison rags, many sick, most half-starved – westward across the snow-scoured landscape of a collapsing empire. Many stragglers were shot or clubbed to death, others dropped and died, leaving the survivors to be herded into the camps of central and western Germany. With the Third Reich in its death throes, the orderly supply of food, fuel, medicine and other essentials collapsed and camp administrators compounded this logistical crisis by willful neglect and murderous brutality. When British forces liberated Bergen-Belsen and the Americans Dachau they came upon unspeakably harrowing scenes that came to encapsulate the utter immorality of the Third Reich. The Soviet armies discovered far worse as they pushed into Poland and encountered the SS's network of extermination camps at Chelmno, Belzec, Sobibor, Auschwitz-Birkenau, Treblinka, and Majdanek. It had been beyond the capacity of the SS adequately to disguise the monstrosity of what had happened: 1.5 million of the 6 million Jews murdered by the Nazis perished at Auschwitz-Birkenau alone.

The road into this abyss was scarcely incidental, even if the details of the so-called "Final Solution" only crystalized into a coherent program at the turn of 1941–2.[18] The National Socialist regime had displayed increasingly radical and deadly anti-Semitic traits from the outset and the Jews of the conquered eastern territories fell victim to the *Einsatzgruppen* (task forces) in the immediate wake of the advancing German armies, first in Poland and then in the Baltic states and Soviet Union. The events at Babi Yar, outside the Ukrainian city of Kiev, remain particularly notorious. On September 29, 1941 Kiev's Jewish community was ordered to assemble for resettlement, only to be marched out of the city to their deaths. *Einsatzgruppe* C reported laconically to Berlin that: "The Sonderkommando 4a in cooperation with Headquarters and two commandos of Police Regiments South executed 33,771 Jews on 29 and 30 September '41 in Kiev,"[19] but this did scant justice to the reality of events. Execution squads ordered one group of victims after another into a deep, naturally formed chasm, where they were ordered to lie face down, and shot. Quicklime was thrown on the dead and dying, no time was wasted in ordering the next batch into the pit, and the exercise was sustained over two full days.

The remaining Jews of Germany and occupied Western Europe were certainly destined for an unpleasant fate, but various options were considered, including deportation beyond Europe – possibly to Vichy-controlled Madagascar – incarceration in ghettos, or a grinding existence in Nazi equivalents of the Soviet Gulag. By late 1941, however, leading Nazi officials in Eastern Europe concluded that the close quarters mass shooting of Soviet and other East European Jews by the *Einsatzgruppen* could not "resolve" the Jewish question, partly because of the corrosive impact on the morale of the executioners themselves. As one officer reported:

> At the beginning my soldiers were not affected. On the second day, however, it was already noticeable that one or the other did not have the nerves to carry out a shooting over a longer time. My personal impression is that during the shooting one has no moral scruples. These appear, however, after several days if one reflects about it quietly in the evening.[20]

The lieutenant in question asked to be excused further execution duty and the mass murder of millions in this direct manner was neither morally nor logistically possible.

However, the pressure to "do something" mounted, for the Polish ghettos were seen as an unnecessary burden and a potential source of epidemic, and the Jewish communities of urban Germany and Austria occupied thousands of homes needed to house ethnic German incomers from the Soviet Union. The pressure grew toward the end of 1941, when the complete annihilation of Europe's Jewish communities was deemed a moral imperative at the highest level as Germany fought both the Soviet Union and the United States. In the Nazi credo the Jews stood behind

Cracow 1938. Old ghetto Entrance.   *R. Vishniac*

Figure 8.2   Before the Holocaust: the Jewish ghetto of Kasimierz, Krakow, photographed by Roman Vishniac.
Source: © Mara Vishniac Kohn, courtesy International Center of Photography.

Bolshevism and also Wall Street and the US government. Thus Adolf Hitler declared to the Reichstag shortly after Pearl Harbor: "We know what stands behind Roosevelt, it is the eternal Jew who believes his time has come, to inflict on us the same grue-some fate as [he has] on the Soviet Union."[21] The murder of the Jews had become an integral part of the Nazi war effort. Hitler refrained from issuing any written order for the mass murder of the Jews – even the domestic euthanasia programme had demanded circumspection – but his intent was no less deadly for that.

On January 20, 1942, Himmler's Deputy, Reinhard Heydrich, chaired a meeting in the idyllic lakeside surroundings of Wannsee outside Berlin, where the modalities of mass murder were clarified by the interested parties. There were, the meeting was informed, 11 million Jews in Europe, from the 3,000 in Portugal, the 4,000 in Ireland, to the 2,300 in Finland and 69,000 in Greece. The largest communities were in the Polish Generalgouvernement(2.284 million) and the Ukraine (2.994 million).[22] "In the course of the practical execution of the Final Solution, Europe [was to] be combed through from west to east,"[23] which was understood to mean the murder of human beings on an industrial scale. The T4 euthanasia program had pioneered gassing techniques using carbon monoxide (vehicle exhaust fumes). The same method was initially used in the extermination camps before a pesticide gas, Zyklon B, which proved briefly but lethally effective in confined spaces, came into general use. By the time of the Wannsee meeting the first carbon monoxide gassings had already begun at Chelmo.

Later, as Auschwitz began its deadly work, many went to the gas chambers oblivious to their fate. When several hundred Jewish factory workers arrived at the camp early one morning in 1942 they were treated considerately, assured that well-paid work was available and asked to take showers. "Now, when you've had your showers, there'll be a bowl of soup waiting for you all," they were promised, but as they entered the "shower room":

> Two SS men slammed shut the heavy iron-studded door which was fitted with a rubber seal, and bolted it. Meanwhile the [NCOs] on duty had gone onto the crematorium roof [and] removed the covers from the six camouflaged openings. Then, protected by gas-masks, they poured the green-blue crystals of the deadly gas into the gas chamber. … It was as though Judgement Day had come. We could clearly hear heart-rending weeping, cries for help, fervent prayers, violent banging and knocking and [to drown out] everything, the noise of … truck engines running at top speed.[24]

Beyond mass murder, these concentration camps also served as part of the SS's slave labor empire. The fitter prisoners were often not killed immediately, but instead hired out to firms that established factories in the neighborhood of the camps. Receiving starvation rations and experiencing grueling conditions, the slave laborers were literally worked to death. Among the companies involved in this macabre process was I. G. Farben (part-owner of the company manufacturing the Zyklon B gas), 23 of whose senior executives faced trial after the war by an American military tribunal, which convicted 13 of their number. If the slave labor program bought its victims a little time, other inmates worked as camp orderlies, some involved in the clearance of bodies from the gas chambers, or the sorting of clothing and even the extraction of gold fillings from the victims' teeth. Again, however, few ultimately escaped death themselves, for it was never the SS's intention to allow any Jews or members of other targeted groups to survive.

This systematic program of mass murder, which engulfed many more beyond its Jewish victims – the Roma and Sinti peoples notable among them – has demanded an explanation beyond the descriptive, but the enormity of events has left historians struggling to arrive at a satisfactory consensus.[25] Whether the Holocaust had been hardwired into German history and society, perhaps even represented *the* course of German history up to 1945, or whether the German historical path had contained other, more likely, outcomes prior to 1933, remains debatable. The anti-Semitism that pervaded many European societies before and during the Second World War undoubtedly contributed to the intensity of the Holocaust, for the Nazis found many non-German collaborators, but the very process of extermination also demanded active participation, tolerance or at the very least apathy on the part of many in German society. Whether these attitudes represented an opportunistic adjustment to the world Hitler and his lieutenants had created, or accorded with the participants' innermost convictions must have varied. Millions of ordinary Germans, after all, simply struggled in remote, self-regarding corners of Germany to endure the privations of the war years as best they could with little or no aware-ness of the mass murder perpetrated in their name.[26]

Despite the sincere, public contrition displayed by postwar (West) Germany and a series of traumatic confrontations with the Nazi past, it has taken the passage of time and generations gradually to wear away the stain of the Third Reich and restore to German nationhood a sense of ethical normality. The transformation of Germany itself into an increasingly multiracial and multicultural society, whose football team has recently depended heavily on the efforts of two strikers of Polish descent, and where many residents have closer ancestral ties to Anatolia or other Mediterranean lands than with the Third Reich, must also relativize any concept of hereditary blood guilt.

Chapter Nine
Europe: An Honorable Legacy?

Since the caesura of the Second World War no major political movement has sought to claim the mantle of heir to Nazism or Fascism, even if the authoritarian regimes of neutral Iberia survived for several decades. Britain had withstood the ambitions of Berlin and Rome and this story of successful resistance served as a national mobilizing myth for two generations or more. If Belgium and the Netherlands could reflect on substantial collaboration with the Nazis, their interwar polities were largely restored, while the Scandinavians had less to excuse and a robust interwar political settlement to build on. A generation of French men and women sought simply to sweep Vichy under the carpet by stressing the legitimacy and continuity of the country's republican traditions, before undertaking a more fundamental reckoning with the past during and after the late 1960s. West Germans (many actually refugees from the east) sought initially to piece together their daily lives, before confronting the past during the later 1960s. Fascist Italy had never fully displaced or even contested the country's deeper ethical and institutional traditions, and the country had possessed the most powerful wartime resistance movement in Western Europe. Postwar political life quickly gelled into a struggle between an American-backed, Christian Democratic majority and Communist (ex-partisan) minority.

In Eastern Europe, East Germany included, the war's end brought greater change. The political and institutional past was swept aside and replaced by a Soviet-style order. The new, Moscow-backed rulers claimed to have resolved their nations' past traumas by establishing Marxist-Leninist regimes in place of the capitalist or even semifeudal past. Fascism and Nazism, Marxist-Leninist ideologues maintained, had been outgrowths of the crisis-wracked, interwar capitalist order, and by resolving the class struggle Soviet societies had lanced this boil. Postwar capitalism was regarded as inherently vulnerable to a fascist or Nazi revival, so allowing the characterization of the Cold War as a struggle between the "peoples' democracies" of the east and the latent "fascism" of the west.

Beyond Europe, the continent's overseas empires soon enough disappeared as the material strength and moral conviction to preside over African and Asian societies and civilizations evaporated. However, the intimations of decolonization had been unmistakable even between the wars and in a host of other ways the upheavals of the Second World War had fractured and shattered the European world, but without leaving the pre-1939 age beyond recall. The list of examples is compelling and long. The evolving structure of European society continued to witness a shift in population from agriculture and the countryside to the industrial or tertiary economy and the town. Urbanization, however, was complemented simultaneously by an ongoing process of suburbanization (made possible by the earlier railway age and the advent of the motor car), which saw the postindustrial class of office workers, public servants and a swelling army of well-educated technicians and professionals look beyond the confined spaces of the traditional city. The mass proletariat of Karl Marx's imagination was already in relative and absolute numerical decline before 1939 and this trend continued in the form of an often traumatic post-1945 process of deindustrialization. The social profile of employment continued to change in another way as women gained additional political, social, and property rights alongside widening access to education and most areas of economic activity. The interwar Jazz Age and the technology to record and market popular music on a mass scale, the beginnings of a consumer society, the expansion of cinema, the extension of educational opportunity, the burgeoning of spectator sports, and many other pre-1939 developments brought with them, among other things, the first intimations of a youth culture and a discrete youth identity. During the 1950s youth indeed became a distinctive generation, initially in the Western world. State involvement in social and economic life, which had been expanding erratically but unmistakably since the later nineteenth century, continued to grow after 1945 as terms such as the "mixed economy" and the "welfare state" entered the general vocabulary. Keynesian economics, its principles laid down during the 1930s, informed most Western governments' economic and fiscal policies. The scientific and technological achievements of the first and second industrial revolutions, which already anticipated the electronic, nuclear, and modern medical eras, were complemented and enhanced. And so on.

International relations also reflected in large measure a process of adaptation and progression from the interwar and earlier periods. The United Nations, we were reminded, owed a considerable debt to the often maligned interwar League of Nations.[1] The liberalization of global trade and the management of currencies were certainly addressed through new institutions and arrangements, such as the World Bank and the General Agreement on Tariffs and Trade, but these too owed as much to the successes and failures, the "lessons," of the past as they did to any form of war-induced tabula rasa. The confrontation with the Soviet Union was nothing new, but in the nuclear age was conducted on more equal terms, and the new "great powers" were either non-European (the USA) or only part European (the Soviet Union). However, the potential for this configuration was clear enough to the decision makers of interwar Europe. If Britain, France and Italy tried in their various ways to address and stem Europe's relative decline,

Hitler strove to reverse the march of history and in failing to do so hastened the triumph of the very forces he abhorred.

Perhaps the most significant continuity, however, lay in the fundamental redefinition of Europe's material and ethical meaning that took on institutional form during the early 1950s. In 1952 France, West Germany, Italy, the Netherlands, Belgium, and Luxembourg signed the Treaty of Paris and so founded the European Coal and Steel Community. The Community created common institutions for regulating the six countries' heavy industrial economies under a common, supranational legal framework, so diluting the principle of national sovereignty. Subsequent efforts to create a common European Defence Community and Political Community failed, but in 1957 the Treaty of Rome, signed by the same six countries, established the European Economic Community and the European Atomic Energy Community, which initiated collaboration in the nonmilitary sector of nuclear power. The Treaty of Rome laid the legal and institutional foundations for today's European Union. The EU's growing range of competences and expanding territory has restored to Europe collectively a weight and presence in global affairs which appeared all but irretrievable in 1945, when 80 million displaced persons struggled across the ruins, silent battlefields, and mass graveyards of a destroyed continent.

This process of European integration was driven in part by efforts to escape from the vicious circle of war and retribution. It served as a French-inspired strategy to accommodate Germany within an increasingly supranational European order, apart from America yet with American approval. It marked a clear departure from the age of the great, imperial powers, but its architects had cut their political teeth during the interwar era. They drew on the initiatives of that time and before, which sought in particular to achieve a fundamental Franco-German reconciliation anchored on a structured and institutionalized pooling of common interests. August and Fritz Thyssen, father and son controlling one of the Ruhr District's great industrial dynasties, had sensed and articulated the possibilities during the twilight years of peace preceding the Great War;[2] a succession of interwar French governments resumed the quest even as they simultaneously sought security from their powerful neighbor by more conventional means,[3] and interwar German governments responded, not just during Stresemann's tenure as Foreign Minister but until the Great Depression swept away the Weimar Republic and the battered hopes and values that had underpinned its creation.[4] And even the French politicians at Vichy hoped forlornly, in the deluded aftermath of abject military defeat, to salvage something of this agenda.

Vichy aside, the erratic and rocky road toward today's Franco-German alliance, which forms the bedrock on which the European Union rests, must constitute one of the definitive yet relatively neglected strands of our continent's pre-1945 history. The earlier stages of this process were certainly met with a mixture of official British hostility and indifference, although the impact on the British collective consciousness was minimal and the subsequent neglect in the Anglophone literature therefore not entirely surprising. Not much has changed since 1945. British news bulletins continue to grant the EU relatively scant attention. Edward Heath (and possibly Tony Blair) apart, British premiers have continued to regard continental Europe with a mixture of indifference, hostility and incomprehension, even if membership of the Union can no longer seriously be called into question.

But in fairness to historians of each and every nationality, during the immediate post-1945 era premonitions of European integration hardly marked the most obvious dimension of Europe's interwar story. An inherently destructive mix of war, economic crisis, and revolution was bound to dominate the stage, alongside political personae of gigantic proportions, called into being by the enormity of events. Churchill, Stalin and Hitler continue to fascinate successive generations of scholars and readers.

However, time and distance can offer fresh perspectives. Alongside these conventional and central narratives stand the more positive forces and efforts that contributed to the emergence of contemporary Europe. As noted above, countless features of current experience, including patterns of consumption, cultural innovation, the texture of private life, scientific and technological innovation, and more, were laid down before 1945. The same applied in the institutional and political world. Businessmen, politicians, diplomats and visionaries from cultural and academic life often proved unequal to, or compounded, a succession of disasters. But their number included those who laid the foundations of the European Union, a body which has come to exercise a profound influence over our lives and public affairs. As its supporters claim with considerable justification, its effect is essentially benign. The pre-1945 strategic alternatives had little if anything to recommend them; today's semicomical, sometimes distasteful, alternatives to European integration appear thinner still.

Notes

1 The European Paradox

1 Edwin Heathecote, "Grand Designs," *Financial Times*, magazine (Jun. 30–Jul. 1, 2007), 24.
2 Georges Dupeux, *French Society* (Methuen, London, 1976), 191.
3 Gerald D. Feldman, *The Great Disorder: Politics, Economics and Society in the German Inflation, 1914–1924* (Oxford University Press, New York, 1993), 858.

2 The Coming of War

1 F. R. Bridge, *From Sadowa to Sarajevo: The Foreign Policy of Austria-Hungary, 1866–1914* (Routledge and Kegan Paul, London, 1972), 353.
2 Ibid., 358.
3 Ibid., 360.
4 Ibid., Document 36, 441.
5 Ibid., Document 36, Enclosure, 442.
6 Mark Cornwall, "Serbia," in Keith Wilson (ed.), *Decisions for War 1914* (UCL Press, London, 1995), 55.
7 Ibid., 84.
8 Quoted in Bridge, *From Sadowa to Sarajevo*, 9.
9 Holger H. Herwig, "Why Did It Happen?" in Richard F. Hamilton and Holger H. Herwig (eds.), *The Origins of World War I* (Cambridge University Press, Cambridge, 2003), 453.
10 R. J. W. Evans, "The Habsburg Monarchy and the Coming of War," in R. J. W. Evans and Hartmut Pogge von Strandmann (eds.), *The Coming of the First World War* (Clarendon, Oxford, 1988), 54
11 Bernard Michel, *Banques et banquiers en Autriche au début du 20e siècle* (Presses de la Fondation Nationale des Sciences Politiques, Paris, 1976), 363–4, 367–8.
12 Fritz Fellner, "Austria-Hungary," in Wilson, *Decisions for War*, 12.
13 Quoted in Fellner, "Austria-Hungary," 13.
14 Fellner, "Austria-Hungary," 14.

15   Evans, "Habsburg Monarchy," 37.

16   Fellner, "Austria-Hungary," 17.

17   Quoted in Fellner, "Austria-Hungary," 15.

18   Fellner, "Austria-Hungary," 16.

19   Cornwall, "Serbia," 81.

20   Quoted in Fellner, "Austria-Hungary," 16.

21   For Germany's role, see pp. 00.

22   Fritz Fischer, *Germany's Aims in the First World War* (Chatto and Windus, London, 1967); Fritz Fischer, *War of Illusions: German Policies from 1911 to1914* (Chatto and Windus, London, 1975).

23   Michael Howard, *War and the Liberal Conscience* (Temple Smith, London, 1978), 72.

24   John A. Hobson, *Imperialism: A Study* (London, 1902).

25   Paul Kennedy, *The Rise and Fall of the Great Powers: Economic Change and Military Conflict from 1500 to 2000* (Unwin Hyman, London, 1988), 196.

26   Ibid., 227.

27   Norman Angell, *The Great Illusion* (Heinemann, London, 1909), discussed here in David French, *British Economic and Strategic Planning 1905–1915* (George Allen and Unwin, London, 1982), 18.

28   French, *British Economic and Strategic Planning*, 87.

29   Ibid., 8.

30   Ibid., 10.

31   Erskine Childers, *The Riddle of the Sands* (Smith Elder, London, 1903).

32   Paraphrased in Niall Ferguson, *The Pity of War* (Allen Lane, London, 1998), 3.

33   Richard Cobb, "France and the Coming of War," in Evans and Pogge, *First World War*, 126.

34   Edouard Detaille, *Le Rêve*, Musée d'Orsay, Paris.

35   Quoted in Klaus Wilsberg, *"Terrible ami – aimable ennemi." Kooperation und Konflikt in den deutsch-französischen Beziehungen 1911–1914* (Bouvier, Bonn, 1998), 314.

36   Maurice Paléologue, *An Ambassador's Memoirs 1914–1917* (Hutchinson, London, 1973), 9.

37   Quoted in Wilsberg, *Terrible ami*, 272.

38   Quoted in ibid., 273.

39   Volker R. Berghahn, *Quest for Economic Empire: European Strategies of German Big Business in the Twentieth Century* (Berghahn Books, Providence RI, 1996), 9.

40   Wilsberg, *Terrible ami*, 276.

41   Quoted in ibid., 234–5.

42   Quoted in ibid., 223.

43   Quoted in Raymond Poidevin, "Le Nationalisme économique et financier dans les relations franco-allemandes avant 1914," *Revue d'Allemagne et des Pays de Langue Allemande*, 28, 1 (1996), 64–5.

44   Poidevin, "Nationalisme," 64–5.

45   Quoted in Wilsberg, *Terrible ami*, 258.

46   Quoted in Hartmut Pogge von Strandmann (ed.), *Walther Rathenau: Industrialist, Banker, Intellectual, and Politician. Notes and Diaries 1907–1922* (Clarendon Press, Oxford, 1985), 185.

47   Quoted in Gerald D. Feldman, "Hugo Stinnes and the Prospect of War before 1914," in Manfred Boemeke, Roger Chickering, and Stig Förster (eds.), *Anticipating Total War:*

The German and American Experiences, 1871–1914 (Cambridge University Press, Cambridge, 1999), 90.

48 Quoted in Frederick L. Schuman, *War and Diplomacy in the French Republic: An Inquiry into Political Motivations and the Control of Foreign Policy* (Whittlesey House, New York, 1931), 182.

49 Schuman, *War and Diplomacy*, 183.

50 Quoted in Wilsberg, *Terrible ami*, 49.

51 Quoted in Pogge, *Walther Rathenau*, 157.

52 Quoted in Ferguson, *Pity of War*, 68–9.

53 Hew Strachan, *The First World War*, vol. 1: *To Arms* (Oxford University Press, Oxford, 2003), 667.

54 Quoted in Ferguson, *Pity of War*, 69.

55 Quoted in ibid., 70.

56 Ferguson, *Pity of War*, 187.

57 Cobb, "France and the Coming of War," 139–41.

58 Quoted in Ferguson, *Pity of War*, 204.

59 Quoted in Heinrich-August Winkler, *Der lange Weg nach Westen, I: Deutsche Geschichte vom ende des Alten Reiches bis zum Untergang der Weimarer Republik* (C. H. Beck, Munich, 2002), 212.

60 Volker R. Berghahn, "War Preparations and National Identity in Imperial Germany," in Boemeke et al., *Anticipating Total War*, 316.

61 John Brett, *Britannia's Realm*, Penlee Gallery, Penzance.

62 George F. Kennan, *The Fateful Alliance: France, Russia, and the Coming of the First World War* (Manchester University Press, Manchester, 1984), 39 and 44.

63 Quoted in ibid., 153–4.

64 Quoted in Henry Kissinger, *Diplomacy* (Simon and Schuster, New York, 1994), 203.

65 Stig Förster, "Dreams and Nightmares: German Military Leadership and the Images of Future Warfare, 1871–1914," in Boemeke et al., *Anticipating Total War*, 350.

66 Ibid., 350.

67 Frank Müller, "The Spectre of a People in Arms: The Prussian Government and the Militarisation of German Nationalism, 1859–1864," *English Historical Review*, 122, 495 (Feb. 2001), 82–104.

68 Quoted in Förster, "Dreams and Nightmares," 358.

69 Quoted in ibid., 366.

70 Strachan, *First World War*, 62.

71 Quoted in Winkler, *Der lange Weg nach Westen, I*, 330.

72 Quoted in Röhl, "Germany," 38.

73 D. W. Spring, "Russia and the Coming of War," in Evans and Pogge, *The Coming of the First World War*, 60.

74 Keith Neilson, "Russia," in Wilson, *Decisions for War*, 106.

75 Strachan, *First World War*, 60.

76 Quoted in Spring, "Russia," 66.

77 Strachan, *First World War*, 50.

78 David Hermann, *The Arming of Europe and the Making of the First World War* (Princeton University Press, Princeton, 1996), 178.

79 Quoted in Paléologue, *Ambassador's Memoirs*, 10–11.

80 Quoted in ibid., 14–15.
81 Paléologue, *Ambassador's Memoirs*, 21.
82 Quoted in ibid., 22.
83 Quoted in Ferguson, *Pity of War*, 58.
84 Quoted in Wilson, "Britain," in Wilson, *Decisions for War*, 184.
85 Quoted in Kennedy, *Rise and Fall*, 232.
86 Quoted in Wilson, "Britain," 190.
87 Quoted in Schuman, *War and Diplomacy*, 230–1.
88 Quoted in ibid., 242.
89 Jean Stengers, "Belgium," in Wilson, *Decisions for War*, 159.
90 Poincaré was, in fairness, born in the town of Bar le Duc, which lay on the River Meuse and on the historic border between Lorraine and the Champagne. However, contrary to the impression left on the unwary reader, this was far distant from the Département of the Moselle, the northeastern and largely German-speaking corner of Lorraine annexed by Germany in 1871.
91 Quoted in Stengers, "Belgium," 158.

3 Fighting the War

1   Quoted in Paul-Marie de la Gorce, *The French Army: A Military-Political History* (Weidenfeld and Nicolson, London, 1963), 102.
2   Martin van Creveld, *Supplying War: Logistics from Wallenstein to Patton* (Cambridge University Press, Cambridge, 1980), 139–40.
3   Strachan, *First World War*, 242.
4   van Creveld, *Supplying War*, 140.
5   Ferguson, *Pity of War*, 208.
6   John Horne and Alan Kramer, *German Atrocities 1914: A History of Denial* (Yale University Press, New Haven, 2001), 96.
7   Thomas Weber, *Hitler's First War: Adolf Hitler, the Men of the List Regiment, and the First World War*, unpublished summarized manuscript (forthcoming, Oxford University Press, Oxford, 2010), 15.
8   Ibid., 31.
9   Strachan, *First World War*, 342.
10 Ibid., 316.
11 Ibid., 335.
12 Ibid., 693.
13 Michael Howard, *The First World War: A Very Short Introduction* (Oxford University Press, Oxford, 2007), 61.
14 Quoted in Paléologue, *Ambassador's Memoirs*, 358.
15 Quoted in ibid., 262.
16 Paléologue, *Ambassador's Memoirs*, 291.
17 Quoted in Horne and Kramer, *German Atrocities*, 82.
18 Jay Winter, *Remembering War: The Great War between Memory and History in the Twentieth Century* (Yale University Press, New Haven, 2006), 97–9.
19 Winter, *Remembering War*, 99–100.

20 Michael Howard, however, stresses the harsher side of the German occupation: Howard, *First World War*, 62.

21 Quoted in Gerd Hardach, *The First World War 1914–1918* (Allen Lane, London, 1977), 80.

22 Quoted in Alistair Horne, *The Price of Glory: Verdun 1916* (Penguin Books, London, 1993), 33.

23 Ibid.

24 Quoted in Howard, *First World War*, 66.

25 Jean Rouaud, *Fields of Glory* (Harvill, London, 1993), 129–30.

26 Horne, *Price of Glory*, 49

27 Ibid., 49.

28 Quoted in ibid., 60.

29 Quoted in ibid., 115.

30 Horne, *Price of Glory*, 188.

31 Quoted in ibid., 188.

32 Ferguson, *Pity of War*, 456.

33 Thus Otto Dix, *Trichterfeld bei Dontrien von Leuchtkugeln erhellt* and *Gastote (Templeux-La-Fosse, August, 1916)* in War Series (1924), National Galleries of Scotland, Edinburgh.

34 Quoted in Horne, *Price of Glory*, 223.

35 Quoted in Ferguson, *Pity of War*, 292.

36 Quoted in Horne, *Price of Glory*, 291.

37 Robin Prior and Trevor Wilson, *The Somme* (Yale University Press, New Haven, 2006), 116.

38 Ibid., 117.

39 David Edgerton, *The Shock of the Old: Technology and Global History since 1900* (Profile Books, London, 2006), 143.

40 Christopher R. W. Nevinson, *That Cursed Wood*, National Galleries of Scotland, Edinburgh.

41 Howard, *First World War*, 89.

42 Quoted in Hardach, *First World War*, 42.

43 Quoted in Margaret Macmillan, *Peacemakers: The Paris Conference of 1919 and Its Attempt to End War* (John Murray, London, 2003), 425.

44 Quoted in Howard, *First World War*, 100.

45 Hardach, *First World War*, 44.

46 Hubert Goenner, *Einstein in Berlin 1914–1933* (C. H. Beck, Munich, 2005), 75.

47 Quoted in Winkler, *Der lange Weg nach Westen, I*, 339–40.

48 Thus for Einstein, Goenner, *Einstein in Berlin*, 75–88.

49 Thomas Weber, Review on H-German (Jan. 2006) of Peter Hoeres, *Krieg der Philosophen: die deutsche und britische Philosophie im Ersten Weltkrieg* (Ferdinand Schöningh, Paderborn, 2004).

50 Jackie Wullschlager, *Chagall: Love and Exile* (Allen Lane, London, 2008), 35.

51 Quoted in Horne, *Price of Glory*, 321.

52 Quoted in de la Gorce, *French Army*, 126.

53 Howard, *First World War*, 107.

54 Quoted in ibid., 123.

55 For a fuller discussion: Heather Jones, "The German Spring Reprisals of 1917: Prisoners of War and the Violence of the Western Front," *German History*, 26, 3 (2008), 335–56.

56 Quoted in Ferguson, *Pity of War*, 314.

57 de la Gorce, *French Army*, 146–7.

4   Ending the War: Revolutions and Peacemaking

1 Hardach, *First World War*, 1.

2 A. S. Hartrick, *Women's Work: On Munitions – Heavy Work, Drilling and Casting*, shown in exhibition "The Great War: Britain's Efforts and Ideals," London, 1917, presented by the Ministry of Information to the National Galleries of Scotland, Edinburgh, Feb. 1919.

3 For a general account of disturbances in Britain caused by food shortages: Bernard Waites, *A Class Society at War: England 1914–1918* (Berg, Leamington Spa, 1987).

4 Ferguson, *Pity of War*, 331.

5 Ibid., 336.

6 Ute Daniel, "The Politics of Rationing versus the Politics of Subsistence: Working-Class Women in Germany, 1914–1918," in Roger Fletcher (ed.), *Bernstein to Brandt: A Short History of German Social Democracy* (Edward Arnold, London, 1987), 92.

7 From the German *hamstern* – to hoard in a hamster-like way.

8 Hardach, *First World War*, 119, table 13.

9 Richard Pipes, *Russian Conservatism and Its Critics: A Study in Political Culture* (Yale University Press, New Haven, 2005), 24. See also Sheila Fitzpatrick, *The Russian Revolution 1917–1932* (Oxford, University Press, Oxford, 1984), 10.

10 Quoted in Pipes, *Russian Conservatism*, 118.

11 Quoted in ibid., 25.

12 Pipes, *Russian Conservatism*, 155.

13 Fitzpatrick, *Russian Revolution*, 13–15.

14 Edward Acton, *Rethinking the Russian Revolution* (Edward Arnold, London, 1990), 15.

15 Quoted in Norman Davies, *Europe: A History* (Oxford University Press, Oxford, 1996), 839.

16 In 1902 Lenin published a seminal essay, "What Is To Be Done?" setting out his revolutionary strategy. See Fitzpatrick, *Russian Revolution*, 25.

17 Hubertus Jahn, "Russia," in Robert Gerwarth (ed.), *Twisted Paths: Europe 1914–1945* (Oxford University Press, Oxford, 2007), 298.

18 Quoted in Fitzpatrick, *Russian Revolution*, 40.

19 Jahn, "Russia," 302.

20 Fitzpatrick, *Russian Revolution*, 41.

21 Ibid., 43.

22 Quoted in Acton, *Rethinking the Russian Revolution*, 24.

23 Fitzpatrick, *Russian Revolution*, 54.

24 Jahn, "Russia," 304.

25 Martin McCauley, *The Soviet Union since 1917* (Longman, London, 1982), 14.

26 Quoted in Davies, *Europe*, 921.

27 Fitzpatrick, *Russian Revolution*, 68.

28 Ferguson, *Pity of War*, 392.

29 Davies, *Europe*, 928.

30 Macmillan, *Peacemakers*, 72.

31 Quoted in Macmillan, *Peacemakers*, 76.

32 McCauley, *Soviet Union*, 26.

33 Fitzpatrick, *Russian Revolution*, 69.

34 Ibid., 76–7.

35 Kennedy, *Rise and Fall*, 361.

36 Jahn, "Russia," 311.

37 See pp. 267–8 below.

38 Quoted in Jackie Wullschlager, "Rooted in Mother Russia," *Financial Times*, Life and Arts section (Oct. 18–19, 2008), 17.

39 John Maynard Keynes, *The Economic Consequences of the Peace* (Macmillan, London, 1920), 19.

40 Cornelius Torp, *Die Herausforderung der Globalisierung* (Vandenhoeck und Ruprecht, Göttingen, 2005), 289.

41 Quoted in Winkler, *Der lange Weg nach Westen, I*, 326.

42 Fischer, *Germany's Aims*; Fischer, *War of Illusions*; Fritz Fischer, *From Kaiserreich to Third Reich: Elements of Continuity in German History* (Allen and Unwin, London, 1986).

43 Winkler, *Der lange Weg nach Westen, I*, 280–1.

44 Quoted in ibid., 290.

45 Frank Lorenz Müller, "'Perhaps Also Useful for Our Election Campaign': The Parliamentary Impasse of the Late Wilhelmine State and the British Constitutional Crisis, 1909–1911," in Dominik Geppert and Robert Gerwarth (eds.), *Wilhelmine Germany and Edwardian Britain: Essays on Cultural Affinity* (Oxford University Press, Oxford, 2008), 86. During this period a power struggle in Britain between the House of Commons and House of Lords over taxation reform was at its height.

46 Winkler, *Der lange Weg nach Westen, I*, 321.

47 Quoted in ibid., 334–5.

48 Quoted in Hans Mommsen, *Arbeiterklasse und Nationale Frage. Ausgewählte Aufsätze* (Vandenhoeck und Ruprecht, Göttingen, 1979), 67.

49 Robert Michels, *Political Parties: A Sociological Study of the Oligarchical Tendencies of Modern Democracy* (Crowell Collier, London, 1962), 359.

50 Paraphrased in John R. Moses, *Trade Unionism in Germany from Bismarck to Hitler, 1869–1933*, vol. 1 (Barnes and Noble, Totowa NJ, 1982), 192.

51 Quoted in Winkler, *Der lange Weg nach Westen, I*, 350.

52 Quoted in Hagen Schulze, *Weimar. Deutschland 1917–1933* (Siedler, Berlin, 1998), 160.

53 Schulze, *Weimar*, 161.

54 William Mulligan, *The Creation of the Modern German Army: General Walther Reinhardt and the Weimar Republic, 1914–1930* (Berghahn Books, New York, 2005), 222.

55 Winkler, *Der lange Weg nach Westen, I*, 380.

56 Gerald D. Feldman, *Army Industry and Labor in Germany, 1914–1918* (Princeton University Press, Princeton, 1966), 523.

57 This was the former National Liberal Party, now led by Gustav Stresemann.

58 Quoted in Winkler, *Der lange Weg nach Westen, I*, 385.

59 Schulze, *Weimar*, 218.

60 Ibid., 221.

61 Quoted in J. Hampden Jackson, *Clemenceau and the Third Republic* (Hodder and Stoughton, London, 1946), 211.

62 Keynes, *Economic Consequences*, 211.

63 Quoted in Macmillan, *Peacemakers*, 469.

64 Quoted in ibid., 477.

65 de la Gorce, *French Army*, 125.

66 Irène Némirovsky, *Suite Française* (Chatto and Windus, London, 2007), 241.

67 *The Scotsman*, magazine (Oct. 27, 2007), 6–7.

68 Quoted in Ferguson, *Pity of War*, 331.

69 See p. 64 above.

70 Richard Bessel, *Germany after the First World War* (Oxford University Press, Oxford, 1995), vi.

71 Max Beckmann, *The Way Home*, part of his Die Hölle (Hell) series of 11 lithographs, National Galleries of Scotland, Edinburgh.

72 Carolyn Grohmann, "From Lothringen to Lorraine: Expulsion and Voluntary Repatriation," in Conan Fischer and Alan Sharp (eds.), *After the Versailles Treaty: Enforcement, Compliance, Contested Identities* (Routledge, London, 2008), 155.

73 Winter, *Remembering War*, 139.

74 Ibid., 140.

75 *The Scotsman* (Nov. 5, 2007), 34–5.

76 Mark Derez, "A Belgian Salient for Reconstruction: People and *Patrie*, Landscape and Memory," in Peter H. Liddle (ed.), *Passchendaele in Perspective: The Third Battle of Ypres* (Leo Cooper, London, 1997), 448.

77 Piet Chielens and Wim Chielens, *De Troost van Schoonheid. De literaire Salient (Ieper 1914–1918)* (Globe, Groot-Bijgaarden, 1996), 17, quoted here in Derez, 'Belgian Salient,' 451.

78 William Nicholson, *The End of the War*, shown in "The Great War," London 1917.

79 Macmillan, *Peacemakers*, 81.

80 Among Pierre Renouvin's many works: *La Première Guerre Mondiale* (Presses Universitaires de France, Paris, 1965).

81 David Stevenson, "French War Aims and Peace Planning," in Manfred Boemeke et al. (eds.), *The Treaty of Versailles: A Reassessment after 75 Years* (Cambridge University Press, Cambridge, 1998), 107.

82 Quoted in Goenner, *Einstein in Berlin*, 72.

83 Jacques Bariéty, *Les Relations franco-allemandes après la Première Guerre Mondiale. 10 novembre 1918–10 janvier 1925. De l'exécution à la négociation* (Éditions Pedone, Paris, 1977), quoted here in Paul Guinn, "On Throwing Ballast in Foreign Policy: Poincaré, the Entente and the Ruhr Occupation," *European History Quarterly*, 18, 4 (1988), 428.

84 Georges-Henri Soutou, "La France et les marches de l'est, 1914–1919," *Revue Historique*, 578 (1978), 387.

85 Anna-Monika Lauter, *Sicherheit und Reparationen. Die französische Öffentlichkeit, der Rhein und die Ruhr 1918–1933* (Klartext, Essen, 2006), 54.

86   Keynes, *Economic Consequences*, 128.

87   Ibid., 131.

88   Ibid., 133.

89   David Dutton, "Britain and France at War, 1914–1918," in Alan Sharp and Glyn Stone (eds.), *Anglo-French Relations in the Twentieth Century: Rivalry and Cooperation* (Routledge, London, 2000), 81.

90   Ibid., 84–5.

91   Ibid., 85.

92   Quoted in Macmillan, *Peacemakers*, 18.

93   Macmillan, *Peacemakers*, 94.

94   It was returned to China in 1922.

95   Peter Krüger, *Deutschland und die Reparationen 1918/19. Die Genesis des Reparationsproblems in Deutschland zwischen Waffenstillstand und Versailler Friedensschluß* (Deutscher Verlags-Anstalt, Stuttgart, 1973), 9.

96   Stevenson, "French War Aims," 96.

97   Edgar Holt, *The Tiger: The Life of Georges Clemenceau 1841–1929* (Hamilton, London, 1976), 226.

98   Keynes, *Economic Consequences*, 119.

99   Paraphrased in Krüger, *Deutschland und die Reparationen*, 137.

100 Quoted in Eugène Darsy, *Les Droits historiques de la France sur la rive gauche du Rhin*, pamphlet (Paris, 1919), 1.

101 Quoted in Franziska Wein, *Deutschlands Strom – Frankreichs Grenze. Geschichte und Propaganda am Rhein 1919–1930* (Klartext, Essen, 1992), 21, n27.

102 Quoted in Macmillan, *Peacemakers*, 209.

103 Quoted in Stevenson, "French War Aims," 100.

104 *The Treaty of Peace between the Allied and Associated Powers and Germany … Signed at Versailles, June 28th, 1919* (HMSO, London, 1928), Part VIII, Annex II, Clause 18, 111.

105 Quoted in Stevenson, "French War Aims," 101.

106 Quoted in Macmillan, *Peacemakers*, 306.

107 Hermann J. Rupieper, *The Cuno Government and Reparations 1922–23: Politics and Economics* (Nijhoff, The Hague, 1979), 53.

108 Macmillan, *Peacemakers*, 474.

109 Quoted in Macmillan, *Peacemakers*, 475.

110 Quoted in Heinrich August Winkler, *Weimar 1918–1933. Die Geschichte der ersten deutschen Demokratie*, 2nd edn. (C. H. Beck, Munich, 1994), 92.

111 de la Gorce, *French Army*, 165.

112 Quoted in Roger Moorhouse, "'The Sore That Would Never Heal': The Genesis of the Polish Corridor," in Fischer and Sharp, *After the Versailles Treaty*, 189.

113 Quoted in Rom Landau, *Paderewski* (Nicholson and Watson, London, 1934), 65–6.

114 Quoted in Moorhouse, "The Sore," 185.

115 Quoted in ibid., 186.

116 Ibid.

117 Quoted in Macmillan, *Peacemakers*, 486.

118 Quoted in ibid., 487.

119   Quoted in Alan Sharp, "Anglo-French Relations from Versailles to Locarno, 1919–1925: The Quest for Security," in Sharp and Stone, *Anglo-French Relations*, 122.

120   Francis L. Carsten, *Revolution in Central Europe 1918–1919* (Wildwood House, London, 1988), 284.

121   Ibid., 53.

122   R. J. W. Evans, "The Successor States," in Gerwarth, *Twisted Paths*, 226.

123   Quoted in Macmillan, *Peacemakers*, 278.

124   Quoted in ibid., 272.

125   Evans, "Successor States," 223.

126   Quoted in Macmillan, *Peacemakers*, 252–3.

127   Quoted in Davies, *Europe*, 935.

128   Ibid.

129   R. J. Crampton, "The Balkans," in Gerwarth, *Twisted Paths*, 241–2.

130   Quoted in Macmillan, *Peacemakers*, 123.

131   Macmillan, *Peacemakers*, 122.

132   Ibid., 133.

133   Quoted in Anthony Adamthwaite, *Grandeur and Misery: France's Bid for Power in Europe 1914–1940* (Arnold, London, 1995), 73.

134   Quotes in Macmillan, *Peacemakers*, 391.

135   Rebecca K. McCoy, "The Société Populaire at Sainte Marie-aux-Mines: Local Culture and National Identity in an Alsatian Community during the French Revolution," *European History Quarterly*, 27, 4 (1997), 447–8.

136   See p. 17 above.

137   Grohmann, "From Lothringen to Lorraine," 159–60.

138   Ibid., 161–2.

139   Quoted in Alvin Jackson, "The Two Irelands," in Gerwarth, *Twisted Paths*, 64.

140   Jackson, "Two Irelands," 65.

141   Ibid., 67.

142   Anne Dolan, *Commemorating the Irish Civil War: History and Memory 1923–2000* (Cambridge University Press, Cambridge, 2003), 3.

143   Jackson, "Two Irelands," 81–2.

144   Thus: Roger Eatwell, *Fascism: A History* (Allen Lane, New York, 1997), xix, 3–4; Roger Griffin (ed.), *International Fascism: Theories, Causes and the New Consensus* (Arnold, London, 1998), x.

145   Thus: R. J. B. Bosworth, "Italy," in Gerwarth, *Twisted Paths*, 174.

146   Martin Clark, *Modern Italy 1871–1982* (Longman, London, 1984), 184.

147   Quoted in ibid., 197.

148   Clark, *Modern Italy*, 198.

149   Ibid., 196.

150   Ibid., 203.

151   Ibid., 218.

152   Bosworth, "Italy," 161.

153   Ibid., 170.

154   Muriel Spark, *The Prime of Miss Jean Brodie* (Macmillan, London, 1961). The fictitious schoolmistress displayed considerable enthusiasm for Mussolini in the classroom, and for that matter for General Franco's Spanish nationalists.

5 Revision and Recovery, 1919–1929

1   Patricia Clavin, "Europe and the League of Nations," in Gerwarth, *Twisted Paths*, 325.

2   For example: Stanislas Jeannesson, "L'Europe de Jacques Seydoux," *Revue Historique*, 299, 1 (1998), 129.

3   Andrew Webster, "Making Disarmament Work: The Implementation of the International Disarmament Provisions of the League of Nations Covenant, 1919–1925," in Fischer and Sharp, *After the Versailles Treaty*, 142–6.

4   Clavin, "Europe and the League of Nations," 353.

5   Karl Kautsky, Max von Montgelas, and Walther Schücking, *Die deutschen Dokumente zum Kriegsausbruch* (Deutsche Verlagsgesellschaft für Politik und Geschichte, Charlottenburg, 1919).

6   Annika Mombauer,*The Origins of the First World War: Controversies and Consensus* (Longman, London, 2002), 58–9.

7   *Die Grosse Politik der Europäischen Kabinette* (Arbeitsauschuß Deutscher Verbände, Berlin, 1922).

8   Holger Herwig, "Clio Deceived: Patriotic Self-Censorship in Germany after the Great War," in Keith M. Wilson (ed.), *Forging the Collective Memory: Government and International Historians through Two World Wars* (Berghahn Books, Providence RI, 1996), 88–9.

9   Ministère des Affaires Étrangères, *Documents diplomatiques français 1871–1914* (Imprimerie Nationale, Paris, 1929ff.).

10 Adamthwaite, *Grandeur and Misery*, 87.

11 G. P. Gooch et al. (eds.), *British Documents on the Origins of the War, 1898–1914* (HMSO, London, 1926–38).

12 Quoted in Mombauer, *Origins*, 69.

13 Mombauer, *Origins*, 63.

14 Among the many: Sally Marks, *The Illusion of Peace: International Relations in Europe, 1918–1933*, 2nd edn. (Palgrave Macmillan, Basingstoke, 2003); Stephen A. Schuker, *The End of French Predominance in Europe: The Financial Crisis of 1924 and the Adoption of the Dawes Plan* (University of North Carolina Press, Chapel Hill, 1976).

15 *Treaty of Peace, 1919*, Part VIII, Annex II, Clause 18, 223.

16 Quoted in David Watson, *Clemenceau: A Political Biography* (Eyre Methuen, London, 1974), 387.

17 Quoted in Adamthwaite, *Grandeur and Misery*, 64.

18 Quoted in ibid., 71.

19 Klaus Tenfelde, "Disarmament and Big Business: The Case of Krupp, 1918–1925," in Fischer and Sharp, *After the Versailles Treaty*, 128.

20 Lauter, *Sicherheit*, 46–7.

21 Stanislas Jeannesson, "French Policy in the Rhineland, 1919–1924," in Fischer and Sharp, *After the Versailles Treaty*, 61.

22 *Treaty of Peace, 1919*, Article 251, 247.

23 See pp. 99–100 above.

24 Quoted in Conan Fischer, *The Ruhr Crisis 1923–1924* (Oxford University Press, Oxford, 2003), 60–1.

25   Feldman, *The Great Disorder*, 428.

26   Gerald D. Feldman, "The Reparations Debate," in Fischer and Sharp, *After the Versailles Treaty*, 70.

27   Gerald D. Feldman, "A Comment," in Boemeke et al., *Treaty of Versailles*, 445. Sally Marks and Stephen Schuker have been prominent among those stressing the opposite in a "can't pay" or "won't pay" debate.

28   Gunther Mai, "'Wenn der Mensch Hunger hat, hört alles auf.' Wirtschaftliche und soziale Ausgangsbedingungen der Weimarer Republik (1919–1924)," in Werner Abelshauser (ed.), *Die Weimarer Republik als Wohlfahrtsstaat … (Vierteljahresschrift für Sozial- und Wirtschaftsgeschichte*, suppl. 81, 1986), 60, n105.

29   Conan Fischer, "The Human Price of Reparations," in Fischer and Sharp, *After the Versailles Treaty*, 84.

30   The Palatinate, lying west of the Rhine to the north of Alsace, was part of Bavaria.

31   Jeannesson, "French Policy," 61.

32   James Henry Penson, *Is Germany Prosperous? Impressions Gained January 1922* (E. Arnold, London, 1922), 117–21.

33   Quoted in Dietmar Petzina, "Is Germany Prosperous? Die Reparationsfrage in der Diskussion angelsächsischer Experten zwischen 1918 und 1925," in Christoph Buchheim, Michael Hutter, and Harold James (eds.), *Zerissene Zwischenkriegszeit. Wirtschaftshistorische Beiträge. …* (Nomos, Baden-Baden, 1994), 246.

34   Quoted in Stanislas Jeannesson, *Poincaré, la France et la Ruhr (1922–1924). Histoire d'une occupation* (Presses Universitaires de Strasbourg, Strasbourg, 1998), 95.

35   Quoted in Fischer, "Human Price of Reparations," 83.

36   Quoted in ibid., 86–7.

37   Georges-Henri Soutou, "Vom Rhein zur Ruhr: Absichten und Planungen der französischen Regierung," in Gerd Krumeich and Joachim Schröder (eds.), *Der Schatten des Weltkriegs. Die Ruhrbesetzung 1923* (Klartext, Essen, 2004), 65.

38   Quoted in Jeannesson, "French Policy," 65.

39   Ibid.

40   Quoted in Jeannesson, *Poincaré*, 116.

41   Soutou, "Rhein zur Ruhr," 66.

42   Ibid., passim.

43   Ibid., 77.

44   Ibid., 81.

45   Fischer, *Ruhr Crisis*, 31.

46   Jeannesson, "French Policy," 66.

47   Quoted in Jeannesson, *Poincaré*, 141–2.

48   Lauter, *Sicherheit*, 286–7.

49   Ibid., 310–11, 313.

50   Fischer, *Ruhr Crisis*, 153.

51   Quoted in Peter Krüger, *Versailles. Deutsche Außenpolitik zwischen Revisionismus und Friedenssicherung*, 2nd edn. (Deutsche Taschenbuch, Munich, 1993),116.

52   Jeannesson, *Poincaré*, 302–3.

53   Quoted in Fischer, *Ruhr Crisis*, 72.

54   Quoted in ibid., 77.

55   Quoted in ibid., 111.

56 Quoted in ibid., 182.

57 Equivalent of a Permanent Secretary in the British civil service.

58 Quoted in Fischer, *Ruhr Crisis*, 183.

59 Ibid.

60 Ibid., 184.

61 Winkler, *Weimar*, 198.

62 Quoted in Fischer, *Ruhr Crisis*, 188.

63 Quoted in Elspeth Y. O'Riordan, *Britain and the Ruhr Crisis* (Palgrave, Basingstoke, 2001), 75.

64 Quoted in Carl Bergmann, *The History of Reparations* (Houghton Mifflin, Boston, 1927), 202.

65 SPD, Center Party, DDP.

66 Quoted in Feldman, *The Great Disorder*, 699.

67 Quoted in Jeannesson, *Poincaré*, 294.

68 William Lee Blackwood, "German Hegemony and the Socialist International's Place in Interwar European Diplomacy," *European History Quarterly*, 31, 1 (2001), 118–20.

69 Quoted in Fischer, *Ruhr Crisis*, 228.

70 Quoted in O'Riordan, *Britain*, 103.

71 Quoted in Fischer, *Ruhr Crisis*, 247.

72 Quoted in O'Riordan, *Britain*, 119.

73 Quoted in Jonathan Wright, *Gustav Stresemann: Weimar's Greatest Statesman* (Oxford University Press, Oxford, 2002), 271.

74 Quoted in O'Riordan, *Britain*, 154–5.

75 Quoted in Bergmann, *History of Reparations*, 254.

76 Adamthwaite, *Grandeur and Misery*, 105.

77 Ibid.

78 Quoted in de la Gorce, *French Army*, 176.

79 Quoted in Adamthwaite, *Grandeur and Misery*, 120.

80 Quoted in Jeannesson, "L'Europe de Jacques Seydoux," 141.

81 Quoted in ibid., 139.

82 Thus Fischer, *From Kaiserreich to Third Reich*, passim.

83 Wright, *Gustav Stresemann*, 1.

84 Ibid., 62.

85 Christian Baechler, *Gustave Stresemann (1878–1929). De l'impérialisme à la sécurité collective* (Presses Universitaires de Strasbourg, Strasbourg, 1996).

86 Wright, *Gustav Stresemann*, 68.

87 Quoted in ibid., 195.

88 Wright, *Gustav Stresemann*, 329.

89 Quoted in ibid., 342.

90 Ibid., 344.

91 Quoted in Adamthwaite, *Grandeur and Misery*, 125.

92 Patricia Clavin, *The Great Depression in Europe, 1929–1939* (Macmillan, Basingstoke, 2000), 92.

93 Quoted in Adamthwaite, *Grandeur and Misery*, 131.

94 Quoted in Wright, *Gustav Stresemann*, 474.

95 Ibid., 476.

96 See p. 152 above.

97 Quoted in Adamthwaite, *Grandeur and Misery*, 132.

98 The author's current research focuses on Franco-German relations during the Great Depression, including the efforts during 1931 and early 1932 to cement rapprochement between the two traditional enemies.

99 Derek H. Aldcroft, *From Versailles to Wall Street 1919–1929* (Allen Lane, London, 1977), 163.

100 Quoted in ibid., 58.

101 Derek H. Aldcroft, *The European Economy 1914–1970* (Croom Helm, London, 1978), 34.

102 Ibid., 36.

103 Aldcroft, *From Versailles to Wall Street*, 101.

104 Derek H. Aldcroft, *Europe's Third World: The European Periphery in the Interwar Years* (Ashgate, Aldershot, 2006), 54–5.

105 Clavin, *Great Depression*, 47.

106 Aldcroft, *European Economy*, 63.

107 Quoted in Clavin, *Great Depression*, 51.

108 Quoted in Aldcroft, *From Versailles to Wall Street*, 150.

109 Clavin, *Great Depression*, 55.

110 See 6.1 below.

111 Peter Demetz, "Introduction: A Map of Courage," in Matthew S. Witkovsky, *Foto: Modernity in Central Europe, 1918–1945* (Thames and Hudson, London, 2007), 1.

112 David Elliot, "A Life-and-Death Struggle: Painting and Sculpture," in Dawn Ades et al. (eds.), *Art and Power: Europe under the Dictators 1930–45* (Hayward Gallery, London, 1995), 276 and 303.

113 Cf. Lutz Becker, "Optimistic Realism: Cinema," in Ades et al., *Art and Power*, 199–245 and Elliot, "Life-and-Death Struggle," 270–6, 279–321, which includes Nazi and oppositional art.

114 Elke Fröhlich, "Joseph Goebbels: The Propagandist," in Ronald Smelser and Rainer Zitelmann (eds.), *The Nazi Elite* (Macmillan, Basingstoke, 1993), 56.

115 Carolyn Lyons, "The Empire's New Clothes," *Financial Times*, magazine (Aug. 25–6, 2007), 25.

116 Aldcroft, *Europe's Third World*, passim.

117 Christopher Hitchens, "Divine Decadence," in David Friend et al. (eds.), *Vanity Fair Portraits: Photographs 1913–2008* (National Portrait Gallery, London, 2008), 13.

118 Sandy Nairne, "Foreword," in Friend at al., *Vanity Fair Portraits*, 6.

119 Graydon Carter, "Foreword," in Friend at al., *Vanity Fair Portraits*, 7.

120 Virginia Button, *Ben Nicholson* (Tate Publishing, London, 2007), 38–40.

121 Ibid., 36.

122 Lucia van der Post, "High on Heal's," *Financial Times*, How to Spend It section (Sept. 5, 2009), 20–2.

123 Quoted in Alain de Botton, *The Architecture of Happiness* (Hamish Hamilton, London, 2006), 55.

124 Ibid., 57.

125   Ibid., 62.

126   Mary Hilson, "Scandinavia," in Gerwarth, *Twisted Paths*, 27.

127   de Botton, *Architecture of Happiness*, 62.

128   Illustration in ibid., 64; included here as the frontispiece illustration.

129   Quoted in Button, *Ben Nicholson*, 42.

130   Witkovsky, *Foto*, 11.

131   Ibid., 12.

132   Iván T. Berend, *Decades of Crisis: Central and Eastern Europe before World War I* (University of California Press, Berkeley, 1998), 3, 24.

133   Witkovsky, *Foto*, 53.

134   Ibid., 71.

135   Ibid., 75, illustration 47.

136   Ibid., 77, illustration 49.

137   In Britain, John Stevenson observes, the female labor force comprised 2.84 million unmarried and just 101,000 married women. Stevenson, correspondence with author, Nov. 19, 2009.

138   W. L. Guttsman, *Workers' Culture in Weimar Germany: Between Tradition and Commitment* (Berg, New York, 1990), 305–13.

139   Witkovsky, *Foto*, 79, illustration 51.

140   Ibid., 161.

141   Ibid., 114.

142   Franz W. Seidler, "Fritz Todt: From Motorway Builder to Minister of State," in Smelser and Zitelmann, *Nazi Elite*, 248.

143   Witkovsky, *Foto*, 115, illustration 94.

144   Iain Boyd Whyte, "National Socialism and Modernism: Architecture," in Ades et al. *Art and Power*, 268.

145   Ludwig Finckh, "The Spirit of Berlin (1919)," in Anton Kaes et al. (eds.), *The Weimar Republic Sourcebook* (University of California Press, Berkeley, 1994), 415.

146   Quoted in Jeffry M. Diefendorf, *In the Wake of War: The Reconstruction of German Cities after World War II* (Oxford University Press, New York, 1993), 54.

147   Ibid., 53.

148   Gerdy Troost, *Das Bauen im neuen Reich*, 3rd edn. (Gauverlag Bayerische Ostmark, Bayreuth, 1941), 73.

149   Diefendorf, *In the Wake of War*, 159.

150   Otto Hochreiter, "Ländliches Leben: Zur Darstellung des Bauern und der alpine Landschaft," in Otto Hochreiter and Timm Starl (eds.), *Geschichte der Fotographie in Österreich* (Museum Moderner Kunst, Vienna, 1983), 414.

151   Witkovsky, *Foto*, 175, illustration 150.

152   Ibid., 71, illustration 41.

153   The film was the successor to *Triumph of Faith*, made to commemorate the 1933 Nazi Party rally.

154   Mary Beth Rhiel, "Riefenstahl, Leni (1902–)," in Dieter K. Buse and Juergen C. Doerr (eds.), *Modern Germany: An Encyclopedia of History, People, and Culture, 1871–1990*, 2 vols. (Garland, New York, 1998), vol. 2, 849.

155   Hitchens, "Divine Decadence," 13.

6   The High Noon of the Dictators

1   Edward Chancellor, *Devil Take the Hindmost: A History of Financial Speculation* (Macmillan, Basingstoke, 1999), 191.

2   Ibid., 200.

3   Ibid., 197–8.

4   Ibid., 215.

5   Quoted in ibid., 219.

6   Quoted in Clavin, *Great Depression*, 110.

7   The global headquarters of the former Halifax Bank of Scotland and of the Royal Bank of Scotland. In the event the impact of the financial crash on the Edinburgh regional economy has turned out to be relatively limited.

8   "End of Laisser Faire?" *Financial Times* (Sept. 27–8, 2008), 32.

9   Overall British unemployment levels remained above 10 percent (ca. 1 million) from 1921.

10   Quoted in Alec Nove, *An Economic History of the USSR* (Allen Lane, London, 1969), 166.

11   Nove, *Economic History*, 168.

12   Ibid., 187.

13   Quoted in ibid., 187.

14   Nove, *Economic History*, 190–1.

15   Ades et al., *Art and Power*, 218–21.

16   Nove, *Economic History*, 198.

17   Ibid., 223.

18   Hartmut Pogge von Strandmann, "Industrial Primacy in German Foreign Policy? Myths and Realities in German-Russian Relations at the End of the Weimar Republic," in Richard Bessel and E. J. Feuchtwanger (eds.), *Social Change and Political Development in Weimar Germany* (Croom Helm, London, 1981), 241–67.

19   George D. H. Cole, *Practical Economics; or, Studies in Economic Planning* (Penguin, London, 1937).

20   Peter Fearon, *The Origins and Nature of the Great Slump 1929–1932* (Macmillan, London, 1979), 58.

21   Clavin, *Great Depression*, 121.

22   Ibid., 130.

23   Tom Kemp, "The French Economy under the Franc Poincaré," in John C. Cairns (ed.), *Contemporary France: Illusion, Conflict, and Regeneration* (New Viewpoints, New York, 1978), 75.

24   Richard Overy, *The Nazi Economic Recovery 1932–1938* (Macmillan, Basingstoke, 1982), 53.

25   Quoted in Clavin, *Great Depression*, 164.

26   Clavin, *Great Depression*, 166.

27   Ernst Feder, Cécile Löwenthal-Hensel, and Arnold Paucker (eds.), *Heute sprach ich mit … Tagebücher eines Berliner Publizisten 1926–1932* (University of Chicago Press, Chicago, 1973).

28   Volker Berghahn, email correspondence, Sept. 4, 2008.

29   As successor to the Second, Bismarckian Reich.

30 John C. G. Röhl, *From Bismarck to Hitler: The Problem of Continuity in German History* (Longman, Harlow, 1970).

31 Fischer, *From Kaiserreich to Third Reich*, passim.

32 Thus Michael Geyer and John W Boyer, "Introduction: Resistance against the Third Reich as Intercultural Knowledge," in Geyer and Boyer (eds.), *Resistance against the Third Reich, 1933–1990* (University of Chicago Press, Chicago, 1994), 1–14.

33 Quoted in Ludwig Hümmert, *Bayern vom Königreich zur Diktatur 1900–1933* (W. Ludwig, Pfaffenhofen, 1979), 208.

34 Ibid., 208–9.

35 Ian Kershaw, *Hitler 1889–1936: Hubris* (Allen Lane, London, 1998), 197–8.

36 Ibid., 210.

37 Ibid., 211.

38 Quoted in ibid., 212.

39 Quoted in Conan Fischer, "Continuity and Change in Post-Wilhelmine Germany: From the 1918 Revolution to the Ruhr Crisis," in Geoff Eley and James Retallack (eds.), *Wilhelminism and Its Legacies: German Modernities, Imperialism, and the Meanings of Reform, 1890–1930* (Berghahn Books, New York, 2003), 204.

40 Cf. Anna Menge, "The Iron Hindenburg: A Popular Icon of Weimar Germany," *German History*, 26, 3 (2008), 358–60.

41 Jesko von Hoegen, *Der Held von Tannenberg. Genese und Funktion des Hindenburg-Mythos* (Böhlau, Cologne, 2007), 263, 271.

42 Wolfram Pyta, *Hindenburg. Herrschaft zwischen Hohenzollern und Hitler* (Siedler, Munich, 2007), 461.

43 Kershaw, *Hitler 1889–1936*, 300.

44 Fröhlich, "Joseph Goebbels," 54.

45 von Hoegen, *Held von Tannenberg*, 152.

46 William Sweet, "Schmitt, Carl (1888–1985)", in Buse and Doerr, *Modern Germany*, vol. 2, 890.

47 Gunther Mai, "National Socialist Factory Cell Organisation and the German Labour Front: National Socialist Labour Policy and Organisations," in Conan Fischer (ed.), *The Rise of National Socialism and the Working Classes in Weimar Germany* (Berghahn Books, Providence RI, 1996), 124.

48 Helen Boak, "National Socialism and Working-Class Women before 1933," in Fischer, *Rise of National Socialism*, 177.

49 Quoted in Barbara Miller Lane and Leila J. Rupp (eds.), *Nazi Ideology before 1933: A Documentation* (Manchester University Press, Manchester, 1978), 122–3.

50 Ibid., 138.

51 Quoted in ibid., 144.

52 Karl Dietrich Bracher, *The German Dictatorship: The Origins, Structure and Effects of National Socialism* (Penguin, Harmondsworth, 1973), 145.

53 Seymour Martin Lipset, *Political Man: The Social Bases of Politics* (Johns Hopkins University Press, Baltimore, 1981), 148.

54 Peter Fritzsche, *Rehearsals for Fascism: Populism and Political Mobilization in Weimar Germany* (Oxford University Press, New York, 1990), 235.

55 Peter Fritzsche, *Germans into Nazis* (Harvard University Press, Cambridge MA, 1998), passim.

56 Jürgen W. Falter, *Hitlers Wähler* (C. H. Beck, Munich, 1991); Dirk Hänisch, *Sozialstrukturelle Bestimmungsgründe des Wahlverhaltens in der Weimarer Republik ...* (Sozialwissenschaftliche Kooperative, Duisburg, 1983). See also Dirk Hänisch, "A Social Profile of the Saxon NSDAP Voters," in Claus Christian Szejnmann, *Nazism in Central Germany: The Brownshirts in "Red" Saxony* (Berghahn Books, New York, 1999), 219–31.

57 Jürgen W. Falter, "How Likely Were Workers to Vote for the NSDAP?" in Fischer, *Rise of National Socialism*, 41.

58 Detlef Mühlberger, *The Social Bases of Nazism 1919–1933* (Cambridge University Press, Cambridge, 2003), 51.

59 Quoted in Kershaw, *Hitler 1889–1936*, 390.

60 Schulze, *Weimar*, 396.

61 Kershaw, *Hitler 1889–1936*, 396–402.

62 Schulze, *Weimar*, 396.

63 Quoted in ibid., 400.

64 Schulze, *Weimar*, 401.

65 Quoted in Pyta, *Hindenburg*, 781.

66 Hermann Beck, *The Fateful Alliance: German Conservatives and Nazis in 1933. The Machtergreifung in a New Light* (Berghahn Books, New York, 2008), 86–7.

67 Quoted in ibid., 89–90.

68 Ibid., 90.

69 Quoted in Kershaw, *Hitler 1889–1936*, 439.

70 Kershaw, *Hitler 1889–1936*, 456.

71 Pyta, *Hindenburg*, 825–6.

72 Hans-Christof Kraus, "Der deutsche Reichstag 1933–45. Zur Geschichte und Funktion eines Scheinparlaments," for 58th Conference of the International Commission for the History of Representative and Parliamentary Institutions, St Andrews (Sept. 2007).

73 Quoted in Robert Gellately, *Backing Hitler: Consent and Coercion in Nazi Germany* (Oxford University Press, Oxford, 2001), 53.

74 Kershaw, *Hitler 1889–1936*, 508.

75 Quoted in ibid., 509.

76 Quoted in Pyta, *Hindenburg*, 849.

77 Quoted in Kershaw, *Hitler 1889–1936*, 525.

78 Norbert Frei, *National Socialist Rule in Germany: The Führer State 1933–1945* (Blackwell, Oxford, 1993), 27.

79 Ian Kershaw, *Popular Opinion and Political Dissent in the Third Reich: Bavaria 1933–1945* (Clarendon Press, Oxford, 1983).

80 For example: Hans Mommsen, *Beamtentum im Dritten Reich* (Deutsche Verlagsanstalt, Stuttgart, 1966); Martin Broszat, *The Hitler State: The Foundation and Development of the Internal Structure of the Third Reich* (Longman, London, 1981).

81 See 7.2 below.

82 Norbert Frei, *1945 und wir. Das Dritte Reich im Bewußtsein der Deutschen* (C. H. Beck, Munich, 2005), 110.

83 Ibid., 114.

84 Mai, "National Socialist Factory Cell," 131.

85 Michael Burleigh and Wolfgang Wippermann, *The Racial State: Germany 1933–1945* (Cambridge University Press, Cambridge, 1991), 293.

86 Mai, "National Socialist Factory Cell," 118.

87 Fröhlich, "Joseph Goebbels," 56.

88 Ibid., 55.

89 Quoted in Detlev J. K. Peukert, *Inside Nazi Germany: Conformity, Opposition and Racism in Everyday Life* (Penguin, London, 1989), 168.

90 John Jay Hughes, "Galen, Clemens August von (1878–1946)," in Buse and Doerr, *Modern Germany*, vol. 1, 364.

91 Daniel Jonah Goldhagen, *Hitler's Willing Executioners: Ordinary Germans and the Holocaust* (Little, Brown, London, 1996).

92 Frei, *1945 und wir*, 128.

93 Burleigh and Wippermann, *Racial State*, 92.

94 Ian Kershaw, *Hitler 1936–45: Nemesis* (Allen Lane, London, 2000), 132–3.

95 Quoted in Richard Overy, *The Morbid Age: Britain between the Wars* (Allen Lane, London, 2009), 93.

96 Ibid., 121.

97 Hilson, "Scandinavia," 25.

98 Michael Burleigh, *Death and Deliverance: "Euthanasia" in Germany c. 1900–1945* (Cambridge University Press, Cambridge, 1994), 212.

99 Burleigh and Wippermann, *Racial State*, 169, 171.

100 Jill Stephenson, *Women in Nazi Society* (Croom Helm, London, 1975); Jill Stephenson, *The Nazi Organisation of Women* (Croom Helm, London, 1980).

101 Stephenson, *Women in Nazi Society*, 118.

102 See Overy, *Morbid Age*, esp. ch. 1.

103 Ross McKibbin, "Great Britain," in Gerwarth, *Twisted Paths*, 48.

104 Figures from Scott Newton, "The 'Anglo-German Connection' and the Political Economy of Appeasement," in Patrick Finney (ed.), *The Origins of the Second World War* (Arnold, London, 1997), 294–5.

105 McKibbin, "Great Britain," 49.

106 Overy, *Morbid Age*, 266–7.

107 Ibid., 270.

108 Quoted in F. L. Carsten, *The Rise of Fascism* (Methuen, London, 1970), 220.

109 Stanley G. Payne, *A History of Fascism 1914–45* (UCL Press, London, 1995), 305.

110 Martin Conway and Peter Romijn, "Belgium and the Netherlands," in Gerwarth, *Twisted Paths*, 85.

111 Quoted in Carsten, *Rise of Fascism*, 209.

112 Ibid., 215.

113 Ibid., 216.

114 Conway and Romijn, "Belgium and the Netherlands," 89.

115 Quoted in Payne, *History of Fascism*, 302.

116 Payne, *History of Fascism*, 423.

117 Carsten, *Rise of Fascism*, 167.

118 Hilson, "Scandinavia," 21.

119 Ibid., 19.

120 Quoted in Hans Kohn, *Nationalism and Liberty: The Swiss Example* (George Allen and Unwin, London, 1956), 129.

121 Payne, *History of Fascism*, 309.

122 Quoted in J. S. McClelland (ed.), *The French Right from de Maistre to Maurras* (Jonathan Cape, London, 1970), 30–1.

123 de la Gorce, *French Army*, 23.

124 Quoted in Stephen Wilson, "The 'Action Française' in French Intellectual Life," in Cairns, *Contemporary France*, 140.

125 Maurice Larkin, *France since the Popular Front: Government and People 1936–1986* (Clarendon Press, Oxford, 1988), 2.

126 Payne, *History of Fascism*, 291–2.

127 Quoted in Larkin, *France*, 2.

128 Ibid., 21.

129 François Caron, *An Economic History of Modern France* (Methuen, London, 1979), 180.

130 Payne, *History of Fascism*, 294.

131 Peter Jackson, "France," in Robert Boyce and Joseph A Maiolo (eds.), *The Origins of World War Two: The Debate Continues* (Palgrave, Basingstoke, 2003), 99.

132 Julian Jackson, *The Popular Front in France: Defending Democracy, 1934–38* (Cambridge University Press, Cambridge, 1990), 288.

133 Joan Tumblety, "France," in Gerwarth, *Twisted Paths*, 125.

134 Kemp, "French Economy," 85.

135 Tumblety, "France," 124–5.

136 Jackson, "France," 103–5.

137 Quoted in Payne, *History of Fascism*, 315.

138 Frances Lannon, "Iberia," in Gerwarth, *Twisted Paths*, 143.

139 Aldcroft, *Europe's Third World*, 140–3.

140 Joseph Harrison, *The Spanish Economy in the Twentieth Century* (Croom Helm, London, 1985), 43–50.

141 Lannon, "Iberia," 144.

142 J. Fontana and J. Nadel, "Spain 1914–1970," in Carlo M. Cipolla (ed.), *The Fontana Economic History of Europe: 6.2, Contemporary Economies* (Collins Fontana, London, 1976), 473.

143 Aldcroft, *Europe's Third World*, 131.

144 Stanley G. Payne, *The Collapse of the Spanish Republic 1933–1936: Origins of the Civil War* (Yale University Press, New Haven, 2006), 6.

145 Ibid., 17.

146 Ibid., 42–3.

147 Ibid. 136.

148 Ibid., 175–80.

149 Ibid., 181.

150 Quoted in Jonathan Haslam, "Soviet Russia and the Spanish Problem," in Boyce and Maiolo, *Origins*, 76.

151 Aldcroft, *Europe's Third World*, 135.

152 Stanley G. Payne, *The Spanish Civil War, the Soviet Union, and Communism* (Yale University Press, New Haven, 2004), 270.

153 Ibid., 241.

154 Marko Daniel, "Spain: Culture at War," in Ades et al., *Art and Power*, 63.

155 Aldcroft, *Europe's Third World*, 135.

156 Daniel, "Spain," 65.

157   Ibid., 69.

158   Lannon, "Iberia," 153.

159   Daniel, "Spain," 105.

160   Bosworth, "Italy," 175.

161   Payne, *History of Fascism*, 217–18.

162   Quoted in ibid., 218. The words were later altered to exclude Mussolini's name.

163   Quoted in Victoria de Grazia, *The Culture of Consent: Mass Organization of Leisure in Fascist Italy* (Cambridge University Press, Cambridge, 1981), 225.

164   Payne, *History of Fascism*, 216.

165   de Grazia, *Culture of Consent*, 20.

166   Payne, *History of Fascism*, 216–17.

167   Ibid., 221.

168   Quoted in Ester Coen, "'Against Dreary Conformism': Giuseppe Bottai and Culture during the Fascist Period," in Ades et al., *Art and Power*, 178.

169   Ibid., 180.

170   Payne, *History of Fascism*, 217.

171   Quoted in Lutz Becker, "Black Shirts and White Telephones: Cinema," in Ades et al., *Art and Power*, 137.

172   Becker, "Black Shirts," 139.

173   Simonetta Fraquelli, "All Roads Lead to Rome: Painting and Sculpture," in Ades et al., *Art and Power*, 133.

174   Quoted in ibid., 135.

175   Quoted in Bosworth, "Italy," 181.

176   Quoted in Paul Webster, *Pétain's Crime: The Full Story of French Collaboration in the Holocaust* (Papermac, London, 1990), 167.

177   Ibid.

178   Quoted in Payne, *History of Fascism*, 228.

179   Ibid., 230.

180   Ibid., 232.

181   John Gooch, "Fascist Italy," in Boyce and Maiolo, *Origins*, 39–40.

182   MacGregor Knox, "The Fascist Regime, Its Foreign Policy and Its Wars: An 'Anti-anti-fascist' Orthodoxy?" in Finney, *Origins*, 162.

183   Quoted in ibid., 163.

184   Evans, "Successor States," 221.

185   Payne, *History of Fascism*, 276.

186   Evans, "Successor States," 223.

187   Paraphrased in Payne, *History of Fascism*, 249.

188   See pp. 201–3 above.

189   Quoted in Jahn, "Russia," 319.

190   Jahn, "Russia," 317.

191   Quoted in ibid., 319.

192   Jahn, "Russia," 320.

193   Alexandr Isaevich Solzhenitsyn, *One Day in the Life of Ivan Denisovich* (Penguin, Harmondsworth, 1963); Alexandr Isaevich Solzhenitsyn, *The Gulag Archipelago, 1918–1956* (Fontana, London, 1974).

194   Jahn, "Russia," 322.

195   See p. 135 above.

196   Detlev Peukert, *The Weimar Republic: The Crisis of Classical Modernity* (Allen Lane, London, 1991), 236–40.

197   Zeev Sternhell, "Fascist Ideology," in Walter Laqueur (ed.), *Fascism a Reader's Guide: Analyses, Interpretations, Bibliography* (Penguin, Harmondsworth, 1979), 372.

198   Matthew Feldman (ed.), *Fascist Century: Essays by Roger Griffin* (Palgrave, Basingstoke, 2008); cf. Laqueur, *Fascism*.

199   For example, cf. Karl Dietrich Bracher, "The Role of Hitler: Perspectives of Interpretation," in Laqueur, *Fascism*, 202; Ian Kershaw, *The Nazi Dictatorship: Problems and Perspectives of Interpretation*, 4th edn. (Arnold, London, 2000), 45; Diethelm Prowe, "Fascism, Neo-fascism, New Radical Right?" in Griffin, *International Fascism*, 307.

200   Richard Overy, "Heavy Industry and the State in Nazi Germany: The Reichswerke Crisis," *European History Quarterly*, 15 (1985), 334.

201   Hannah Arendt, *The Origins of Totalitarianism* (Allen and Unwin, London, 1967).

202   Alan Bullock, *Hitler and Stalin: Parallel Lives* (HarperCollins, London, 1991).

203   Dagmar Barnouw, *Visible Spaces: Hannah Arendt and the German-Jewish Experience* (Johns Hopkins University Press, Baltimore, 1990).

7   The Return to War

1   See pp. 262–3 above.

2   Overy, "Heavy Industry," 334.

3   Cf. Runciman quoted in Paul Vyšný, *The Runciman Mission to Czechoslovakia, 1938: Prelude to Munich* (Palgrave Macmillan, Basingstoke, 2003), 312.

4   Quoted in Vyšný, *Runciman Mission*, 8.

5   Vyšný, *Runciman Mission*, 13.

6   Quoted in ibid., 18.

7   Kershaw, *Hitler 1936–1945*, 91.

8   Quoted in Vyšný, *Runciman Mission*, 320.

9   Igor Lukes, "Czechoslovakia," in Boyce and Maiolo, *Origins*, 172.

10   Quoted in Iain Macleod, *Neville Chamberlain* (Frederick Muller, London, 1961), 231.

11   Quoted in Lukes, "Czechoslovakia," 174.

12   Paraphrased in Macleod, *Neville Chamberlain*, 237.

13   Macleod, *Neville Chamberlain*, 250.

14   Davies, *Europe*, 993.

15   Kershaw, *Hitler 1936–1945*, 179.

16   Anita J. Prazmowska, "Poland," in Boyce and Maiolo, *Origins*, 161.

17   Zachary Shore, *What Hitler Knew: The Battle for Information in Nazi Foreign Policy* (Oxford University Press, New York, 2003), 114.

18   Quoted in Teddy J. Uldricks, "Soviet Security Policy in the 1930s," in Finney, *Origins*, 175.

19   Geoffrey Roberts, however, emphasizes German efforts to woo the Soviet Union during the summer of 1939: Geoffrey Roberts, *The Soviet Union and the Origins of the Second World War: Russo-German Relations and the Road to War* (Macmillan, Basingstoke, 1995), 73.

20 Quoted in Davies, *Europe*, 997.

21 Quoted in Kershaw, *Hitler 1936–1945*, 205.

22 A. J. P. Taylor, *The Origins of the Second World War* (Penguin Books, London, 1964).

23 For a discussion of these theories see Kershaw, *Nazi Dictatorship*, chs. 4 and 6.

24 Tim Mason, "Intention and Explanation: A Current Controversy about the Interpretation of National Socialism," in Gerhard Hirschfeld and Lothar Kettenacker (eds.), *The Führer State: Myth and Reality. Studies in the Structure and Politics of the Third Reich* (Klett-Cotta, Stuttgart, 1981), 23–42.

25 Richard Overy, "Germany, 'Domestic Crisis' and War in 1939," *Past and Present*, 116 (Aug. 1987), 155; see also 153.

26 For the Mason–Overy debate: Tim Mason, "Comment 2: Debate. Germany, 'Domestic Crisis' and War in 1939," *Past and Present*, 122 (Feb. 1989), 205–21; Overy, "Germany, 'Domestic Crisis' and War," 138–68, and Richard Overy, "Reply: Debate. Germany, 'Domestic Crisis' and War," *Past and Present*, 122 (Feb. 1989), 221–40.

27 Overy, "Germany, 'Domestic Crisis' and War," 155; cf. Overy, "Heavy Industry," 313–40.

28 Kershaw, *Nazi Dictatorship*, chs. 4 and 6; Jonathan Wright, *Germany and the Origins of the Second World War* (Palgrave Macmillan, Basingstoke, 2007).

29 Gerhard L. Weinberg (ed.), *Hitler's Second Book: The Unpublished Sequel to Mein Kampf* (Enigma, New York, 2003).

30 Gerhard L. Weinberg (ed.), *Hitlers zweites Buch: Ein Dokument aus dem Jahr 1928* (Deutsche Verlags-Anstalt, Stuttgart, 1961), 69; cf. the extended treatment of this theme in Richard Bessel, *Nazism and War* (Weidenfeld and Nicolson, London, 2004).

31 Weinberg, *Hitlers zweites Buch*, 60.

32 Quoted in Overy, "Germany, 'Domestic Crisis' and War," 142.

33 Quoted in Peter Neville, "British Appeasement Policy and the Military Disaster in 1940," *World War II Quarterly*, 6, 1 (2009), 6.

34 The author's current research focuses on this "prehistory" of the post–Second World War European Union, which has a Franco-German axis at its heart.

35 Anthony Adamthwaite, "France and the Coming of War," in Finney, *Origins*, 81–2. Similar ideas had been floated during 1931–2 and had been put into effect before the First World War. See pp. 00 above.

36 Quoted in ibid., 82.

37 See p. 16 above.

38 de la Gorce, *French Army*, 254.

39 Quoted in ibid., 255.

40 Quoted in Adamthwaite, "France and the Coming of War," 80.

41 Quoted in de la Gorce, *French Army*, 279.

42 Here quoted in Stephen A. Schuker, "France and the Remilitarization of the Rhineland, 1936," in Finney, *Origins*, 273.

43 Quoted in ibid., 234.

44 Charles de Gaulle, *Vers l'armée de metier* (Berger-Levrault, Paris, 1934), here cited in de la Gorce, *French Army*, 256.

45 François-Poncet in Ministère des Affaires Étrangères, *Le Livre jaune français. Documents diplomatiques 1938–1939* (Imprimerie Nationale, Paris, 1939), Document 18, 30.

46 Adamthwaite, "France and the Coming of war", 83.

47 Gerhard L. Weinberg, "Munich after 50 Years," in Finney (ed.), *Origins*, 411.

48 Adamthwaite, "France and the Coming of War," 84.

49 The Europe of the great Frankish Emperor Charlemagne which by ca. 800 AD extended from Rome to today's Netherlands, and from the River Elbe to the Pyrenees.

50 Sidney Aster, "'Guilty Men': The Case of Neville Chamberlain," in Finney, *Origins*, 64.

51 Neville, "British Appeasement Policy," 8.

52 Leo McKinstry, *Spitfire: Portrait of a Legend* (John Murray, London, 2007).

53 Quoted in Aster, "'Guilty men,'" 63.

54 Keith Grahame Feiling, *The Life of Neville Chamberlain* (Macmillan, London, 1946), 359; cf. Williamson Murray, "Britain," in Boyce and Maiolo, *Origins*, 123–4.

55 Quoted in Martin Gilbert, "Horace Wilson: Man of Munich?" *History Today*, 32 (1982), 6.

56 Aster, "'Guilty Men,'" 70–1.

57 Quoted in ibid., 64; cf. Weinberg, "Munich," 410.

58 Quoted in David Dilks, "'We Must Hope for the Best and Prepare for the Worst': The Prime Minister, the Cabinet and Hitler's Germany, 1937–1939," in Finney, *Origins*, 43.

59 Quoted in ibid., 44.

60 Quoted in Aster, "'Guilty Men,'" 75.

61 Shore, *What Hitler Knew*, 101.

62 Davies, *Europe*, 1000–1; cf. Prazmowska, "Poland," 163.

63 Richard Overy, *1939: Countdown to War* (Allen Lane, London, 2009), 103.

64 Gamelin, Feb. 1940, in de la Gorce, *French Army*, 289.

65 Fred Taylor (ed.), *The Goebbels Diaries 1939–1941* (Hamish Hamilton, London, 1982), 16.

66 Quoted in Wright, *Germany and the Origins*, 151.

67 Quoted in Winkler, *Der lange Weg nach Westen*, II, 74.

68 Wright, *Germany and the Origin s*, 154.

69 Winkler, *Der lange Weg nach Westen II*, 75.

70 Quoted in Kershaw, *Hitler 1936–1945*, 245.

71 Quoted in ibid., 247.

72 Quoted in Davies, *Europe*, 1003.

73 See pp. 00 above.

74 de la Gorce, *French Army*, 283.

75 Quoted in Julian Jackson, *The Fall of France: The Nazi Invasion of 1940* (Oxford University Press, Oxford, 2003), 80.

76 Quoted in de la Gorce, *French Army*, 285.

77 de la Gorce, *French Army*, 286.

78 Quoted in Jackson, *Fall of France*, 84.

79 Ibid., 85.

80 Ibid., 84.

81 Paraphrased and quoted in Richard Overy, *Why the Allies Won* (Pimlico, London, 1996), 29.

82 Overy, *Why the Allies Won*, 31.

83 Ibid., 46–7.

84 Quoted in Winkler, *Der lange Weg nach Westen*, II, 76.

85 Cf. Gorce, *French Army*, 299.

86 Quoted in Jackson, *Fall of France*, 27.

87 Quoted in de la Gorce, *French Army*, 272.

88   Ibid., 273.

89   Ibid., 274.

90   Quoted in Wright, *Germany and the Origins*, 160.

91   Newton, "Anglo-German Connection," 311.

92   Quoted in Jackson, *Fall of France*, 32.

93   Ernest R. May, *Strange Victory: Hitler's Conquest of France* (Hill and Wang, New York, 2000).

94   Quoted in Jackson, *Fall of France*, 99.

95   de la Gorce, *French Army*, 299.

96   Max Clauss, *Zwischen Paris und Vichy. Frankreich seit dem Waffenstillstand* (Deutscher Verlag, Berlin, 1942), photo facing page 17.

97   Kershaw, *Hitler 1936–1945*, 297.

98   Quoted in Winkler, *Der lange Weg nach Westen*, II, 76.

99   Kershaw, *Hitler 1936–1945*, 300.

100 Keitel quoted ibid., 300.

101 Quoted in Kershaw, *Hitler 1936–1945*, 300.

102 Winkler, *Der lange Weg nach Westen*, II, 77–8.

103 Thomas J. Laub, *After the Fall: German Policy in Occupied France, 1940–1944* (New York, Oxford University Press, 2009).

104 Quoted in Julian Jackson, *France: The Dark Years 1940–1944* (Oxford University Press, Oxford, 2003), 132.

105 Jackson, *Fall of France*, 234.

106 Quoted in Webster, *Pétain's Crime*, 73.

107 Jackson, *France: The Dark Years*, 139.

108 de la Gorce, *French Army*, 315.

109 William L. Shirer, *Berlin Diary 1934–1941* (Sphere Books, London, 1970), 355–6.

110 Quoted in Kershaw, *Hitler 1936–1945*, 304.

111 Michael Postan, *British War Production* (HMSO and Longman, London, 1952), 108.

112 Bill Jamieson, "Scotland's War: The Dawn of Conflict," *The Scotsman* (Sept. 2, 2009), 15.

113 Quoted in Macleod, *Neville Chamberlain*, 304.

114 de la Gorce, *French Army*, 326.

115 Quoted in ibid., 327.

116 Kershaw, *Hitler 1936–1945*, 365.

117 Quoted in de la Gorce, *French Army*, 328.

118 Davies, *Europe*, 1010.

119 Quoted in Kershaw, *Hitler 1936–1945*, 334.

120 Hitler quoted in ibid., 336.

121 Quoted in Winkler, *Der lange Weg nach Westen*, II, 88.

122 Quoted in Wright, *Germany and the Origins*, 178.

123 Van Creveld, *Supplying War*, 174.

124 Overy, *Why the Allies Won*, 187.

125 Warren F. Kimball, "The United States," in Boyce and Maiolo, *Origins*, 145.

126 Quoted in Winkler, *Der lange Weg nach Westen*, II, 90.

127 Kershaw, *Hitler 1936–1945*, 364.

128 Davies, *Europe*, 1028.

8   Europe Eclipsed

1   Overy, *Why the Allies Won*, 182.
2   Ibid., 201–3.
3   Ibid., 207.
4   Quoted in ibid., 43.
5   Quoted in Kershaw, *Hitler 1936–1945*, 529.
6   Quoted in Kyle Jantzen, "White Rose," in Buse and Doerr, *Modern Germany, II*, 1070; for a biography of Sophie Scholl, Frank McDonough, *Sophie Scholl: The Real Story of the Woman Who Defied Hitler* (History Press, Stroud, 2009).
7   For a recent account of the German war in the east: Ben Shepherd, *War in the Wild East: The German Army and Soviet Partisans* (Harvard University Press, Cambridge MA, 2004). A classic exposition of the dynamics of racialist annihilation by German army units is found in Christopher R. Browning, *Ordinary Men: Reserve Police Battalion 101 and the Final Solution in Poland* (Harper Perennial, New York, 1993).
8   Overy, *Why the Allies Won*, 141.
9   Ibid., 156.
10 Roger Moorhouse, *Killing Hitler: The Third Reich and the Plots against the Führer* (Jonathan Cape, London, 2006), 2.
11 Van Creveld, *Supplying War*, 230; cf. Charles Whiting, *Patton* (Ballantine Books, New York, 1970).
12 Quoted in Peter D. Stachura, "President Franklin D. Roosevelt and the Poles, 1941–1945," in Peter D. Stachura (ed.), *The Warsaw Rising, 1944* (Centre for Research in Polish History, University of Stirling, Stirling, 2007), 61.
13 Peter D. Stachura, "Introduction," in Stachura, *Warsaw Rising*, 17.
14 Quoted in Davies, *Europe*, 1041.
15 Quoted in Kershaw, *Hitler 1936–1945*, 725.
16 Joanna K. M. Hanson, "The Civilian Population and the Warsaw Rising," in Stachura, *Warsaw Rising*, 55–6.
17 That is, the lands to the east of the rivers Oder and Western Neisse which form the current Polish-German border.
18 Among the many accounts of this road to genocide, Mark Roseman, *The Villa, the Lake, the Meeting: Wannsee and the Final Solution* (Allen Lane, London, 2002) provides a recent and excellent summary.
19 Quoted in Steve Hochstadt (ed.), *Sources of the Holocaust* (Palgrave Macmillan, Basingstoke, 2004), 110.
20 Quoted in ibid., 122.
21 Quoted in Winkler, *Der lange Weg nach Westen, II*, 93.
22 Figures from Wannsee Conference minutes, here from Roseman, *The Villa*, 111–12.
23 Quoted in Roseman, *The Villa*, 113.
24 Quoted in Hochstadt, *Sources of the Holocaust*, 229–30.
25 Among classic English-language works: Christopher R. Browning, *The Path to Genocide: Essays on Launching the Final Solution* (Cambridge University Press, Cambridge, 1992); Lucy S. Dawidowicz, *The War against the Jews, 1933–1945* (Holt, Rinehart and Winston,

New York, 1975); Raul Hilberg, *The Destruction of the European Jews*, 3 vols (Holmes and Meier, New York, 1985).

26   Cf. Jill Stephenson, *Hitler's Home Front: Württemberg under the Nazis* (Continuum International, London, 2006).

9   Europe: An Honorable Legacy?

1   See pp. 143–4 above.
2   See pp. 18–19 above.
3   See pp. 109, 152, 171–2, 176, 178–9, 281 above.
4   See p. 179 above.

Bibliography

Acton, Edward. *Rethinking the Russian Revolution*. Edward Arnold, London, 1990.

Adamthwaite, Anthony. "France and the Coming of War." In Finney, *Origins*, 78–90.

Adamthwaite, Anthony. *Grandeur and Misery: France's Bid for Power in Europe 1914–1940*. Arnold, London, 1995.

Ades, Dawn, Benton, Tim, Elliot, David, and Whyte, Iain Boyd (eds.). *Art and Power: Europe under the Dictators 1930–45*. Hayward Gallery, London, 1995.

Aldcroft, Derek H. *The European Economy 1914–1970*. Croom Helm, London, 1978.

Aldcroft, Derek H. *Europe's Third World: The European Periphery in the Interwar Years*. Ashgate, Aldershot, 2006.

Aldcroft, Derek H. *From Versailles to Wall Street 1919–1929*. Allen Lane, London, 1977.

Angell, Norman. *The Great Illusion*. Heinemann, London, 1909.

Arendt, Hannah. *The Origins of Totalitarianism*. Allen and Unwin, London, 1967.

Aster, Sidney. "'Guilty men': The Case of Neville Chamberlain." In Finney, *Origins*, 62–78.

Baechler, Christian. *Gustave Stresemann (1878–1929). De impérialisme à la sécurité collective*. Presses Universitaires de Strasbourg, Strasbourg, 1996.

Bariéty, Jacques. *Les Relations franco-allemandes après la Première Guerre Mondiale. 10 novembre 1918–10 janvier 1925. De l'exécution à la négociation*. Éditions Pedone, Paris, 1977.

Barnouw, Dagmar. *Visible Spaces: Hannah Arendt and the German-Jewish Experience*. Johns Hopkins University Press, Baltimore, 1990.

Beck, Hermann. *The Fateful Alliance: German Conservatives and the Nazis in 1933. The Machtergreifung in a New Light*. Berghahn Books, New York, 2008.

Becker, Lutz. "Black Shirts and White Telephones: Cinema." In Ades et al., *Art and Power*, 137–9.

Becker, Lutz. "Optimistic Realism: Cinema." In Ades et al., *Art and Power*, 199–245.

Berend, Iván T. *Decades of Crisis: Central and Eastern Europe before World War I*. University of California Press, Berkeley, 1998.

Berghahn, Volker R. *Quest for Economic Empire: European Strategies of German Big Business in the Twentieth Century*. Berghahn Books, Providence RI, 1996.

Berghahn, Volker R. "War Preparations and National Identity in Imperial Germany." In Boemeke et al., *Anticipating Total War*, 307–26.

Bergmann, Carl. *The History of Reparations*. Houghton Mifflin, Boston, 1927.

Bessel, Richard. *Germany after the First World War*. Oxford University Press, Oxford, 1995.

Bessel, Richard. *Nazism and War*. Weidenfeld and Nicolson, London, 2004.

Bessel, Richard, and Feuchtwanger, E. J. (eds.). *Social Change and Political Development in Weimar Germany*. Croom Helm, London, 1981.

Blackwood, William Lee. "German Hegemony and the Socialist International's Place in Interwar European Diplomacy," *European History Quarterly*, 31, 1 (2001), 101–40.

Boak, Helen. "National Socialism and Working-Class Women before 1933." In Fischer, *Rise of National Socialism*, 163–88.

Boemeke, Manfred F., Chickering, Roger, and Förster, Stig (eds.). *Anticipating Total War: The German and American Experiences 1871–1914*. Cambridge University Press, Cambridge, 1999.

Boemeke, Manfred F., Feldman, Gerald D., and Glaser, Elizabeth (eds.). *The Treaty of Versailles: A Reassessment after 75 Years*. Cambridge University Press, Cambridge, 1998.

Bosworth, R. J. B., "Italy." In Gerwarth, *Twisted Paths*, 161–83.

Boyce, Robert, and Maiolo, Joseph A. (eds.). *The Origins of World War Two: The Debate Continues*. Palgrave Macmillan, Basingstoke, 2003.

Bracher, Karl Dietrich. *The German Dictatorship: The Origins, Structure and Effects of National Socialism*. Penguin, Harmondsworth, 1973.

Bracher, Karl Dietrich. "The Role of Hitler: Perspectives of Interpretation." In Laqueur, *Fascism*, 211–25.

Bridge, F. R. *From Sadowa to Sarajevo: The Foreign Policy of Austria-Hungary, 1866–1914*. Routledge and Kegan Paul, London, 1972.

Brock, Michael. "Britain Enters the War." In Evans and Pogge, *The Coming of the First World War*, 145–78.

Broszat, Martin. *The Hitler State: The Foundations and Development of the Internal Structure of the Third Reich*. Longman, London, 1981.

Browning, Christopher R. *Ordinary Men: Reserve Police Battalion 101 and the Final Solution in Poland*. Harper Perennial, New York, 1993.

Browning, Christopher R. *The Path to Genocide: Essays on Launching the Final Solution*. Cambridge University Press, Cambridge, 1992.

Buchheim, Christoph, Hutter, Michael, and James, Harold (eds.). *Zerrissene Zwischenkriegszeit. Wirtschaftshistorische Beiträge. Knut Borchardt zum 65. Geburtstag*. Nomos, Baden-Baden, 1994.

Bullock, Alan. *Hitler and Stalin: Parallel Lives*. HarperCollins, London, 1991.

Burleigh, Michael. *Death and Deliverance: "Euthanasia" in Germany 1900–1945*. Cambridge University Press, Cambridge, 1994.

Burleigh, Michael, and Wippermann, Wolfgang. *The Racial State: Germany 1933–1945*. Cambridge University Press, Cambridge, 1991.

Buse, Dieter K., and Doerr, Juergen C. (eds.). *Modern Germany: An Encyclopedia of History, People, and Culture, 1871–1990*, 2 vols. Garland, New York, 1998.

Button, Virginia. *Ben Nicholson*. Tate Publishing, London, 2007.

Cairns, John C. (ed.). *Contemporary France: Illusion, Conflict, and Regeneration*. New Viewpoints, New York, 1978.

Caron, François. *An Economic History of Modern France*. Methuen, London, 1979.

Carsten, Francis L. *Revolution in Central Europe 1918–1919*. Wildwood House, London, 1988.

Carsten, Francis L. *The Rise of Fascism*. Methuen, London, 1970.

Carter, Graydon. "Forward." In Friend et al., *Vanity Fair Portraits*, 7.

Chancellor, Edward. *Devil Take the Hindmost: A History of Financial Speculation*. Macmillan, London, 1999.

Chielens, Piet, and Chielens, Wim. *De Troost van schoonheid. De literaire Salient (Ieper 1914–1918)*. Globe, Groot-Bijgaarden, 1996.

Childers, Erskine. *The Riddle of the Sands*. Smith Elder, London, 1903.

Clark, Martin. *Modern Italy 1871–1982*. Longman, London, 1984.

Claus, Max. *Zwischen Paris und Vichy. Frankreich seit dem Waffenstillstand*. Deutscher Verlag, Berlin, 1942.

Clavin, Patricia. "Europe and the League of Nations." In Gerwarth, *Twisted Paths*, 325–54.

Clavin, Patricia. *The Great Depression in Europe, 1929–1939*. Macmillan, Basingstoke, 2000.

Cobb, Richard. "France and the Coming of War." In Evans and Pogge, *The Coming of the First World War*, 125–44.

Coen, Ester. "'Against Dreary Conformism': Giuseppe Bottai and Culture during the Fascist Period." In Ades et al., *Art and Power*, 178–80.

Cohrs, Patrick O. *The Unfinished Peace after World War I: America, Britain and the Stabilisation of Europe, 1919–1932*. Cambridge University Press, Cambridge, 2006.

Cole, George D. H. *Practical Economics; or, Studies in Economic Planning*. Penguin, London, 1937.

Conway, Martin, and Romijn, Peter. "Belgium and the Netherlands." In Gerwarth, *Twisted Paths*, 84–110.

Cornwall, Mark. "Serbia." In Wilson, *Decisions for War*, 55–96.

Crampton, R. J. "The Balkans." In Gerwarth, *Twisted Paths*, 237–70.

Daniel, Marko. "Spain: Culture at War." In Ades et al., *Art and Power*, 63–107.

Daniel, Ute. "The Politics of Rationing versus the Politics of Subsistence: Working-Class Women in Germany, 1914–1918." In Roger Fletcher (ed.), *Bernstein to Brandt: A Short History of German Social Democracy*. Edward Arnold, London, 1987, 89–95.

Darsy, Eugène. *Les Droits historiques de la France sur la rive gauche du Rhin*. Pamphlet. Paris, 1919.

Davies, Norman. *Europe: A History*. Oxford University Press, Oxford, 1996.

Dawidowicz, Lucy S. *The War against the Jews, 1933–1945*. Holt, Rinehart and Winston, New York, 1975.

de Botton, Alain. *The Architecture of Happiness*. Hamish Hamilton, London, 2006.

de Gaulle, Charles. *Vers l'armée de métier*. Berger-Levrault, Paris, 1934.

de Grazia, Victoria. *The Culture of Consent: Mass Organization of Leisure in Fascist Italy*. Cambridge University Press, Cambridge, 1981.

de la Gorce, Paul-Marie. *The French Army: A Military-Political History*. Weidenfeld and Nicolson, London, 1963.

Demetz, Peter. "Introduction: A Map of Courage." In Witkowsky, *Foto*, 1–7.

Derez, Mark. "A Belgian Salient for Reconstruction: People and *Patrie*, Landscape and Memory." In Liddle, *Passchendaele in Perspective*, 437–58.

Diefendorf, Geoffrey. *In the Wake of War: The Reconstruction of German Cities after World War II*. Oxford University Press, New York, 1993.

Dilks, David. "'We Must Hope for the Best and Prepare for the Worst': The Prime Minister, the Cabinet and Hitler's Germany, 1937–1939." In Finney, *Origins*, 43–62.

Dolan, Anne. *Commemorating the Irish Civil War: History and Memory 1923–2000*. Cambridge University Press, Cambridge, 2003.

Dupeux, Georges. *French Society, 1789–1970*. Methuen, London, 1976.

Dutton, David. "Britain and France at War, 1914–1918." In Sharp and Stone, *Anglo-French Relations*, 71–88.

Eatwell, Roger. *Fascism: A History*. Allen Lane, New York, 1997.

Edgerton, David. *The Shock of the Old: Technology and Global History since 1900*. Profile Books, London, 2006.

Eley, Geoff, and Retallack, James (eds.), *Wilhelminism and Its Legacies: German Modernities, Imperialism, and the Meaning of Reform, 1890–1930. Essays for Hartmut Pogge von Strandmann*. Berghahn Books, New York, 2003.

Elliot, David. "A Life-and-Death Struggle. Painting and Sculpture." In Ades et al., *Art and Power*, 270–6.

Evans, R. J. W. "The Habsburg Monarchy and the Coming of War." In Evans and Pogge, *The Coming of the First World War*, 33–55.

Evans, R. J. W. "The Successor States." In Gerwarth, *Twisted Paths*, 210–36.

Evans, R. J. W., and Pogge von Strandmann, Hartmut (eds.). *The Coming of the First World War*. Clarendon, Oxford, 1988.

Falter, Jürgen W. *Hitlers Wähler*. C. H. Beck, Munich, 1991.

Falter, Jürgen W. "How Likely Were Workers to Vote for the NSDAP?" In Fischer, *Rise of National Socialism*, 9–45.

Fearon, Peter. *The Origins and Nature of the Great Slump 1929–1932*. Macmillan, London, 1979.

Feder, Ernst, Löwenthal-Hensel, Cécile, and Paucker, Arnold (eds.). *Heute sprach ich mit … Tagebücher eines Berliner Publizisten 1926–1932*. University of Chicago Press, Chicago, 1973.

Feiling, Keith. *The Life of Neville Chamberlain*. Macmillan, London, 1946.

Feldman, Gerald D. *Army Industry and Labour in Germany, 1914–1918*. Princeton University Press, Princeton, 1966.

Feldman, Gerald D. *The Great Disorder: Politics, Economics and Society in the German Inflation, 1914–1924*. Oxford University Press, New York, 1993.

Feldman, Gerald D. "Hugo Stinnes and the Prospect of War before 1914." In Boemeke et al., *Anticipating Total War*, 77–95.

Feldman, Gerald D. "The Reparations Debate." In Fischer and Sharp, *After the Versailles Treaty*, 69–80.

Feldman, Matthew (ed.). *A Fascist Century: Essays by Roger Griffin*. Basingstoke, Palgrave, 2008.

Fellner, Fritz. "Austria-Hungary." In Wilson, *Decisions for War*, 9–25.

Ferguson, Niall. *The Pity of War*. Allen Lane, London, 1998.

Finckh, Ludwig. "The Spirit of Berlin" (1919). In Kaes et al., *Weimar Republic Sourcebook*, 414–15.

Finney, Patrick (ed.). *The Origins of the Second World War*. Arnold, London, 1997.

Fischer, Conan. "Continuity and Change in Post-Wilhelmine Germany: From the 1918 Revolution to the Ruhr Crisis." In Eley and Retallack, *Wilhelminism*, 202–18.

Fischer, Conan. "The Human Price of Reparations." In Fischer and Sharp, *After the Versailles Treaty*, 81–95.

Fischer, Conan (ed.). *The Rise of National Socialism and the Working Classes in Weimar Germany*. Berghahn Books, Oxford, 1996.

Fischer, Conan. *The Rise of the Nazis*, 2nd edn. Manchester University Press, Manchester, 2002.

Fischer, Conan. *The Ruhr Crisis 1923–1924*. Oxford University Press, Oxford, 2003.

Fischer, Conan, and Sharp, Alan (eds.). *After the Versailles Treaty: Enforcement, Compliance, Contested Identities*. Routledge, London, 2008.

Fischer, Fritz. *From Kaiserreich to Third Reich: Elements of Continuity in German History*. Allen and Unwin, London, 1986.

Fischer, Fritz. *Germany's Aims in the First World War*. Chatto and Windus, London, 1967.

Fischer, Fritz. *War of Illusions: German Policies from 1911 to 1914*. Chatto and Windus, London, 1975.

Fitzpatrick, Sheila. *The Russian Revolution, 1917–1932*. Oxford University Press, Oxford, 1984.

Fletcher, Roger (ed.). *Bernstein to Brandt: A Short History of German Social Democracy*. Edward Arnold, London, 1987.

Fontana, J., and Nadel, J. "Spain 1914–1970." In Carlo M Cipolla (ed.), *The Fontana Economic History of Europe: 6.2 Contemporary Economies*. Collins Fontana, London, 1976, 460–529.

Förster, Stig. "Dreams and Nightmares: German Military Leadership and the Images of Future Warfare, 1871–1914." In Boemeke et al., *Anticipating Total War*, 343–76.

Fraquelli, Simonetta. "All Roads Lead to Rome: Painting and Sculpture." In Ades et al., *Art and Power*, 130–6.

Frei, Norbert. *National Socialist Rule in Germany: The Führer State 1933–1945*. Blackwell, Oxford, 1993.

Frei, Norbert. *1945 und wir. Das Dritte Reich im Bewußtsein der Deutschen*. C. H. Beck, Munich, 2005.

French, David. *British Economic and Strategic Planning 1905–1915*. George Allen and Unwin, London, 1982.

Friend, David, Hitchens, Christopher, and Pepper, Terence. *Vanity Fair Portraits: Photographs 1913–2008*. National Portrait Gallery, London, 2008.

Fritzsche, Peter. *Germans into Nazis*. Harvard University Press, Cambridge MA, 1998.

Fritzsche, Peter. *Rehearsals for Fascism: Populism and Political Mobilization in Weimar Germany*. Oxford University Press, New York, 1990.

Fröhlich, Elke. "Joseph Goebbels: The Propagandist." In Ronald Smelser and Rainer Zitelmann, *Nazi Elite*, 48–61.

Gellately, Robert. *Backing Hitler*. Oxford University Press, Oxford, 2001.

Geppert, Dominik, and Gerwarth, Robert (eds.). *Wilhelmine Germany and Edwardian Britain: Essays on Cultural Affinity*. Oxford University Press and German Historical Institute London, 2008.

Gerwarth, Robert (ed.). *Twisted Paths: Europe 1914–1945*. Oxford University Press, Oxford, 2007.

Geyer, Michael, and Boyer, John W. (eds.). *Resistance against the Third Reich, 1933–1990*. University of Chicago Press, Chicago, 1994.

Gilbert, Martin. "Horace Wilson: Man of Munich?" *History Today*, 32 (1982), 6.

Goenner, Herbert. *Einstein in Berlin 1914–1933*. C. H. Beck, Munich, 2005.

Goldhagen, Daniel Jonah. *Hitler's Willing Executioners: Ordinary Germans and the Holocaust.* Little, Brown, London, 1996.

Gooch, G. P., et al. (eds.). *British Documents on the Origins of the War 1898–1914.* HMSO, London, 1926–38.

Gooch, John. "Fascist Italy." In Boyce and Maiolo, *Origins*, 32–51.

Griffin, Roger (ed.). *International Fascism: Theories, Causes and the New Consensus.* Arnold, London, 1998.

Grohmann, Carolyn. "From Lothringen to Lorraine: Expulsion and Voluntary Repatriation." In Fischer and Sharp, *After the Versailles Treaty*, 153–70.

Guinn, Paul. "On Throwing Ballast in Foreign Policy: Poincaré, the Entente and the Ruhr Occupation," *European History Quarterly*, 18, 4 (1988), 427–37.

Guttsman, W. L. *Workers' Culture in Weimar Germany: Between Tradition and Commitment.* Berg, New York, 1990.

Hamilton, Richard F. "On the Origins of the Catastrophe." In Hamilton and Herwig, *Origins*, 469–506.

Hamilton, Richard F., and Herwig, Holger H. (eds.). *The Origins of World War I.* Cambridge University Press, Cambridge, 2003.

Hänisch, Dirk. "A Social Profile of the Saxon NSDAP Voters." In Szejnmann, *Nazism in Central Germany*, 219–31.

Hänisch, Dirk. *Sozialstrukturelle Bestimmungsgründe des Wahlverhaltens in der Weimarer Republik.* Sozialwissenschaftliche Kooperative, Duisburg, 1983.

Hanson, Joanna K. M. "The Civilian Population and the Warsaw Rising." In Stachura, *Warsaw Rising*, 47–56.

Hardach, Gerd. *The First World War 1914–1918.* Allen Lane, London, 1977.

Harrison, Joseph. *The Spanish Economy in the Twentieth Century.* Croom Helm, London, 1985.

Haslam, Jonathan G. "Soviet Russia and the Spanish Problem." In Boyce and Maiolo, *Origins*, 70–85.

Hermann, David. *The Arming of Europe and the Making of the First World War.* Princeton University Press, Princeton, 1996.

Herwig, Holger H. "Clio Deceived: Patriotic Self-Censorship in Germany after the Great War." In Keith M. Wilson (ed.), *Forging the Collective Memory: Government and International Historians through Two World Wars.* Berghahn Books, Providence RI, 1996, 87–127.

Herwig, Holger H. "Why Did It Happen?" in Hamilton and Herwig, *Origins*, 443–68.

Hilberg, Raul. *The Destruction of the European Jews*, 3 vols. Holmes and Meier, New York, 1985.

Hilson, Mary. "Scandinavia." In Gerwarth, *Twisted Paths*, 8–32.

Hirschfeld, Gerhard, and Kettenacker, Lothar (eds.). *The Führer State: Myth and Reality. Studies in the Structure and Politics of the Third Reich.* Klett-Cotta, Stuttgart, 1981.

Hitchens, Christopher. "Divine Decadence." In Friend et al., *Vanity Fair Portraits*, 12–15.

Hobson, John A. *Imperialism: A Study.* London, 1902.

Hochreiter, Otto, and Starl, Timm (eds.). *Geschichte der Fotografie in Österreich.* Museum Moderner Kunst, Vienna, 1983.

Hochstadt, Steve (ed.). *Sources of the Holocaust.* Palgrave Macmillan, Basingstoke, 2004.

Hoeres, Peter. *Krieg der Philosophen: die deutsche and britische Philosophie im Ersten Weltkrieg.* Ferdinand Schöningh, Paderborn, 2004.

Holt, Edgar. *The Tiger: The Life of Georges Clemenceau 1841–1929.* Hamilton, London, 1976.

Horne, Alistair. *The Price of Glory: Verdun 1916.* Penguin Books, London, 1993.

Horne, John, and Kramer, Alan. *German Atrocities 1914: A History of Denial.* Yale University Press, New Haven, 2001.

Howard, Michael. "Europe on the Eve of the First World War." In Evans and Pogge, *The Coming of the First World War,* 1–17.

Howard, Michael. *The First World War: A Very Short Introduction.* Oxford University Press, Oxford, 2007.

Howard, Michael. *War and the Liberal Conscience.* Temple Smith, London, 1978.

Hughes, John Jay. "Galen, Clemens August von (1878–1946)." In Buse and Doerr, *Modern Germany,* vol. 1, 364.

Hümmert, Ludwig. *Bayern vom Königreich zur Diktatur – 1900–1933.* W. Ludwig, Pfaffenhofen, 1979.

Jackson, Alwin. "The Two Irelands." In Gerwarth, *Twisted Paths,* 60–83.

Jackson, J. Hampden. *Clemenceau and the Third Republic.* Hodder and Stoughton, London, 1946.

Jackson, Julian. *The Fall of France: The Nazi Invasion of 1940.* Oxford University Press, Oxford, 2003.

Jackson, Julian. *France: The Dark Years 1940–1944.* Oxford University Press, Oxford, 2001.

Jackson, Julian. *The Popular Front in France: Defending Democracy, 1934–38.* Cambridge University Press, Cambridge, 1990.

Jackson, Peter. "France." In Boyce and Maiolo, *Origins,* 86–110.

Jahn, Hubertus. "Russia." In Gerwarth, *Twisted Paths,* 297–324.

Jamieson, Bill. "Scotland's War: The Dawn of Conflict." *The Scotsman* (Sept. 2, 2009), 15.

Jantzen, Kyle. "White Rose." In Buse and Doerr, *Modern Germany,* vol. 2, 1070.

Jeannesson, Stanislas. "French Policy in the Rhineland, 1919–1924." In Fischer and Sharp, *After the Versailles Treaty,* 57–68.

Jeannesson, Stanislas. "L'Europe de Jacques Seydoux," *Revue Historique,* 299, 1 (1998), 123–44.

Jeannesson, Stanislas. *Poincaré, la France et la Ruhr (1922–1924). Histoire d'une occupation.* Presses Universitaires de Strasbourg, Strasbourg, 1998.

Jones, Heather. "The German Spring Reprisals of 1917: Prisoners of War and the Violence of the Western Front," *German History,* 26, 3 (2008), 335–56.

Kaes, Anton, Jay, Martin, and Dimendberg, Edward (eds.). *The Weimar Republic Sourcebook.* University of California Press, Berkeley, 1994.

Kautsky, Karl, von Montgelas, Max, and Schücking, Walther (eds.). *Die deutschen Dokumente zum Kriegsausbruch.* Deutsche Verlagsanstalt für Politik und Geschichte, Charlottenburg, 1919.

Keiger, John F. V. "France." In Wilson, *Decisions for War,* 121–49.

Kemp, Tom. "The French Economy under the Franc Poincaré." In Cairns, *Contemporary France,* 65–91.

Kennan, George F. *The Fateful Alliance: France, Russia, and the Coming of the First World War.* Manchester University Press, Manchester, 1984.

Kennedy, Paul. *The Rise and Fall of the Great Powers: Economic Change and Military Conflict from 1500 to 2000.* Unwin Hyman, London, 1988.

Kershaw, Ian. *Hitler 1889–1936: Hubris.* Allen Lane, London, 1998.

Kershaw, Ian. *Hitler 1936–1945: Nemesis.* Allen Lane, London, 2000.

Kershaw, Ian. *The Nazi Dictatorship: Problems and Perspectives of Interpretation*, 4th edn. Arnold, London, 2000.

Kershaw, Ian. *Popular Opinion and Political Dissent in the Third Reich: Bavaria 1933–1945*. Clarendon, Oxford, 1983.

Kershaw, Ian. "'Working towards the Fÿhrer': Reflections on the Nature of the Hitler Dictatorship," *Contemporary European History*, 2, 2 (1993), 103–18.

Keynes, John Maynard. *The Economic Consequences of the Peace*. Macmillan, London, 1920.

Kimball, Warren F. "The United States." In Boyce and Maiolo, *Origins*, 134–54.

Kissinger, Henry. *Diplomacy*. Simon and Schuster, New York, 1994.

Knox, MacGregor. "The Fascist Regime, Its Foreign Policy and Its Wars: An 'Anti-Anti-Fascist' Orthodoxy." In Finney, *Origins*, 148–68.

Kohn, Hans. *Nationalism and Liberty: The Swiss Example*. George Allen and Unwin, London, 1956.

Krüger, Peter. *Deutschland und die Reparationen 1918/19. Die Genesis des Reparationsproblems in Deutschland zwischen Waffenstillstand und Versailler Friedenschluß*. Deutsche Verlags-Anstalt, Stuttgart, 1973.

Krüger, Peter. *Versailles. Deutsche Außenpolitik zwischen Revisionismus und Friedenssicherung*, 2nd edn. Deutsche Verlags-Anstalt, Munich, 1993.

Krumeich, Gerd, and Schröder, Joachim (eds.). *Der Schatten des Weltkriegs. Die Ruhrbesetzung 1923*. Klartext, Essen, 2004.

Landau, Rom. *Paderewski*. Nicholson and Watson, London, 1934.

Lane, Barbara Miller, and Rupp, Leila J. *Nazi Ideology before 1933: A Documentation*. Manchester University Press, Manchester, 1978.

Lannon, Frances. "Iberia." In Gerwarth, *Twisted Paths*, 136–60.

Laqueur, Walter (ed.). *Fascism: A Reader's Guide. Analyses, Interpretations, Bibliography*. Penguin, Harmondsworth, 1979.

Larkin, Maurice. *France since the Popular Front: Government and People 1936–1986*. Clarendon Press, Oxford, 1988.

Laub, Thomas J. *After the Fall: German Policy in Occupied France, 1940–1944*. Oxford University Press, New York, 2009.

Lauter, Anna-Monika. *Sicherheit und Reparationen. Die französische Öffentlichkeit, der Rhein und die Ruhr 1918–1933*. Klartext, Essen, 2006.

Lepsius, Johannes, et al. (eds.). *Die Grosse Politik der Europäischen Kabinette*. Arbeitsausschuß Deutscher Verbände, Berlin, 1922–27.

Liddle, Peter H. (ed.). *Passchendaele in Perspective: The Third Battle of Ypres*. Leo Cooper, London, 1997.

Linton, Derek S. "Preparing German Youth for War." In Boemeke et al, *Anticipating Total War*, 167–87.

Linz, Juan J. "Some Notes towards a Comparative Study of Fascism in Historical Perspective." In Laqueur, *Fascism*, 3–38.

Lipset, Seymour Martin. *Political Man: The Social Bases of Politics*. Johns Hopkins University Press, Baltimore, 1981.

Lukes, Igor. "Czechoslovakia." In Boyce and Maiolo, *Origins*, 165–75.

Lyons, Carolyn. "The Empire's New Clothes," *Financial Times*, magazine (Aug. 25–6, 2007) 25–7.

Macleod, Iain. *Neville Chamberlain*. Frederick Muller, London, 1961.

Macmillan, Margaret. *Peacemakers: The Paris Conference of 1919 and Its Attempt to End War.* John Murray, London, 2003.

Mai, Gunther. "National Socialist Factory Cell Organisation and the German Labour Front: National Socialist Labour Policy and Organisations." In Fischer, *Rise of National Socialism*, 117–36.

Marks, Sally. *The Ebbing of European Ascendency: An International History of the World 1914–1945.* Arnold, London, 2002.

Marks, Sally. *The Illusion of Peace: International Relations in Europe, 1918–1933*, 2nd edn. Palgrave Macmillan, Basingstoke, 2003.

Mason, Tim. "Comment 2: Debate. Germany, 'Domestic Crisis' and War in 1939," *Past and Present*, 122 (Feb. 1989), 205–21.

Mason, Tim. "Intention and Explanation: A Current Controversy about the Interpretation of National Socialism." In Gerhard Hirschfeld and Lothar Kettenacker (eds.), *The Führer State: Myth and Reality. Studies in the Structure and Politics of the Third Reich.* Klett-Cotta, Stuttgart, 1981, 23–42.

May, Ernest R. *Strange Victory: Hitler's Conquest of France.* Hill and Wang, New York, 2000.

McCauley, Martin. *The Soviet Union since 1917.* Longman, London, 1982.

McDonough, Frank. *Sophie Scholl: The Real Story of the Woman Who Defied Hitler.* History Press, Stroud, 2009.

McKibbin, Ross. "Great Britain." In Gerwarth, *Twisted Paths*, 33–59.

McKinstry, Leo. *Spitfire: Portrait of a Legend.* John Murray, London, 2007.

Menge, Anna. "The Iron Hindenburg: A Popular Icon of Weimar Germany," *German History*, 26, 3 (2008), 357–82.

Michel, Bernard. *Banques et banquiers en Autriche au debut de 20e siècle.* Presses de la Fondation Nationale des Sciences Politiques, Paris, 1976.

Michels, Robert. *Political Parties: A Sociological Study of the Oligarchical Tendencies of Modern Democracy.* Crowell-Collier, London, 1962.

Ministère des Affaires Étrangères. *Documents diplomatiques français 1871–1914.* Imprimerie Nationale, Paris, 1929ff.

Ministère des Affaires Étrangères. *Le Livre jaune français. Documents diplomatiques 1938–1939.* Imprimerie Nationale, Paris, 1939.

Mombauer, Annika. *The Origins of the First World War: Controversies and Consensus.* Longman, London, 2002.

Mommsen, Hans. *Arbeiterbewegung und Nationale Frage. Ausgewählte Aufsätze.* Vandenhoeck und Ruprecht, Göttingen, 1979.

Mommsen, Hans. *Beamtentum im Dritten Reich.* Deutsche Verlagsanstalt, Stuttgart, 1966.

Moorhouse, Roger. *Killing Hitler: The Third Reich and the Plots against the Führer.* Jonathan Cape, London, 2006.

Moorhouse, Roger. "'The Sore That Would Never Heal': The Genesis of the Polish Corridor." In Fischer and Sharp, *After the Versailles Treaty*, 185–95.

Moses, John. *Trade Unionism in Germany from Bismarck to Hitler 1869–1933*, 2 vols. Barnes and Noble, Totowa NJ, 1982.

Mucha, Sarah (ed.). *Alphonse Mucha: Celebrating the Creation of the Mucha Museum, Prague.* Malcolm Saunders, Prague, 2000.

Müller, Frank. "'Perhaps Also Useful for Our Election Campaign': The Parliamentary Impasse of the Late Wilhelmine State and the British Constitutional Crisis, 1909–1911." In Geppert and Gerwarth, *Wilhelmine Germany*, 67–87.

Müller, Frank. "The Spectre of a People in Arms: The Prussian Government and the Militarisation of German Nationalism, 1859–1864," *English Historical Review*, 122, 495 (Feb. 2007), 82–104.

Mulligan, William. *The Creation of the Modern German Army: General Walther Reinhardt and the Weimar Republic, 1914–1930*. Berghahn Books, New York, 2005.

Murray, Williamson. "Britain." In Boyce and Maiolo, *Origins*, 111–33.

Nairne, Sandy. "Forward." In Friend et al, *Vanity Fair Portraits*, 6.

Neilson, Keith. "Russia." In Wilson, *Decisions for War*, 97–120.

Némirovsky, Irène. *Suite Française*. Chatto and Windus, London, 2007.

Neville, Peter. "British Appeasement Policy and the Military Disaster in 1940," *World War II Quarterly*, 6, 1 (2009), 5–22.

Newton, Scott. "The 'Anglo-German Connection' and the Political Economy of Appeasement." In Finney, *Origins*, 293–315.

Nove, Alec. *An Economic History of the USSR*. Allen Lane, London, 1969.

O'Riordan, Elspeth. *Britain and the Ruhr Crisis*. Palgrave, Basingstoke, 2001.

Overy, Richard. "Germany, 'Domestic Crisis' and War in 1939," *Past and Present*, 116 (Aug. 1987), 138–68.

Overy, Richard. "Heavy Industry and the State in Nazi Germany: The Reichswerke Crisis," *European History Quarterly*, 15 (1985), 313–40.

Overy, Richard. *The Morbid Age: Britain between the Wars*. Allen Lane, London, 2009.

Overy, Richard. *The Nazi Economic Recovery 1932–1938*. Macmillan, Basingstoke, 1982.

Overy, Richard. *1939: Countdown to War*. Allen Lane, London, 2009.

Overy, Richard. "Reply: Debate. Germany, 'Domestic Crisis' and War in 1939," *Past and Present*, 122 (Feb. 1989), 221–40.

Overy, Richard. *Why the Allies Won*. Pimlico, London, 1996.

Paléologue, Maurice. *An Ambassador's Memoirs 1914–1917*, trans. Frederick A. Holt. Hutchinson, London, 1973.

Parker, R. A. C. "Alternatives to Appeasement." In Finney, *Origins*, 206–21.

Payne, Stanley G. *The Collapse of the Spanish Republic, 1933–1936: Origins of the Civil War*. Yale University Press, New Haven, 2006.

Payne, Stanley G. *A History of Fascism 1914–45*. UCL Press, London, 1995.

Payne, Stanley G. *The Spanish Civil War, the Soviet Union, and Communism*. Yale University Press, New Haven, 2004.

Penson, James Henry *Is Germany Prosperous? Impressions Gained, January 1922*. E. Arnold, London, 1922.

Petzina, Dietmar. "Is Germany Prosperous? Die Reparationsfrage in der Diskussion angelsächsischer Experten zwischen 1918 und 1925." In Buchheim et al., *Zerrissene Zwischenkriegszeit*, 241–62.

Peukert, Detlev J. K. *Inside Nazi Germany: Conformity, Opposition and Racism in Everyday Life*. Penguin, London, 1989.

Peukert, Detlev. *The Weimar Republic: The Crisis of Classical Modernity*. Allen Lane, London, 1991.

Pipes, Richard. *Russian Conservatism and Its Critics: A Study in Political Culture*. Yale University Press, New Haven, 2005.

Pogge von Strandmann, Hartmut. "Germany and the Coming of War." In Evans and Pogge, *The Coming of the First World War*, 87–123.

Pogge von Strandmann, Hartmut. "Industrial Primacy in German Foreign Policy? Myths and Realities in German-Russian Relations at the End of the Weimar Republic." In Bessel and Feuchtwanger, *Social Change*, 241–67.

Pogge von Strandmann, Hartmut (ed.). *Walther Rathenau: Industrialist, Banker, Intellectual, and Politician. Notes and Diaries 1907–1922*, trans. Caroline Pinder-Lacraft. Clarendon Press, Oxford, 1985.

Poidevin, Raymond. "Le Nationalisme économique et financier dans les relations franco-allemandes avant 1914," *Revue d'Allemagne et des Pays de Langue Allemande*, 28, 1 (1996), 63–70.

Postan, Michael M. *British War Production*. HMSO and Longman, London, 1952.

Prazmowska, Anita J. "Poland." In Boyce and Maiolo, *Origins*, 155–64.

Prior, Robin, and Wilson, Trevor. *The Somme*. Yale University Press, New Haven, 2006.

Prowe, Diethelm. "Fascism, Neo-Fascism, New Radical Right?" In Griffin, *International Fascism*, 305–24.

Pyta, Wolfram. *Hindenburg. Herrschaft zwischen Hohenzollern und Hitler*. Siedler, Munich, 2007.

Renouvin, Pierre. *La Première Guerre mondiale*. Presses Universitaires de France, Paris, 1965.

Reynolds, David. "1940: Fulcrum of the Twentieth Century?" In Finney, *Origins*, 434–56.

Rhiel, Mary Beth. "Riefenstahl, Leni." In Buse and Doerr *Modern Germany*, vol 2, 848–49.

Riddel, Paul. "This Isn't a New Great Depression – and It Mustn't Turn into One," *The Scotsman* (Oct. 8, 2008), 28.

Roberts, Geoffrey. *The Soviet Union and the Origins of the Second World War: Russo-German Relations and the Road to War*. Macmillan, Basingstoke, 1995.

Röhl, John C. G. *From Bismarck to Hitler: The Problem of Continuity in German History*. Longman, Harlow, 1970.

Röhl, John C. G. "Germany." In Wilson, *Decisions for War*, 27–54.

Roseman, Mark. *The Villa, the Lake, the Meeting: Wannsee and the Final Solution*. Allen Lane, London, 2002.

Rouaud, Jean. *Fields of Glory*, trans. Ralph Manheim. Harvill, London, 1993.

Rupieper, Hermann J. *The Cuno Government and Reparations 1922–23: Politics and Economics*. Nijhoff, The Hague, 1979.

Schuker, Stephen A. *The End of French Predominance in Europe: The Financial Crisis of 1924 and the Adoption of the Dawes Plan*. University of North Carolina Press, Chapell Hill NC, 1976.

Schuker, Stephen A. "France and the Remilitarization of the Rhineland, 1936." In Finney, *Origins*, 222–45.

Schulze, Hagen. *Weimar. Deutschland 1917–1933*. Siedler, Berlin, 1998.

Schuman, Frederick L. *War and Diplomacy in the French Republic: An Inquiry into Political Motivations and the Control of Foreign Policy*. Whittlesey House, New York, 1931.

Seidler, Franz W. "Fritz Todt: From Motorway Builder to Minister of State." In Smelser and Zitelmann, *Nazi Elite*, 245–56.

Sharp, Alan. "Anglo-French Relations from Versailles to Locarno, 1919–1932: The Quest for Security." In Sharp and Stone, *Anglo-French Relations*, 120–38.

Sharp, Alan, and Stone, Glyn (eds.). *Anglo-French Relations in the Twentieth Century: Rivalry and Cooperation*. Routledge, London, 2000.

Shepherd, Ben. *War in the Wild East: The German Army and Soviet Partisans*. Harvard University Press, Cambridge MA, 2004.

Shirer, William L. *Berlin Diary 1934–1941*. Sphere Books, London, 1970.

Shore, Zachary. *What Hitler Knew: The Battle for Information in Nazi Foreign Policy*. Oxford University Press, New York, 2003.

Smelser, Ronald, and Zitelmann, Rainer (eds.). *The Nazi Elite*. Macmillan, Basingstoke, 1993.

Soutou, Georges-Henri. "La France et les marches de l'est, 1914–1919", *Revue Historique*, 578 (1978), 341–88.

Soutou, Georges-Henri. *L'Europe de 1815 à nos jours*. Presses Universitaires de France, Paris, 2007.

Soutou, Georges-Henri. "Vom Rhein zur Ruhr: Absichten und Planungen der französischen Regierung." In Krumeich and Schröder, *Der Schatten des Weltkriegs*, 63–84.

Spark, Muriel. *The Prime of Miss Jean Brodie*. Macmillan, London, 1961.

Spohr Readman, Kristina. "Finland and the Baltic States." In Gerwarth, *Twisted Paths*, 271–96.

Spring, D. W. "Russia and the Coming of War." In Evans and Pogge, *The Coming of the First World War*, 57–86.

Stachura, Peter D. "Introduction." In Stachura, *Warsaw Rising*, 17–20.

Stachura, Peter D. "President Franklin D. Roosevelt and the Poles, 1941–1945." In Stachura, *Warsaw Rising*, 61–77.

Stachura, Peter D. (ed.). *The Warsaw Rising, 1944*. Centre for Research in Polish History, University of Stirling, Stirling, 2007.

Steinisch, Irmgard. "Different Paths to War: A Comparative Study of Militarism and Imperialism in the United States and Imperial Germany, 1871–1914." In Boemeke et al., *Anticipating Total War*, 29–53.

Stengers, Jean. "Belgium." In Wilson, *Decisions for War*, 151–74.

Stephenson, Jill. *Hitler's Home Front: Württemberg under the Nazis*. Continuum International, London, 2006.

Stephenson, Jill. *The Nazi Organization of Women*. Croom Helm, London, 1980.

Stephenson, Jill. *Women in Nazi Society*. Croom Helm, London, 1975.

Sternhell, Zeev. "Fascist Ideology." In Laqueur, *Fascism*, 315–76.

Stevenson, David. "French War Aims and Peace Planning." In Boemeke et al., *Treaty of Versailles*, 87–101.

Stevenson, John, and Cook, Chris. *The Slump: Society and Politics during the Depression*. Cape, London, 1977.

Strachan, Hew. *The First World War*, vol. 1: *To Arms*. Oxford University Press, Oxford, 2003.

Sweet, William. "Schmitt, Carl (1888–1985)." In Buse and Doerr, *Modern Germany*, vol. 2, 890–1.

Szejnmann, Claus-Christian. *Nazism in Central Germany: The Brownshirts in "Red" Saxony*. Berghahn Books, New York, 1999.

Taylor, A. J. P. *The Origins of the Second World War*. Penguin, London, 1964.

Taylor, Fred (ed.). *The Goebbels Diaries 1939–1941*. Hamish Hamilton, London, 1982.

Tenfelde, Klaus. "Disarmament and Big Business: The Case of Krupp, 1918–1925." In Fischer and Sharp, *After the Versailles Treaty*, 113–31.

Torp, Cornelius. *Die Herausforderung der Globalisierung*. Vandenhoeck und Ruprecht, Göttingen, 2005.

The Treaty of Peace between the Allied and Associated Powers and Germany ... Signed at Versailles, June 28th 1919. HMSO, London, 1928.

Troost, Gerdy. *Das Bauen im neuen Reich*, 3rd edn. Gauverlag Bayerische Ostmark, Bayreuth, 1941.

Tumblety, Joan. "France." In Gerwarth, *Twisted Paths*, 111–35.

Uldricks, Teddy J. "Soviet Security Policy in the 1930s." In Finney, *Origins*, 169–78.

van Creveld, Martin. *Supplying War: Logistics from Wallenstein to Patton*. Cambridge University Press, Cambridge, 1980.

van der Post, Lucia. "High on Heal's," *Financial Times*, How to Spend It section (Sept. 5, 2009), 20–4.

von Hoegen, Jesko. *Der Held von Tannenberg. Genese und Funktion des Hindenburg-Mythos*. Böhlau, Cologne, 2007.

Vyšný, Paul. *The Runciman Mission to Czechoslovakia, 1938: Prelude to Munich*. Palgrave Macmillan, Basingstoke, 2003.

Waites, Bernard. *A Class Society at War: England 1914–1918*. Berg, Leamington Spa, 1987.

Watson, David. *Clemenceau: A Political Biography*. Eyre Methuen, London, 1974.

Weber, Thomas. *Hitler's First War: Adolf Hitler, the Men of the List Regiment, and the First World War*. Oxford University Press, Oxford, 2010.

Weber, Thomas. Review on H-German (Jan. 2006) of Hoeres, *Krieg der Philosophen*.

Webster, Paul. *Pétain's Crime: The Full Story of French Collaboration in the Holocaust*. Papermac, London, 1992.

Wein, Franziska. *Deutschlands Strom – Frankreichs Grenze. Geschichte und Propaganda am Rhein 1919–1930*. Klartext, Essen, 1992.

Weinberg, Gerhard L. (ed.). *Hitler's Second Book: The Unpublished Sequel to Mein Kampf*. Enigma, New York, 2003.

Weinberg, Gerhard L. (ed.). *Hitlers zweites Buch. Ein Dokument aus dem Jahr 1928*. Deutsche Verlags-Anstalt, Stuttgart, 1961.

Weinberg, Gerhard L. "Munich after 50 Years." In Finney, *Origins*, 402–13.

Whiting, Charles. *Patton*. Ballantine Books, New York, 1970.

Whyte, Iain Boyd. "National Socialism and Modernism: Architecture." In Ades et al., *Art and Power*, 258–69.

Wilsberg, Klaus. *"Terrible ami – aimable ennemi." Kooperation und Konflikt in den deutsch-französischen Beziehungen 1911–1914*. Bouvier, Bonn, 1998.

Wilson, Keith M. "Britain." In Wilson, *Decisions for War*, 175–208.

Wilson, Keith M. (ed.). *Decisions for War 1914*. UCL Press, London, 1995.

Wilson, Keith M. (ed.). *Forging the Collective Memory: Government and International Historians through Two World Wars*. Berghahn Books, Providence RI, 1996.

Wilson, Stephen. "The 'Action Française' in French Intellectual Life." In Cairns, *Contemporary France*, 139–67.

Winkler, Heinrich August. *Der lange Weg nach Westen, I. Deutsche Geschichte vom Ende des Alten Reiches bis zum Untergang der Weimarer Republik*. C. H. Beck, Munich, 2002.

Winkler, Heinrich August. *Der lange Weg nach Westen, II. Deutsche Geschichte vom "Dritten Reich" bis zur Wiedervereinigung*. C. H. Beck, Munich, 2002.

Winkler, Heinrich August. *Weimar 1918–1933. Die Geschichte der ersten deutschen Demokratie*, 2nd edn. C. H. Beck, Munich, 1994.

Winter, Jay. *Remembering War: The Great War between Memory and History in the Twentieth Century*. Yale University Press, New Haven, 2006.

Witkowsky, Matthew S. *Foto: Modernity in Central Europe, 1918–1945*. Thames and Hudson, London, 2007.

Wright, Jonathan. *Germany and the Origins of the Second World War*. Palgrave Macmillan, Basingstoke, 2007.

Wright, Jonathan. *Gustav Stresemann: Weimar's Greatest Statesman*. Oxford University Press, Oxford, 2002.

Wullschlager, Jackie. *Chagall: Love and Exile*. Allen Lane, London, 2008.

Wullschlager, Jackie. "Rooted in Mother Russia", *Financial Times*, Life and Arts section (Oct. 18–19, 2008), 17.

Zeman, Z. A. B. "The Balkans and the Coming of War." In Evans and Pogge, *The Coming of the First World War*, 19–32.

Index